MIKE COLAMECO'S
FOOD LOVER'S GUIDE
TO NYC

AN INSIDER'S GUIDE TO NEW YORK CITY'S
GASTRONOMIC DELIGHTS

WILEY

JOHN WILEY & SONS, INC.

"A true gastronome should always be ready to eat,

just as a soldier should always be ready to fight."

—Charles Pierre Monselet

Published by John Wiley & Sons, Inc., Hoboken, New Jersey
Published simultaneously in Canada

No part of this publication may be reproduced, stored in a retrieval system, or transmitted in any form or by any means, electronic, mechanical, photocopying, recording, scanning, or otherwise, except as permitted under Section 107 or 108 of the 1976 United States Copyright Act, without either the prior written permission of the Publisher, or authorization through payment of the appropriate per-copy fee to the Copyright Clearance Center, Inc., 222 Rosewood Drive, Danvers, MA 01923, (978) 750–8400, fax (978) 646–8600, or on the web at www.copyright.com. Requests to the Publisher for permission should be addressed to the Permissions Department, John Wiley & Sons, Inc., 111 River Street, Hoboken, NJ 07030, (201) 748–6011, fax (201) 748–6008, or online at http://www.wiley.com/go/permissions.

Limit of Liability/Disclaimer of Warranty: While the publisher and author have used their best efforts in preparing this book, they make no representations or warranties with respect to the accuracy or completeness of the contents of this book and specifically disclaim any implied warranties of merchantability or fitness for a particular purpose. No warranty may be created or extended by sales representatives or written sales materials. The advice and strategies contained herein may not be suitable for your situation. You should consult with a professional where appropriate. Neither the publisher nor author shall be liable for any loss of profit or any other commercial damages, including but not limited to special, incidental, consequential, or other damages.

For general information on our other products and services or for technical support, please contact our Customer Care Department within the United States at (800) 762–2974, outside the United States at (317) 572–3993 or fax (317) 572–4002.

Wiley also publishes its books in a variety of electronic formats. Some content that appears in print may not be available in electronic books. For more information about Wiley products, visit our web site at www.wiley.com.
Library of Congress Cataloging-in-Publication Data:

Colameco, Mike.
 [Food lover's guide to NYC]
 Mike Colameco's food lover's guide to NYC : an insider's guide to New York City's gastronomic delights.
   p. cm.
 Includes index.
 ISBN 978-0-470-04443-8 (pbk.)
 1. Restaurants—New York (State)—New York--Guidebooks. 2. Grocery trade—New York (State)—New York—Guidebooks. 3. New York (N.Y.)—Guidebooks. I. Title. II. Title: Food lover's guide to New York City.
 TX907.3.N72C63 2009
 647.95747—dc22
                              2008044561
Cover Design: Jeff Faust

Front cover photos: top row: 1) Black Star/Alamy, 2) dk/Alamy, 3) Author photo by Yen Dang, 4) Fancy/Veer/Corbis, 5) Image Source/Jupiter Images

Bottom row: 1) City Hall restaurant © courtesy City Hall, 2) JupiterImages.com, 3) Russel Kord/Alamy, 4) Black Star/Alamy

Back cover: 1) ©iStockphoto.com/hidesy, 2) ©iStockphoto.com/Jancouver, 3) ©iStockphoto.com/bluestocking, 4) Author photo by Yen Dang

Spine photos: top; ©iStockphoto.com/Terraxplorer, bottom; ©iStockphoto.com/CostinT

Printed in the United States of America

10 9 8 7 6 5 4 3 2 1

Contents

Acknowledgments

I owe much to many, starting with the unwavering support of my family and friends, my grandmother Nancy DiRenzo, who was such a great cook, the chefs who were my mentors over the years, and the restaurant owners and the countless working chefs and cooks in NYC today who allowed me access to their dining rooms and kitchens. To my editor, Justin Schwartz, who discovered me on PBS and thought I might have a book or two in me. And of course to the revolving team of companions who night after night joined me in all kinds of weather for the thousands of meals required as research.

But I also need to acknowledge New York City itself, this magical place where I moved to in January 1982. The great E.B. White in his short sweet paean, "Here is New York," wrote of the multitudes who arrive here every day as strangers, who come from somewhere else, have pulled up their stakes and have chosen New York as had I, seeking sanctuary, or fulfillment, or some greater or lesser grail...the city of final destination, the city that is a goal....Commuters give the city it's tidal restlessness; natives give it solidity and continuity; but the settlers give it passion. And whether it is a farmer arriving from Italy to set up a small grocery store in a slum, or a young girl arriving from a small town in Mississippi to escape the indignity of being observed by her neighbors, or a boy arriving from the corn belt with a manuscript in his suitcase and a pain in his heart, it makes no difference: each embraces New York with the intense excitement of first love, each absorbs New York with the fresh eyes of the adventurer, each generates heat and light to dwarf the Consolidated Edison Company.

Those words written in a midtown hotel room during a heat wave one summer day in 1948, ring as true today as they did then. For many, New York City represents promise and potential. It's a city of remarkable diversity and relentless optimism, brimming with opportunity and confidence, where the great American ideal of egalitarianism is still very much alive and well.

I hope you enjoy the book, and find it useful, but most importantly enjoy this city for all that it has to offer in the world of food, wine, and beyond.

Introduction

I've used and trusted a few very good guidebooks over the years; my copies of various editions of the great Patricia Wells' *Food Lover's Guide to Paris* are well worn, with notations scrawled in the margins and check marks I've added noting which of her recommendations proved to be priceless. Invariably, over many visits, I agreed with her judgment and sensibility. Years back I felt the same way about Pauline Kael's movie reviews in the *New Yorker*. Faced with a plethora of seemingly good choices, I prefer to turn to someone whose good taste, broad experience, and informed opinions save me the time and expense of having to guess or gamble. In reading current New York restaurant guides, I'm struck by how similar they've all become—dumbed-down and bland, lacking passion, voice, or any recognizable point of view. While these pocket-sized volumes may be useful for checking phone numbers, dress codes, and addresses, their generic three-sentence descriptions of thousands of restaurants fail to provide anywhere near enough information on which to base a sound decision. You're given no sense of the places, the food they serve, or the people behind them. My guide was written to fill that void.

The New York restaurant scene has evolved dramatically over the last decade. For the most part it has moved downtown and has become more casual. Neighborhoods that several years ago had almost no restaurants, such as the Lower East Side, NoLIta, and the meatpacking district, are now some of the hottest areas in the city. Tribeca has become the wealthiest zip code in Manhattan, and it seems everyone wants to be south of 14th Street these days. Upping the ante, visionary chefs such as Nobu Matsuhisa, Jean-Georges Vongerichten, Thomas Keller, and Alain Ducasse have opened restaurants here that continue to push the envelope, restaurants that stand among the best anywhere, adding to New York's stature as a magnet for world-class talent.

That said, I'd also argue that more than a few innovative restaurants from previous decades that are consistently voted to the top of these "best of" lists year after year are in large measure coasting on their reputations. The food press and the legions of publicists employed by the chefs and owners tend to act solely as cheerleaders and sycophants, creating an echo chamber of positive feedback wherein if enough people say it's good, well, then it has to be. Take, for example, Zak Pelaccio. While I have no doubt that he can cook, I've also had some really bad meals at both the Fatty Crab and 5 Ninth, where the cooking is remarkably inconsistent and the staff scatterbrained, distracted, and just plain poorly trained. Perhaps an even better example would be David Chang, who indeed has a certain dazzle and imagination, but Ssam Bar may have been the most overhyped restaurant of the year back in 2007. After he won the coveted James Beard Rising Star Chef award that year, he honestly proclaimed amazement, and stated that he felt as if he was living a real-life scene from *The Truman Show.* His honesty and self-effacement were a breath of fresh air in an industry that teems with unchecked egos, though later fluff pieces in *GQ* and elsewhere made me wonder. In truth, it has been my experience that the talent pool in New York is so deep that there are many excellent chefs working on the fringes, in restaurants that operate under the radar yet provide food and service equal to and often better than those celebrated handful who are the darlings of the media year in and year out.

The opinions expressed in this book come from a lifetime of experience in the business. I started cooking at age 13 in the Philadelphia suburbs and worked in kitchens through junior high, high school, and two years of college prior to attending and graduating from the Culinary Institute of America in 1982. I moved to New York the day after graduation and spent the next decade working in some very good kitchens here as a cook, sous chef, and executive chef.

As was the case for many chefs and restaurateurs of my era, while working in New York during the 1980s, all my summer vacations were organized around European restaurant tours. Reservations were made months in advance, and we'd dine throughout France, Italy, Germany, Switzerland, Spain, and England, at nearly all the Michelin three-star restaurants, many of the two-stars, and countless wonderful, unheralded local restaurants featuring authentic, rustic regional cuisines. In those days there was nothing like that in America. In order to develop, to train your palate and aesthetic, traveling through Europe and working at stages in various restaurants there was a must. In our business there are no post-graduate degrees that matter; essentially it comes down to travel, dining out, cooking in different kitchens under great chefs, and then trying to re-create the flavors from memory while developing your own original style. Over the years (and after many thousands of dollars invested in travel expenses and meals taken here and there) one develops a trained palate and a veteran's sense of how restaurants should be run, both in the front and back of the house.

The entries included in this book are new restaurants of merit, as well as the places I've frequented over the years that still, after many visits, maintain my interest and stand out in a city with so many options. I've tried to be selective as best I know how. I don't rate restaurants; if they are in this book, I simply like them very much. Ratings tend to be arbitrary, unreliable, and utterly subjective. I am a huge fan of good food and am an unabashed omnivore; I live to eat. I've tried to cover as many options as possible in all price ranges. Should you have $5 or $500 to spend on a meal, you'll learn where to find New York's best, from hot dogs, pizza, dumplings, and sandwiches to bistros, delis, ethnic options, and twelve-course tasting menus.

Methodology

There is a new and somewhat disturbing trend these days—everyone wants to be the first to review a new place. Blogs, Web sites, and the younger generation, who get most of their restaurant information from such Web sites, have pushed the envelope. Simply post a construction permit in the window and Eater.com or Curbed.com has it posted as a story by the day's end, with rumors about who's involved, the expectant crowd, the scene, and what it may be like on opening night. Once open, any new restaurant within a week can expect to have been covered by Eater, RestaurantGirl, Gothamist, NYMag.com, the Strong Buzz, Citysearch, and a dozen other new sites, replete with photos, descriptions, and verdicts. If being first in the door is that important, then none do it better than these and their ilk. I'll give blogs credit where due—in some cases these postings are a testimonial to the experience of the average customer, as opposed to the experience of professional restaurant reviewers, who are often favored by better tables and, in some ways, better food. In theory, the bloggers have democratized restaurant criticism. By reading about their experiences, one may be able to derive some valuable information about a restaurant: the scene, the service, the food, and the vibe. Though I caution that some of the bigger, most active Web sites are run by people who are in contact each and every day with the big New York City restaurant publicists, who want them in early and are more than willing to pay for the meal—"comp" them, in industry parlance—and in return expect favorable press, I only see blogs becoming more and more popular.

That said, there are opinions and then there are informed opinions. When I read some of the writing and many of the threads on chat boards, I'm struck by the lack of experience, the lack of familiarity with ingredients and styles, and the general amateurishness of the "criticism." I prefer to give a restaurant time; often there is an organic growth and learning curve required until the restaurant gets it right. In opening a restaurant, there are a lot of moving parts. It takes a while for the kitchen staff to coalesce and work well as a team, to learn the menu and style, to get a feel for the equipment, and to execute under the pressure of a busy night. It takes time to locate the right ingredient purveyors and time again for the front of the house to learn the room and menu and to work with the kitchen staff and chef effectively as a team. Ask anyone who has ever been involved with a new restaurant opening and they'll tell you—it takes a while. Restaurants mature and develop much in the way that most new enterprises do, but these days in this business there is no such thing as a dress rehearsal or a soft opening, though to my mind there should be a grace period. As an analogy, Broadway plays open up in Providence, Pittsburgh, Philadelphia, or New Haven, and have dozens of performances there to work out the logistics and figure out "live" what is good and what's not as good, what works and what doesn't. They shift and change and polish their act before they make their Broadway debut. Restaurants too need a gestational period to develop, mature, and get it right.

The role of the modern restaurant critic has changed from the service it was a generation ago to more of a modern stylistic commentary these days. I'm not against blogs or Web sites. Many of them are accessible and well designed, and some are even very well written. But I still question how sound the judgments are, how informed the opinions are, and how reliable these instant verdicts, based on one or two early visits, really can be. Writing well is one thing, but really understanding cooking, process, ingredients, wines, service, and the subtle nuances of the restaurant business is quite another. In reading many of these blogs over the last few years, I've come to wonder what qualifications many of these critics bring to the table, aside from being clever, having good writing skills, and displaying a snarky, quick wit. Perhaps, in this increasingly blogosphere-dominated world, old-school qualifications as such are beside the point—though I hope not.

As open-minded as we all strive to be in our opinions, for each of us there are simply some qualities that we admire over others, and in making judgments, we weight these accordingly. This may be even more true with food, chefs, dining rooms, and styles of cooking—objectivity is nearly impossible. Take, for example, a big trend in 2007: young, well-trained chefs, fresh off long apprenticeships in some of New York's best kitchens, set out on their own, opening small, relatively humble eateries all over town—places such as Shorty's 32, Dell'anima, Bar Blanc, Smith's, and Market Table, to name a few. What characterized these restaurants were the humble reach and the scope and design of the menus. These chefs had worked in three- and four-star restaurants but were now seeking affordable rents for smaller settings to pursue their own projects in a city where that is increasingly difficult to do. They weren't aiming for the bleachers—they just wanted to cook good, simple, honest food. And in many cases, they were the ones doing the actual cooking on the line each night. That's a trend I champion, and that's why you'll see many of those restaurants in this book. Call it a bias, fine, but I welcome this new informality and the idea of chefs paring down ambitions and concentrating on cooking, often doing the lion's share of the cooking themselves.

I've dined at every restaurant in this book multiple times, generally once without being announced and again after speaking with the chef and owner, often spending time with them in the kitchen. Sometimes on these follow-up visits I get a bill, and other times I don't. Being comped, or dining as a guest of the house, has no effect on my opinions. Free food doesn't curry favor. It can be argued effectively for a variety of reasons that critics should never eat free, that in fact they should order off the menu, pick their own food, dine with friends who do the same, and in this way replicate the experience of an "average" diner. I agree with this philosophy. However, as we all know, the major restaurant critics in town are employees of newspapers or magazines and as such have generous expense accounts. They dine out five or six nights a week and never actually pay out of their own pockets for any meal they eat; their publishers pay for them. For you and me, dining out costs money, real money, our money, and I believe that it does make a difference in terms of value and perception. I'm generally a lot less picky if I'm spending someone else's money or eating for free. We all are; it's only natural.

As far as getting special treatment once they know me, sure I do, but let's be honest about anonymity. As determined as New York restaurant critics are to remain unrecognized and dine like everyone else, any good restaurant has head shots of all the major restaurant critics posted in the kitchens and tucked discreetly by the reservation book. Restaurants keep lists of the various aliases critics use to book tables as well as what they tend to eat and drink and the size of the parties they characteristically dine with. Whether they like to admit it or not, most critics are recognized on their first or second visit. I know of a very famous restaurant that combed through all of Frank Bruni's reviews from his first year at the *Times* and found a pattern in his likes and dislikes regarding certain ingredients and cooking styles. When Mr. Bruni dined at this establishment, it was no surprise that the tasting menus he was offered often included many of those same ingredients, flavor combinations, and cooking styles for which he'd shown a personal preference in the past.

Outing a Former Critic

As William Grimes is no longer the restaurant critic for the *New York Times,* I can write this without blowing his cover. Below is his description from one restaurant.

While veteran critics such as Mimi Sheraton, Gael Greene, and Ruth Reichl often went to elaborate lengths to disguise themselves with makeup, wigs, body padding, and even entire theatrical outfits in order to go unrecognized, they often were spotted by alert front-of-the-house staff nonetheless. And really, how much difference does it make? Critics come

WILLIAM GRIMES/*NEW YORK TIMES* FOOD CRITIC

Weight: Thin

Dress: Conservative dresser, sometimes a little more casual depending on venue

Hair: Thin, longish, graying slightly, messily parted on the side

Looks: Looks a little professorial, wears fairly thick rounded wire-framed glasses, contacts maybe, long thin nose, slightly weak chin

Ordering: Will pay close attention to wine list, often tries several glasses or bottles

Reservation Aliases (such a list would have included phone numbers)

1. Arthur Davis
2. Alan Ward
3. Ron De Feo
4. Peter Nichols
5. Marilyn Minden
6. Peter Richards
7. Gary Wells
8. Franc De Falco
9. Robert Kugel
10. Paul Moore
11. Alex Ward
12. R. Roberts
13. Alan Barker (from his most recent reservation)

Credit Card Names:

William Grimes
Nancy Grimes
Paul Moore
Richard Roberts
James Stevens (from his most recent reservation)

to eat with friends, often in groups of four or five. Even if the restaurants they visit know they are coming, they have no idea ahead of time what they may order. So a good restaurant need not worry—they make great food every night for every customer, and simply take even more care for a critic. At establishments where discipline and quality ingredients are lacking, can they make old fish fresh again? Can they turn average choice meat into dry-aged prime? Can ill-constructed sauces be improved upon in just a few minutes? Or what if several of the young cooks, the weakest links on the kitchen chain, were unsupervised, showed up late, or simply had too much work to do in too little time, and several main courses or appetizers were not prepped correctly that day? By the time the food is ordered, it's too late. Nothing can be done.

You simply can't make bad food good just for a critic. You can't suddenly teach an undisciplined kitchen discipline for serving one table. I think too much is made of this idea that critics can receive food that is that much better than what the restaurant serves others. Yes, critics can get special service, and yes, only the best and most trusted cooks or the chef him- or herself may personally cook the meal, but can the results change drastically compared to what other diners get? No, not really. In cooking for VIP clients, great restaurants will shine, average ones will do their average best, and the others will stumble or worse.

A Brief History of Modern Chefdom

The job description, associated prestige, and public awareness of restaurant chefs in America has changed dramatically in the last quarter century. The image of an anonymous, ruddy-faced, portly man, hat tilted to the side, long apron drawn over starched whites, tirelessly tending to the stoves, chopping, dicing, stirring, tasting, and supervising his brigade, seems almost quaint now. Yet there are still quite a few chefs whose days are spent exactly this way. In one sense, today's chefs will certainly do more paperwork than their predecessors did—scheduling, ordering, and designing new menus, all the while keeping a watchful eye on the revenue side and managing food and labor costs percentages. Yet, more significantly, the reach of the modern chef has expanded well beyond the kitchen. In addition to the chef being directly involved with the training, education, and supervision of the cooks, the industry today encourages the chef to be equally involved with the wait staff. This change certainly has made restaurants more interesting places to visit. This specific aspect of modern chefdom, the chef's role out of the kitchen, is the hallmark of the modern restaurant era, effectively breaking down the wall between the front and back of the house that had existed for centuries.

Historically this is a very new phenomenon, though when we look back in history we can point to three chefs who were pivotal to this change: Antoine Carême, Auguste Escoffier, and Fernand Point. It took Carême and then Escoffier to write what would become the recipes that solidified French haute cuisine. Carême is considered the first celebrity chef, and his book *L'Art de la Cuisine Française,* in six volumes, was the first treatise of its kind. On Carême's shoulders, the great Escoffier wrote *Le Guide Culinaire* in 1903, a book that is still in print, graces the shelves of most chefs I know, and is an oft-used reference text in culinary schools. These two chefs, their work, and their recipes created the basis for what is considered classical French cuisine, still taught and practiced today in cooking schools and kitchens around the world. But it was the great chef Fernand Point who would usher in the modern era.

Point's philosophy on cooking, simply put, was to buy the very best ingredients, process them minimally, cook and season them perfectly, and don't get in the way. The "market chefs" of today, including Alice Waters, Dan Barber, Bill Telepan, and Peter Hoffman, to name just a few, are following in Point's footsteps. His emphasis that food should taste like what it is, that the pure flavors of ingredients shouldn't be masked or altered, was the foundation for the next generation of chefs and the best of what is taking place around New York today. Prior to Point, French cooking was very heavy and driven by complicated techniques that involved transforming or masking the ingredients (at least in part because much of this style of cooking developed prior to refrigeration). Read old cookbooks and they'll have you poach a whole salmon for an hour and a half or longer. The art of cooking in those days balanced the needs of hygiene and food safety, using proteins that were often well past their prime, with end goals of flavor. Point's emphasis on freshness, local ingredients, and a far lighter style of cooking presaged what we now have come to accept as the modern style.

Not surprisingly, many of the most influential French chefs of the 1960s and 1970s traveled to Viennes, France, as young men to work under Point at his restaurant, La Pyramide. These young Frenchmen—including the brothers Pierre and Jean Troisgros, Paul Bocuse, Bernard Loiseau, Alain Chapel, Louis Outhier, François Bise, and Raymond Thuilier, to name just a few—became the chefs who would in turn train the first generation of the great American chefs to follow. Today, more than 50 years after Point's death, his shadow still looms large. Thomas Keller's favorite cookbook was written by Point and given to Keller as young man by the obscure but talented French chef Roland Henin. Alain Ducasse, arguably one of the most influential chefs of this era or any other, was himself a disciple of Chapel, who trained with Point. New

York's own darling Jean-Georges Vongerichten studied under both Outhier and Bocuse, two of Point's best-known protégés.

However, the most important change that Point brought to bear outside of cuisine was to create the new role of chef/owner, so common in the industry today, where chefs commonly change into clean whites, often over dress shirt and tie, and work the dining room during service. Point was the first chef to do this. He placed the chef in the limelight, dealing directly with customers and working the dining room floor. He broke down that last barrier separating chefs from their dining public. All working chefs today owe a debt of gratitude to Point for liberating them from the kitchen side of those swinging doors. The dining public too should be grateful to Point, for making chefs and their kitchens accessible.

Chefs as Brands

It is not at all uncommon for chefs today to have publicists and media trainers, do television and radio appearances, cook live at benefits, and write books, all the while promoting their restaurants and themselves. For the first time in American history, the names of many chefs are common knowledge. This is due in large part to a groundswell of public interest and respect for all things food-related that coincided with the popularity of cooking as entertainment, a genre initially introduced by PBS and then expanded greatly by the Food Network and cable TV. The phenomenon of the star chef was born. Though they represent a tiny fraction of the industry, these chefs are brand-building jet-setters, backed by financiers with very deep pockets. Their names, and to some degree their reputations, are attached to multiple projects, often across multiple time zones if not continents. They have retail product lines of sauces, soups, marinades, and frozen pizzas, as well as signature lines of pots and pans, knives, and other kitchen gadgets. As the rapper Jay Z put it, "I'm not a businessman, I'm a business . . . man," and surely he knows all about branding and self-promotion. But the restaurant business differs greatly from the entertainment business—it's about consistently great service in pleasant surroundings, paired with great food. Historically, the reason most chefs ran a single establishment and stayed put in their restaurants was to ensure this quality each and every night. This time-tested model remains a very reliable formula to guarantee consistency. It's fair to ask who is doing the cooking and supervising the cooks if the chef is not in the kitchen. A while back, I interviewed the great British chef Marco Pierre White for my *Food Talk* program on WOR Radio, and he stated flat out that when he began to travel and leave his base kitchen while customers were spending thousands of dollars a night at his restaurant and he was not there to cook for them, he felt he was a fraud. It's the main reason he closed the restaurant. I suppose it's an old-fashioned ethic, but he and I both agreed that a chef's place is in his or her own kitchen and that customers deserve to know who is doing the cooking.

While the modern chef has the potential to earn an income that's many multiples of what his predecessors could dream of, it comes at a cost to customers. Delegation in the workplace is a fine idea, but as chefs spread themselves thin, the cooking at their various outposts reflects this. For me, the best restaurants are the ones where the chef is on premises. Yes, I know, some interesting and important exceptions come to mind—Per Se, Alain Ducasse, Daniel Boulud, and Jean Georges, among others—but there are exceptions to every rule, and later on I'll explain how these talented few manage to pull it off where most others fail. Businesses run best when the brains and talent behind the operation are present to maintain standards, inspire excellence, and take part in the creative process, pushing the group effort further. Orchestras perform best under great conductors; as talented as the Yankees in their best season were individually, it was Joe Torre who pulled them all together and brought out the best in them as a team. When chefs overreach, their restaurants start to run like franchises. Call me old-fashioned, but I still prefer to eat in places where the chef is present.

New York Today

New York City is considered by many to be the restaurant capital of the planet. The last 25 years have been a golden age in terms of the quality of cooking and the number of new restaurants and restaurant neighborhoods that have blossomed all over town. Those of us who have been a part of this scene—as cooks, chefs, or the dining public—have witnessed firsthand one of the most remarkable eras in the history of cuisine. When Americans decide we are interested in something, as we have in the last few decades with food and wine, we move fast. A culture that was eating canned vegetables, TV dinners, and Wonder bread a generation ago can now boast of its world-class bakeries, artisanal cheeses, organic farms, heirloom fruits and vegetables, heritage-breed livestock, pristine day-boat line-caught fish, diver scallops, wild mushrooms from all over the country, microbreweries, and fine wines. Cooking schools are springing up everywhere, with waiting lists to get in. What was once considered a blue-collar dead-end career now attracts talent from across the board. Working-class kids from small-town America are joined by Ivy League graduates and well-paid professionals who walked away from lucrative jobs, all lining up for the opportunity to peel carrots at the French Laundry, Charlie Trotter's, or Le Bernardin.

America has become food-obsessed, and no place more so than New York. Nowhere else will you find the sheer number of restaurants combined with this city's ethnic diversity. In terms of talent, pick any one of New York's top 50 restaurants, move it to any other city in the country, and it would very likely be the best restaurant in town. Our great restaurants are now, for the first time, equal to the superb Michelin three-star establishments abroad. It's no surprise, then, that Michelin chose New York for its first-ever American guide. What has come together in the last 25 years is a critical mass combining remarkable domestic ingredients, an international talent pool of mature chefs all cooking in their prime, and an enthusiastic cooperative public willing to fund it all—in short, the magical confluence of commerce and creativity. While some may bemoan the rise of the $44 lamb chop, the truth is that cooking in New York has never been better than it is today, and the restaurant scene has never been more vibrant or diverse.

As for that diversity, you can eat virtually anything from anywhere within 45 minutes of midtown. This is one of the city's great distinguishing features. While New York always has been home to immigrants, these populations have soared over the last decade. Among the first businesses they open are restaurants, for that taste of home. While one can surely eat very well in Paris, it's all about French cuisine there, and ethnic options are limited—a little Moroccan here, a few Chinese restaurants, but who goes to Paris for Italian food or sushi? You can eat incredibly well all over Italy, but is there a single Korean restaurant to be found anywhere in Rome? Throughout New York's long history, it has attracted immigrants from both inside the country and abroad whose talent, ambition, and vision have enriched and informed this cultural fabric unique among urban centers. No wonder, then, that this city, which has long been a world center for banking, advertising, publishing, and the arts, the city that hosts the United Nations, is also the United Nations of the food world. The most recent New York census revealed that 2.9 million New Yorkers are foreign-born. In Elmhurst, Queens, immigrants comprise 7 out of 10 residents, making it one of 17 neighborhoods where the majority of the population was born outside the United States. Amidst all this culinary and cultural cross-pollination, it's no surprise that a snapshot of the city from 2006 reveals that for years the owner of the venerable Eisenberg's Sandwich Shop, in the Flatiron district since 1929, was Korean; the fellow who made your pizza at Totonno's, one of the city's best pizzerias, in business since 1924, is from Tibet; and those great frothy egg creams at the Lower East Side fixture Gem Spa are now expertly prepared by Jay Naryane, from Gujarat, India. Some of the best handmade pasta in the city is being made daily by well-trained chefs from Mexico or Peru. Your sushi and sashimi at the three-star Hatsuhana may have been made by a native of Puebla, Mexico. The great caviar, smoked salmon, and sturgeon at Sable's Smoked Fish on the Upper East Side were purchased and hand-cut by the owner, born and raised in Hong Kong. The opening chef at Marseilles, a French Moroccan restaurant in the theater district, was from the Dominican Republic. One of the best Persian restaurants in town is led by a chef who hails from Thailand. Oh, and by the way, I recently met an American chef who prepared wonderfully authentic Korean meals nightly during her stint as the executive chef at Woo Lae Oak in SoHo. Well, folks, that's New York.

Of late the scene has moved casual and downtown in a big way. The old established residential neighborhoods such the Upper East Side have fallen out of favor as a younger generation of New Yorkers, both singles and those with families, now increasingly choose to live and dine downtown. Most of the more interesting restaurant openings these days are below 23rd Street. The Lower East Side and the West Village are hotbeds of talent, while uptown giants such as Le Cirque now struggle for relevancy. Things have changed radically since the mid-1990s—dining is becoming more casual, and as the crowds skew younger, they are looking for different things from restaurants. Designers now pay attention to all aspects of dining rooms, from color schemes to lighting, to ensure that people look good and feel comfortable. In many ways the new informal restaurant scene has replaced the old club scene, where guys go to meet girls, and vice versa. Food matters, but so does the vibe, the sound track, the bar, the scene. Like it or not, for many diners it's about seeing and being seen. This younger generation of restaurant-goers brings an energy and velocity to the restaurant scene unique to their generation, along with their likes, dislikes, and peculiar tastes. In time, I suppose, as they age, the scene too will mature to suit their sensibilities and tastes, all of which is good, healthy, and normal. I don't resist or lament these changes. In fact, I'm thrilled that "kids" today (FYI, in my book that's anyone under 40) take restaurants and dining out so seriously and spend as much time, energy, and money on it as they do. It keeps the scene improving and evolving each and every day.

Selection Criteria

Choosing which establishments would be included in this book was no easy task in such a great culinary city. First and foremost, there has to be a certain "New Yorkness" to the place. I look for how and where each establishment fits into the greater fabric of its era, neighborhood, ethnicity, and place. This immediately rules out national restaurant chains and stores, as well as franchises or theme restaurants that, while maintaining a New York address, could just as easily be housed in a strip mall in Cincinnati. As previously stated, I also prefer establishments where the owners and chefs are hands-on and can be found working most days at the store. Not that this in and of itself is a guarantee of anything—goodness knows there are plenty of terrible restaurants with the owners present each and every day, and chefs toiling long hours who still somehow haven't learned how to cook. But in the right hands, with proper staff training and supervision, great restaurants thrive under the stewardship of working professionals, owners who are present. I look for restaurants that reflect the personality and point of view of the owners and chefs, and as such are far more interesting and worth visiting. Anyone who has ever been employed in the food service industry knows that the staff simply performs better under the watchful eye of an owner who works the floor. The cooks are more mindful, more careful, less likely to take shortcuts or serve mistakes when the owner is on hand, in and out of the kitchen, forever checking the plates and tasting things. Chefs who spend time working the pass or cooking in their own kitchens during service maintain a level of consistency lacking in those places where the chef is frequently absent.

I'm not a fan of restaurants where ownership views them as simply another business, delivering a generous return on their investment. For me restaurants are very different from dry cleaners, pharmacies, muffler shops, or nail salons. It is perfectly reasonable for businessmen with certain acumen to turn to food service and see opportunity, but the restaurants they create invariably are missing something. They lack soul. While Steve Hanson or Jeffrey Chodorow may be the two most successful restaurant operators in the city, nearly all of their restaurants leave me cold.

As to the food itself, I ascribe to the philosophy of the great chef Fernand Point, who once stated that at its best, "food should taste like what it is." Chefs should purchase the best ingredients, understand their natural flavors and characteristics, decide on the best way to prepare them for each dish, combine elements on a plate that work harmoniously, cook them as best they can, and not get in the way. It's not so different from the essence of the Hippocratic oath: do no harm. If you have great ingredients, then you should cook them with respect. At the end of the day it's all about turning the simplest ingredients into the sublime. I'm not a fan of designer food, of foam and dots and flavorless squiggles of sauce here and there. Tall food was a silly construct. Tasteless microgreens and pretty hydroponic salads are a waste of space on the plate. Pointless, inedible garnishes should be outlawed. Turning the familiar into the bizarre should be left to novelists, playwrights, filmmakers, and other artists.

So there you have it. Those are my terms. If you like good food, regardless of whether your budget is $5, $40, or $500, then stay with me and read on.

The RESTAURANTS

Abboccato

212-265-4000
136 West 55th Street, between
Fifth and Sixth Avenues
Casual to business
Reservations
Moderate to expensive
All major credit cards accepted
Breakfast, lunch, and dinner
seven days a week
N, Q, R, W trains to 57th Street
station

This was the third New York City restaurant opened and run by the ambitious Livanos family, Greek immigrants who started in the diner business on Long Island and now own three excellent restaurants, Oceana, Molyvos, and Abboccato, all within a few blocks of one another in midtown. It's easy to walk past this place housed midblock between Sixth and Seventh Avenues and just next to the entrance to the Blakely Hotel, formerly the Gorham Hotel, an older brick-front midlevel business hotel directly across the street from the City Center performance space. The dining room is narrow and long, running deep into the building, with the kitchen to the rear. There are a few tables on the sidewalk, and a few more in the front near the windows, but most of the room is down a few steps past the bar. It tends to be dark, even at lunch, with no natural light, and the crowd skews older, with many business types in suits. The ceiling is low, beamed, and covered with white stucco, the walls covered in brick, stone, white leather, and beige leather, accented with natural wood, and lit by lamps made from wrought iron arranged here and there. Though all new, it kind of has a sixties feel to it, like split-level houses—not really my scene, but the food is very good.

Chef Jim Botsacos, who works around the corner at Molyvos, is billed as the chef-partner, but the day-to-day cooking here is done by the talented Jake Addeo, the chef de cuisine. Jake worked and studied in Italy, then returned to New York to work in two fine restaurants: Felidia under Lidia Bastianich and Esca under Dave Pasternak. His training in those kitchens shows here. His pastas are all very good, and he has a deft hand with seafood as well. Fritto misto arrives presented in a folded white napkin, a small tower of mixed polenta-laced deep-fried fish, squid, shrimp, whiting, and clam strips, topped with shards of pickled white onion and fried parsley. Ricotta gnocchi, with a light, fresh tomato sauce accented with julienned basil, are perfect, like little clouds, light and flavorful; the pink sauce is mild and almost sweet. The crudo plates are very nice, a nod to his days with Dave Pasternak. Sea urchin in its shell gains richness from the addition of an olive oil gelato, cut by the sweet acidity from slices of Meyer lemon confit. Fluke arrives drizzled with olive oil, snapper topped with shards of hot pepper, all very nice. Try the ravioli of beets and gorgonzola in season, or the spaghettini with razor clams and their juice, crunchy sautéed dried bread crumbs, and thin slices of botarga to round it all out. The spaghetti alla chitarra, made with many extra egg yolks and cut over drawn wires, is a specialty of Abruzzo, and here is toothsome, rich, and delicious paired with clams, foie gras, and fresh ricotta, bound by a walnut-sage balsamic butter sauce. In winter months, the braised meats stand out. Tripe braised and then pressed and grilled is nice, the veal shank is excellent, and suckling pig braised in milk with a smooth potato puree does the trick.

The wine list is good, a bit on the expensive side but well put together, and all Italian save for one Champagne. Desserts are solid. Panna cotta is served a variety of ways, usually with fruit. The warm, light fried bomboloni, paired with fruit and vanilla mascarpone, are a nice dessert to share. The staff are good, some a bit young and green, but they try hard. In this part of town, a short walk to theaters and offices, Italian cooking at this level is very hard to find.

Aburiya Kinnosuke

212-867-5454
213 East 45th Street, between Second and Third Avenues
Casual to dressy
Reservations
Moderate
All major credit cards accepted
Lunch and dinner Monday–Friday, dinner Saturday and Sunday
4, 5, 6, 7, S trains to 42nd Street/Grand Central station

I'm really not sure how to describe this place. I have no reference for this kind of food, but apparently a lot of Japanese businessmen and expats do, as they pack it nightly. This style of dining and restaurant is known as Izakaya and allows the dinner guests to create a casual small-plate-based tasting menu derived from top-shelf ingredients, as well as some rather odd cuts along the way mixing fried foods with broiled and Robata charcoal grilling.

The room is clean and well lit, and it features shades of beige, blending rice paper with natural wood and small hanging curtains for private booth dining. I'm told these places are very popular in Japan: the menu is essentially a broad selection of good but, to us, odd snack foods designed to accompany alcohol consumption, with larger, more substantial dishes of rice or noodles to end the meal. The menu is large and mostly unfamiliar; the main feature, though, is grilling, which you can do tableside on one of the charcoal-fired shichirin grills, or they can grill for you in the kitchen. Tableside grilling has never been my thing, even at the many Korean BBQ places around town, where it seems every table is in the midst of a galbi cook-off. I prefer to have my food cooked in the kitchen by the chefs, not by me tableside. Here you are given either fish or meat, with the instruction to coat it with red miso and chopped scallions and then wait. That's not my idea of precision, so I'll pass.

Instead, try the items cooked in the kitchen off the robata grill, from which weird but delicious cuts such as salmon neck, pork cheek, sea eel, and tuna collar emerge, cooked and plated, for your enjoyment. Start with dried shark fin (fukahire)—for me this was a first, and at this place I'm sure you'll have a few firsts as well. Black sesame tofu arrives almost custard-like in a small ceramic bowl with little wooden spoons; the sea salt served on the side brings out the flavor nuances nicely. The home-made tofu basket is another great starter. The texture is delicate, and the sea salt really opens up the flavors. If they have Berkshire pork simmered in brown sugar and soju, order it. The chicken meatballs (tsukune) are very popular, but I can't figure out quite why. Instead try the vegetable side dishes, either simmered, steamed, pickled, or preserved, such as the carrots, burdock root, bamboo shoots, or crunchy lotus root braised in a soy-based sauce. The foil-wrapped salmon is darn good, as are matsutake mushroom tempura and the eel hotpot (I love eel). They have a kaiseki tasting menu that I've heard is very, very good, but as of this writing I have yet to try it. For dessert, try the custard-smooth sesame pudding. The sake collection is impressive.

The service is spotty if you don't speak Japanese, but I can live with that. In some ways, as the place caters mainly to Japanese expats, it makes it that much more authentic in an era when generic ethnic dining is more than trend.

Adour

212-720-2277
2 East 55th Street, in the St. Regis Hotel, between Fifth and Madison Avenues
Dressy
Reservations
Expensive
All major credit cards accepted
Dinner seven nights a week
E, V trains to Fifth Avenue/ 53rd Street station; 4, 5, 6, N, R, W trains to Lexington Avenue/59th Street station

I was a huge fan of the old Ducasse restaurant when it was on the 58th Street side of the Essex House—it was, on any given night, the best res-taurant in town. But that run was rather short-lived. The opening was a PR and conceptual disaster and initial reviews were tepid at best, though four stars did come later on. It took New Yorkers a long time to warm up to the place, and in truth it took Ducasse a long time to learn that we do things differently here. Sadly, it closed in 2005 after five years. So when news came that Ducasse was reopening in the old Lespinasse space, I was thrilled. Lespinasse was a legendary room, where chef Gray Kunz, followed by Christian Delouvrier, earned four stars and cooked some of the best food New Yorkers have even eaten.

But Adour was never meant to re-create the old Ducasse, nor Lespinasse. Its aim is to be more casual, less upmarket. The name comes from a river that ran through the Landes regions of southwestern France, where Ducasse was born and raised on a small working farm. In all fairness, I've had only a few meals there, and they took place right after the restaurant opened in February 2008, so they still needed to get some kinks out.

By way of comparison, it's nearly impossible not to compare Adour with Bar Boulud across town. Both opened just a month or so apart, both are the efforts of great chefs, and both are wine-centric in concept. That said, Daniel Boulud is a New York chef. He understands this city and its ways like very few others, and so Bar Boulud strikes the perfect tone in terms of design, concept, and delivery. The space is grand yet casual, the lines in the dining room are clean, the effect is open and minimal, the food is wonderful, and the atmosphere is relaxed. Adour is done up in the Ducasse style, an elite line extension of an ultra-luxury brand. David Rockwell was the architect, and the room, gilded and rich, in no way resembles the room that housed Lespinasse before it. Wherever you sit you'll be flanked on all sides by backlit glass walls, behind which the extensive wine collection is on display in temperature-controlled caves. Comfortable banquettes form the perimeter, with free-standing tables in the center. There are lots of curving custom wood installations, alcoves, and leather upholstery; the ceiling is framed by thick, grand moldings, the restaurant interior walls are formed from floor-to-ceiling glass panels decorated with a pattern of vines and their leaves etched in platinum leaf, and a large chandelier frames the center of the room.

You enter up the stairs from the street past the more public Astor Court restaurant, and then past the small (four-seat) interactive wine bar or "library," where you can eat and drink, matching wines to your food utilizing a space-age touch-screen menu set into the bar. This screen allows you to explore wine and food pairings by region and varietals simply by moving your fingers across a screen—quite a nifty toy. The main dining room is around the corner, with four smaller "lounges"—a bit more private, each with three tables—set off on the corners. Service is formal and the staff well trained. The look and feel is of luxury dining anywhere on the planet; I don't get a sense of New York today when I'm there. This space has no exterior windows, so once seated, you are transported from midtown New York to Ducasse-land.

The official concept here is cuisine designed with wine in mind. Each and every dish was tested to be very wine-friendly. To that end, the sommelier accepts the challenge of pairing a single bottle of wine, or a single varietal, with the whole meal, claiming that the food not only can work with a single bottle but in fact show off the range of the wine across all the courses. As to the food, it's very good as the menu was designed by the old chef from the previous Ducasse location, Tony Esnault, who has since been replaced by Joel Dennis, his longtime sous chef who was formerly of TRU in Chicago. The plates are busy, but the cooking always shows great precision and accuracy. The wine list is strong, courtesy of wine director Thomas Combescot. Early on the food seemed a bit forced, a bit too thought out, the kitchen a bit tight and nervous; I'd suspect that as of this printing, the kitchen is more relaxed and the whole concept has gelled and matured. In visiting this restaurant, expect to spend a good deal of money but enjoy dish after dish prepared with great thought given to ingredient selection, combinations, cooking methods, and balance. The word *refinement* perhaps sums it up best.

Needless to say, for its first month or two, the restaurant played host to every major chef, food writer, critic, and foodie in town. During one of my visits the first week they were open, Wylie Dufresne was dining with his wife, and Paul Liebrandt was seated directly behind me. A few nights later you'd find François Payard, Gabriel Kreuther, Michael Romano, and husband-and-wife team Karen Page and Andrew Dornenburg, armed with an infrared digital wine thermometer to be certain their glasses of Champagne were exactly 43.5°F (they were). While I wish the place in general had a more relaxed feel to it, I can assure you that the food and service will be beyond reproach.

Alfama

212-645-2500
551 Hudson Street, at the
corner of Perry Street
Casual
Reservations
Moderate
All major credit cards accepted
Dinner Monday–Friday, lunch
and dinner Saturday and
Sunday
1 train to Christopher Street
station

As good as Spanish food is, it took New York City a long time to warm to it and for decent Spanish restaurants and tapas bars to open and stay in business. So perhaps Alfama is an early entry into what may be the Portuguese push. The food in Portugal is very good, driven of course by ingredients, and features seafood, especially cod.

The exterior of this restaurant is painted a bright white that almost reminds you of the sun-bleached whitewashed stucco buildings in coastal European towns. Deep blue awnings are set above the large windows. You enter through an old-fashioned wooden doorway on the street corner and into the main room. When the weather permits they have tables outside beneath those awnings. The interior is bright and cheery, with a good-sized cherrywood bar and tables and chairs filling out the room. It is a neighborhood hangout, so even on slow nights it does a decent business with West Village locals. The Portuguese for generations have been great sailors and fishermen. Many of the Portuguese families that moved to North America hundreds of years ago established our great East Coast port towns such as New Bedford and Gloucester as commercial fisheries. In fact, this establishment is named after an ancient Portuguese fishing village. The flavors are big here, the portion sizes decent, and the prices reasonable.

Start with caldo verdo, a rich soup with chunks of potato, collard greens, and slices of chouriço sausage, or the big bowl of steamed top neck clams in a briny broth scented with garlic, fresh cilantro leaves, and lemon juice. Shrimp are marinated in red pepper paste, then pan-seared and served over a white bean salad with citrus accents. Little meatballs are formed from pork and shrimp, a combination the Chinese love to play with as well. Here they are served over a rich tomato-based Macanese sauce, a nod to the Portuguese seafarers of yore who visited Macau. A flambé of chouriço comes on its own cast-iron mini-stove, but even better is the selection of smoked sausages served with garlic-infused olives and good bread. Bacalhau, salt cod, an Old World staple famous in Portugal and elsewhere, is offered three ways. My favorite is the dish billed as Bacalhau Espiritual, the fish pureed, blended with potato and small shrimp, and served under a gratin crust of dried, seasoned bread crumbs and São Jorge cheese. Skate wing is dusted with paprika, sautéed, served with a mix of pearl onions, peppers, mushrooms and tomatoes, and garnished with a cheese fondue. If it's meat you're after, try the stone-grilled filet mignon, or better yet the rabbit braised in Madeira served over lentils laced with carrots, turnips, pepper, peas, and garlic confit.

The wine list, put together by Tarcisio Costa, features a great selection of Portuguese reds and whites, as well as more than 40 different bottles of port to choose from. Service is good, though it seems English is a second or third language for most on the floor. Check for weekday deals such as the Monday three-course $25 prix fixe menu. There's live entertainment on Wednesday nights after eight, with fado singers and a very slight upcharge for the talent.

Alto

212-308-1099
11 East 53rd Street, between
  Madison and Park Avenues
  (behind the Pink store)
Dressy
Reservations
Expensive
All major credit cards accepted
Lunch and dinner Monday–
  Friday, dinner Saturday
E, V trains to Fifth
  Avenue/53rd Street station

This had been Chris Cannon's and Scott Conant's place along with L'Impero (now Convivio) in Tudor City before Scott departed for the Hamptons, then returned to NYC in 2008 with the opening of Scarpetta on 14th Street off Ninth Avenue. Now chef Michael White is in charge; for years he was the executive chef of Fiamma downtown and is highly regarded as a talent in his own right. The room is a bit stuffy and formal for my taste, but I suppose it suits the uptown clientele and business crowds who flock here. I have had the chef make meals for me on several occasions, when I was with other food press and chefs, and can report those meals were some of the most memorable I've had in years. In short, this midwesterner knows how to cook Italian food. There are no windows in the dining rooms and hence no views save for the towers of wine bottles stacked behind glass and backlit. The effect is dramatic, but the entire feel, with small rooms and limited sightlines, is rather sterile and essentially bland.

The food is anything but bland, however, and that's what matters most to me. This is Italian food from the Alto Adige region, the haute cuisine of Italy. Refinement is key, and in some ways its modernism distracts me. I'd prefer a bit of the rustic simplicity you find downtown at Peasant, or at their new space Convivio, but that said, order well and you'll do fine here. Start with Michael's crudo appetizers, excellent fish paired minimally with one or two more ingredients and drizzled with lovely olive oils, or the stunningly good sweetbreads, Milanese style, cut thin, lightly breaded, then flash-fried till crisp on the outside and creamy in the center—next visit I'll be tempted to ask for a double order as a main course. The pastas are all first-rate as well. A simple plate of spaghetti with a fresh tomato-and-basil sauce is as good as it gets anywhere, here topped with finely grated Parmigiano Reggiano as they do in the north. My rustic roots still lean toward pecorino Romano cheese with tomato sauce, but I'm a peasant at heart. Smoked pappardelle with a chunky rich lamb ragù and shaved fried ricotta salata could be a meal in itself, which is also true of the guinea hen agnolotti with sliced prosciutto, here finally pecorino cheese adding salt and bite. A thick slab of European turbot arrives perfectly cooked on top of caramelized leeks, onions, endive, and lentils—this is a very good dish too. Halibut, this time from our waters but another excellent firm-fleshed fish, is set in a mussel broth, again with leeks (popular in Italy's north) and sauced with an emulsion of potato and olive oil. Look for game dishes in the winter—boar and venison, as well as lamb, steak, and veal. If you have time and pockets, have the chef do a tasting for you; this is when the kitchen really shines.

The wine list is impressive, courtesy of Cannon, a veteran of the New York restaurant scene and Chef White's business partner in the project and major wine buff. That said, the list can get expensive fast. The service is formal, sometimes a bit stiff, but good. Desserts are modern and well executed by the new pastry chef, Heather Bertinetti, a CIA graduate; she spent considerable time working at both Per Se and Gramercy, where the pastry programs are excellent. Michael took over the kitchen in the summer of 2007, has been reviewed, and I suspect now can relax a bit and have fun. I look for this place and Convivio to do nothing but get better under his tenure.

Amy Ruth's

212-280-8779
113 West 116th Street,
   between Seventh and
   Lenox Avenues
Casual
No reservations
Inexpensive to moderate
All major credit cards accepted
No alcohol served
Breakfast, lunch, and dinner
   Monday–Thursday, 24 hours
   a day Friday and Saturday,
   brunch and dinner Sunday
2, 3 trains to 116th Street
   station; B, C trains to 116th
   Street station

Among the crop of new restaurants to open in Harlem since the mid-1990s, Amy Ruth's is one of the very best. It's original chef-owner, Carl Redding, a New York native, grew up spending summers at his grandmother's house in rural Alabama. While his other siblings were out doing chores in the yard, young Carl felt that the bugs, heat, and oppressive Alabama sun were too much and opted instead to stay indoors and help his grandma with the kitchen work. It was there at Amy Ruth's side that he learned to cook, and learned very well indeed. Carl is one of those larger-than-life personalities, gregarious, armed with a thousand-watt smile.

Even though Carl recently sold Amy Ruth's to open up a new restaurant in the Bronx, this place may still have the best version of chicken and waffles now that Wells' and Pan Pan are both closed. If you have never had this dish, trust me, you must. It features crisp-skinned, lightly floured chicken served on wonderful fresh waffles and topped with real Vermont maple syrup and whipped butter, should you desire. This is one of my son's favorite meals. Since the early days Carl has expanded the waffle genre to an entire menu section featuring fried whiting and waffles, steak and waffles, sautéed apples and waffles, chocolate waffles, strawberry waffles, and cinnamon waffles with fresh ripe bananas and pecans.

Carl is one of the very few chefs I've met who have actually created a "new" dish. One night, Carl told me, he was having dinner at an Italian restaurant with the Grammy Award–winning singer Jennifer Holliday when she asked him to come up with a new dish just for her. Not being a man to shy from a challenge, Carl went straight back to his kitchen that night at 2 AM and began work on what would become the Soulvioli, a soul-food version of ravioli. It's really a great dish. Carl makes pasta dough from sweet potatoes, which he then fills with a savory mix of long-braised collard greens or black-eyed peas, all bathed in an herb-flecked sweet potato butter sauce.

I suggest that you go with a crowd to sample as many dishes as you care to share. Don't miss the chicken and dumplings, fork-tender braised short ribs, rich oxtail stew, smoked ham hocks, BBQ pigs' feet, smothered steak with green peppers and onions, or the fried or smothered pork chops. Seafood is done in a similar southern style. Of note are the salmon croquettes, fried or pan-seared shrimp, fried whiting, fried or baked catfish,

CHICKEN AND WAFFLES

For those of you not familiar with the dish, chicken and waffles is a staple of urban African American cuisine. A few years back, while filming the pilot for my PBS show, we were able to do a piece on Wells' just a week before it closed for renovation. Sadly, it never did manage to reopen. Ms. Wells was getting up in years, the investors got other ideas, and another Harlem landmark was gone. But I was thrilled to have met her and to have learned directly from her the answer to a question I'd had for years: how did chicken and waffles come to Harlem, anyway?

As told to me by Ms. Wells, her husband had been working in restaurants in Florida just prior to coming to New York. Arriving in the mid-1930s, he desperately wanted to run his own restaurant. In those days Harlem had a lot of restaurants, and he wanted to do something different: a place that served breakfast, lunch, and dinner and would be open nearly 24 hours a day. He remembered a dish from his youth growing up in the coastal South, served to commercial fishermen who came off the boats and into the docks tired and hungry at all times of day: fried chicken served over great waffles and drizzled with Vermont maple syrup. It's really a perfect all-around meal, as it combines a bit of breakfast, lunch, and dinner all together. In the early days at Wells', Mr. Wells literally had to give it away to get people to try it. Every day a sign went up in the window reading "Free chicken and waffles, come inside," and soon the place was packed day and night. It was a famous haunt for all types of people, from the Rockefellers to Sugar Ray Robinson, Sinatra to busloads of Japanese tourists. Live bands would perform, and the dance floor on any given night was full of happy couples enjoying dinner and swing dancing, as I found them on my last visit just prior to the restaurant's closing.

crab cakes, and bourbon-cured salmon with peach butter. From among the various side dishes, go straight to the fluffy and lightly buttered stone-ground grits from Dothan, Alabama, the long-cooked smoky braised collard greens, or the dense baked macaroni and cheese. Save room for the homey desserts: dig into the terrific peach cobbler, pineapple coconut cake, bread pudding, red velvet cake, or sweet potato pie.

Note that they do not serve any alcohol here but do have great homemade lemonade.

Annisa

212-741-6699

13 Barrow Street, between
    West 4th Street and
    Seventh Avenue South

Casual

Reservations

Moderate

All major credit cards accepted

Dinner seven nights a week

1 train to Christopher Street
    station; A, C, E, B, D, F, V trains
    to West 4th Street station

This is Anita Lo's restaurant, one of very few owned and operated by a woman chef. Initially her partner was Jennifer Scism, also a fine cook, who ran the dining room while Anita oversaw the menu and the kitchen. Anita trained at Bouley and then Chanterelle, and then was the chef at the short-lived Mirezi, where her passion for modern fusion cooking was very well received. The wine list here was partially the work of Roger Dagorn, the great master sommelier from Chanterelle, and focuses exclusively on wine produced by female vintners or vineyard owners. (*Annisa* means "women" in Arabic.) The room is small and squarish, with a little bar area up front; up a few steps you'll find the main room, decked out primarily in white. Like the room, the menu is small but clean and well focused, full of seasonal ingredients put together with imagination and an open mind. Anita likes to play with contrasting flavors and textures, so instead of pairing tomatoes with goat's-milk feta, she ups the sweetness factor by using grapes, a nice foil for the salty, assertive cheese. Then she throws dill and lightly roasted pine nuts into the mix for two more notes that blend well and provide edge and contrast to an otherwise simple dish.

Cultural lines too are crossed: Shanghai-style soup dumplings are stuffed with, among other things, foie gras, and garnished with crunchy, clean-tasting jicama to sort things out. Roasted chicken breast gets a lot of help from its stuffing of pigs' feet, and filet of beef, my least favorite cut, gets much help from a thin coat of mustard seed, which provides texture and flavor to the otherwise pallid piece of meat. Fish is always done well here, it seems. One recent menu featured hake, a much-overlooked fish in the cod family, that was pan-seared and set over a mix of sliced braised Chinese pork belly, slow-cooked white soybeans, and a broth of Manila clams bound with butter. The supporting staff on this plate included a lovely Yorkshire pudding enriched with bone marrow and oxtail (now there's a nice cut for you) and two types of mustard just in case.

The staff are all very well trained and enthusiastic; the wine list, again courtesy of Mr. Dagorn, is well thought out and fairly priced. Desserts are simple and homey in the way found at well-run small restaurants, which rarely have pastry chefs and have learned to work within the limits imposed by kitchen space and talent—individual apple tarts on puff pastry with good rich caramel sauce, or deep-fried sesame-studded mochi served wrapped in a napkin with pineapple-and-coconut dipping sauce.

There is a nice modern sensibility to the place, it's quiet and romantic, and the food reflects the intellect and mixed cultural heritages and aspirations of the talented chef who designed it.

Anthos

212-582-6900
36 West 52nd Street, between Fifth and Sixth Avenues
Casual to dressy
Reservations
Expensive
All major credit cards accepted
Lunch and dinner Monday–Friday, dinner Saturday
E, V trains to Fifth Avenue/53rd Street station, or B, D, F, V trains to 47th–50th Streets/Rockefeller Center station

Restaurant Dona was among the best new restaurants to open in 2006. Restaurateur Donatella Arpaia and chef Michael Psilakis teamed up to produce what was the most ambitious Greek restaurant in New York. Then the building that housed Dona was sold and the lease not renewed, and Dona was shuttered suddenly in early 2007 after a nine-month run. Arpaia, never known as faint of heart, quickly got back on her feet, found a new space nearby, and opened Anthos with Psilakis. So in many ways Dona was the dress rehearsal for this, their latest collaboration. Not surprisingly, the food here has been very, very good from the start.

Like Molyvos before it, Anthos is Greek food being cooked at a level not found before in New York. Frankly, I'm not sure that a restaurant like this exists anywhere in Greece either. This is Greek cooking via Psilakis' vision of what modern Greek cuisine could be, a sort of culinary Esperanto melding Greek and Mediterranean ingredients with international modern techniques and refinement to create new dishes—studies of a sort, deconstructions and reconstructions of the classics of Greek cuisine. What I find remarkable is that Psilakis is entirely self-taught. Donatella knew him from an Italian restaurant he ran on Long Island, working the front of the house. One day after his chef was a no-show, he decided to teach himself how to cook. That was less than eight years ago. Here he decided to reinvent Greek cuisine—to modernize it, if you will.

Take, for example, the dish that combines baby pork chops, braised pork belly, grilled lahanodolma fennel, and avgolemono foam. Each element of the dish refers back to the Greek culinary tradition—the use of pork, the cooking methods, the sauce—but the dish that is set before you is one giant step removed from that tradition. Each ingredient is given separate careful treatment, the whole far greater than the sum of the parts. The baby pork chops are cooked medium rare, tender and rich-tasting, from heritage-breed stock; the belly is braised then crisped; and the foam is a whisper of lemon and egg.

The room is a long rectangle, the tables spaced comfortably apart. The volume level is pleasantly low even when it is packed full, which it has been since it opened. The staff are well trained, as they are in all Arpaia's restaurants, the crowd a well-heeled, well-dressed mix of New Yorkers and the international crowd who spend a good deal of time here in town.

Where the chef shines brightest is in his smallest plates, one-bite creations. It's here that he gets to do what he likes best. Talented chefs love to play with these small plates, following the Kelleresque philosophy that after three bites of anything we really stop tasting. There are over a dozen flights of plates, ranging in size from one bite to maybe three or four, all of which share the distinction of containing remarkable layers of flavors and textures. Raw tuna belly is brushed with mastic oil and topped with a sliver of lemon confit, grains of sea salt, and a single sprig of rosemary. Taken in one bite, the layers of flavors and textures work beautifully together. A single BeauSoleil oyster set in its shell is garnished with romaine jus, a small arrowhead cut of that same lettuce, slices of radish, and a pink peppercorn. Again, layers and layers reveal themselves as you chew, slurp, and swallow. A small bowl of tiny raw pink botan ebi prawns is paired with crumbled feta and spicy basil in a pool of clear tomato consommé that was clarified not with heat but frozen with gelatin, then allowed to thaw clear. This is not your grandmother's Greek cuisine. These small-plate combinations are expensive, ranging from the low teens to just under $20, but the ingredients are unimpeachably fresh and the preparation accurate; you could just as well stay in this section of the menu and arrange an entire meal. I have.

But then you'd miss that great pork tasting plate, or the remarkable earthenware crock containing spicy shellfish stew. It starts with rendered merguez sausage and pairs razor clams with halved shrimp in their shells, tiny clams, and mussels in a rich broth redolent of saffron dotted with orzo. It's accompanied by a long slice of crisp paximathi toast, topped with rich creamed cheese and a dollop of caviar, then dipped into the broth. The menu is market-driven and changes daily, but you'll always find pork, steak, lamb, and half a dozen excellent seafood selections to choose from.

The wine list is very good; the sommelier, Bruce Yung, is very helpful in navigating you through a wide selection of wines you may not be familiar with, such as the sparkling Emery Grand Prix Brut (Athiri) from Rhodes, the Harlaftis Argilos Nemea, or the Skouras Megas Oenos, a blend of cabernet sauvignon with aghiorgitiko. One night we had an excellent Belgian Regenboog Wostyntje mustard ale, a perfect match with the tasting flight of seafood meze.

Desserts, courtesy of the Canadian-born, nearly self-taught pastry chef Bill Corbett, are a fitting end to a great meal. After a stint at WD-50, he is in full form here. Try the bougatza, which is kataifi with a slender slice of goat-cheese cheesecake, goat's milk caramel, and poached plump golden kumquats, or the baklava trio, which includes pistachio baklava, a honey custard and brown sugar tuile walnut cake, and cinnamon ice cream.

For the time being, this is not only the best Greek restaurant in New York but also a fine choice for a great meal, a most ambitious and successful undertaking, and a real standout in a city where that's a lot easier said than done. Arpaia and Psilakis should be watched, as they now run three very good restaurants together—Anthos, Mia Dona, and Kefi—with more concepts in the works.

Artichoke Basille's Pizza and Brewery

212-228-2004
328 East 14th Street, between First and Second Avenues
Casual
No reservations
Inexpensive
Cash only
Seven days a week noon–11 PM, later on weekends
L train to First Avenue station; 4, 5, 6, L, N, Q, R, W trains to 14th Street/Union Square station

Bad pizza is everywhere, but good pizza I'll travel for. I take the crosstown bus just for this place, on a funky strip of East 14th Street. It's primarily a takeout-only hole-in-the-wall; however, there is a small wooden counter affixed to the wall, allowing for, say, four courteous guests to dine indoors, standing elbow to elbow, as I've often done. The pizza is available by the slice or as whole pies, and they usually have four varieties: a square thin-crusted Sicilian, a round Neapolitan, the signature thick-crusted artichoke version, and occasionally a special, like the interesting crabmeat pie on a recent visit.

As New York pizza places go, this one is very, very good, and to my mind a real bargain. A slice of the artichoke pie costs $4 and is in itself a meal. With a thick, chewy, slightly charred crust, this pizza is topped with a creamy cheese mix that may be béchamel sauce or just seasoned creamy ricotta with a puree of artichokes, another cheese or two, and leaves of spinach strewn through it. It's an acquired taste, but I love it. The Sicilian is much more traditional, with a thin, well-charred crust topped with a thin layer of good tomato sauce and a mix of mozzarella, pecorino, and Parmesan cheeses. The Neapolitan is the classic Margherita, with tomato, fresh basil, and mozzarella. The owner, Francis Garcia, hails from Staten Island, where he worked with his cousin Sal Basille at his eponymous eatery. They also offer (when available) their signature stuffed artichokes, meatballs on skewers, sautéed broccoli rabe (which can be had, if you're lucky, as a sandwich), and other odds and ends from the urban southern

Italian culinary lexicon. I also give them points for the entertaining banter between the cashier and the pizza boys, most recently centered around Nissans versus Hondas, 9/11 theories, and Bigfoot and UFOs, as well as the kitschy decor, highlighted by the leg lamp in the front window and the amateur Kennedy boys painting adorning the wall.

Artie's Delicatessen

212-579-5959
2290 Broadway, between
82nd and 83rd Streets
Casual
Reservations
Inexpensive
All major credit cards accepted
Breakfast, lunch, and dinner
seven days a week
1 train to 79th Street station

For many years legendary restaurant impresario Artie Cutler wanted to open an old-style New York deli. He was the brains behind Carmine's, Dock's, Ollie's, Virgil's, Gabriella's, and Jake's, but his untimely death midcareer left that dream to be realized by his wife, her brother, and partners Jeffrey Bank and Chris Metz. Opened in 1999 a few blocks from Barney Greengrass and Zabar's, this is, surprisingly, the only "old-style" deli on the Upper West Side except for Fine & Shapiro on 72nd Street— surprising because this neighborhood has historically been home to a large Jewish population. Well, with Ratner's now closed, New Yorkers have fewer and fewer options to choose from.

The place was built to look as if it had been here for years. Rows of red-cased salamis hang from the ceiling à la Katz's, there is counter seating as well as banquettes and tables, and a familiar heavy-plastic-sheathed three-page menu will please deli fans. For me, pastrami is as good a place as any to judge a deli. Here it is good, and at $8.95 a sandwich a bargain really, but it lacks the characteristic heavily seasoned, smoky crust of the same meat served at Carnegie or Katz's. My sense is that it may have been wet-cured at some point. On the other hand, on my most recent visit the corned beef was very good. For *fressers* they have a brisket Reuben for $9.95 that is worth checking out. They offer a minimum of four soups daily, including a decent version of matzo ball soup and chicken with kreplach.

They serve traditional deli comfort foods, such as braised flanken in the pot served with mushroom barley soup. Stuffed cabbage is always a good choice, and where else these days can you find broiled calf's liver with sautéed onions, braised tongue with sweet-and-sour sauce, or the combination platter of stuffed cabbage, potato pancakes, and pierogis? All this plus open-face hot sandwiches, a good variety of cold meat sandwiches, the usual deli section of bagels and smoked fish, decent burgers and hot dogs, and a children's menu to boot.

Desserts are on display in the glass-front refrigerator and include decent rugelach, New York–style cheesecake with or without fruit toppings, rice pudding, black-and-white cookies, a tall and moist carrot cake, hamantaschen, and Linzer tarts. Though they have beer and wine, I'd suggest washing all this food down with a Dr. Brown's soda (they have the increasingly hard-to-find diet Cel-Ray).

Arturo's

212-677-3820
106 West Houston Street, at Thompson Street
Casual
No reservations
Inexpensive
All major credit cards accepted
Dinner seven nights a week
1 train to Houston Street station; B, D, F, V trains to Broadway/Lafayette Street station

Arturo's is a family-run, multigenerational business, a vestige of what was once a vibrant Italian American neighborhood that thrived in Greenwich Village. Now run by a brother-and-sister team who live nearby, the place is a classic with a funky old New York feel to it. While they have a full menu with appetizers and pastas, the pizza is the draw here. At the heart of this place is the ancient coal-fired pizza oven in the kitchen. Fewer and fewer places have coal-fired ovens, and this one dates back to when the coal deliveries were dropped off by trucks directly into the basement. This warhorse of an oven produces an intense and even heat, and the pizza that comes out has a nice char, almost burnt, with a smoky-tasting, thin, crisp, salty crust. Some toppings are good, some very good, others not so great, and though there is an ongoing and never-ending debate among New York pizza fans as to who does the best this and that, Arturo's is on many folks' top-10 list, and for good reason. One of my favorites is the clam pie with the shelled calms hidden beneath the cheese. Also good are the sausage, meatball, calamari, and basic mozzarella.

There is a full bar, which gets very busy, and the place can get packed, especially on weekends. Some nights there they have live entertainment, and that, plus the funky décor, goofy artwork on the walls, great pizza, and an overall jovial New York vibe to the place, make it a classic.

A Salt & Battery

212-691-2713
112 Greenwich Avenue, just north of West 12th Street
Casual
No reservations
Inexpensive
All major credit cards accepted
Seven days a week 11:30 AM–10:30 PM
1, 2, 3 trains to 14th Street station

In what appears to be a hub for British-themed food stores, this part of the West Village is home to the Spotted Pig, Myers of Keswick, and Tea and Sympathy next door, coincidently run by the same folks as this fine fish-and-chips place. It's a tiny storefront designed mostly for takeout, but if you've been to Britain and really miss great fish and chips, this is the place for you. Or if you've never been to Britain at all and want to try this specialty, look no further. The room is very small, with stools set before a stainless-steel counter should you decide to eat in. In England, they often use sand shark or dogfish filets, but here they use several fish varieties: cod, haddock, sole, whiting, and something billed as "a load of shrimps." There is the option to make your own "chip buttie," a sandwich consisting of fries slathered in tartar sauce and maybe fish too on a buttered roll. Actually it's quite good. They also serve battered sausages—sort of a British version of a corn dog, I suppose—and something called mushy peas. To finish it all off, try a deep-fried battered Mars bar, which again is pretty darn good. The fried stuff gets wrapped in newspaper for easy carryout.

If you're not in a fish mood and can't make it a few blocks west to Myers of Keswick to try the meat pies there, steak and kidney, chicken and mushroom, and beef and onion are offered here at $6.50 apiece. Of course they serve soda, mostly British, such as Shandy, Tango, Tiger, and the unforgettable dandelion and burdock, as well as a few great beers— Boddingtons and Newcastle Brown Ale both come to mind. Essentially this is a great place for a quick drink and a bite at bargain prices, and the food is very decent to boot.

L'Atelier de Joël Robuchon

212-350-6658
57 East 57th Street, in the Four Seasons Hotel, between Park and Madison Avenues
Casual to dressy
Reservations
Expensive
All major credit cards accepted
Dinner seven nights a week
4, 5, 6, N, R, W trains to Lexington Avenue/59th Street station; F train to 57th Street station

By way of background, Joël Robuchon was considered by many to be the best chef of his generation working in France. Through the 1980s and 1990s, he ran the esteemed three-star Michelin restaurant Jamin in Paris, at various locations. Some of the best chefs working in New York trained under him there—Eric Ripert and David Bouley, to name just two. He was known to be a taskmaster, moody, and very difficult to work for. In short, he was a perfectionist who strove each day for each meal service to put the best food possible in front of his customers. The bread for each meal was baked just prior to service, the herbs for the plates chopped only at the last second, and mistakes were never served. It was rumored that the young men who worked for him were driven to tears; some had their hair turn gray during their stint in that kitchen. To say it was stressful was to put it mildly, but perfection in this business is hard to come by, and he put more pressure on himself than on his cooks. I had the pleasure of eating at Jamin when it was located on rue Longchamp—the food was as beautiful and perfectly cooked as one could imagine, but somehow, to my taste, it was almost too polished, too perfect. It lacked a degree of soul. At the age of 50, exhausted and tired of playing for the Michelin star system, he closed Jamin at the top of its game and "retired."

I ran into him later at a food event in Cannes, and he spoke of the changing scene and the Michelin pressure. He stated that he no longer knew what it took to get three stars and that it wasn't so much about the food as about other things. He wanted to do something different, and a few years later he opened the first L'Atelier on the rue de Montalembert, on the Left Bank in Paris. The concept was revolutionary: it broke down the walls between the kitchen and the dining room, quite literally. It was designed like Japanese sushi restaurants, where you sat at a bar and ordered the food, mostly small plates, while the cooks worked out in the open right in front of you, interacting with you, placing the finished plated food before you just as they do in Japan. It broke new ground and liberated the chef from the burdensome requirements of the formal gilded dining rooms that need 20-odd cooks per service and countless wait staff to take orders, clear plates, pour wine, and dote. Here it finally was just about the food and the customer. He took this model on the road, opening first in America in Las Vegas, and then here in the stunning Four Seasons Hotel.

You enter from 57th Street, walk up the grand center staircase, turn right past the bar, and go further back up another small set of stairs. To the right is the main dining counter. The bar will seat 20 or so guests, and there is room for another 20 or so at tables just before the bar. My suggestion is to eat at the bar, where you can see the cooks working and experience the restaurant as it was designed to be.

The chef here is Yosuke Suga, a recent James Beard award winner, a protégé of Robuchon, and a disciplined, talented chef indeed. The food is in true Robuchon style, close to flawless. The small jewel-like presentations look as if every plate was just made for a magazine shoot. But somehow I still sense a certain lack of soul to this kind of perfection. It's like listening to the finalists at the Van Cliburn competition—surely the playing is perfect, but you wait for the one moment that transports you, that one that gets past the notes on the page and delivers music into the realm of magic.

There are several menus to choose from. You can simply order à la carte, picking the small plates that interest you, or you can opt for the three-course express for $54 or the full-blown seven-course tasting menu at $190, with an additional $125 to pair it with wine. A brilliant signature dish pairs alternating layers of smoked foie gras with caramelized eel, along with a dollop of whipped cream dusted with red pepper from the south of France. Day boat scallops arrive set in their shell, perfectly cooked and glistening, topped with seaweed-flavored butter flown in from Bordier's in Brittany. A single filet of rouget arrives with the crisped skin facing up, bouillabaisse style, in a clear, full-flavored broth redolent of fennel and saffron, garnished with baby artichokes, snap peas, and cauliflower florets. Amadai, a Japanese fish, is sautéed and served with sunchokes, lotus root, and light blue shiso flowers in a yuzu-accented ramen-style broth. Slow-roasted vegetables, each distinct and perfectly cooked to retain flavor, are served with milky, rich buffalo mozzarella. Squab breast appears in a traditional role, pan-seared to medium rare, accompanied by sautéed cabbage and bacon lardons with a light jus as accent. Sweetbreads cooked perfectly, lightly browned on the exterior and creamy in the center, are served skewer style on a sprig of laurel, with small stuffed romaine leaves. Tête de veau here is a pinwheel of veal tongue, crisped and served with a splendid version of the traditional ravigote sauce.

The desserts follow the style of the previous courses: small plates, compositions really, and variations on a theme. For the one billed as pamplemousse (French for "grapefruit"), small grapefruit segments are set amongst a gelée of olive oil, mint sorbet, a clear wine gelée, and sugared almonds. A small baba is split and topped with a sabayon flavored with thyme, pineapple, and rum, next to a small round of caramel ice cream. Fruit soup, an excellent lighter choice, here is a small bowl containing a lemongrass-scented broth of fruit and syrup and a scoop of basil-lime sorbet atop a bed of miniature diced hard fruits. The one billed as cherries jubilee–style features that stone fruit poached in flavored simple syrup and set atop a light soufflé made entirely of egg whites, with a bitter almond ice cream as counterpoint.

The wine list is deep and as expensive as the food. Service is spotty, as is the case with all New York hotels; the union is strong, and some of the staff are much better than others. During a recent meal when I asked our waiter about our food, he lacked a good answer, and instead of asking the kitchen he just guessed, and for the most part guessed wrong. That said, this is certainly one of the best dining rooms in New York, different in many ways, as was Robuchon's intention, and certainly deserves a visit should you have the money to spare.

August

212-929-4774

395 Bleecker Street, between
West 11th and Perry Streets

Casual

No reservations

Moderate

All major credit cards accepted

Lunch and dinner seven days
a week

1 train to Christopher Street
station; A, C, E, B, D, F, V trains
to West 4th Street station

The space is rather small, and the fact that they don't take reservations kept me away for some time, but I live in the area, walk by all the time, and took my chances when the room seemed less than full. There is a bar area to the back right, with tables up front and along the brick and distressed plaster walls. A small wood-burning brick oven, left there by the previous tenant, is utilized for the menu. There's also an outdoor garden with an all-weather glass enclosure atop it. The ceiling is arched and coated in cork to deaden the sound, one assumes, though when the place is busy noise is still an issue. The food is honest and straightforward, and I know lots of chefs who eat here for that very reason. The chef here for many years was Tony Liu (formerly of Babbo), replaced in 2008 by Terrence Gallivan; the owner is Jason Hennings, and the room they run is a very good place to tuck in for a meal should the wait not be too long. The menu is not overly ambitious, but they deliver on the promise of very good food at fair prices, a lesson many restaurants should take to heart. No artifice, no striving—this is simple food made with good ingredients and properly seasoned.

During the summer months, order the signature house white gazpacho, made with ground almonds and grapes, drizzled with good fruity olive oil, and topped with tiny croutons. The kitchen uses small black cast-iron vessels for a fair number of dishes that go into that wood-fired oven, similar to what Frank DeCarlo does at Peasant with ceramic vessels. So the food is cooked quickly, and the flavors meld together and have an added smoky quality from time to time. Start with blistered peppers, the chunky meat charred and drizzled with good garlic-scented olive oil and a sprinkle of sea salt. Octopus and potatoes alla plancha are good too, the octopus crisp and the potatoes a nice sponge for the olive oil. Hake, a fish from the cod family that is often overlooked, is slow-roasted. Its mild, flaky flesh is paired with chorizo and a succotash of corn, lima beans, and fresh chanterelles. The baby back lamb ribs, Provençal style, are long on flavor, the fatty rib meat succulent after being hot-smoked.

The wine list is very decent with good values in the $20–$40 range. If you can get in for brunch, do. All the food is good, especially the burger, the steak and eggs, the gravlax scrambled eggs, and the eggs en cocotte out of that oven in various styles. The best time to try August may be midafternoon or for an early dinner, unless you are lucky. With the food this good at these prices, anytime after 7 PM you should expect a wait.

Aureole

Note: In mid 2009 Aureole moved to a beautiful new location in The Bank of America Building on Bryant Park. The new chef is Christopher Lee, formerly of Gilt; I expect it to be as good or better than it ever was.

212-319-1660
One Bryant Park, between Fifth and Sixth Avenues
Dressy
Reservations
Expensive
All major credit cards accepted
Lunch and dinner Monday–Friday, dinner Saturday
7, B, D, F, V, S trains to 42nd Street/Bryant Park station

Charlie Palmer opened this restaurant in 1988 with his then partner, Steve Tzolis, who still is a big behind-the-scenes player in the restaurant industry. Charlie was fresh off his successful run at the famed River Café, in the post–Larry Forgione, pre–David Burke era, and with all the good press that place generated, Charlie was one of the rising-star American chefs of that generation. Born and raised in humble surroundings upstate, he was introduced to cooking by his high school home economics teacher, who first showed him how to bake, and in doing so kindled his love for cooking. After graduating from the CIA, he came to New York and worked, as did many others, under the tutelage of Jean-Jacques Rachou, a great chef and culinary mentor to a long list of young American cooks of that era, at his famed restaurant La Côte Basque. So back in 1987 with Charlie's newly minted fame and Steve and his partner Nicola Kotsoni's funding, they bought this beautiful brownstone together, where Charlie lived upstairs and cooked below. It was a significant restaurant of the era, with professionals such as Mike Bonadies running the dining room and a strong cast in the kitchen under Charlie.

But it's hard to keep things fresh in a business where a 10-year run is considered a huge success. Chefs have come and gone from that kitchen, as has management, and these days Charlie and his family live mostly in northern California, where he has a Relais & Châteaux property. But Aureole won't just go away. Charlie won't let it; it's his baby, after all, and in fact there is already a deal in place to move it in 2009 into a brand-new bank building, steps off 42nd Street in midtown.

On a good night, this still can be a lovely and civilized place for dinner. From the beginning this was billed as new American cooking, but much has changed since 1988, and most of what takes place around town these days is market-driven, seasonal, fresh, and cooked by Americans. So at Aureole, more than ever, it's more a new American style that reminds one of old French, which is fine too.

A full-flavored disk of tuna tartare comes with a side of pommes gaufrettes, as may steak tartare. Sautéed foie gras, interestingly enough, is paired with a small spiced malted waffle, caramelized pears, roasted hazelnuts, and blackberries. Another interesting dish features excellent firm-fleshed, thin-sliced shards of oakwood-smoked salmon served with a poached egg and a salad of bitter greens set off with horseradish and dill dressing. Here the familiar pairing of salmon and dill is offset yet balanced by the rich, runny egg yolk, the crispness of the greens, and then the hit of horseradish—a nice play on flavors, texture, and tradition.

As is common these days (thanks, I suspect, to Thomas Keller), Maine lobster arrives slow-poached in beurre fondue, then set in an open ravioli, the skins just folded over. The sauce is a lobster reduction topped with sweet corn foam and a nice piece of hen-of-the-woods mushroom, giving the plate some heft and woodsiness. The pan-seared striped bass with crabmeat and an English mustard cream didn't do much for me, but the turbot roasted on the bone, the thick white flesh rich-tasting, held up well with the white bean puree, braised artichokes, and cured olives that rounded out the dish. Meat lovers will be more than happy with the veal T-bone, accented with fresh thyme, garnished with poached bone marrow and braised endive, and set above a lovely, sticky old-school Madeira sauce. Or opt for the honey-glazed squab—order it medium rare—its gaminess offset by the apple beignets, stuffed cabbage, and fondant-style fingerling potatoes.

They feature a seven-course tasting menu for $95; wine pairings are additional. Desserts here are uniformly good. Pumpkin brown butter financier eats well and screams new American. If they have the sweet corn French toast with roasted plums, slightly sweetened fresh ricotta, and corn ice cream, get it; it's wonderful. The wine list is big, impressive, and expensive.

Babbo

212-777-0303
110 Waverly Place, between
  Sixth Avenue and
  MacDougal Street
Casual
Reservations
Moderate to expensive
All major credit cards accepted
Dinner seven nights a week
A, C, E, B, D, F, V trains to West
  4th Street station; N, R, W
  trains to 8th Street station

While Mario Batali is all over the place these days with restaurant projects, books, TV appearances, and his peripatetic lifestyle, when you dine at Babbo, you remember why he became famous in the first place. He can cook, he loves big flavors and layers of them, and he loves his lipids, the more the merrier. As I recall, Babbo was Frank Bruni's first review for the *New York Times*. My sense of the review was that he loved the food and gladly awarded it three stars, but the rock-and-roll sound track and party atmosphere each night kept it from getting four.

The place chugs along with or without Mario in the kitchen, and trust me, it's mostly without. Frank Langello is the day-to-day chef, and he's a darn good one at that. You'd be hard pressed to find a menu more stacked with flavor than the one here. The list is big and full of good choices.

From the antipasti section you can't go wrong with the fresh sardines set over caramelized fennel and then drizzled with lobster oil. That's the way they cook here—anyone else would have put the excellent plump sardines over the sweet and crunchy fennel and said it was perfect, but here they thought they needed more. They oven-roast and then slow-cook the lobster bodies with olive oil until that oil picks up the lobster flavor and red color, adding one more flavor kick. They do wonders with offal here, and the lamb tongue vinaigrette with marinated chanterelles and a three-minute egg is superb. The meat is tender, firm, and rich-tasting, the mushrooms provide a woodsy background, and the egg yolk blends and balances the flavors while adding mouth feel and richness.

Pigs' feet, a favorite cut of the chef's, are braised and then deboned, breaded, and fried thin and crisp, Milanese style, with "rice beans" and arugula for contrast. Any of the salumi, either house-made or made by Mario's father in Seattle, are well worth checking out too. With over a dozen pastas to choose from, it's never easy to pick one. In truth, I haven't had that many, but they all sound great and the ones I've had were just that. The maccheroni alla chitarra, a typical Abruzzi style that my grandmother used to make, are chewy from all the egg yolks required by the recipe— nearly a dozen per pound of flour. Then they are tossed with house-made oven-dried plum tomatoes, rich and deeply flavored, accented with some red chiles, and topped with shaved botarga for a nice, salty fish kick. The gnocchi with braised oxtail is a showstopper too and could be a meal for any reasonable person. The sauce, a braising liquid, is rich, meaty, and dense. The gnocchi are a perfect light foil for the rich meat. And the beef cheek ravioli, in a sauce enriched with squab liver and shaved black truffles, will have you dreaming of them and wanting more.

The list of main courses is meat-heavy, but the thick slab of grouper set over braised then grilled leeks and warm imported Treviso radicchio, bitter and crunchy, set off with a pancetta-laced vinaigrette, is a good fish choice. You'll find duck, squab, quail, and guinea hen, as well as rabbit, veal sweetbreads, heritage-breed pork, and Colorado lamb chops, as well as several items for two, such as the thick charred ribeye and the deconstructed osso buco.

The wine list has always been very good, and these days, with Joe Bastianch involved so heavily in wine importation, it's even better. It's an all-Italian list with value across the board, one of the best Italian wine lists in New York. For carb cravers they even have an all-pasta tasting menu, a bargain with six pastas plus dessert for $69 per person. Of course they offer a tasting menu with eight courses for $75 plus wine for another $50, and to me that's another real bargain in this town for food this good. Come hungry, come with meat lovers, and save room for dessert.

The pastries, by Gina DePalma, are as good or better than any you'll find in Italian restaurants here or in Italy, from the dense, moist, and utterly delicious chocolate hazelnut cake with orange sauce to the delicate custard-like saffron panna cotta with quince, pink peppercorns, and quince sorbetto. Or if you're too full, order the great little flavor-packed biscotti for the table, a perfect ending to what will have been a nearly perfect big meal. The place gets loud, so be prepared, but roll with the punches, throw your diet out the window, and my guess is you'll have had one of the best meals you've had in quite some time.

Bacaro

212-941-5060
136 Division Street, between Orchard and Ludlow Streets
Casual
No reservations
Moderate
All major credit cards accepted
Dinner Tuesday–Sunday
F train to East Broadway station

Bacaro opened in late 2007. I first got a chance to have a few meals there in late February 2008 and can now report that it is one of my favorite restaurants in town. It is Frank DeCarlo's homage to Venetian cuisine, specifically its bar food. As he did with Peasant, his other place on Elizabeth Street, Frank built this space mainly by hand—his hands, that is. The project took nearly three years to complete. Other chefs cobble together investors and hire architects and designers. Frankie DeCarlo looks for good long leases in up-and-coming neighborhoods, then grabs a shovel and wheelbarrow and gets to work. This is not an easy place to find the first time you visit; it's a bit off the grid. Division Street runs from Essex Street all the way to the Bowery, but it begins just a few yards east of the front door of the restaurant. The gentrification of the Lower East Side keeps pushing lower and further east all the time, and here it collides with Chinatown. This space used to house a fish tank store on the first floor and an illegal gambling den in the basement, and from the bones of these ruins Frank has created one of the most beguiling and romantic restaurants anywhere in the city.

You enter into the small upstairs room with its marble-topped bar and a smattering of small tables and chairs. To get downstairs you descend via a beautiful custom cast-iron staircase into a subterranean room with another bar and another, somewhat larger dining room. Then there is a series of small semiprivate alcoves, some with just a table or two, going off the main room at odd angles, including one that by its relation to the front door must be under the sidewalk. The ceilings are all left open and unfinished, revealing the century-old dark wooden beams. The walls are mostly brick and stone; the tables—some for two, others for four, with a few larger ones thrown into the mix—are all different, some of old wood, others with marble tops. Lighting upstairs comes from a Venetian chandelier, and downstairs for the most part is courtesy of the many candles adorning the tables. In some ways it reminds me of Allen and Delancey, another romantic spot where the food is great, the room is cast in a lovely candlelit glow, and the crowds skew young and arrive late into the night.

The menu works from small plates to slightly larger ones, with nearly 20 offerings in total. There is no traditional division of starters followed by pastas and mains, just a series of choices. Octopus is braised and then grilled and tossed with halved fingerling potatoes, olives, parsley, and good olive oil. The meat and cheese platter comes with thin slices of prosciutto, speck, bresaola, coppa salami, sliced apples, pears, breadsticks, and Asiago cow's-milk cheese. The classic sarde in saor, or soused sardines, is an old Dalmatian dish that found its way to Venice; the story goes that shepherds used to carry the dish with them away from the coast and eat it days later. Whole head-on sardines are first fried until done, then cooled and covered with a mix of sautéed onions, vinegar, and oil, and allowed to marinate. The firm meat comes right off the bones, and the vinegar and onions are a nice foil for the rich fatty meat. Salt cod is creamed, then placed in the center of a nice flat plate of creamy polenta enriched with fontina cheese.

If you have a few people at the table, you must order the plate of fritto misto—it's nearly perfect. Vegetables and seafood arrive in a pile, crisp and golden, the flavors bright and distinct. The breading, a combination of seltzer and 00 flour, remains crisp for a long, long time, and all this dish needs is the lemon wedges that it comes with and a good glass of prosecco to wash it down. House-made potato gnocchi are light yet firm and taste of good cooked potato. Bathed in a light brown butter sauce, they pick up the flavors of the porcini mushrooms, the only other element of this simple yet satisfying plate. Along the same lines, pasta with clams is just that: clams steamed in their shells, their natural juice bound by good olive oil, to which the kitchen adds some chopped parsley, a few hot pepper flakes, and some of the starchy pasta cooking water, making this another winner for any argument in favor of simple cooking. Risotto al nero di seppia arrives al dente and black from the cuttlefish ink it is made with. In the center of the plate is a single tiny cuttlefish; the dish is rich with flavor and satisfying. Braised duck leg is set over creamy stewed white beans, and the other meat option is braised tender pork shank served over polenta. The menu is fish-heavy—this is Venetian cuisine, after all. The prices start at $6 for a good soup of pasta and beans and top off at $18 for the pork shank dish, with most of the menu in the low to mid-teens.

The wines are mostly from Trentino, Alto Adige, and work perfectly with the food. Desserts are like those at Peasant: simple, straightforward, and satisfying panna cotta, fruit tarts, and gelati. The staff are well trained; Frank's wife, Dulci, is often in the room to make sure. As they don't take reservations, the easiest time to secure a table is early, before 7:30. After that the place fills with a young, hip Lower East Side crowd who seem to get the food and the vibe, and add to it.

Back Forty

212-388-1990
190 Avenue B, just south
    of 12th Street
Casual
No reservations
Moderate
All major credit cards accepted
Dinner seven nights a week,
    brunch Saturday and Sunday
L train to First Avenue station

Chef Peter Hoffman, an early pioneer of the ever-popular and growing market-driven menu movement, opened Savoy to much-deserved acclaim back in 1990. He comes from the school of bright, quirky cooks who worked in New York City back in the early 1980s, including Barry Wine, David Waltuck, and Len Allison and his wife, Karen Hubert, who ran Hubert's on East 22nd Street, where Hoffman cooked as a young man. His cooking at Savoy reveals a fine mind, well-trained palate, and excellent technique, as well as a sensibility for ingredients and combinations that work naturally and appear simple, though they are not always as simple as they seem. When he opened just outside of Soho back in 1990, it was a very different neighborhood, and in opening Back Forty here on Avenue B, he seems prescient in again being a bit of a pioneer. But not exactly—Hearth is not far away, nor is Momofuku, Momofuku Ko, Ssam Bar, and others. The neighborhood has limits in terms of styles and price points, however, and his simple, inexpensive menu deals with both issues head-on. The space is larger than it seems; fronting on the street, it spreads out over two rooms. The off-white walls are decorated with simple farm implements, tools, and various vintage Americana; the bare wooden tables are set with knives, forks, spoons, and a paper napkin on a place mat that doubles as the menu. The staff are young and energetic, and the kitchen manages well under the eye of former Savoy sous chef Shanna Pacifico.

The Maine shrimp and bacon beignets sounded better than they tasted—they were mostly beignet, bathed in a sweet-and-sour chili sauce. I wished they had more kick from either the shrimp or the bacon, but alas, after several bites I gave up and moved on to the excellent salad of Beluga lentils tossed in a nice mustard vinaigrette accented with tarragon. The cranberry bean salad was also very nice, the portion on the large side, the beans cooked firm but perfectly, plated amidst radicchio leaves and feta cheese chunks enrobed in a ground spice mix redolent of coriander seed. Oven-roasted Brussels sprouts arrived warm and seared atop a soubise-like sauce, made from slow-cooking shallots with cream. Accents of orange zest added a nice citrusy note to the rich, nutty cabbages. On one visit early on, I had just returned from Alba, Italy, where twice I had cotechino sausage, and here the house-made version, set over a slaw of cabbage, brought a smile to my face. Rotisserie chicken, quartered and rubbed with a spice mix, was good, moist and flavorful. The grass-fed heritage bacon burger was very good, and the BLT with fancy smoked bacon is well worth the trip. The french fries are done right: twice-fried, they arrive warm and crisp, tossed with rosemary and sea salt. The buttermilk onion rings are as good as the ones they serve at BLT uptown, with a thick breading crisped by hot oil, the onion steamed and sweet within. Desserts are simple. I loved the apple pie with vanilla ice cream, the apple cider doughnuts, the root beer float, or, for the ambitious and hungry, the stout float spiked with blackberry brandy syrup.

The house cocktails are good. Try the one made from Concord grapes and gin. The wine list is short, fairly priced, well selected, and almost entirely made up of organic and biodynamic wines from the United States and Europe. Two people can dine well here, ordering what they want off the menu, with a bottle of wine and dessert to boot, for well under $100, and that's getting harder and harder to do these days.

Baldoria

212-582-0460
249 West 49th Street, between Broadway and Eighth Avenue
Casual
Reservations recommended
Moderate to expensive
All major credit cards accepted
Lunch and dinner Monday–Friday, dinner Saturday and Sunday
1, C, E trains to 50th Street station; N, R, W trains to 49th Street station

This was supposed to be the midtown alternative for all of us who can't get into Rao's. It isn't Rao's, but it's not bad either. It has a tongue-in-cheek, mobbed-up, old-school Italian vibe. A doorman is posted like a lookout out front, joined by a bunch of guys in funny suits who could just as well be *Sopranos* extras, puffing away on cigarettes and cigars and waiting for Matthew Ianniello to pull up any minute and tell the story about how Joey Gallo got whacked that night at his place downtown, but he was in the kitchen and didn't see a thing.

Baldoria spreads out over two floors with a nice-sized bar and a jukebox on the first floor, and live entertainment, yet another jukebox, and a raw bar upstairs. The clientele range from wanna-be wise guys to pre- and post-theater diners, the bridge-and-tunnel crowd on the weekends, and a smattering of out-of-towners looking to spot someone famous. When the place is packed, it's fun, the crowd and the staff joking back and forth like some 1940s movie, and Frank Pellegrino Jr. working the floor like he owns the place, which he does, no small thanks to Dad and Rao's larger-than-life reputation.

The menu for the most part is lifted straight out of Rao's with a few additions. Good starters are the cold seafood salad, a mix of squid, mussels, shrimp, lobster, and crab. For crunch they add small dice of celery and red bell peppers, all bathed in a rich vinaigrette of olive oil and lemon juice. Smoky house-roasted bell peppers à la Rao's arrive set off by pine nuts and plump sweet raisins. The famous house salad is chopped lettuce tossed with crunchy shaved fennel, cucumber, red onions, radicchio, and cherry tomatoes, with a bracing red wine vinaigrette. Grilled octopus, when it's not overcooked, is another excellent starter, set atop a small pile of sautéed broccoli rabe with minced garlic and olive oil.

The pastas are surprisingly strong for a place that does this kind of volume. Al dente penne arrive tossed with braised eggplant, fresh basil, and a rich tomato sauce alla Siciliana. Linguine with shrimp and arugula, in a pan sauce of fresh cherry tomatoes and lots of chopped, garlic is another good choice. Spaghetti with clams is typical; try instead the chewy, fresh-made pappardelle with porcini and truffle oil in a rich mushroom cream sauce.

Osso bucco was dry and tired one night, but the sausage with pepper and onions was reliably good, as was the calf's liver Venetian style, with onions, white wine, a splash of vinegar, and fresh chopped parsley. The wine list is just okay, but the martinis are very good. Desserts are nothing special. On slow nights it all seems a bit surreal, like somehow you arrived way too late for the party, but overall this can be a fun place to eat, especially when the place is rocking and Frankie junior is singing for you.

Bangkok Café

212-228-7681
27 East 20th Street, between
   Broadway and Park Avenue
Casual
Reservations
Inexpensive
All major credit cards accepted
Lunch and dinner seven days
   a week
6, N, R, W trains to 23rd Street
   station

This casual little place exists mainly for takeout, but they have a few tables with tablecloths, and the small, humble, carpeted room is actually rather nice in a homey sort of way. The staff are gracious and the food for the most part tastes very good and clean.

They offer prix fixe lunch and dinner specials that are real bargains but also limit what you can have from the menu to a set series of options. I'd suggest you pass on the deals and go à la carte, spending a few more dollars but ordering exactly what you like. Try anything with the green curry paste, as aside from the usual layers of flavor, these dishes have a nice chili pepper kick to them missing in most other places. Start with kra prow, a dish of stir-fried shrimp with red curry redolent of good fresh

Thai basil, or the pad see yu, a broad noodle stir-fry, again loaded with Thai basil, crunchy vegetables, and slices of good boneless chicken meat. The pad Thai is very nice, sweet and crunchy with a good chili kick at the end. Duck dishes are flavorful, especially the crispy duck salad. In fact, it's hard to go wrong off this menu—even the item billed as pineapple fried rice is good.

Bánh Mi Saigon Bakery

212-941-1541
138-01 Mott Street, between Hester and Grand Streets, in the back of the jewelry store
Takeout only
Inexpensive
Cash only
Tuesday–Sunday 10 AM–7 PM
6, J, M, Z, N, Q, R, W trains to Canal Street station

How they got a certificate of occupancy for this place I'll never know, but some of the best banh mi sandwiches to be had anywhere in New York are found here, at a booth tucked away in the back portion of a jewelry store on Mott Street. The place is run by a couple, Kevin and Nina, who had another location under the Manhattan Bridge for a while but moved here. I think the jewelry store owner is a relative. It's announced by a blue awning and nothing more, so you'd never know it was here unless someone told you. This sandwich is a product of the French colonial occupation of Vietnam, essentially a melding of the two countries' culinary traditions in one simply delicious sandwich. From the French side comes the roll, originally a baguette or something like it (the Vietnamese use a bit of rice flour in the mix), then mayonnaise applied to it, and then pork pâté, usually found buried amidst the other ingredients. From the Vietnamese side comes the roast BBQ pork—here it is nem nuong style—long sprigs of fresh cilantro, sliced hot jalapeño peppers, and various pickled vegetables, including carrots and cucumber. These are offered in only two styles, spicy or regular; try both. The bread is warm and crisp, heated to order in a toaster oven. The fillings vary from warm to room temp to cold; bite down and the crust cracks, the dough warm and faintly yeasty. Then the insides ooze, fats melt, vegetables crunch, and the flavors follow in big waves. Soon you're smiling and digging in for another bite. It's hard to have any more flavor packed into such a small package or find any more value in a meal than this; last I checked they were $3.25 apiece and worth multiples of that.

Barbetta

212-246-9171
321 West 46th Street, between
    Eighth and Ninth Avenues
Casual
Reservations
Expensive
All major credit cards accepted
Lunch and dinner seven days
    a week
1, 2, 3, 7, S, N, Q, R W trains to
    42nd Street/Times Square
    station; A, C, E trains to 42nd
    Street/Port Authority Bus
    Terminal station

While it's often said that this place has been there forever, here it's true—in 2006 Barbetta celebrated its 100th anniversary. I don't have any idea what West 46th Street looked like in 1906, but these days, as the entire neighborhood is going upscale, it turns out that Barbetta was way ahead of its time. This strip of 46th Street is the theater district's official restaurant row, with over a dozen choices in the one block bounded by Eighth and Ninth Avenues. Woody Allen filmed inside this place, and Rhoda's apartment from the TV sitcom was right across the street. With Lattanzi and Becco, both good options, a few doors down, why choose the stuffy dining room at Barbetta? Because the food is very good. If you like, dine in the lovely backyard garden when it's open. To my taste the dining room is overly wrought, with its gleaming chandeliers, rose-colored walls, dozens of candles, and heavy furniture, but the garden in the rear is a jewel. This is one of the best outdoor dining spots in all of New York. Set beneath mature trees, with a gurgling fountain and nice stone floors, this spot is perfect in season for al fresco dining. Most of what passes as outdoor space in New York is a joke—the tables set on Sixth and 57th at Rue 57, or the ones on 14th Street at Vento? Please. We've outlawed smoking in New York restaurants, so who wants to dine while inhaling bus exhaust fumes? They may as well put tables outside the Port Authority. At Barbetta, it works the way it should. Aside from the occasional siren or car alarm, you'd never know you were in midtown.

Stick with homemade pastas and simple dishes and you'll do fine. Run by the same Piedmontese family, the Maioglios, for its entire existence, Barbetta features white truffle dishes in season and other Piedmontese specialties.

Bar Blanc

212-255-2330
142 West 10th Street,
    between Waverly Place
    and Greenwich Street
Casual
Reservations
Moderate to expensive
All major credit cards accepted
Dinner Tuesday–Sunday
1 train to Christopher Street
    station; A, C, E, B, D, F, V trains
    to West 4th Street station

Bar Blanc opened in late December 2007 as part of an interesting trend that started earlier that year and continues mostly downtown, where you'll find a spate of talented young chefs opening their own restaurants, often partnering with front-of-the-house managers, all of whom have done good long apprenticeships at top New York City eateries. In the case of Bar Blanc, we have four graduates of Bouley University. The original opening chef, César Ramirez, was chef de cuisine for years at Bouley, and his replacement and former Bar Blanc sous chef, Sebastiaan Sijp, is another Bouley grad. The partners, Didier Palange and Kiwon Standen, also did long stints working at Bouley.

This spot they have chosen on West 10th has been seemingly cursed with a prior series of openings and closings, so much so that the über-cynical, naysaying bloggers who prognosticate daily on Eater predicted doom as well for this venture. I'd disagree.

The long narrow space is done up in black and white, mostly white, hence the name. The walls have so many coats of high-gloss white paint they seem to glow. The bar itself is of white marble, the tables, chairs, and banquettes are upholstered in white, and even the backlit mural in the rear is mostly white accented with black geometric patterns.

I visited a few times soon after they opened, and while the front-of-the-house staff needed a bit more time to iron out the wrinkles, overall the level of service was good and improving. Ditto the wine list. It's difficult with a limited budget to open a new place and have much left over for an extensive wine list; here the list is relatively small but well put together, with a selection from around the planet.

The menu is small: four appetizers, four mains, and four pastas. That said, my tuna duo was a lovely study in contrasting and complementing flavors and textures: one tuna was a slow-cooked tuna belly, confit style, the other a tartare. Another plate paired tender boneless rabbit meat, again almost confit style, with sautéed sweetbreads and small mounds of fresh ricotta. Perfectly cooked seared scallops needed little more than the good olive oil they were dressed with and lozenges of candied orange. A simple cheese-filled ravioli was just right, lightly sauced. The understated simplicity of this dish is a signature of a certain strain of authentic Italian cooking in which less is more. A dish of baby pig, referred to on the menu as "porcelet," arrived in parts—the belly braised and crisped, a loin lightly smoked, a terrine done up head-cheese-style, all with defined flavors and well seasoned. The only dish I didn't like was a slow-cooked salmon filet set atop a sauce made of sweet tomato confit accented with vanilla. To me, the rich, fatty meat needed acid and perhaps crunch for complement, not sweet and vanilla, but that's a minor quibble.

The desserts are very good for a place this size, as they actually are able to hire a pastry chef. The Meyer lemon soufflé was nice, as was the pear parfait. While the prices were a bit high in the beginning, I suspect over time they'll come down a bit; the cooking, already being done on a high level, will only get better, as will the service. I look for this to be yet another excellent restaurant in a neighborhood rich with great choices.

Bar Boulud

212-595-0303
1900 Broadway, at the corner
  of 64th Street
Casual
Reservations
Moderate to expensive
All major credit cards accepted
Lunch and dinner Monday–
  Friday, brunch and dinner
  Saturday and Sunday
1, A, C, B, D trains to 59th
  Street / Columbus Circle
  station; 1 train to 66th Street
  station

Daniel Boulud is the best example of a New York–based chef-proprietor who has been able to sustain multiple operations in this city while maintaining consistent, unassailable quality at them all. His signature restaurant, Daniel, stands elite among the short list of best in town while doing a volume night after night that would crush others less able. Café Boulud has been a standout on the Upper East Side for some time now, refined and inventive. DB Bistro Moderne, in the midtown theater district, is better by a long shot than it needs to be. And while Bar Boulud began as a wine bar, it rises well above that genre. Opened in January 2008, Bar Boulud instantly became one of the best restaurants on the Upper West Side, which finally is emerging from its long-standing reputation as a culinary black hole. It should also be noted that for fans of great French cooking who grieve the closure of so many of our city's classic old-school French restaurants such as La Caravelle, La Côte Basque, and Lutèce, in Bar Boulud they'll have a new champion of fine pedigree to carry on that rich culinary tradition. This place is situated on Broadway directly across from Lincoln Center and thus is guaranteed a pre-theater crowd most nights; I suspect it will have a long and fruitful run.

The room is a bit odd, long and narrow, like a shrunken, tightened airplane hangar, but the architects make great use of the space, and the setting has a sense of drama. The entire wall running the length of the left side is sheathed in a backlit curtain of small crushed limestone cased in a fine metal mesh. Small framed Rothkoesque prints made from red wine stains on linen line the walls. The high ceiling is vaulted, the sightlines are open, and the room is softly but well lit; the tables are natural oak, deuces and four-tops up front, booths to the right, lining that wall. When you're seated at the booths, the comfortable chairs set you a little higher than most, which is nice—to me, too many other banquettes have adults sitting too low at the table, like children requiring a phone book to get the right height. A long communal table with a charcuterie bar anchors the center of the space, with more tables to the rear.

As we've come to expect with Daniel Boulud, the food is top-notch, really much better than it has to be at a wine bar, which is why this place appears here listed as a restaurant and not a wine bar. The wine list is superb, as it has been put together by Daniel Johnnes, the man who runs the wine program at Daniel and who spent decades as a buyer and educator while running the wine programs for restaurateur Drew Nieporent and his Myriad Group. While Burgundy-centric, there are excellent, delicious, and affordable wines from the Rhône as well. It is in pairing those wines with the solid cooking here that the magic begins. Most noteworthy is the charcuterie, courtesy of a recent arrival, the Parisian master Gilles Vérot, whose forcemeats are to that genre what Cuban Davidoffs used to be to the cigar world: the gold standard. Pâté making is part art, part craft, utilizing the entire animal, head to tail, cheap cuts mixed with good ones. Even the bones are used for the glace that often binds these meaty mosaics, turning lesser pieces of the animal, even trim, into the sublime. To achieve this, he layers whole recognizable cuts, such as a duck or partridge breast, within a mix of meats from various animals—duck, pheasant, partridge—ground at varying textures, coarse to fine, with the additions of pork fat, pork meat, duck fat, spices, seasoning, and sometimes a little alcohol. They are assembled, packed into terrines, some bordered with pastry crusts, and then slow-baked in the oven in water baths, allowed to cool, and pressed and refrigerated for days or even weeks before being sliced. Here they are served at the perfect temperature, a rarity—cool but not cold. I'd guess they are plated at around 50° to 55°F, just as they should be, so that you can taste the product. The charcuterie tasting plate alone is worth the trip. But then you'd miss the rest of the menu, which would be a shame.

The appetizer billed as frisée Lyonnaise may be the best version of frisée lardon in town. Here that classic boasts the addition of buttery soft, rich sautéed chicken livers. The boudin blanc and noir are perfect cool-weather items, plump, juicy sausages bursting with clean flavor—the noir or blood sausage plated with caramelized apples, the blanc with creamy truffled potatoes. While the menu leans toward classic heavy fare, you can find lighter dishes too, like the Chatham cod, slow-poached in olive oil, garnished with fresh Louisiana shrimp and quail eggs, or the homemade linguine with cuttlefish, razor clams, olives, and lemon in a briny clam broth doused with good extra-virgin olive oil. Fans of beef tartare will love the one here, hand-cut to order from Black Angus top sirloin and served with French-cut waffled potato chips. Fish and chips at Bar Boulud means lightly battered grouper served with root vegetable chips and a rich, tangy mustard sauce. Fatty, thick slabs of Scottish salmon stand up well to the syrah-based red wine butter sauce, enriched with chunks of rendered, crisped bacon and salsify and laced with sage.

But to my mind, the real stars are the classics of the old French canon, such as the boeuf aux carottes. Here a disk-shaped chunk of flatiron steak is braised until it is falling-apart tender, the sauce a deep, rich, dark reduction of the cooking liquid, the meat set over a sweet, smooth carrot puree and a simple onion confit. The coq au vin arrives as several drumsticks and thighs, the skin's deep brown color a testament to the day it spends in a red wine marinade and the subsequent slow cooking in that wine. The meat is enrobed in a sticky, rich reduction of the braising liquid with some parsley added, a few forkfuls of hand-rolled pasta, and the classical garnish of lardons, mushroom caps, and pearl onions.

They offer some great cheeses in various flights, sides of fries, potatoes Lyonnaise style, cauliflower gratin, and so on. The menu in total has great balance and something for everyone. Prices are reasonable, with appetizers in the teens, most mains in the mid-twenties, and sides at $6 each. Desserts are great, so save room. Again here you'll find the theme of French classics; the pear-based tarte Pont Neuf, a gâteau Basque with a rich custard studded with brandied cherries, and a selection of coupes and glaces served in tall glasses, layering ice creams and sorbets with crunchy feuilletines, gingerbread biscuits, or roasted pineapple. While for the opening the menu was rich and hearty, I expect that in warmer months as they open the front and have outdoor seating, lighter fare will follow. I also expect that this place will be an instant destination in this neighborhood, and above all one of the great temples to old-school French cooking now so scarce in modern New York. Expect good service, great food and wine, and prices that are more than fair considering the quality of the ingredients and preparations.

Barney Greengrass

212-724-4707
541 Amsterdam Avenue, just north of 86th Street
Casual
No reservations
Moderate to expensive
Visa, MasterCard accepted
Breakfast and lunch until 4 PM Tuesday–Friday, until 5 PM Saturday
1, B, C trains to 86th Street station

If you think you know lox and bagels but have yet to visit Barney Greengrass, think again. To the best of my knowledge, this is the only deli of its kind in New York, with the possible exception being the venerable Russ and Daughters downtown on East Houston Street, but down there it's all takeout—they don't have seating for customers. They are both fish delicatessens, or in old New York parlance "appetizing" restaurants, specializing in the best smoked and cured fish from around the world. Nicknamed the "Sturgeon King," Barney Greengrass has been in business, run by the same family, for over a hundred years. Like its neighbor Citarella, a few blocks to the south, Barney Greengrass was originally located in Harlem but moved to the Upper West Side in the early 1900s. In the mid-1980s Gary Greengrass, Barney's grandson, began to take over from his father, Moe, who remained a constant presence at the store until his last days, working behind the counter or seated in the dining room schmoozing with old-timers and doing great card tricks.

Here you'll find some of the best smoked fish to be had anywhere. If you are looking for a gold standard for the genre, this is it. I've never gotten a completely good explanation as to why the smoked fish here is better than at nearly all the competition. Gary just rolls his eyes and says, "We pay more, we have longtime relationships with our purveyors, they know what we want, and we're very picky." Okay, so who am I to argue?

There are two dining areas: a smaller one in the middle of the store, tucked between the fish counter and the bagel counter, and a larger one, to the left in a separate room. The décor is bare-bones basic—Formica tables, paper napkins, vintage refrigerators, etched glass displays, wooden chairs, a dropped ceiling, and walls adorned with vintage water-stained wallpaper depicting street scenes from New Orleans. Why street scenes from New Orleans in a New York Jewish deli? I'm told by a reliable source (Gary) that they were on sale when they last did the room, back in the 1930s.

The menu is divided into appetizers, platters, side dishes, specialties, and egg dishes. It's hard to go wrong. All the cured smoked salmon, from the salty belly lox variety and pastrami style to the standard eastern and western nova, are superb, buttery, fresh—what all other smoked salmon strives to be. Sturgeon, as is to be expected, is wonderful. I've taken to eating it plain on white bread with a schmear of butter. Sable is oily and rich; the whitefish is flaky, moist, fresh, and lightly smoked, and when prodded with a fork simply falls off the bones. The whitefish salad is very good, with diced celery and plenty of fish, not too sweet, and not too much spread. The chopped liver, in my opinion, vies for the best in the city—it's a great lunch choice on rye with onion for $9. The scrambled egg dishes are favorites of the regulars, all with a bagel or bialy on the side. There is a selection of egg sandwiches—sturgeon and egg, nova and egg.

If you need meat, they offer pastrami, tongue, salami, or corned beef and egg sandwiches. Herring cured several ways make a good side dish. Try it pickled in cream with onions, or as a mound of homemade chopped herring, sweet matjes, salty schmaltz, or broiled kippers. Their borscht is top-notch, and if you have room for dessert, try the chocolate babka, crumbly, moist, sweet, and quite the finish. The place is not cheap— expect to spend $30 per person to eat well—but you will eat well indeed, and I doubt you'll ever have better fish that that found here.

Bar Stuzzichini

212-780-5100

928 Broadway, between 21st and 22nd Streets

Casual

Reservations

Moderate

All major credit cards accepted

Lunch and dinner seven days a week

N, R, W, 6 trains to 23rd Street station

Forget the Italian Pottery Barn interior and concentrate on the food and service. Heck, Morandi, seemingly packed all the time, has those cheesy wicker-clad chianti bottles all over the place, and their food is half as good as what's served here. This place was last Komagashi, and the transformation includes leather banquettes, round marble tables, and large wooden chandeliers with exposed bulbs hanging overhead. Rustic, I suppose, is the theme. The chef, Paul DiBari, worked with Kurt Gutenbrunner at Wallsé for a while, and that's a good solid kitchen The word *stuzzichini* derives from the verb *stuzzicare*, meaning "to pick" or "to choose," in this case among small tapas-like plates. It's a nice way to eat, and at places like this, it's often some of the best food on the menu.

The appetizers are sorted into five categories—vegetables, fish, fried, cheese, and salumi—and can be ordered à la carte as you see fit or in a groups of five for $22, which is a nice way to put a small meal together. Start with the grilled sardines, Sicilian style, served with pine nuts and raisins, or the lightly battered salt cod fritters (assuming you like salt cod, that is—I must admit I've never found a salt cod dish anywhere that I much liked). Fresh clams simply steamed, their broth enriched with good butter, are hard to argue with, as are the Roman-style artichokes, fried crisp with multiple textures, the outer leaves crisped and crunchy, the heart chewy and moist. All they need is a good splash of fresh lemon juice to work their magic.

In the early spring they offer puntarella, a great bitter green tossed with a bracing anchovy-rich vinaigrette. Off-season the same idea works almost as well with chicory. Stuffed chickpea fritters remind me of my grandmother's cooking, as does the toothsome orecchiette, paired with peas and bound with a touch of heavy cream and Parmigiano Reggiano.

If it's bigger plates you want, try any of the pastas offered—they are uniformly good—or the tomato-braised short ribs. Though this cut of meat is common these days all over town, it's a satisfying choice when the weather turns cold, its richness to some extent offset by the mildly acidic tomato sauce. Tuna steak, usually as bland a fish as there is, here is marinated in basil oil and topped with a pesto-like mix for a needed flavor fix.

The owner, Carolyn Renny, makes all the desserts; while dessert has never been Italian cuisine's strong suit, here some of the more rustic offerings are very good. The orange-scented olive oil pound cake is always nice, as is the mucca, an Italian version of the root beer float. Here scoops of chocolate and vanilla gelato are smothered with the Italian bitter cola chinotto to good effect. If all else fails, share an order of the good cannoli, arriving in threes and dusted with powdered sugar; they are perfect with an after-dinner espresso. The wine list has well over 100 bottles, all of Italian origin and many priced in the $30–$50 range, as well as 20 or so available by the carafe. Service is good, and the value is even better; with that combination, I hope Bar Stuzzichini has a good long lease.

Basta Pasta

212-366-0888
37 West 17th Street, between Fifth and Sixth Avenues
Casual
Reservations
Moderate
All major credit cards accepted
Lunch and dinner Monday–Friday, dinner Saturday and Sunday
4, 5, 6, L, N, Q, R, W trains to 14th Street/Union Square station

I heard about this place from an Italian immigrant, the great saxophone repairman Roberto Romeo, whose shop is upstairs in a small building on West 46th Street. A native of Verona, Italy, he knows his pasta. I was there with my friend Bill Evans, who was picking up his soprano sax, one day when we all got to talking about—what else?—food. Roberto told me about this great place off Union Square where these Japanese guys made pasta as well as Italians do. He's one of the best repairmen in the business, and he's Italian, so I figured he knew what he was talking about, and he was right. The original Basta Pasta opened in Tokyo in 1985, and this place followed five years later. The Japanese are great technicians. They have French bakeries that are just like French bakeries in Paris, and in this case the pasta is all house-made and all very good. The open-kitchen idea comes from the *Iron Chef* TV program, which inspired the original owners to open in the first place.

The menu is laid out in typical Italian style, with antipasti, primi piatti, secondi piatti, griglia, and desserts. Start with the grilled squid, ringlets tossed with okra, endive, mullet roe, tomatoes, and pistachios. The tuna Tataki features pan-seared rare tuna slices topped with an interesting wasabi tartar sauce. All of the pasta courses are good, but I especially like the toothsome garganelli paired with chicken thigh meat and okra in a vegetable ragù. If the uni is fresh, the spaghetti with sea urchin in pink sauce is darn good too. Or opt for the traditional pappardelle with braised eggplant and tomatoes; veal ravioli with prosciutto, mozzarella cheese, and tomatoes; fusilli Bolognese; or the weird but good spaghetti with flying fish roe and chopped shiso.

For main courses, the Berkshire pork chop is good, as is the crisp-crusted veal Milanese and panko-crusted free-range chicken over Italian couscous (fregola) mixed with fresh peas and Parmigiano Reggiano.

Desserts are okay—plates of this and that dusted or drizzled with something or other. Service can be uneven but is usually good. The staff is all Japanese, and one day I had dinner there early, after many of them must have returned from a wine tasting. Everyone had wine on their breath, as well as red-stained lips and teeth. How Italian!

Bellavitae

212-473-5121
24 Minetta Lane, off Sixth
   Avenue
Casual
Reservations
Moderate
All major credit cards accepted
Dinner Tuesday–Friday, brunch
   and dinner Saturday and
   Sunday
A, C, E, B, D, F, V trains to West
   4th Street station

For years and years this place operated as La Bohème, named not after the opera but for Bohemia, that long-gone characterization of Greenwich Village, the Greenwich Village of De Kooning and Kerouac, of Allen Ginsberg, Bob Dylan, Phil Ochs, Jimi Hendrix, and Joni Mitchell, of Beat writers and bohemians, poets, artists, hippies, and dreamers. But the bohemian opts now for the good life, the kids grew up, and Bohème became Bellavitae. Fitting, as this part of town is no longer a place for dreamers unless they have a nice trust fund to tap. The Village remains one of the strongest real estate markets in all New York, charming always but now very expensive. But not all is gloom and doom. La Bohème had its day and has been improved upon by Bellavitae, a very good Italian restaurant, serious, as they should be, about Italian ingredients.

The new owner didn't have to change much: the bar is still to your left as you enter, those wide center-cut yellow pine plank floors exposed beneath you as before, the main dining room to the rear, with another bar area, the wood-burning oven, and the open kitchen framing the back. The walls are brick with framed pictures, the lighting soft, the clientele eclectic. The man behind this, Rolando Beramendi, has been very active in the Italian specialty foods import business in New York for years, supplying many of the city's top restaurants with exotic and hard-to-find olive oils, vinegars, artisanal pastas, rice, olives, and even honey. Not surprisingly, these same items are showcased here on the menu; some are even for sale. This place is like many of these new wave Italian restaurants in New York in that the food is simply prepared and the ingredients are excellent—they remind me very much of the places I love to dine at in Italy. Italian food is at its heart simple food. The chef is Darren McRonald, who worked at Chez Panisse and elsewhere, but here at Bellavitae that Chez Panisse influence is what I sense the most. After all, sometimes simple is the hardest thing to do.

Start with the grilled radicchio wrapped in pancetta. The radicchio here is flown in fresh from little farms around Treviso, wrapped like a cigar in paper-thin strips of pancetta, grilled, and drizzled with 12-year-old balsamic vinegar tableside. At first taste it's salty and bitter, but soon the flavors meld and the lovely porky quality of the pancetta takes the edge off these bitter greens, allowing the sweetness of the vinegar to emerge. Asparagus gets the same treatment when they don't have radicchio available, but I prefer it with the greens. I found the tiny fried meatballs a little greasy on several visits, but the crostini layered with creamy gorgonzola and then drizzled with chestnut honey from Lake Como was a huge winner. For fans of chicken liver, try the Tuscan-style version served here, soft and mashed with anchovies and pureed garlic, the flavors framed again by a splash of vinegar (good chefs know that acidity has a way of polishing flavors). Little fried risotto balls come in several varieties; the saffron-scented version is good, but I preferred the ones spiked with tomato and smoked mozzarella.

The pastas are uniformly good. Fettuccine is paired with tiny zucchini cut in rounds and cooked nearly to a confit, the flavor rich and almost nutty, tossed with an onion brunoise, a good dose of fruity olive oil, sea salt, and cracked pepper—very simple and very good. Toothsome bucatini is served with a variety of shellfish in their own broth, enriched with olive oil and chopped parsley, and eggy, rich garganelli are paired with a good, thick, meaty Bolognese sauce. To this add main courses of grilled fish and meats. Steak in the European style is sliced thin, a small potion by our standards, and topped with a good herby salsa verde. Fritto misto of this and that is good as well—rabbit one night, mixed seafood another, all garnished with thin slices of fennel bulb, dusted with semolina, and flash-fried along with slivers of Meyer lemon that have received the same treatment. In winter months good braises are paired with creamy polenta, and the pizza oven sees even more use.

Desserts are okay, though never a strong point in Italian cuisine. A decent chocolate semifreddo, moist and airy panettone, and very good gelato may be the best choices. The wine list is good and nearly exclusively Italian, offering a good selection of many hard-to-find choices from small producers.

Bella Napoli

212-683-4510
130 Madison Avenue,
between 30th and 31st
Streets
Casual
No reservations
Inexpensive to moderate
All major credit cards accepted
Seven days a week from 11 AM
6 train to 33rd Street station;
N, R, W trains to 28th Street
station

If you're looking for a much better than average local pizza place, it just got a bit easier, as Bella Napoli has opened a second location on Seventh Avenue in Chelsea. It's not just a pizza place; they serve a pretty large selection of pastas and salads as well, but I can only vouch for the pies. I'm not big on lots of toppings on pizza. I prefer the classic Margherita with just tomato sauce, basil, and good mozzarella, which they do very well here. The pies have thin, well-charred crusts and the tomato sauce is good and full-flavored but not overly seasoned with dried oregano and the like.

They do a big volume, so the pizza comes right out of the oven and never sits very long waiting for a home. Unlike many of the fancier places around town, here you can stop in and just get a slice or two and not have to order an entire pizza. They also make some very good Italian sandwiches, hero-style (or hoagies, as they say where I come from). The meatball, sausage, breaded veal cutlet, eggplant, and chicken heroes are all a pretty darn good meal for under $8 a pop, a value that's hard to beat these days. Lots of folks rave about the lasagna, baked ziti, and stuffed shells, but I've never tried them. Honestly, most neighborhood pizza places stink, but this is easily one of the best you'll find in New York.

Ben Benson's

212-581-8888
123 West 52nd Street,
between Sixth and Seventh
Avenues
Casual to dressy
Reservations required
Expensive
All major credit cards accepted
Lunch and dinner Monday–
Friday, dinner Saturday and
Sunday
1 train to 50th Street station;
N, R, W trains to 49th Street
station

Is there really a Smith behind Smith and Wollensky? Does a Gallagher work at Gallagher's anymore? Where is the Spark at Sparks? And who the heck are Maloney & Porcelli anyway? Well, rest assured that there is a Ben Benson, and he can be found daily at the eponymous Ben Benson's, located steps off Sixth Avenue on 53rd Street, just past the Rochester Big and Tall store, where perhaps a few of Ben's frequent customers find their suits. Ben, a Brooklyn native raised on Long Island, was half the team that started the original TGI Friday's way back when, and then the original Smith and Wollensky's in 1979, working as a partner with the founder and current owner, Alan Stillman. They parted ways amicably, as Alan wanted to drive the company to open franchises throughout the country, and Ben had other ideas. In 1982 Ben opened his own shop in midtown, and 25 years later it's still packed nightly. While the trend in steakhouses has been to franchise the successful brands, Ben resists. One day over coffee, Ben confided that he too had had offers to open in Boca Raton, Vegas, and elsewhere, but as he put it, "I live in the neighborhood, I walk to work, I love this place, I love being here every day, I enjoy being with my customers. Boca? Heck, I don't want to go south of 34th Street."

This place is more than just another steakhouse, and is much better than most in many ways and for many reasons. Their version of creamy New England clam chowder puts many seafood houses to shame. The appetizer of stone crab claws is excellent—well cooked, fresh, sweet, and moist. Try the hearts of romaine with Caesar dressing and freshly grated Parmesan as a starter, or the Maryland jumbo lump crab cakes as appetizers or entree, lightly bound, crisped on the outside, and full of delectable crabmeat. The large menu lists 34 entrees in all, including the standard selection of meats, which here are all USDA prime and dry-aged. There is a section of Italian classics, including chicken Parmesan, scaloppini of veal Milanese, and shrimp scampi, which are all okay, albeit served on overcooked pasta. The lemon pepper chicken is popular, as is the dry-rubbed grilled skirt steak, roast pork tenderloin, carved prime rib, and poached salmon platter.

Order fried chicken at Ben Benson's and be prepared to take half home. Here you get the whole bird as a single portion; a 3½-pound fryer is butchered individually for each incoming order, dredged in buttermilk, coated with seasoned flour, and cooked to order. It's well worth it, but allow 20 to 25 minutes. Daily specials include Monday's excellent chicken pot pie, Tuesday's roast turkey with trimmings, Wednesday's beef stew with noodles, Thursday's roast beef hash, and Friday's lobster cakes—if you aren't hungry yet, check your pulse. All the sides are uniformly superior. The hash browns are the gold standard, with a crisp dark golden brown exterior revealing a moist, almost creamy potato center laced with onions and red and green peppers. The wild mushrooms arrived creamy and herbed, a good mixture of well-seasoned sautéed mushrooms bound in reduced heavy cream. Sautéed or creamed spinach scores high marks; Ben really does taste the creamed spinach every day. Or try the steamed asparagus or broccoli.

There is a boisterous bar scene every night, and a few tables are scattered there as well. But the handsome wood-paneled main dining room is the place to eat. The wait staff are all seasoned pros, many of whom have worked here for decades. The wine list is very well put together to work with this food, with a broad assortment and a range of price points. This is one of my favorite classic American restaurants in the country. It's the kind of place you can bring foodies, friends from out of town, your great-aunt from Topeka, and kids, and everyone will be happy.

Big Wong King Restaurant

212-964-0540
67 Mott Street, between
  Bayard and Canal Streets
Casual
No reservations
Inexpensive
All major credit cards accepted
Lunch and dinner seven days
  a week
6, J, M, Z, N, Q, R, W trains to
  Canal Street station

If you're a fan of congee, this is the place. Cantonese is the style, and they're open for breakfast, lunch, and early dinner. Don't let the bare-bones dining room scare you off. The place is usually packed with regulars, 85% Chinese, and half of them, it seems, come here for the congee. It's served with a long fried piece of dough, best described as a savory cruller of sorts, known as yu za kuei, or you tiao. I'm not a huge fan of congee; I didn't grow up eating it, but for those who did, this place is a little taste of home. As you enter and wait in line for seats to clear at any of the communal tables, you'll see the roast duck and pork hanging just before you, and the cooks at work preparing dishes from them.

Any of the fried rice, lo mein, or noodle dishes are very good. The lo mein is served using thin noodles, which I usually eschew, but here they taste great. Fried rice dishes are also generous and flavorful. The noodle soups taste great and have a good amount of meat within them, especially considering the bargain-basement prices. Try the egg noodles in beef broth with shrimp dumplings, or any of the roast meats; duck and pork are excellent, simply presented chopped or sliced and served over a bed of warm rice drizzled with soy sauce. You can eat well here for under $10 per person, and that's hard to beat. Yes, the tables are cramped, and the waiters yell across the room at each other like seagulls fighting over cheese fries on the boardwalk, but who cares? For food this good at these prices, I'm in.

Blaue Gans

212-571-8880
139 Duane Street, between
  Church Street and West
  Broadway
Casual
No reservations
Moderate
All major credit cards accepted
Seven days a week 11:30 AM–1 AM
1, 2, 3, A, E trains to Chambers
  Street station; R, W trains to
  City Hall station

Originally opened as Le Zinc, this was Karen and David Waltuck's casual alternative to Chanterelle. They sold the space to Kurt Gutenbrunner in 2006, and little has changed between the last two owners. The space is fine as these things go, long and not too narrow, with a good high ceiling and walls hung with large mirrors and a nice collection of artsy movie posters. The zinc bar to your right as you enter is long and broad, and in a jam it's a perfectly fine place to eat too. With the kitchen in the rear, traffic flow is minimal, and the space feels as if it could be in any major city. In other words, it has a nice timeless European quality about it.

The food here has never been better, billed as German-Austrian, and the kitchen is led by Martin Pirker, who worked with Kurt for years at Wallsé. This is Kurt's casual spot, with Café Sabarsky uptown and Wallsé in the West Village being more of his signature locations, with prices to match. I love it here for lunch, especially since you can eat a darn good three-course meal for under $20. The dinner menu isn't much more expensive. This is, after all, still a heavy local neighborhood spot, and while the neighborhood has changed—it is now the most expensive zip code in New York—the idea is still the same. Hence the crowd that assembles here on any given day is a mix of men in suits and well-dressed women who work in the neighborhood, old-time locals in khakis and colored T-shirts, and trustafarians in board shorts.

Upon being seated, you're given a dish of hand-cut chunky rye bread and a spread of soft creamy Liptauer cheese blended with onions, paprika, and herbs. Beef consommé isn't easy to make. It's time-consuming and expensive, and the one served here in the cooler months, poured tableside over semolina and calf's liver dumplings, makes you wish more places offered it. It's a great starter, managing to be hearty, delicious, satisfying, and light all at the same time. Or try the famed smoked trout; here the filets are skinned and boned, the meat blended with crème fraîche to lighten it, then spread between layers of thin crepes, torte-style. From this they cut wedges that are plated with baked baby beets, a salad of frisée, and shaved horseradish. It's a great study in contrasts of texture and a wonderful melding of flavors, the crêpes and filling smoky, sweet, and light, the beets tasting of the earth, the frisée bitter, and the radish supplying the needed crunch and edge. For lunch the schnitzel sandwich is a bargain at $14 with fries, as are the pork and beef sausages served with excellent sauerkraut for $8. If I'm hungry, I opt for the jaegerschnitzel, a boneless pork medallion pounded thin and flash-sautéed, set over a sauce of heavy cream reduced with quartered mushrooms, garnished with fingerling potatoes.

For dinner, if you're brave and hungry, start with the goulash soup—it is a revelation—or the big bowl of steaming mussels. Who knew that boiled beef, here billed as kavalierspitz, could be so good? Slow-braised until fork-tender, it is paired with creamed spinach and an apple horseradish. If I'm not mistaken, I've had this same dish at Wallsé as part of a tasting menu. Venison too gets the goulash treatment, the flavorful chunks of game slow-cooked in a rich braise thick with paprika and set alongside puffy light spaetzle. Yes, it does seem that the menu favors hearty fare over light, but that is the hallmark of this style of cuisine.

Desserts are first-rate, made by pastry chef Pierre Reboul, who oversees all of Kurt's dessert menus. In between the classic seasonal fruit strudel and sachertorte, you'll find great items such as the poached quark dump-lings floating in an orange-scented fruit soup, or kaiserschmarren, essentially a warm pancake sprinkled with powdered sugar and topped with apple compote. The wine and beer list was put together by Aldo Sohm, who won the Sommelier of the Year award in 2006. Last I checked, he had moved on and was overseeing the beverage program at Le Bernardin. Needless to say, the list is thick with enough great selections and surprises from both Austria and Germany to keep anyone happy. Of all of Kurt's efforts, this may be my favorite, as the relaxed vibe, great food, and easy-to-take prices hit just the right balance.

BLT Market

212-521-6125
1430 Sixth Avenue, in the Ritz-Carlton Hotel, at the corner of Sixth Avenue and Central Park South
Casual to dressy
Reservations
Expensive
All major credit cards accepted
Breakfast, lunch, and dinner seven days a week
N, R, W trains to Fifth Avenue/ 59th Street station; 1, A, C, B, D trains to 59th Street/ Columbus Circle station; F train to 57th Street station

By the time BLT Market opened in the late summer of 2007, chef Laurent Tourondel had morphed from being a very good chef into an international brand. He has five restaurants in New York City alone, and twice that many projects going on spread over several continents, including several other BLT Markets in various Ritz-Carlton locations. To that add cookbooks and a lifestyle magazine, and it would seem from his energy and potential that he's just getting started. This hotel has changed hands several times over the last few decades; now it is at its most polished in recent memory. The dining room used to be Atelier, but that project was closed and renovated prior to opening as BLT Market, a fine addition to the New York scene and, with its market-driven cuisine, a concept in tune with the times. You can enter the space past the hotel bar off the main lobby or directly off the street via the Sixth Avenue side, just steps off Central Park South. That Sixth Avenue entrance is a very good idea, as fussy New Yorkers on their way to dinner, with just a few exceptions, famously loathe being asked to walk through hotel lobbies and bars, with all their riffraff.

The room is nice and bright with big windows that open up onto the street and even some decent outdoor seating on Sixth Avenue, weather allowing, though the charm of dining al fresco here is totally lost on me, what with all those horse-drawn carriages just north, the usual traffic on that corner, and a bus stop a few steps south. I'm not sure anyone except the brave, the uninformed, naive tourists from out of town, or the desperately hungry will be takers for those tables. Stay inside, and the chances are that on any given night you'll eat very well too. I'm not a fan of all Tourondel projects. I really like BLT Steak, and BLT Prime too is good, but BLT Fish downstairs is a complete disaster, and upstairs too has been a disappointment lately, slipping a lot in my opinion since it first opened.

Here the menu is good, small, and well focused, changing daily. The left side states the month and is followed by a list of "peak in season" ingredients utilized by the dishes offered throughout the menu. You'll learn that October is good for sunchokes, salsify, matsutake mushrooms, and mustard greens, and you'll find nearly all of those on your excellent appetizer plate of roasted langoustine tails, set atop pan jus and a nice matignon of vegetables. The mustard greens appear in their infancy as microgreens, and fresh hearts of palm from Hawaii are cut on a mandoline in long thin shards and set atop the plate. Or opt for the big salad starter, maybe too big, of duck confit, taken off the bones and tossed with good greens including watercress, a few excellent aged goat cheese beignets, and a sweet honey-mustard vinaigrette. A half bottle of Olivier Leflaive's excellent Chassagne-Montrachet did the trick. Little bowls of rock shrimp risotto followed, the chewy Arborio rice redolent of good shellfish stock, and the addition of cauliflower florets and shaved black truffles raised the ante considerably. This is my kind of good-tasting food. A single manicotti, the simple crêpe rolled and filled with a duxelle of wild mushrooms, sits in a pool of reduced heavy cream thick with mushroom flavor accented by fresh sage and beurre noisette, and garnished with sautéed miniature mushroom caps. A glass of fumé blanc and a crisp Pouilly-Fuissé paired well with these dishes. Wild salmon here is first hot-smoked, then finished in the oven and served as a semi-smoked filet garnished with Honeycrisp apples, American caviar, and shards of good Schaller & Weber bacon. Fatty, rich Alaskan black cod is marinated in acacia honey, then cooked under the salamander and served in a cast-iron casserole, crisp and brown on top, rich and creamy at the center, set atop a nice puree of butternut squash, also listed in the "peak season" section, and quickly sautéed spinach. A 2005 Bethel Heights pinot noir from the Willamette Valley married well with both dishes.

Desserts too are all good, the list mercifully short, with just a half-dozen choices, but nary a clinker in the list. The hazelnut Paris-Brest with chocolate cappuccino is fine. The rich moist Macintosh apple cake with calvados cream and a scoop of Vermont crème fraîche flavored with lavender honey is sturdy and delicious. The chestnut nougat sundae arrived in a tall parfait glass that held enough dessert for two or more reasonable people, the various ingredients layered and dripping with chocolate cream, while the chocolate coconut layer cake set next to a scoop of rum ice cream will please any lover of coconut layer cakes, or just fans of good desserts.

At the opening, Laurent brought in his A-team. The floor staff are excellent and the cooks, led by chef de cuisine David Malbequi, are all very conscientious. The team as a whole works like a well-oiled machine. We'll see if they can hold this high standard as Tourondel moves on to other projects, there is the usual turnover, and the complications of running a seven-day-a-week, full-service restaurant in a busy Manhattan hotel take their toll. For now, it's a lovely spot to eat very well and a welcome addition to this midtown north neighborhood.

BLT Prime

212-995-8500
111 East 22nd Street, between Park Avenue South and Lexington Avenue
Casual
Reservations
Expensive
All major credit cards accepted
Dinner seven nights a week
6 train to 23rd Street station

Years back this place was Restaurant C.T., where the young French chef Claude Troisgros was cooking great food in a neighborhood that had yet to arrive. Working with him in that kitchen was a young Laurent Tourondel. Post-C.T., Rocco DiSpirito opened Union Pacific here, and by then the neighborhood was ready. The place was very busy, but Rocco apparently got bored and had aspirations well beyond cheffing. Hence the return of Tourondel and this, his most unabashedly meat-centric steakhouse. The room is nice. You enter off the street past the bar to your right. The main room features a glass skylight to the left; to the right, frosted glass reveals the once open kitchen. Tables and chairs are set far enough apart to distinguish this as an "adult" dining room. Cocktails and the wine list are courtesy of Fred Dexheimer, the young man who oversees all the beverage programs for the BLT restaurants.

This can be one of the best steakhouse options in town. They offer lots of meat in different cuts: prime and Angus, dry-aged to various degrees, both domestic Wagyu and Japanese Kobe beef, and a half-dozen or more house-made sauces: béarnaise, Roquefort, peppercorn, chimichurri, red wine reduction, three mustards, horseradish, etc.

Portions are big. The excellent spinach salad could be a meal. It arrives tossed in a large bowl with baby spinach sharing the company of sliced button mushrooms, crumbled double-smoked bacon, and Maytag blue cheese, all in a creamy dressing—as good a spinach salad as I've had in years. The grilled double-cut bacon isn't as good as Luger's, but the roasted baby beets with goat cheese were very good, as was the crab cake. The truth is that meat is meat, and at any great steakhouse, you can have an amazing cut and then return the next day and be disappointed by the exact same thing. All animals are different and carcasses vary, even within prime, but the side dishes here, as they are at BLT Steak, are head and shoulders above what you'll get in most every other old-school steakhouse. The fish is just so-so; I recommend you order meat. If not steak, then opt for the excellent chicken or the veal chop, and try the sides too. The onion rings are perfect; various wild mushroom varieties come sautéed or braised; the blue cheese tater tots are addictive; the fries are crisp, dark, and delicious; and the creamy pudding-like gratin is good too.

After all this, who has room for dessert? But should you be brave, the crêpe soufflé is excellent, and the lemon meringue pie is too. Should you be entirely crazy, opt for the rich, moist, dense cream-cheese-topped carrot cake with a scoop of ginger ice cream for good measure. The cocktail program is strong, the wine list blends Old and New World styles, and if Fred is on the floor, have him help you make a choice.

BLT Steak

212-752-7470
106 East 57th Street, between Park and Lexington Avenues
Casual to dressy
Reservations
Expensive
All major credit cards accepted
Dinner seven nights a week
E, V trains to Lexington Avenue/53rd Street station; 4, 5, 6, N, R, W to Lexington Avenue/59th Street station

Forget the name—it stands for Bistro Laurent Tourondel. All I can figure is that the chef, who is French, didn't know that this was actually the name of a famous sandwich, and then it was too late; everyone was afraid to tell him. Tourondel, who had been known in New York for his talent with seafood at the now closed but fondly remembered Cello, opened this spot to instant success with his business partner Jimmy Haber, who had the space, formerly Pazo. Haber has an eye for talent and also financially backs Patricia Yeo with her various New York projects, while several of those, including this one, have now become part of the BLT franchise. Haber and Tourondel run the very successful BLT Fish in Chelsea (formerly Yeo's three-star AZ) and BLT Prime in the Flatiron (formerly Rocco DiSpirito's Union Pacific). They know their clientele and saw a window of opportunity here for a new, more modern steakhouse with a refined menu prepared by a talented team in the kitchen. Steakhouses like this (and Tom Colicchio's Craftsteak) are built by chefs who use classical steakhouse ingredients and cooking as a base but then vastly improve on them, moving the popular genre into the modern era.

They have refined the dining room at BLT since it opened, and it is quite comfortable now—gone is that odd long black table for communal seating. You enter off 57th, with the bar area to your left. To the rear, the square dining room is lined with banquettes against the walls and comfortable leather chairs positioned before beautiful polished ebony tables with plenty of seating in the center of the floor. The well-lit room has a blackboard in the rear listing the day's specials and wines by the glass.

Is the meat at BLT as good as that at Peter Luger's? No, but the comparisons stop there. Everything else is better, tons better. While a meat eater will be more than happy here with the wide selection of beef, lamb, pork, veal, and chicken, seafood lovers will also leave with smiles on their faces. The menu is well designed and well executed, from the colossal plump Gruyère-infused Yorkshire pudding that greets each diner to the varied appetizers of raw and cured fish, plump and meaty crab cakes, and interesting seasonal salads. Having a real chef in the kitchen of a steakhouse makes a tremendous difference. He knows how to cook, and his cooks know how to cook and are all taught well and supervised.

The plates come out of this kitchen clean, hot, cooked accurately, and well seasoned. The à la carte sides include assorted sautéed wild mushrooms (shiitake, hen-of-the-woods, bluefoot, morels) sautéed with shallots and bathed in butter, cream, and herbs. Dig into the towering stack of perfectly battered onion rings or any the half-dozen excellent potato options, including exemplary crisp and salty frites, chunky flavorful hash browns, and creamy smooth mashed. There is the signature foie gras and the brioche BLT, assembled with applewood-smoked bacon and oven-roasted tomatoes, although I for one do not like toasted sliced brioche and always have a glass of water nearby, as I nearly inevitably choke on those nasty crumbs. A selection of seasonal soups include a delicious bacon-studded New England clam chowder. Steak cuts vary and usually feature an American Kobe flatiron steak, New York strip, ribeye, and hanger steak, all offered with your choice of sauce: béarnaise, red wine, peppercorn, three mustards, blue cheese, or horseradish. Not in the mood for a grilled steak? Try the braised short ribs, lemon rosemary chicken, pot-au-feu, the crispy Moulard duck breast, or the juicy and pink two-inch-thick Niman Ranch organic pork chops.

Seafood selections are based on market availability, but you'll often find grilled swordfish, tuna, Dover sole, or the whopping 3½-pound lobster, cooked carefully, seasoned well, and offered with a choice of several sauces.

Save room for the desserts. Unlike at most steakhouses, there really is a pastry chef in the kitchen. Go traditional and try the wonderfully rich and moist carrot cake, the rarely seen and delicious crêpe soufflé resting in a pool of citrus sauce, or the orange-raspberry sundae, served in a tall glass studded with nougat glacé, candied nuts, and crunchy meringue.

Blue Hill

212-539-1776
75 Washington Place,
between Sixth Avenue and
Washington Square
Casual to dressy
Reservations
Expensive
All major credit cards accepted
Dinner seven nights a week
A, C, E, B, D, F, V trains to West
4th Street station

Blue Hill is one of my favorite restaurants in the Village, if not the city as a whole. It strikes the perfect balance between very good food, attentive service, and a relaxed downtown vibe. On a recent hot July night, I had dinner there in short pants and a golf shirt, while the men at the table next to mine were dressed in suits and ties. They seemed shocked that another fellow entered the room in shorts and an untucked T-shirt, hugged the maître d', and was seated. "He must be a friend of the owner," one guessed. I knew better—shorts are okay here, not to worry. Chef Dan Barber, the man behind Blue Hill, is one of the few top-tier working chefs today who is actually from New York City. Born and raised on the Upper East Side, a product of private schools, he spent his summers growing up in the Berkshires at a family farm with the same name as the restaurant. Up there, they ate what they raised, and it didn't hurt either that his father was a gourmand in his own right, having eaten in many of the best restaurants both here and abroad. The fruit didn't fall far from the tree, yet with Dan's privileged background, a career in investment banking or a partnership at a law firm would have seemed more appropriate. But unlike many wealthy New York kids, Dan is without pretense. Nothing about his mannerisms suggests his pedigree. He's a straight-up, old-school hard worker in a business where that still matters. He worked in Europe, cooking in some good kitchens, and then cut his teeth back in New York at the original Bouley. David was a taskmaster, and that was a tough kitchen to work in, while a fertile training ground for many top chefs around the city today.

Dan opened Blue Hill in the spring of 2000, and the place has done very well since. For years the real day-to-day cooking was done by Juan José Cuevas (now chef de cuisine at Ed Brown's excellent restaurant Eighty-one), and these days Trevor Kunk runs the kitchen. Dan's other restaurant, Blue Hill at Stone Barns, in Westchester, is where he spends most of his time nowadays and is well worth a visit, even a detour. There Dan has a full-blown working organic farm that supplies both restaurants nearly year round with seasonal produce as well as Berkshire pork, chickens, lamb, and other ingredients.

A recent summer meal started with a pairing of Junma Ginjo sake and Hitachino Nest White Ale, also Japanese, made from rice, alongside several courses including a summer gazpacho, heirloom tomato concassé with tomato sorbet and Parmesan foam, and black bass crudo laced with powdered Espelette peppers. A plate of summer vegetables was a study in flavor and texture: it carried blanched haricots verts; paper-thin slices of baby fennel; slivers of marinated Kuroda carrots; broccoli florets; the most flavorful baby zucchini I've ever had, raw and cut into long thin strips; and that same squash lightly grilled with the flowers still on. A warm heirloom tomato soup was a perfect midsummer course, featuring at least half a dozen varieties of tomatoes, all raw, peeled, and seeded, ranging from sweet to tart, red to yellow, and set adrift in a bowl of tomato water laced with orange zest, tarragon, and chervil. Next came three fresh-smoked large shrimp set on a paper-thin slice of warm pork belly—its buttery richness a good foil to the lean shrimp—and sprinkled it with toasted pine nuts and micro arugula. It was paired with an '04 Buty, a mix of sémillon and sauvignon blanc from the Columbia Valley. I couldn't go a meal without trying some of the great pork. This evening it was presented two ways on one plate, first as a medium-rare loin, sliced in medallions, with a tall square of the belly braised and then crisped at the top. Sharing the plate were curlicues of baby bok choy, sautéed chanterelles, a lozenge of braised white eggplant topped with a layer of tomato concassé, and little perfect spheres of cucumber flesh. Everything on that plate, like most of the rest of the meal, was grown on the farm 30 miles to the north and harvested within the last 48 hours.

The wine pairings featured two vintages of La Maestra from Ruston, the 2001 and 2002, made from a mix of cab, merlot, cab franc, and petit verdot, organically grown, of very limited supply, and in a word, superb. Two desserts that stood out were a tall glass filled with summer fruit as a parfait, and another plate of warm, steaming chocolate bread pudding. The room is very nice, simply adorned and comfortable. The crowd on any given night may include students from NYU (whether with the money and good taste to splurge here, or celebrating something with their parents in tow and the bill taken care of), guys and gals in business suits, locals from the neighborhood, tourists from around the globe, and a chef or two. All are treated very well here and will eat well too.

Bobo

212-488-2626
181 West 10th Street,
at Seventh Avenue,
unmarked door, steps
down from the sidewalk
Casual
Reservations
Moderate
All major credit cards accepted
Dinner seven nights a week
1 train to Christopher Street
station; 1, 2, 3 trains to 14th
Street station; A, C, E, B, D,
F, V trains to West 4th Street
station

For many years, New Yorkers of a certain age knew this place as the longtime home of John Clancy's, a very good seafood restaurant with a loyal following that in the late 1980s moved to John Clancy's East up on East 63rd Street. The space has since been several different restaurants, but none nearly as good as its current incarnation, Bobo. Oddly, the place is named after a word that political journalist David Brooks coined, which is short for "bourgeois bohemian," though that does seem to describe the crowd to some extent. There is no sign outside; you just take a few steps down from the sidewalk and enter the subterranean bar/dining area, with a few tables lit by candles. The bartender spins vinyl off an old turntable, supplying the restaurant's funky, eclectic old-school sound track. Upstairs is where you'll find the main dining rooms and a back garden, weather allowing. Both floors are done up in a collection of antique odds and ends and have rather low ceilings, as the building is very old. There are exposed brick walls, a nonworking fireplace, two large curtained windows facing the avenue, and a mix-and-match assortment of tables and chairs. Aside from the two glass-beaded chandeliers in the front, most of the light comes from the dozens of candles about the place. When it's full, which is most nights after seven, it can be noisy, but the food and the atmosphere are fun, and worth the trip down here. It reminded me a bit of both Allen and Delancey and Bacaro, two other new restaurants with loads of candles, exposed bricks and beams, an antique feel, and very good food, drawing hip young crowds nightly.

The original chef at Bobo, Nicolas Cantrel, a young Frenchman, is now gone, replaced in early 2008 by Jared Stafford-Hill, who had been cooking at Hearth and who in turn was replaced later that same year by Patrick Connolloy. The owner, Carlos Suarez, is on the floor most nights, greeting guests and taking care of the front of the house. The menu is relatively small but with good balance; starters are priced in the low teens, main courses in the mid- to upper twenties. The wine list is small but good, with a mostly European selection. A recent winter menu offered a rich soup made of roasted winter squash and studded with smoked duck, and a very good winter salad of shaved fennel, thin-sliced celery, and flat-leaf parsley, set over a small pool of Greek yogurt and tossed in a lemon-based vinaigrette, a nice contrast of crunch, cream, and acid. Another good starter had raw marinated bay scallops set in a deep bowl over lightly cooked and then marinated crunchy baby beets and fennel;

the citrusy marinade component played nicely off the earthy beets, fennel, and sweet scallop meat.

Cod is served with braised leeks and a fine rich olive tapenade; what's called a lamb pot-au-feu is in reality a boneless braised shoulder, the meat soft, flavorful, and tender, shaped in a ring mold and topped with an herbed crumb gratin, alongside boiled winter vegetables, the whole doused with good lamb jus poured tableside for effect and accompanied by a small crock of Dijon mustard, which works well with the meat and vegetables. Berkshire pork has the belly braised and then crisped, served alongside good cabbage and potatoes. That same pork will be found utilized in an appetizer of assorted charcuterie, a nubbly and coarse-grained house pâté, and excellent rillettes as well.

You can opt for a small cheese plate with some fine selections from nearby Murray's, a good choice to end the meal, or go for sweets such as the rich chocolate pot de crème with warm madeleines, or the less sweet pear upside-down cake with a good pear sorbet for extra measure. There is talk of expanding the restaurant up one more floor, but in the meantime put this one on your list if you're looking for a romantic, funky setting with a great sound track, a young crowd, and very decent straightforward cooking.

Bonbonnière

212-741-9266
28 Eighth Avenue, between
   West 12th and Jane Streets
Casual
No reservations
Inexpensive
Cash only
Breakfast, lunch, and early
   dinner seven days a week
A, C, E, 1, 2, 3, trains to 14th
   Street station; L train to
   Eighth Avenue station

Okay, I'll admit that the food here is just so-so, and barely that. With that established, Bonbonnière is a classic West Village hangout with a mix of artsy types, cops, trust fund slackers, delivery people, occasional celebrities, and a host of locals, many whom it would appear have been eating here for years and live in those increasingly scarce $300-a-month rent-stabilized apartments that still exist nearby. In an area going upscale at a fast clip, eclectic places like this are a real throwback to a time when the West Village was more Village and less attitude. (Each day, a few blocks south of here, a bus parks and unloads passengers for the daily *Sex and the City* tour.) New York has also lost many old-time diners of late: the Cheyenne, the Market, and the Moondance are all history. So a place where anyone can tuck into a familiar meal of ham and eggs at any time of day, or have grilled cheese, decent soup, and a cup of joe in good company, has my vote. This is essentially a diner by any other name—the room is long and narrow, with tables scattered about and seating on stools at a counter. The cooks prepare most of the food in the open diner-style kitchen, using the flat-top grill and Frialators. I'm there for breakfast—$8 will get you two eggs any style, weak coffee, toast, hash browns, and bacon, sausage, or a thin hamsteak. Part of the appeal is that the whole place fronts a section of Eighth Avenue, just south of 14th Street, with ringside seats to the sidewalk. It's classic New York people watching. And who knows who you'll find eating next to you? One morning halfway through my eggs and toast I noticed Ethan Hawke and a few friends at a table nearby.

Bonsignour

212-229-9700
35 Jane Street, off Eighth Avenue
Casual
No reservations
Inexpensive
All major credit cards accepted
Seven days a week 8 AM–8 PM
1, 2, 3, A, C, E trains to 14th Street station; L train to Eighth Avenue station

More hole-in-the-wall than restaurant, this little shop exists primarily for takeout, and while there are a few tables inside and a bench outside, they are more often than not filled with regulars. In what may be one of the smallest storefronts in the city you'll find some pretty darn good food. Mornings here are busy, with great inexpensive bargains like the strong-brewed Illy brand coffee, bagels, homemade muffins, Danish, and a great frittata of the day straight out of the oven. The efficient staff are all exceedingly pleasant, the sound track is good, and the vibe decidedly West Village.

The prices are more than fair, with plain bagels selling for under a dollar and good toasted bagels with cream cheese at $1.50. Egg sandwiches are in the $3–$4 range, the other pastries in the $3 range. For lunch they have a decent small selection of sandwiches and salads. I especially like the roast beef with watercress, Dijon mustard, and tomato. The hot meat loaf sandwich is a treat, as are the Cubano and the avocado and Swiss melt. To this add a good selection of salads and a pretty decent chicken soup to boot. With food this good at these prices, it's no wonder the place is busy all day long. Weather permitting, it's a great place to grab a meal to go and enjoy in any one of the many small parks nearby.

Boqueria

212-255-4160
53 West 19th Street, off
  Sixth Avenue
Casual
No reservations
Moderate to expensive
All major credit cards accepted
Seven days a week noon–
  midnight
4, 5, 6, L, N, Q, R, W trains to
  Union Square/14th Street
  station

Neither the chef, Seamus Mullen, nor owner/partner Yann de Rochefort is Spanish. Yet since this is New York, where seemingly anything is possible, this is one of the best places for tapas in the city. The dining room has a long, deep rectangular layout, bar to the front right, seating filling out the rear. The walls are tiled and the seating along the banquettes is rather high—even the legs of tall folks dangle—but it works somehow, and this arrangement is comfortable. By 8 PM each night the place is generally packed and buzzing. This location had previously been an Alsatian restaurant called L'Acajou, but they never did these numbers. New Yorkers have slowly warmed to Spanish food; pioneering restaurants such as Solera struggled at first, but now, because the food is delicious, simple, and approachable, places like this are packed nightly. They're popular also because small-plate dining is a nice way to eat. You can construct a meal around lots of little courses with glasses of good wine to match, courtesy of the sommelier Roger Kugler, and never get bored.

Should you arrive in a group of four or more, order small plates and split the big ones. There are many winners to be reckoned with. The lunch and dinner menus change almost daily and are broken down into a tapas section, all under $10 per plate, followed by embutidos, which is a variety of hams and sausages in the same price range, media raciones (or half portions) served on larger plates in the low teens, and raciones (main courses), good for sharing, priced in the high teens to low twenties. The offerings follow the market, but if they have suckling pig on the menu, jump on it. Braised lamb shank in various guises is also great, as is the whole turbot.

I often start with slices of serrano ham set on good toasted sliced bread with rings of chorizo on the side. The house mixed green salad features a blend of decent greens, shaved paper-thin artichokes, sliced shallots, grape halves, and a pink-hued romesco vinaigrette. The small lunch salad of baby arugula served with canned ventresca, an imported confit of tuna belly bathed in olive oil with guindilla peppers and small black olives, is a mini-meal in itself.

The bite-sized fried croquetas, essentially mini-fritters, are addictive; the fillings change daily, but they are all lightly breaded, then fried crisp, and often liquid at the center. Some days it's the trio of mushroom duxelle fritters, or another made from pureed salt cod and potato or braised pork belly, each perched on thin schmears of various purees: fig beneath the cod, a lemon hollandaise under the pork, and an herbed cream beneath the mushroom.

As the kitchen is open all day, this is a great spot to drop in for a light snack, hang with friends over wine and small plates, or come for dinner and graze with a friend, a date, or a small crowd. The more the merrier, as you get to order more food and have lots of variety; most everything that comes out of the kitchen is very good. Should you arrive after 8 PM, expect to wait a while for a table, but it's worth it.

Bouchon Bakery

212-823-9366
10 Columbus Circle, in the Time Warner Building, third-floor atrium
Casual
Reservations
Inexpensive to moderate
All major credit cards accepted
Monday–Friday 8 AM–9 PM, Saturday 10 AM–9 PM, Sunday 10 AM–7 PM
1, A, C, B, D trains to 59th Street/ Columbus Circle station

The entire Time Warner Building enterprise has seen its share of calamities: a fire occurred at Per Se just five days after it opened, Jean-Georges Vongerichten's V Steakhouse folded, Charlie Trotter's supposed seafood restaurant never even opened its doors, and Café Grey is now shuttered. But everything Thomas Keller has done here has been absolutely first-rate.

I like the pastry counter for lazy late weekday breakfasts. Show up around 9:30 AM and it's pretty quiet. They have little round marble tables with stools and a long marble bar with more seating. Copies of the *New York Times* are there gratis for perusing. The coffees are all very good, as are the hot teas and iced tea. The croissant is among the top two or three in the city, not as buttery and sweet as the ones at Petrossian, more in the style of Millet in Paris. All butter, yes, but crisp and dark brown on the bottom, feathery light in the center. Alongside French classics such as pain au chocolat, almond croissant, pain aux raisins, and seasonal fruit Danish, they have American classics including fabulous sticky buns, perfect muffins, and even little crustless sandwiches of house-made cashew butter and apricot jam on dense homemade pain de mie, pressed and served golden brown and warm. The cookies are spot-on: chewy and densely flavored oatmeal raisin, a layered peanut butter variety, the Thomas Keller Oreo (or TKO), delicious bite-sized signature chocolate Bouchon cakes, and macaroons that are picture perfect—the caramel variety is worth a trip across town. For lunch the sandwiches are uniformly superior, well thought out, well put together with top-tier ingredients, and served on great bread. A tuna niçoise, simple and lovely, comes on a small ciabatta; roast pork tonnato is laced with shards of pickled red onion, topped with tuna aioli, and served on slices of thick crusted rustic loaves; a vegetarian sandwich pairs roasted red peppers with grilled eggplant, portobello mushrooms sliced thin, and arugula, again on a ciabatta roll.

In the dining area they have more hot soups, more salads, a great salmon rillette made from fresh and smoked salmon, lovely pâtés served with cornichons and perfect little slices of baguette grilled on both sides and buttered, maybe the best ham and cheese croissant in town, a decent cheese plate, and superb dessert courtesy of Sébastien Rouxel. The éclairs are as good as those at the old Fauchon, the banana tart a gem. I could go on and on, but in truth I've eaten here dozens of times, and all the pastries are superb, among the best to be had anywhere. The service is professional, and I've never had a bad meal. While some say it's pricey, I'd counter that you'd be hard pressed to find better food than this at these prices anywhere in the city, and you could easily spend far more and eat not nearly as well.

Bread

212-334-1015
20 Spring Street, between
  Mott and Elizabeth Streets
Casual
No reservations
Inexpensive to moderate
All major credit cards accepted
Breakfast, lunch, and dinner
  Monday–Friday, brunch and
  dinner Saturday and Sunday
6 train to Spring Street station;
  J, M, Z trains to Bowery station

This is the first of what I assume will become many Bread locations around town. There is already another, much larger second store at the site of the old Barocco in Tribeca, but I like this one better, as its quirkiness fits well into this neighborhood. Of late NoLIta has become a great place to eat very well, with an abundance of projects fueled by talent, ambition, and a public that can't seem to get enough. Just around the corner from Peasant and that lovely wine bar below, this place offers just what its name suggests: great bread and the things that we put between the slices. The bread, courtesy of Balthazar Bakery, is absolutely top-notch, the kind of stuff you couldn't get in New York until a few years back. The slow natural fermentation of the dough and the good ovens they bake them in yield a thick, chewy, dark crust and deeply flavored, moist, rich bread beneath.

To this wonderful bread add great fillings, and you have the makings of the perfect sandwich. Soft and chewy ciabatta comes slathered with rich yellow imported butter, paper-thin slices of prosciutto, and fresh mozzarella cheese. Remember sardine sandwiches? They were once a staple of every decent delicatessen in the country and are now all but extinct, but they make a return appearance here. This time that good fish carries a Sicilian passport and is packed for export in tins topped off with a rich olive oil. The sandwich pairs a row of those little fish combined with sliced ripe tomatoes whose acid offsets the fish's naturally rich, oily flesh, and a schmear of spiced mayonnaise makes the whole better than the sum of the parts. Drippy, fishy, creamy, yummy, and good for you too, loaded with omega-3 fats. Italian canned tuna, the only kind you'll find in my house, is served with mixed greens and sliced tomatoes, with a citrus vinaigrette. Grilled eggplant and zucchini come with fresh tomatoes, arugula, and quality olive oil. The fontina panini is a minimalist construct: crunchy on the outside, nutty and buttery in the middle, and delicious.

Aside from sandwiches, the tiny kitchen at this 32-seat location offers decent meatballs and a thick, hearty tomato soup seasoned with grated Parmesan cheese. The menu and selections change frequently, but the concept and execution remain solid. It's inexpensive, casual, and well thought out, with delicious little bites of this and that to share. Wines are served by the glass, nearly all in the $5–$10 range; the selections are good and work well with the food. At night candles add a bit of romance to the cramped quarters—the crowds get thick. I prefer the late breakfast and late lunch, between the rushes, where you can linger over your meal with the newspaper without a dozen hungry people eyeballing your progress.

Brooklyn Diner

212-581-8900
212 West 57th Street,
  between Seventh Avenue
  and Broadway
Casual
No reservations unless you're
  a big shot
Moderate
All major credit cards accepted
Breakfast, lunch, and dinner
  seven days a week
N, Q, R, W trains to 57th Street
  station; 1, A, C, B, D trains to
  Columbus Circle/59th Street
  station

Shelly Fireman is a Bronx-bred New York restaurant guy, and this is his tribute to Brooklyn's past, although these days Kings County's present and future seem pretty bright. A big mural and historic photographs cover the walls, the menu is written in a Jewish-Italian tongue-in-cheek style, like the breakfast item dubbed Mixed Marriage, which is a fried egg set in challah bread with tomato sauce, Italian sausage, and fried cubes of polenta. Of all his places around town—at last count he had four others nearby—this is the only one I frequent, and that said, I basically just come for the big breakfasts.

Set up to look like a classic rail car, the diner is entered a few steps up from the sidewalk off 57th Street. There is usually a greeter there who actually greets you. A bar is to the right, and the L-shaped seating loops from your right by the bar to the main dining room on the left. All seating is in comfortable banquettes.

For breakfast the coffee is very good, fresh and strong, and the portions generous to say the least. Pancakes are excellent, fluffy in the center and firm from the grill. They have one laced with Valrhona chocolate chips, another served with fresh fruit and whipped butter, and all arrive with a small ramekin of real maple syrup. Omelets are good, and they even do a tasty one with just egg whites. For the health-conscious you can get a big bowl of fresh berries, but if you're not counting calories, go all out. The steak and eggs is an 8-ounce skirt steak served with fried polenta (they don't do hash browns?) and eggs over easy with challah toast. The smoked salmon plate has a generous amount of the real thing, sliced thin, covering the plate, and served with a toasted bagel and cream cheese. There is some kind of French toast that resembles two thick slices of moist cake studded with candied fruit and nuts, served with whipped butter and a little carafe of Vermont maple syrup; this sits halfway between a huge dessert and a really over-the-top breakfast. For lunch or dinner try the excellent hamburgers or long custom-made hot dogs dubbed "15 bites."

Or stick with the comfort food theme and have a good slab of meat loaf, a very good roast beef sandwich served in a custom-made bun with noodle kugel, or a rich wedge of bacon-studded mac and cheese. Some of the desserts are very good. The strawberry cheesecake is a prime example of the genre; layer cakes are best when fresh, and all of them are simply too big, but isn't that why you're here in the first place? Start your diet when you go home. They serve mixed drinks, beer, and wine, or you can get a classic Dr. Brown's Cel-Ray or a decent egg cream to wash it all down.

Bubby's

212-219-0666
120 Hudson Street, between
   North Moore and Beach
   Streets
Casual
Reservations
Moderate
All major credit cards accepted
Breakfast, lunch, and dinner
   Monday–Friday, brunch and
   dinner Saturday and Sunday
1 train to Franklin Street station

Chef-owner Ron Silver, while justly famous for his pies, actually started out training to be a regular chef, not a pastry chef. Somewhere along the way he decided he'd like to win a pie contest—you know, the state fair kind, beating out talented but less savvy housewives and grandmothers. What he discovered was that pies aren't so easy, and upstate housewives and grandmothers happen to be superb pie and crust makers. Well, he didn't win, but maybe we did. Fast-forward to today, and what you have here is a wonderfully simple little restaurant-bakery serving honest, unpretentious food and very good desserts, with pies at the forefront. And don't miss brunch.

For breakfast, look for fresh-squeezed juice, great coffee, and lovely sour cream or banana walnut pancakes with real maple syrup. Eggs and sides are all good, and they make one of the best versions of huevos rancheros this side of the Mississippi. To that add excellent grits, homemade granola, and thick-cut custardy French toast, and you get the picture. For lunch they offer a good range of soups, salads, burgers, and sandwiches, and on warmer days they have tables on the sidewalk facing Hudson. The dinner menu is big, with loads of options from the soup and salad side, dozens of good vegetable and starch sides, decent fried chicken, better-than-decent meat loaf, and creamy mac and cheese. Service is friendly and casual. They serve mixed drinks, wine, beer, and very good milk shakes and malteds, but please save room for dessert. If they have coconut cream pie, get it; it may be the best you've ever had. Any of the fruit pies in season will be fine; he shops for fruit nearly every day and is very picky. The banana cream pie and chocolate cream pie are delicious too, as are the pecan pie variations and the lemon meringue. This is a popular neighborhood hangout, is kid-friendly, and offers the right mix of value and quality to keep it going strong for a long time to come.

Bull & Bear

212-872-4900
**570 Lexington Avenue,
   at the Waldorf-Astoria**
Business attire preferred
Reservations suggested
Moderate to expensive
All major credit cards accepted
Lunch and dinner Monday–
   Friday, dinner Saturday and
   Sunday
E, V trains to Lexington Avenue/
   53rd Street station, 6 train to
   51st Street station

Bull & Bear is the kind of place you can walk past a hundred times and not really notice. Situated on the back side of the famed Waldorf-Astoria, from the outside it appears to be yet another dark wood-paneled bar, a watering hole for suits after hours. But go inside and walk past the bar, veer right into the room beyond, and you'll find a very good steakhouse tucked inside, absent the bar's clamor.

The specialty here is a New York exclusive, dry-aged prime Certified Black Angus, this being the only establishment in town serving this meat in that form. So let's decode that. Prime is the top grade awarded by the USDA, and it is dry-aged a minimum of 21 days to develop flavor and tenderness. That leaves us with the type of beef used. These cattle come from the Certified Black Angus program, in which cattle must test as at least 50% Black Angus, one of the great American cattle breeds for steaks. So do order steak, and you'll be rewarded, because this is very good beef: the 14-ounce New York strip, 24-ounce porterhouse, ribeyes full of concentrated beef flavor, and filet mignon, tender and well charred.

Crab cakes are plump and moist, and the grilled fish—salmon, snapper, and Chilean sea bass—generously portioned. Giant jumbo shrimp, a half dozen, are plated with a good vinaigrette of fennel, orange, and extra-virgin olive oil. This being New York, a good Dover sole meunière is on the menu, and Maine lobster can be had by itself at 2½ pounds per, or as part of a classic surf-and-turf that pairs a 1½-pound lobster with a 6-ounce filet mignon. The side dishes are uniformly well done. Hash browns are individually cooked in black steel pans and arrive crisp and crunchy, golden on the outside, the moist interior laced with caramelized onions. Typical wedge salads are available as starters, or a good alternative is the crunchy, cheesy, salty Caesar salad; try the hearts of romaine too. Vegetable sides are large and typical of the steakhouse theme: broccoli, asparagus, and creamed spinach, which is actually very good. In a throwback to the old days, they have regular daily specials à la Ben Benson. Some of my favorites are the whole roasted chicken on Monday, the famed Waldorf chicken pot pie on Tuesday, braised short ribs with spaetzle on Thursday, and the roast Long Island duck with red cabbage, lentils, carrots, and parsnip on weekends.

The wine list is decent, albeit pricey, with some good selections from California and abroad by the glass, and a few reasonably priced offerings by the bottle if you know what you're looking for. That said, there is only one nebbiolo under $100 a bottle and far too few burgundies to speak of. Bordeaux starts at $70 for a 2002 De Pez, a sleeper of a vintage, sandwiched between the great 2000 vintage and the heat-wave-induced early harvest of 2003 that came after, and quickly escalate to $200 and beyond. Desserts, baked in house, are what you'd expect: big, sweet, and traditional. The cheesecake is good, as is the carrot cake. If you're looking for an alternative to your regular steakhouse, dine here. You'll have chosen well, and I suspect you'll return.

Butter

212-253-2828
415 Lafayette Street, between East 4th Street and Astor Place
Casual to dressy
Reservations
Moderate to expensive
All major credit cards accepted
Dinner Monday–Saturday
N, R, W trains to 8th Street station; 6 train to Astor Place station

This sprawling club-like space was originally conceived as Belgo, a Belgian-inspired restaurant that came and went quickly and led to Butter, which is at its core a more modest and market-driven restaurant with a very good chef in the kitchen. That chef, Alex Guarnaschelli, took over when things were tough, and her early days here included many trips to the local Food Town for ingredients, due to early credit issues with purveyors. These days that's not a problem. Business is good, the ingredients are still sourced from markets (but most likely that would be the farmers' market in Union Square), and the food is better than ever.

When I first ate here, I didn't know what to make of the place. We arrived around 7:30 and walked past the empty bar to the back room, which at that time of night held only a few other diners. Gradually it filled up, and by the time we left it was packed with 20- and 30-somethings, five guys at one table, six girls at another, couples too, but mostly all relatively young. That is the new downtown restaurant scene—part food, part club, a place for guys to meet girls, and girls to meet guys as well. Who knew? A decade ago that was the province of bars and nightclubs, but all around town these days, it's restaurants too.

You enter the space, which is narrow but deep and impressive, past the backlit bar and up into the main dining room with loads of natural cedarwood paneling, not just on the walls but also on the vaulted, barrel-shaped ceiling. The rear wall is covered by an enormous translucent photograph of a sun-dappled birch forest. I'm not sure why this is, or what it is supposed to inspire, but it is interesting. The seating consists of good comfortable banquettes lining both sides of the room and large freestanding tables at the center. It turns out there is also a lounge downstairs where DJs spin tunes after hours, and that too may explain the young late crowd—after dinner, they can head downstairs to throw a few back and meet the girls from table 11. The servers too are young and friendly; ours was a young chap from Berkeley, California, and what he lacked in polish he made up for in charm.

The chef, New York born and bred, graduated from Barnard College with a major in art history but was soon cooking with Guy Savoy in Paris, then Daniel Boulud here, a brief stint with the very talented Joachim Splichal in L.A., and then back to New York. Her food is straightforward, led by ingredients, and interesting. A starter of braised veal shank garnished with fried sweetbreads and served with salsa verde suggests that she is not shy about laying big flavors and textures side by side. Fresh Florida shrimp are served over wilted arugula with a small salad of citrus fruits and splashed with a good pistachio oil.

A nice pink, well-seasoned foie gras terrine arrived simply plated with a homemade kumquat compote and brioche toast points. Sautéed calamari came Italian-style, mixed with fresh cranberry beans and oregano. Fresh cavatappi pasta was sauced in a light herbed cream and studded with small sections of sausage and little bits of tomato. A large slab of oven-roasted halibut came in a nice broth made from a squash emulsion, with pan-roasted asparagus on a side dish. Classic coq au vin came with braised crisped pork belly, cipollini onions, and white button mushrooms in a good rich reduced braising liquid—again big flavors put together. Fresh wild-caught Montauk striped bass is given the steak treatment, au poivre and served atop a salad of shaved fennel and blood oranges alongside a small mound of sautéed wilted spinach. The menu is large, with a dozen starters and a dozen entrees; essentially there is something here for everyone.

Desserts are good. On my last visit we had an apple upside-down tart with a cranberry orange sablé crust and a side dish that amounted to a vanilla calvados milk shake. A dark chocolate mint cake comes with

Bailey's ice cream, and a very good chocolate semifreddo is spiked with Hawaiian sea salt and caramel. The wine list is good, the room is fun, the vibe is casual, and the food is better than it needs to be. Compliments to Chef Guarnaschelli.

Café Boulud

212-772-2600
20 East 76th Street, between
Fifth and Madison Avenues
Casual to dressy
Reservations
Expensive
All major credit cards accepted
Dinner Sunday and Monday,
lunch and dinner Tuesday–
Saturday
6 train to 77th Street station

Before Daniel Boulud moved back to the old Le Cirque space on 65th Street, this was Daniel. It has always been a very good choice in this neighborhood, and of late an incubator and launching pad for talent. Daniel, perhaps more than any other chef in New York, has had a lot of good cooks pass through his kitchens, and one way to retain top talent is by giving them opportunities for prized gigs such as the restaurant chef job at Café Boulud. Andrew Carmellini was there for years; these days the kitchen is run by another Boulud protégé, Gavin Kaysen.

The room is rather old-school and nondescript, the ceiling low, the décor done in shades of beige; I suppose the best way to describe it is to say that it's soothing. While it's less gilded than Daniel, it's also a lot easier to land a reservation, and you can eat very well here, as it's easily one of the best restaurants on the Upper East Side.

The menu for some time has been divided into four sections, each with a small list of options; seasonal, classic, vegetarian, and global are the themes. I'd stick with the seasonal and classic dishes, and don't miss the pasta either. That's where the kitchen shines. In some ways the seasonal and classic menus are hard to tell apart, as the classics are modernized here, and the market-driven seasonal menu is still at its core very French. Appetizers start in the high teens and run right up into the high twenties fast. Entrees start in the mid-thirties and go up from there, but this is the Upper East Side, after all, and just steps off Fifth Avenue no less, the epicenter of the 10021 zip code crowd.

They offer a dish billed, tongue in cheek, as "biscuits and gravy." Well you won't find this on the breakfast menu at Shoney's, that's for sure. Here what arrives is a shimmering, tender slice of braised glazed pork belly, foie gras, silky smooth creamed spinach, and the aforementioned gravy, which turns out to be a sticky, rich reduction, essentially a sauce périgourdine studded with black truffles.

While I love French cooking, I've felt the French never quite understood pasta. It's like a language they can't speak well, no matter how hard they try. Perhaps it's too simple and the French chefs overthink it, or maybe it's genetic. So when Andrew Carmellini, an Italian American from Ohio, was here, the pastas were excellent, and I can report that they still are, though now with a bit more of a French accent. Lovely little hand-cut agnolotti offered as a starter or a main are filled with a winter squash puree and served with sweetbreads, well coated with a butter-enriched pan reduction sauce, fried sage leaves, glazed pearl onions, and chunks of rendered slab bacon. A lighter starter is the peekytoe crab salad, the sweet rich crabmeat paired with crunchy watermelon radish, sliced cucumber and fennel, and a clementine-based vinaigrette.

The cooking here is all done with restraint and finesse. Take the main-course selection of Vermont guinea hen, the breast slow-cooked sous vide, slightly gamy but tender, almost like chicken, the flavor slowly coaxed out of the good meat. The leg meat is crisped, the dark meat standing up well to this treatment, and the contrast in texture is welcome. To this add creamy polenta studded with sautéed wild mushrooms, buttery braised green cabbage, a slab of sautéed foie gras for good measure, and a simple pan jus. Or on the lighter side, try the pan-seared John Dory—the rich white-fleshed fish is cooked perfectly and set atop a simple shellfish broth dotted with clams and mussels of various pedigrees, along with chunks of good prosciutto providing a touch of richness to an otherwise well-balanced seafood composition.

The staff is formed in that classic Daniel mold: professional, well dressed, well groomed, and slightly formal, and they know the menu. The wine list is deep and expensive. The desserts here are worth saving room for, and the list is broad, with nearly a dozen offerings put out each day by the very talented Raphael Haasz. In season, the poached pear belle Hélène, a classic old-school dessert here modernized, is as good as you'll find anywhere. The pear, poached in white wine, simple syrup, and aromatics and allowed time to sit in that mixture, is tender and flavorful, plated with a scoop of toasted almond ice cream and a rich warm chocolate sauce. Each meal ends with a plate of warm madeleines.

The crowd is true to the neighborhood, well heeled and a bit snooty for my taste. I was often the worst-dressed diner in the place, and there were enough diamonds, gold, and face-lifts on display to help you remember which part of New York City you were dining in, in case you'd forgotten. That said, the food here rivals the food at Daniel, and that makes it one of the best restaurants north of 57th Street.

Café Katja

212-219-9545
79 Orchard Street, between
   Broome and Grand Streets
Casual
No reservations
Inexpensive
Most major cards
Dinner seven nights a week,
   4 PM–1 AM
F, V trains to Second Avenue
   station; B, D trains to Grand
   Street station

In what is now becoming a familiar tale, a couple of guys who worked at swank places uptown decided they wanted to open their own spot—downtown, of course, and small. At Café Katja, the guys in question are chef Erwin Schrottner, whom I'd met around town at various events, and his business partner, Andrew Chase. Most nights both can be found working this tiny room. Erwin is Austrian, and the food served here is simple, satisfying Austrian fare—herring, roasted beets, cheeses, spaetzle, potatoes, loads of cured pork, wurst tasting plates—all of which works perfectly well with the great beer list, short wine list, and even schnapps.

I've been known to schlep all the way down to Russ and Daughters just for their excellent herring, so when I see it on a menu, which is rare, like here or at Aquavit uptown, I leap. This underrated, underappreciated little swimmer arrives cured, boneless, oily, and salty and is addictive alongside a cucumber potato salad, a good foil for the fish, and a dollop of sour cream laced with good hot mustard. Or try any of the sandwiches, such as creamy Liptauer cheese set against crunchy sliced radish and fresh thyme, or Emmenthaler cheese with smoked ham and sliced hot peppers, or my favorite, house-made liverwurst with sweet pickled onions.

Don't miss the wurst plates, Austrian salumi on parade. Blood sausage is paired with crunchy Savoy cabbage and glazed sautéed apples, or the satisfying slab of head cheese, gelatinous and studded with flavorful meat bits, alongside a dollop of fig jam. They have excellent house-made pretzels served with cheese and meat spreads, or plockwurst, a soft salami-like cervelat made of beef and pork, garnished with house-cured pickles and again Liptauer cheese. If that's not enough, then go for the spaetzle, a light, chewy dumpling first boiled, then sautéed and crisped, served as a side dish if you so choose, with carmelized onions and cheese, or alongside some very rich goulash.

If you really need dessert, do the Linzer torte; it's good and not too sweet. Beers on tap and by the bottle are lovely with this style of food, the bubbles helping to cleanse the palate and refresh it for the next bite. The wine list, though small, is tight, inexpensive, and again works well with this food. If I lived nearby, I suspect I'd dine here a lot, and would weigh a few more pounds for that pleasure.

Cantoon Garden

212-964-2229
22 Elizabeth Street, between Bayard and Canal Streets
Casual
No reservations
Inexpensive to moderate
All major credit cards accepted
Lunch and dinner seven days a week
6, J, M, Z, N, Q, R, W trains to Canal Street station

Chinatown can be a tough place to decide where to eat. We all have our four or five favorites that we visit during the year, where we tend to order the same things over and over again. But how do you decide on a new spot to try? Reviews, which are infrequent? Recommendations from friends? It's easier if you work in the area and can experiment at lunch, when there are tremendous bargains, but for those of us who schlep all the way down to Chinatown for dinner from the outer reaches of the city or the greater metro area, we tend to bet on sure things and visit our usual haunts.

I try to look for new spots based on how many Chinese people are eating there and how few Westerners. I figure the Chinese know their own food a heck of a lot better than I do, so if a place is filled with Chinese customers, it must be doing something right. On a recent visit to Cantoon Garden I was seated next to a table of three uniformed officers from the New York City Police Department, two men and a woman, all Chinese American—surely another good sign.

It's a big square room, well lit, with many round wood-grain Formica communal tables. It's busy for both lunch and dinner, and for lunch it's a real bargain. Each day they have a $5.95 lunch special that includes soup and a main course. Or order off the lunch à la carte menu, and for around $15 two of you will eat very well. It's one of the best deals in town for lunch, bar none.

The menu is a huge document broken down into sections, essentially a list of traditional Cantonese-style greatest hits: various noodle varieties and fried rice constitute an entire page, congee and seafood another. This leads us to the steamed section, followed by beef, pork, chicken, vegetables, sizzling-plate, fish, hibachi-style, noodle soup, and finally rice in casserole, totaling well over 250 choices.

Among the various noodle choices, the lo mein is good: chewy, thick, yellow, locally made, and tasting of the pan it was cooked in, a good thing. The long noodles mixed with cut scallions, fresh bean sprouts, and Chinese chives are well seasoned. Chinese eggplant, a $3 lunch side dish, is quartered, cut into two-inch lengths, and flash-cooked; it arrives heaped onto an oval platter, just done, with a slight resistance at the center, tossed with minced pork, scallions, garlic, and a mix of sauces including a good fish sauce. Water spinach in season is offered a variety of ways, and all are very good. Sautéed snow pea leaves are great. Bean curd Szechuan-style is a mini-meal in itself. The specialty here is fresh fish scooped live from the tank. They usually have rock bass, also known as tautog. Try it steamed and topped with julienned vegetables and dipping sauce. Live crabs, here billed as "steamed big crab with ho fun and garlic," are cooked whole and brought to the table for dissection alongside a steaming bowl of very good chicken and abalone soup. One day after a late lunch, I watched as the chef sat at a table with three friends and enjoyed that crab dish along with steamed whole fish and heaping plates of noodles and vegetables, all washed down with tea and a bottle of Hennessy. While this may not be the best Chinese restaurant in the neighborhood, it's a good, steady performer that I highly recommend.

Capsouto Frères

212-966-4900
451 Washington Street,
   at Watts Street
Casual
Reservations
Moderate
All major credit cards accepted
Lunch and dinner Monday–
   Friday, brunch and dinner
   Saturday and Sunday
1, A, C, E trains to Canal Street
   station

The Capsouto brothers, for whom this place was named (there are three of them, Jacques, Samuel, and Albert), were some of the earliest restaurant pioneers in Tribeca. The restaurant opened in the early 1980s, pre-Montrachet, pre-Odeon. It was a pioneering "loft-style" dining room, with a high ceiling and exposed bricks and beams. They built the place themselves, pretty much by hand, with pieces gathered from here and there—the bar came from a place upstate, the wall behind the bar from a barbershop in Queens, and the mirrors from auctions around town.

The food is very old-school French and is consistently good within that genre. Start with a vegetable terrine Provençal, layering eggplants and peppers, or the lovely cheese soufflé. For main courses, the poached salmon with herbed vinaigrette is a good light choice, but I usually go with dishes such as the navarin of lamb, veal or beef stews, classic duck confit, or the daily specials, like the excellent cassoulet served here in the winter months. The simpler dishes—calf's liver with a sherry wine vinegar sauce, sautéed sweetbreads with mushroom ragout, steak aux poivre with frites—remind me of the solid classical cooking that was once a staple in French kitchens all over town but is now harder and harder to find in New York.

Desserts are good—the soufflé especially, and don't miss the superb apple tarte Tatin, a caramelized confit of butter-tender apples encased in a flaky crust. The wine list is good and fairly priced, as Jacques Capsouto is quite the sommelier. Overall, this Tribeca pioneer has aged well, and the prices are very low considering the quality of the food. It is worthy of a visit anytime you are in the mood for good, simple old-style French cooking.

Caracas Arepa Bar

212-228-5062
91 East 7th Street, between
  First Avenue and Avenue A
Casual
No reservations
Inexpensive
All major credit cards accepted
Lunch and dinner seven days
  a week
6 train to Astor Place station

For me this is more of a lunch or light dinner spot, as arepas, good as they are, and even preceded by the very hearty Peruvian soup chupe caraqueño, still leave me wanting a meal. But the prices are very fair, the quality is good, the food is usually very fresh, and a friend of mine who is from Venezuela likes the arepas served here. There are at least a dozen varieties. My favorites have been the Muchachos, with grilled chorizo, white cheese, hot peppers, and sautéed sweet peppers; chunky chicken and avocado; roasted shredded pork shoulder with tomato and mango sauce; or shredded beef with sweet plantains, black beans, and aged cheese. That last option can be had as a stand-alone lunch or as a dinner platter billed as Pabellón Criollo, a decent-sized meal for $14. The place is East Village budget all the way: exposed brick, tin ceiling, simple wooden chairs and tables, young crowd, another space next door for table service. For side dishes, try the yoyos, little deep-fried balls of cooked plantain wrapped around white cheese, or the guasacaca with chips, essentially a Venezuelan riff on guacamole, good especially with the cold Tona lager from Colombia. There are a few bottles of wine listed, soda, and a mimosa or two, but to my mind beer works best with this simple food.

Carnegie Deli

800-334-5606
854 Seventh Avenue, between
  54th and 55th Streets
Casual
No reservations
Moderate
Cash only
Lunch and dinner seven days
  a week
N, Q, R, W trains to 57th Street
  station; 1, A, C, B, D trains to
  59th Street/Columbus Circle
  station; B, D, E trains to
  Seventh Avenue station

If you need three reasons to visit the Carnegie Deli, here they are: pastrami, corned beef, and cheesecake. On any given day, the quintessential deli sandwiches served here rank among the best in the city, and therefore the best in the country. In fact, a fair number of other delis around town and around the country use Carnegie's cured meats for their sandwiches, because this is one of the last places that really cure and smoke their own meat. The real secret to this place lies across the Hudson River tucked away in the shadows of the Meadowlands, on Washington Avenue in Carlstadt, New Jersey, where they run a state-of-the-art smokehouse and bakery. Their corned beef, made from beef brisket, is cured there in thousand-pound batches. The pastrami, taken from an unusual cut known as the navel, is dry-rubbed with a spice mix that includes loads of cracked coriander, then smoked for four hours over southern hickory wood in 1,200-pound batches. These meats are then shrink-wrapped, dated, labeled, and shipped out, to be cooked for a minimum of three to four hours in a steam table until fork-tender.

The discussion of who has the best this or that is a silly one, especially when it comes to meats such as pastrami, corned beef, or prime steaks. Meat varies from night to night and from place to place, just as cattle vary animal to animal, and each carcass is unique. One day Katz's may be the best, hand-cut and lovely; another day it could be Carnegie's, machine-sliced and fork-tender. Really, it just depends on the piece of meat. But if you want to taste the gold standard for these classic deli-style sandwiches, go straight to either place. The shtick at Carnegie is size: the sandwiches often weigh over a pound and are simply way too much food for any reasonable person to consume. The sandwiches are expensive, and there is a $3 charge to split them, but go ahead and split one anyway. For around $18 you'll get two of the best sandwiches you've ever had. Or do what I do: order one, take half home in a carry-out bag, and you'll have enough meat left over for a few great breakfasts of corned beef hash. The bread they use is a good fresh rye, also baked in New Jersey. The pickles are a mix of sour and half sour. I suggest you eat the corned beef with mustard, but enjoy the pastrami plain, for what it is. The flavor is intense, and mustard really masks some of that nuance.

There are two dining rooms, both bare-bones affairs with wooden seats and Formica tables, lit by fluorescent lights above. If it's available, the room to the right at the rear is a little more pleasant for my taste. The wait staff are gruff and rude in that unique New York style, but inside they are all sweethearts. They have worked here for years and have that seen-it-all attitude. The walls are lined with 8-by-10 head shots of once-famous actors, performers, news anchors, sports figures, and politicians.

The combo sandwiches are great: the tongue is excellent, the turkey breast is excellent, and don't even ask about the Reuben—there is enough fat and salt on that plate to ruin your diet for the next month, but it's great if you can handle it or find someone to share it with. As to the rest of the menu, it's rather uneven. Skip the stuffed cabbage, way too sweet for me. Chicken in a pot is good. Matzo ball soup . . . well, don't get me started, but the one they used to serve at the old Second Avenue Deli was much better. The burgers are decent, and one day a British woman seated next to me ordered a bacon sandwich. What arrived must have been a full pound of cooked bacon crammed into two slices of bread. She ate the whole thing and loved it. The blintzes are better than average, and the desserts are good.

The cheesecake recipe came from the original Lindy's, where Jeff Jensen's dad worked as a pastry chef. Jeff runs the operation in Carlstadt. It is a classic New York cheesecake, with cream cheese, eggs, cream, and flavorings, baked in three stages: it's baked once to set the crust, baked again at high temperature to get the brown color on the top, then removed from the oven, allowed to cool, and baked a third time at a lower temperature in a water bath to set the custard. The layer cakes are all made from scratch; I like the chocolate and the coconut best. Wash it all down with some Dr. Brown's soda or a beer.

Chanterelle

212-966-6960
2 Harrison Street, at Hudson Street
Casual to dressy
Reservations
Expensive
All major credit cards accepted
Dinner seven nights a week, lunch and dinner Tuesday–Friday
1 train to Franklin Street station

Trusting their instincts, aesthetics, and talent, Karen and David Waltuck have run this jewel of a restaurant for over a quarter century. Blessed with the restaurant equivalent of perfect pitch, they sprang out of nowhere in 1979, during the early days of SoHo, opening the restaurant at its original location on the corner of Grand and Greene. David had studied marine biology, then briefly attended cooking school and worked here and there—Le Petit Ferme, the Empire Diner—basically teaching himself how to cook while deciding he wanted his own place. Karen had studied anthropology, worked in fashion, and agreed to take this leap of faith. When they'd been open barely a month, Gael Greene, then a very influential critic at *New York* magazine, wrote a glowing review, and the phone started ringing off the hook.

In stark contrast to what was going on elsewhere in the New York restaurant scene—think big and splashy: the Russian Tea Room, the Palace, Maxwell's Plum, Tavern on the Green—their tiny room in those days was spare and European. Lace curtains hung from brass rods midway down the tall windows. No art adorned the walls, there were only seven or eight tables, and they had no liquor license or air-conditioning, yet reservations were booked months in advance. They moved south in 1989 to the ground floor of the former Mercantile Exchange, a space that allowed them to expand the dining room quite a bit and vastly improve the kitchen and wine cellar. But this room still reminds one of their early days. The warm peach walls of the SoHo spot are now a soft glowing yellow, the tall ceiling framed with thick white moldings and centered by an elegant brass chandelier; the gorgeous floral arrangements are still Karen's work, as are the handwritten menus, which change monthly. The restaurant scene has changed dramatically since 1979. Critics have come and gone, but the legions of fans who pack this place nightly appreciate the simple originality of the food, the superb wine list, and the refined service.

The entrance foyer is adorned with menu covers designed by famous patrons over the years, a reminder that this has been a downtown restaurant for a long time, when the cheap lofts of Soho and Tribeca attracted artists of all stripes: choreographers, musicians, poets, and painters. You'll see Matthew Barney's stunning geisha head, Vija Celmins' spiderweb, and covers by Ross Bleckner, Allen Ginsberg, John Cage, Francesco Clemente, Merce Cunningham, Donald Evans, April Gornik, and Jasper Johns, to name just a few.

Over the years I've had meals here that were superb and others that I didn't like as much. The menus change monthly, and David follows his own course. His food is mostly simple, not fussy. The technique and flavors are straightforward and reflect the seasons and the market availability of meat, fish, and produce.

The only menu item that he can't seem to get rid of is the white seafood sausage, which has been a signature dish since the early days. David had read about the seafood sausage at the famed Michelin three-star restaurant Taillevent in Paris, wondered what it was like, and created his own version. Years later, he would dine at Taillevent and discover a totally different sausage from the one he had created. Chef Dan Barber's father, who is quite the gourmand, is the only other person I know of who has had them both, and he prefers David's version, a testimonial to his originality and talent. The menus are small, six or seven appetizers and the same number of main courses, followed by a great cheese cart should you wish, four desserts, and a tasting of ice creams or sorbets. A recent menu had lobster bisque flavored with sauternes and curry; quenelles of salmon with truffles set over a pool of lettuce cream; a wonderful free-range chicken pot pie with truffles and vegetables; and a mixed grill of Moulard duck with a béarnaise sauce partially made with emulsified duck fat—yummy!

The format is à la carte. Six-course tasting menus are offered for around $100; add $60 for the wine pairings. Roger Dagorn, one of the most widely respected sommeliers in America, is in charge of the wine cellar and is often on hand in the dining room to assist you. Trust him—his judgment is flawless. The cheese cart is one of the best in the city, and all the staff on the floor know the cheeses well. I should mention that the dining room staff here is very good at knowing what type of service you want, and delivering. Should you require a lot of attention, explanations, etc., you've got it. But if you know the food and wine and want to have a conversation without being interrupted, you'll never notice them. That's what service is supposed to be about.

Kate Zuckerman, the pastry chef, is to my mind is one of the best working pastry chefs in New York City. Her plates are great to look at, but they taste even better than they appear, combining textures and colors, balancing sweetness with acidity, revealing the very bright mind behind the sound technical foundation.

Charles' Southern Style Kitchen

Note: This venue is closed.

212-926-4313
2841 Frederick Douglass
Boulevard, at 151st Street
Casual
Reservations
Inexpensive
All major credit cards accepted
Lunch and dinner Wednesday–
Sunday
B, D, A, C trains to 155th Street
station

Some of chef-owner Charles Gabriel's earliest memories are of being taken along with his mother and her sisters while they picked cotton in the Carolina fields. Many days, weather permitting, he would be set on a blanket with a jug of water and a toy or two to amuse himself, and as his mother and his aunts finished each row of cotton, they'd check on him. He is part of an older generation of New Yorkers who grew up poor and black in a segregated South that no longer exists, and who migrated north while young to look for work and improve their livelihood. He also remembers the big weekend family gatherings, when he'd spend a lot of time in the kitchen with those same ladies, learning how to cook southern-style.

He was employed in the theater district for years before venturing out on his own by selling fried chicken, greens, and homemade pies from a park bench in Harlem one summer. He'd prepare these dishes at home starting at 4 AM and take them out each day for sale. As winter approached, a woman he knew in the neighborhood asked how he was planning to manage this in the cold months ahead, and offered the use of an idle lunch truck she owned that had been parked indoors for years. He cleaned the truck, got it running, painted it, and began his stint selling soul food from this mobile marketplace for a few years. At the urging of his growing fan base he decided to sign a lease and get a permanent address in a small store on Eighth Avenue between 151st and 152nd Streets. Now his empire stretches across half the block with two restaurants. These days he does takeout in one store, and the other has one of the best sit down all-you-can-eat buffets in the city, serving breakfast, lunch, and dinner seven days a week.

His fried chicken is some of the best in New York. He buys the birds fresh daily at the market in the Bronx, dry-marinates them, then dredges them in seasoned flour before frying them in batches in a large black steel pan out back. The whole cooking process takes between 15 and 20 minutes, and should you be there when they are putting fresh chicken in the buffet, grab some and you'll see why I like it so much.

But don't stop there: his giant braised turkey wings are delicious, as are the oxtail stew, beef short ribs, smothered pork chops, BBQ pork ribs, and chopped BBQ. For fish, he makes a good salmon cake, and offers fried porgies or whiting. Side dishes include superb slow-cooked collard greens with smoked turkey wings, okra and tomatoes, black-eyed peas, baked macaroni and cheese, sweet potatoes, and four varieties of rice, as well as coleslaw, potato salad, macaroni salad, and cake-like corn bread. The lemonade is homemade from fresh lemons, the iced tea house-made as well. Desserts include layer cake, sweet potato pie, peach cobbler, and banana pudding, and last I checked, the all-you-can-eat dinner buffet was offered for $12 per person. Come hungry and with company.

Chat Noir

212-794-2428
22 East 66th Street, between
  Madison and Fifth Avenues
Casual to dressy
Reservations
Moderate
All major credit cards accepted
Lunch and dinner Monday–
  Friday, brunch and dinner
  Saturday and Sunday
6 train to 68th Street station

It's getting harder and harder to find decent traditional French cooking in New York. For decades the French ruled the restaurant scene. The best places to eat were Lutèce, La Côte Basque, La Caravelle, La Grenouille, Chantilly, and Le Périgord. Now they are mostly all closed, and the style of food and service too is a thing of the past. That's a shame, because French cuisine is one of the great cuisines of the world, and the French have a keen understanding of good service and style too. So when this place opened, bucking that trend, I had to check it out. Housed on a beautiful block, steps off Fifth Avenue, in the ground floor of a brownstone, it has an intimate salon-like appeal. The walls are cream-colored, the banquettes red, the lighting partly from bronze sconces. Suzanne Latapie, who had worked for a dozen years at La Goulue around the corner, is in charge of the dining room, and she's a pro. The menu caters to a certain segment of the Upper East Side crowd, namely, ladies who lunch, as well as fans of good French bistro food.

Starters include good goat cheese paired with roasted beets in a nice vinaigrette, a less-than-memorable tuna tartare, Maryland lump crabmeat paired with guacamole, steamed mussels with garlic butter, endive and Roquefort tossed with walnuts and dates, and grilled asparagus in season. Several of these can be ordered as either an appetizer or a main course.

The main courses that I liked best were the lunchtime salad niçoise, served here with imported canned ventresca tuna, packed in olive oil and tender as butter. For some strange reason, at night that same salad is served incorrectly with a seared fresh tuna steak instead of the tastier canned variety. Why, I have no idea. The steak frites is good, as are the roast chicken with mashed potatoes and sautéed spinach for $26 and the lamb medallions wrapped in phyllo and plated with very good eggplant caviar and hummus for $27. Salmon is grilled; farm-raised dorade is bland as always but helped by the sun-dried tomato rub. Daily specials include chicken paillard, steamed mussels, soft-shell crabs in season, cheese soufflé, sautéed skate, and cold poached salmon. The wine list is good, service friendly, prices nearly fair, and the cooking consistent. In a neighborhood of overpriced, overhyped eateries, Chat Noir is a solid find.

Chinatown Brasserie

212-533-7000
380 Lafayette Street
Casual
Reservations
Moderate to expensive
All major credit cards accepted
Lunch and dinner seven days
a week
N, R, W trains to Prince Street
station

The trustafarian team responsible for both Lever House and Lure tapped veteran Chinese food expert Ed Schoenfeld as a consultant to open this ambitious project in 2006. Ed, a Brooklyn native, was drawn to Chinese cooking as a teenager and was part of the team that helped create Shun Lee, Auntie Yuan, and Pig Heaven, among other notable spots. He's traveled extensively to China and knows the food as well as any non-native could ever hope to. He discovered chef Joe Ng, who was doing excellent dim sum in Benson-hurst/Sunset Park. The menu has drifted a bit since it opened, but mostly for the better, with the kitchen putting out some very good Cantonese specialties alongside Chinese classics such as Peking duck. A little long on design for sure, the open room has steel support columns, hanging red Chinese lanterns, a polished dark wood floor, comfortable bentwood seats, and curving high-backed dark leather banquettes. The bar sits to the right, and the large room opens out to the left in a familiar arrangement. Downstairs there is another dining room of equal size, which I assume is used for banquets or when the place gets very busy upstairs. In the warmer months they have plenty of seating at small tables on the sidewalk, which in their part of town makes for some great people watching.

The specialty is their excellent dim sum, which arrive both steamed and pan-fried. Joe is considered one of the great chefs today in New York doing what is known as the new modern-style dim sum. They make their own dumpling skins, which are paper-thin and very light. The chef makes the fillings, and often he stuffs them as well. The designs are intricate, the skins multicolored, and the garnishes clever. But most importantly, the flavors are as clean, fresh-tasting, and bright as the presentation. While I usually take my dumplings pan-fried, the steamed dumplings here are outstanding due to these delicate house-made skins, some translucent, others with shapes and outlines designed into them. The quality of the dumplings here far surpasses many of the standard dim sum served elsewhere.

They also have a new BBQ chef. The St. Louis ribs, though one night they were oddly redolent of cinnamon, are good nonetheless. The Peking duck at $48 is not cheap, but it is darn good. The pancakes that come with it are delicate and house-made. The duck is crisped, full of flavor, sliced thin, and served with hoisin sauce and julienned scallion and cucumber as garnish. If you have a table of four or more and are hungry, give it a try. Orange-flavored beef is a good twist on that standard, with rich-flavored filet mignon cut into large chunks, then quick-sautéed, glazed, and served with sautéed peppers; it may actually have me ordering that cut of meat, which I usually avoid at all costs. Sliced roast duck is sautéed with a sweet-and-sour celery-cabbage mix and is full of flavor. The noodle dishes and fried rice are all very good too, though a bit expensive. On the lighter side, either the steamed farm-raised branzino or the red snapper is perfect set atop a pool of light homemade soy sauce and julienned vegetables.

The wine list is good, the beer selection is as well, and the staff are helpful. I'd say that the food here, though a tad pricey, is as good or better than at many of the older Cantonese stalwarts down by Canal Street. I just wish they had a few more Asian waiters and a little less attitude.

Chin Chin

212-888-4555
216 East 49th Street, between
Second and Third Avenues
Casual
Reservations
Moderate to expensive
All major credit cards accepted
Lunch and dinner Monday–
Friday, dinner Saturday and
Sunday
6 train to 51st Street station;
E, V trains to Lexington
Avenue/53rd Street station

Usually when I want Chinese food, I hop on the subway and head downtown, where the prices are much lower, the food is excellent, and the dining rooms and service are utilitarian at best. But there are hosts of New Yorkers who don't want to leave the comforts of their uptown neighborhoods or have guests staying in nearby hotels. Or perhaps they simply like the fancy version of Chinese dining, modern sleek rooms with linen on the table, wine lists, and attentive service, and they don't mind spending a lot extra for it. So it is for them that places such as Mr. Chow, Shun Lee Palace, and Chin Chin exist.

To be honest, it really is nice to eat well-turned-out Chinese food in something other than a dormitory environment. After all, Chinese cuisine is great food, so why not dine in a fittingly grand setting? I learned of this place back in 1987, when I was the chef at the Ritz-Carlton on Central Park South and the legendary bartender at our signature restaurant, the Jockey Club, one Norman Bukofzer, told me to give it a try. He knew the owners and raved about the just-opened eatery. Turns out he was correct, as he usually is. Here the room is sleek, clean, and modern with off-white walls, softly lit from recessed fixtures above and decorated with vintage black-and-white photographs of the extended Chin family. Each wall is lined with high-backed dark wood banquettes, with freestanding four-tops running down the center of the room. The bar is at the front, the kitchen to the rear, and we recognize this instantly as a traditional New York dining room layout.

The menu is large and divided into predictable sections: hot and cold appetizers, soups, noodles, vegetables, seafood, meat by species, and a house specialty, Peking duck. Let's start there. Outside of the Peking Duck House on Mott Street, my favorite, this is one of the best ducks to be had anywhere in the city, crisp-skinned, nearly without fat, the meat moist and flavorful, the texture almost like a confit. The thin crêpe-like pancakes served with it arrive soft and warm, with little piles of julienned cucumber and scallion and a very good hoisin sauce. The duck can be ordered à la carte or as a complete meal with set side dishes for two, including soup, fried rice, a vegetable, and dessert, for $34 per person. Not bad at all for the quality. Should you not want duck, try the excellent crispy fried squid or the minced squab in lettuce pockets. Here my other favorite dark-meat bird, usually a challenge to debone and devour, is served boneless, shredded, wrapped in lettuce, and very easy to eat.

Among the cold appetizers, jellyfish arrives cut in long strands like linguine dressed with a sauce accented with vinegar, hot peppers, and fish sauce, yet slightly sweetened. This is mostly a textural dish: the crunch of the mild fish goes well with the hot, salty, sweet, and sour sauce. The dumplings are all good and nearly greaseless. Among the noodles, the chow fun, broad and chewy pappardelle-like noodles, arrive paired with minced beef; the lo mein is good; and the Singapore-style mai fun, thin strands of rice noodles, is studded with julienne pork, red and green peppers, onions, scallions, and dried shrimp, all laced with an accent of curry powder. Lamb, an oddity in most Chinese restaurants, is offered either as boneless medallions with Chinese string beans or as a curried stew. Tea-smoked duck is excellent and refined, and I love the Hong Kong pork filets, less refined but delicious.

Lobsters are offered a half-dozen ways, including the always delicious Cantonese-style; roll up your sleeves and don't miss a bite of food. Whole fish come steamed or fried. I love the black bass fried, the skin scored and crisp, topped with loads of ginger and shredded scallions in a light fish sauce.

Desserts are okay; I stick with ice cream or fresh fruit. The wine list is also okay but seriously needs updating. Wines are divided by color and then characteristic. For white, it's crisp to mild and fruity to big and bold, and all with the various oak gradations duly noted. But why no German whites, which work so well with this food? And there are far too few offerings from the Loire Valley, Austria, or northern Italy. Reds are laid out the same way, with tannins measured alongside oak and body character. But from France you have no choices between the often mediocre Château de la Chaize Beaujolais at $27 and the Talbot at $110, the next French wine on the list. And who in their right mind orders Opus One or Lafite-Rothschild with this kind of food? Well, Smith and Wollensky is just around the corner, and this *is* the East Side. All in all, the flavors here are clean, the food well prepared, the room civilized, and the service very good; Jimmy Chin and his brother, attentive owners, are nearly always on hand. If you don't mind shelling out the extra bucks, just think what you're saving on cab fare down the FDR to Mott Street.

Cho Dang Gol

212-695-8222
55 West 35th Street,
  between Broadway and
  Fifth Avenue
Casual
Reservations
Moderate
All major credit cards accepted
Seven days a week 11:30
  AM–10:30 PM
1, 2, 3, B, D, F, V, N, Q, R, W
  trains to 34th Street station

If you thought tofu was boring, you're wrong. My case in point is this restaurant. This place specializes in dishes centered around great, fresh homemade tofu. It has a very different menu than most of the other Korean restaurants in this neighborhood. Three days a week in the back of the dining room, the tofu chef is at work using a large cauldron, where they cook the soy in order to make tofu. Starting with fresh soybeans that have been soaked overnight, then crushed to render soy milk, water is added and the whole mixture is put over a flame to be simmered, stirred, skimmed, and then strained to separate the soy milk from the remains of the crushed beans. This milk is then reheated, and to it they add an enzyme that causes a chemical reaction, resulting in curds. It is then cooked further until just the right moment, when the heat is cut off and the curdled mix is removed, strained, and brought downstairs. It is then poured into a cheesecloth-lined mold and set in a large square wooden press. Pressure is added, squeezing off excess water, until the whole block is firm enough to yield a cube of tofu that can be cut.

Back upstairs, you can have that fresh tofu in a dish called cho dang sol son doo boo kimchi, a simple plate of large squares of tofu, warmed and sprinkled with seaweed, set alongside a dozen or so slices of warm braised pork belly, a small pile of kimchi, and two dipping sauces. Or try an even simpler option, juk suk yang nyum doo boo, large squares of steamed tofu served with a special soy dipping sauce. You'll also find those great Korean pancakes presented with a mix of assorted vegetables, tofu, and sliced or ground pork. In the soups and casserole section of the menu, you'll find soft tofu, delicious mixed with various seafood stews and vegetables. A standout is the kong bi ji, combining ground soybeans with white kimchi and ground pork. There is a section of the menu mixing rice, in this case healthy brown rice, with vegetables, seafood, beef, pork, and tofu in hot stone bowls, and a few of the best dishes on the back of the menu are listed as entrees or special casseroles. Try the cho dang ssam jung sik, for two people, featuring a delicious mix of sliced pork with squid, assorted seasonal vegetables, and a huge pot of soy-based stew. Or the mo doo boo nak ji bok um, spicy octopus tossed with noodles, chunks of vegetables, and tofu, served on a hot stone plate.

The room is clean and spare, with lots of natural wood and an industrial cement floor. Service is sincere and very polite. The menu overall is very healthy, and you can wash it all down with tea, beer, soju, or mag gul li, a cloudy Korean rice wine. Come with friends, as this is a menu that needs to be explored and shared by ordering a good variety of plates and being surprised. It's not the cheapest place in this part of town, but the fresh tofu becomes habit-forming, and it's worth the extra few dollars.

City Bakery

212-366-1414
3 West 18th Street, between Fifth and Sixth Avenues
Casual
No reservations
Inexpensive to moderate
All major credit cards accepted
Monday–Friday 7:30 AM–7 PM,
Saturday 7:30 AM–6:30 PM,
Sunday 9 AM–6 PM
4, 5, 6, L, N, Q, R, W trains to
14th Street/Union Square
station

As if this Union Square neighborhood were in need of yet another good spot to buy ingredients, meals, or just snacks, this little stretch of West 18th Street, with both City Bakery and Cupcake Café across the street, reminds us that in New York, enough is never enough. City Bakery is everything cafeteria-style dining can be when done right. Which is to say that you can walk in any time of day, any month of the year, and find very well-prepared hot and cold foods, excellent baked goods, a variety of beers and wines, and assorted other beverage choices, in a nice, clean, spacious environment in which to sit back and enjoy them. Maury Rubin, the owner, moved City Bakery to this space in 2001, just a couple of blocks from the original location, and in doing so, greatly expanded the room. You enter off 18th Street into a space framed by the large glass windows facing the sidewalk at the front. There is seating up front at small tables with stools and counters, then plenty more seats along the walls on both sides around the center counter, and room for another 50 or 60 upstairs in the open mezzanine.

To the rear is a U-shaped self-serve buffet, with the daily offerings, priced by the pound, which change seasonally. For breakfast they have excellent hot oatmeal, warm bread pudding, cornmeal mush, salami and eggs, and thick sweet slabs of great French toast. On the lighter side there are always bowls full of fresh fruit, granola, yogurt, and pastries à la European hotel breakfasts. For lunch and early dinner they segue into a mix of hot and cold dishes, seasonal salads, pastas, potato dishes, sides, and hot dishes in bain-maries that include main courses of meat and fish prepared under the supervision of chef Ilene Rosen. The center of the store is where the bulk of the pastries and hot and cold beverages are dispensed. In the colder months they serve an excellent hot chocolate, which can be topped with their addictive homemade marshmallows. In the warmer months there are several fresh fruit juices, flavored iced teas, lemonade, and chilled coffees to quench your thirst.

Some of my favorites are the potato kugel, dense macaroni and cheese, salt-and-pepper chicken wings, and heirloom tomato sandwiches in the summer months. The ice creams are custom-made for them, and nearly all the pastries sold are first-rate. In short, I can't think of a better upscale salad bar in the city, or a nicer place to simply kill some time during the day sipping coffee, having a snack, and catching up on some reading.

City Hall

212-227-7777
131 Duane Street, between Church Street and West Broadway
Casual
Reservations
Moderate to expensive
All major credit cards accepted
Lunch and dinner Monday, breakfast, lunch, and dinner Tuesday–Friday, brunch and dinner Saturday
R, W trains to City Hall station; 1, 2, 3, A, C trains to Chambers Street station

The menu at City Hall is written in a certain familiar New York vernacular, melding the old with the new. Appetizers such as chicken soup with matzo balls, carrots, and dill stand alongside offerings of iceberg wedge salads, tuna or salmon tartares, fried calamari, and oyster pan roasts. The food here rarely dazzles, but this is an excellent choice if you are looking for well-prepared, straightforward cooking drawn from first-rate ingredients, including excellent dry-aged prime steaks, locally caught seafood, and organic vegetables. It offers attentive service, a user-friendly menu, and a dining room housed in a beautifully renovated space.

In this stately old cast-iron building on Duane Street, the site of a former shoe factory dating back to 1854, chef-owner Henry Meer has created a stunningly contemporary space and a menu based on updated classic New York City chop house cuisine. I first met Henry, a native of the Upper East Side, in cooking school in the 1980s. Back then he impressed me as a serious and ambitious young man. After graduating in 1982, he spent the next fifteen years training under two of the best chefs in the city, cooking for J. J. Rachou at La Côte Basque and then as a sous-chef for the famed André Soltner at Lutèce. From these two greats Henry learned his work ethic. Both Rachou and Soltner were old-school chefs, putting in 80-hour weeks, working at the stoves every day for lunch and dinner.

The dining rooms at City Hall feature open structural beams and soaring ceilings lined with large backlit durotrans vintage photographs of old New York street scenes and turn-of-the-century black-and-white photos of chefs, peddlers with pushcarts, food stalls, butchers, and beer joints, all selected by Henry from the archives of the New York Public Library. As you enter the restaurant past the podium to the right, there is a very nice bar space with a few tables around it; to the left is the main dining room, with its partially open kitchen visible at the rear, through a long rectangular pass. The dining room has a small semicircular oyster bar in one corner, housing several small steam-jacketed kettles like those at the Grand Central Oyster Bar. Here the tiered stacks of iced seafood combinations are prepared out in full view of the room, assembled to order. The square street-level room is large, open, and inviting, with plenty of comfortably spaced seating at tables cut from beautifully grained, unadorned blond Belgian pearwood; high-backed banquettes anchor the space in the center of the room. The food is classic American cuisine, updated and very well executed.

As either starters or main courses, an entire section of the menu is devoted to those tiered seafood platters, featuring fresh-shucked oysters, clams, mussels, crabs, lobsters, razor clams, and scallops—veritable high rises of shellfish on ice. Old-fashioned salads are brought up to date here: a chopped Cobb salad is topped with sliced grilled beef, avocado, and asparagus; a crunchy, garlicky Caesar is dressed with fresh-grated Parmigiano Reggiano; and a wonderful iceberg wedge is topped with crumbled Maytag blue cheese dressing or Moscow mayonnaise, a variation on Russian dressing, sprinkled with crumbled applewood-smoked bacon.

Here one afternoon, thanks to the chef's suggestion, I discovered one of the best hamburgers in town. The large patty is formed from their own meat mix (ground in-house), grilled, and served on a homemade onion bun baked in the basement kitchen. The burger is set beside a pile of crisp and greaseless twice-fried, hand-cut french fries.

Next to the main kitchen and plainly visible in the dining room is a lit glass-front refrigerator in which you'll see an assortment of tagged, dry-aged prime meat waiting to be butchered. New York strips, Delmonicos, filets, hangers, and skirt steaks are all top-notch; the meat here is better than in most of New York's top steakhouses. The seafood selection varies with seasonal availability, but a recent menu included grilled Atlantic salmon with béarnaise sauce, peppered tuna steak, and roast monkfish with a Dijon hollandaise. Vegetables in season come from a private organic farm in Bridgehampton, Long Island.

The wine list is very well thought-out, focusing on a broad variety of American producers. House-made desserts include a red velvet cake, classic New York cheesecake, chocolate soufflé, crème brûlée, and baked fruits topped with streusel. I should mention that downstairs, City Hall has one of the nicest private party rooms in all New York. Situated below street level, part of this subterranean space extends beneath the sidewalk. Those sandblasted stone slabs forming the ceiling above you are in fact the bottom sections of the hand-cut granite squares forming the century-old walkway. This beautifully renovated, completely private space is an excellent choice for parties or weddings, with the real City Hall just a few blocks away.

Cookshop

212-924-4440
156 Tenth Avenue, at 20th
  Street
Casual
Reservations
Moderate
All major credit cards accepted
Lunch and dinner Monday–
  Friday, brunch and dinner
  Saturday and Sunday
C, E trains to 23rd Street
  station

Friends of mine had been raving about this place—well, not exactly raving; let's say extolling its virtues—to me for years before I first visited it. The virtues are the casual neighborhood setting and vibe, combined with reasonable prices, good service, and sensible home-style, down-to-earth cooking, and for my money that's enough.

The room is L-shaped, the ceiling covered with strips of oak, which helps to soften the sound level. Even when the place is full, which is about every night at 8 PM, you can actually have a conversation without shouting. It's a novelty increasingly hard to come by at a lot of the newer restaurants these days, especially places like this, which seat well over 100 guests at a time. The setting is spare, with hard wood chairs set before plain square oak tables, but it's consistent with the overall tone, which is accessibility and sustainability. The chef is Marc Meyer. He cooks what he likes to eat and keeps it simple too. He runs this place and his other space, Five Points, with his wife, Vicki Freeman, and their business partner Chris Paraskevaides. The menu is informed by the market and the season, and whenever possible it champions sustainable agriculture and animal husbandry. A chalkboard in the dining room lists the current roster of the chef's favorite farmers.

Start with the spicy fried grits, addictive little crunchy balls of well-seasoned cornmeal that work well with just about any aperitif, including beer. I am a bluefish fan and consider it one of the most underrated fish in our waters; here it is marinated, then smoked and served with a variety of accompaniments. Last I was here, the firm smoky filets were paired with a salad of dressed dandelion and spiced lady apples. The squid served here, another of my favorite underrated fish (which happens to be plentiful off our coasts), comes from Montauk and is flash-grilled, set atop a tumble of frisée, and garnished with black olives, aioli, and seasoned crunchy bread crumbs. Fried duck livers are another great starter, again set atop bitter frisée and then balanced out with crunchy Honeycrisp apples and lovely creamy Maytag blue cheese.

There are always three or four salads to choose from as starters, middle courses, or a light dinner. The Hudson Valley organic chicken salad, served with green olives, toasted almonds, golden raisins, and bracing zinfandel vinaigrette, makes a great light dinner selection for $15. Out of the stone oven comes a pizza of the day, and usually a roast fish or meat as well. Keeping with casual, they offer sandwiches as entrées for lunch. The burger here is good, but I'd go for the fried catfish sandwich slathered with a slaw of savoy cabbage, a creation dubbed Tabasco rémoulade, and a pile of potato chips, all for $15. The pastas of the day are hit-and-miss. They always have a good, fresh fish, and for meat lovers, if they have it, try the tri-tip steak, also known as a Newport steak, a great well-marbled cut taken from the bottom of the sirloin, paired with mashed fingerling potatoes, a big spoonful of salsa verde, and arugula salad for a very decent $22. At night they have a selection from the kitchen's rotisserie, usually a chicken. One recent night it was Hudson Valley rabbit served with creamy polenta, sautéed oyster mushrooms, and a drizzle of pumpkinseed pesto. Side dishes are $5 and well worth it for vegetable lovers. Try the great kale and lemon or the cake-like jalapeño corn bread.

Do save room for desserts—they are very good too. The roasted pear bread pudding with "buttery dates" and thick brandy cream sauce is addicting. Ditto the warm apple turnover or the peppermint-stick hot-fudge sundae. Wines are well chosen, and there are many very good offerings from smaller producers in the $25–$50 range.

Overall, New York City needs a lot more restaurants like this and others that are along the same lines—Pearl Oyster Bar, Prune, Little Owl, Crispo, and Peasant, to name just a few. They play to the crowd, but don't cook down to it. Cookshop is proof positive that a chef with personality, ability, and vision can create an interesting menu around very well-selected ingredients and serve well-thought-out plates of darn good food at reasonable prices.

Cooper's Tavern

212-268-8460

481 Eighth Avenue, at West
35th Street, inside the
New Yorker Hotel

Casual

Reservations

Moderate

All major credit cards accepted

Lunch and dinner seven days
a week

1, 2, 3, A, C, E, B, D, F, V, N, Q,
R, W trains to 34th Street
station

That Cooper's Tavern is included in this book may have more to do with where it is than what it is. Not that it's a bad choice or that the food is so-so—neither is true. It's just that in this heavily trafficked midtown neighborhood just steps from Penn Station and Madison Square Garden, there are very few other choices outside of Korean restaurants and Keens. That said, if you're attending an event at the Garden, missed your train, or just for some odd reason want to hang out in this part of midtown, you can do far worse than here. The place opened in late 2007, and in many ways it still looks and feels like a midlevel hotel restaurant anywhere in the United States. The L-shaped dining room has a bar up front with a few flat-screen TVs, usually tuned to sports. The main dining area is just past that and is done hotel-style in tones of beige. The staff is good—I suppose they're card-carrying union holdovers from whatever this was before it was Cooper's. On some nights the crowd dining here can also remind you of the fact that you're in a hotel, as on a few of my recent visits the families and couples seated around me had that "we're not in Kansas anymore" look about them. But you can still eat well.

The energetic chef is Julian Clauss-Ehlers, who was at Zitoune and then Links before setting up shop here. For starters, the signature dish of steamed littleneck clams with chunks of chorizo in a fennel, tomato, and white wine broth is decent, with ficelle to dip into the broth should the spirit move you. Fried squid served wrapped in a napkin frites-style were a bit soggy for me. Instead try the shrimp variations, featuring three potsticker dumplings, three poached shrimp with cocktail sauce, and three fried tempura-style with a tamarind-based dip. Of the various starter salads, the Caesar was my favorite, and for main courses they also feature a Cobb salad and an Asian-style chopped salad with diced shrimp and cashews, daikon, and shreds of fried Asian pasta.

For main courses, the fish and chips made with cod is good, and the falafel-crusted salmon has fans too. I'd come back anytime just for the heritage-breed Berkshire pork chops, a huge portion featuring two bone-in chops stuffed with onion confit and set over a hearty white-bean ragout studded with root vegetables (a meal in itself) for the bargain price of $26. The 20-ounce rib steak is great, as is the porterhouse for two, with meat as good as you'll find in many steakhouses around town. The skyscraper burger, a 12-ounce disk topped with crisped bacon, grilled portobello mushrooms, smoked Gouda, crispy fried onions, and slice of tomato, comes with a fork and knife and a side of fries. It's a darn good burger. Add a good beer, and that's dinner for around $22.

Desserts are actually better than they need to be. For whatever reason, they come in small portions, priced accordingly at $4 per plate, which encourages overordering. I liked the banana bread and butter pudding, and especially the absurd but undeniably good Cooper's sundae, which is essentially a mixture of ice cream, cheesecake, chocolate chip cookies, fresh berries, a raspberry sauce, and even some whipped cream for good measure. The wine list is decent and fairly priced. I hope this place hangs around for a while because the food is much better than you'd think walking past the rather pedestrian New Yorker Hotel, and in this neighborhood, as mentioned, it's slim pickings if you're not a fan of Korean. I just hope they fix the heavy metal front door, which on cold windy winter nights is almost impossible to open.

Corton

212-219-2777
239 West Broadway, between North Moore and White Streets
Casual
Reservations
Expensive
All major credit cards accepted
Dinner Monday–Saturday
1 train to Franklin Street station

Officially opened in late September 2008, this high-profile project had been in the works for quite some time and was the source of lots of speculation, especially among the press and blogs. The reason is simple and twofold: the space it occupies was home for many years to the legendary, groundbreaking restaurant Montrachet, where in 1985, a then 29-year-old Drew Nieporent teamed with a relatively unknown chef named David Bouley, introducing great French food to the Tribeca of the mid-eighties while creating a new, casual, "downtown" style of service with moderate prices. David was out within a year and has since gone on to write his own page in the history of New York restaurants, and Nieporent expanded his Myriad Group throughout the 1990s, while Montrachet, under the direction of a handful of different chefs, just got old, became less relevant, and grew tired, eventually closing its doors for good a few years back.

It reopened as Corton, where again we have a very talented team in place with Nieporent at the helm and Paul Liebrandt in the kitchen. Unlike Bouley, Liebrandt is a partner in the process, and that simple detail may in the end make all the difference in the world. Paul is a hugely talented young chef, a Brit, and a protégé of Marco Pierre White. Paul burst onto the scene a while back with a three-star review at the short-lived Atlas, then bumped around cooking here and there until he opened Gilt to mixed reviews a few years back. As with many talented young artists, he tended to be a bit self-indulgent and didactic, and was in need of a culinary editor. He may have found the perfect partner in Nieporent. I was at Corton on opening night and suspect that this restaurant will both be critically well received and have lasting power, in spite of the difficult economic times in which it opened.

What was wrong with Montrachet has been fixed, from the gloomy, odd-shaped dining room to the less-than-inspired food in its later years. There's a spanking new state-of-the-art kitchen to boot. This was a complete makeover. The new space is quiet and civilized, with a bar past the entrance to your right, and essentially an open, well-lit dining room to the left and rear. The carpet and banquettes are beige, and the walls are white with a bas-relief theme of vines and small birds. Lighting is courtesy of several sources, including a series of long thin tubular glass chandeliers that remind me of the Lippold sculpture above the bar in the Grill Room at the Four Seasons. A long, narrow slit is cut through the wall that separates the kitchen from the main room, giving diners a glimpse of the chef and his kitchen staff. The wine list is exclusively French, with an emphasis on Burgundy.

The menu is offered as three courses à la carte for $76, or a seven-course preset tasting menu for $110, preferably ordered by the entire table. My inclination is always to go with tasting menus, as they are more varied and give the kitchen a chance to really shine. Either way there is a lot to like on both menus. Jerusalem artichokes are turned into an incredibly silky velouté-style soup, dotted with peekytoe crab. Lightly smoked pasta is served with shaved black truffles in a cream sauce and finished with aged gouda. A creamy, smooth torchon of foie gras arrived pink at the center and wrapped in a borscht gelée accented with blood orange.

Veal sweetbreads are slowly cooked, and dotting the plate around them is a just-set, slow-cooked Violet Hill Farm egg, braised carrots, and a drizzle of Moroccan argan oil. Maine lobster is poached in butter and served garnished with sautéed chanterelles and a lobster jus redolent of hazelnuts. From the tasting menu, a lobe of Pacific uni was set in a bracing Meyer lemon gelée with foamed cauliflower; the small spoon that accompanies this dish arrived chilled. Also from the tasting menu, amadai fish was set over a citrus-laced coconut broth, punctuated with confit cloves of black garlic, redolent of licorice, and Serrano ham. Lamb loin was lovely, paired with a boneless section of braised neck meat, seasoned with the Moroccan spice mix known as ras el hanout, and set above a pool of chocolate mint jus. From the à la carte menu, a lobe of center-cut squab breast is wrapped in good bacon and then slow-cooked sous vide style, served with a chestnut cream and a light milk jus accented with gingerbread spices. With this meal they suggested a bottle of Gevrey-Chambertin, a 2004 Domaine Harmand-Geoffroy "En Jouise," that matched very well with all the plates.

Desserts were beautiful, courtesy of pastry chef Robert Truitt. Caramel brioche accented with passionfruit puree, coffee, and banana was better than it sounds. The white sesame cream with huckleberries and salted toffee was lovely, and the bitter chocolate fondant with chestnut puree was another winner. Service is professional, as expected. Within months of the opening, all the critics' verdicts were in, and for once I agreed with them all. Four stars from Adam Platt of *New York* magazine, 6 stars from *Time Out New York*, and a glowing 3 stars from Frank Bruni of the *New York Times*. I've spent some time in the kitchen observing Paul and his crew and can tell you that with the review stage of the restaurant behind them, they can now relax and concentrate on cooking and are doing so with precision and finesse matched in few other kitchens in town. Nieporent more than anyone wants this place to work and regain its luster. With Paul as a chef/partner and all the combined talents they bring to the table, I wish it well and fully expect that this will be seen as one of the most important and successful openings of the year.

Counter

212-982-5870
105 First Avenue, at 7th Street
Casual
Moderate
All major credit cards accepted
Dinner Monday–Friday, lunch and dinner Saturday and Sunday
F, V trains to Second Avenue station; 6 train to Astor Place station

There aren't a lot of vegetarian restaurants in this book because, quite frankly, I don't like them. Counter is an exception. The mood is cheery, not serious or dour. They serve beer and wine, and the food for the most part stands out and tastes very good. The room is small and open, featuring a tile floor and circular bar, and the staff are young and East Village friendly. The menu is broken down into several sections: mezze, appetizers, soups and salads, entrees, sandwiches, and sides. Aside from being vegan, all the food here is organic, not surprisingly, and the flavors are big and bold. From the mezze section try the lovely warm corn beignet served with a creamy rémoulade dipping sauce, or the walnut and lentil panini, the chunky rosemary-accented puree served on chewy ciabatta slathered with eggless aioli. Yum. I'm one of the few foodies I know who actually likes veggie burgers, so I tried their mock meatloaf, and it was very good. The thick slab, chewy from lentils combined with wild rice, is served with some kind of brown meatless gravy, mashed potatoes, and roasted vegetables. I could feel myself getting thinner, healthier, and younger the whole way through. One night the feather-light potato-almond gnocchi, served with an herbaceous lemony sage butter, was as good as could be had in any first-rate Italian kitchen in Manhattan, and better than most. Cauliflower risotto was a good, playful take on this dish, served with polenta and an herbed arugula emulsion. The real surprise entrée was the cassoulet. I love good cassoulet and really could not imagine this classic southern French white bean stew, which normally takes two or more days to make and is studded with duck confit, slab bacon, sausages, and ham, being anything near as good as the meat version, but I was wrong.

The cassoulet here is remarkable, and not just for its meatlessness. Here they slowly braise excellent white beans with an herbaceous vegetable broth, accented with chunks of root vegetables and tomato. Hand-cut french fries come with three dipping sauces, one laced with Moroccan harissa paste, then organic ketchup, followed by rosemary-garlic aioli, all very good, as are the fries. For dessert try the poached pear in spiced red wine, the root beer float, or, in season, the strawberry shortcake with homemade vanilla ice cream. This is among my favorite vegetarian eateries anywhere. There is a good selection of beer and biodynamic wines and perhaps soon, pending a liquor license, organic spirits to add to the list.

Craftsteak

212-400-6699
85 Tenth Avenue, between
15th and 16th Streets
Casual to dressy
Reservations
Expensive
All major credit cards accepted
Dinner seven nights a week
A, C, E trains to 14th Street
station; L train to Eighth
Avenue station

As I've mentioned, sometimes it takes restaurants a year or more to mature. The more ambitious the restaurant the longer the maturation time, and Craftsteak is a perfect example. As you may already know, I'm a big fan of steakhouses. I love good American beef, and I especially like the steakhouse concept when serious chefs get involved—places such as BLT, the short-lived 7 Square, and Michael Lomanico's Porterhouse, to name a few recent examples.

So when Tom Colicchio, one of the most talented chefs on the scene today, opened Craftsteak in early 2006, expectations were very high. Inexplicably, he made the same mistakes with Craftsteak that he made when he opened the original Craft nearly a decade earlier: the menu was way too big and way too complicated. The dining public wants to be given a menu that provides them with relatively simple choices, from which they can make informed decisions, and then eat dinner. We don't want to be presented with a document that is way too long (it still is), requiring dozens of decisions (fewer, but still too many), involves loads of questions for the wait staff, and perhaps even necessitates a bit of USDA beef research prior to ordering. The opening menu had no less than five types of beef offered, and then those five varieties were aged in gradations from 21 days to 40+. Add to that dozens of sauces and sides (including vegetables that were offered either roasted, sautéed, braised, or pureed), and so essentially one had to decide from well over a hundred possible variations offered on the menu.

To add to the problem, Colicchio, who now presides over a small empire of restaurants, has no choice but to delegate and trust. I'm not certain that the opening chef, Damon Wise, was really up to the task. The style of cooking, the sheer size of the menu, and the repertoire of recipes, many dating back to Tom's Gramercy days and Marco Canora's early stint at Craft, made the burden unwieldy. And as was often the case with Craft, the food and presentation were too carefully wrought, often too pared down, too precious, too careful. The press panned Craftsteak nearly universally, and in some ways it deserved it.

That said, there was a lot of talent in that kitchen. Wise had Matt Accarrino as a sous-chef for the first year, along with pastry chef Catherine Schimenti, both of whom I remembered from their days working in the kitchens at Per Se, and both major talents in their own right. Many of the line cooks were good, disciplined veterans of New York kitchens; the potential for greatness was there. These days Accarrino and Schimenti are both in L.A. running yet another Craft, and the kitchen here is under the watchful eye of Shane McBride, whom I first met when he worked with Christian Delouvrier at Lespinasse (and who was also the chef at 7 Square prior to its sudden demise).

A year into the project, Craftsteak had vastly improved, found its stride, and on a good night stands out as one of the very best steakhouses in New York City. That said, the menu is still way too big, with over fifty side dishes alone. This results in uneven performance at times, and on many nights the 86 board (the list of items they are out of) can grow long. With high kitchen turnover and a general shortage of experienced cooks citywide, some of the line cooks seem green, and mistakes are more common than they should be, especially in the oversalting of certain dishes.

The building, the back of the old Nabisco complex, is set on a bleak corner just off the West Side Highway, on the far western outskirts of the meatpacking district, opposite a gas station and car wash. It's well worth the trek, and with Del Posto flanking the northern corner, this is the best block for food in the area. The dining room, designed by Bentel and Bentel, is sleek and modern with Hudson River views. It is an open space, with the long slate bar up front. The main dining room has high ceilings and clean sight lines. Lighting is courtesy of long fluorescent bulbs hung vertically in sleek black metal fixtures. A huge mural of the High Line neighborhood and the Manhattan skyline dominates the back wall. In the front there is a lounge before the bar where you are offered either the entire menu or a simple, pared-down bar menu, as you choose. To the right sits a raw bar with more seating. The staff is very efficient and well trained.

The current menu is long but manageable. It starts with a great selection of shellfish: half a dozen varieties of oysters from each coast; standards such as chilled Maine lobsters, a Maine shrimp cocktail, and Florida stone crab claws; raw sashimi-quality fish; and French sardines served in a variety of guises. To this add a half dozen very nice salad options, a selection of American charcuterie, and unusual steakhouse hot appetizers such as sautéed sweetbreads, braised pork belly, batter-fried bone marrow set over a porcini ragout, or luscious Maine crab fondue over buttery pureed potatoes.

The steaks are either standard American corn-fed prime, grass-fed free-range, or Wagyu from the United States or Japan. Among the corn-fed steaks, the strip is offered aged for 28 days, 42 days, or (believe it or not) 56 days. They use Brandt beef as well as beef from Knight Ranch, both excellent producers of traditional corn-fed beef. The best steak on the menu may be the grass-fed New York strip from Montana Ranch, with the grass-fed strip from Parker Ranch Hawaii a close second. Some steakhouse aficionados will rue the fact that the steaks here are not broiled, as is so common elsewhere. Here they cook them in cast-iron sauté pans, basting with foaming spoonfuls of herbed butter; this cooks them simultaneously on both the top with that hot butter and the bottom in contact with the hot pan. The results are as good as and in some cases better than broiling, which can leave a thick charred crust that can conceal the quality of the beef (a good idea at some steakhouses). To round out the menu, there are items like a whole roast Muscovy duck, roasted free-range chicken, New Zealand venison saddle, Berkshire pork chops, and three or four seasonal fish offerings to choose from.

The sides can be great. Vegetables are roasted or sautéed, including dandelion greens, baby onions, ramps, and white and green asparagus in the spring. Potatoes are offered a half dozen ways, and there are beautiful compositions of assorted sautéed or braised wild mushrooms: porcini, baby shiitake, hen-of-the-woods, and morels. The Parker House rolls each table is given are delicious, the wine list is excellent, and the desserts are superb. Made-to-order fried doughnuts are perfect—yeasty, sweet, and light. Moist, delicious red velvet cake is served deconstructed with a garnish of candied beet sorbet. They may offer the best carrot cake anywhere, and if you like peanuts, try the peanut butter cup, set in chocolate, sprinkled with sea salt, garnished with peanut brittle, and served with caramel ice cream. You also have a choice of three ice creams, three gelatos, and three sorbets, all fine examples of their type.

Expensive, sure, but so is great beef. But all things considered, on a good night, this very well may be among the very best steakhouses in New York City.

Crif Dogs

212-614-2728
113 St. Marks Place, between
    First Avenue and Avenue A
Casual
No reservations
Inexpensive
All major credit cards accepted
Seven days a week noon–2 AM
6 train to Astor Place station;
    L train to First Avenue station

This is the funky hot dog joint one would hope to find in the East Village. Step down off the sidewalk from St. Marks and into this basement room decorated with vintage action figures, movie posters, flat-screen TVs showing old surf or Mafia movies, and classic, old-school video games like Ms. Pac-man, Galaga, and Centipede, which you can play while waiting for your order. The name comes from one of the original founders, Chris; Crif is what Chris sounds like when you have a hot dog in your mouth.

As the story goes, two Jersey guys were living in Manhattan and longing for a Jersey-style deep-fried hot dog but couldn't find one anywhere in New York. They got tired of driving across the George Washington Bridge to Callahan's all the time, so they did some research (combing through Callahan's dumpster after hours, along with the one at Rutt's Hut in Clifton) to find out who made their hot dogs so good. Then this space became available, and New York got its first Jersey dog stand, with a twist. Instead of just offering the normal fried dog with the typical toppings, which you can get here (sauerkraut, relish, onions, mustard), they came up with some of their own creations.

The Crif dog itself is a beef and pork blend, lightly smoked with a snap to it. If you want to order it plain with mustard, it's very good at $1.75 a pop. But I say go right for the Spicy Redneck at $3.50, a house dog wrapped in bacon, deep-fried, and topped with chili, coleslaw, and jalapeño peppers. Or try the Chihuahua for $3.25, bacon-wrapped and deep-fried, topped with sliced avocados and sour cream. For breakfast they offer the Good Morning Dog, yet again bacon-wrapped, fried, and this time topped with melted cheese and a fried egg. They of course have a corn dog, and they offer a veggie dog as a nod to all the vegetarians in the neighborhood, as well as great sides like tater tots topped with melted cheese, and chili cheese fries. The place is a classic—they serve soda, shakes, and beer to boot. It's hard to go wrong with a menu like this when you have a craving for delicious junk food. My kids love the place, and guess what—so do I.

Note that one of the city's great cocktail lounges, PDT (which stands for Please Don't Tell), is entered via the walk-in phone booth against the wall at Crif Dogs. Space there is very limited, and the cocktails are amazing.

Crispo

212-229-1818
240 West 14th Street, between Seventh and Eighth Avenues
Casual
Reservations
Moderate
All major credit cards accepted
Dinner seven nights a week
1, 2, 3, A, C, E trains to 14th Street station; L train to Eighth Avenue station

On the inside of the swinging door that connects the kitchen to the dining rooms of Crispo, the door that faces the kitchen staff all day and through which the wait staff must pass, there is a large brass plaque with the word PRIDE etched on it. Fitting, as that one word reflects the spirit of this place better than any other. Frank Crispo has been a part of the New York restaurant scene since the early 1980s. A Philadelphia native, he came straight to New York City after graduating from the Culinary Institute and trained like so many others of that generation with the venerable Jean-Jacques Rachou in the kitchens of La Côte Basque. While other Côte Basque alumni quickly became household names in New York culinary circles—Charlie Palmer, Rick Moonen, Todd English, Henry Meer, Waldy Malouf, and Sam Hazan, to name a few—career success was more elusive for Frank. Just as gifted as any of the others in the kitchen, he simply didn't get the breaks. He opened the pioneering Andiamo on the Upper West Side in 1989 only to have it fail, the result of a bad business partnership that cost him years to recover from. It took him over ten years to get back on his feet, and when he signed the lease on this place, formerly Quatorze, he gutted and rebuilt the space, which took nearly a year and half. The light fixtures are the thick-filament style, the same as used to be common in the old New York subway cars, and the paneling in one small dining room was removed piece by piece from an old Bowery hotel. The broad pine floors are from a warehouse in Brooklyn, and the river stone waterfall was built by his hands from stones exhumed from the basement below. The bar is to your right as you enter, the main room and kitchen are to the rear, and out back is another room that doubles as great outdoor seating in the summer and can be sealed with a retractable roof and heated during the colder months. This has become an excellent neighborhood restaurant, a great choice for fairly priced, homemade Italian food.

Most of the pastas served here are made fresh each day. Frank can be seen most nights working the hand-cranked Berkel slicer, doling out paper-thin cuts of excellent prosciutto, to be paired with chunks of Parmigiano Reggiano and draped over creamy warm polenta, or topping a dish of fresh trofie pasta twists swimming with tiny green peas in a sweet butter sauce. For starters, try a bowl of the house-made eggplant caponata, slathered over slices of good crusty bread, fried risotto balls, fresh roasted peppers paired with capers and anchovies, pickled roasted beets, a plate of mixed olives, assorted cheese plates, or the lovely fresh bufala mozzarella with chiffonade of fresh basil and olive oil.

All the pastas are excellent, from the simple plate of spaghetti with fresh tomato sauce, basil, and pecorino cheese to the ravioli stuffed with Swiss chard and fresh ricotta or his excellent version of the classic spaghetti carbonara.

Entrees vary with the season. Fish items include grilled whole fish, crisp-skinned sautéed sea bass, cuttlefish stew, and braised monkfish in a rich tomato sauce. In the winter his pork shank diavolo is a meal in itself. Osso buco comes in a light broth some days, while other times the broth is dark and rich. Veal is always good here, as is the hanger steak, and the crisp chicken paired with baby artichokes and roast garlic shines.

Desserts are house-made and are decent but I always end my meal here with a plate of just-fried zeppole, arriving at the table dusted with sugar, steaming hot, set alongside a bowl of dark chocolate dipping sauce. Service is good and the kitchen consistent, as is expected when the owner is always on hand. If you are looking for reasonably priced, well-executed Italian food, put Crispo on your short list.

Cru

212-529-1700
24 Fifth Avenue, at 9th Street
Dressy
Reservations
Expensive
All major credit cards accepted
Dinner Monday–Saturday
N, R, W trains to 8th Street
    station

This space has had many restaurant incarnations over the years, but in my mind the cooking has never been better than it is today at Cru. This is easily one of the best restaurants in the city today. The chef is Shea Gallante, a talented young American who learned his craft working in the kitchens of the old Bouley. He's part of a growing group of young, well-trained, homegrown talents that have been incubating here in New York's top kitchens over the last decade and are just now stepping forward into the spotlight with their own style, leading kitchens that a generation ago surely would have been under the baton of chefs from France, Germany, Switzerland, or Italy. In fact, it was at this address during the 1980s that the French chef Michel Fitoussi, fresh off his stint at the Palace, then the city's most expensive restaurant, was wowing New Yorkers with some decent food and lots of blown-sugar baubles. Times surely have changed, and the style of cooking is distinctly modern American.

The name Cru stems from the fact that the owner, Roy Welland, is a famed wine collector, and his fabled cellar is very much front and center here. The French word *cru* describes wines from very specific vineyards and plots of land. When seated, you're presented with the restaurant menu and not one but two thick, leather-bound wine catalogues, one for red wines, the other devoted to whites. There are more than 65,000 wines to choose from in total. Astonishing, yes; confusing, indeed; ridiculous, of course. But nearly all the bottles are from his private collection, and he owns the restaurant. So there we have it—big kids, big toys, big sandbox. The good news is that the attentive, well-trained staff can help you pair wines with your meal; just give them guidelines on pricing and style preferences. Needless to say, the place attracts wine geeks like flypaper attracts flies, and on any given night you'll see them there, elbow to elbow, purple-lipped, gathered at the bar sipping, sniffing, and swirling fancy glasses of this Bordeaux or that Burgundy and commenting in wine-speak.

The room is rather formal, done in shades of beige and dark brown, the wood-paneled walls adorned with lit oil paintings set in heavy frames. White linen tablecloths with fresh flowers, heavy silver, lovely show plates, lit candles, and the well-heeled crowd set the tone for the food, which is very serious and very good.

The menu is divided into two sections, with a very nice three-course prix fixe menu for around $75 per person, with a lot of good choices and mercifully few supplements. Or you can opt for the seasonal tasting menu, seven smaller courses at $110, with wines to match for another $72 per person. Either way, there are lots of great choices and nary a bad one to be found on the entire document.

A recent dinner started with an amuse-bouche of whipped burrata cheese, with a touch of blueberries, scented with basil, drizzled with 25-year-old balsamic vinegar, and set in a tiny pastry shell. It was followed by a crudo tasting; these vary nightly but are well worth ordering. Ours was a trio starting with a tartare of Japanese amadai fish (basically a Japanese sea bream) paired with shiso flowers, a hint of yuzu, pitted tiny gaeta olives, and white miso, alongside bigeye tuna loin and fatty hamachi belly, all beautiful, miniature compositions of melding flavors and contrasting textures. Filet of halibut was slow-cooked nearly confit, then set in a broth scented with saffron, verbena, and baby ginger foam. Skate came turned on its side, a section of the wing twirled like a pinwheel, garnished with European canned tuna belly, tiny lardons of double-smoked bacon, and spring garlic. This was paired with a great and inexpensive rarity of a wine, a Cassis Blanc Domaine du Bagnol from the south of France—proof that fantastic bargains still exist. My favorite fish dish was seppia cut long and thin, as if it had been sliced on a mandoline, paired with Vaucluse white asparagus, tart pomelo lozenges, long shards of red Italian chicory, and a squid-ink-based vinaigrette, playing the bitter crunch of the leaves against the sweet smooth seppia. Pasta here is handmade. The liquid corn tortellini, sweet and chewy, set beneath a black pepper Parmesan foam, were lovely and light, as were the little ricotta cavatelli with tiny chunks of sweet veal sausage, Black Forest ham, and ramps. The best were the little ravioli filled with cheese and nettle puree, paired with a 2000 La Spinetta Gallina Barbera d'Alba.

The meat course featured a medallion of tender, grain-fed veal loin with glazed favas, porcini, and a dark green organic parsley puree, and breast of poulard baked in buttermilk and herbs, set atop braised red cabbage, tiny baby carrots, and celery root jus.

Desserts are all à la carte and excellent. A standout was the Honeycrisp apple beignet, feather-light like a little puffy doughnut, served with salted vanilla ice cream, a sabayon made from stout, and candied walnuts. My dining companion had a dessert that was a kind of candy store redux: a delicious chocolate peppermint bombe, a small bar of hazelnut crunch, mocha chip ice cream, and braised sour cherries. We started the meal with a fino manzanilla sherry with the crudo, and ended with an Emilio Lustau Tintilla de Rota.

The food here is modern and accurate, tastes great, and is beautifully presented, with an emphasis on contrasting textures and balanced flavors while utilizing the best, freshest seasonal ingredients from around the world. In short, this is an excellent example of a modern chef approaching his prime at work, with a staff and wine list to match the food.

Curry Leaf

212-725-5558
99 Lexington Avenue,
 at 27th Street
Casual
Reservations
Inexpensive to moderate
All major credit cards accepted
Lunch and dinner seven days
 a week
6 train to 28th Street station

Curry Leaf is owned and operated by Aziz Osmani, a neighborhood fixture who for years has been the owner of the venerable Kalustyan's market right up the street. He also runs the place called Rice on the corner. He's a very good businessman, knows the limits of this neighborhood in terms of value and price point, and in Curry Leaf strikes the right balance. I've always asked for advice on where to eat real traditional Indian foods in New York, and those who answer honestly, including Aziz, advise me to get invited to an Indian expat's home for a real authentic Indian dining experience. Until that happens, we have many good choices that come close.

The menu here is a mix of Indian and Pakistani cuisines, with a good selection of vegetarian choices as well as spicy braised dishes, simple tandoori meats, deep-fried specialties, and homemade breads. Ignore the silly salad plate of chopped iceberg lettuce, sliced cucumbers, and wedges of generic tomato; someone must have convinced Aziz that Americans like free salads. Head straight into the menu and there you'll find many good choices. For starters, the samosas are all good, packed with the concentrated flavors of spiced ground meats or vegetables, and fried light and crispy. For some these may be a meal in and of themselves. Also good is mulligatawny soup, a British-Indian hybrid of sorts, or the fried vegetable and cheese platter with its dipping sauces. Chicken tikka is good, but better with sauce. The lamb vindaloo packs a punch. Braised okra arrives with a clear flavor (and no slime), and the eggplant side dishes are all excellent. The staff are helpful, and the room is clean and bright, though a bit generic. Trust me, on this stretch of Lexington, you could do far worse.

Dae Dong

212-695-3873
17 West 32nd Street, between Broadway and Fifth Avenue
Casual
Reservations
Moderate
All major credit cards accepted
Lunch and dinner seven days a week
1, 2, 3, B, D, F, V, N, Q, R, W trains to 34th Street station

There are so many good places to eat on this one-block stretch of 32nd Street between Broadway and Fifth Avenue that you'd have to try very hard to have a bad meal. That said, in this part of town I tend to be a creature of habit and go to certain restaurants to eat very specific dishes—house specialties, I suppose you could call them. I'll go to Gahm Mi Oak for the seol long tong, kimchi, chilled meat platters, or warm salad of cow knee. I'll visit Hyo Dong Gak, now called Shanghai Mong, just for a bowl of ja jang myun and jam pon, Kum Gang San for their tripe soup, hae jong gook, and Cho Dang Gol for their large variety of fresh tofu dishes. In the summer when New York is swelteringly hot and I'm not in the mood to sit over a tableside BBQ grill and break into a sweat cooking my own galbi, nor do I want to slurp from a large bowl of steaming broth loaded with beef short ribs, daikon, and noodles, I long for lighter fare and especially cold dishes. The Koreans have absolutely addictive cold noodle dishes and soups, many of them based on chewy, long buckwheat noodles called naeng myun. This style of Korean cooking originated in North Korea in and around Pyongyang before the war, and loosely melded Chinese cooking with traditional Korean. These noodles, usually house-made in restaurants that feature them, are a mixture of buckwheat flour, high-gluten flour, and a splash of vinegar and seltzer water, mixed initially in a commercial mixing bowl and then by hand. The dough is stretched and then cut into long, thick noodles, so long that the only way to eat them is to slurp them up and bite them off. It's not a bad idea to ask your server to precut them, which they gladly do with a pair of scissors.

The room is square with a bar up front. Above each table there is a copper hood system to draw off the BBQ smoke. The banquettes are comfortable, many equipped with a flat-screen TV playing a Korean version of MTV. The crowd is mostly Korean, and the staff is very helpful and welcoming to all. Order naeng myun and within minutes a large ceramic bowl arrives filled with noodles surrounded by a clear chilled beef broth, topped with thin slices of chilled brisket that had been cooked in that broth, julienned crisp Asian pears, cucumber, and daikon, slices of white cabbage, and half of a hard-boiled egg. While the wait staff may suggest you add some vinegar and mustard (apparently it's customary), I skip it; the vinegar is that nasty white industrial stuff better suited for cleaning windows, and the mustard just makes the dish taste like, well, mustard. Tuck your napkin in and slurp away happily until the contents of the bowl are gone. The noodles are chewy, the broth mildly beef-flavored, and the vegetables add crunch and coolness, a nice foil to the richness of the brisket meat. A seriously good one-bowl meal if ever there was one.

Another dish on that menu, hamhung naeng myun, is much spicier and features noodles made from sweet potato tossed with red chile peppers, bell peppers, and a paste of ground garlic, ginger, onions, honey, and sesame seeds, all bound by sesame oil and here again topped with sliced brisket, pickled daikon, pear, cucumber, and half of a hard-boiled egg. The balance between the peppery paste and the relief from the vegetable garnish is what makes this dish. The other menu items are good traditional BBQ—dishes like bibimbap and jaep jea—but I always order the naeng myun and never regret it. The owner, Jung-Hyun Kim, has been in the restaurant business since his youth in Korea. He has a bigger branch in Flushing, Queens, and at one point had a place in Paraguay as well. All of his restaurants feature this one dish. In fact, he based his career on the popularity of naeng myun, his favorite, which his mother prepared for him as a child.

Daisy May's BBQ

212-977-1500

**623 Eleventh Avenue,
at 46th Street**

Casual, BYOB

Reservations

Inexpensive to moderate

All major credit cards accepted

Lunch and dinner seven days
a week

1 train to 50th Street station;
N, Q, R, W trains to 49th
Street station; A, C trains to
42nd Street/Port Authority
Bus Terminal station

As of this writing, the four best BBQ places in New York are RUB, Daisy May's, Hill Country, and Dinosaur. Anyone of them is capable of producing competition-grade BBQ right here in Manhattan. This is a relatively new phenomenon. Six or seven years ago there really was no good BBQ here, and now we have world-class options. The man behind this place is Adam Perry Lang, a professionally trained chef and CIA grad with years of experience in the kitchens of Le Cirque and Daniel. In other words, he can cook seriously good food, seriously complicated food, but got the BBQ bug while working a stint in the Southwest.

Often the seemingly easiest things to do are really the hardest. Think good baguettes or great pizza dough—conceptually simple, actually very hard. There are a lot of factors that go into making great BBQ, from the choice of equipment to the choice of the meats themselves. Then there are the spice rubs, cooking times, and ever-changing environment. How loaded is the oven? Some days the weather is dry and cool, other days it's hot and humid. These are all variables that need to be factored in.

The oven here is of the dual-fuel (gas and wood) variety, with large trays that rotate like paddleboat wheels, making great use of the relatively small size. I've seen baking ovens like this before, but never a smoker. The temperature is controlled to within a tenth of a degree, and the oven is constantly on. Adam tries hard to get first-rate ingredients, often sourcing from individual farms for his pork, lamb, and beef. Heritage breeds are preferred, as are animals that have been humanely raised. The space runs down 46th toward the river and is larger than it looks at first glance. Takeout orders are taken in the front, but in the rear is a small wood-paneled dining room with three long communal tables and two flat-screen TVs to keep you amused. All the sandwiches are under $10 a pop, half a rack of ribs is $11.50, sides are $3 to $4, and combination plates are in the mid-teens with two sides included. I'd opt for the $25 tasting menu, which offers a selection of cuts—ribs, butt, chicken, pulled pork, beef brisket—plus sides and corn bread. You'll see which items you like most, and that will help guide you next time around.

Another suggestion is to go with a big group and order ahead some of the real house specialties, like the half pig, whole pig, or whole pork butt. All of these are brought to the table, where you are given rubber gloves and bibs, and the rest is up to you. The whole pig cooks moister than the half and feeds 10 to 12 people well. If you've never been to a pig roast, here's your chance. It is removed from the oven whole and split, brought to the table on a long wooden cutting board where the crisp browned skin is peeled back revealing the tender white meat, smoky and delicious. Here too he uses heritage species, and It shows in the flavor.

I love his baby back ribs and pulled pork. The sides are okay, but that's not the point; you come here for the BBQ. Adam also has a fair number of pushcarts around the city offering limited versions of these dishes with soups and sides as well. There is one on Wall Street that I hit on my way out from work at least once a month for a sandwich and soup special to take home. Though Adam Perry Lang was a seemingly unlikely candidate to throw his hat into the BBQ arena, we're all lucky he did, as he makes some of the best around.

Daniel

212-288-0033
60 East 65th Street, between Park and Madison Avenues
Dressy
Reservations
Expensive
All major credit cards accepted
Dinner Monday Saturday
6 train to 68th Street station

Chef Daniel Boulud, of the eponymous restaurant Daniel, is one of the preeminent chefs in the United States. He's a force of nature, a whirlwind, full of enthusiasm, talent, optimism and energy. This restaurant is one of only five restaurants given four stars by the *New York Times*. Daniel also runs three other very good restaurants: Café Boulud, ten blocks to the north, DB Bistro Moderne in the theater district, and Bar Boulud on the West Side, as well as a busy catering business, Feasts and Fêtes, with a downtown space planned for opening mid-2009. To that list add his own line of pots and pans, knives, books, a Café Boulud in Palm Beach, and his restaurant in Steve Wynn's new gambling palace in Las Vegas.

Of all the four-star restaurants in New York City, Daniel far and away does the most volume. Most nights the restaurant has been booked full for two months in advance and will do upward of 300 covers. That's a large number of diners in a business where increased volume has a diminishing effect on quality. Many of the top-ranked European restaurants do far less than half that. And yet somehow, in spite of the volume, the kitchen at Daniel puts out very interesting dishes, accurately cooked and well seasoned, plate after plate, table after table, all night long.

After several years at the helm of Le Cirque, Daniel left that restaurant to open his own place in what is now Café Boulud, where he was awarded four stars again. When Sirio Maccioni decamped and moved to the Palace Hotel, the original Le Cirque space became available, and Daniel, never short of ambition, pounced. Backed by Joel Smilow, he gutted the space, nearly tripling its size. They built separate kitchens on two floors and bought state-of-the-art equipment, the best money could buy. His new kitchen was among the finest anywhere in New York City, complete with one of the handful of custom-made Bonnet stoves to be found in New York, windows facing a courtyard and providing natural light, high ceilings, and an elevated duplex-style chef's office, dubbed the Skybox, to oversee it all.

A recent five-course tasting menu included as starters a spicy carrot-tomato broth with shrimp, octopus, squid, avocado, mint, and lime—essentially a very well-dressed ceviche. Or the tuna tartare seasoned with wasabi and crisp mini batons of cucumber and radish, topped with osetra caviar and a drizzle of Meyer lemon coulis, paired with a Vouvray demi-sec, Domaine Philippe Foreau 2000. This was followed by a very Provençal turn: fried zucchini blossoms stuffed with Dungeness crab, served with a spicy tomato marmalade and zucchini pesto. Roasted sea scallops arrived with fresh summer beans, late-season asparagus, marinated cherry tomatoes, and a refreshing pine nut and basil pesto broth paired with a 2000 Vincent Girardin premier cru Saint-Aubin.

Fish courses were the famed signature paupiette of black sea bass, wrapped in a crisp potato skin, set over a Syrah butter sauce and paired with braised leeks, a dish Daniel has had on the menu since his Le Cirque days, still very good and all too often poorly imitated. Skate was stuffed with a chanterelle duxelles and garnished with a chanterelle fricassee, creamy spinach, and bordelaise sauce, matched with a fine 1998 Stolpman Santa Ynez Nebbiolo.

Broiled squab arrives medium rare, with a slab of sautéed foie gras, peppered nectarines, turnip confit, and baby spinach. Rack of lamb is coated with a crust that includes brunoise lemon zest and is garnished with a spoon of caramelized eggplant with a honey and black olive panisse, alongside a glass of the fine 1995 Château Sociando-Mallet Haut-Médoc.

The cheese cart is a viable alternative to dessert and always features perfectly ripe cheeses at optimal temperature, mixing hard with soft, creamy with veined, and an assortment of goat milk cheeses, all offered with fresh baked breads, dried fruits, nuts, and compotes.

The wine program is under the direction of Daniel Johannes, who for years worked with Drew in that same capacity for the Myriad Group. The list here is very expensive and very impressive—this is, after all, a destination restaurant with prices that match the quality and expectations.

The desserts are some of the best in the city, composed and plated à la carte, involving elements that contrast with and complement each other in both flavor and texture. A mango sorbet vacherin with a citrus meringue and verbena ice cream is one example; another is the gorgeous milk chocolate mousse bombe and the accompanying 1996 Capezzana Vin Santo Riserva.

There are a dozen or so restaurants in New York that embody the best of this modern era. This is one of them and well worth splurging on for a special occasion.

Degustation

212-979-1012
239 East 5th Street, between Second Avenue and the Bowery
Casual
Reservations
Moderate
All major credit cards accepted
Dinner Monday–Saturday
F, V trains to Second Avenue station; 6 train to Astor Place station; N, R, W trains to 8th Street station

The first time I visited this place I forgot my reading glasses, could not read the menu, and wasn't sure what to make of it. A friend had to act as my seeing-eye menu reader. It was December and asparagus was listed on the menu twice, which troubled me. The place was really small too. We arrived early and sat at the bar, which is the only place to sit, and within 30 minutes the place was packed and I felt cramped. The space is well designed, sleek, and vibey with its black slate walls, sushi-style two-decker wooden bar, and open kitchen, but it's not a romantic dining scene unless your idea of romance is touching elbows with strangers and talking sideways over your shoulder to your date. We ordered a few items, picked a bottle of inexpensive rosé to drink, and settled in. The food was better than I thought it would be, more accurate, well seasoned, and surely better than it read on the menu, which is always good. I hate menus that oversell and underdeliver, and hence I came back for more the next time with glasses on.

We started with croquetas, little fried balls formed from salt cod and potato and set over an herbed puree, and they were very good indeed, better than in most of the good tapas places around town—an encouraging start. This was followed by grilled squid. The body sack was stuffed with braised short ribs and charred, the smoky finished product set over braised lentils—another winner. An item billed as warm mushroom salad turned out to be great. A bowl arrived containing at least five different varieties of mushrooms, some sautéed, some grilled, all with big clean individual flavors, with a big piece of tempura-battered and deep-fried hen-of-the-woods on top, set next to a few strips of lamb bacon, the whole garnished with a touch of chopped dill. I love mushrooms done right, and this is a plate that I'd come back for again and again. Last we had a "cannelloni" of roasted red pepper stuffed with earthy taleggio cheese mixed with a version of the Majorcan vegetable stew called tumbet, another winner.

The menu is divided into three sections, all small plates, but the ones farthest left are smallest and least expensive, those in the center are a little bigger (well, sometimes), and to the right are the larger plates, none of which is really very large. If you're hungry, this place can get expensive, as you'll tend to order four to five plates per person, and with a wine by the glass or the bottle, you're pushing $70 to $80 apiece for dinner. The dessert section is small, often just three choices, and the wine list is okay, not great. Service varies too, as you sit at a bar with just sixteen seats, the cooks working before you, and there are just two servers for the room; that's a bit of a stretch. I know I sound ambivalent, but the truth is I've never had a bad dish here, though I do avoid the ones that sound silly or are covered with foam. It's a good serious little place to drop in for a bite of often very good food, but not my idea of a restaurant for a bigger meal or intimate conversation.

Dell'Anima

212-366-6633
38 Eighth Avenue, at Jane Street
Casual
Reservations
Moderate
All major credit cards accepted
Dinner seven nights a week until 2 AM
A, C, E, 1, 2, 3 trains to 14th Street station; L train to Eighth Avenue station

This little restaurant is the kind of place I like to champion. It's small and intimate, the owners are nearly always there, and they have youth, passion, energy, and good training on their side. It was opened in the fall of 2007 by two young veterans of the New York restaurant scene: Joe Campanale, who worked as a sommelier at Babbo, and his partner, Gabriel Thompson, who I remember from his days in the kitchens of Le Bernardin—not a bad little resume. The focus is simple Italian food, not unlike what you'll find a few blocks to the south at another tiny spot I love, the Little Owl. The room is small, with just fifty seats, but seems even smaller than that. Weather permitting, they have outdoor seating as well, on the West 4th Street side, a quintessential tree-lined, narrow West Village street. Aside from the individual tables, you can eat at the bar and at a high counter directly across from the chef and his open kitchen.

The menu starts with bruschetta, which I would normally skip, but here they offer a few that are noteworthy, such as the one with bone marrow custard with gremolata salad; another with chickpeas and preserved lemons; the mantecato, with a hint of garlic and chopped parsley; and the romanesco, polished with the addition of a few drops of lime juice. I adore veal sweetbreads and here they did not disappoint, arriving nicely browned and tender, almost creamy at the center, set atop a parsley root puree and glossed with a brown butter sauce redolent of lemon juice and studded with capers. Baby arugula leaves carry a lemon-based vinaigrette and are topped with shaved Parmigiano Reggiano, a nice clean salad, as is the one combining endive with anchovies and sharp sheep's milk cheese pecorino. I think my grandmother would have loved this one too.

The pasta offerings here are all usually very good, handmade daily, and meant to be taken as a middle course, not a main, as is customary in Italy. I found the pastas too big for that; you might share them or consider them as a main course, as they are all very good. The pappardelle Bolognese is good. The buckwheat pizzoccheri are cut like broad, frilly pappardelle and tossed with potatoes, Brussels sprouts, garlic, and fontina cheese.

The selection of main courses is usually small, half a dozen or fewer. If they have striped bass, get it. Gabriel's time at Le Bernardin pays off, as he shows a sure hand with fish. Here it is cooked perfectly, the skin crisped well and browned, the flesh just set, silky, meaty, and rich, yet still very moist, atop a puree of broccoli rabe and garnished with a tapenade-like olive relish—good simple food. On colder nights you can't go wrong with the braised lamb shank set over creamy polenta, or the wild boar braised in red wine and again paired with creamy, cheesy polenta. The dish billed as chicken fra diavolo is excellent. Here the bird is marinated in some sort of pepper-based spice mix, then sautéed skin side down and finished flesh side down just to cook the meat to the center, retaining its crisp skin. Beneath it there is a pool of rose-colored chicken stock, thickened slightly with butter that just carries the hot pepper theme.

There are always a few vegetable side dishes, and the wine list is good and growing all the time, with real value in the $20–$40 range. Service is fine, the prices are more than fair, and two people can eat very well with a bottle of wine for around $100 total, prior to tipping. I can only assume that the place will just get better as time goes by.

Del Posto

212-497-8090
89 Tenth Avenue, at 16th Street
Casual to dressy
Reservations
Expensive
All major credit cards accepted
Dinner seven nights a week
A, C, E, 1, 2, 3 trains to 14th
Street station; L train to
Eighth Avenue station

This restaurant is a collaboration between two of New York City's best Italian chefs, Lidia Bastianich and Mario Batali. To that mix add the third partner, Lidia's son Joe, who is an MBA, a chef by training, and a wine importer of some renown. Then there is the lease for this enormous space, rumored to have been purchased in 2004 at the pre-1980s level of just over $130,000 per year—that's the kind of numbers restaurateurs can only dream of these days, though after a scuffle with the new landlord they negotiated a new, higher (though still way below market) rent. Add in some good press, and what you have here is that rarest of rare birds in this industry: a money-making machine. You also have a very nice restaurant housed in one of the grandest spaces in town.

You enter off the avenue into a large foyer, coat check to your right, greeter straight ahead. Up a few steps and you're in the main room proper with its soaring 40-plus-foot ceiling, a lovely marble staircase to the rear, and a comfortable large bar and lounge area off to the left. There is an upstairs dining room, essentially a mezzanine, that wraps around the open main floor below. There is plenty of room between the plush tables and comfortable chairs, and the place is never noisy, no matter how busy it gets. It reminds me of the old grand hotel dining rooms that, for the most part in this city, are all gone. There's glitz for sure, with lots of polished marble, thick custom carpets, carved mahogany, small elegant lamps, soaring columns, heavy fabric, large windows, and an insular sense that while you're still very much in New York, you are, at least for the duration of this meal, cosseted and far removed from its noise, clutter, pace, and occasional harshness. And for this effect they have been criticized by many. Mario's other places are like his own private nightly parties, replete with booming rock music and snarky young foodie types yelling at one another across tables (and sometimes across the room) while downing big glasses of good wine before plates of very good food, usually loaded with offal and pork fat. If those places are all about the food, here they're going for something else—great food, but served in a grand room and in a much more formal fashion. This place, they say, is too Vegas, too suburban, too sterile, not Bataliesque at all; so be it.

The staff here are numerous and the headwaiters all good at what they do. Upon seating you, they offer several choices of good warm bread and a ramekin of fresh farm butter and another of lardo, essentially pure white pork fat, a Batali flourish. The chef is Mark Ladner, a Lupa alumna, and a very good chef in his own right.

Start with the good plate of beef and veal carpaccio, the meat pounded thin, drizzled with olive oil and grated horseradish, and set against a crisp salad of baby mustard greens blended with soft and silky lamb's-tongue lettuce. Or the salumi misti, a Batali specialty, a large plate with a variety of house-cured meats: sopressata, bresaola, speck, and mortadella. Or opt instead to just begin with any of the excellent pasta dishes served here.

If they have it, opt for the feather-light sheep's milk ricotta gnudi, made with sweet spring peas and served in a cream sauce studded with pink peppercorns, their little crunch a nice touch to offset the quenelle-like richness of the gnudi. The item billed as wild mushroom lasagna arrives two to a plate, small envelopes made from sheets of cooked pasta, folded over a cooked fine dice of porcini and the mushroom supporting chorus, and tossed lightly in a mushroom cream reduction with a touch of good grated Parmesan cheese to bring it all together. Agnolotti dal plin, the small stuffed pasta delicate, the meat filling light and flavorful, tossed with a little of the cooking liquid and enhanced by browned butter and grated Parmesan cheese, were as good as I remember them being on my most recent trip to Alba, Piedmont, where in the best local restaurants they are served with great pride as a beloved regional specialty.

The meat dishes are very good; here they do a lot of business with the local purveyors such as the La Frieda boys, who have some of the best cuts in town. The pork chop, moist and richly flavored, is excellent. The spring lamb is tender, with that nice lanolin bite from the lamb fat, the various cuts pink where they should be, and off-the-bone tender where that should be the case. If you have the inclination and money, they have a rare restaurant cut, a bone-in veal chop for two. It will remind you of why many Italians love veal. The meat is seared on the outside, then slow-roasted pink though the center, the deckle meat fatty and addictive, the sauce made from a veal reduction, strengthened with reduced Barolo. They like showmanship here, and the excellent bollito misto is rolled through the dining room in a glorious chariot where the various cuts, including the best cotechino I've had in New York, are removed, sliced, and plated tableside and then drizzled with just a touch of the poaching bouillon.

Fish lovers will not be disappointed. You'll find a good selection of some of the best fish available, from the turbot served with an Italian version of succotash featuring sweet corn and little chanterelles to slow-baked slabs of wild salmon set over a ragout of root vegetables. They offer tasting menus and wine pairings, and an assortment of cheese plates and other offerings. The wine list is superb, albeit expensive, but compliments to Mr. Bastianich for depth, variety, and regional strength. It holds its own as one of the best Italian wine lists anywhere in New York. For an Italian restaurant, the desserts too are far better than what you'll find around town. As I've said, Italians aren't the best bakers on the planet, and in Italy desserts are often just fruit, or a nibble and an afterthought. Here there is none of that: try the silky chocolate caramel bar served with peanut butter powder and salted caramel gelato, or the Meyer lemon tart with just the right balance—sweet, yes, but not too sweet, and with just enough pucker. To this they add a luscious, rich, and light lemon cream chiboust and a quenelle of lemon verbena sorbetto.

The crowd does skew older, and on some nights it may also weigh heavily toward those traveling into town from the suburbs—yes, the dreaded bridge-and-tunnel types, but get over it. The food is solidly good, the room dignified and elegant, with service and prices to match the setting. Maybe this is Mario for grown-ups.

Dennis Foy

Note: This venue is closed.

212-625-1007
313 Church Street, between Walker and Lispenard Streets
Casual
Reservations
Moderate to expensive
All major credit cards accepted
Dinner Monday–Saturday
A, C, E trains to Canal Street station; 1 train to Franklin Street station

A self-taught blue-collar chef from South Philly, Dennis is a thirty-year veteran of the greater New York–New Jersey metro restaurant scene. I first met him years back at Mondrian, where the young Tom Colicchio was cooking with him in the mid-1980s and the food was very, very good. Since then Dennis has opened up well-received restaurants on both sides of the Hudson: Townsquare and then the Tarragon Tree in Chatham, New Jersey; EQ in New York City; Foy's at Bay Point Prime, back at the Jersey shore; and now this space, right in his own neighborhood, which had previously been Lo Scalco. I don't like the room much—those strange bright-colored arches seem more in line with a McDonald's play area—but I do like the cooking. Joining Dennis in the kitchen is Raj Dixit, who had worked as a sous-chef at the Ryland Inn and is a very talented chef in his own right.

The food is straightforward and not too fussy. For starters the tian of crab is a good choice, a nod to the niçoise style, here essentially a very lightly bound crab cake cooked in a ring mold, seasoned mostly with chive butter. Potato gnocchi, light and toothsome, are served with porcini mushrooms and bound with a simple sauce accented with chives, sage, a hint of garlic, and Parmesan foam. The salad of roasted beets pairs the beets with a small tangle of frisée, endive, blood orange sections, and candied walnuts. In the colder months, beautifully slow-cooked braised short ribs, full of flavor and retaining their beefiness while being fork-tender, are set alongside braised red cabbage and pan-braised baby carrots. Boneless loin of lamb is roasted, then set next to corn squash, some broccoli rabe, and an old-style black pepper gastrique.

Kimberly Bugler is the pastry chef and, for the most part, the desserts are well executed and taste as good as they look. The chocolate dome is lovely for people who can't get enough chocolate. I especially liked the black plum financier, nestled alongside a fruit compote and a scoop of aged rum ice cream. The wine list is good and growing, and the front-of-the-house service is efficient and friendly, with Dennis usually joined by his wife in the dining room. The paintings on the walls are all the work of the chef, who in his spare time is an avid painter.

Devin's Fish and Chips

212-491-5518
747 St. Nicholas Avenue,
  between 146th and 147th
  Streets
Casual
No reservations
Inexpensive
Cash only
Lunch and dinner seven days
  a week
A, C, B, D trains to 145th Street
  station

If you're a fan of fish and chips, there are a few places that do it right. A Salt and Battery in the West Village comes to mind, as does this place. Here the fish of choice is whiting, a fish that I adore and buy every chance I get when I see it in the market. The New York coastal waters used to be full of these fish, similar in a way to ling and its big brothers scrod and cod, but just as flaky, white-fleshed, delicate, and delicious. The space is small and does mainly takeout, but there are a few chairs by the counter where you can sit. The thin breading appears to contain a bit of cornmeal and some dried spices, but the fish is always straight out of the fryer, steaming and crisped well. They also have crabs, calamari, and other varieties of fish that I like but which are hard to find, such as porgies and croakers, both local fish—delicate, clean-tasting, and a fraction of the price of the overtouted competition so popular among mainstream American fish eaters. For under $10 you'll get a whole fish and two sides, such as good rice and beans, which for the young and the thin can actually be a meal for two. If you live in the area, give it a try; as these places go, it's among the best, with fresh fish all the time and good understanding of correct frying protocol.

Dirt Candy

212-222-7732
430 East 9th Street, between
  Avenue A and First Avenue
Casual
Reservations
Moderate
All major credit cards accepted
Dinner, Tuesday–Sunday
6 train to Astor Place station;
  N, R, W trains to 8th Street
  station

The first time I ate here was the night of the 2008 presidential election, just a few weeks after they opened. I'm not a vegetarian and tend not to frequent vegetarian restaurants, but that night after a small party Tom Colicchio was hosting at CraftSteak, I wanted to slip away somewhere where there was no TV set. Plus I'd already had my beef fix. In the company of another food writer who is a famous meat eater not known to eat vegetables at all, we hopped into a cab and went to this oddly named little jewel. It's a small, neat, well-lit room, seating maybe 25 people, with the open kitchen visible at the rear. Three tables line the wall to the left, which is covered with a natural wood surface made from recycled wood chips. To the right is a banquette, and the remaining seats are beneath a backlit frosted glass panel. About the name: I suppose if you are of a certain stripe, you're allowed to refer to vegetables as "dirt candy."

Truth be known, I love to cook and eat vegetables—most chefs do—and because of dietary concerns, I eat a lot more of them lately than I used to, and am none the worse for it. That said, there is sometimes a preciousness and an almost palpable anti-meat evangelical "religiosity" in the vegetarian movement, all too often combined with a monochromatic blandness to many of the restaurants. Dirt Candy is one of a few notable exceptions and is now one of my favorites in the city. These folks aren't on a mission to change you or the world; they just want to cook well in this idiom. The chef, Amanda Cohen, worked in a small handful of some other very good vegetarian/vegan places in town, and here she is stepping into the spotlight. This is very good food that doesn't play it safe and nibble around the edges of flavor, concept, or execution. It's in your face and full-flavored, and it offers layers of texture and flavor with confidence, not apologies.

Take her riff on the Greek salad; it combines the usual diced tomatoes, shaved fresh fennel, good olives, cucumber, and feta, all lined up together and topped with a row of panko-breaded, deep-fried trumpet mushrooms. The side of the plate is drizzled with lemon mayonnaise, and off to one side sits a small pile of pink pickled onions, best immediately applied to the salad. Crunch from the fennel, a perceived meatiness from the mushroom, acid from the tomato, coolness from the cukes, salt and creaminess from the cheese . . . well, you get it—a very satisfying dish that one can eat and never think of as vegetarian. We started the night with deep-fried, jalapeño-studded hush puppies, piled high and served with maple butter—this could be a first course at a steakhouse. The carrot risotto was another great dish. There are many risotto variations requiring no meat, but this one, made with carrot juice and then loaded with shaved fresh carrots, carrot dumplings, and carrot curls, all bound at the end with good cheese, cream, and butter, left me wanting more. A salad included panini-esque cheese croutons and little lollipops—bamboo skewers each with a single lozenge of grapefruit that had been dipped in blond caramel. The sweet crunch and then a burst of fresh grapefruit juice was a nice alternative to vinaigrette. Another winner was the stone-ground grits, laced with pickled sliced shiitakes and holding a deep-fried poached egg. Once broken, the yolk spills out, enriching the grits. Who needs meat with food like this?

Desserts too are very, very good, courtesy of the pastry chef Debbie Lee, who had worked with Pichet Ong prior to this. Who can resist popcorn-flavored pudding served with a side of hazelnut caramel popcorn, or warm ricotta fritters with a sweet-and-sour green tomato marmalade and a dollop of olive oil ice cream, or her not-too-sweet chocolate cake with chocolate chili ice cream and smooth, creamy sweet potato sorbet? With a very nice small wine and beer list and earnest service, this could well be my favorite vegetarian eatery in New York at the moment.

DoSirak

212-366-9299

30 East 13th Street, between University Place and Fifth Avenue

Casual

Reservations

Inexpensive to moderate

Cash only

Lunch and dinner Monday–Friday, dinner Saturday and Sunday

4, 5, 6, L, N, Q, R, W trains to 14th Street/Union Square station; F, V trains to 14th Street station

This little family-run Korean restaurant is a rare find these days, outside of the traditional 32nd Street neighborhood. The food is simple, honest, and humble, and the prices are really a bargain, especially inexpensive for the West Village. The name means "lunch box" in Korean. A few steps up from street level, the room is small but clean and well lit, with a bar at the rear and tables set up front by the large windows. The dumplings come fried or boiled and are good either way. Jeon, or pancakes, are served in two styles: haemul pajeon, made from rice flour, cooked on a griddle till crisp, and studded with seafood, squid, mussels, octopus, scallops, and shards of scallions, and kimchijeon, again made with rice flour, mixed with fresh kimchi. Both are good dipped in soy sauce mixed with a little vinegar. Bibimbap is served either hot or cold in a ceramic bowl and is loaded with vegetables and bean sprouts and topped with an egg. The ssam here—small sandwiches filled with grilled, marinated rib eye, small spinach salads, and soy beans, and wrapped in lettuce leaves—are far better than the ones at the overhyped Ssam Bar across town. More traditional dishes include nakji bokkeumbap, octopus or squid sautéed in a hot red pepper sauce with chunks of julienned vegetables served over steamed rice or thick buckwheat noodles, and japchaebap, translucent noodles made from potato starch, tossed with a mix of sautéed vegetables, seasoned with soy and sesame oil, and served over a scoop of rice. In the summer the cool buckwheat noodle salad, momill muchim, is refreshing, dressed with carrots, sliced cabbage, and julienned cucumbers. The joulmyeon, thicker noodles with more cabbage, bean sprouts, and a hard-boiled egg, makes for a great lunch or light dinner. The food is healthy, tasty, and inexpensive, and the staff is friendly; they even serve beer and wine to wash it all down.

Dovetail

212-362-3800
103 West 77th Street,
   between Columbus and
   Amsterdam Avenues
Casual
Reservations
Moderate to expensive
All major credit cards accepted
Dinner seven nights a week, tea
   service Saturday and Sunday
   afternoons
1 train to 79th Street station; B,
   C trains to 81st Street station

One by one, seriously good restaurants are finally opening up on the Upper West Side. Early 2007 saw two great examples: Chef Ed Brown's first solo effort, Eighty One, which he started after decades heading up some of New York's best kitchens, and Dovetail, under the direction of the youthful chef John Fraser. I first met John back in 2000 when we were filming an episode for my PBS series at the French Laundry in Yountville, California. After his West Coast stint, he returned to New York and worked at Compass and Snack Taverna in the Village. However, here at Dovetail he is cooking at his best. The place over the years had been an Ethiopian restaurant and then something forgettable before the new team took over, gutted the entire space, and installed a simple casual dining room on the second floor and a state-of-the-art kitchen below.

Just steps off Columbus Avenue, you enter the brownstone into a foyer behind which lies the bar and the dining room, though there are two large tables downstairs, in front of the kitchen, for busy nights or private parties. The design is by Richard Bloch. The tables are well spaced, and a large brick support arch runs exposed down the center of the room; the floor is carpeted in beige, and the walls too are done in a beige material, perhaps to keep the noise level low. The ceiling is backlit, and the tables are a polished dark wood set without linen. The comfortable chairs provide the only color in the room, with their pastel green cushions. The crowd is typical Upper West Side, which is to say casually dressed and mostly older.

Each meal starts with a witty amuse-bouche: a raw piece of tuna is set in a vodka-laced jelly accented with salmon roe, capers, and sour cream—a nice play on the Jell-O shot, I suppose. This is followed by the house bread, several individual miniature loaves of corn bread, fresh from their cast-iron baking dish and laced with cheese. The opening menu listed ten appetizers ranging in price from $12 to $16, followed by eight main courses from the high twenties to the mid-thirties, with good balance across the board.

An excellent clam chowder comes spiked with chunks of good chorizo sausage, diced potato, and fresh clams. A salad based on Brussels sprout leaves was interesting; the leaves were slightly crunchy but obviously blanched ahead of time, perhaps cooked whole like cabbage, then peeled off, their color a bright green, their flavor mild and paired with thin-sliced Bosc pears, shards of Serrano ham, and cauliflower puree.

108   MIKE COLAMECO'S FOOD LOVER'S GUIDE TO NYC

Sweetbreads were coated with panko, flash-fried, dusted with powdered fennel, and set in a mustard-based sauce; they were crunchy and light on the exterior, rich and creamy at the center—for sweetbread fans, of whom I am one, it's a pleasant little dish indeed. Salmon is quick-cooked on a plancha, then sauced with a classical sauce, gribiche, laced with horseradish and American black caviar, the rich salmon responding well to the brine and kick of the sauce. Lamb's tongue was done muffuletta style, a play on a sandwich; the meat is cut thin, layered with cheese, and rolled, the thin crust taken with it. It reminded me a bit too much of good cold cuts and little more, but the Idaho potato gnocchi were lovely, a half dozen light and fluffy quenelles sauced with boneless veal short ribs, slow cooked, taken off the bone, and then returned to their excellent braising liquid, studded with diced carrots and enriched with foie gras butter and prunes.

Interesting main courses included excellent plump, fresh dry-sautéed sea scallops with parsley root puree, grapefruit lozenges, and a good rich Hollandaise sauce. Slow-braised Berkshire pork belly, which is cropping up all over town these days, was set in a light reduction of the braising liquid, accented with sautéed maitake mushrooms, a swirl of braised kale, and a poached egg, a lot of food when taken together. Venison loin arrived as ordered, cooked medium rare and sliced in three, above a good venison jus with a puree of yams, sautéed cabbage, and braised chestnuts. Dishes like this reflect the time spent in Keller's Yountville kitchen, which, though thoroughly modern, never strays too far from French classical cooking. Roasted sirloin was sliced into chunks and paired with a lasagna of beef cheeks and king trumpet mushrooms. Loin of lamb, wrapped in caul fat, comes sliced into two large disks set over a crunchy winter tabbouleh and a stuffed grape leaf—good lamb enriched with the addition of whole-milk yogurt. The five-course $65 tasting menu represented good value, and the $38 three-course Sunday dinner is a complete steal.

Desserts are excellent. The pastry chef, Vera Tong, is young and talented; she worked with John at Compass, and they complement each other stylistically. The almond soufflé tart is light and airy with fine color across the top. Bread-and-butter pudding is garnished with banana and rum sauce. Bread pudding comes with bacon-flavored caramel, which I liked but others did not, but everyone loved the chocolate hazelnut strudel. They have a respectable wine list and an extensive sherry list. In fact, our dessert came with a sherry pairing. While I was there very soon after the opening, I suspect this place will be well received and well reviewed and will become a fixture in a neighborhood screaming for more serious eateries.

East Side Poultry

212-288-7777
1522 First Avenue, between
79th and 80th Streets
Takeout only
Inexpensive to moderate
All major credit cards accepted
Seven days a week 11 AM–9 PM
6 train to 77th Street station

This far East Side location, a takeout-only joint, has some of the best roast and fried chicken in the city. Roast chicken is one of those great, cheap easy meal solutions when it's done well. The trouble is that far more often the birds are overcooked or have been held warm for too long, and the meat has the consistency and flavor of sawdust. For whatever reasons, East Side Poultry gets it right most of the time. You can get chicken, turkey, duck, or Cornish game hen, sold by the pound, along with a slew of soups and sides, and be home enjoying the meal within minutes. The fried chicken is very good, the chopped liver is too, the chicken-in-a-pot is decent, the mac and cheese is serviceable, the various vegetable soufflés are actually decent, and they even have steamed vegetables if you're watching your weight. For lunch half a chicken and two sides will set you back $6.99, and they deliver. For dessert try the simple old-school chocolate pudding, bread pudding, fruit Jell-O, or rice pudding and you'll be transported back to the 1960s. When convenience and comfort food are required menu items and a serviceably low budget defines the goal, this is the place.

Eighty One

212-873-8181
45 West 81st Street, between
Columbus Avenue and
Central Park West
Casual
Reservations
Moderate to expensive
All major credit cards accepted
Dinner seven nights a week
B, C trains to 81st Street
station; 1 train to 79th Street
station

It opened in late February 2008, carved out of what had been unused space on the ground floor of a hotel, and I suspect that restaurant Eighty One will be among the most important restaurants in this neighborhood for some time. The Upper West Side is finally seeing serious players opening some very good restaurants—Kefi, Dovetail, and Bar Boulud, to name a few—but very few of those have Eighty One's ambitions. And those ambitions come directly from chef/owner Ed Brown. Ed is a seasoned veteran and has been cooking on a high level in New York for years. His first big break was a two-star review from Bryan Miller, then food critic for the *New York Times* when Ed was the chef at Marie Michelle; he was all of 23 years old. Prior to that he had worked at the Maurice under Christian Delouvrier and then spent a few years with the great French chef Alain Senderens at the legendary three-star Michelin restaurant Lucas Carton. He worked for Restaurant Associates in New York, opening Tropica, then left briefly to open Judson Grill, and then was back again with RA to run the Sea Grill, one of New York's best seafood houses. But most chefs dream of opening their own place someday, and Eighty One is that dream for Ed. Here he has assembled an A-team of other New York veterans. In the kitchen he has chef Juan Cuevas, who had been running the kitchen of Blue Hill downtown. For his wine program he tapped Heather Branch, a California transplant who had been running the wine program at Craftsteak Vegas prior to coming east and doing the same at Dona and then Aureole.

The restaurant is located in the Excelsior Hotel, with the entrance off 81st Street, opposite the Museum of Natural History. Once through the door, you walk past a small lounge area set with a few sofas, stools, and small tables. The long wood bar sits just past this to the right, flanked by the corridor that leads you to the main dining room proper, which is set within the back section of the building and opens up, stretching further out to the left. The ceiling is covered with beige fabric-textured backlit acoustic baffles, the tables are spread well apart by today's often cramped standards and are set with white linen, the chairs are of cloth and leather with pumpkin-colored fabric, banquettes at the center of the room mix with free-standing tables, and more banquettes line the walls, which are trimmed in a rich red fabric. Structural columns break the sight lines. Large sprays of flowers sit above the centered banquettes. Wines are kept in climate-controlled storage, visible through large backlit glass doors lining the far wall of the room, heading toward the kitchen. The floor plan is mostly open; the space has a large, modern, spacious feel to it. It is the nicest, most civilized, most grown-up dining room on the Upper West Side.

The food is modern, well conceived, seasonal, and market-driven. Ed's been at this for some time in New York, and his supply chain includes small farmers and fishermen and specialty houses that can supply him with heritage-breed pork, cattle, and poultry. A good example would be the starter of poached hen's egg, the yolk a deep orange color, the egg slow-poached at low temperature for over an hour until the proteins are barely set and custard-like. The supporting cast on the plate includes sautéed milk-fed veal sweetbreads from Vermont and Berkshire pork trotters, slow-braised, set atop a disk of toasted brioche, the whole tossed in a veal jus reduction mounted with butter and herbs. The flavors were so pure and clear, I asked for a soup spoon to clean the bottom of my plate. Baby squid from Montauk are quick-cooked on a planche, then tossed with garlic chips, smoked paprika, leaves of flat parsley, and a splash of good olive oil; simple, yes, but with great ingredients, that's all you really need.

Tuna tartare comes studded with big-flavored Sicilian pistachios, chervil, good olive oil, accents of sesame and ginger, and a touch of chili for a little kick. Berkshire pork belly, these days found all around town, is braised, then crisped, and served with a small mound of Beluga lentils, Banyuls vinegar, and two delicious, rich-tasting greens, soft and herbaceous sheep sorrel and Malabar spinach. Once again, a rather simple dish, but the quality of ingredients and cooking make the end product greater than the individual parts. A luxurious treat from the tasting menu is a thick-cut slab of excellent smoked salmon, first soaked in milk, then slow-cooked and served warm. It is a nod to an old Senderens menu item, but here it is garnished with lemon and lime zest, cucumber, and a dollop of golden osetra caviar; at $39, it's an indulgence, but a dish I suspect you'll never forget. Try the warm ravioli of foie gras and scallops, simply served glossed with thyme-accented beurre blanc, flavored with vin jaune from the Arbois, another nod to chef Senderens. Ed and Juan love to cook sous vide, and their osso bucco is done this way. The meat is taken off the bone and the muscle slow-cooked for hours at low temperature. When done, it is plated with celery heart gratin, Brussels sprouts leaves, and sautéed black trumpet mushroom and set atop Anson Mills grits, organic South Carolina grits that are essentially made in the style of polenta and then at the end studded with Jasper Hill cheddar cheese. Heather accompanied it with a Margerum syrah, a bottle from a year when only 60 cases were made, and at Eighty One she has 20 of those 60. The wine, a southern Rhône varietal, married perfectly with the rich meat and flavor profiles of the plate.

John Miele is the pastry chef, another seasoned veteran who spent nearly a decade in the kitchen at Aureole in New York. His dessert compositions offer contrasts in texture and flavors: sweet balanced with sour, smooth and creamy textures accented with crunch, acids set against rich cream bases for accent and focus. A pear tart is prepared like a tarte Tatin, over rich crumbly pastry. A spoon of reduced pear cider joins the scoop of frozen sour cream to round out the plate. The Meyer lemon frozen soufflé is smooth and crystal free, silky, sweet, and sour all at once, studded with Sicilian pistachio nougat and served with a scoop of pomegranate sorbet. I'm confident that this restaurant will quickly mature into the most casually civilized dining room on the Upper West Side with food to match. In Eighty One the West Side finally gets a long-awaited place for grown-ups who like good food and conversation and for the younger generation looking for creative cooking and great ingredients, in a setting to match.

Eisenberg's Sandwich Shop

212-675-5096
174 Fifth Avenue, between
22nd and 23rd Streets
Casual
No reservations
Inexpensive
All major credit cards accepted
Monday–Friday 6:30 AM–8 PM,
Saturday and Sunday 8 AM–6 PM
N, R, W trains to 23rd Street
station

Eisenberg's is the type of sandwich shop that used to be found all over America. You'd sit on swiveling stools before a long marble counter, and the cooks worked right in front of you, assembling sandwiches, salads, desserts to order. Drinks were prepared in the same manner— they'd mix seltzer with other flavorings to create colas, root beer, lemon and lime rickeys, egg creams, milkshakes, and various ice cream floats. But then Norman Rockwell fell out of fashion, fast food and rock-and-roll arrived, and America's eating habits changed. Precious few of these establishments are left anywhere these days. So it's a bit odd to find this endangered species surviving, in fact thriving, on Fifth Avenue in the red-hot Flatiron district of midtown Manhattan. It's been in business at the same location since 1929, and as far as I can tell that's the same well-worn black marble countertop they had on opening day. Just as you'd expect, the waitress, who has been there forever, knows the customers by name, knows what they like, knows the names of their children and spouses, takes phone orders from local merchants, and is part waitress, part sales-girl, and part counselor.

Open for breakfast and lunch only, this is one of New York's greatest bargains, and a culinary time capsule all rolled into one. The menu follows a familiar path. Soup of the day: chicken noodle, split pea, matzo ball, borscht, or vegetarian vegetable, all between $2.15 and $2.75 per cup, crackers included. Egg salad (delicious), tuna salad (ditto), chicken salad, chopped chicken liver, bacon, and so on—these are truly the model for the genre, again all at around $6 per sandwich. To this add the grilled section: grilled cheese, ham and cheese, tuna melt, etc., and a fairly decent version of pastrami and corned beef, albeit sliced thin ahead of time and held warm in a bain-marie, but still very good, especially at $6.25 a sandwich. Take that, Carnegie Deli!

I like the egg creams here, which are at once sweet from the chocolate syrup and a little tart from the seltzer, foamy and delicious. After spending way too much money at ABC Home & Carpet nearby, stop by here for lunch to repair. As a footnote, in typical modern New York fashion, Eisenberg's was owned for years by a very smart Korean man named Steve Oh, who recently sold it to Josh Konecky, a New Yorker exiting the printing business who worked in the neighborhood, was a frequent customer, and just didn't want to see the place closed.

Elettaria

212-677-3833
33 West 8th Street, between
  Fifth and Sixth Avenues
Casual
Reservations
Moderate
All major credit cards accepted
Dinner seven nights a week
A, C, E, B, D, F, V trains to West
  4th Street station

This stretch of 8th Street is in need of reinvention. For years it was home to cheap sneaker stores, head shops, tattoo parlors, and places specializing in belts and T-shirts. But change is on the way, with a very good wine store a few doors down, a nice wine bar, and now Elettaria, which happens to be the Latin word for green cardamom. Chef Aktar Nawab spent years working at various Craft restaurants, where he met and worked with Noel Cruz, who is now his business partner and who oversees the interesting wine list, modern cocktail/bar program, and the front of the house. The room reminds me of two other downtown rooms I like a lot, Freeman's and Allen and Delancey, combining materials, textures, and colors that evoke an upstate farmhouse chic. A large plate-glass window with the restaurant's name etched on it fronts 8th Street and looks straight down the length of MacDougal. Past the doorway, you enter the lounge and bar area, with the bar proper to your left, and some additional tables to the right offering an alternative to dining in the main room, which is straight ahead. A long communal table runs down the center. This seemingly single table is actually divided up into many groups of reservations as the night progresses: a deuce next to a four-top, a larger party of six toward the back—in other words, the seating in this section is flexible. Along the perimeter is seating via comfortably upholstered banquettes that is a bit more private, providing space between the tables and arranged accordingly in rows of two. The open ceiling was created from dark-stained, rough-hewn barn wood, the walls are of brick with red velvet curtains, there is an eclectic mix of homey oil paintings, and the room is lit from the fixtures above as well as by small lamps set here and there. The back of the restaurant features the centerpiece of the whole space, the open kitchen, which is well lit and framed by a wall of olive-green ceramic tile, before which sit the stoves, stainless-steel hoods, and worktables the cooks use to prepare your meal. I like the effect. The kitchen is clean, and the cooks work quietly with concentration, their movements economical, their work stations neat and organized. Should you need the rest rooms, you'll pass the far end of the line and nearly walk through the pastry station on your way downstairs. The staff is young and, for the most part, know the menu. There is an excellent tiki-themed cocktail list, which comes courtesy of shared mixologists from both Freemans's and Death and Co., and the wine list is divided by style and food pairing, instead of varietal or country of origin.

   The food reflects Nawab's Indian American heritage, combining spices and textures that blur traditional recipe lines and cross borders, if not continents. For example, he makes samosas, stuffed pastries (often veg-etarian) that are a traditional Indian snack or first course, but here they are stuffed with braised rabbit, coconut sambar, and a tamarind-based vinaigrette. Another example of this is the crabmeat resala, a traditional Eastern Indian dish, usually hot and spicy and flavored with cilantro. Here jumbo lump crabmeat is served warmed in a faintly creamy sauce set above a slow-cooked base of onion, soubise-style, flavored with turmeric and sprinkled with basil seeds and deep-fried herbs for crunch and flavor, as well as a couple of gnocchi for good measure. A spring menu had pan-seared diver sea scallops set over a bright green parsley puree, rich braised boneless oxtail meat, and crunchy sautéed ramps, accented by roughly chopped cilantro leaves. The sweetness of the scallops was a good comple-ment to the rich meat, and both were offset by the fresh parsley puree. Another winner was the classic French bavette cut of steak, also known as the flap cut, a thin muscle often taken from the sirloin section, or short loin; it resembles a skirt steak or flank steak. Here it is cooked fast, served medium rare, sliced thin over sautéed oyster mushrooms and paired with pan-roasted turnips seasoned with fenugreek.

For dessert, I loved the milk doughnuts, resembling Indian rasmalai, flavored with rosewater and set beside ginger custard and yogurt gelato. If it's available, try the coconut tapioca pudding, garnished with banana fritters. Initial reviews of this restaurant were very mixed, partly because the food itself is challenging to dissect, conceptually process, and under-stand; it doesn't fit into easy molds for comparison and therefore presents an open and inviting target for criticism. But I disagree. I really like the space, the bar, the cocktail program, the wine list, and the food, and I trust that there are enough of us to support this venture and the talented team that has put it together.

Eleven Madison Park

212-889-0905
11 Madison Avenue, at 24th Street
Casual to dressy
Reservations
Expensive
All major cards
Lunch and dinner Monday–Friday, brunch and dinner weekends
6, N, R, W trains to 23rd Street station

Perhaps opening multiple restaurants is a bit like raising a large family, in that birth order seems to have an impact. Your firstborn always get loads of attention. You dote on that child while you're learning on the fly. You also expect a lot, and so firstborns tend to be overachievers. With each subsequent child, you gain a bit of confi-dence and relax, and at some point the rules change. With our youngest, we are usually less stringent and more forgiving. Younger children are allowed to stray a bit more. And so it is then that my initial impres-sions of Eleven Madison Park must have been from its somewhat ambivalent high school years. Of all Danny Meyer's restaurants, this was my least favorite—the least consistent and to my mind even occasionally mediocre. Then came Swiss-born chef Daniel Humm to the rescue. Prior to this gig, he had worked as the chef at Campton Place in San Francisco, a longtime incubator of talent. Since his arrival at Eleven Madison Park, the food has become much more refined, the kitchen more disciplined, and the flavors more clear and extracted. I've never loved the room, though many do. A former bank, it is all about soaring ceilings, loads of polished marble and bronze, long sight lines, and great views of the park across the street, but somehow I find it a cold-feeling space, even when full.

However, all of this can be ignored or forgotten once the food starts to arrive. Below are notes from a recent visit to celebrate an old friend's birthday on a snowy winter night. We were a ten-top, not an easy table to manage, and by our choice, with some arrivals coming in from out of town, we were seated late on a busy Saturday night. We started with an appetizer billed as heirloom beets with fresh Lynnhaven chèvre. I was expecting some nice roasted beets with a little salad and some good cheese, right? Wrong. What arrived were two white ceramic spoons set on a custom-made plate, each holding a small sphere, one white, the other the color of purple beets, with liquid centers that release the concentrated flavors of goat cheese and beet. Well, that got my attention. I've seen this technique before, made famous by the Spanish chef Ferran Adrià, where sodium alginate is added to a liquid, in this case beet juice, then released via a piping bag or kitchen syringe as a liquid into a bath of calcium carbonate. The chemical reaction causes a thin skin to form on the outside while the center of the sphere remains entirely liquid. The next course, billed as diver scallop en chaud-froid, had me wondering if we'd stepped back in time. Chaud-froid, for those of you too young to remember, goes back to the cuisine of Escoffier, where dishes especially for banquets were cooked, then cooled and enrobed with an aspic or decorative glaze and served cold. Set before me was a pretty plate featuring one medium-rare scallop, its sides wrapped with a ribbon of celery root. The scallop was topped with a perfectly round, thin disk of shaved black truffle; braised leeks and a truffle cream rounded out the plate. A lovely miniature construction like a composition in the spirit of J. S. Bach, each element was carefully balanced against the others, and it was perfectly cooked and seasoned, a dish complete as plated, needing nothing more, and served with a great sake from Akita prefecture.

The real winner to my mind that night was the plate of the European fish known as loup de mer. The small center-cut fillets were cooked, skin on, with no color, glazed in coconut cream, and set over a complex shellfish reduction laced with Madras curry—clean, bright flavors, light and refreshing, served with a glass of good, dry mineral-laden 2007 Châteauneuf-du-Pape blanc by Raymond Usseglio. This was followed by a butter-poached lobster tail, which these days, thanks to Thomas Keller, is the go-to method of cooking lobster in many fine kitchens. The tail was topped with a thick, rich sabayon of dried cèpes, the sauce butter-based and laced with orange juice and zest, a dose of foam accented by star anise, and a single poached dried fig, its sweetness playing well off the good firm lobster meat. I found the 2005 Mersault Clos des Meix Cha-vaux Latour-Labille, served as the companion wine, to be surprisingly overly oaked. What followed as a meat course was a firm, dark chunk of boneless short ribs, Black Angus the breed, glazed with a reduction of the cooking liquid, set against Jerusalem artichokes—a pleasure to eat with a glass of good Clos de la Cure St-Emilion grand cru, 2000.

The wine director, John Ragan, has done a great job cleaning up and expanding the impressive wine list. The wait staff are all well versed and can help with pairings if asked. Cheese followed, then a dessert of white miso sorbet with roasted pineapple and caramelized puffed rice, then a tier of excellent mignardises. Service was spot-on, and the meal, though quite expensive, was well worth the tab considering the broad reach of ingredients and technique, steady execution, and flawless delivery. The wandering child finally grows up and makes good.

El Malecón

212-927-3812
4141 Broadway, between 175th and 176th Streets
Casual
Reservations
Inexpensive
All major credit cards accepted
Lunch and dinner seven days a week
A train to 175th Street; 1 train to 168th Street station

Of all the great New York restaurant bargains, El Malecón ranks somewhere near the top. It's hard to order anything off this menu that isn't very good, so no wonder the place is packed all day long every day. They opened two more locations that are just as busy. This is a Dominican restau-rant in one of the prime Dominican neighbor-hoods in the city. After the big wave of Puerto Rican immigration in the 1950s and 1960s, the next big wave of Spanish-speaking people was the Dominicans. By the mid-1980s, a good percentage of cooks in most New York restaurants were either Puerto Rican or Dominican. So not surprisingly, this story involves a hardworking Dominican family, the Gomezes. It all started when the sister wanted to open a coffee shop; there she started serving rice and beans, and then the coffee shop morphed into a restaurant. Her two brothers pitched in, the menu grew, the reputation grew, and soon it was a very busy spot. But the winters in New York can be cold and tough, and the sister wanted to move to Florida where the weather is better, so she sold the place to her two brothers. They ran it with their mom; they had to for legal reasons, since both the boys were still in their teens, and Pablo Gomez, the younger of the two, was all of seventeen years old, working seven days a week while attending college full-time. These folks weren't short of ambition.

Fast-forward a few years, and the place expanded. On a good week they sell 8,000 roast chickens, some of the best in New York. Cooked on a large rotisserie, these birds are bought fresh daily at the market, gouged with a knife so the marinade can penetrate, then wet-marinated in a secret sauce containing lots of lemon and lime juice, herbs, garlic, and spices for 48 hours. The cooked bird is perfectly moist and with a pronounced flavor to boot. The paella is very good; ditto for the meatballs special. The chicken chicharrón is crisp and flavored with that same marinade. Mofungo is a Dominican specialty made with twice-fried plantains, and here it is irresistible. The crisped slices of plantain are mashed with a mortar, combined with pork cracklings, fried cheeses, garlic, and spices, and then inverted in one piece onto the plate. It's a meal in itself, but have it with the chicken and a salad and you need not eat again that day. If you don't like rotisserie chicken (and why not?), try the chicken breast with garlic sauce—it's great. The goat stew is wonderful, and the rice and beans, as expected, are tender with deep, rich flavors. Asopao, a tomato-based rice stew, is filling as well, the pepper steak makes great use of a less-than-prime piece of beef, and the cubano sandwich makes a good lunch. If you have room, try the corn pudding for dessert, the flan, or the mix of orange juice and milk, morir soñando, that resembles a melted Creamsicle. The staff is very friendly, the place is clean and well run, they serve alcohol, and for roughly $15 a person, you'll eat better here than at many of the fancier places downtown for triple the bill.

El Paso Taqueria

212-831-9831
1642 Lexington Avenue, between 103rd and 104th Streets
Casual
No reservations
Inexpensive
Cash only
Lunch and dinner seven days a week
6 train to 103rd Street station

The barrio, once a Puerto Rican stronghold, is now home to a growing Mexican American community. Not surprisingly, the original El Paso Taqueria location is the one on Lexington Avenue, the barrio; a second location on Park Avenue is the only one that serves beer and wine. What both have in common is very good Mexican food at very reasonable prices. There are chalupas, enchiladas, flautas, burritos, and of course soft tacos formed from excellent corn tortillas and filled with a variety of options, including Mexican-style chorizo, beef, chicken, marinated pork, tripe, and salted preserved beef. The daily specials are a real draw and vary from roast pork on the bone with a tomato-based sauce, to the dark, rich stew mole poblano. If you're hungry, start with a bowl of pozole, a soup of stew-like richness studded with pork and dried corn, best finished tableside with a squirt of lime juice or two.

Emilio's Ballato

212-274-8881
**55 East Houston Street,
between Mott and
Mulberry Streets**
Casual
Reservations
Moderate
All major credit cards accepted
Lunch and dinner Monday–
Friday, dinner Saturday and
Sunday
B, D, F, V trains to Broadway/
Lafayette Street station;
6 train to Bleecker Street
station

This place is situated midblock on the south side of busy Houston Street, and I'd walked past it hundreds of times over the years without ever thinking of going in for a meal. It's a funny part of Houston and a transitional neighborhood as well. While Soho continues to gentrify, this strip of Houston reminds you of when the area was still called Hell's Hundred Acres for the sweat-shops that occupied the upper floors of the buildings and the many fires that tore down the narrow, hard-to-access cobblestone streets. The restaurant was originally run by John Ballato, who took a chance on what was at the time a very dicey neighborhood and strove to make great food, believing New Yorkers would come for that; they still do all these years later. The first time I ate there, I was the guest of my old friend Rick Ciccotelli, the owner of Cento Foods, who met me one July night with his wife and daughter and a well-known San Marzano tomato packer from Sarno, Italy, just outside Naples, who was visiting New York. I was stunned at how good, simple, and genuine the food was. This is the kind of place I like, with a real sense of New York and neighborhood and a chef-owner who seems to be always there and enjoys running a restaurant and cooking. His enthusiasm is contagious, and the food is surprisingly good.

The main dining room is small, with just a half dozen tables. There is a VIP room out back for visiting celebs, and I'm told it has its own sepa-rate entrance. The walls are covered with a hodgepodge of art and photo-graphs and an autographed piece by Andy Warhol, who must have spent some time hanging out here. The proprietor is Emilio Vitolo, a thick, gre-garious fellow also from Sarno. His food is honest and straightforward.

Start with a plate of sliced San Daniele prosciutto with chunks of good aged Parmigiano Reggiano cheese, or sliced warm house-made mozzarella with tomatoes in the summer months. The pasta varies depending on the day but are all homemade, and the sauces good and rich. Tagliatelle, the broad soft noodles, are an excellent sponge for the rich porcini sauce covering them. The simple dish of spaghetti with fresh tomato sauce and just-torn basil reminds one of why good pasta prepared well is so beloved. Fish of the day is good, the rack of lamb is very good, and the sausage with broccoli rabe is nearly as good as my grandmother's. Save room for dessert as well, because they have some of the best cannoli in New York. Service is fine, Emilio will take care of you, and the wine list too is decent.

Ethos

212-253-1972
495 Third Avenue, between 33rd and 34th Streets
Casual
Reservations
Moderate
All major credit cards accepted
Lunch and dinner Monday–Saturday
6 train to 33rd Street station

Ethos is one of the better Greek restaurants in Manhattan, and best of all, it's located in Murray Hill, a neighborhood in need of good eateries of any ilk. Kostas Avlonitis, who worked for decades at the well-loved Taverna Roumeli in Astoria, was tapped as the consultant for this space. Keep it simple and you'll eat well, and what is simpler than whole grilled fish, the specialty of the house?

Start with the garlicky tzatziki accompanied by very good pita bread. Toasted beets are good as well, set over skordalia, a garlic spread. In fact, all the little spreads are for the most part a good way to begin the meal. Melitzanosalata, roasted eggplant puree blended with parsley, oregano, lemon juice, and good olive oil, is light yet rich. The sharp feta tyrokafteri is blended with hot and sweet roasted peppers. Or go for the hot appetizer of lovely giant Greek lima beans, braised in a rich tomato sauce. The simple but delicious grilled calamari is garnished with nothing but lemon juice, olive oil, and chopped herbs. Octopus and calamari are cooked in a small clay pot. The grilled chicken and lamb kabobs seemed dry and overcooked to my taste, but the braised baby lamb, again in a clay pot with tomatoes, small potatoes, herbs, and kefalograviera cheese, was a winner.

For sides, the steamed dandelions are great if they have them, as are the slow-stewed rustic-style string beans. The wine list is small but decent. Explore the Greek wines. Still relatively unknown here, they provide good value and work well with the menu. The room is nice, with an open kitchen; the staff is friendly and the prices are reasonable. All in all, for midtown east Greek, this is hard to beat.

F&B Güdtfood

646-486-4441
269 West 23rd Street, between Seventh and Eighth Avenues
Casual
No reservations
Inexpensive
All major credit cards accepted
Seven days a week 10:30 AM–9 PM
1, C, E trains to 23rd Street station

With two locations in midtown and plans for many more, F&B is the dream child of two European expats, a Brit, Nicholas Type, and a German, Till Horkenbach, who now call New York home. As to the name, well, even the owners aren't really certain where it comes from. Okay, maybe it's short for frites and beignets, which they do serve here, or perhaps it stands for food and beverage, as in hotel talk, stemming from the days when Nicholas attended hotel school in Switzerland. What it means to me is a European take on great cheap eats, and that's exactly what Nicholas had in mind, re-creating the Danish street food of his student days.

With walls painted robin's egg blue, a uniformed staff behind the brushed stainless-steel counter, small stools facing the slim Formica countertops that line each wall, and the Brit pop techno–New Age sound track, it's as if I've stepped off 23rd Street into a kiosk in Copenhagen. This stretch of Chelsea is still a work in progress. Yes, they're selling million-dollar condos all around here, but it remains a funky and cheap retail neighborhood in many ways. F&B sits across the street from Burritoville and Boston Chicken and in a row of eateries that includes a Ben and Jerry's, Big Booty Bread Company, Starbucks, Murray's Bagels, and Dunkin Donuts; price points mean everything here, and cheap rules.

There's just plain cheap and then there's good cheap, and this is very good cheap. My favorite menu item is the Great Dane hot dog for $3.50. They use an imported thin pink frank from Denmark. It has a nice casing that snaps when you bite it. Underneath the frank they lay down some ketchup, a schmear of rémoulade, mustard, and then the dog, which is topped with a layer of delicious sweet-and-sour cucumber pickles and sprinkled with crispy brown roasted and dehydrated onions. Sounds weird, but it really works; this is one great hot dog. Other dogs include the Bare Bones, with a choice of sauerkraut, mustard, or ketchup; the Bavarian, a veal and pork bratwurst with mustard and sauerkraut; the Barcelona, with beef sausage, tomato, guacamole, and cheese; and even a great selection of tofu-based veggie dogs topped with hummus, carrot salad, black olives, or sweet corn relish.

Non-dog options include a variation of steak frites, with strips of beef joining great crispy, salty fries packed into an upright paper container that looks like a beverage holder. Or the Viking Roll, which is a toasted hot dog bun with a beer-battered cod filet, topped with chopped tomato and horseradish. Or chicken frites, a meal that my kids love, which are strips of breaded fried chicken mixed with sweet potato fries and a sweet Thai chili dipping sauce. In the mood for vegetables? Do try the deep-fried haricots verts drizzled with garlic butter; it's another winner. For dessert, have the classic freshly made beignets dusted with powdered sugar (a steal at three for $1), apple beignets, or the churros, all very good.

This is one of the very few fast-food joints in town that have a liquor license. There is a nice assortment of beers, including some very good ones from Belgium, as well as those cutesy little Pommery Blue POP Champagne bottles if you're so inclined. Yes, the papaya joints are cheaper, but the selection here is different and mostly very good. The crowd predictably skews young, and why not? In an area surrounded by $2,000 studio apartments, who has any real money left for food?

Felidia

212-758-1479
243 East 58th Street, between Second and Third Avenues
Casual but well-dressed
Reservations
Expensive
All major credit cards accepted
Lunch and dinner Monday–Friday, dinner Saturday and Sunday
4, 5, 6, N, R, W trains to Lexington Avenue/59th Street station

It's easy to forget that before Lidia Bastianich became a household name, thanks to her hugely successful PBS series, she was a very good chef running this very good restaurant. Unlike many TV chefs these days, Lidia actually knows both how to cook and how to run a business. This is one of the best Italian restaurants in New York. Expensive, yes, but busy all the time, and consistently above average.

This block was once home to dozens of northern Italian restaurants, including Casa d'Oro, Gian Marino, Buona Tavola, Caesars East, Le Fenice, Brunos, Girafe, La Camelia, Anche Vivolo, and Tre Scalini, very few of which are still in business today. The neighborhood changed, tastes changed, the restaurant scene moved downtown, and traffic patterns on this block make parking nearly impossible most days. Delivery trucks clog the way, and forget driving here at rush hour, due to the bridge traffic. Rents too have been a factor. Not surprisingly, Lidia did the smart thing and bought the building back in 1980 for a whopping $575,000. Housed in a midblock brownstone building, the restaurant is spread over two floors. You enter and walk past the small bar area into the main dining room downstairs, or up the stairs to the second-floor room with a huge window overlooking 58th Street.

The day-to-day chef who oversees this excellent kitchen and maintains the consistency here is Fortunato Nicotra. The big menu is broken down into sections: appetizers, primi piatti, soups, fish, and meat and poultry. The scope is Italian and mostly from the north, with appetizers priced from the mid- to high teens, pastas $20 and up, and main courses almost exclusively in the $30 range. Start with a plate of three livers prepared three ways: chicken liver is served over white polenta, duck liver is paired with vin santo, and goose foie gras is served mantecato style, a specialty of Istria, her home region. There is a very good selection of house-made salumi: dry-cured, thin-sliced pork loin, duck breast prosciutto, a bresaola of venison, and goose terrine, all served with pickled vegetables.

The pastas offered, and there are usually at least ten different plates to choose from, are made from either artisanal Italian dried varieties or homemade fresh daily. I tajarin con l'anitra is dense, toothsome pasta (thirty egg yolks per pound), cut like spaghetti and paired with a suave braised shredded Hudson Valley moulard duck. An unusual combination that I loved was the ravioli con cacao e pere, pear and pecorino cheese ravioli glossed with a light cream sauce and sprinkled with black pepper and more aged pecorino cheese.

This restaurant does a good job with fish, as it should—Italy is, after all, surrounded with water and has a great tradition of regional seafood cookery. Here a bracingly rich zuppa di pesca is paired with couscous and drizzled with Ligurian extra-virgin olive oil. Pan-seared Long Island fluke is served in a light mushroom tomato broth, garnished with royal trumpet mushrooms and celeriac puree, again drizzled with a fruity Tuscan Capezzana extra-virgin olive oil.

For meats, there is a semi-boneless Vermont quail served saltimbocca style, with prosciutto and a sauce made from pan drippings and Marsala wine. Calf tripe is slow-cooked in a tomato broth, parmigiana-style, and paired with polenta crostini. I had the tripe with a German riesling one night, at the suggestion of the sommelier, and much to my surprise they worked very well together. During the winter season guanciale di manzo, or beef cheeks, are braised in a sauce of red wine, veal stock, onions, and dried porcini mushrooms and plated with smoked mashed potato and pan-roasted shiitake mushrooms.

I've never found desserts to be the strong suit of Italian cooking, but here they are well worth trying. A ricotta torte is served with an almond amaretto crust and caramelized Bartlett pears. A light chocolate and almond flour cake is set beside a ball of Venetian spiced ice cream, sauced with a glazed sweetened red wine reduction. A blueberry-studded white cake is garnished with fresh blueberries, poached in lemon syrup, and served with white yogurt ice cream.

The wine list is broad and expensive. There are wines by the glass starting at $10. The list itself starts at $29 per bottle for a run-of-the-mill wine from Molise and goes straight up with deep listings for brunello, barbaresco, and other big Italian reds. For connoisseurs with deep pockets it's a treat, but I'd appreciate more wines on the lower end of the spectrum for those of us who love Italian wine but lack the funds for Gaja.

15 East

212-647-0015
15 East 15th Street, between
  Fifth Avenue and Union
  Square
Casual
Reservations
Moderate to expensive
All major credit cards accepted
Lunch and dinner Monday–
  Friday, dinner Saturday
4, 5, 6, L, N, Q, R, W trains to
  14th Street/Union Square
  station

This space used to be Tocqueville before they expanded and moved a few doors down the same street. The owners are still the same, Marco Moreira and Jo-Ann Makovitsky, who run this place with the very talented sushi chef Masato Shimizu, formerly of Jewel Bako, further downtown. Years back, Marco Moreira was the sushi guy at Dean and Deluca, and he learned his craft in São Paulo, Brazil, which, it just so happens, has one of the largest expat Japanese communities anywhere on the planet. Growing up there, he ate loads of great sushi and learned how to prepare the fish professionally as well. This is no Buddakan or Morimoto. The room is intimate and small but not cramped, and the sushi varieties offered are well focused and of excellent quality. The bar seats nine, and the tables around the room fit another few dozen guests, allowing the chefs to concentrate and service the room while taking great care in preparing the fish and other specialties.

The menu itself is rather large, I thought, offering a mix of à la carte specialties, both hot and cold, as appetizers and entrees, as well as a good selection of sushi and sashimi by the piece, or priced as flights by the platter. I love good-quality salmon roe, and here it's firm, sweet, and briny, marinated in sake, and served in a champagne glass as a starter. Another great starter is an item billed as kakiage that mixes shrimp with root vegetables and raw onion, formed into little patties and then sautéed much like a latke, plated alongside artisanal sea salts and wedges of key lime. If you want to splurge, order the appetizer of bluefin tuna sashimi, served with a creamy sauce studded with caviar, blending the salty with the rich and fatty tuna belly meat—a very satisfying option for $22. Two main courses that stood out were the tasting of wild salmon five ways, and a magret duck breast smoked over Hojicha tea leaves and served with a rich pumpkinesque kabocha squash puree.

I usually just stick with the sushi offerings, divided by species. Fatty bluefin tuna belly is hard to pass up, even at $12 per piece, but don't miss the more unusual offerings found here, such as isaki, or gruntfish; Japanese barracuda, or kamasu; ishi garei, known as stone flounder; or the selection billed as silver fish, which includes several varieties of mackerel, as well as Japanese sardines and whiting (iwashi and kisu, respectively). To all this add salmon, shrimp, varieties of shellfish, crab, and traditional rolls—unagi, anago, hamachi, and such—as well as fish roe. Essentially you can build a very nice meal around very fresh fish for about $75 per person. If you want dessert, try the almond tofu or the rice pudding

124   MIKE COLAMECO'S FOOD LOVER'S GUIDE TO NYC

tempura à la mode. You'll find that 15 East is a welcome addition to this neighborhood, and frankly a great choice of a variety of traditional Japanese food, regardless of neighborhood.

First Avenue Pierogi and Deli

212-420-9690
130 First Avenue, at 8th Street
Casual
Takeout only
Inexpensive
All major credit cards accepted
Seven days a week 9 AM–8 PM
F, V trains to Second Avenue station; 6 train to Astor Place station; N, R, W trains to 8th Street station

When you find yourself in the mood for pierogi, stuffed cabbage, borscht, and bigos, this is the place to come to. The pierogi come with a variety of fillings, from fruit in season to various meats, sweet cabbage, stewed prunes or apricots, carrot and mushroom, and the classic potato and cheese, which is great with sautéed onions, caraway seeds, and a side of sour cream or applesauce. They are available for around $4.50 a dozen, making this a great bargain meal. They are simple to prepare, either dropped into simmering water for a few minutes or sautéed like potsticker dumplings. The bigos is a mixture of cabbage, sauerkraut, tomato sauce, dill, spices, and smoked pork and makes an excellent standalone meal, a sort of Eastern European choucroute. Borscht, as expected, is superb. The place is owned by Wieslawa Kurowycky, an aunt of Jerry Kurowycky, who used to run the late, great, but sadly shuttered smoked meat market formerly just a few steps away.

Flor de Mayo

212-663-5520
2651 Broadway, between 100th and 101st Streets
Casual
Reservations
Inexpensive
All major credit cards accepted
Seven days a week noon–midnight
1 train to 103rd Street station; B, C trains to 103rd Street station

This is a Peruvian-Chinese restaurant, yet another twist on the Spanish-Chinese styles that we see here and there all over New York, especially the Upper West Side, like the famed Caridad a few blocks away. The room is narrow but bright and clean, with slatted wooden dividers separating one side from the other. The tables have dark Formica centers trimmed in plain wood, the walls are brick, the air-conditioning is strong, and the service is very pleasant, a mix of Peruvian and Chinese waiters who work the room in white shirts and black trousers. The crowd is a mix of security guards on break, a table of big guys in from Long Island, well-dressed middle-aged Asian women dining alone, moms with strollers, and teenagers and college kids plugged into iPods—a typical Upper West Side mix.

Nearly every table on my first visit seemed to be eating the lunch special, half a roast chicken with rice and salad. The menu is huge, with well over 150 choices (which is crazy): eight soups, ten variations on fried rice, seven chow meins, a Peruvian section, twenty items billed as chef's suggestions, a big Hong Kong section, an entire page labeled "Spanish food" that has another fifty-plus items, and the daily specials. Over the course of several visits, I've tried a handful of dishes, a few from each section, and can report that they were uniformly very good. But that roast chicken is the star. There are a fair number of Hispanic restaurants, especially Dominican places further uptown in Washington Heights, that specialize in marinated, spit-roasted chicken that is at once flavorful, relatively crisp-skinned, and especially moist. I'd say that these places serve better chicken than 90% of the high-end eateries in town. And I'd posit that the secret, if there is one, is the combination of the marinade and the rotisserie style of cooking chicken in bulk. One of these days I am going to order that gadget from Ron Popeil that I see on TV; there is something great about rotisserie chicken. For $6 you get a half a chicken, for $7.25 half a chicken plus either yellow rice or plantain and a salad, and for $8.75 a cup of soup, half a chicken with fried rice, and a salad. Now that's what I call a great deal. The chicken is very good, flavorful, fresh, and very moist, and it comes with a vinegary dipping sauce laced with scallions, onions, and hot pepper. The fried rice has pork, shrimp, and beef, and the salad is shredded iceberg with a tomato. This is one of New York's great deals. The ropa vieja is delicious, as is the Peruvian seco de res, another slow-cooked beef dish, here served with a rich sauce flecked with much cilantro.

I don't know how that small kitchen handles all those menu items, but the place is usually very busy, and the food absolutely solid, especially at this price level.

Food Sing 88 Corp.

212-219-8223
2 East Broadway, between
  Catherine and Oliver Streets
Casual
No reservations
Inexpensive
Cash only
Seven days a week 9:30 AM–10 PM
6, J, M, Z, N, Q, R, W, trains to
  Canal Street station

This is one of the best Fujianese noodle shops in all Manhattan. The Fujianese arrived in this neighborhood in large numbers back in the late 1990s. Soon there appeared noodle stalls, such as Super Taste and Sheng Wang, that raised the bar with both hand-pulled noodles and hand-peeled noodles, essentially little slivers cut from the dough ball with a sharp blade. Most of these places are so downmarket, catering only to locals or students, that I am loath to recommend them, but Food Sing, just steps from Confucius

Square, has more appeal and is a very good little restaurant. The place is very well lit, as in too bright. The walls are painted white, the tables are black Formica, and the chairs are of the bent-steel-and-black-plastic variety.

I come here for the part of the menu devoted to Lanzhou noodle dishes, named after a city in Gansu. You can witness these noodles being stretched and pulled by hand at several spots in the area, including this one. Try the house special, hand-pulled noodles, a dish that will set you back a full $6. Like your grandmother's chicken noodle soup, Vietnamese pho, or the dishes at the great soba or ramen joints around town, noodle soup speaks to the soul. Here the noodles are served long and uncut, and by long I mean three feet or more, so be prepared to slurp and splatter. Tuck in your tie, place a napkin in your collar, grab the chopsticks, lean down, and go to work. This is not first-date food. The house special soup reeks of beefiness and is studded with sliced brisket, beef tendon, slivers of tripe, and tenderloin. The seafood version is fifty cents more and utterly delicious, swimming with shrimp, scallops, fish balls, squid, and fresh clams. For $4.50, have the pork bone noodles—the rich broth contains noodles, plus center-cut pork marrow bones with some meat attached—and get ready for some serious slurping.

Other noodles to try, should you have a large group or be looking for variety, are the line noodles, also known as thread noodles, which are like angel hair and very thin, or the broad, flat ho fun, a rice-based noodle. The menu is limited, as are the beverage choices. You can bring your own beer. Go for the noodles and for well under 10 bucks per person, you're out the door and sated.

The Four Seasons

212-754-9494
99 East 52nd Street, between Park and Lexington
Jacket required
Reservations required
Expensive
All major credit cards accepted
Lunch and dinner Monday–Friday, dinner Saturday
E, V trains to Lexington Avenue/53rd Street station; 6 train to 51st Street station

Were legendary restaurants ascribed legendary personalities, the Four Seasons surely would be Cary Grant: elegant in middle age, stunningly handsome, urbane, impeccably dressed, larger than life, altogether a study in refinement. In this era of the modern restaurant, it has few peers in terms of influence, reputation, and longevity. If you've never eaten there, you must. It is one of the greatest of all American restaurants, featuring solid cooking, professional service, and an absolutely gorgeous dining room. It is also worth mentioning that this restaurant, more than any other, is a living link to the origins of what we would consider today modern American cuisine. As it approaches its fiftieth anniversary, its story is the story of the American culinary evolution. As the name implies, back in 1959 when they first opened, the menu changed with each season, a practice that was really unheard of at the time. Back in the 1960s, it was one of the very first restaurants in New York to use fresh herbs, fresh vegetables, and fruit in season, and it's featured local American ingredients since opening. The famous barrel tasting dinners pioneered the emergence of excellent new California wineries in what was once a snobby, Eurocentric New York wine world.

Choose the Grill Room for lunch and witness one of the great New York power dining rooms. National politicians, CEOs, famous actors and actresses, authors and their agents and publishers, divas, and assorted movers and shakers all break bread here. Many have taken lunch here several times a week at the same table for years. For dinner, I'd suggest the Pool Room, centered around a gurgling square Carrera marble pool. Here you'll dine under a soaring 22-foot ceiling, flanked by floor-to-ceiling windows on two sides and three-inch-thick panels of old-growth French walnut lining the interior walls, a million dollars' worth of rare wood in 1950s money.

The menus aren't informed by the trend of the moment, but rather follow a more traditional path of research, experimentation, and recipe development by refinement. Appetizers feature one of the best chilled seafood platters to be had anywhere. Consider their classic pink foie gras terrine, served with quince and kumquat jam, cooked in a bain-marie and seasoned perfectly, the mildly acidic quince a brilliant foil to the richness. Or there are the bison carpaccio, topped with mixed microgreens and drizzled with a fine vinaigrette; buttery sliced prosciutto di Parma paired with the bold fruitiness of papaya; and lightly smoked Scottish salmon, perfectly carved tableside, served with toast points, capers, and onion brunoise.

Main courses feature an assortment of seasonal seafood—halibut, lobster, scallops, and cod—grilled, sautéed, or as specials, as well as classic Dover sole, boned tableside, or crispy sautéed Maryland crab cakes in a pool of mustard sauce. Meats include top-notch prime aged steaks and a classic steak tartare, ground in-house and served with crisp, salty frites. In the cooler months, enjoy the fork-tender braised short ribs, the loin of venison with porcini, spinach spaetzle, and wild berry sauce, or the excellent meaty Colorado lamb chops. For decades they have been buying their beautiful, plump Long Island ducks from the same source; they are served for two and carved tableside, paired with wild rice, a baked apple in pastry, and a gastrique-based demiglace with a classic fruit reduction.

The original pastry chef was the legendary Albert Kumin, who I was lucky to have had as an instructor at culinary school. His chocolate velvet cake recipe from the 1960s is still on the menu and is a must-have. The soufflés are made to order, are delicious, and require 15-plus minutes, as the wait staff will surely inform you ahead of time. They also offer fruit tarts, crème brûlée, and assorted ice creams and sorbets, and they still use that crazy cotton-candy machine should the occasion require it.

Gam Mee Oak

212-695-4113
43 West 32nd Street, between
   Broadway and Fifth Avenue
Casual
No reservations
Inexpensive to moderate
All major credit cards accepted
Open seven days a week from
   7 AM–4 AM
1, 2, 3, B, D, F, V, N, Q, R, W
   trains to 34th Street station

This is one of the very few "hip" Korean dining rooms in New York. Open for business with the same menu nearly 24 hours a day, it's sound system often features classic Miles Davis or John Coltrane. This long, narrow room on the first floor of the Carlton Hotel features postindustrial architecture, with an open, high ceiling revealing commercial plumbing and ductwork. The brick walls were left partially exposed and showcase, gallery-style, the artwork or photography of Korean American artists (the works are also for sale). Tables are odd-shaped natural crosscuts of mature trees coated with heavy polyurethane. When the original proprietor, Hyung Kee Choi, opened Gam Mee Oak, he wanted to re-create something he'd seen in Korea—a restaurant with a small but tightly focused menu that would offer a few hard-to-find, homey Korean dishes accompanied by wonderful homemade kimchi. I must mention that several years back, Mr. Choi and his wife were divorced, and she now runs the place. It's really not quite what it used to be under his stewardship, but it's still very good. The kimchi recipe was provided by an elderly woman he knew from Seoul, and the recipe is top secret, I'm told. This restaurant actually employs a special kimchi chef who does little else but prepare kimchi and oversee the aging room in the basement, a sort of subterranean wine cellar where vats of kimchi are stored to ferment. If for no other reason (and there are many other good reasons), visit Gam Mee Oak for its wonderful kimchi, cut with stainless-steel scissors tableside, followed by its signature soup, sul long tang. I've had this hearty soup for breakfast, lunch, and dinner, and at 2 AM on the way home from the last set at the Village Vanguard. The broth alone takes 48 hours to make, and it all starts in the open kitchen at the rear of the long, narrow dining room, where two 100-gallon stockpots simmer day and night. In each cauldron, hundreds of pounds of beef bones simmer and are eventually combined with thick slabs of beef brisket, all slowly surrendering their essence to make this soup.

Place your order and within minutes a hot ceramic bowl of this steaming milky white broth, with the addition of some rice, rice noodles, and thin-sliced beef brisket, is set before you. On each table you'll find a bowl of chopped scallions and another of coarse sea salt. To the broth you add these two ingredients to suit until you have it just right, then enjoy. I've gotten into the habit of dipping a few shreds of kimchi into the broth, wrapping them around some submerged rice, and eating part of the soup in that manner. The owner does this, and it's delicious, adding yet another flavor element to the broth. This really impresses the staff as well; you're an instant insider.

A good section of the menu features what amounts to Korean charcuterie. Modum soon dae, a Korean-style kielbasa served sliced at room temperature, is made from ground pork, onion, scallion, garlic, cabbage, sweet potato noodles, and sweet rice; it's excellent. Another winner is the Korean-style blood sausage, a version of boudin noir that is rarely seen in any other Korean restaurant. For the timid, try something less exotic: the soo yuk, warm brisket sliced paper-thin and laid out in a fan shape around the perimeter of the plate, surrounding a pile of shredded scallions in vinaigrette, which act as a delicious salad counterpoint to the rich meat. One of my absolute favorite dishes anywhere is the dogami moochim, described on the menu as "gelatin of cow knee cooked with Korean vegetables," which translates on the plate to a mixed salad of watercress, cucumber, julienne carrots, and sliced hot peppers, tossed with warm, silky, gelatinous chunks of beef cartilage, all bathed in a red-pepper-based vinaigrette. I could see this dish in a much smaller form appearing on any number of four-star menus, it's that good.

As a starch alternative to rice, order the perfect bin dae duk, three little crispy fried pancakes made from ground mung beans, carrots, onions, scallion, bean spouts, and minced pork, cooked on a hot griddle and drizzled with oil to ensure a crisp skin. A non-meat choice might be chojang ohinguh, perfectly cooked squid served with a dipping sauce. Or try the modum bossam, a heap of raw oysters paired with cooked sliced pork belly, pickled bok choy, and spicy-hot shredded radish. Wash all this down with a good assortment of international beers or hot roasted barley tea.

Gascogne

212-675-6564
158 Eighth Avenue, between
    17th and 18th Streets
Casual
Reservations
Moderate
All major credit cards accepted
Dinner Monday, lunch and
    dinner Tuesday–Sunday
1 train to 18th Street station;
    1, 2, 3, A, C, E to 14th Street
    station; L to Eighth Avenue
    station

Gascogne is named after the remote, hilly, flinty part of southwest France — a region, in all honesty, that even the French don't visit much. Bordeaux sits to its northwest; you'd most likely fly into the Gascogne region via the city of Toulouse, to the east; and the prettier beaches of Perpignon, about an hour or so southeast, see far more visitors. But I have toured the area a few times and love the food, the Armagnac, and the proud folks who live here. It reminds me, I suppose, of rural Kentucky, where generations of families live, hunt, fish, make bourbon, don't travel much out of the region, and don't give a hoot who comes to visit. This is the home of D'Artagnan and the tradition of the musketeer. The food is big and bold-flavored and meat-heavy: duck, foie gras, cèpes and other mushrooms, and that great vegetable soup garbure. To my mind, this is cold-weather food, best consumed in the months between early October and late April.

The space spreads out over two floors, with a dining room upstairs and another down that leads as well to a garden, lovely in warmer months and, thanks to a canopy, very comfortable on cool nights as well. It has a funky bistro feel with painted brick walls, French posters, objets d'art, brass chandeliers, bare light bulbs, dried flowers, and old wine bottles as decoration. The staff is friendly and outgoing, as you'd expect from an established neighborhood spot like this.

Baked mussels with garlic butter is a good starter, garlicky and rich; soak up the leftover butter with crusty bread. Sautéed wild mushrooms are served warm over puff pastry vol-au-vent—old-school, sure, but delicious. The light brown cream sauce infused with herbs has a great mushroom flavor. Or try the chilled rabbit terrine, the forcemeat well seasoned, studded with canned black truffles and set within a frame of sauternes aspic.

Foie gras is offered in two guises, one as a $23 tasting plate with a terrine, prunes stuffed with foie mousse, dried fruits, and truffles, and the other featuring a large slab of foie gras, sautéed and served with a honey-poached pear. Both are good choices and can be shared as a middle course. While I hate to say this, skip the fish. They offer a few each night, but opt instead for the very good cassoulet, the white beans redolent of tomato and meat, and of course a bit of fat, especially from the duck confit and good garlic sausage that make this plate such a treat. Or try the confit, the cured leg meat fork-tender and well seasoned, or the magret, the breast crisped yet medium rare, sliced thin over a sauce made from the sturdy local Madiran wine. They have veal kidneys, rack of lamb, and a good faux fillet if you are in a conservative mood. All entrees are very fairly priced at $25.

Desserts are okay. Let's face it, with a small restaurant like this, it's hard to employ a full-fledged pastry chef. But the crêpes Suzette are good, and the Armagnac and prune mousse is very good. If you've never had Armagnac, here they have one of the best selections in the city, with offerings from some very good houses including Castarede, Laubade, and Darroze. They are not cheap, but trust me, French chefs in the know prefer them to their dainty and faint-hearted cousins the cognacs. As an entry level, try the VS or VSOP blends for starters, but if you're ready to go all out, look for the ones that are at least 20 years old and aged in oak, where the flavors really start to open up and smooth out. The wine list is full of good buys from the region, many not very well known, whites such as Jurançon Sec and Pacherenc and reds such as Madiran, Cahors, and Buzet.

On cold winter nights, with the wind blowing down from the park or across the Hudson, I am drawn to this place and this style of food, rich, bold, and meaty, and the dark, tannic wines that pair so well with those dishes.

Gilt

212-891-8100
455 Madison Avenue,
  at 50th Street
Dressy
Reservations
Expensive
All major credit cards accepted
Lunch and dinner Monday–
  Friday, dinner Saturday
E, V trains to Fifth
  Avenue/53rd Street station;
  N, R, W trains to 49th Street
  station

Housed in one of the most beautiful rooms in the city, this was once a wing of the old Villard mansion. Built in 1885, designed by McKim, Mead and White for the railroad financier Henry Villard, it was later occupied by the Archdiocese of New York prior to being folded into what is now the Palace Hotel, which sits directly behind and above the courtyard off Madison Avenue. This space had most recently been Le Cirque 2000, until Sirio Maccioni found dealing with the ever-changing hotel management to be too much. In marched chef Paul Liebrandt, flush with investors' cash, and Gilt was born. I'm not crazy about what they did to the room. The dining room floor seems to be made of beige dimpled rubber, reminiscent of those old cheap footballs, and that same flooring curves its way a foot or so up the wall. The bar area is set next to an odd, igloo-esque sculptured half wall. The dining room tables stand on see-through Plexiglas tubes. All that postmodern effect is set jarringly against some of the most lovely old carved woodwork, wainscoting, and turn-of-the-century decoration to be found in any New York public space. As had happened before with Paul, his tenure was short-lived—here his departure was perhaps hastened by some lukewarm reviews and a huge debt that required a full house each night. He's a big talent, and he's back now cooking better than ever at Corton downtown. But into Gilt marched the new team, headed by chef Christopher Lee, who worked at Daniel, at Jean Georges, and most recently as the chef at the highly touted Stephen Starr eatery in Philadelphia, Striped Bass. The pastry chef is David Carmichael, who worked with Christopher at Daniel and then for the Livanos family at Oceana before a brief stint at the doomed latest incarnation of the Russian Tea Room. In late 2008, Christopher left to open the new Aureole for Charlie Palmer, and his longtime sous chef Justin Bogle has taken over the reins.

Compared to what Paul was doing, the current menu is much more straightforward, a bit more simple and streamlined, but the cooking is very consistent and quite often very good. The kitchen is a grand tiled space, with a high ceiling, a separate glassed-in pastry station, and not one but two Bonnet stoves, among the finest in the world and rarities in New York City. The prices are also down from what they'd been at Le Cirque 2000: a three-course menu for $78 or five courses for $105, wine pairings additional. They are obviously playing for a broader audience in both price and scope, but the food is not dumbed down at all. In most cases it's darn good.

The menu is broken down into hot and cold starters, main courses divided into land and sea selections, and desserts. The tasting menu follows the à la carte menu for the most part, and supplements are rare. Creamy fresh burrata cheese is served with paper-thin shards of grilled sourdough and set in peppery balsamic vinaigrette. The wine pairing was a 1999 Domaine Ganard Chassagne-Montrachet premier cru Morgeot. Two small fillets of Mediterranean dorade are served escabeche-style, hot-cured in a bracing vinaigrette, garnished with black olives, tomato confit, baby artichokes, and nubbins of tangy feta cheese. With this they poured a lovely 2005 Reichsgraf von Kesselstatt Piesporter Goldtropfchen Riesling, Kabinett. Fresh artichoke soup does a great job capturing the essence of that elusive artichoke flavor. Here it's all artichokes, barely creamed, flavored with spring onions, a swirl of verdant parsley pesto, and slivers of guanciale, and garnished with three tiny California snails, individually breaded and fried, then set on a thin metal skewer laid across the rim of the plate.

A real winner was a small plate of fresh-caught Alaskan spotted prawns, just barely cooked, stacked one atop the other and set over a garnish of tiny dice of something billed as smoked ham potato hash (was it potato or ham?), piquillo peppers, chives, chervil, and a light sauce made from salt cod. A small house-made bratwurst was very good, but the mixed plate of Australian lamb, combining a sliced medium-rare rack with a ragout made from the braised shoulder, garnished with earthy Swiss chard, golden raisin falafel, and Moroccan Saumur-style lemon jus, stole the show. The pour here was a powerful 2001 Ceretto Barolo Brunate.

David Carmichael is a very good pastry chef. In spring, his rhubarb crumble is excellent, as is the chocolate constellation, featuring various chocolate orbs filled with creams and purees. The Black Forest mousse is good, but the apple confit paired with pistachios and saffron is a knockout. Service is earnest. They want this place to succeed, and you can tell. All in all, the beautiful room, simplified food, and easier-to-bear price point bode well for the longevity and make it a very good choice for this part of town.

Gobo

212-255-3242
401 Sixth Avenue, between Waverly Place and 8th Street
Casual
Reservations
Moderate
All major credit cards accepted
Lunch and dinner seven days a week
A, C, E, B, D, F, V trains to West 4th Street station; 1 train to Christopher Street station

This is a nice upscale spot serving very good vegetarian cuisine on a strip of Sixth Avenue that is stuck in time in the Greenwich Village of the 1960s and 1970s, with head shops, fast-food franchises, and tattoo parlors. Now upscale restaurants are joining their ranks. This place comes with a vegetarian pedigree. Gobo is run by David and Darryn Wu, whose parents opened the original Zen Palate. The room is nice, upscale, even sleek, with an open kitchen, rows of tables down the center, hanging square yellow-shaded lamps, and a wall of banquettes. Unlike some vegetarian places around town, here they have a liquor license and serve beer and wine, as well as freshly squeezed juices, to go with the food.

The menu is big and, as far as vegetarian menus go, diverse. You can create a good meal by sticking with the quick bites and small plates sections; the two combined offer more than two dozen choices, including marinated tofu, spring rolls, pan-seared spinach dumplings, scallion pancakes, creamy avocado tartare with wasabi lime dressing, lettuce wraps, and pan-roasted vegetables, mostly all priced below $10 per plate. For traditional main courses, I liked the nori-wrapped tofu in a Thai red curry sauce, the thin and chewy Singapore-style mai fun noodles with vegetables, the soy cutlet with black pepper sauce, and the organic king oyster mushrooms with black bean sauce scented with basil. Add another dozen soup and salad selections, sturdy sides of brown rice or yucca fries, friendly staff, and the typical loyal mild-mannered vegetarian customers, and you get the idea—this is the kind of place you could bring Liv Tyler to lunch.

Good Enough to Eat

212-496-0163

483 Amsterdam Avenue,
   between 83rd and 84th
   Streets

Casual

No reservations

Inexpensive to moderate

Breakfast, lunch, and dinner
   seven days a week

1 train to 86th Street station;
   B, C trains to 81st Street station

Through the Upper West Side's culinary ice age, Good Enough to Eat went about its business quietly. For over twenty-five years, this little homey outpost on Amsterdam Avenue has operated under the radar of the food press. Like its celebrity cousin Sarabeth's, located a few blocks to the south, Good Enough to Eat originally opened in 1981 with just 10 tables and moved to the current location in 1989, doubling their size. The brainchild of chef Carrie Levin, no relation to Sarabeth Levine, here they serve an interesting version of what I'd call The Berkshires meets Manhattan, an amalgam of home-made culinary Americana. To Sarabeth's Laura Ashley-esque polish, Good Enough to Eat was like your working class hippy cousin in old jeans and faded flannel. For whatever reason, Sarabeth's was celebrated in the press, and Good Enough to Eat just quietly went about its business, developing a loyal and passionate neighborhood following. Sarabeth's, while wonderful in its day, has since been sold and to my mind is not nearly as good; skip it and head straight to Good Enough to Eat.

The room is a bit funky. You enter off Amsterdam, directly into the dining room, separated by three feet of white picket fence from a small bar to your left and the simple wooden tables and chairs before you. Exposed brick and loads of farm and roadside memorabilia adorn the walls and ceiling—a spade here, a lace doily there, and lots of spotted cows in one form or another.

What I like most about this place is that everything is truly homemade, the way it should be but these days so rarely is. Breakfast is always packed with locals lined up for great pancakes with real maple syrup, eggs and omelets, hot cereals, and an assortment of muffins and freshly baked goods. Lunch and dinner menus offer the familiar, but here they do it the way it should be done, not the way it usually is.

Gotham Bar and Grill

212-620-4020
12 East 12th Street, between
University Place and Fifth
Avenue
Casual
Reservations
Expensive
All major credit cards accepted
Lunch and dinner Monday–
Friday, dinner Saturday and
Sunday
4, 5, 6, L, N, Q, R, W trains to
14th Street/Union Square
station

For over two decades this restaurant has reigned as one of the most popular dining rooms in the city, and its chef, Alfred Portale, is one of the most widely praised in the industry. Great review followed great review; they've won enough James Beard awards to fill a small chest; and an impressive lineage of chefs have worked there over time and gone on to glory, further adding to the legendary status of Gotham as a training ground for star chefs. Yet from the beginning I've remained on the sidelines, arms folded, wondering why the big fuss. While the food is very pretty and consistently prepared, I've never been moved by it. For the most part it's been good, even very good, but to my taste, rarely does it rise to the realm of great in the current New York restaurant scene, which in terms of talent has moved forward with great velocity since the mid-nineties. Part of that problem may be the sheer volume of customers the restaurant feeds each day for both lunch and dinner: upward of 400 each day, limiting the kitchen's ability to reach, except perhaps for the daily specials, and yielding a less-than-inspiring brand of paint-by-numbers, sauté-and-plate, assembly-line designer cooking.

This was the first restaurant opened by Jerome Kretchmer, also known as Bobby Flay's restaurant partner, with whom he opened Mesa Grill years back when Bobby was a little-known chef. Kretchmer had worked in politics and ran the sanitation department under the Lindsay administration. When Gotham opened, the loft-like, open room design was new, and to run the kitchen he hired cookbook writer Barbara Kafka as a consultant. The menu was a sort of French-Moroccan amalgam, composed of rather odd-tasting dishes served on black plates.

Business, needless to say, was not good. Changes needed to be made, and to the rescue came the young chef Portale, with new plates, a new menu, much better cooking, and the advent of tall food (a trend better left forgotten; fortunately, it seems to have run its course here). The idea of using ingredients not necessarily for flavor but for their structural integrity as weight-bearing supports to create towering vertical plates sounds more like architecture than cooking to me.

Portale knew how to design beautiful presentations, often drawing his plates prior to cooking them. As a young man he wanted to be a jeweler, and he had a great inherent sense of presentation and visual esthetics. After graduation from cooking school, he worked in France with Michel Guérard, the creator of cuisine minceur, at his legendary three-star restaurant in Eugénie-les-Bains. He was slated to work in Paris with Alain Senderens, but instead he returned to New York, where he worked with another brilliant French chef, Jacques Maximin. Fueled with inspiration, and having honed his technique after those two great jobs, he set to changing the food at Gotham and, in so doing, put his stamp on a new modern style. There was great passion and energy in this visually stunning, French-inspired American cuisine. In those early days, Alfred worked the stoves, cooking, tasting, plating, and working day and night. He pushed the cooks to refine their craft, to season, to taste, to be consistent. In the context of what was going on in the New York culinary world of 1985, his daring, innovative menus broke new ground, combining solid French technique with his refined visual style. The food critics, including the veteran Gael Greene, were dazzled, and soon three-star-review followed three-star-review, going on for twenty-plus years.

But success comes with a price, and as Portale began to delegate in the 1990s, taking nights and weekends off, his very capable sous-chefs, starting with Bill Telepan, began to do more and more of the actual cooking and hands-on supervising, and of late a certain smugness has replaced the earlier brilliance.

Not that the food here isn't good; it is, and it can be very good, but it is expensive, the portions tend to be small, and the menus have a certain sameness from season to season and year to year. The front-of-the-house staff is well trained and attentive, and they know both the menu and the wine list, which is a fine document. The salad portion of the menu is invariably interesting, albeit a carryover from the tall-food days. Lobster and avocado salad towers above the plate, with the sliced avocado base wrapped with lobster claw meat, concealing fingerling potatoes and beets, all beneath a vertical spray of greens bathed in a lemongrass vinaigrette. Hamachi salad is a play in texture and flavor, pairing the rich tuna meat with thin-sliced fennel and crunchy Asian pear in a polished vinaigrette made from an emulsion of orange oil, soya, and yuzu juice. A thin slice of Muscovy duck and foie gras terrine is paired with a little stack of perfectly cut haricots verts, a spoonful of lentil salad, a few pickled pearl onions, and a port glaze; I just wish there were more of it for $19. The chilled seafood salad has been on the menu forever and no longer merits attention; skip it and try the warm skate salad or one of the seared foie gras presentations instead.

Seafood entrees are all uniformly well done; the roasted Maine lobster tail with escarole and fingerling potatoes is very good, as is the sturdy and firm-fleshed pan-seared halibut, holding its own against sautéed morels, buttery English peas, and tiny Yukon gold potatoes. Pork from Snake River Farm is paired with creamy soft polenta, fava beans, roasted plums, and rhubarb. A single crisp-skinned, medium-rare roast squab sits on a bed of greens with sautéed pancetta in a pool of balsamic caper sauce. It's a good acidic foil to the meat's richness, but again, for $36, I'd love more.

The desserts are very well conceived and executed, such as the tiny lemon meringue tart, essentially lemon curd housed in a thin round pastry shell, the curd topped with a piped border of tiny meringue dollops. Fanciful creations like the very grown-up macadamia nut ice cream sandwich, or the s'more, combining a warm chocolate tart with a graham cracker crust, toasted vanilla marshmallow, and sour cream sorbet, are entertaining and delicious.

To paraphrase the great playwright Edward Albee from a 2005 interview, musing on the continued interest in and yet another revival of his 1961 classic, *Who's Afraid of Virginia Woolf?*—if something is dubbed an "instant classic" and enough people refer to it as a classic over time, then it just becomes one. And so it is with Gotham Bar and Grill. It's hard to argue with success—this is one of the city's most beloved eateries. Do visit it and have that reference point, but the 1980s were a long time ago, the quality of cooking has risen substantially in New York, and we have many more great choices now.

Gramercy Tavern

212-477-0777
42 East 20th Street, between
Park Avenue South and
Broadway
Casual to dressy
Reservations except for the
Tavern Room
Expensive
All major credit cards accepted
Lunch and dinner seven days
a week
6, N, R, W trains to 23rd Street
station

Of all of Danny Meyer's very good restaurants, this has been consistently the best year in and year out with small lapses here and there. Gramercy combined Meyer's genius for hospitality with Tom Colicchio's great cooking. Though Tom is no longer involved with the kitchen, it still bears his signature style. These days the kitchen is under the watchful eye of Michael Anthony after his long stint at Blue Hill at Stone Barns. The market-driven food is as good as at Blue Hill and in some ways maybe even better, as it has gone a tad leaner style-wise than Tom's food was. Colicchio's style offered big bold flavors, both meats and fish served well seared and accented with liberal use of salt and then layers of lipids—butter, olive oil, goose fat. Anthony's style shows more restraint, less pan-searing and roasting, and more delicate techniques such as braising, poaching, and cooking sous vide. This is partly due to the influence of Dan Barber, by way of Juan Cuevas at Eighty One, and Julian Alonzo at Brasserie 8½. Since it opened, Gramercy has been a quintessential New York destination, and in my experience, it is nearly impossible not to eat well here.

Meyer, a native of St. Louis, opened Union Square Café to great acclaim when he was all of 27 years old. At that time he was living above Gotham Bar and Grill during its legendary early days and was a frequent diner there. That was the kind of place he wanted to own: busy, professionally run, trend-setting, and very modern. If opening restaurants were like composing music, Meyer, it seemed, had perfect pitch. Gramercy was his second place after opening the hugely successful Union Square Café, and here he tapped the young but already veteran New York chef Tom Colicchio, a working-class Italian American kid from suburban northern New Jersey. The first time I sampled his cooking was at the short-lived Mondrian in the early 1980s, housed in the former Playboy Club. Dennis Foy was billed as the chef, but it was Colicchio who possessed the real talent in that kitchen. I was a young chef in New York back then and traveled frequently to Paris and throughout Europe on dining vacations, as did many young chefs of that era. At this early stage in his career, you could see that his talent was considerable. The food reminded me of some of the best meals I'd had overseas, and was far better than nearly all of what was being done in top kitchens around New York.

After Mondrian closed, I dined a few times at the short-lived Rakel, where Colicchio was Thomas Keller's sous-chef. His emergence at Gramercy Tavern was worth the wait. From the beginning, the food at Gramercy was excellent. As Colicchio focused more on his various Craft restaurants, the kitchen here drifted a bit, so when Michael Anthony took over, a remake was needed. To my taste, it just keeps getting better. The service is professional, the two dining rooms are very comfortable, and the customer mix is egalitarian in a way that I wish I saw in more New York restaurants. In some ways I prefer the more casual tavern room, where they take walk-ins only and the service is excellent. You can wait for your table at the long bar to the side of the room.

The flavors are big and honest, the combinations on the plate suggest culinary intelligence, and the execution is nearly flawless. The nightly menu, as is often the case with most restaurants these days, changes frequently, often week to week, based on seasonal ingredients. For starters, I'm a huge fan of the charcuterie plate, which combines house-made mortadella with disks of excellent head cheese, salami-style salumi, and cured duck breast, garnished with a fruit compote and pickled vegetables, served with toast. Pair it with a decent burgundy, Côtes du Rhône, or Beaujolais and you can't go wrong. Silky-smooth chicken liver mousse is accompanied by braised baby turnips and slow-cooked Swiss chard stems, an idea I love, as the earthy minerality of chard is best expressed in the stem.

On the lighter side, brook trout is slow-roasted, the sweet freshwater fish set against a slightly acidic cipollini puree and doused with a pickled onion vinaigrette, a nice foil to the trout. Pappardelle served with a braised lamb ragout is hard to argue with, the meat tender and flavorful, the braising liquid rich and perfectly suited for that broad chewy noodle. Preserved lemon and beet greens round out this plate. In colder weather, the plate of sliced smoked kielbasa set over spaetzle and diced browned butternut squash is a sure bet. Pair that with one of the great aged beers they stock at the front bar. In warmer months, there is a dish of slow-cooked halibut, the meat just cooked, the proteins almost custard-like, set over a herb-scented broth, studded with pole beans and favas, a lovely spring-summer food that leaves room for dessert.

Here the desserts have always been among the best in town. Homey and done in an American vernacular, the pastry program is these days presided over by Nancy Olson, a native of North Dakota. The peach pie is picture-perfect, the crust rich and crumbly and the concentrated peach filling not too sweet or gooey; the garnish of lemon verbena ice cream strikes a lovely balance with the rich peaches. Ditto the blackberry streusel cake, moist and studded with fruit. The blackberry lime sorbet works well alongside it. I love coconut and I love tapioca, so I jumped at the coconut tapioca pudding with passion fruit and coconut sorbet, garnished further with a caramel made from passion fruit and a drizzle of cilantro syrup. Fargo's loss is New York's gain. If all else fails, have the small plate of cookies to share at the table—they too are wonderful.

Service is, as with all of Danny Meyer's places, spot on. The beverage program is among the best in the city, from the perfectly crafted cocktails through the beer and wine lists and the digestifs to end the meal. Well over a decade since it first opened, Gramercy is still a New York benchmark.

Grand Central Oyster Bar and Restaurant

212-490-6650
89 East 42nd Street, at
  Vanderbilt Avenue,
  in the basement of Grand
  Central Station
Casual
Reservations
Moderate
All major credit cards accepted
Monday–Friday 11:30 AM–9:30 PM,
  Saturday noon–9:30 PM
4, 5, 6, 7, S trains to 42nd
  Street/Grand Central station

While this is for the most part a restaurant, and a fairly decent one too, I could have included it here as a wine bar. Why? Well, as restaurants go, this isn't really a standout. It's more a piece of New York history, a link to the days when oyster bars were common, as was the tasty bivalve itself that once thrived in our tidal bays, rivers, and estuaries. From Cape May to Montauk, up the Hudson, and down through the lower bays, the Atlantic coastal waters once teemed with them. The oysters are, for the most part, history, but this space remains, and it's a lovely public dining hall. You enter from Grand Central into a room with tables set cafeteria style beneath high vaulted ceilings covered with beautiful decorative Guastavino tiles. Beyond the main room, you'll find the "saloon," which doubles as a bar area, and here (and everywhere else in this place) you can have a glass of any wine on the menu, and the wine list is better than the food. It's not that the food isn't good—it's just that the place does some serious volume each day and also seafood cooking has moved on and modernized, and places such as Esca, Oceana, the Sea Grill, and of course Le Bernardin do it to perfection. But if by chance you missed your train and have to wait, or if you simply have a hankering for simpler fare—grilled, fried, or sautéed fish, with slaw and vegetables, a great selection of raw oysters on the half shell, or those little oyster pan roasts made individually in tiny steam-jacketed kettles right in front of you—then this is the place.

I'd say go for the fresh shucked oysters on the half shell. Mix the varieties, from the sweet, small, melon-like West Coast Kumamotos to the brinier warm- and cold-water natives of the Atlantic, and wash them down with—what else?—a glass of good muscadet, a Picpoul de Pinet, or perhaps a glass of Iron Horse Russian River bubbly. From the Loire, the Coulée d'Argent Vouvray sec is delicious, as is the S. Kunz trocken from the Mosel, which pairs well with many of the simple sautéed fish here. The list is fairly broad and decent, including a good number of reds and even three very nice sakes by the glass, like the super Ichishima Shuzo Dream junmai daiginjo from Nigata, Japan, for $20 a pour. While the food plays second fiddle to the space, the wine list is more than adequate. If you choose the food carefully to match the wine, consider a meal at Grand Central Oyster Bar as a real classic New York experience.

Grand Sichuan St. Marks

212-529-4800
19-23 St. Marks Place,
at Third Avenue
(and elsewhere)
Casual
Reservations
Moderate
All major credit cards accepted
Lunch and dinner seven days
a week
6 train to Astor Place station;
N, R, W trains to 8th Street
station

At last count there were four or five restaurants sharing this same name around town. All are owned by the same people, and all are very, very good, especially if you like hot food. At the heart of many of the dishes is the famed, and for a while illegal, Sichuan peppercorn. Not all the dishes are hot, but many are, and a good place to start is with the dan dan noodles. The bowl arrives with fresh room-temperature noodles tossed with minced pork and sliced pickled vegetables, and bound by a hot red sauce that grows hotter as you progress. The soup dumplings are always good, too, loaded with ground pork and crab, and plump with that meaty braising liquid contained within the dumpling. Little dumplings in red oil are another good starter, as are the cold cucumber in scallion sauce and the sliced jellyfish tossed with spicy vinegar sauce.

Kung pao chicken is wonderful—the meat is diced and then wok-fried with peanuts, chunks of celery, red peppercorns, and Shaoxing wine; it's got a lot going on, texture- and flavor-wise. Another dish featuring celery pairs the crunchy, cooling vegetable with long slices of smoked tofu sautéed together; the combination works well as a middle-course palate cooler. If they have those curly little pea shoots, order them sautéed with garlic and hot oil, a delicious vegetable side dish. Sliced pork with "home special sauce" is very good as well; here the tender pork is tossed in a sauce made with miso paste, studded with fermented black beans, chunks of Chinese celery, and sliced green pepper. The tea-smoked duck is great, but if you're really brave, order the chong qing dry spicy chicken. I saw it first at a table near me filled with Chinese Americans, and ordered it after watching them finish the bowl. What arrives is a mix of seemingly 50% chicken and 50% red peppercorns, screaming hot off the wok. Just the steam coming off the plate is enough to get your eyes watering from the heat. With your chopsticks, carefully pick out the chicken pieces, scallions, or ginger, and eat them one by one slowly. Soon, I assure you, you'll be sweating, fanning your open mouth to cool it off, and reaching for that glass of tea, beer, ice water, or all of the above.

The sliced cured pork with dried string beans is great, as is most of the menu. Come with friends and order as much variety as you can—that's the best way to experience these places. One menu item was a runner-up for my annual weird menu translation. I didn't order it, but maybe you will. It's billed as "Associated Cured Food in Hot Wok." In any case, all the locations of this restaurant are good and worth a visit, especially if you like it hot, really hot.

Gray's Papaya

212-799-0243
2090 Broadway at 72nd
    Street (and elsewhere)
Casual
No reservations
Inexpensive
Cash only
Seven days a week, 24 hours a day
1, 2, 3, B, C trains to 72nd
    Street station

An offshoot of the original Papaya King across town, the theme here is the same. This store was the first one, but now they have identical outposts all over town. The building it sits in is a dump, but you can't argue with great, cheap, crisp grilled dogs, served with typical topping options and various fruit drinks, for prices that are laughably low. The hot dogs are less than a buck apiece, and for under $3 you can get two dogs and a drink. Not surprisingly, all the locations are busy at all hours of the day. There is no seating; you either take the dog out and eat it while walking or pony up to one of the slim Formica counters, rest your elbows, and dig in. Either way, it's hard to go wrong with the quality/price ratio here.

Great N.Y. Noodle Town

212-349-0923
28 Bowery, at Bayard Street
Casual BYOB
Reservations
Inexpensive to moderate
Cash only
Seven days a week 9 AM–4 AM
B, D trains to Grand Street
station; 6, J, M, Z, N, Q, R, W,
trains to Canal Street station

While some may complain about the falling quality of the food found in Manhattan's Chinatown (and the superior versions now available in Jackson Heights or Elmhurst, Queens, or in Sunset Park, Brooklyn), I find places like N.Y. Noodle Town to be uniformly consistent and satisfying. Easy to find on the brightly lit corner of Bowery and Bayard, in typical Chinatown fashion the décor is a joke: too bright, too much Formica, too many mirrors, communal style tables, and too noisy when busy, which is often. Yet for serious food lovers, all of this is soon forgotten once the plates start to arrive.

Hong Kong–style noodles dishes alongside roast duck, roast pork, and on occasion roast suckling pig, combined with really good seafood, make this a destination for many. Any of the noodle soups or soups with dumplings are full-flavored and can be a meal in themselves, arriving in big steaming bowls, laden with vegetables, thick chewy noodles, and many with the addition of chopped pork. The salt-baked seafood (deep-fried, actually), especially the shrimp and soft-shell crabs in late spring and early summer, alone are worth the trip. This technique involves frying the seafood, in some cases twice-frying it, in an addictive salt crust. When you order the shrimp this way they are served whole still in their shells, which are meant to be eaten, so don't peel them or you'll miss the beauty of the dish. Whole sea bass or tautog is braised and served in a delicious broth; steamed fresh flounder serves the delicacy of this fish's meat well; and the shrimp dumplings arrive hot, plump, and moist. If you like well turned-out lo mein, order any of the varieties here. Recently I questioned a waiter about a dish billed as boiled beef tendon. He said he thought I wouldn't want it and was nice enough to bring me a piece to sample to be certain. It was exactly what I wanted, served traditional-style with simple boiled noodles.

Order any of the roast meats, duck, pork, or BBQ pork chopped and served over white rice—simple and excellent. And did I mention cheap? This is one of the great bargains in a part of New York where you can still eat very, very well for under $20 per person if you know where to go and what to order.

Grifone

212-490-7275
244 East 46th Street,
between Second and
Third Avenues
Casual to dressy
Reservations
Moderate to expensive
All major credit cards accepted
Lunch and dinner Monday–
Friday, dinner Saturday
4, 5, 6, 7, S trains to 42nd
Street/Grand Central station

If you are a fan of old-school formal Italian restaurants—think Parioli Romanissimo, Il Nido, Lello, and the like—then this is the place for you. Grifone seems to have been here on this stretch of East 46th Street forever; well, twenty-odd years is forever in restaurant terms. It was originally opened in 1986 by Nello Trauzzi and Joseph Bicocchi, the same folks who ran Girafe back then on East 58th Street, when it was a restaurant row of sorts, with well over a dozen eateries dotting both sides of the street, and all thriving through the 1970s and late 1980s. Due to changing tastes, traffic patterns, and rents, most of the old places now are shuttered, but Grifone persists down here, a dozen blocks to the south, serving a classic New York version of northern Italian food.

The space reminds us that this is what most restaurants used to look like before the big, boxy, showy ones became popular. You enter the main dining room past two carved wooden griffons into a rather narrow space with a low ceiling. Banquettes line the walls, and a mirror above them helps the room seem less cramped. The lighting is soft but not too dark, and the color selection is mostly pastel variations of peach. The tables are set with starched linen, napkins folded so as to stand up on the table like little peacocks (remember that?), and the wait staff are all clad in formal wear.

I'd be lying if I told you that the long menu is anything but familiar, even clichéd these days. They are not treading new ground in this kitchen. Appetizers include grilled portobello mushrooms, stuffed braised whole artichokes, imported mozzarella di bufala with fresh tomatoes and basil, thinly sliced smoked salmon and prosciutto with melon . . . are we yawning yet?

Well, not so fast. The roasted peppers with anchovies and mozzarella are very good, and the baked clams are better than what 90% of the steakhouses in New York serve, as are the Caesar salad and the endive salad with beets. The pasta selection has some real standouts as well. The tagliatelle with porcini in season are lovely, as are the thick, meaty perciatelli matriciana Roman-style and the fusilli puttanesca, sharp and fishy with a good edge to it. Tortellini are plump and delicious, stuffed with Swiss chard and ricotta cheese, and that old saw, tortellini with prosciutto and fresh peas in a cream sauce, reminds me of how much I really love these old-style dishes. The pasta portions are very decent, and none is priced over $20.

Veal is the featured meat, and it is prepared as chops and thinly pounded scaloppine in at least a dozen different ways. If you've never had a great veal Milanese-style, try the one here. It's crisp and light, tender, and full of flavor. The other variations remind us of how well this rather bland but tender cut of meat serves as a sponge for flavors around it, hence the tradition and the great dishes that result. For fish they have the usual suspects—salmon, shrimp, sole, tuna, swordfish, branzino. Instead try the zuppa de pesce, which may be nearly as good as the version served across town at Esca. I'd skip the beef dishes—Sparks is right down the street for that jones—and opt for the chicken instead. Their version of chicken scarpariello is the model of what this dish can be, as is the thickly breaded Francese and the lighter Gabriella, with fresh artichoke hearts and thinly sliced mushrooms adorning a simple white wine pan sauce.

The wine list is good, a bit on the expensive side, but for whites try the lovely greco di tufo by Mastrobernardino, a fine example of this grape from Avellino, just north of Naples, rich in minerality and redolent of sulfur from the volcanic Vesuvian soil nearby. For reds it gets harder to choose in the low end, but if you want to shell out a few bucks, the 1995 Lagrein from Steinraffler at $90 a pop is delicious. Desserts are mainly an afterthought; opt for something light, and made with fruit if possible. Service is very polished; though these days some may find it too formal, I for one don't mind a bit.

Italian restaurant cooking has come a long way since this place first opened over twenty years ago, but it still merits a visit for the no-nonsense, serious cooking coming out of this kitchen.

Gusto Ristorante e Bar Americano

212-924-8000
60 Greenwich Avenue, off Seventh Avenue at the end of Perry Street
Casual
Reservations
Expensive
All major credit cards accepted
Lunch and dinner Monday–Friday, dinner Saturday and Sunday
1, 2, 3 trains to 14th Street station; A, C, E, B, D, F, V trains to West 4th Street station

Shortly after this restaurant opened, people kept telling me I'd have to try it. The year was 2005, and the owner was Sasha Muniak, who owns the Mangia chain, which I don't like. The chef was Jody Williams, who had worked as a chef in New York after spending some years cooking around Italy, and with whom I really wasn't familiar, so I gave it a try. The food was very Italian in a good way: simple, ingredient-driven, and homey. But then we get a scene all too common in New York these days...chefs on the move. Williams left to head up the kitchen in Keith McNally's latest effort, Morandi, and has since moved on to

Gottino, a lovely wine bar in Greenwich Village. Her replacement, Amanda Freitag, who also did a brief stint at 'Cesca uptown, has departed as well, and is heading up the kitchen downtown at Jimmy Bradley's Harrison. Then for a while in early 2008, the kitchen at Gusto was overseen by Anne Burrell, formerly of Centro Vinoteca, who is now also gone from both places to work on a TV career, and these days the actual chef doing the day-to-day cooking is longtime sous chef Saulito Montiel.

This style of pared-down, simple cooking is often lost on most chefs here and underappreciated by the greater American public who have grown used to a version of Italian cuisine that never existed in Italy but thrives here. Jody Williams got it, and apparently so do the crowds that flock here nightly. As this is a Greenwich Village restaurant, the crowd is very varied, including twentysomethings who blog about food, young professionals, artsy types, middle-aged couples, and dapper gray-haired longtime Village residents who know a good thing. I'm not crazy about the room itself. Upstairs the main dining area is inexplicably divided in half by a huge stairwell leading to the basement room below. It makes for an odd flow of traffic, to say the least, with the large bar area on one side and the dining area separated by that stairwell on the other side of the room. It's mostly black-and-white tile on the floor, white brick on the front walls, the back a shade of peach. There is ample, comfortable seating, a mix of banquettes and tables, with a huge chandelier toward the rear, centering the upstairs room. I should mention that this room can be very, very loud. It's one of those places that can resemble a raucous party, complete with a Rolling Stones soundtrack. Downstairs is a smaller room, which I don't like much, but some may find more intimate.

As for the food, most everyone loves the fried artichokes, crisp and flavorful, served with a lemon wedge, but at the end of the day, they are just Roman-style fried artichokes. The salad of fava beans and escarole, on the other hand, is very good. The large portion arrives piled high; the crunchy beans play well against the rough, slightly bitter escarole, tossed in a citrus vinaigrette, laced with fresh mint, and doused with salty, crunchy pecorino cheese; for some this could be a summer meal in itself. All the pastas, mostly house-made, are solid and done in an Italian manner—lightly sauced, with the emphasis on the quality of the pasta itself, enhanced by the ingredients they are paired with. Linguine with clams is a good example. Forget the horrid, tasteless white sauce served all over town. Here it's just good al dente pasta, tossed with the natural briny oceanic juice rendered from the clams themselves, a good jolt of fruity olive oil, chopped parsley, and a turn or two of fresh pepper—perfect. Or try the spinach malfatti, ricotta dumplings that resemble little green pillows, tasting of fresh spinach and bathed in a rich sage butter.

The fritto misto of seafood is good, the fish dusted with flour and then fried white and crisp in the Italian style, served with a lemon wedge. I liked the grilled octopus, tossed with shards of celery bathed in good olive oil laced with oregano and small olives, as well as the fried zucchini blossoms stuffed with mozzarella cheese, and the focaccia variations. My only complaint is that it all seems a little pricey. Sicilian meatballs were very good, made from a mix of pork and veal, pine nuts, and raisins in a rich dark tomato sauce, but it's really just a bowl of terrific meatballs and a little sauce for $18. On a recent visit my waiter suggested a special of roast goat with potatoes. Sounded good, and it was, served with a jus from the pan drippings and chunks of browned potato. But I wished I had more of the goat's meatier sections and a few less nearly meatless ribs. When the bill came, that roast goat set me back $29, making it one of the most expensive entrees. I thought goat and potatoes was cheap peasant food. The wine list is good, with some nice choices in the $20–$40 range The desserts are nice as well.

Haandi

212-685-5200
113 Lexington Avenue, between 27th and 28th Streets
Casual
No reservations
Inexpensive
All major credit cards accepted
Lunch and dinner seven days a week
6 train to 28th Street station; N, R, W trains to 28th Street station

This is one of my favorite ethnic eateries in New York. It's totally lowbrow, unpretentious, utilitarian, and cheap. For $10, you can eat very, very well. On this strip of Lexington Avenue, right out front of Haandi, sits a mini-fleet of yellow cabs and Lincoln town cars parked day and night, seven days a week. There are a fair number of Pakistani and Indian expats who work as livery drivers in the city, and they come here to take a break and for a taste of home. I've bumped into customers here who have taken the subway in from Queens to get takeout and then return to their apartments, because Haandi has that authentic home-cooked appeal.

You enter by walking up a few well-worn steps from the Lexington Avenue sidewalk into a square room with Formica tables and wooden chairs. Hanging from the ceiling up front is a TV featuring Bollywood movies or Indian soap operas. Aside from the mix of livery drivers are students from Baruch down the street, some locals, and folks like me looking for a great bargain.

Forgive me for this rather odd review format, but I'll describe the place exactly as I experience it. You place your order at a glass-shielded counter where the food is displayed in chafing dishes and hotel pans, sitting within a simmering bain-marie. While there is a menu of sorts above on the wall in the rear, I'm not sure it coincides with what they serve in those dishes. I simply look at what other people are eating and then take a guess as to what is in each dish. The majority are slow-cooked braises of lamb, beef, chicken, or vegetables, stews really, with a little layer of fat floating on top (which is a good sign), bones and chunks of meat revealing themselves here and there on the surface, and the braising liquid often is a thick brown gravy. So go for it and order—a little of this stew, a little of that, some chicken tikka to play it safe, and soft bread to wipe it all up with. Grab a few napkins, seat yourselves, and dig in. I've almost never had anything here that I didn't like. True, I'm an omnivore, but I can't be totally wrong based on the fact that a good percentage of the crowd that packs this place daily carry Pakistani or Indian passports.

Hakata Tonton

212-242-3699
61 Grove Street, between
  Seventh Avenue and
  Bleecker Street
Casual
Reservations
Inexpensive to moderate
All major credit cards accepted
Dinner seven nights a week
1 train to Christopher Street
  station; A, C, E, B, D, F, V
  trains to West 4th Street
  station

I'd first read about this place in the *Village Voice,* and then just a few days later Josh Ozersky of Grub Street told me we just had to go and check it out. Easy enough, as I live in the neighborhood and happen to be a huge fan of pigs' feet, known as tonsoku, which are the house specialty. I'm not at all certain what the restaurant's name refers to. I do know that Hakata is the largest city in northern Kyushu, an island in southern Japan just north of Okinawa, and part of their cuisine features pigs' feet. As to Tonton, well, that's anybody's guess. The place used to be called Taka and had one of New York's few female sushi chefs, but that closed and this is what has emerged. Himi Okajima runs the place, which opened in the fall of 2007. Prior to this he had a similar venture in Japan where he introduced collagen cuisine, I kid you not. Forget face creams and fancy bars of soap—the way to perfect, youthful skin is now pigs' feet. Hey, I'm in. If this is what it takes to get people to eat this delicious, protein-filled delicacy, bring it on. Chefs in the know have been cooking with pigs' feet forever. The French have the famous pied de cochon—it's added to stocks for the natural collagen and gelatin content— and Alain Senderens had it as a central ingredient in the "ravioli of three feet" at his three-star Michelin temple to fine dining, L'Archestrate. Here in the far West Village, it arrives in more humble guises as parts of dumplings, spring rolls, pastas, braises, and soups.

On cold nights, try the tonsoku hot pot designed for two, featuring spinach, onions, scallions, and dried mushrooms in a pleasant broth studded with the meat and fat of pigs' feet. This could be one of my new favorite late-night soups. Gyoza are especially good with the addition of the fatty, protein-laden meat contained within. The Chinese-inspired shu mai dumplings, steamed and shaped round like a flower, arrive two per plate with a vinegar-based soy dipping sauce and again the distinct, sticky richness associated with trotters. Korean-style cold buckwheat noodles, known as naeng myeon, are dressed with a nice spicy red pepper sauce, perhaps a nod to the famed Korean red pepper paste known as kochujiang.

I love the simple, grilled tonsoku presented off the grill, unembellished and served with just sea salt on the side. Yum, pass the bone marrow. Service is good, and beer, sake, or shoyu works well with the rich fatty food. Obviously this is not a place for those with offal issues, anyone with a calorie or fat phobia, vegetarians, or the culinarily faint of heart. But if, on the other hand, you are an omnivore and a big fan of culinary curios, especially those done well and focused keenly, then this may be a place for you.

HanGawi

212-213-0077
12 East 32nd Street, between
 Fifth and Madison Avenues
Casual
Reservations
Moderate
All major credit cards accepted
Lunch and dinner seven days
 a week
B, D, F, V, N, Q, R, W trains to
 34th Street station; 6 train to
 33rd Street station

Entering HanGawi is like being transported to another world, a sanctuary of calm in the heart of bustling midtown, just steps off Fifth Avenue. It is one of my favorite vegetarian restaurants in New York. It is run by the Chois, a husband-and-wife team, who represent a shrinking Korean vegetarian population, with ties to its past. These are Buddhist vegetarians, and for them, this restaurant is a calling, a ministry, as much as it is a business. You enter off 32nd Street via heavy antique wooden doors, remove your shoes (a Korean custom), and are then seated on soft brightly colored cushions set on the polished wooden floor. The tables are low-slung, and the cushions can be used to sit on or lean on, your choice. The sound level is very low and the place has a pronounced calming effect. The softly lit room features earth tones, antique pottery, and loads of natural wood, and there is a unique sense of ease and balance.

The menu draws ingredients from across Korea, featuring rare dried roots and ferns from the mountains, assorted grains and tubers, and exotic seaweeds from the coast. For mushroom lovers, and I'm one, an entire portion of the menu features mushrooms, including a beautifully simple dish of sautéed maitake, with asparagus in the spring. There are also abalone mushrooms served on a stick, crispy mushrooms served with sweet-and-sour sauce, or the mushroom sizzler served on a hot stone. There are daily selections of vegetarian broths and porridges, a half dozen tofu options to choose from—custard-like creamy tofu served in clay pots, fried firm tofu, tofu pizza—plus vegetarian dumplings and assorted Korean bean pancakes. This is really a celebration of meat-free textures, contrasts, and flavors. Add to this a great tea selection to partner with the food, and it is indeed vegetarian paradise.

Hearth

646-602-1300
403 East 12th Street,
  at First Avenue
Casual
Reservations
Moderate to expensive
All major credit cards accepted
Dinner seven nights a week
L train to First Avenue station;
  4, 5, 6, L, N, Q, R, W trains
  to 14th Street/Union Square
  station

If you consider, as I do, that the best New York restaurants are essentially graduate school programs for aspiring chefs, then it's not hard to figure out that Hearth springs from the Colicchio school of cooking. The clues are the menu's market-driven food, well-executed cooking, big bold flavors, and a very well thought-out wine list. Chef-owners Marco Canora and Paul Grieco as well as pastry chef Lauren Dawson all worked together at Craft. Here, as at Craft, the food is modern Italian-influenced, ingredient-driven, and for the most part very well executed. The wine list, put together by Grieco, is excellent; service strives to match the food and sometimes even does. There are two comfortable dining rooms, one in the front, which sits alongside 12th Street, and one in the rear, which is smaller and includes a few stools at a small bar facing the open kitchen. The crowd, as expected in the downtown neighborhood, tends to be young, hip foodies.

A roasted beet salad arrives spread long across a slender plate: baby beets dressed in a good olive-oil-based vinaigrette, small fronds of fries connecting the beets with chunks of gorgonzola and chopped candied hazelnuts. In the cooler months, ribollita combines black cabbage, white beans, heirloom cauliflower, and shaved parmesan. Sweet raw bay scallops are topped with rich raw sea urchin and then drizzled with excellent extra-virgin olive oil, the three flavors and textures combing to create a very pleasant effect. Cabbage stuffed with sweetbreads and veal arrives lighter than expected, small packets swimming in a veal broth garnished with tiny pastina. A dish that appeared at my table one night and was consumed so quickly I almost don't remember it combined slices of roast sturgeon, a very firm and meaty fish, with sliced prosciutto, escarole, black olive paste, and smoked garlic. A dish I remember more clearly off that midwinter menu was the roast loin of venison set next to a single venison sausage on a bed of braised red cabbage, garnished with finely diced spiced poached pear and pine nuts. Pastas here are another winner; that night was the duck pappardelle, with black olive and rosemary, in a rich wine sauce, and a simple bowl of pasta with beans and parmesan cheese.

Desserts seem to be getting better all over town, with an explosion of talent in that "other" kitchen, and Hearth is no exception. I'd go back for chocolate trifle with gianduja mousse and a dollop of fresh whipped cream anytime, but I'm a sucker for that sort of thing. The perfectly light goat's milk panna cotta with kiwi and tangerine is another good option, as are the made-to-order cider doughnuts, a brightly flavored lemon meringue tart with a side of huckleberry compote, and the favorite at our table one night, the malted pudding—yes, think Ovaltine with chocolate wafers. Alongside the dessert menu is an excellent short list of dessert wines to match. Speaking of wines, the beverage list here is a fine little document. It includes a good selection of excellent beers and Normandy ciders, and offers a variety of choices in the form of 3-ounce "tastes," plain old 6-ounce glasses, and of course bottles. It's a very good, broad, but tight list, well laid out and divided very intelligently into categories. It starts with a great selection of sparkling wines, then German Rieslings, followed by grüner veltliner from Austria and the great wines of the Loire, and continues in this manner, white followed by reds, all listed by varietal and country, with not a bad bottle to be found on the list and many unusual selections such as the extraordinary Clos de Gamot from Cahors, made mostly from pre-phylloxera malbec vines. Like many of the wines on its list, I suspect this already very good establishment will continue to get better with age.

Hill Country

212-255-4544
30 West 26th Street, between
   Fifth and Sixth Avenues
Casual
No reservations
Moderate
All major credit cards accepted
Lunch and dinner seven days
   a week
1, F, V, N, R, W trains to 23rd
   Street station

Hill Country opened in mid-June 2007, and expectations were high. The team behind it had a lot of competition BBQ experience, and in an already somewhat crowded field, many felt Hill Country may emerge as the best. Who knows, but at this point it's a darn good choice if you're looking for Texas-style BBQ and really good country music. Meant to be a paean of sorts to the Austin, Texas, scene, and specifically Kreuz Market in nearby Lockhart, Hill Country mixes traditional smoky BBQ with great live music, cafeteria-style service, long wooden communal tables, wood floors, cords of hardwood stacked in the rear, and lots of exposed brick, along with two bars on two floors and a casual "y'all come on in" vibe. The space is big and seats well over 250 when both floors are full, making it the biggest BBQ place in town, and perhaps the most ambitious to date.

There are a few people who brought this together, and they include the pit master, Long Island native Robbie Richter; Rick Schmidt of Kreuz Market, who brought with him a half-burnt log to start the pit at Hill Country; Big Lou, a former NYPD officer and understudy of Adam Perry Lang; and Marc Glosserman, who handled the business end of things. The ovens come from Texas, three big black steel monsters nearly as big as some Manhattan studio apartments. The ovens are dual-fuel (hickory wood and gas) paddle smoke pits capable of turning out a thousand pounds of BBQ per day per oven. The sausage comes directly from Kreuz, the ice cream is Blue Bell, a cult Texas brand, and among the sodas they have Big Red, which tastes like sweet bubblegum to me. They offer many Texas beers and even four wines from the Lone Star State. These days, Richter is working with Zak Pelaccio at his BBQ place in Williamsburg, and Big Lou runs Steve Hanson's Wildwood BBQ on Park Avenue South.

The service style is reminiscent of Katz's on Houston Street. You enter, walk past the bar toward the service counter in the center of the room, and order your meats (which are sold by weight). The meat is then carved to order, placed on thick brown butcher paper, and wrapped up for you to transport it to your table, where you'll unfold the paper and just dig in, Texas-style. You're given a little card to hold on to where they tally the prices. Beverages and sides can be had via the wait staff, and you pay on the way out.

The meat menu is small and tight: they have brisket, ribs, sausage, chicken, Cornish hen, other cuts like the mammoth boneless beef shoulder, and even racks of lamb. To this add a lot of sides. The hot selection includes baked beans with burnt beef trimmings, beer-braised pinto beans, red chili, corn pudding, mac and cheese, sweet potatoes mashed with bourbon, and even an old-fashioned string bean casserole with button mushrooms like Mom used to make. From the cold side they have deviled eggs, potato salad, coleslaw, cucumber salad, sliced sweet pickles, and a farmer's market salad. If you have room for dessert, try the brownies, pudding, fruit cobbler, or that famous Blue Bell ice cream.

Bottled beer may be the beverage of choice, but the selection of bourbons is deep and impressive. I prefer to dine downstairs and take in the great eclectic live bands that play here regularly. One night early on, David Byrne hopped up onstage for an impromptu mini concert. Overall the BBQ is very good, the vibe fun, the crowd young and noisy, and the music a real plus. After a few minutes in that room, you'd swear you weren't in New York anymore, and sometimes that's a good thing. Is it the best? I'll leave that to someone else, but between RUB, Daisy May's, Dinosaur, and Hill Country, we have four great choices now that on any given night may deserve to be called the best of the best in New York City.

Hop Kee

212-964-8365
21 Mott Street, between Mosco and Worth Streets
Casual
No reservations
Moderate
Cash only
Seven days a week 7 AM–4 AM
6, J, M, Z, N, Q, R, W trains to Canal Street station

I'll confess, I've been eating at Hop Kee since I first came to New York in 1982, so I have a soft spot for this place. This subterranean dining room features Cantonese food, and when it's busy, the line snakes up the stairs and out onto the sidewalk above. There are two dining rooms, both rather dumpy, with lots of Formica tables, vinyl seating surfaces, fluorescent lights; the waiters are grumpy; the bathroom is a scandal—in short, it's vintage Chinatown. Come hungry and come with friends.

Salt-and-pepper shrimp or squid are great starters. The shrimp are twice-fried in their shells, extra crunchy from the cornstarch coating, moist and chewy, and set on a bed of shredded lettuce with sliced hot peppers. The squid are made from the dried variety and are equally impressive. Mussels, clams, or sea snails come paired with a gooey addictive black bean sauce, all very good. Extra sauce goes well on top of rice. The dumplings are fresh, plump, and satisfying. For main courses, pan-fried whole flounder is delicious; be sure to eat everything, including the little cartilage-like collar that rings the fish where the flesh line meets the fins. In good sushi restaurants they save this part for VIP customers. Peking-style pork chops are very good, crisply fried and coated with another sauce that's a winner, as is the steamed whole fish in a ginger coriander broth.

Il Cortile

212-226-6060
125 Mulberry Street, between Hester and Canal Streets
Casual
Reservations
Moderate
All major credit cards accepted
Lunch and dinner seven days a week
6, J, M, Z, N, Q, R, W trains to Canal Street station

There really just aren't that many good restaurants down in Little Italy any more. The neighborhood has become more and more Chinese as Chinatown moves north of Canal, and the remaining Italian restaurants increasingly cater to the tourist trade; the price points have become so low, it's hard to do any serious food. On any given day here, there are dozens of restaurants advertising $12 three-course lunch deals. While Il Cortile is nowhere near my favorite Italian restaurant in New York, for these parts it's among the best. As a footnote, this was the place where they'd take cast members from *The Sopranos* who were going to be written out of the script; their characters would get whacked, but the actors got dinner at Il Cortile.

The space sprawls out and is composed of several dining rooms and a garden. The décor is gaudy, but this is Little Italy, after all, so expect columns, Romanesque statues and frescoes, stained glass, and loads of potted plants. The staff is friendly, the menu relatively straightforward, and I especially like the starters and pastas. The chilled seafood salad is nice, blending cooked scallops, squid, conch, and shrimp in a light lemony vinaigrette. The scaciatta is very good, a deep-dish quiche of sorts with a flaky crust, the rich custard filling holding sausage bits, artichoke hearts, and fresh mozzarella. The hot fried shrimp appetizer too is good, the shrimp dusted with a thin coat of Wondra flour, flash-fried, and then tossed with olive oil, lemon, and a splash of vinegar.

For pasta, try the trusty spaghetti puttanesca, the sauce rich and tart, the pasta al dente, or the orecchiette tossed with slow-cooked eggplant, fresh chopped tomatoes, and salty, firm ricotta salata. On Sundays they do the traditional classic cavatelli in a rich meaty red sauce, with tender rolled braciole, sausage, meatballs, and braised pork. The rest of the menu features fish, chicken, beef, veal, and pork in various predictable guises; the veal is good and tender, as is the pork. Otherwise it's a bit hit-and-miss, but you can do well with an assortment of starters followed by pasta, and leave it at that. For dessert head over to Ferrara around the corner.

Indian Taj

212-982-0810
181 Bleecker Street, between
MacDougal and Sullivan
Streets
Casual
No reservations
Inexpensive
All major credit cards accepted
Lunch and dinner seven days
a week
A, C, E, B, D, F, V trains to West
4th Street station

On the rare occasions that I get a car service in New York, it's not unusual for the drivers to be young Indian or Pakistani expats, and I always ask them where they eat. So after an event one night, heading home, a young Punjabi who was about to take his first vacation in years, eight weeks off and heading back home, told me about this place. A few weeks later I stopped by, and of course he was right. It wasn't great, but it was very good, and at lunch with the $9.95 buffet, it was hard to go wrong. The place is frequented by Indians living in New York and a fair number of NYU students and teachers who know good food and value.

The vegetable and meat samosas are good, light, and clean-tasting; the chicken pakoras, made from seasoned ground chicken meat redolent of cumin, onions and green chiles, are blended, battered, and then fried into large brown lumps, served with chutney on the side. From the tandoor, the chicken tikka is good, as are the lamb chops and the malai kaba, chicken tenders marinated first in yogurt. The breads are good. I like the oily, garlicky naan, served warm, and the lach partha, flaky from much butter in the recipe. For main courses, try the vindaloo and ask for it hot; they may oblige. Vegetarians, of course, have a lot of good options here as well. They have no liquor license but offer lassi, chai, and a good assortment of soda and fruit-based drinks. Amidst all the bars, horrible restaurants, and assorted retail nonsense on this strip of Bleecker, Indian Taj is a keeper.

Insieme

212-582-1310
**777 Seventh Avenue,
at 51st Street**
Casual to dressy
Reservations
Moderate to expensive
All major credit cards accepted
Dinner Monday–Saturday
1 train to 50th Street station;
N, R, W trains to 49th Street
station

Although the talents behind Insieme are the same team that created and run Hearth downtown, I prefer the food at Insieme. My first meal there, just a few months after they opened in 2007, was one of the best I had had anywhere in New York that year. The space on the Seventh Avenue side of the Michelangelo Hotel had previously been an outpost of the Cipriani restaurants, and then Lemoncello, which I never had a chance or inclination to visit. This stretch of Seventh Avenue, really an extension of Times Square north, is heavily populated year round by tourists, with many hotels, including the giant Hilton, Marriott, and Sheraton, to name just a few, located steps away. It's also a convenient area, with many offices nearby, and in the north end of the theater district. The chef is Marco Canora, and his business partner, who works the floor and oversees the beverage program, is Paul Grieco. The room is adequate, nothing special, a bit on the bland side, but comfortable, a long beige rectangle with curtained windows lining the walls at street level and nice recessed lighting. A small bar anchors one end, and the tables, while a bit cramped, still allow a degree of privacy.

The menu is divided into two distinct sections, one traditional, the other contemporary. After several visits, I favor the traditional menu, but frankly it's hard to find a missed step on either side. From the traditional side, the fine Mediterranean fish rouget arrives marinated and cured, skin on, with pickled vegetables, excellent olive oil, and sprinkled with sea salt. Another selection from this menu was a beautiful hand-cut beef tartare, the meat well oiled and spread into a long thin rectangle, the meat flavor enhanced with the addition of a fine dice of porcini, seasoned with sea salt, cracked pepper, and minced chervil, the plate garnished with a half dozen paper-thin toasted slices of a good thin roll. From the contemporary side, a lovely starter billed as fish crudo melded dice of raw, lightly marinated salmon belly, hamachi, yellowfin tuna, and Barron Point oysters, tossed together and seasoned with very good olive oil and a touch of salt, and served in an oversized frozen shot glass made from ice. Again from the contemporary side, a chamomile-perfumed farfalle was paired with fresh baby morels, diced sweetbreads, and squash, one of the best pasta dishes I'd had in quite some time. From the modern menu try the lamb four ways, which I hope becomes a classic and stays on the menu. Here you'll get a roasted lamb chop, grilled saddle, braised and pressed breast, and sausage, tossed with more fresh morels, spring garlic, and spiced chard. But the big winner of my first night was the boiled-meat main course with assorted condiments. In a bowl of rich brown broth arrives a breast of organic chicken, perfectly cooked and butter-tender, a piece of beef, rich and meaty, firm, yet tender, and a disk of good sausage, accompanied by small plates containing horseradish cream, salsa verde, and finely diced mustard fruits. For me, the perfectly cooked meats and the rich broth they were served with needed no garnish whatsoever.

At both Hearth and Insieme, the wine lists are excellent documents, offering fine choices in all price ranges. One night during our tasting menu, Grieco selected wines for the table, and when we got the bill, none of the wines, which were all excellent, were over $12 per glass, with many below the $10 level. For dessert, it's hard to pass up fried-to-order bombolini, crisp, warm, light, and delicious. In the spring, opt for anything made with rhubarb. Here it's braised and turned into the filling for a modern "cannoli." Or try the dense orange-flavored ricotta torte (really a cheesecake variation), the simple fresh strawberries with whipped cream, or the chocolate gianduja bar, redolent of hazelnuts and utterly delicious.

As good as this restaurant was at the beginning, it continues to get better and ranks as one of the best Italian eateries in a city of many, offering enough selections, both classic and modern, to please any good palate.

Ippudo NYC

212-388-0088
65 Fourth Avenue, between
9th and 10th Streets
Casual
No reservations
Moderate
Visa, MasterCard
Lunch and dinner seven days
a week
6 train to Astor Place station;
N, R, W trains to 8th Street
station

One of the best ramen houses in New York City, Ippudo is the first U.S. branch of a Japanese institution. It's these kinds of places that I always refer to when arguing how well one can eat in the city for very little money. Good ramen in good broth is a real treat. Past the bar, the main room opens up, with tables at a dining counter, a wall of booths, and larger communal tables scattered on the floor in between. Bright, spacious, noisy, and usually packed, this isn't a date spot or a room for lingering, but what ramen shop is? Where it does deliver is seriously good noodles, fairly priced, starting in the very low teens. The real stars to my mind are the original Shiromaru classic at $13, a rich pork broth studded with good noodles, Berkshire pork belly, shredded cabbage, and scallions, which can be had as is or jacked up with more pork for an extra $3. In colder months, try a new entry rolled out in the fall of 2008, the Kogashi Miso, made with roasted miso that almost smells like truffles. The dark, rich broth is packed with braised pork, spinach, fish cake, and a hard-boiled egg, and is then topped with a good 1/8 inch of a meaty oil slick that adds a whole new layer of richness. Komo Ttsukemen is a noodle dish with no broth. Here the darker wheat-bran based noodles are served cold alongside medium rare, room-temperature sliced duck with a dipping sauce. Not in the mood for soup alone? Try the Saiko-style grilled Berkshire pork glazed in miso, or the decent shrimp tempura. Expect large crowds at peak times, due to the quality-to-price ratio and East Village location. They have beer and sake, and the kitchen is open till 1 AM on weekends.

Jaiya Thai

212-889-1330
396 Third Avenue, between
28th and 29th Streets
Casual
Reservations
Inexpensive to moderate
All major credit cards accepted
Lunch and dinner seven days
a week
6 train to 28th Street station

This place is run by Pok and Wanne Pokpoonpipat, who started out with a place in Queens; they now have a branch out in Hicksville, Long Island, as well. The Murray Hill location is a simple room with Thai art and figurines decorating the off-green walls, which are lit by small sconces. The tables are covered with tablecloths topped by a clean sheet of glass, and the staff are kind and welcoming in typical Thai fashion. The menu has a fair amount of non-Thai dishes that are Indian curries; apparently the Elmhurst location was a favorite of Indians living nearby. That said, the Thai dishes are all for the most part good, and some, especially the curries, can be hotter than one has come to expect in American Thai eateries; it appears that they are more than willing to spice your food per your request.

As is customary, they offer discounted lunch and dinner specials, with limited options, so if you are on a budget, that may be the way to go, and you can still eat well. But I like to order off the menu, so start with the pad Thai here, or any of the good soups. I really liked the one billed as spicy seafood. The steaming hot broth was loaded with shrimp and shellfish and could have been a meal by itself. For mains, the pork with curry paste and string beans was brimming with flavor, as was the shrimp with chili and basil leaves. The seafood selections are good, especially the Thai version of fried squid and peppery hot mussels with fresh chili sauce. Vegetarians will be happy, as there is a large section of the menu devoted to them, including a list of starters, middle courses, and main courses as well.

They have a full bar, but to my taste beer works best with this food. If you order your food spiced hot here, expect to get it that way, and keep an ice cold beer nearby—you may need it.

Jarnac

212-924-3413
328 West 12th Street,
  at Greenwich Street
Casual
Reservations
Moderate
All major credit cards accepted
Dinner seven nights a week
A, C, E, 1, 2, 3 trains to 14th
  Street station; L train to
  Eighth Avenue

There is something very Parisian about this place, partly due to the simple fact that this West Village neighborhood has such a European feel to it, with many old cobblestone streets running at odd angles off the normal grid, and a healthy stock of small older buildings that simply allow more sky to come through. It doesn't hurt either that Jarnac's owner, Tony Powe, a British expat raised in Jarnac, France, had just that idea in mind. This type of restaurant is an increasingly rare bird in New York City these days: a small, intimate neighborhood place serving very decent French food at reasonable prices and with much charm. The chef since opening in 1999 has been Maryann Terillo, a seasoned veteran with loads of experience under her belt. She loves to cook, and it shows.

The menu changes very often and keeps with the seasons and the market. Braises, grills, roasts are on the menu in the winter months; ramps, fava beans, asparagus, and soft-shell crabs herald the spring; chilled soups, mixed salads, tomatoes, and eggplant are paired with simple grills during the summer; and loads of mushrooms, game, and heartier vegetables are back on board throughout the autumn.

In the warmer months, try the velvety creamed carrot soup, accented with ginger and garnished with a dollop of thick Greek yogurt. Billed as a starter but a great light entrée choice is the Jarnac BLT, where thick slabs of Eckerton Farms heirloom tomatoes share the stage with crisped pancetta and arugula on good bread, slathered with a smooth and spicy homemade mayonnaise. In cooler months, the duck rillette is fine spread over toasted baguette, and roasted beets are often available tossed with assorted mixed greens, seasonal beans—favas in the spring, string beans in the summer—and good goat cheese.

I really like the deep-fried soft shells in May and June, at once crispy and sweet at the center, set over broad homemade pasta, tossed simply with fresh tomato and basil chiffonade. Her braised leg of lamb is a treat, a dish we don't do much at home. Here the meat, tender and full-flavored, is served with braised artichokes and Moroccan-style preserved lemons, a good bright accent to the richness of the braising sauce. Bistro classics like duck confit and pan-seared skate with olive tapenade are fine choices, as is the odd dish like fried duck eggs over sautéed wild mushrooms over brioche.

Desserts follow in the same tradition, simple, house-made, and good. Fresh apricots are roasted, which helps concentrate the flavor of this fruit. The accompanying poached figs and vanilla gelato make this dish a winner. The blueberry tart is lovely, as are the peach crumble in the summer and the bread-and-butter pudding with black fig gelato all year long. The wine list starts in the $30 range and offers some good choices from smaller producers around the world, courtesy of the consultant Jonathan Ray. A great little Portuguese red, Herdade de Muge, for $32 works well with the heartier meat dishes, as does the Cusuamo Rosso made from the nero d'Avola grape from Sicily, rich with big soft tannins. In the $40 range for whites, the Sablet 2004 Côtes de Rhône, made with clairette and roussanne grapes, is crisp and clean, with notes of green apple skin. For a few dollars more, the versatile pinot gris, here hailing from Montinore Vineyards in Oregon, has lovely minerality, good crispness, more of the green apple skin melding with grapefruit rind, and pear.

I should mention that they have a very good cognac selection, should you have interest after your meal. Little French bistros like this are getting harder and harder to find in New York, and Jarnac should be on your short list. If you're told there is a two-hour wait at the Spotted Pig just south of here, head to Jarnac. You'll be surprised.

Jean Georges

212-299-3900
1 Central Park West, in the lobby of the Trump Hotel at Columbus Circle
Dressy
Reservations
Expensive
All major credit cards accepted
Lunch and dinner Monday–Friday, dinner Saturday
1, A, C, B, D trains to 59th Street/Columbus Circle station; N, Q, R, W trains to 57th Street station

Jean-Georges Vongerichten, or JG as he's known to insiders, is perhaps the busiest, highest-paid chef on the planet. He has dozens of restaurants bearing his various brand names, and projects working, or in the works, on nearly every continent. While he was born and raised in Alsace, France, the German quadrant of that country, his palate and culinary sensibility veer toward Asia, where in his younger days he spent a good deal of time working as an executive chef in major hotels in Bangkok, Singapore, and Hong Kong. He also worked for the great French chef Louis Outhier in the south of France. Outhier's restaurant, L'Oasis, in La Napoule, just outside Cannes, was one of the great kitchens in its day, and Outhier himself was a disciple of that modern culinary giant, chef Fernand Point. But despite all that Frenchness in his resume, the food at Jean Georges is the least French of all the great New York restaurants. Rattle off the list for yourself: Per Se, Bernardin, Daniel, Ducasse, Bouley, Le Cirque; in all these kitchens, the shadow of Escoffier looms large. But at Jean Georges, the food is much less anchored in that tradition and is noticeably lighter and cleaner. Broths are used in place of rich sauces, and spices, chile peppers, and deft use of citrus notes define flavors more than butter, meat-based sauces, and wine reductions.

He evolved gradually to this style of cooking after he arrived in New York via Boston. I remember the food at his restaurant Lafayette in the old Drake Swiss Hotel, where he first earned four stars from the *New York Times*, and was known in those days to cook everything—soups, stocks, sauces, even blanching his vegetables—in Evian water, claiming he could taste the difference; they went through truckloads of the stuff. These days, his best restaurant is far and away this signature location on Columbus Circle. The entrance is off Central Park West, and the restaurant is divided into two rooms, really two different restaurants: the first and more casual, arranged around the bar area, is Nougatine. Past that, facing the Time Warner Building, is Jean Georges proper. The room was redone in 2007 and is spacious and comfortable, well lit by day from the large south-facing windows, and softly lit at night from the strange, large light installation hanging from the center of the ceiling, part H. G. Wells, part Calder.

If you're looking for bargains, they have a weekday lunch special, a three-course $28 menu with smaller portions of certain menu items, but nonetheless identical food at a great price. The dinner menu is prix fixe at $98 for four courses, with two other tasting menus for $148: one is dubbed the Jean Georges menu, essentially a greatest hits compilation, the other is seasonal, and both are seven-course flights.

A good starting point may be the dish billed as yellowfin tuna ribbons. Normally I have no interest in these tuna tartare variations, but this one is truly great. Tuna from the center of the loin is cut in long strands like percatelli pasta and tossed in an oil-based mix including a very good sesame oil and thinly sliced radish. It's then topped with scoops of avocado tableside, and a soy-based vinaigrette redolent of fresh ginger is poured around the bottom of the bowl, a great mix of flavor and texture. This idea of having beautiful presentations plated and set before you that you then must stir together before you eat them is unique to this restaurant. In truth, if you were to taste each element on the plate by itself, they would be just okay, but when mixed on the plate and taken as a whole, the flavors coalesce and just explode. The best example of this may be the dish of sea trout sashimi. It arrives in a tall, narrow soup bowl. One side is painted a bright green, rising from the bottom to the top; this is the dill puree. At the bottom you'll find diced, raw sea trout, then a scoop of red trout eggs, some horseradish, a dollop of yellow lemon foam, and squiggles of sea trout skin that, once removed from the fish, were rolled like a cigar, frozen, then sliced in little rings and flash-fried until crisp. Each item alone is really nothing special, but when you stir it all up and take a taste, wham! There it goes. . . lemon and salt, crunch and herbal relief, fish meat and horseradish—it's all balance and angles, and as such a marvel.

Perhaps the most traditional item on the appetizer side is the foie gras terrine, but not so fast. Here the terrine is formed and cured, and then shaped in a PVC pipe, forced out, cut into small towers set atop a matching thin round of brioche, then topped with turbinado sugar and brûléed with a blowtorch before being plated with a spoonful of sweet-and-sour dried cherry compote, candied pistachios, and white port gelée. Plump Santa Barbara sea urchins are set atop black bread, stacked three to an order, topped with a single slice of jalapeño and a splash of yuzu, and arrive like some fancy offering from a New Age appetizing store.

The fish here for the most part are cooked on a plancha. Gulf shrimp are wrapped in smoky bacon, set atop the planche, and served with a papaya mustard, really more a house-made chutney. Arctic char is sautéed, then slow-cooked at low temperature before being plated next to a schmear of miso-laced potato puree, and sauced with a Granny Smith apple jalapeño broth, the sweet hot apple broth contrasting well with the rich fatty fish. Sweetbreads are dusted with licorice powder, pan-seared and braised, then served with a grilled pear and a sauce made from brown butter and fresh lemon juice. The squab dish here is essentially a remake of the classic duck à l'orange, done Jean Georges style. First the bird is deboned, lightly smoked, and seasoned with cardamom and five-spice mix. Then it is cooked under a salamander, skin side up, and plated over diamond-shaped raw Asian pears and candied tamarind, all served with a sauce, really a broth, redolent of star anise—modern, clean, light, and bursting with flavor.

Desserts are courtesy of the brilliant pastry chef Johnny Iuzzini, and are ordered by theme. If you want chocolate, you'll get it four ways on four small plates set in quadrants. Strawberries in season, ditto. This methodology allows Johnny to play, experiment, and have fun. So you never tire of one big thing, one taste sensation, and each construct tends to play off the other, based upon texture, flavors, temperature, and style. The service staff is very good, professional but relaxed, and the wine list is excellent and not overbearing. The open kitchen and the cooks are not quite as polished as in the other great New York kitchens. With all the projects JG has going on, occasionally he hires a line cook who needs more time—mistakes do happen here. But the core team has been with him for years, and of all the great New York restaurants, this one is by far the most relaxed and the least pretentious. It sends out food that is stylistically apart from everyone else's and international in reach, and as such is well worth multiple visits.

J. G. Melon

212-744-0585
1291 Third Avenue, between 74th and 75th Streets
Casual
No reservations
Moderate
Cash only
Seven days a week 11 AM–4 AM
6 train to 77th Street station

Oh yeah, I can see the eyes rolling already. "Why in the world did he include this place in his book?" I know, I know, this is after all a famed preppy watering hole for overprivileged Upper East Side frat boys and their crew. But it's been around a while, has a classic neighborhood bar feel to it, and still serves some darn good burgers. And please note I'm not writing this review at 3 AM after a night out binge drinking. Fact: great burgers are now taken seriously in New York culinary and foodie circles, and many a very good chef has opened or considered opening a burger joint. Think Shake Shack, BLT Burger, BRGR, and Pop Burger. Essentially what I'm getting at is this: if Corner Bistro has legions of fans (and I'm not sure the burgers are worth anywhere near all that praise) and that burger joint in the Parker Meridien Hotel gets top honors all the time (which I'll never, ever understand), then for that reason alone, J. G. Melon deserves its props for what are still good juicy burgers, very decent cottage fries, and a good selection of cold beer to wash it all down with.

The room is smallish, long and narrow, the old tin ceiling a nice touch. The seating is minimal, mostly on stools, and the tables are cramped, so most nights and lunchtimes, it's very crowded with a line out the door. The crowd varies depending on the time of day, from the young and the younger to well-dressed middle-aged and gray-haired couples who enjoy the standard (though not especially inspiring) American bar food menu served here, preceded by the very good bloody Marys. As far as burgers go, and I'll stop there, you can do far worse, so if you're in the area and that's what you crave, you'll be rewarded.

Jimmy's No. 43

212-982-3006
43 East 7th Street, between Second and Third Avenues
Casual
Reservations
Moderate
All major cards
Bar (with snacks) seven days a week noon until late; full menu available after 5:30 PM
6 train to Astor Place station; N, R, W trains to 8th Street station

The Jimmy in question is the chef-proprietor, Jimmy Carbone, who presides most nights over a series of individual electric hot plates that are all he has to cook with, except a few convection ovens out back The kitchen is minuscule. The space (or should I say spaces) spreads out like some odd haunted house, reaching through narrow halls and arched doorways. The décor, if one could call it that, is randomly ironic. The crowd skews young—after all, the place is in the East Village   and the beers and food are pretty darn decent. If you didn't know the place was here you'd pass it by, as you need to descend down a flight of steps to enter the main bar room. Here we have another case of an ambitious young chef who wanted a place in Manhattan, was willing to make any space work, and in this case succeeded.

The formula is good—simple, hearty dishes, meat-centric and braise-heavy—but what did you expect to come off electric hot plates? I was here one night for a bacon, cheese, and beer tasting. All the rooms were full when, out of nowhere, a fire department enforcement officer walked in and closed it for some sort of fire code violations. It remained closed for over a week until they could sort things out. This is a tough town to run a business in.

Back to the food. You'll find homey dishes like shepherd's pie topped with grits, beef stew made with Victory India pale ale, cheddar and corn soup, braised heritage-breed Violet Hill pork belly, veal cheeks, oxtail stew, razor clams steamed in sake, a salad made from faro tossed with radicchio and Moroccan-style preserved lemons, salumi plates garnished with excellent pickled vegetables courtesy of Rick's Picks, sliders with ground meat from grass-fed cattle, and a good cheese plate that changes nightly.

The beer list is awesome. On draft they usually offer a dozen choices, many from small breweries such as Six Point, High and Mighty, Tröegs, Steenbrugge, Brooklyn Brewery, and Young's. These can be had in small pilsner glasses, half-liter steins, 13-ounce Belgian goblets, pints, or 20-ounce UK imperials. For bottled choices, you'll find more than half a dozen from Belgium alone, with a small assortment from Germany, France, Italy, the UK, and the USA, including a few large bottles like the fabulous ⅗-liter Scotch ale from Smuttynose, and a few "vintage" brews. All in all, this is a good place for the post-college crowd to commune, grow up, and develop good palates trained on great beers paired with very decent market-driven gastropub offerings from one of New York's least likely kitchens.

Joe Jr. Restaurant (THIRD AVENUE)

212-473-5150
167 Third Avenue, between 15th and 16th Streets
Casual
No reservations
Inexpensive
All major credit cards accepted
Seven days a week 6 AM–midnight
4, 5, 6, L, N, Q, R, W trains to 14th Street/Union Square station; L train to Third Avenue station

There are two Joe Jr.'s. A long time ago they used to have the same owner, but no more. That said, what hasn't changed is the old-time diner/coffee shop quality offered at both. New York City used to have more diners and coffee shops before the real estate market went ballistic. Moondance, a longtime SoHo staple, was sold for the ground it sat on; it was moved lock, stock, and barrel and is now in Wyoming somewhere. Many others have been razed or converted to other uses. People's tastes have changed as well in this town. Delis are now nearly extinct, and places like Joe's seem more fit as location shoots for an *Odd Couple* episode: Felix pays the check, gathers his umbrella, walks out, and hails a passing Checker.

The food is what it should be, the coffee brewed weak and kept hot too long, the eggs cooked close to right, the bacon some days crisp and other days not really. The overall appeal is its classic New York coffee shop vibe: a very friendly staff, prices that are affordable to most everyone, and, I suppose, value in a nutshell. The eggs and omelets are all between $5 and $7, including potatoes and toast. Nearly every sandwich, from the tuna melt to the classic jelly and cream cheese, are under $5, triple-deckers under $8. The burgers are decent, better than many that get a lot of press these days. Broiled or fried chicken, chopped steak, and calf's liver entrees are under $10, and the most expensive item on the menu is the $15 Romanian steak. If you live nearby, if you're shopping in Union Square and want to avoid the yuppie hangouts nearby, or perhaps if you find yourself stumbling out of a concert at Irving Plaza before midnight, give Joe Jr. a try; it delivers grandly on the reliable coffee shop promise.

Joe Jr. (SIXTH AVENUE)

212-924-5220
482 Sixth Avenue,
   at 12th Street
Casual
No reservations
Inexpensive
All major credit cards accepted
Seven days a week 6 AM–1 AM
1, 2, 3, F, V trains to 14th Street
   station; L train to Sixth
   Avenue station

I'd walked right past this coffee shop a hundred times, I must confess, between picking up bagels at Murray's just a block north and then heading down to Jefferson Market or Citarella for more goodies. Then one day I thought, "I have to try this place." There are great espresso bars nearby, and many very good restaurants, but once in a while it's hard to pass up a great coffee shop. I also worry that places like Joe Jr., which seemingly have been here forever, are going the way of the dinosaur. Soon they will exist only in memory. Like Bonbonnière nearby, but maybe better, this shop is a classic. The eggs and omelets, pancakes, or French toast variations will run you between $5 and $10 with sides and weak coffee. They serve Belgian waffles all day long if you have serious munchies.

For a great lunch or light dinner, the London broil sandwich is a bargain at under $10. I ask you, when was the last time you had a cream cheese sandwich served on date nut bread? Like the other Joe Jr., they serve real sardines here, surely a canned fish in need of a comeback. Sardines are good for you and inexpensive, and back in the day, every coffee and sandwich shop had them. (Consumption back in the 1960s was nearly a million cans a year in the New York market.) I love them on white or rye, with a little onion, some lettuce, and good mustard. For under $12 you can have an open-faced hot sandwich of sliced Romanian steak with potatoes and brown gravy, plus vegetables or a half cup of soup. All the sandwiches, including the triple-deckers and the Reuben, are under $10. The burger list is extensive and priced between $5 and $10 a pop with fries. Hot meat plates are retro to the bone: liver with bacon and onions, London broil with mushroom gravy, and roast turkey with cranberry sauce. To this add those big salads with all sorts of chopped-up cheese and ham, and even chocolate pudding or very good rice pudding for dessert. I hope this place never closes.

John's of Bleecker Street

212-243-1680
278 Bleecker Street, between
Morton Street and
Seventh Avenue South
Casual
No reservations
Moderate
Cash only
Lunch and dinner seven days
a week
1 train to Christopher Street
station; A, C, E, B, D, F, V trains
to West 4th Street station

A Greenwich Village institution that still after all these years makes some very decent pizza pie. Is it the best? No, not by a long shot. The goalposts have moved, and places like Una Pizzeria Napoletana and others now make some of the best pizza in the world right here in New York. But John's, often dismissed by bloggers and the press, still turns out hundreds of nice, charred thin-crust pies with good toppings every day, day after day. The large pizzas start at $14 and are enough at 8 slices to feed two hungry adults. The décor is vintage chic but authentic. The walls are adorned with what never passed as art but years later still amuses: one scene depicts rowboats in what appears to be a cavern, while another of the bay of Naples seems still unfinished. The wooden banquettes are covered with knife carvings, people's initials, more "art" renderings of this and that (some not mentionable in mixed company), and graffiti, although someone did a nice bird portrait carved in the back of the wooden chairs by the front door.

I've never had anything other than the pizza here, so I can recommend only that, with soda or beer, but for the most part that's enough. It is a pizzeria, after all. The staff is nice, a bit quirky, but this is the Village, so don't mind if they are a bit brusque on occasion; it's part of the flavor of the place. But the pies, again, are good—better than good, in fact, as they are consistently fully cooked through, with a good char on the bottom and the outer circle of dough. The tomato sauce is clean-tasting and the toppings for the most part of decent quality as well. Could the dough have more gluten development and be chewier? Yeah, sure, but that aside, as these things go, it's a decent choice and a neighborhood classic.

Katz's Delicatessen

212-254-2246
205 East Houston Street,
at Ludlow Street
Casual
No reservations
Inexpensive to moderate
All major credit cards accepted
Monday–Tuesday 8 AM–9:45 PM,
Wednesday–Thursday 8 AM–
10:45 PM, Friday–Saturday
8 AM–2:45 AM, Sunday 8 AM–
10:45 PM.
F, V trains to Second Avenue
station

Mention delis and every New Yorker has an opinion. While some believe that Katz's is way overrated, I find the pastrami here consistently some of the best in New York. I've always loved delis. My first restaurant job was at Hal Willner's father's deli, Hymie's, in Merion, Pennsylvania. At 13 I was hired as a bus boy, and when a prep cook called in sick I was promoted. My early memories of laying out deli trays with Murray the caterer and snacking on excellent nova, sable, and whitefish are a big part of the reason I got into the restaurant business in the first place. Katz's has been in business since 1888, and for most of that time it's been right here on the corner of Houston and Ludlow. The Lower East Side of Manhattan was a haven for newly arriving Jewish immigrants in the early 1900s and historically has been home to many great delis. That tradition would continue through the 1970s, but then slowly, one by one, they started closing. Bernstein's on Essex Street went, followed by Ratner's, and then in 2006 the 2nd Avenue Deli closed (though it since reopened on East 33rd Street). Of all those famous names in the area, only Katz's and Russ and Daughters survived. The dining room here is much bigger than the one at the 2nd Avenue Deli, but the menu is much smaller, with the primary focus on sandwiches. I'd guess that 90% of the sales here are pastrami, corned beef, brisket, or hot dogs. I can venture up to midtown for classics like cholent, picha, stuffed derma, and the legendary chicken in the pot at 2nd Avenue, but should I want a great deli sandwich downtown, I come straight here.

Entering Katz's is like stepping into a time warp. It's an old-style cafeteria. There are two ways to order. You can sit and ask for a menu and a waiter, but who does that? Or you take a ticket from the fellow working the door, approach the long counter, and get in one of the lines. I like the ritual here—you join dozens of others waiting in line, looking up at the menu board. When you order one of the hot sliced meat sandwiches, they hand-slice the meat right in front of you, and even give you a piece or two to nibble on while you're waiting. Eventually you hand the guy behind the counter your card, and they mark on it what you ate: one sandwich, one soda, one order of fries, etc. You then take your tray, find a table with some free seats, eat, and pay on the way out after the cashier reads your card. You can tip the countermen if you want; it's a nice idea, and there's always a cup with a few bills in it as a suggestion. I once asked the counter guy at Carnegie if I could taste the pastrami while I was waiting, and he said, "No, you kidding? We don't give away free food here." Needless to say, I didn't go back for well over a year after that. But here they give you a taste and make you feel right at home.

To the right are hot dogs, knoblewurst, knockwurst, and chili. The grilled hot dogs are excellent, with a nice snap when you bite into them. Garnished with a little mustard and sauerkraut, they're a perfect snack. Or ignore your doctor's advice and go for the hefty knoblewurst. This is a classic garlic sausage split, grilled, and eaten on a roll with a schmear of mustard. While they do have soups, salads, and an assortment of cold sandwiches, don't bother. Stick with the hot dogs, wurst, pastrami, corned beef, brisket, or Reuben. They still have some of the best cured meats in

New York. Unlike Carnegie uptown, the portions here aren't way too big. Come hungry and you can finish your sandwich, nibble on a good sour pickle, wash it all down with a Cel-ray, and be on your way for well under $20 per person.

The crowd is always a great mix, composed of the regulars, usually big overweight guys of all races and nationalities, mixed with local Chinese families, students, tourists, and suburbanites who drive in for a sandwich and an experience they can't get anyplace else.

Keens Steakhouse

212-947-3636
72 West 36th Street, between Fifth and Sixth Avenues
Casual
Reservations
Expensive
All major credit cards accepted
Lunch and dinner Monday–Friday, dinner Saturday and Sunday
1, 2, 3, B, D, F, V, N, Q, R, W trains to 34th Street station

With the steakhouse craze in full bloom, it's easy to forget about places such as Keens, which has been going about this steak and chop business since 1885 and even before that as part of the Lambs club. That and the fact that these days, the neighborhood around West 36th Street has seen so many changes since the place first opened, and functions now as the northern boundary of Manhattan's Koreatown.

But close your eyes and think back to the turn of the 20th century, when places like this all over New York were open, but to men only. In 1901 a young lady who stood her ground right here at Keens won women the right to eat at this establishment alongside the men; that young lady with no shortage of gumption was Lillie Langtry. In the modern world of fancy-pants steakhouses with big-name publicists, it's easy to overlook this place, and that would be a shame. In fact, many of the newer chains and modern steakhouses should come spend some time here and see how it should be done. I should mention that the owner is a NYC physician turned restaurateur who also runs Elephant & Castle in the Village as well as Noho Star downtown, and that the chef is a very serious cook who spent a good deal of time working with Barry Wine at the four-star Quilted Giraffe as part of his training.

The steaks here are very good, but steaks vary in the best of places now, as these days prime dry-aged meat is scarce, to say the least, and everybody is having trouble getting the best cuts. So it is a problem to judge any steakhouse by one or two meals or one or two steaks, as they are hit-and-miss even at the best places. But here they do use only prime meat. The chef selects it himself at his packer's place in the Bronx and also oversees the aging of the meat on premises.

Keens sits on the south side of the block in a low-slung three-story building with the restaurant and bar spreading out over what appears were several contiguous buildings. The ceiling is low and hung with antique stemmed churchwarden pipes, the woodwork is really old, and the floors are of various materials, including well-worn tiles as you approach the bar and lounge to the far right. All of the rooms upstairs and down are perfectly good places to eat, with nary a bad table in the house. The staff is all seasoned, the drinks are big and strong, and the value is there. This is a seriously good steakhouse.

If it's steak you must have, be my guest. They can range from good to excellent, depending always on the carcass; that's just the way it is. I'd suggest you try instead the signature mutton chops. While no longer mutton, they are big, juicy, flavorful Colorado lamb chops with the rib flap meat left on, hanging down off the sides like lamb bacon, and are delicious. Or for a real knockout, order the roast beef hash off the pub menu for a mere $16.50. It just may be the best in the city, and a classic dish to boot. It arrives a completely crisped and golden brown orb, seared fully from long cooking in cast iron, chunks of potato and large chunks of prime rib melded together by butter and fat. This is the hash of your dreams.

For starters, the oysters Rockefeller are good, as are any of the oysters on the half shell. The crab cakes are decent too, and I actually enjoy the silly wedge salads slathered in dressing. Iceberg lettuce is utterly delicious in certain applications, and with a few ounces of good thousand island or blue cheese dressing, it's perfect.

The steaks are the usual varieties: strip, porterhouse, filet mignon, and prime rib, which I really like in spite of all the foodies who claim it to be a silly cut. Prime rib, like all standing carved roasts, has its appeal in its rich beefy flavor and lack of outer char. Juicy, tender, and with the right amount of deckle, it's utterly delicious swimming in the au jus sauce. Seafood . . . well, order it if you must. The sides here aren't bad either. Try the good creamed spinach, sautéed escarole, or carrots in brown butter (Keens is only place I know that has this dish) just in case you're not getting enough cholesterol from the protein side.

The wine list is short and could be better; the domestic selection is better than the Old World offerings. For dessert, try the red berry bibble, the chocolate cake courtesy of Lady M Confections, the Iowa caramel custard, or, if you can manage it, the excellent butterscotch sundae. This classic New York steakhouse is woefully overlooked by foodies, bloggers, and the press in general and most certainly deserves a visit.

Burgers

New York has always had decent burger options, historically found in good neighborhood bars, steakhouses, diners, and independent chains that have concentrated on burgers. such as Jackson Hole and the well-named Burger Heaven. Of late, serious chefs have come to reconsider this quintessential American sandwich for its culinary possibilities and price-to-pleasure ratio, which these days makes sense. To that end, I've listed a selection of the best burgers in town, some found at places that just do burgers, many coming out of kitchens that have talented chefs in charge, serving seriously great burgers to match.

But let's define a burger. I'm not talking about blending braised short ribs with foie gras or dotting ground ribeye with diced black truffles. That's not a burger. A burger is simply a well-seasoned ground meat patty either cooked on a flat-top griddle or grilled over a flame or under a radiant-heat broiler, and served on a soft bun with condiments. Cheese is optional. The essence of any burger is the ground meat used in its preparation. A few wholesale meat distributors have made ground meat mixes a house specialty. La Frieda Meats is one. Operating 24 hours a day, this third-generation family-run business custom-grinds blends for many of the best burgers in town. Historically burger meat was just a simple mix of ground chuck with fat added in particular ratios and sold on that basis: 80% meat and 20% fat, or for leaner burgers, 85% meat and 15% fat. These days ground chuck may still be the base, but for their custom blends, La Frieda adds a percentage of ground brisket, short ribs, aged ribeye cap meat, hanger steak, beef cheek, and bavette cut. Some chefs will add pork fatback and even ground lamb to the mix in search of the perfect burger. These meat grinds and the burgers made from them are a vast improvement over the inferior and less expensive commodity ground meat found in the supermarket and used by many less ambitious establishments.

Anthos, 36 West 52nd Street, 212-582-6900: lunch menu only, unconventional, made with seasoned ground lamb and feta cheese, $20.

Big Nick's, 2175 Broadway, at 77th Street, 212-362-9238: old-school Greek diner with a 10-page menu, open 23 hours a day, great burgers starting at $9.25.

Blue 9, 92 Third Avenue, between 12th and 13th Streets, 212-979-0053: old-school and cheap, the burgers here start at $3.30.

Blue Smoke, 116 East 27th Street, 212-447-7733: custom-ground meat from La Frieda, $11.95.

Brgr, 287 Seventh Avenue, between 26th and 27th Streets, 212-488-7500: ground meat from naturally raised cattle, burgers starting at $7.

Café Cluny, 284 West 12th Street, 212-255-6900: custom-ground meat from La Frieda, lunch or brunch, $15.

City Burger, 1410 Broadway at 39th Street, 212-997-7770: offers custom-ground Black Label La Frieda burgers made from prime dry-aged meat and trim for $11.99, regular ground meat for $4.95.

City Hall, 131 Duane Street, 212-227-7777: custom-ground meat from La Frieda on a house-made onion bun, $16.

Corner Bistro, 331 West 4th Street, 212-242-9503: custom-ground meat from Ottomanelli, $5.50, $6.50 for the famed Bistro burger with bacon and cheese.

Five Napkin Burger, 630 Ninth Avenue, between 44th and 45th Streets, 212-757-2277: great burgers starting at $4.95.

Irving Mill, 116 East 16th Street, 212-254-1600: ground beef with pork fatback added, $16.

Island Burgers and Shakes, 766 Ninth Avenue, between 51st and 52nd Streets, 212-307-7934: loads of burger variations and toppings, with a basic burger starting at $6.75.

Keens, 73 West 36th Street, 212-947-3636: available only at the bar from the pub menu, $15.

The Little Owl, 90 Bedford Street, at Grove Street, 212-741-4695: custom-ground meat from La Frieda, offered as a bacon cheeseburger, $16.

Marc Forgione, 134 Reade Street, 212-941-9401: custom-ground meat from La Frieda, with a lot of hanger steak meat incorporated, $14.95.

Market Table, 54 Carmine Street, off Bedford Street, 212-255-2100: custom-ground meat from La Frieda, cheeseburger $16.

Ottomanelli Grill, 1424 Lexington Avenue at 93rd Street, 212-426-6886: an 8-ounce patty for $5.95.

Patisserie des Ambassades, 161 West 22nd Street, 212-255-5101: beef burger with cheese and a fried egg, $8.

P. J. Clarke's, 915 Third Avenue, at 55th Street (and elsewhere), 212-317-1616: starting at $8.90.

Pop Burger, 58-60 Ninth Avenue, between 14th and 15th Streets, 212-414-8686: bite-sized, served in pairs for $6, excellent portobello veggie burger.

Prune, 54 East 1st Street, 212-677-6221: made from ground lamb, served on an English muffin, $12.

Rue 57, 60 West 57th Street, corner of Sixth Avenue, 212-307-5656: custom-ground dry-aged meat from La Frieda, on a ciabatta bun with Roquefort cheese, $13.95.

Sassy's Sliders, 1530 Third Avenue, at 86th Street, 212-828-6900: old-school malt shop, bite-sized, made of beef, turkey, or veggie, starting at $1.09 apiece.

Shake Shack, Madison Square Park, Broadway and 23rd Street (and elsewhere), 212-889-6600: custom-ground meat from La Frieda, starting at $4.75.

The Spotted Pig, 314 West 11th Street, at Greenwich Street, 212-620-0393: custom-ground meat from La Frieda, with blue cheese, $17.

The Stoned Crow, 85 Washington Place, off Sixth Avenue, 212-677-4022: a subterranean NYU bar hangout with pool table, burger with cheese, $12.

Tavern on Jane, 31 Eighth Avenue, at Jane Street, 212-675-2526: an 8-ounce patty for $9.

Telepan, 72 West 69th Street, 212-580-4300: offered as part of the $22 two-course lunch or brunch menu.

The Waverly Inn, 16 Bank Street, at Waverly Place, 212-243-7900: best at lunch or early dinner when tables can be had, a burger for $13.

Wollensky's Grill, 201 East 49th Street, at Third Avenue, 212-753-0444: $16.

Kyo Ya

212-982-4140

94 East 7th Street, between
First Avenue and Avenue A,
downstairs

Casual

Reservations

Moderate to expensive

All major cards

Lunch and dinner Monday–
Friday, Saturday dinner only

F, V trains to Second Avenue
station; 6 train to Astor Place
station

I was tipped off about this place by a few Japanese ex-pats who know I love good food, otherwise I would have never found it. It's in the basement space of a small tenement, with no signage as best I can tell. Once inside, the space is clean, neat, and minimally decorated, and the staff polite and helpful and perhaps a little stiff, but this is, after all, a Japanese place, in spite of the East Village address.

The menu combines the small dishes and large variety found in the best izakaya places around town, but here the cooking is more refined. The ingredients seem pristine, and they offer a 10-course minimum kaiseki menu that must be ordered at least a day in advance, featuring imported hard-to-find Japanese specialties. From the cold appetizer side, try the dish billed as yoba and uni Yoshino style. It arrives in a small white ceramic bowl containing a fresh, clean-tasting, custard-like lobe of sea urchin set atop a tofu skin in a pool of clear, pleasant broth garnished with julienned black seaweed—great textures and flavors that play well off each other, minimalist with just the right balance. Another starter had sliced soy-braised duck, glazed and shimmering, the salty sweet soy glaze playing well off the fatty duck skin and meat. Off the hot side, an appetizer of Berkshire pork belly, perhaps the most popular meat of the year around town, was slow-braised and sliced, served in the dark brown, fat-glossed braising liquid, topped with a few slow-cooked wild white mushrooms with small caps on long stems. Mushroom tempura was great too, crisp, greaseless, and tasting of strong fresh fungus, salted on the way out of the kitchen.

For mains off a special list, we had a plate featuring a variety of sea urchin, Californian and Japanese origin, with several species of tuna sashimi and tuna belly. Though black cod cooked in miso may seem ubiquitous these days, when done well, as it was here, it is a perfect pairing, the soft, silky, fatty, somewhat bland West Coast fish enriched by the miso marinade and glaze. The cod is sliced in small pieces and served three or four per serving atop a long light green leaf set on a beige ceramic plate. Delicious and on the light side, a dish billed as seasonal fish netsuke offers a mix of seafood, slow-cooked and served in a faintly sweet soy-based poaching liquid; I love good, fresh fish and found this delicious. I am a huge fan of monkfish liver, the foie gras of the sea, and here it comes just cooked, warm and medium-rare against a sauce that serves as a textural and flavor foil, made from shredded daikon radish. Monkfish appears again, this time the tail meat cut into small medallions and flash-fried, plated with a variety of toppings and dipping sauce.

For dessert, try the black sesame ice cream, three small quenelles served with a few shortbread-style cookies, or the mochi and custard bowl. They have a good selection of sake and beer, both perfectly matched to the food. So the fish is as fresh as you'll find anywhere in town and can be had simmered, glazed, or fried, the meats are all of fine pedigree, the cooking across the board is very well executed and precise, and the seasonings are accurate. All in all, this is one of my favorite Japanese places in town.

L'Absinthe

212-794-4950
227 East 67th Street, between Second and Third Avenues
Dress well, but no jackets required
Reservations
Expensive
All major credit cards accepted
Lunch and dinner Monday–Friday, brunch and dinner Saturday and Sunday
6 train to 68th Street station

After the closures of Lutece, La Caravelle, and LCB Brasserie, restaurants offering traditional French cooking became scarce in New York. Then in the spring of 2008, Alain Ducasse opened Benoit, and the Serafina group brought us Brasserie Cognac. But when I'm looking for an upscale alternative to the bistros and brasseries around town, I still turn to L'Absinthe, which may be the best of them all. Drawing on the lineage of New York's French restaurants from the previous generation, places such as Le Pavillon, Lutèce, La Côte Basque, and La Caravelle, L'Absinthe remains stalwart, part of a shrinking breed serving classical cuisine, run by French chefs who are in the kitchen each and every day for each service. It's no surprise here that the chef-owner, Jean-Michel Bergougnoux, spent over a decade working with André Soltner at Lutèce, who, like Jean-Michel, lived directly above the store. Sad to say, these old-school French restaurants have fallen out of fashion with today's dining public. Yet here on 67th Street, on the well-heeled Upper East Side, there are enough fans of this food to keep the chef busy every day for lunch and dinner.

The noon seating is a typical Upper East Side mix: the ladies-who-lunch crowd, well-dressed, tan, and fit, sharing the room with business types from nearby midtown offices. The menu, in a nod to the times, offers a good selection of lighter choices, mixed in with the typical offerings of hearty fare one would expect at a place like this. Try the Provençal-influenced plate of grilled sardines with marinated white anchovies, shards of zucchini, and sun-dried tomato, bathed in an arugula vinaigrette. Or opt for the à la carte chilled seafood platters, assembled from your choice of East or West Coast oysters, clams, imported French crevettes grises when available, periwinkles, whelks cooked in their shells, razor clams, lobster, and cooked mussels. The warm lobster tart with crisped chorizo, set in a pool of pesto-enriched lobster emulsion, for some may be a meal in itself.

Among lunch entree choices, you'll find very good lamb chops served with addictive goat cheese fritters, roast striped bass with béarnaise sauce, assorted omelets (who does that anymore?), croque-monsieur with salad, and a very good beef tartare with frites. The dinner menu expands on the lunch menu, with specials, heartier fare, and larger portions. Try the great roast free-range chicken, carved tableside, or the buttery confit of rabbit leg and loin, slow-poached in olive oil and served with artichokes barigoule, black olive tapenade, and braised fresh fava beans. Desserts are house-made, very good, and typical of the genre. There is a classic tarte fine chaude, a thin glazed warm apple tart with vanilla ice cream, the soufflé du jour, and a very good baba soaked in excellent old rum, or for a lighter option, the frozen raspberry parfait.

I come for dinner and usually order off the brasserie classics section of the menu, old-fashioned, hard-to-find dishes that alone are well worth the trip here. In winter months there is often a meat special wrapped in puff pastry à la Wellington. I had a great venison loin steak, topped with a venison and foie gras forcemeat, studded with black truffles, perfectly cooked, sealed in puff pastry and set in a pool of sticky rich sauce périgourdine, a veal stock perfumed with truffle juice, reduced to a glace, then garnished with more black truffles. Jean-Michel's chilled terrine of quail and foie gras, encased in a thin pastry sheet and served with port wine aspic, reminds me of why this type of food was so popular for so long, and also why it is disappearing. Simply put, very few chefs know how to make these kinds of dishes anymore; they require considerable technique, many steps, and a lot of time, the opposite emphasis of most modern restaurant cooking, which focuses on volume and is much less labor- and technique-intensive. Unctuously rich dishes served here, including pied de cochon and tête de veau, are rarely seen on this side of the Atlantic. These specialties showcase the old-fashioned craft of taking humble, inexpensive ingredients such as pigs' trotters and calf's head, basically discarded cuts, and turn them into something fabulous. That was part of the art of the old cuisine; nothing on the animal was wasted, and the most humble ingredients were transformed into the sublime.

La Nacional

212-627-4770
239 West 14th Street,
   between Seventh and
   Eighth Avenues
Casual
Reservations
Moderate
Cash only
Lunch and dinner seven days
   a week
1, 2, 3, A, C, E trains to 14th
   Street station; L train to
   Eighth Avenue station

Let me start by explaining that this really isn't a restaurant in the normal sense of the word. It is the public dining room located on the ground floor of the Spanish Benevolent Society, a non-profit organization founded in 1868. Housed on the north side of 14th Street between Seventh and Eighth Avenues, it's very easy to miss; save a Spanish flag hanging out front, there is no sign for the restaurant. To find it, you step down from the sidewalk and enter the building beneath the normal parlor floor entrance, walk a little ways down a hall, and enter the first of two rooms, a well-lit bar with a TV set and some chairs strewn about. Tara Berman, the opening GM for Bouchon Bakery uptown, first told me about the place, and one night after I had had dinner with Frank Crispo at his restaurant located almost directly across the street, he took me over to La Nacional to introduce me to the chef, Lolo Manso. These days, it is hard to imagine an unknown restaurant of merit in New York, but this may be one of the very few. The tapas are really good and truly authentic. The paella is up there with the best in the city, which makes sense, as this place is open nearly exclusively to feed expat Spaniards living in or traveling through New York.

The bar area usually features soccer matches in season, and the spare dining room located in the front, facing the sidewalk, is fine with me. You eat off polished wood tables and sit on simple chairs in a room done in a shade of ochre with a bluish purple ceiling. The dining room is quieter than the bar, which is usually full of regulars who use the place as a hangout.

Lolo is self-taught. A Spaniard, he came to New York, worked for a while at Solera, and then became the chef here. The food is simple, like Grandma would make—if you had a Spanish grandma who could cook, that is. Start your meal with an order of shrimp in garlic sauce. The shrimp taste of shrimp, and the sauce is redolent of garlic. Sop up any leftover with the bread and you can't go wrong. Fried squid is a personal favorite of mine wherever it is done well, as it is here. The squid rings are crisp and barely floured, arriving golden brown and with a clean, fresh flavor. Or opt for the simple grilled squid, presented cut in sections and doused with good Spanish olive oil and a white wine and parsley reduction. Codfish croquettes are flash-fried, crisp little balls, light, tasty, and well-made, and flavored with the fish and garlic in balance. Filets of white anchovies are set atop thin slices of manchego cheese and topped with a sliver of roasted red pimiento. Paper-thin slices of cured tuna are topped with chopped garlic, pimiento, and onion and bathed in good green olive oil. Anchovies appear again, this time fresh and boneless, lightly battered and fried, paired with quartered artichoke hearts that received the same crisp-fried treatment.

The item billed as a tortilla is actually a frittata of sorts, baked in a large round and then cut into pie-like slices, filled with cooked diced potato and served with two sauces; this in itself could be lunch. Octopus, imported from Spain, comes grilled and doused with olive oil, Spanish paprika, and sea salt on the way out of the kitchen. The flavor, rich and complex, reminded me of good fresh snails. Whole sardines are grilled and of course come in a pool of olive oil, with chopped parsley. The good, simple desserts are house-made. The wine list has improved markedly with the addition of a part-time sommelier/manager. Many good choices can be had for under $10 a serving, with most glasses of red selling for $6 to $7 per glass and whites and rosés at $5. Service is amiable and genuine. Overall, this is a bargain, the food is good, and I just hope it doesn't ever get too busy and change.

La Pizza Fresca

212-598-0141
31 East 20th Street, between Broadway and Park Avenue South
Casual
No reservations
Moderate
All major credit cards accepted
Lunch and dinner Monday–Saturday, dinner Sunday
6, N, R, W trains to 23rd Street station

This place exists in its own unique culinary universe, falling somewhere between a full-blown, full-service pizzeria, which it is, and a very decent Italian restaurant that has a killer wine list. I suppose in my experience I've found that places like this exist with more frequency in and around Naples, but here on our fair shores, it's a rather unique combination. The softly lit room is nice, with exposed brick walls and tables with tablecloths; it's decorated thematically with wine-themed odds and ends, including paper labels, bottles, empty wine crates, spent corks, and the like.

The pizza is done in the Neapolitan style, flash-cooked in a very hot wood-fired oven, the crust thin almost like a cracker and well charred. All the pizzas here are very good, but beyond that, try the pastas, especially the ones with seafood. The chef is Alessandro Cargioli, hailing from Liguria, and his other half in the kitchen is the great pizza maker Alejandro Rivas. They are joined by Massimo Vitino, a native of Lombardy, who oversees the excellent wine program. A sommelier in a pizza place? Now you know why I'm a bit confused, as it is really much more than just a great pizzeria.

You can start the meal with a simple plate of sautéed spinach with garlic and olive oil, or a bowl of steamed mussels and clams in a wine-laced broth. Of the pasta dishes, I love the penne paired with smoked baby eggplant, slices of pancetta, and shards of ricotta salata, or the light gnocchi with Friulian speck in a wild mushroom sauce. They have some decent entrees, like the Niman Ranch pork chop with a balsamic glaze reduction and potato puree, or the chicken breast Milanese-style, lightly breaded and flash-fried over rosemary-laced roasted potatoes.

But you have to have pizza. My favorites are the basic Margherita and the puttanesca, as I love anchovies. They range from just $9 for your basic pie to $19 for the monumental pizza topped with robiola cheese from Alba, Parmigiano, and fontina, plus preserved porcini mushrooms and paper-thin slices of San Daniele prosciutto. The wine list is insane for a place like this; I can think of dozens of restaurants that should come here to learn about balance, with great value in the under-$50 range and fairly priced classics like those super Tuscans from the vineyards of Gaia. The place is under the radar and doesn't have a publicist, but it's as good as or better than many of the bigger, better-known Italian eateries around town.

Lassi

212-675-2688
28 Greenwich Avenue
   between Charles and
   West 10th Streets
Casual
No reservations
Moderate
All major credit cards accepted
Tuesday–Sunday noon–10 PM
A, C, E, B, D, F, V trains to West
   4th Street station; 1 train to
   Christopher Street station

This may be the smallest restaurant in New York, with four—that's right, four—stools. It must exist, I'd surmise, solely for takeout. The storefront is exactly six feet wide and it's easy to miss as you're walking down Greenwich Avenue, so look for the little red neon sign in the window or you'll go right past the place. The name comes from the yogurt-based drink, of which they offer a good variety, made from low-fat yogurt, a little sugar, and natural seasoning. The owner and chef is Heather Carlucci-Rodriguez, who previously had been a pastry chef at Veritas and L'Impero prior to this twist of fate. By way of explanation, she simply loved Indian food and was motivated by cooking with an Indian pastry student named Purva Sudan, whom she once taught while doing summer pastry classes for the ICE on 23rd Street. This meeting of minds and interests gave seed to the idea of creating a down-home, simple, honest family-style Indian eatery unlike any that exists in New York, and to that end she has succeeded. The space is very small, barely 10 feet wide, with brick walls painted white and a small bar counter to the left with those four stools. A long black mirror sits above the bar, and the kitchen and takeout area are to the rear.

The style is Punjabi cooking, which some consider India's finest. The region sits just south of Kashmir, in the far northwestern corner, and dairy, specifically cream, butter, curds, buttermilk, and ghee, is a prominent feature. Wheat, not rice, is the grain of choice, and a specialty is the stuffed paratha breads featured here at Lassi. These are griddle-cooked stuffed flatbreads, and they can be simple and quite delicious. Start with the rajmah chawal, an Indian version of rice and beans. Here the red kidney beans are slow-simmered with onions, tomatoes, green chiles, turmeric, garam masala, and cilantro, and have a lovely aromatic quality. The rice acts as a sponge for the sauce. The paratha, nearly all vegetarian (there's cauliflower, potato, daikon, paneer, or braised goat), are served with boondi raita, chickpea dumplings set over yogurt.

For lunch, they feature a $10 special that includes a tall glass of lassi, a small bowl of the daily soup, and one paratha—quite reasonable, sensible, healthy, and filling. The lassi flavorings vary but usually include mango, coconut, rose, cardamom, coffee, and lemon blossom. If you live in the area, takeout is an option, or try to snag one of the seats and eat the paratha hot off the griddle.

La Taza de Oro

212-243-9946
96 Eighth Avenue, between
   14th and 15th Streets
Casual
No reservations
Inexpensive
Cash only
Monday–Saturday 6 AM–10 PM
A, C, E, 1, 2, 3 trains to 14th
   Street station; L train to
   Eighth Avenue station

One of the neighbors in my building raved to me about this place; he was right on. While this whole neighborhood has gentrified (a fancy Balducci's sits across the street, an HSBC bank is next door), this place sits here as if frozen in time, circa 1965, with prices to match. There is a corrugated tin awning over the sidewalk, painted in the bright colors of the Puerto Rican flag. Way uptown, places like this are more common, but down here, this is really one of the last. The reason the restaurant is still here is that the restaurant owner also owns the building, and that's great news for all of us looking for great authentic ethnic food at bargain prices in Manhattan. It's seemingly always bustling; they do takeout all day long as well. The sound track is salsa, and the menu changes a bit every day but is very big and ambitious, with a long list of daily specials posted in the window. You sit at the bar, or at one of a half dozen tables flanking the wall. At the bar, it helps to speak Spanish, as often the wait staff, especially in the morning, are non-English-speakers. Two eggs any style with bacon, sausage, or ham, alongside a decent version of hash browns, not crispy but soft chunks of potato laced with paprika and bits of onion and pepper, with a cup of coffee, comes to $3.75. The fresh oatmeal is soupy and sweet, and the ham and egg sandwich served on a long thin fresh roll is $2.50—no wonder it's always busy.

The standard menu each day includes variations of pork cutlets, fried, baked, smothered, or braised. Ditto with the chicken, and add crispy, crunchy chicken chicharrón. Just behind the counter, in those lidded hotel pans set in the long steam table each day, you'll find a choice of beef stew, pot roast, braised pigs' feet, excellent ropa vieja (shredded beef), and those chicken and pork variations. I love the mondongo, a rich tomato-laced tripe soup brimming with chunks of that tender offal, alongside large pieces of potato and yucca; it's an acquired taste but delicious. Arroz con calamares, a simple combination of rice cooked with squid, is a meal in itself. All the main-course dishes come with a side of rice, yellow or white, and beans, white or black. A late lunch here for me usually doubles as dinner, and I'm a big eater.

Service is fast and efficient, though no one ever seems rushed. Desserts are simple; the red-topped flan is very good, the rice pudding is very sweet, and I'm a sucker for the coconut cream custard. Sodas are all Latin affairs, flavored with guava, mango, and the like. (They don't serve alcohol.) Equal in import to the food is the fact that this place is such a mainstay for its regular Latino patrons, many of whom work nearby, and the mix of middle-class New Yorkers from the neighborhood who know a good thing when they find it. Everyone seems to know everyone else, and Spanish is the language of the house. The owner is usually up front by the cash register or seated on a sofa by the front window with a few friends, discussing the news of the day. I hope this place never closes, because it's a classic.

Le Bernardin

212-554-1515
155 West 51st Street, between
Sixth and Seventh Avenues
Formal, jackets required
Reservations required
Expensive
All major credit cards accepted
Lunch and dinner Monday-
Friday, dinner Saturday
B, D, F, V trains to 47th–50th
Streets/Rockefeller Center
station; N, R, W trains to
49th Street station; 1 train
to 50th Street station

Le Bernardin is one of the most influential restaurants to have opened in America in the last 50 years. While today in good restaurants all across the country, servers are trained to ask customers how they would like their fish cooked, this was the first restaurant where that concept was introduced, the first restaurant that served a piece of fish medium rare on purpose. The dish was salmon filet, served in a lightly creamed fresh tomato sauce, accented with sorrel and mint, and brought to the table in a lidded china casserole custom-made just for this dish at this restaurant. The year was

1986. Menu items that are now ubiquitous throughout the country, including tuna tartare and salmon carpaccio, were invented here. Species of fish once obscure—monkfish, black sea bass, and skate—gained in popularity thanks in large part to being featured on their early menus. Without exaggeration, this restaurant singularly changed the way professional and home cooks alike select, handle, and cook fish. Le Bernardin ushered in the era of modern seafood cookery.

This was the first nonsmoking restaurant in New York, decades before it became law. It also holds the distinction of being the longest-running four-star-rated restaurant in New York City, having maintained that status, unblemished, for more than 20 years since Bryan Miller, then the food critic for the *New York Times,* penned his review barely eight weeks after their opening in the spring of 1986. Critics have come and gone, other four-stars have lost their luster, some have lost their stars, while others have closed, but Le Bernardin continues to perform at a very high level to a packed house nightly.

It was opened by the team of pioneering chef Gilbert Le Coze and his sister Maguy, who oversaw the dining room, a working arrangement they had shared since 1972 in Paris where they earned two Michelin stars at their previous Le Bernardin, named after a nearby abbey on the quai de la Tournelle. Gilbert and Maguy grew up in the hospitality business. Their parents ran a small restaurant and inn in Port-Navalo, on the Brittany coast, where fish and fishing were a way of life. When they announced their plans to move to New York and open in the brand-new Equitable Tower building, word spread quickly through the restaurant community that this would be the opening of the year. Gilbert hired two New York veterans, Eberhard Muller and Dominick Cerrone, to help run the kitchen, train and hire staff, and select purveyors. Prior to opening, Muller and Le Coze visited many of the best seafood restaurants in the Northeast and toured the big fish markets, where, to Le Coze's surprise, the quality of the fresh fish he found was superb. But these were fish varieties he was not familiar with, so they did a lot of experimenting in fine-tuning their recipes. The philosophy was, and still is, to consider each species for its unique characteristics. Is the flesh firm or flaky, fatty or lean, sweet or mild? Then determine the best way to cook it, and the best sauces to serve with it to accent, complement, and emphasize the unique qualities of the fish on the plate. To execute this, they had to train their cooks in an all-new way of cooking fish. They designed a system wherein when each new order arrives in the kitchen, the fish is immediately removed from refrigeration and allowed to slowly come to room temperature. Then, at the last possible moment, the fish is cooked, often on one side only, placed on a hot china plate and allowed to finish cooking on the way out to the dining room. This style emphasizes the split-second accuracy required in cooking fish, which, it turns out, is a lot harder to cook correctly than meat.

One of the best dishes that has been on and off the menu for quite a while is the tuna from the almost raw section of the menu. Here they take perfectly toasted baguettes, brushed with fruity olive oil, covered with a thin layer of prepared foie gras terrine, and sprinkled with chives, and cover them with paper-thin sheets of buttery yellowfin tuna. In each bite, you have crunch, followed by that fruity lipid, a hint of heat from the chives, and lastly the rich marriage of the buttery foie gras with the fatty tuna, which lingers on and on, pure pleasure. Raw diver scallops are cut very thin, shingled on the plate to form a circle, drizzled with just extra virgin olive oil and a splash of fresh lemon juice, maybe a touch of cayenne, and topped with chopped chives and a few grains of sea salt. Tuna carpaccio arrives covering the entire plate, coated with a thin layer of lime-ginger emulsion. A superb dish from a few years back, one of my all-time favorites here, was the Spanish mackerel and caviar tartare. Here humble mackerel gets the royal treatment. It is diced very small and combined with osetra caviar, chopped chives, capers, cornichons, a little corn oil to bind it, a touch of sea salt, white pepper, and lemon juice. The mixture is then formed into a small dariole, or ring, placed in the center of the plate, and served with a sauce ravigote. In another wonderful dish, thin, folded rounds of poached celeriac act as open ravioli "pasta," filled with a mixture of lobster, shrimp, and langoustine, bathed in an incredibly rich sauce thickened with a foie gras butter and truffle emulsion. Disks of boneless halibut are poached until just done. On each is placed a slice of sautéed foie gras, topped with a few peeled, seedless grapes, and at tableside finished with a sauce made with a reduction of good port and sherry vinegar, finished with butter and then whisked, resulting in a very dark brown, almost sticky sauce, a perfect balance of sweet, sour, and rich.

A recent meal in the summer of 2008 started with an appetizer of two thin slices of smoked salmon flanking a quenelle of osetra caviar. Aldo Sohm, one of the great sommeliers working in the United States, paired that with a Shizuku Junmai Daiginjo sake. A few courses later, a perfectly cooked pan-seared diver scallop was set atop a sauté of braised morels and chanterelles, served with a 2000 Daniel-Etienne Defaix Chablis premier cru Vaillons. Chablis is often overlooked and misunderstood. Though made from the now ubiquitous chardonnay grape, it is unique, and 2000 was a very good year. This wine had a pronounced steely, mineral quality, citrusy notes, and a hint of anise, perfect with the rich scallop meat and woodsy mushrooms. This was followed by a baked lobster with late-season asparagus and a variation of tangy sauce gribiche. To my mind, it posed an odd wine pairing problem, which was solved by Sohm with a glass of 2006 Domaine Boyet-Martenot Mersault Tillets, again from the same grape as before, but an entirely different wine. This was a beautiful chardonnay, imported by Michael Skurnik, with a crisp, citrusy, mineral nose. It was a great match with the lobster.

The cheese plate too posed a challenge. To pair with a rich, creamy, veined Fourme d'Ambert, garnished with bits of bacon, soy caramel, and gingersnap, Sohm reached for a rather obscure vin jaune, or "yellow wine," from the Jura region of France, just by the Swiss border. These partially oxidized wines are aged in sherry barrels and pair well with blue cheese and foie gras. Sohm works wonders with his wine pairings, so my suggestion is to opt here for the tasting menu. It's worth the extra dollars for the full Le Bernardin experience.

Desserts are always superb, and these days with Michael Laiskonis in charge, they are as good as ever. A pineapple charlotte has thin slices of poached pineapple forming the outer ring, and inside sits a just-set buttermilk panna cotta, topped with a lacy tuile, onto which they set a small round of cassis sorbet. Paper-thin tart pastry holds a light parfait made from yuzu and ginger, with a lid of caramel tuile. The chestnut bombe has a classic old-school look. The bombe arrives centered on the plate, an imposing half sphere dusted with cocoa and filled with a chestnut, almond, pistachio, and nougat glace, and the plate is drizzled with maple, rum, and vanilla syrup. At a recent meal, I had a single dessert, a silky rich boule of chocolate olive oil ganache, made from dark Amedei chocolate, served over brioche toast, sprinkled with Maldon sea salt, and paired with a small glass of 2002 Austrian Muskat Ottonel Trockenbeerenauslese number 4, courtesy of Alois Kracher—that alone could have been dessert.

Le Bernardin is very expensive and still has a dress code for men, which I really don't understand, and may seen stuffy to some. But all in all, it is still the gold standard for seafood restaurants in America and continues night after night, 20 years after it opened, to deliver some of the best food, wine, and service to be found in all of New York.

Le Cirque

212-644-0202

151 East 58th Street, at Lexington Avenue, in the Bloomberg Building

Formal; jackets required in main dining room, not required in the wine bar area

Reservations

Expensive

All major credit cards accepted

Lunch and dinner Monday–Friday, dinner Saturday and Sunday

4, 5, 6, N, R, W trains to Lexington Avenue/ 59th Street station

It would be unimaginable to list the great restaurants of New York and not include Le Cirque, but through the last decade, during which it moved several times, it seemed that perhaps its best days might have been behind it. Through the 1970s, 1980s, and 1990s, this was the quintessential power dining scene. Under proprietor Sirio Maccioni, the greatest of his generation, this restaurant was a launching pad for famous chefs such as Daniel Boulud and Alain Sailhac before him. Everyone who mattered in New York society ate here, and everyone who wanted to be a part of that gilded scene did their best to secure a table. But after Le Cirque 2000 closed, many thought Sirio should just retire at the top of his game, with his pockets full. But with most greats, calling it quits is the hardest thing to do, and he has three sons who seem to want to continue the legacy. So with the help of someone looking for a famous anchor tenant, a rumored $14 million was pumped into this latest Le Cirque incarnation, which opened in 2006 to a great shrug. Has Le Cirque lost its relevance in today's New York dining scene? With all of the talent cooking in the city these days, and the emphasis on the downtown scene and more casual dining, why should anyone care about this restaurant, or the line of black limos double-parked out front all night long, or the awkward dining room that comes off at times as hushed and pretentious, filled nightly with a well-heeled, Botoxed, surgically improved, bejeweled, older clientele garbed in formal attire? As to the menu and the food, besides being very pricey, it is a bit schizophrenic, as clearly the young chef wants to, and indeed can, cook modern food, but the bulk of the older Le Cirque clientele still wants roast chicken, Dover sole, osso buco, and steamed spinach.

Truth be told, even in the heady old days the food was never great, but the star power in the dining room was undeniable. Back then the chef would cook for a few VIP tables whose plates were showered in truffles and the like, while the rest of the room ate from the cafeteria. These days, while once unthinkable, the place actually struggles for legitimacy, as there are just so many good kitchens in New York, and Le Cirque is feeling the squeeze, at one point actually hiring a consultant to help right the ship. That said, as of 2007, a very talented new young chef was in charge, the food was for the most part better than ever, and on a good night, the room had a buzz that is quintessentially Upper East Side New York, though it is still terribly expensive to dine here. Appetizers start in the low twenties and can hit $40. Main courses start there and waltz into the $50 range without blinking an eye. Opt instead for the $145 tasting menu, where the chef and his crew can really shine. You'll get a seven-course tour, and many of the best dishes are on this part of the menu.

Set just inside the courtyard of the Bloomberg building, the dining room is sleek, modern, and yet odd all at once. The space curves, following the elliptical outline of the building footprint, and that makes it seem awkward, like two or three different spaces that don't quite come together as one. Inside, the ceiling soars what must be 20-plus feet above you, and there is lots of polished wood paneling, plush carpeting, curved glass, and steel all the way around. To the right, the bar is big and comfortable, and beyond it is a very decent, casual, though pricey modern wine bar, serving excellent wines from this deep cellar by the glass, paired with some of the best wine bar food in New York. The dining room to the left is comfortable and spacious, maybe even too spacious, with the kitchen partially open to the rear.

The opening chef, who had been the chef at Le Cirque 2000, was Pierre Schaedelin, but he got mediocre reviews, and there was much grumbling that he never should have opened this restaurant in the first place. He's gone now and was replaced by Christophe Bellanca, a young energetic Frenchman, who had worked with Marc Meneau at La Pyramide and Chapel before coming here at the suggestion of Thomas Keller. His cooking was very good, excellent even, but at these prices it must be all that and more, every night, for every plate, as we have come to expect that level of cooking at places such as Per Se, Ducasse, Le Bernardin, Jean Georges, and Daniel, to name just a few. In late 2008, Christophe was replaced by Craig Hopson, whose food I'd enjoyed when he was cooking at Picholine and then downtown at One if by Land. He was still getting settled in when I dined here last in early 2009, but the food was lovely and will just get better. The notes that follow are from several meals over the course of 2007 and 2008.

If the zucchini flowers are on the menu, get them. Delicate, ethereal, light, almost transparent, they are stuffed with a zucchini mousse scented with parmesan and mint. Off a tasting menu one night, a jewel of a plate arrived carrying disks of perfect raw tuna topped with transparent sheets of tomato gelée, joining two separate but equally delicious compositions. Within a double chicken consommé, the dark brown liquid perfectly clear, accented with kaffir lime and rich tasting, swam three tiny ravioli filled with wild mushrooms. A long slender leg of king crab sits next to a stuffed "cannelloni," a thin slice of Granny Smith apple acting as the sheet of "pasta," alongside a shellfish bavaroise atop deep green watercress coulis, all decorated with a paper-thin, crisp milk tuile.

Tiny sweet bay scallops followed, done in a Provençal style, with a small potato confit; this was paired with a plate of slow-cooked Icelandic cod, meaty and flaky, flecked with black sesame seeds, garnished with rather bland white asparagus, orange confit, galangal, and fresh soybeans. The trio of beef, a winner, pairs a lightly grilled calotte, the cap meat of the rib-eye, next to a deep dark slice of red-wine-braised short rib, with a single ravioli of oxtail on a bed of superb onion confit drizzled with sticky rich veal stock reduction.

Desserts lean on the classical canon. An excellent napoleon is served with a strawberry sorbet. For fans of light, crisp meringue, there is a perfect vacherin with yogurt-lime ice cream and fresh berry compote. Floating islands, meringue again but this time soft and silky, are poached in milk, then drizzled with caramel, set atop a rich vanilla-flecked crème anglaise. And there is chocolate poire belle Hélène, a century-old creation named after the Offenbach operetta: a peeled, cored whole pear is slow-poached in vanilla syrup, flecked with a brunoise of fresh diced pear, and then drizzled with semisweet chocolate sauce.

The wine list is very good and very expensive, and in what may be a trend these days, both the helpful sommeliers are young women. The wait staff, a mix of seasoned Americans and Europeans, try their best to be good, and mostly succeed. If you want to see what's left of the old New York power dining scene, you'll find it here: handsome older men in $5,000 suits, with pencil-thin, tanned wives, joined by earnest under-studies glad to be part of the scene on someone else's dollar. Sirio was a giant in his day, starting in this industry at the very bottom as an immigrant busboy at Delmonico's, then in short order becoming a captain at the Colony. He has written his own chapter in the history of the New York restaurant scene, and I wish his sons all the best, as he will be a very hard act to follow and the weight of this place a heavy load to bear.

L'Ecole

212-219-3300
462 Broadway at Grand Street
Casual
Reservations
Moderate
All major credit cards accepted
Lunch and dinner Monday–Friday, dinner Saturday
6, J, M, Z, N, Q, R, W trains to Canal Street station

The meals prepared here are cooked by culinary students; essentially this is their final class prior to graduation. The servers are outside contractors brought in by the school to work the dining room. The food is good, sometimes even better than good, as a chef instructor is in place to prevent any mistakes from being served.

The menus change every few weeks in keeping with the seasons. The prix fixe lunch at $24 may not be the greatest bargain in town, but the five-course $34.50 dinner is a pretty good deal by any measure. The room, which is set out on two levels, is nice and bright, with high ceilings and decent space between tables. Up front is a small bar, to the rear a few semicircular banquettes. Service is good, and because of the low prices and classroom dynamic, little shortcomings can be forgiven. The menu usually includes a few classics: braises, roasts, and stews in the colder months, chilled terrines, pistou, chilled soups, and salads in the warmer ones. One highlight is the bread. The baguettes, baked daily and served here and only here, may be the best in all New York. I only wish they sold them retail, but they don't, so this could be the only restaurant that I'd recommend based solely on the bread basket. Desserts are very good, and the wine list decent and mostly French. Overall, in this part of town, or any part for that matter, the dinner deal offered here is hard to beat.

Les Halles

212-679-4111
411 Park Avenue South, between 28th and 29th Streets
Casual
Reservations
Inexpensive to moderate
All major credit cards accepted
Seven days a week 7:30 AM–midnight
6 train to 28th Street station

Though touristy and often overhyped, in part thanks to the mythical involvement of the celebrity chef author Anthony Bourdain, this is still one of my favorite restaurants for casual French dining. Every night scores of regulars gather here for the reliable, inexpensive, and consistently satisfying brasserie fare. I only wish there were more restaurants in New York that offered reasonably priced, well-executed food with friendly service in a great, convivial dining room. I was there for dinner with Swedish friends the night of the 2000 presidential election. When news broke that Gore had taken Florida, the mood turned gleeful, with cheers and high fives all around and people hugging in the aisles, everyone buying everyone else drinks into the late evening. Our mild hangovers the following morning seemed the least of our concerns.

Les Halles opened a few years after the pioneering Park Bistro, which was then across the street on this odd stretch of Park Avenue South. Back in the early 1980s this neighborhood was deserted at night except for drive-through traffic and streetwalkers congregating under the lamps. The duo that opened Les Halles, José de Meirelles and his partner Philippe LaJaunie, had been working at Park Bistro when one day they spotted a For Rent sign across the street. With just a few dollars between them, they signed the lease and opened a short time later. During the renovations, they discovered that behind the Sheetrock, the dropped ceilings, and the linoleum flooring was the basis for a turn-of-the-century brasserie straight from the Latin Quarter. In nearly perfect condition were the original checkered black-and-white-tiled floors, partially tiled walls with period wooden wainscoting, a nearly double-height ceiling featuring beautiful plaster moldings—in short, an instant classic, as if preserved intact in amber. As it turns out, the place was built back in the twenties as a wholesale fruit and vegetable store, hence the tile floors and food-themed ornamental plaster. From day one, Les Halles looked as if it had been there forever.

Opening night, not knowing what to expect, they were so busy they ran out of food by 8:30 and had to turn away the crowds. More than 20 years later, the place has been full nearly every night since, and now there is a Les Halles downtown, one in D.C., and another in Miami Beach. They offer breakfast from 8 AM, and then the same simple menu from noon to midnight. The kitchen never closes, so you can stop by for a meal any time of day.

Appetizer choices include steaming bowls of plump mussels in white wine, redolent of fresh thyme, snails in garlic butter, thick slices of their house-made rustic duck pâté, a good version of French onion soup, duck confit, smooth and creamy rillettes, and a few simple salads, including a solid version of frisée aux lardons, all served with wonderful sourdough bread. The entree list features a reliable steak frites using the traditional French cut, the bavette. This thin steak cut from the short loin is a bit chewy but very flavorful and best ordered grilled rare to medium-rare. Try the excellent onglet, with an almost organ-like flavor, served with a shallot red wine reduction or a béarnaise sauce. Steak au poivre is a good choice here; they use the delicious rump steak known in French as the pointe de culotte or pièce de boeuf.

Grilled tuna is served with sautéed vegetables and an emulsion of olive oil and lemon; salmon, sliced thin and broiled, is served with the same sauce plus basil; and plump scallops come with a Champagne sauce. Rounding out the menu are the typical brasserie offerings of Moroccan lamb sausage (merguez), braised pied de cochon pané, boudin aux pommes (blood sausage with caramelized apples), nightly specials such as choucroute, and a decent cassoulet. Most of the entrees come with their excellent frites, made the old-fashioned way, first blanched at low temperature, then cooked the second time at 375°F until they are very crisp and golden; they go through hundreds of pounds a day, and these are some of the best to be found anywhere in the city.

Add to the mix a great, inexpensive, and well thought-out wine list. Look for wines from excellent smaller Beaujolais producers including Pascal Granger and Bernard Dalicieux. From the Rhône try the 1990 J. Vidal-Fleury Crozes-Hermitage for $25; the 1989 E. Guigal Côte-Rôtie for $60; and the classic dark and spicy 1990 Vieux Telegraphe

Châteauneuf-du-Pape for $49. Smaller French country wines at bargain prices work very well with this food: try the 1989 Château de Haute-Serre Cahors for $23.50 and a 1990 Bandol Mas de la Rouvière for $27.50.

In the front they have a small retail butcher shop selling the same meat they use at the restaurant: great steaks, free-range chicken, boudin, and assorted pâtés by the pound. They have recently expanded, taking over the identical space next door, which was actually the other half of the original vegetable market; hence the authentic décor is the same.

Lexington Candy Shop

212-288-0057
1226 Lexington Avenue,
    at 83rd Street
Casual
No reservations
Inexpensive
All major credit cards accepted
Seven days a week 7 AM–7 PM
4, 5, 6 trains to 86th Street
    station

The official phone number is Butterfield 8-0057, and that gives you an idea of what this place is about—in a word, history. This is an old-fashioned New York sandwich shop, like Eisenberg's in the Flatiron District. There are very few of these left. The men behind the counter wear long white buttoned coats atop button-down shirts and ties. The L-shaped dining room is set around a long bar with circular spinning stools and looks much as it did 60 years ago. The menu is similar to what it was in the 1950s: traditional breakfast offerings, followed by sandwiches, soups, salads, and the like, and some old-fashioned soda fountain cuisine, sundaes, and floats. Most of it doesn't rise much above the ordinary, but some of it does, and for those things and the ambiance, it's well worth a visit.

Orange juice is squeezed fresh by hand for each glass, pulp strained out if you like, and don't miss the classic jelly omelet—mine has to be grape. Otherwise the breakfast offerings are fine, eggs, omelets, pancakes, muffins, etc., but for some odd reason they don't serve hash browns. The ice cream scooped here is the great Bassetts from Philadelphia, made in a creamy whipped style that is nearly impossible to find these days in New York City. It's lighter and less dense than Häagen-Dazs or Ben and Jerry's, yet very rich, buttery, and full-flavored. I've had it scooped fresh at the counter of their original Bassetts stand within Reading Terminal Market in Philadelphia, a tradition since 1885, where it was for many years made fresh daily. This is the only place I know of in New York that serves it. They make soda the old-fashioned way, by mixing flavored syrups with seltzer for each order. In a city rife with Starbucks, coffee shops, and dessert emporiums, I can think of no better spot to park myself over a root beer float or a jelly omelet than right here.

Little Giant

212-226-5047
85 Orchard Street,
   at Broome Street
Casual
Reservations
Moderate
All major credit cards accepted
Lunch and dinner Wednesday–
   Friday, brunch and dinner
   Saturday and Sunday, dinner
   Monday
J, M, Z trains to Bowery
   station; F, V trains to Second
   Avenue station

I love little spots like this that are run by chefs who like to cook. Think Prune, Little Owl, the first version of Pearl Oyster Bar, and you get the idea—an odd little space with a cramped open kitchen in which the cooks bump into each other, a dining room that seats maybe 25 people, a small but well-focused menu of modest reach with prices to match, and a great sound track. I'll take these places over the Spice Market any day of the week. Like Prune, Little Giant started as a dinner-only restaurant, then added brunch, then lunch, and now it's busy all day long.

Opened in 2004 by Julie Taras and Tasha Garcia, this is a labor of love. They did much of the demolition and even some of the construction themselves. A former shoe store, the room is set on the corner with large windows looking out onto the street. Once a down-on-its-heels neighborhood home to immigrants and then nearly abandoned as they moved on, Orchard Street and the surrounding blocks are now being transformed into a vibrant, chic area, with seemingly every other building under scaffolding and undergoing renovations. New storefronts include shops selling hip clothes, skateboards, and custom-made, artsy jewelry, as well as a smattering of lovely, quirky eateries like this and Bacaro, just few blocks to the south. The homey dining room features lots of pale wood and exposed brick walls. The menu changes with the season, and the specials and ingredients often come from local farmer's markets.

The menu is small but not too small. You can choose from a half dozen starters and a few salads that are actually very interesting. In the warmer months, an item billed as salad pairs roasted beets with heirloom kabocha squash, set over sautéed organic black kale, a nice piece of cow's milk cheese, and a sprinkle of toasted pistachios. Another sets blood orange lozenges against arugula, chunks of Maytag blue cheese, a good two-year-old imported prosciutto, sweet tiny taggiasca olives from Liguria, and roasted dates. In the summer when it's really hot, try the assorted pickle plate as a cold starter, or in cooler months the starter of house-made sausage, served with caramelized onions and crusty bread.

For meat-eaters, try the bavette, a rather obscure but very flavorful cut of meat taken from the short loin; it's like a cross between the hanging tenderloin, or onglet, and a skirt steak—bloody, a bit chewy, and full of flavor. Here it is served with two steakhouse classics, creamed spinach and a small mound of onion confit. Or you can opt for the swine of the week, which, as the menu states, varies from braised and glazed Berkshire pork belly to beer-braised and curried pork butt set alongside a slaw made from jícama and fennel, with a tomatillo relish to cut the richness. Tasmanian sea trout, a salmonesque red-fleshed fish that I love, is served with parsnip puree, fried parsnip chips, and pan-roasted Brussels sprouts. For side dishes, try the maple-roasted Brussels sprouts, the very good mac and cheese, or the deviled eggs; is this the place that started the deviled egg craze?

For dessert, jump at the sticky toffee pudding or the egg cream and vanilla float. The wine list is small but decent, and the friendly staff do their best to navigate the tight space.

The Little Owl

212-741-4695
90 Bedford Street, at the corner of Grove Street
Casual
Reservations
Moderate
All major credit cards accepted
Dinner Monday–Friday, brunch and dinner Saturday and Sunday
1 train to Christopher Street; A, C, E, B, D, F, V trains to West 4th Street station

Chef Joey Campanaro grew up in a row house in South Philadelphia and summered with his family in Wildwood, New Jersey. It was there that he got his start in the restaurant business, washing pots at the age of 13 in a town better known for its boardwalks and cheese fries than its Bordelaise. He continued cooking through his teens and eventually landed a job at DiLullo's in Center City Philadelphia when Frank Crispo ran that kitchen. It was there that he met Jimmy Bradley, the owner of the Red Cat, Harrison, and Mermaid Inn, who was also cooking in that fine kitchen in those days. After a few years, Crispo left and returned to work in New York, as did Bradley, and Campanaro followed, working for a while with Jonathan Waxman. He spent a few years in Los Angeles in charge of the corporate dining rooms for MGM by day while working for the very talented Joachim Splichal at Patina Catering by night, eventually returning to New York to open the Harrison with his old friend Jimmy Bradley. It was there that I first sampled Joey's cooking. The Harrison was the first new restaurant to open in New York in the immediate aftermath of 9/11, an opening made even more complicated by the fact that it was located on a strip of Greenwich Street that was then an acrid, smoky war zone, just a few blocks north of what had been the World Trade Center. His food was good, boldly flavored, and not too complicated, and the Harrison did well. He moved on but continued working with Harrison owners Jimmy Bradley and Danny Abram at Pace, and then, like many ambitious young chefs, left a secure job to go out and look for his own spot.

I bumped into him one day at Burkina on Houston, a favorite haunt of mine a few doors down from Russ and Daughters and Katz's, where I buy hip-hop themed T-shirts for myself and my two sons. He was excited about opening this place, and after a few meals at the Little Owl, I think we should all be excited too. His maître d' and business partner is Gabriel Stulman, with whom he worked previously at Pace. It's a rare thing these days that the chef of a restaurant would actually cook your meal, but here in the tiny space, with an even tinier kitchen, that's what happens for every customer, every night. This is one of the smallest restaurants in the city; it reminds me of Casanis (now Prune) when it first opened, but Little Owl is even smaller, with just two men, Joey and his longtime sous-chef, Gustavo Machuca, doing all the prep and cooking. They work off one six-burner stove, a small grill, and a fryer, with the pleasant aromas from the kitchen often wafting into the dining room, adding to the seduction. They have 30 seats, with room for 4 more at the bar. Restaurants like this are now ever more common as chefs look for cheap rents in Manhattan; places like Shorty's 32, Market Table, and Dell'Anima come to mind. And often the small kitchen spaces the cooks must work in define the limits of the menu, and in doing so, provide good value and seriously good simple homey food. The walls facing the street are composed of large glass windowpanes, with great views of the streetscape and surrounding neighborhood, drawing your eyes outward and relieving the congested feel of the space. Inside, tables and chairs are scattered about, the ceiling is high and tin-plated, and the room is lit by an assortment of hanging lamps with bottles of wine stored here and there, taking advantage of any free wall space. Nightly the crowds spill out onto Bedford Street, and once the room is full, usually starting around 7 PM, it's like stepping into a noisy party.

This part of the West Village has an antique, almost European feel to it, with lots of older, narrow four-story brick townhouses facing quiet tree-lined streets that run at odd angles to the normal New York City grid. Directly across the street there's a four-story wood-frame house dating back to the early 1800s; on its roof the owners have placed one of those plastic owls designed to scare away pigeons and other birds, and it is from that owl that this place takes its name. There is a welcome civility to these streets that's totally absent from the meat market scene just several blocks north, and this restaurant stands in contrast to those 300-seat factories they bill as restaurants up there.

Joey's menu is defined by the space, forcing him to create a simplified, pared-down version of what he had done elsewhere. Often, as is the case here, simplification is a good thing. Pan-roasted boneless sardines, $9, arrive warm and crisp, nestled on a bed of sliced sugar snap peas sautéed with cauliflower, all tossed with a citrus vinaigrette. Joey's basic seasoned salt mix includes a touch of hot pepper and ground coriander, which adds a depth and a bit of fire to all the dishes served here. House-made ricotta cavatelli, $11, nearly enough to be a dinner portion, are served with crunchy, delicious fresh fava beans and chewy chunks of rendered, smoky pork belly, all set in a pool of light tomato sauce, topped with pecorino cheese and scented with fresh basil. In the early summer months when they are available, soft-shell crabs are lightly floured and deep-fried crisp, served over a bed of sautéed asparagus, and bound with salsa verde.

A fist-sized pork chop, weighing in at well over a pound and a bargain at $19, is seasoned with ground fennel, pan-seared and then oven-roasted, glazed with the pan juices and Parmesan cheese, and set atop a nest of sautéed dandelion greens. The dish billed as crispy chicken, $17, is a boneless frenched breast attached to a boneless thigh, all cooked entirely on the skin side. This renders much of the chicken fat out of the skin, yielding a crackling crust beneath, to which the moist silky meat stands in contrast. A grilled New York strip steak, $26, is topped with radicchio and pancetta tossed in a balsamic vinaigrette. Side dishes at $7 include braised greens, butter beans tossed with escarole, addictive asparagus, home fries in season, and mashed potatoes.

They don't serve liquor, as a school sits on the opposite corner, but the wine list is good and growing, the selection arranged by Gabriel Stulman. Desserts are okay—flans, fresh fruit beignets, assorted ice creams—but a glass of port with a small plate of cookies works fine after the big flavors that came before. The staff is friendly, the room welcoming. If you're looking to share very tasty yet simple food with 20-some other diners in one of New York's classic old neighborhoods, this is the place.

Lombardi's

212-941-7994
**32 Spring Street, between
Mott and Mulberry Streets**
Casual
No reservations
Inexpensive to moderate
Cash only
Lunch and diner seven days
a week
6 train to Spring Street station;
N, R, W trains to Prince
Street station

Who has the best pizza in New York? Who knows? Who cares? We have a lot of very good choices, and Lombardi's is still one of them. Yeah, yeah, yeah, I can hear the pizza police screaming at me. I know that in 2006 they changed the dough a bit, they now use a sheeter of some sort, and the edge of the crust on the pie is different, but it's still darn good. And let's not forget that this is, after all, the granddaddy of all New York pizzerias, opened in 1905 by Gennaro Lombardi at the original location just a few doors down the block, 15½ Spring Street. The spot was primarily a grocery store where he also did some baking, including his great pizza pies. So the claim has often been made that New York City was the birthplace of pizza in America, and that Lombardi's was the very first pizzeria, but I'll leave that to the legions of food historians to decide. What we also know as fact is that Lombardi trained a lot of very good *pizzaioli*, including John Sasso of John's, Anthony Pero of Totonno's, and Patsy Lancieri of Patsy's, to name a few.

What matters most is that the pies served here all day long are fine examples of what good pizza can be in the right hands, made with the right ingredients, and out of the right ovens—here the oven is coal fired and over 100 years old, one of the few remaining in the city, grandfathered by code, as is the one at Arturo's, a few blocks away on Houston. They are cherished by pizza makers for the good, steady heat they generate, resulting in a crisp, fully cooked crust, with a slightly burnt tinge to the bottom, and characterized by those bubbles of dough forming here and there along the top. The rooms here are pleasant, with tin ceilings, whirling ceiling fans, exposed brick walls, comfortable seats and banquettes, a full bar, and an all-Italian sound track to boot. Service is good, the staff mostly young and very friendly, and the crowd is a mix of longtime locals, older folks who come in from the 'burbs where these pies don't exist, local businesspeople, and tourists after the real thing.

The pizzas come in two sizes: large, which is 18 inches and cut into eight slices, or small, 14 inches yielding six slices. Hungry guys can eat a small pie no problem—I do all the time. Sensible folks may split one; I suggest you come as a group, and order a few. They do serve salads, but—no offense—skip them and order pizza. The sauce here is made from imported Italian San Marzano tomatoes; it is good though a bit sweet. The toppings start with the simplest basic pie, featuring thin slices of good fresh melted mozzarella cheese with just a sprinkling of grated Romano cheese and a chiffonade of fresh basil. To this you can add pancetta (excellent), sliced sausage from excellent sausage maker Giovanni Esposito on Ninth Avenue, very good homemade meatballs, anchovies, roasted peppers, onions, fresh mushrooms, pitted olives, and more. Order whatever you like—it's really hard to go wrong here.

They also serve an excellent white pizza, the round of dough simply topped with mozzarella, fresh ricotta, and Romano, accented with oregano, basil, fresh black pepper, and garlic oil. It's very good as well. The signature dish, which shouldn't be missed, is the odd-sounding fresh clam pie. Here they use local, shucked-to-order littleneck or topneck clams, which dot the surface along with chopped garlic, fresh basil, some oregano, and a sprinkle of Romano cheese, all glistening with good olive oil. The pie is crisp, crunchy, salty, mildly oceanic, and, due to the Spartan topping, cooked through well on the top and bottom, giving a lovely chewy bite, mouth feel, and true pizza flavor.

While they do delivery, it's the worst way to eat pizza, as the pies steam in those cardboard boxes and get soggy immediately. So skip your cheesy local corner pizza joint and the half-cooked, soggy pies they dish out, and hop in a cab or take the subway to any of the great New York pizzerias. Be glad that they are here and that you have the good taste to enjoy them. You'll never look at pizza the same way again.

Londel's

212-234-6114
2620 Frederick Douglass
  Boulevard, at 140th Street
Casual to dressy
Reservations
Moderate
All major credit cards accepted
Lunch and dinner Tuesday–
  Saturday, brunch on Sunday
B, C trains to 135th Street
  station

As Harlem gentrifies, $2 million brownstones and Starbucks have become common and many of the older restaurants, clubs, and businesses have closed, Wells' Famous and Copeland's sadly among the recent casualties. Londel's, which opened in 1994 and happens to serve some pretty decent old-fashioned soul food in a beautiful stretch of town, is one of the better places to eat—better, I think, than Sylvia's and closer in quality to what they do so well at Amy Ruth's and Charles Southern.

From the street, you can't miss the trim black awning running the length of the front, with the name spelled out in white letters across the outline of a black bow tie. The proprietor, Londel Davis, favors bow ties and crisp suits, maybe the result of spending a career in a blue NYPD uniform, or maybe just out of a natural tendency to dress well. You enter the bar room with framed photographs of famous New York politicians and entertainers lining the walls. The main dining room has a dark hardwood floor, and walls with period wainscoting are painted lime and burgundy.

The food is a mix of southern styles, including some Cajun dishes. Start with the fried whiting fingers, crisp and flavorful; this is one of my favorite North Atlantic fish. Or try the good crusted crab cakes, set in a mustard cream sauce just like we used to do at the Four Seasons years back. Whiting appears again, fried, as an entree, or if you prefer, they have an excellent blackened catfish, a fried shrimp platter, or sautéed salmon topped with coriander butter. On the meat side of the ledger, I love the fried chicken, with or without the waffles, or opt instead for the smothered pork chops, the moist meat buried beneath a mound of slow-cooked braised onions.

You can't come here and not try the slow-cooked collard greens, nor the heavy but good mac and cheese and the candied yams. The appetizers are all mostly under $10, and the entrees in the high teens and low twenties. For dessert, try the sweet potato pie, peach cobbler, or formidable bread-and-butter pudding with rum and caramel sauce; it's almost as good as the bread pudding at Ben Benson's. On weekends, they have live jazz, and when the weather allows, the windows open out onto the street, which adds a nice effect. The wine list is good, beer too works with this food, the staff couldn't be nicer, and Harlem is all the richer for this classic, old-style soul food eatery.

Mai House

212-965-0171
186 Franklin Street, between Greenwich and Hudson Streets
Casual
Reservations
Moderate to expensive
All major credit cards accepted
Lunch and dinner Monday–Friday, dinner Saturday
1 train to Franklin Street station; A, C, E trains to Canal Street station

Tribeca restaurateur Drew Nieporent has had this space for some time now under various guises. First it was Zeppole, with chef Frank Crispo in charge, then the space became Tri-Bakery, with those hulking baking ovens still stored in the basement. In 2006 he tapped Michael Huynh, who had been running Bao 111 to great acclaim on the Lower East Side, the idea being that Vietnamese cuisine was, and still is, underrepresented in New York City. The room is large and roughly L-shaped, with a long bar to your right, along with some tables in the front area where the once-open kitchen now sits behind carved wooden screens but is still backlit and partially in view. The main dining room is to the rear. It is on the large side. The walls are various shades of beige, the tables well spaced, the banquettes comfortable, and the ceiling high.

The cooking has improved since it first opened; as expected, the collaboration between Nieporent and Huynh took time to coalesce. These days Huynh is also involved with a restaurant called Bun, which he opened with the Main Street Restaurant Group in the NoLIta area, nearby Soho and Chinatown. The menu at Mai House is divided up as follows: appetizers, meat, seafood, noodles, rice, and various dishes billed as sides. From the appetizer section, the shrimp rolls are good, clean-flavored, and light, with a hazelnut-flavored dipping sauce. Skip the frog legs, lollipop style; the frog legs themselves are of the frozen, institutional variety, and no matter what one tries to do to them, they remain undistinguished. Instead opt for the sweet Taylor Bay scallops in a spicy bacon-studded curry sauce, or either of the spring rolls, presented in transparent rice wrappers and served with variations on the Vietnamese fermented fish sauce known as nuoc mam.

Another winner is the thin-sliced marinated strips of lamb meat wrapped around sugarcane and grilled, a dish that carried over from Bao 111; initially served here with beef short ribs, it is now even better with lamb. Or try the Wagyu beef cheek stew, studded with chunks of lotus root, a cauliflower puree, and pickled ramps in a spicy beef broth. Braised Berkshire pork belly is rich and delicious, set atop pickled red cabbage and a sauce based on coconut milk. The sweet-and-sour red snapper arrives whole, head on, standing upright, seemingly swimming on your plate freeze-frame style, topped with a sweetish sauce based on tomatoes and Chinese celery. Clams in beer is another winner, featuring fresh Manila clams in a broth of their own juices, Tiger beer, lemongrass, Thai basil, and hot peppers.

Among the rice and noodles section, the duck fried rice is good, but the real winner is the bon bo hue, featuring rice noodles in a spicy, rich beef broth with pigs' feet and the rich meat from beef shanks. Sautéed water spinach, creamy soft Chinese eggplant, or crispy sautéed long beans all make for great sides. The wine list is good, and beer works very well with many of these dishes, as does some of the sake offered here. Desserts too are decent but tend to be hit-or-miss.

Michael Huynh's life is a great American story. He escaped Vietnam via a dangerous weeklong trip on a small boat and arrived in the United States after being picked up at sea by the U.S. Navy. He lived for a while with an Italian American family upstate and worked in their pizzeria before coming to New York City. His sense of flavor, inspiration, and cooking style no doubt come from his mother, with whom he worked in her kitchen each day as a young boy growing up.

Man Doo Bar

212-279-3075
2 West 32nd Street, between
Fifth Avenue and Broadway
Casual
No reservations
Inexpensive
All major credit cards accepted
Lunch and dinner seven days
a week
N, Q, R, W, B, D, F, V, 1, 2, 3
trains to 34th Street station

This narrow storefront boasts some of the best dumplings in New York. That much is clear from the restaurant's name, which translates literally from Korean as "dumpling bar." From the front window, day and night passersby can see the dumplings being handmade and cooked to order. The menu is broken down into six sections: appetizers, soups, dumplings, rice dishes, noodle dishes, and special dishes. A dozen or so varieties of fresh dumplings are prepared each day and offered pan-fried or steamed, as well as incorporated into soups and other dumpling-based dishes. Hey, they called it Dumpling Bar, right? Mixed with the dumplings are an assortment of Korean classics such as bi bim bop, hot rice served sizzling in a earthenware bowl, topped with various steamed vegetables and roots, ground beef, hot pepper paste, and a sunny-side-up egg, a meal in itself. Or japchae, warm clear sweet potato noodles served with sautéed vegetables and minced pork.

This, as are most Korean establishments, is very kid-friendly and usually has a great mix of Korean and non-Korean diners attracted by the quality and very low prices. One of the owners was an architecture student, and the design is minimal and modern all at once. He told me that architecture and cooking have a lot in common: "In building we all use the same materials—two-by-fours, Sheetrock, rebar, concrete—we just design the structures differently. In cooking, it's the same. We all share the same ingredients and with them we simply create different recipes." Why didn't I think of that?

Margie's Red Rose

212-491-3665
267 West 144th Street, between Seventh and Eighth Avenues
Casual
No reservations
Inexpensive
Cash only
Monday–Saturday 6 AM–7:30 PM, Sunday 6 AM–4 PM
A, C, B, D trains to 145th Street station; 3 train to 148th Street station

Margie's is often overlooked in the list of great soul food restaurants in New York, and I don't know why. It's got a real down-South diner vibe, with red vinyl banquettes, a jukebox, and ceiling fans. Margie does the cooking, and it's first-rate southern. The fried chicken is as fine an example as you'll find most anywhere. Her collard greens too rank up there with the best I've had, including those at Charles Southern and Amy Ruth's. Pancakes for breakfast are terrific, and the fried fish—whiting, if you're lucky—is to my mind some of the best you'll find in town, crisp, light, and greaseless.

Desserts are simple and good—fruit cobblers and lemon layer cake, all washed down with very good iced tea. Come early, as the place is known to close if and when Margie feels like she needs a break, but do visit. With Copeland's gone and Harlem gentrifying by the minute, who knows how much longer Margie's will be here, but as long as it is, this is the closest thing to real old-time southern hospitality I've ever seen in New York.

The Market Diner

212-695-0415
572 Eleventh Avenue, at 43rd Street
Casual
No reservations
Inexpensive
All major credit cards accepted
Seven days a week, 24 hours a day
A, C, E trains to 42nd Street station

This diner was built during the Jetsons era, circa 1963, so yes, the theme is space-age, not rail car. The exterior's spaceship-esque curving stainless steel walls and the funky decor inside are worth a visit just in themselves. The food, you ask? Not bad. The place closed for a while between 2007 and 2008 and was re-opened by the Tsinias family in December 2008. Stick with the Greek specialties or the simple stuff and you'll be pleasantly surprised. They have parking out front to boot. So if you're heading home to Jersey or Westchester around 3 AM and need a quick bite, it's a natural stop prior to the West Side Highway or Lincoln Tunnel for anything from greasy eggs and bacon to decent roast pork and moussaka. The desserts are displayed as they should be, perpetually spinning in a refrigerated glass display case. They have a liquor license and make decent cocktails and weak coffee, and with prices this cheap, you have no excuse not to give it a try while it's still here, as we have lost so many of the great old New York diners over the last few years.

Market Table

212-255-2100
54 Carmine Street, between
  Bedford and Bleecker Streets
Casual
Reservations
Moderate
All major credit cards accepted
Lunch and dinner Monday–
  Friday, dinner Saturday
1 train to Houston Street station;
  A, C, E, B, D, F, V trains to
  West 4th Street station

In the space that had formerly been Shopsins (now in the Essex Market), this lovely little spot opened in the fall of 2007. I watched it unfold weekly as I'd pass by to visit the great guitar maker Rick Kelly, whose famous guitar store is just a few doors down the street and who has been kind enough to build a few lovely electrics for me over the years. I also knew the owner Joey Campanaro, who runs the popular Little Owl a few blocks to the west, so I'd pop my head in and see how things were going as the job progressed. This place shares a landlord with Little Owl; he is a die-hard New York foodie who helped put this deal in place from the outset. For the job of chef, they tapped Mikey Price, an old acquaintance who had been cooking at the Mermaid Inn on the Lower East Side. Here the concept was simple: part market, part restaurant, with the market selling essentially the same restaurant-quality ingredients that the restaurant uses, and, for a while at least, an exclusive retail opportunity to offer the fine meats from the previously wholesale-only La Frieda Meats down on Washington Street.

You enter the store with its glass counter to the rear in front of the open kitchen. Here you'll find some pre-packed meat, meat to be cut, and some specialties and prepared dishes. Sometime during 2008 the market itself disappeared and gave way to more tables and seats as the restaurant was busy from the get-go. The open kitchen, visible to the rear, serves as the main restaurant kitchen. The main restaurant space proper is through the archway to the right. Both spaces have a farmhouse feel, with exposed brick walls, high ceilings, and exposed ductwork and beams. The dining room features natural wood tables and chairs, devoid of cloth or padding—modern farmhouse Shaker chic. From the beginning, the place has been very busy, and deservedly so. The food is simple, honest, and straightforward, featuring very good ingredients and accurate cooking.

These guys know how to get the most out of a small space (visit Little Owl), and here the menu is interesting and uniformly executed from what amounts to six burners, a fryer, a little grill, and a couple of cooks, including the chef, pulling it all together.

Start with their Caesar salad variation, here garnished with great crispy fried calamari. Why didn't anyone else think of that before? Or the braised short rib appetizer with onion-studded rösti potatoes and horseradish cream. Or maybe the diver scallops, appearing very retro here wrapped in good bacon and served with heirloom tomatoes and cucumber cream. I love skate, and I love it done in the meunière style, pan-fried and golden brown, set in browned lemon butter with capers, sautéed string beans, and bacon lardons. Seriously, that's exactly the kind of food I make at home. Lamb shank, a workhorse entree, is, as expected, tender and flavorful, with its potato gratin side. Roast chicken celebrates the good bird cooked right. Crab cakes, which I'm picky about, deliver the right balance between good sweet crabmeat and just enough breading, mayonnaise, and seasonings to hold them together. Try the burger—as mentioned, the meat mix is from La Frieda, which also supplies Shake Shack and the Spotted Pig, to name just a few. The Philly hoagies at lunch are a tribute to Campanero's Philadelphia past (and my own as well).

Price doubles as the pastry chef, so these are good, well-executed cook's desserts: chocolate banana bread pudding with caramel sauce, pineapple rhubarb upside-down cake, fresh strawberries and warmed Nutella, a daily fruit torte of one kind or another, and an assortment of ice creams and sorbets. The wine list is good and growing, and as a kicker, there is no corkage fee on any one bottle you bring with you. How long that will last I don't know, but bring a bottle and drink well for as little as $3 a person; in New York that ain't easy. The team behind this place is solid, as is the concept. I suspect they may shrink the market portion of the space down and perhaps add a few more tables, as the restaurant is filled to capacity nearly every day and night, but we'll just have to wait and see.

Menchanko-tei

212-986-6805
43-45 West 55th Street,
between Fifth and Sixth
Avenues
Casual
No reservations
Inexpensive
All major credit cards accepted
Seven days a week 11 AM–
midnight
N, R, W trains to Fifth Avenue/
59th Street station; E, V
trains to Fifth Avenue/
53rd Street station

If you've just spent a few hours shopping at Saks, Bergdorf's, or Henri Bendel or soaking up all that art at the new MoMA and have worked up an appetite, you're in luck. Menchanko-tei, a few steps away on West 55th Street, is one of my favorite stops for an inexpensive, quick, delicious noodle fix in this ultra-luxe midtown retail strip. The long, narrow dining room is always bustling with Japanese customers who know good ramen when they taste it. There are some stools at the small bar area to the left, usually taken up by single diners, with additional seats at the little pine tables that line the walls, and more seats again to the rear. In typical Japanese fashion the service here is polite, brisk, and efficient.

The house specialty is handmade fresh ramen noodles created from a wheat base, seasoned with Mongolian sea salt, and blended with spring water. The menu is small and well-focused, based on a few delicious broths, with noodle and topping variations. These are all served in preheated ceramic bowls and eaten with chopsticks and large wooden spoons, good for slurping. I always have a hard time making up my mind—everything on the menu is very good, and invariably I find myself looking over the shoulders of other diners to see what they are having, which only makes it worse, as everything looks (and tastes) great.

The signature steaming Menchanko bowl features toothsome egg noodles in a well-flavored soy-based broth, enriched with smoky dried bonito shavings, shiitake mushrooms, and seaweed, and topped with scallions, shrimp, diced firm tofu, fried tofu, bits of chicken, and clam meat. The Nagasaki chanpon has thin ramen noodles floating in a rich broth, topped with al dente stir-fried vegetables, tossed with chunks of shrimp, clams, and thin-sliced roast pork. The Hakata ramen is wonderful on cold winter days; here the ramen is served in a very rich cloudy white broth, topped with slices of that same simmered pork, assorted mushrooms, ferns, and vegetables.

As any fan of the film *Tampopo* knows, while these soups feature great noodles and toppings, it's really all about the broth. Here the broths are made from slowly simmered chicken, pork, vegetable, and soy bases, which form great character and richness. There is no MSG added. This is a great choice for a quick lunch, late breakfast, or light pre-theater dinner, and as a bonus, all these soups are under $10 per portion.

Mia Dona

212-750-8170

206 East 58th Street, between
Second and Third Avenues

Casual

Reservations

Moderate

All major credit cards accepted

Lunch and dinner seven days
a week

4, 5, 6, N, R, W trains to
Lexington Avenue/59th
Street station

This is the latest venture from the team of Donatella Arpaia and Michael Psilakis, who run this restaurant as well as Anthos and Kefi. Back in 2006, they opened the short-lived Dona, a Mediterranean restaurant that was a critical success, but the building was sold and their lease terminated. They then opened Anthos, which is more his restaurant than hers and was another big critical success, where Psilakis was able to create a menu showcasing his version of modern Greek cuisine. Here at Mia Dona, it's all about her Italian American roots. This stretch of 58th Street used to be a restaurant row back in the 1970s and 1980s. These days, with Felidia right across the street, it's much quieter, but Mia Dona may change that.

The space sits midblock, and you enter past the bar and front dining room. Beyond this you'll find the middle room and then the wood-paneled library out back. As of this writing the place is still quite new, but I've already had a few very good meals. And as good as the food is, the prices are very fair, with most appetizers in the single digits and low teens, pastas in half courses for $10 to $12 and full portions in the high teens, and the main courses starting in the high teens. Roast chicken is just $17, and an excellent pork chop with frisée, lardons, and a farm egg is $19; in other words, by today's standards, this is a bargain.

A great starter is the large plate of grilled squid, set over a very well-seasoned caponata, with a brioche pressed panini-style and a garnish of toasted pine nuts, pickled eggplant, and diced tomato—for $9, that's quite a plate of food. Even simple dishes here, like baked clams oreganato, are spruced up; the bread crumbs are pre-sautéed and golden brown, and between the crumbs and the mollusks sits a thin sheet of lardo for richness, with a dollop of stracchino cheese thrown in for good measure. Rabbit is slow-cooked confit style, then removed from the bone, tossed in mustard, breaded, and deep-fried golden brown; it's garnished with salt and vinegar and served with deep-fried crispy fingerling potatoes and a side of cucumber rémoulade for dipping.

For pasta, the homemade gnudi are hard to beat, light as a feather and glossed with truffle butter, with sautéed wild mushrooms, crisped slices of speck ham, and deep-fried sage. The bucatini are made using a Torchio pasta press, which forces the semolina-and-water dough through a die. Chewy and dense, the bucatini are rounded out with smoked boneless chicken legs, guanciale, and radicchio. Bigoli comes with slow-cooked broccoli rabe, sautéed with pepperoncini, with lentils added for more richness. Polpettone, or Florentine meatloaf, is made from a rich, light, and flavorful forcemeat; the six-minute runny egg at the center adds a touch of drama to the whole. The mixed grill is another winner, pairing lamb chops, braised lamb riblets, cotechino sausage, and a marrow bone, topped with gratin bread crumbs, all set over a bracing mint-accented salsa verde.

Desserts are simple and good, like the maple-syrup-laced panna cotta with maple walnut ice cream and candied walnut crumbs, or the Sicilian ice cream sandwich, a play on s'mores, with chocolate gelato, caramel, marshmallow, and salty cashews in supporting roles. The wine list, as expected, works well with the food, and the staff is trained in that Donatella style, efficient and good. With food this good and prices this fair, I expect Mia Dona to have a good long run.

Miss Mamie's Spoonbread Too

212-865-6744
366 West 110th Street, between Manhattan and Columbus Avenues
Casual
Reservations
Moderate
All major credit cards accepted
Lunch and dinner seven days a week
B, C trains to Cathedral Parkway/110th Street station

Facing the south end of Morningside Park on West 110th Street, Spoonbread Too is the creation of Norma Jean Darden. One of eleven children born to a family in Wilson, North Carolina, and granddaughter of a freed slave, Charles Henry Darden, she was raised by her parents in northern New Jersey, where her father was a physician. Darden attended the Northfield Mount Hermon boarding school and graduated from Sarah Lawrence, one of very few women of color to have done so in the early 1960s. An actress turned Wilhemina fashion model turned caterer, she has a passion for cooking that has deep family ties. In 1981, together with her sister Carole, another Sarah Lawrence grad, she published the family memoir and cookbook titled *Spoonbread and Strawberry Wine*. This restaurant features many of the family recipes described in that book.

Named after their mother, Mamie Jean Sampson Darden, and styled to resemble her Alabama kitchen, the restaurant has an awning outside that tells it all: "Take out, eat in . . . home cookin' to go." Tables are arranged over the red-and-white tile floor. The clientele is an interracial mix of Columbia students and staff, locals, BET employees, politicians, and the occasional celebrity. The food is as advertised, like meals in her mom's kitchen, served here with a Motown sound track. Mondays feature live music, the Sunday brunch is a classic, and aside from takeout food, they also have a great catering company for parties around town.

Start with the fluffy, light cake-style corn bread, slathered in butter, and move on to vegetable soup made with grilled chicken or popcorn shrimp, both good starters. For a main course, I like the fork-tender braised short ribs, a recipe that includes beef stock and pickling spice. There is crisp fried chicken, BBQ ribs, and for those who can't make up their minds, a sampler platter of chicken, ribs, and shrimp, said to be former president Bill Clinton's favorite. Thick pork chops are smothered in a rich onion-infused gravy, and chicken is offered in several more guises, including BBQ and jerk style. Sides, at $2.50 apiece, include rich, spicy mac and cheese seasoned with a bit of cayenne, fried sweet potatoes, candied yams, long-cut string beans, and braised greens, all followed by those big, rich southern-style desserts: coconut layer cake, sweet potato pie, various fruit cobblers, and the addictive Miss Mamie's banana pudding. They don't serve alcohol, but the iced tea and homemade lemonade work just fine.

This is a good choice for very decent soul food in New York. The neighborhood is lovely, and there are many good walks you can take in any direction afterward to work off that big meal and take in the sights.

Momofuku Ko

No phone, reservations by Internet only at http://reservations.momofuku.com
163 First Avenue, between 10th and 11th Streets
Casual
Moderate to expensive
All major credit cards
Lunch Friday, Saturday, and Sunday, dinner seven nights a week
L train to First Avenue station; 6 train to Astor Place station

David Chang's meteoric rise from relative obscurity to becoming one of the hottest chefs in America in a mere 12-month period is nothing sort of remarkable. In spring 2007 this culinary bad boy and media darling won the James Beard Rising Star Chef award; in spring 2008 Momofuku Ko was awarded three stars by the *New York Times* and four stars by Adam Platt at *New York* magazine, and Chang was given full-blown profiles in both *GQ* and the *New Yorker*, as well as being selected as the keynote guest chef at the annual *Food and Wine* culinary lovefest in Aspen. I can recall very few chefs whose careers experienced so much fame so fast, except maybe Rocco di Spirito. Let's hope Chang's star burns brighter and longer. Part of this is simply the media world we live in, which needs fresh faces and good stories on a daily basis. Chang is a Korean American from suburban Washington, D.C. His dad was in the business, and he did not want his son to do the same. David worked as a line cook at Daniel and Craft, and those who worked beside him recall a cook of average talent and not much more. Time will tell if all this praise has merit or if he's a footnote three years from now, but at present, he's about as hot as it gets.

That said, this little, tightly focused restaurant is Chang's best effort to date, and in many ways, Momofuku Ko captures the spirit of the day, as trends go in New York dining. I've always felt that his Ssam Bar was way overhyped, despite the legions of fans and almost cult-like following, and the same can be said for his noodle shop nearby. But here at the tiny Ko outpost, there is some serious cooking going on, though getting a table is still the biggest problem. For starters, the place seats only a dozen diners at any one time. Reservations are nearly impossible to secure, as they are offered a week in advance, via his Web site starting at 10 AM each day— they are gone literally in the time it takes to hope you're lucky and click the mouse.

But should you be one of the lucky dozens, for $85 per person you will actually have a bargain on your hands for food this good. As to the spirit of the day, the restaurant scene has moved downtown and is more casual. Here you have both. Add to that the fact that traditional barriers, both hierarchical and literal, between kitchen and customers are removed. The cooks here both cook your food and then serve you directly. You sit on stools with no backs, perched before a spare blond wooden bar, facing the open kitchen, and the rhythm of the meal is set by you and the cooks working before you. For historical reference, the great French chef Joël Robuchon became the pioneer of this style of cooking and service in Western cuisine when he closed his famed Jamin and then a few years later opened his first L'Atelier Joël Robuchon on Paris's Left Bank nearly a decade ago, with an open kitchen and a similar style of service.

At Ko you are seated at the bar; set before you are chopsticks (tips resting on a cork), a simple white folded napkin, a glass of water, and a leather-bound beverage list. Though Korean American by birth, David has worked in Japan, and here the cooking, plating, overarching theme, and culinary aesthetic strongly suggest his focus, or at least his interest, is now on Japanese cuisine. Each day the menu is set; you have no choices. The food arrives plated as miniatures, little studies, or variations on a theme. At a recent meal, a small amuse-bouche arrived, essentially an Ivy League chicharrón cut of heritage-stock pork belly, seasoned with Japanese togarashi spice mix. This was followed by miniature house-made English muffins, lardo melted on top and then sprinkled with sea salt and chopped chives. Next was a course of raw scallops, sliced and set over a pool of spiced buttermilk. The dish was sprinkled with poppy seeds and batons of chive, and perhaps a drizzle of roasted poppy seed oil. The rich, sweet scallop meat played beautifully against the buttermilk, and the seeds provided textural contrast and a burst of nutty flavor as bonus. A signature kimchi consommé, with dark clear broth, captured the spice and pickled notes in that ubiquitous Korean side dish and was served over an oyster on the half shell with crisped pork belly. Koreans often pair thick slices of chilled, fatty pork belly with raw oysters, so this theme really speaks to Chang's roots.

Perhaps my favorite dish featured a slow-cooked egg, done sous vide for maybe 50-plus minutes in a warm-water bath, allowing the proteins to just barely set, like a runny custard. This egg was spooned over onions cooked soubise-style, essentially diced very small, then slow-cooked until they are soft and sweet, but white, not caramelized. To this plate they added a large spoonful of domestic hackleback caviar, characteristically a little muddy-tasting, plus a sprig of chervil and the smallest potato chips I've ever seen, cut from fingerlings and fried crisp. The shaved foie gras torchon with riesling jelly, lychee, and pine nuts was too out there for me; I would have preferred the torchon as such cut in proper lobes and the jelly as diced garniture, but I'm a bit old-fashioned in these matters. The flavors and mouthfeel were there; I'm just not a fan of eating powder. Another winner was the slow-cooked (rumored to be cooked for 24 hours) boneless short ribs of beef, which are then deep-fried and served with grilled scallions, a disk of pickled daikon, and a garnish of pickled white mustard seeds. There was also a glazed baby carrot with a half spoon of rich jus, again a lovely dish reflecting Chang's Korean roots and his modern sensibility.

As to dessert, I've never had the apple pie at McDonald's, but I know it looks somewhat like what I was served at Ko, and maybe this speaks to the chef's suburban American roots. Cooked apples were encased in a pastry envelope, which was then deep-fried and served with a scoop of sour milk ice cream and salty, toasted miso. It was a lovely play on flavors, textures, and culture in general. If you can get a table here, do so. If Chang can cook at this level in a bigger store, I'll look forward to it, for here during this meal, it did appear, at least at moments, that all that praise may indeed have some merit.

Momofuku Ssam Bar

212-254-3500
207 Second Avenue,
    at 13th Street
Casual
No reservations
Moderate
All major credit cards accepted
Lunch and dinner seven days
    a week
L train to Third Avenue station

As noted in the entry on Momofuku Ko, over a short span David Chang went from a chef few had ever heard of to one of New York's stars. His funky noodle bar, Momofuku, had opened to broad praise, while the second effort, Ssam Bar, stumbled badly at first, due in large part to the fact that it offered only a small menu of little Korean soft sandwiches, called ssam, for most of the night. He was winging it, the focus was blurry if there was a focus at all, and the place nearly folded. But when word got out about another menu being served only after 11 PM, the place took off like a rocket. Soon that broader and far more interesting late-night menu was offered during the earlier hours as well, showcasing Chang's brand of Asian fusion cookery. It helps in this neighborhood to stay open very late and to capture that certain elusive, perhaps indefinable East Village/Lower East Side foodie vibe. Early on, dining with a friend, I suggested we book an 8 PM reservation and was told I was crazy. "We'll sit down at 10, earliest. C'mon, it's Ssam Bar, man," was his reply. It turns out that an 8 PM dinner at Ssam Bar is a hipster's culinary equivalent of the 4:30 senior-citizen Blue Plate specials offered in Orlando eateries. He was right—the place was still filling up by 10 PM, and I recognized a few chefs and restaurant PR types eating there as well. When we left after midnight, it was packed.

The room is long and narrow, relatively well lit, even late at night, and nearly entirely paneled with a dark stained wood—both the walls and the ceiling are sheathed in it. Seating comes by way of industrial wooden rectangular blocks painted black. A bar runs the length of the slate-floored room, small tables fill the balance of the space, and the modern stainless-steel open kitchen is visible to the rear. The napkins are paper, and the chopsticks are of the industrial, inexpensive bulk variety stored in round containers scattered over the bar. The sound track is on the loud side and hip, and the crowd young.

The menu is broken down in many little sections, with headings such as raw bar, small dishes, country hams, seasonal offerings, offal, fish . . and of course ssam, those little addictive soft rolls. That said, the menu changes a lot; items come off the menu it would appear when David or his chefs become bored making them. Many of the dishes are a nod to the chef's Korean American heritage. Kimchi finds its way into sandwiches, stir-fries, and braises, the long rice noodle duk gook pops up unexpectedly here and there, and aggressive seasoning with red pepper paste, fish sauce, and salt is a hallmark. One of the best starters is the Hokkaido sea urchin, plated alongside a cloud of whipped tofu that has been infused with pungent yuzu, topped with shards of julienned scallion, and concealing a small mound of pearl tapioca that has been cooked in lychee juice. Unctuous, textural, variant—the three elements play off each other beautifully. Under the offal category is the warm veal head terrine, an inspired version of the French tête de veau. Here the terrine is sliced paper-thin, nearly covering the plate, dressed with a light red-pepper-based vinaigrette and served garnished with shaved fresh fennel bulb and grilled toasted baguette. In season, the fried Brussels sprouts just explode with flavor. They are quartered, fried, and then tossed in a bracing spiced vinaigrette laced with fish sauce, red chiles, and mint, then sprinkled with fried puffed rice for a little extra crunch on top of the bold flavors and textures below. A dish billed as braised rice cakes utilizes the aforementioned chewy barrel-shaped Korean rice pasta duk gook. It is cut into one-inch lengths and tossed with coarsely ground pork sausage meat removed from its casings, spoonfuls of chopped kimchi, and chunks of braised collard greens, all tossed together in a thick meaty stew-like affair.

Except for some plates being salty, which happens with Korean food, in general the cooking is bold and big-flavored. But the fusion touches work well, and the menu is one of the more ambitious and successful of its kind to be found anywhere in town. However, as is often the case with young ambitious chefs who are on a roll, I wish the kitchen here were more disciplined, and that some of the dishes that do make their way onto the menu were better vetted and less experimental. They have a good, small selection of beers including excellent Hitachino white and red rice ales, a half dozen good choices of sake, and a small, somewhat pricey wine list offering a well-chosen variety of sparkling, red, and white wines from $40 and up. The servers are earnest, young, and as hip as the crowd. Come for a late dinner—you'll eat well, and the energy is infectious.

Naples 45

212-972-7001
200 Park Avenue, at East 45th Street, in the MetLife Building
Casual
No reservations
Moderate
All major credit cards accepted
Breakfast, lunch, and dinner Monday–Friday
4, 5, 6, 7, S trains to Grand Central station

I'm not exactly sure who all is going to schlep up to the MetLife building for good pizza, but if by chance you happen to live or work in the area, then this place is a real find. When you think of Restaurant Associates, now called the Patina Group, pizza may not be what comes to mind. While they do run some very good restaurants around town, most notably the Sea Grill, the Brasserie, and Brasserie 8½, and some not-so-great ones as well, they just happened to have opened a very good pizza joint right here in the midst of all these midtown office buildings. With three very well-built wood-fired ovens, they can also do volume, as witnessed during any weekday lunch. Then again, pizza is one of the original Neapolitan fast foods. With ovens that can get as hot as 700°F, a good thin-crust pie can cook in a minute or less. They use only Italian 00 wheat flour, imported San Marzano tomatoes, even Italian sea salt and some kind of alkaline-enhanced water to ensure a pizza like you may find on a good day in Naples. To that end, they've succeeded.

I like my pizza simple, so I opt for the basic tomato, mozzarella, and basil topping—the classic Margherita. The cheese melts to a creamy finish, the sauce is lean-tasting, the crust is charred with a bit of chew—in short, for this neighborhood, you'd be hard pressed to find a pie as good within a mile or so in any direction. So should you find yourself in the mood for pizza after visiting MoMA or shopping on Madison Avenue, or just plain want to try very good pizza where you least expect to find it, this is the place.

New Bai Wei Gourmet Foods

212-966-9203
130 Division Street, between Allen and Ludlow Streets
Casual
No reservations
Inexpensive
Cash only
Lunch and dinner seven days a week
F train to East Broadway station

What I love about this city is illustrated in typical New York fashion on this little stretch of Division Street, where you'll find not only some of the best cheap Fujianese food but, just a few doors further east, some of the best Venetian food as well. For great Venetian small plates, visit Bacaro, but let's say you have only $10, want lunch for two, and want to keep some change; then look no further than New Bai. Their lunch special offers a choice of four dishes plus rice and soup for $2.75 per person. That's not a misprint. This is a bare-bones place, the clientele almost always exclusively Asian, but the food tastes decent, and for that price your only real alternative is hot dogs. Hit the steam table out front and grab the salted shrimp with the shells still on. The hacked-up duck and the ribs are okay, but honestly, a lot of what is for sale I could not with any certainty identify, aside from categories like vegetables, fish, or meat. That said, for a $3 lunch, I'm not complaining.

New Chao Chow

212-226-2590
111 Mott Street, just north of Canal Street
Casual
Reservations
Inexpensive
All major credit cards accepted
Seven days a week 8 AM–10 PM
6, J, M, Z, N, Q, R, W trains to Canal Street station

I've heard different theories on how this place got its name. It's either a specific regional cuisine, or perhaps a restaurant named after a specific Chinese dialect known as chiu chow, or the name of a specific subgroup of Chinese who live in Guangdong province around the port town of Shantou. In any case, it seems to be an offshoot of mainstream Cantonese cooking, with influences from elsewhere including Vietnam. The room is generic in the worst sense: bright, noisy, and not so clean, with communal tables of worn Formica and waiters who might speak little or no English, but who cares? Whatever the case may be, the food here is very good, and definitely a little different. They specialize in noodle soup, among other things. On my first visit, I ordered what everyone else was having. I like to do that—look around and see what the regulars are doing. It was a soup called "broth noodles," or mee pok ta; on the menu, it's listed as Chao Chow noodle soup. It's a steaming bowl of rich broth full of housemade chewy noodles and your choice of protein, usually mixing both pork and seafood. You can order this with fish balls, stick rice (that's how it's printed on the menu), duck stick rice, beef ball stick rice . . . you get the idea. The possibilities go on and on and include one listed as chao chow combination soup, which includes organ meats. Yes, that's the one I get a lot.

The roast duck here is good too, not your typical crisp-skinned brown variety but rather an orange-hued bird, redolent of sweet soy sauce and served with a fish-based vinaigrette, similar to Vietnamese nuoc mam, but laced with garlic and ginger. The hae cho, or deep-fried stuffed roll, is really tasty as well, as are the more typical varieties of noodles—various types of lo mein and mai fun. Maybe the best thing about the place, aside from the fact that the food really tastes great, is that it is so cheap. You can eat very well here for under $10 for lunch and $15 for dinner. In fact, if you know how to order, you can eat well for half that. The noodle soups average under $4 per bowl, the quarter duck over rice costs exactly $4, and soft noodles and stir-fries are all around $5. Many of these could be a meal in themselves, making this a standout and one of the best bargains in Chinatown, an area already rich with great food at discount prices.

New Green Bo

212-625-2359
66 Bayard Street, between
  Mott and Elizabeth Streets
Casual
No reservations
Moderate
Cash only
Seven days a week 11 AM–11 PM
6, J, M, Z, N, Q, R, W trains to
  Canal Street station

Now called Nice Green Bo, this restaurant's signature soup dumplings, crab shau lon bau, have gotten lots of press, and even after eating them repeatedly over the years, I still think they deserve it. Known as double traif to my nonobservant Jewish friends, these wontons are filled with broth and ground pork mixed with crabmeat; you must try them. The trick in making these involves incorporating a rich, gelatinous, flavorful pork stock with the ground pork while they are still both at room temp, then chilling the whole mix together, meat and stock. When the ground meat is cold, the rich stock becomes solid, like meaty gelatin, and the dumplings proper can be formed with it. As the dumplings for each order are heated, the previously solid, chilled stock separates from the meat and fills the insides of the dumplings with this rich "soup," plus the ground pork and crab forcemeat. Be careful when eating them, as the broth inside is very hot when served. I let them cool for a while before I eat them, then pop them in my mouth whole and let the whole thing kind of ooze, but others with more sense and less patience pick them up in a soup spoon, poke a little hole in the dumpling, let the broth run out a bit while blowing on it, and then go to town. However you choose to eat them, they are a real treat. The various platters of chilled preserved meats with dipping sauce are very good as well. Pressed pork belly sits aside silky white pieces of drunken chicken and braised beef. Meatballs in Shanghai red sauce are wonderful. Zucchini blossoms are stuffed with a white fish and deep-fried; crispy eel is a must. And ask for the fried yellow fish, a specialty, when available.

All the dumplings are first-rate, and most days you can see them being made right out front, behind the cash register. Scallion pancakes are a good side order, as are the crispy duck, Shanghai cabbage, Singapore noodles, and garlic eggplant. Truth be told, I've never had anything from this menu that I didn't like. The service varies; ignore it. (This is Chinatown, folks!) Just come hungry, order as much as you can eat, roll up your sleeves, and dig in. To many this is still considered the best Shanghai restaurant in Chinatown.

New Malaysia Restaurant

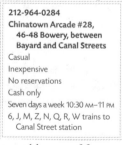

212-964-0284
Chinatown Arcade #28,
   46-48 Bowery, between
   Bayard and Canal Streets
Casual
Inexpensive
No reservations
Cash only
Seven days a week 10:30 AM–11 PM
6, J, M, Z, N, Q, R, W trains to
   Canal Street station

The food here represents a mix of cultures and cuisines, including Indian, Thai, and Chinese. Situated in a little alleyway next to a noodle stall, it can be spotted easily enough, as the sign in front hangs from the ceiling. The food here is more than decent and very inexpensive, and packs a lot of flavor into each plate. Expect curries of various stripes sharing the table with coconut milk, noodles, various proteins, and big round lumps of fragrant rice. The space is small, the lighting bright, and the tables wood-grained Formica, but for under 10 bucks you can eat well. Roti canai is a milky, curry-based soup with green chiles and a side of fresh grilled flat bread. Another appetizer of squid with crunchy water spinach is a winner and can be a whole meal at just under $8. Fried spring rolls are filled with meat and vegetables and arrive crisp, nearly greaseless, and well seasoned.

Indonesian-style fried rice is delicious, studded with peas, chiles, and scrambled eggs and flecked with chicken meat; add a splash of fresh lime juice and you're set to go. I really like the dish billed as char kway teow, broad noodles (like Chinese chow fun) that are pan-seared and lightly coated with sauce, tossed with small flavorful shrimp, bean sprouts, scallion tops, more chiles, and minced meat. Singapore-style chow mei fei, or fried rice noodles, comes pan-seared, nearly dry, laced with curry powder, and topped with julienned peppers, scallions, onions, and slivers of roast pork. There is a huge section as well of noodle-based soups, fish, chicken, or beef, some curried, all flavorful and priced under $5 per bowl. Curried beef brisket is a good main, as are the chicken rending, the whole deep-fried red snapper in belacan sauce, the skate steamed in banana leaf, or, for the brave, the curried fish head casserole.

Nicky's Vietnamese Sandwiches

212-388-1088
150 East 2nd Street, between
   First Avenue and Avenue A
Casual
No reservations
Inexpensive
Cash only
Seven days a week 11 AM–10 PM
F, V trains to Second Avenue
   station

Theresa Dang named this store after her four-year-old son, who is often there with her and her husband behind the counter. Theresa's father ran a successful Vietnamese sandwich shop in the Sunset Park section of Brooklyn in the 1990s, a time when Sunset Park became a very Asian neighborhood. Her dad made only one thing, but he made it very well: the Vietnamese banh mi sandwich, which he sold to long lines of customers who queued up every day. For whatever reason, the Sunset Park store closed and Teresa did not want that to be the end of Dad's banh mi legacy, so she and her husband hunted around for cheap rents in neighborhoods where the same concept might work, specifically lower Manhattan. The East Village seemed perfect: the right mix of people, proximity to Chinatown, and relatively affordable rents. So here they landed, in what was once a tiny skateboard shop, and on any given day, the four of them, Nicky, Mom, Dad, and Grandpa, can be seen behind the counters, making one of the best sandwiches you'll ever have anywhere, for $4.50 a pop. For Brooklynites, they have a branch on Atlantic Avenue that I'm told is just as good.

The banh mi sandwich is a cross-cultural phenomenon harking back to the French occupation of Vietnam. As with any great dish, the beauty results from the simple interplay between the flavors and textures, all balanced to achieve a perfect harmony. All that needs to be there is there, and nothing extraneous is added. In Vietnam, the bread originally was a Vietnamese version of a small French baguette, with some rice flour thrown in with the bread flour. In the case of Nicky's, a bakery in Brooklyn makes these perfect little football-shaped mini-baguettes that have a very crisp crust, plenty of air, and not too much bready dough inside.

These rolls are split, then warmed in a little toaster oven, and filled with a slather of mayonnaise, a slice of French-style liver pâté, minced cooked pork, Vietnamese ham, julienned pickled carrots, pickled cucumbers, a few slices of jalapeño, and a small bouquet of cilantro. Folks, it's heaven. The first bite is all crunch, through the crust and into that warm center. Then the flavors reveal themselves in layers, first, the livery rich pâté, then the oily minced pork and salty ham, all of this polished by the acidulous carrots, crisp cool cucumber, a hit of jalapeño, and finally that burst of cilantro. You cannot eat just one (or at least I can't).

They also have a meatless version with marinated, grilled portobello mushrooms that is a nod to this neighborhood, which is home to many vegetarians. The spring rolls are very good, with their transparent, thin rice paper wraps and cool crisp lettuce and shrimp center, dipped in that funky fish sauce, laced with slightly sweetened vinegar. But I just go for the addictive banh mi, which you simply can't go wrong with.

Nobu

212-219-0500
105 Hudson Street, at
  Franklin Street
Casual to dressy
Reservations
Expensive
All major credit cards accepted
Lunch and dinner Monday–
  Friday, dinner Saturday and
  Sunday
1 train to Franklin Street station

This is one of the most important sushi restaurants on the planet. Chef Nobu Matsuhisa is that rare thing, a real culinary visionary, a true innovator. As the story goes, the chef was lured to New York from L.A. by actor Robert De Niro, who raved about his menu, which features unique sushi, sashimi, and ceviche creations. De Niro encouraged New York restaurateur Drew Nieporent to visit Nobu's Los Angeles restaurant, Matsuhisa, which was very busy and highly regarded. Nobu was beginning to emerge nationally as a rising star, but nothing could have prepared him for what the opening of Nobu in New York in 1994 would do for his career. Originally, the Tribeca Grill space was to have been Nobu, but when they flew him out east to look at it, Matsuhisa said it was simply too big. So when a space right around the corner became available, Drew and his all-star cast of backers, including De Niro, grabbed it.

I'm not an architect; David Rockwell is, and he designed the dining room. I don't know what to make of it except to say that it is different from any other I've sat in before. As one would expect of a sushi bar, there is a prominent bar with workers on one side and customers on the other. Around that bar is a U-shaped room with some sliding Japanese-style doors to the rear, separating several private dining rooms. Rough-hewn wooden pillars, actual birch tree trunks, run from the floor to the ceiling at odd angles. Some of the interior walls are covered with river stones, and the partially finished open ceiling leaves me with the impression of an outdoor Hawaiian seaside resort after a hurricane. But what do I know? The food, on the other hand, is excellent.

Nobu started young as a sushi chef apprentice in his native Japan, working his way up the ranks. When he was 24, he took an offer to open a sushi restaurant in Lima, Peru, which is where he began to develop his unusual international style, featuring ceviches, cooked dishes, and partially cooked dishes alongside traditional sushi and sashimi. If budget doesn't constrain you, go all out and try the omakase tasting menu, which can get very expensive very fast depending on how many courses you have. It starts at $100 per person, but many spend double or triple that before they are done. Option B is to simply order à la carte and sample an assortment of local and imported raw, marinated, and cooked fish of the highest quality.

Among the cooked dishes, the signature black cod in miso marinade is always fabulous; the rich, fatty flesh melts like custard beneath the miso glaze. Or try the yellowtail with jalapeño, the fat tuna pairing well with the acidity and heat of the pepper. Tiradito Nobu-style is a another nod to the chef's days in Peru, and the fettuccine of squid with asparagus has squid cut long and thin standing in for the pasta and tossed with crunchy asparagus in a light soy-based sauce. Lobster with wasabi pepper sauce is a nice turn on one of the most overrated crustaceans of all time, though I prefer that same sauce with his halibut cheeks. His lobster ceviche is lovely, the meat taken from the tail, and for whatever reason, this time the flesh seemed sweeter simply wrapped in bibb lettuce leaves and accented with fresh cilantro and brunoise red onions. His unusual salads, such as the baby spinach salad with fresh fluke sashimi, or the lobster salad with shiitake mushrooms and Nobu spicy lemon dressing, serve as great appetizers. Or simply order sushi and sashimi à la carte, and you'll enjoy some of the best-quality, freshest fish available in all New York.

Save room for the desserts, which include banana sesame harumaki and the chocolate bento box. The delicious mochi are balls of great ice cream wrapped in a chewy dough of sweet rice flour, weird but very good.

As Nobu spent time working in Japan, Peru, Argentina, Alaska, and L.A., his is an international style of sushi, not bound by tradition—his brand of culinary Esperanto. The chef is very creative and has a superb palate for pairing flavors, textures, and temperatures in new and inventive ways, and the good sense to know when enough is enough and not overthink the dishes. It can be very expensive if you eat like I do, and you'll need reservations, which can be maddening, as the place is packed every lunch and dinner service all year long. That leads to the number one problem with the place: the service. If you are a known regular or some sort of celebrity, they'll dote. If not, the wait staff seems to take some kind of pleasure in making you feel invisible or worse. But I can get past that for the great food.

Big hint: Next Door Nobu is literally next door, and it is just as good. Next Door only does dinner, but the food all comes out of the same kitchen, same ingredients, same fish, just a lot less hype and attitude. It is an excellent alternative, which is exactly what it was supposed to be. Or head up to the branch on 57th Street, where the room is far more spacious and the food is just as breathtaking.

Nomad

212-253-5410
78 Second Avenue, between 4th and 5th Streets
Casual
Reservations
Inexpensive to moderate
All major credit cards accepted
Dinner Monday–Thursday 4–11 PM, Friday and Saturday to 12 AM, Sunday 3–11 PM
F, V train to Second Avenue Station; 6 train to Astor Place Station

The great pastry chef and chocolatier Jacques Torres told me about this place one day. The small room is done in authentic Moroccan style, with ochre walls (some decorated with murals), a terra-cotta floor, accents of custom-made wrought iron, a small selection of imported Berber pottery, stained-glass lanterns, wooden archways, and carved wooden screens adding to the effect. The Middle Eastern sound track and candlelight close the deal—Marrakech meets the East Village. In warmer months, they have a small outdoor garden with additional seating. The owner is Mehenni Zebentout, an Algerian with a law degree who wanted to open a place like this for years, and now finally has. The food is very good. Small plates of vegetables and spreads with flat bread make a great starter, as do the small triangle-shaped filled phyllo pastries known as bourekas. They have the best pastilla I've had outside of Morocco, the pastry light and flaky. The filling is chicken, not squab as is traditional, but the meat is moist and flavorful and enriched with ground almonds and solid seasoning. The signature Merguez sausage is superb as well, offered in various guises throughout the menu—don't miss it. The tagines and couscous are all very good.

Save room for the lovely little house-made cookies, courtesy of Salima, the owner's wife. It's hard to find good Moroccan or Algerian food in New York, but here you will do just that.

Norma's

212-708-7460

118 West 57th Street, between
Sixth and Seventh Avenues,
in the Parker Meridien Hotel

Casual

Reservations

Expensive

All major credit cards accepted

Seven days a week 6:30 AM–3 PM

N, R, Q, W trains to 57th Street
station; B, D, E trains to
Seventh Avenue station

Initially I didn't know what to think about a place that does nothing but serve brunch seven days a week. I mean, we're talking brunch, nothing else. No lunch, no dinner, no pre-theater, just brunch. And what the heck is brunch anyway, an excuse to eat too much food that's bad for you and be drunk by 2 PM? Brunch is silly, chefs hate it—it's a culinary aberration relegated to just a handful of spots around town, and then only on weekends. Well, I guess I'm the idiot, because the place is absolutely packed, and that's Monday through Friday; don't even try to get in on weekends, when they do 600-plus covers a day and the line to get in runs out the door, down the stairs, and spills into the lobby below. After several visits, I have concluded that if it's brunch you must have, then this is the perfect place in which to have it. This is brunch on steroids. Everything they do is over the top. The room, modern with lots of wood accents, tan leather, and flattering lighting, is usually 50 percent tourists, many staying at the Meridien, joined by others who by now have heard about the place that serves the $1,000 omelet. Yeah, that's right, and they actually sell a few every month to numbskulls with money to burn. Technically it's a $1,000 frittata, made with a whole Maine lobster and 10 ounces of sevruga caviar. You'd think for $1,000 you'd at least get golden osetra or beluga. But forget that dish and let's talk about what us regular folks can expect.

You start with a tall shot glass filled with a complimentary fruit smoothie, one day guava, another strawberry, always good and creamy. Order coffee and you have your own glass pot, French-press style, brought to your table. Orange juice is freshly squeezed daily, and if you don't like pulp, they strain it.

A good example of what they do here starts with the menu item listed as a "wazza." While a perfectly good waffle is usually good enough for me, at Norma's that's just where they start. Take a perfectly good waffle, then cover it with sautéed sliced banana topped with banana compound butter, brown butter, powdered sugar, and a drizzle of Grand Marnier for good measure. Or they start with a waffle studded with berries that have been folded into the batter. After the waffle is cooked, it is topped with sliced banana, then covered with a dome of Hollandaise sauce laced with raspberry coulis, which is finally dusted with sugar and brûléed under the salamander. On to the Valrhona chocolate brioche French toast. Here a chocolate brioche is made by adding cocoa powder to the flour, then each thick slice is filled with Valrhona chocolate, dipped in egg, sautéed, and served, topped with whipped cream and powdered sugar with that deep rich chocolate now acting as a molten liquid center.

The classic New York mixture of lox and scrambled eggs here is presented in two split croissants, filled with fluffy scrambled eggs, a touch of onion, and big chunks of smoked salmon. A breakfast quesadilla is stuffed with scrambled eggs, applewood-smoked bacon, and guacamole. Even pedestrian hash is given the treatment. Instead of corned beef or roast beef, they take shredded duck confit and toss it with onion, chunks of potato, and peppers, all topped with two poached eggs. Simpler, less exotic options include the usual array of omelets, homemade applesauce with potato pancakes, eggs Benedict, egg-white frittata, and a huge fruit plate. It's so much food at midday that you'll probably find dinner an afterthought. It can get expensive—figure on $30 per person plus tip—but it will be the brunch that afterward all others will be measured against.

Nougatine

212-299-3900
1 Central Park West, at Columbus Circle, in Trump Hotel
Casual to dressy
Reservations
Expensive
All major credit cards accepted
Breakfast, lunch, and dinner Monday–Friday; breakfast, brunch, and dinner Saturday and Sunday
1, A, C, B, D trains to 59th Street/Columbus Circle station

Though a bit expensive, this may be one of the best deals in town, essentially a discount version of the famed Jean Georges located right next door. Though the food at Nougatine comes from a different kitchen downstairs, the philosophy, polished technique, execution, and fine ingredients that make Jean Georges outstanding are all on display here in this less formal setting. The man behind it all needs no introduction; Jean-Georges Vongerichten is one of the preeminent chefs working in American today. Of all the restaurant projects that he is involved with around New York, and there are many, Jean Georges and its sibling, Nougatine, are my favorites. These two represent his philosophy of cooking and aren't far-reaching attempts at Chinese food or a downtown club scene, as some of the others are. Here the flavors are well defined and clean, mixing sweet with sour. Many dishes have a slight heat from the subtle use of hot pepper, and the deceptively complex layers of flavors build on one another. On most days it is here that Jean-Georges spends his time, and his presence in this kitchen and his supervision account for a good deal of the consistency.

You enter off Central Park West, next to the lobby of the Trump Hotel. The room is to the left, off a small lobby with a greeter and a coat check. The dress code is slightly more formal than I'd like it—no shorts, sneakers, or sandals in the summer—and part of this has to do with Jean Georges next door. All of the diners who eat there must pass through this room, so in a sense, it's an attempt to set a slightly formal tone. There is a zinc bar where you can pass time while waiting for your table, and if you can't secure a table, you can eat very comfortably at the bar. The floor is marble that resembles nougat, the ceiling is high, and the décor tasteful and modern, blending anigrewood, beige leather, and stainless steel. To the rear, an open kitchen is separated from the dining room by a chest-height partition. The menu is rather small and undersells the food. There is a five-course prix fixe menu for $68, or à la carte with prices ranging from single digits to the low forties for the most expensive entrees. In terms of price and value you will eat far better here for considerably less than at many other highly touted restaurants around town.

Jean-Georges spent part of his early career working in the Orient, specifically Thailand and Hong Kong, and his skill in incorporating Asian accents into his cuisine is on display here. A salad of peekytoe crab and asparagus arrives set in a pool of clear orange melon water, spiced with hot pepper powder. The asparagus is cut lengthwise paper-thin and intertwined with sweet crabmeat to form a tall disk in the center of the plate. Raw sashimi-grade tuna is cut in medium dice and paired with tomato lozenges, and topped with crisps of julienned, deep-fried sea trout skin. Fluke, again sashimi style, arrives with grapefruit sorbet and spiced powdered yuzu. Foie gras brûlé arrives as a thick two-inch-high cylinder, cut from a torchon, pink, deveined, minimally seasoned, and caramelized on the top, set on a crouton, and garnished only with a schmear of cherry mustard and a small tumble of micro arugula.

One of my favorite dishes was simply billed as slow-cooked cod. Here a center-cut filet of Chatham cod arrives just barely cooked at the center, the meat custard-like and flaky. This is achieved by slow-cooking the fish in a 200°F oven. Once cooked, the filet is set atop a broth that looked like pistou, the Provençal soup, but turned out to be based on fresh pineapple juice. The natural acidity played off the natural sweetness. The broth is then spiced with smoked hot pepper, seasoned with a cilantro puree, and studded with small diced zucchini. The excellent individual elements all worked together to raise the overall effect, as it should be with great cooking. And they do simple well too. A Berkshire pork chop cooked medium rare, simply seasoned and dusted with cumin, was set on a bed of sautéed wilted mustard greens; it required nothing else.

Johnny Iuzzini does desserts for both restaurants and is a huge talent in his own right. He is one of the best pastry chefs working in Manhattan today. The wine list is great, sharing the cellar with the signature restaurant next door. Service too is refined. So if you're looking for Jean

Georges lite, or a great meal pre-theater, or perhaps are in this neighborhood and just want a casual bite of very good food at very fair prices, this place makes a fine choice.

Oceana

212-759-5941
1221 Avenue of the Americas, between 48th and 49th Streets
Business casual
Reservations
Expensive
All major credit cards accepted
Lunch and dinner Monday–Friday, dinner Saturday
B, D, F, V trains to 47th–50th Streets/Rockefeller Center station; N, R, W trains to 49th Street station

The Livanos family has several other very good restaurants in New York, but this is their crown jewel. For well over a decade Oceana has consistently been one of New York's best seafood restaurants, initially under chef Rick Moonen, followed by Cornelius Gallagher, and these days it's even better than ever with Ben Pollinger running the kitchen. The new version of Oceana, which is set to open in the fall of 2009, is on the ground floor of the McGraw-Hill Building on Sixth Avenue. The space is larger and more casual, and the menu reflects that with somewhat more traditional dining options at various price points with large iced tiered seafood platters now part of the fare. That said, the crew is the same, and if you want to order à la carte or from the tasting menu, here's an idea of what you might expect.

Service is professional under the watchful eye of the maître d' and part owner, Paul McLaughlin, a seasoned New York City professional who cut his teeth years back on the floor at Le Bernardin during their opening years.

Ben has worked around town for a while and was a chef de cuisine at Tabla under Floyd Cardoz just prior to taking over at Oceana. His plates feature seafood but are compositions of many ingredients. His sashimi of white and red tuna arrives as a cylinder coated with burnt scallions, creamy spicy vegetables, and a soy sauce that has spent 20 years aging in oak casks. Florida stone crab is seasoned with fresh herbs and cumin, bound with crème fraîche, covered with thinly sliced avocado, and formed into a sphere. An étouffée of West Coast oysters melds the flavors of these sweet briny bivalves with diced Black Forest ham, brunoise celery, and hon shimeji mushrooms bound in a chowder of razor clams.

Like many of this city's top chefs, Pollinger gets his ingredients from local purveyors; he also gets overnight shipments of pristine ice-packed seafood from Maine, Florida, Europe, Hawaii, and Japan. A typical Oceana plate combines flavors, textures, and cooking techniques. Take, for example, his halibut. He slow-poaches a thick square-shaped center cut of Atlantic halibut in clarified butter, sets this on a bed of braised

French beluga lentils seasoned with shallots and thyme, tops the fish off with sliced rings of carrots braised and then glazed in a carrot juice reduction, and finally sauces the plate with pork roasting juices. The thick white flesh of Australian barramundi is sautéed and served southern-style, with Japanese yams, braised collard greens, julienned black trumpet mushrooms, and candied pecans in a foamy sauce accented with applewood-smoked bacon jus. A thick firm round disk of Australian swordfish comes paired with slightly bitter braised red endive, sweet rosemary-onion marmalade, the slightly sour note of sorrel, and a sauce of smoked preserved quince—a well-executed balancing act of sweet, sour, and texture.

The pastry chef until recently was David Carmichael, another Daniel alumnus, who was at Oceana for over a decade. He left for the ill-fated Russian Tea Room and is now at Gilt, but his replacement is Jansen Chan, also very good. A signature dessert is a play on textures, featuring black-pepper-laced meringue and both sticky rice and puffed caramelized rice as garnish to his excellent frozen banana mousse; the chocolate-covered chocolate chip pecan bar is good as well. A lighter but lovely choice would be the blueberry mochi cake with coconut-flavored tapioca and a bracing lime sorbet.

The wine list is very well matched to the food, and though prices creep toward the high end, there are good choices throughout the price range. For $50 per person wines can be paired with the $78 tasting menu, and this is a very good idea.

As mentioned, Oceana is slated to move in late summer or fall 2009 to bigger, more modern digs a few blocks away on Sixth Avenue, on the ground floor of the McGraw-Hill building. The new space will have more seats and be a bit more casual, but I suspect that Pollinger, Chan, and the rest of the team will work hard to make certain that Oceana remains one of the best seafood restaurants in New York.

Odeon

212-233-0507
145 West Broadway,
    at Thomas Street
Casual
Reservations
Moderate
All major credit cards accepted
Lunch and dinner Monday–
    Friday, brunch and dinner
    Saturday and Sunday
1, 2, 3 trains to Chambers
    Street station

And so it was that years back two visionary expat Englishmen, brothers Keith and Brian McNally, created the first hip, modern dining room south of Canal Street. It was really the only thing down there back then. SoHo had a few spots—Raoul's, Chanterelle (before it moved to its current Tribeca location), and Teddy's, or whatever it was called then, a Latin-themed restaurant with blue martinis. While further downtown in the financial district there were old-style restaurants such as Harry's at Hanover and Fraunces Tavern, those catered almost exclusively to the Wall Street crowd, mostly men in suits, drinking and smoking after work in wood-paneled clubby rooms Monday to Friday, which were empty by 9 PM.

Odeon was something entirely new—artsy, edgy, hip, and open till the wee hours of the morning. It was early New York bistro at its best. The crowd was young and good-looking, an egalitarian mix of local artists, the crew from *Saturday Night Live* after hours, entertainers, musicians, parvenues, strivers, and New York trust fund types—essentially the cast of characters inhabiting the pages of *Bright Lights Big City*, much of which was actually based on the Odeon scene and its clientele. The early Odeon menu was presided over by the young, talented chef Patrick Clark, and it was much like it is today, featuring modern American/French bistro dishes. While recent visits suggest that the restaurant hasn't exactly kept up with the times, in 1984 it was a big deal.

Still open daily and serving dinner past midnight, it always seems to be very busy. These days you'll find adequate versions of comfort food classics, such as French onion soup, steamed mussels with white wine, grilled hanger steak, and a decent steak frites, roast half chicken, and pan-seared salmon. While these dishes are by no means new, and in fact seem ubiquitous around town, Odeon is still a little slice of New York history, with a very downtown vibe, good for both people-watching and a reasonable meal, and therefore worth the visit.

Old Town Bar and Restaurant

212-529-6732
45 East 18th Street, between Park Avenue South and Broadway
Casual
No reservations
Moderate
All major credit cards accepted
Lunch and dinner seven days a week
4, 5, 6, L, N, Q, R, W trains to 14th Street/Union Square station

Long before this area was dubbed the Flatiron neighborhood, and even before the famous Fuller Building that gave the area its name was built, there was an Old Town Bar and Restaurant. I wasn't there in 1892 when it first opened as Viemeister's, but I did live in this neighborhood in the mid-1980s, and this was one of the few places open at night. There was no restaurant scene here, and not much of a bar scene either. On this particularly dreary and dark block this was the only place open after 6 PM, it seemed. But it stayed open late, and some nights after work I'd pop in for a drink or two. If you like the old and the authentic, the minute you walk in these doors it will be love at first sight. The place has changed little over the past century. Drinks are served across the same mahogany bar; the tin ceiling is original, as are the well-worn wooden floors, beveled glass, wood cabinets, and tall dark wood banquettes framing the booths (which have secret compartments for hiding drinks during Prohibition). This place is among the oldest continuously operating bars in New York, along with McSorley's, Chumley's, the White Horse, and the Ear Inn, to name a few.

The crowd varies from 20-somethings who have just discovered the place to grizzled old veterans, guys in suits, and everyone in between, depending on the time of day or night. The food . . . well, the beer is good and cold, the drinks strong, and the burgers very decent. It's on my burger list partly because they are simply good, but also because they seem to taste even better when eaten in this classic room. The kitchen is in the basement, so all the food arrives from behind the bar via ancient dumbwaiters. I think the bathroom fixtures are original too. Check the place out because it's a classic.

Olieng

212-307-9388
644 Tenth Avenue, between 45th and 46th Streets
Casual
Reservations
Moderate
All major credit cards accepted
Lunch and dinner seven days a week
A, C, E trains to 42nd Street/ Port Authority Bus Terminal station; C, E trains to 50th Street station

One of the best Thai restaurants in town, along with Pam Real Thai just a few blocks away, this place is tiny, with just seven tables; the narrow storefront is cozy, to say the least. But if you like good Thai food, come early for dinner (lunch is always too busy) and you'll be in for a treat. The staff is very nice, and the room, while small, allows just enough space between tables for a bit of privacy. Don't come here for a romantic night out unless that solely depends on good food, in which case you'll have chosen well. The room has wood paneling up to the level of the tables, then features exposed brick walls with a few mirrors thrown in to help ease the space constraints. The kitchen to the rear is fast and the cooking accurate.

Start with one of the interesting soups. The tom yum koon blends together the flavors of lemongrass, shrimp, and mushroom, accented with a good dose of fresh lime juice. The tom kha gai is based on coconut milk and enriched with chunks of chicken, mushrooms, and again lime juice. Or start with the salad billed as yum neur yang, made from sliced marinated skirt steak, flash-grilled, then set over chopped tomato, onions, and cucumber, accented with good fresh sliced mint and polished with fresh lime juice. Or try the lab, a heap of ground meat—chicken, pork, or beef, your choice—blended with crispy rice, mint, more lime juice, and a very hot chili sauce. While the pad thai is excellent, the dish listed as ladnar is also very good. Here thick chewy broad noodles are tossed with either shredded beef or chicken and bound with Chinese-style oyster sauce and Chinese broccoli. They offer some great combination dishes with rice, where you can choose your protein from chicken, beef, duck, pork, shrimp, calamari, or tofu. The pra ram long song matches your choice with a coconut-milk-based peanut curry sauce laced with vegetables; order this hot, it's excellent. Or try the pad bai ga prow, where the dish is started by sautéing Thai basil in oil; its flavor leaches through that oil and is therefore present throughout the dish, marrying the flavors of the pork, sautéed peppers, scallion, onions, and chili paste.

Seafood dishes are built around salmon, snapper, catfish, and the combination of shrimp, scallops, and squid. Among my favorites is the pla pattaya, where lightly breaded deep-fried snapper filets are covered with a seafood sauce, combining little shrimp, scallops, peppers, onions, Thai basil, and chopped scallions. They do not yet have a liquor license, but they will provide glasses should you bring beer or wine, and as always with Thai food, I find beer the best choice. This is one of my favorite Thai restaurants in town; I just wish it had a few more seats.

One if by Land, Two if by Sea

212-255-8649
17 Barrow Street, between Seventh Avenue and West 4th Street
Casual
Reservations
Moderate to expensive
All major credit cards accepted
Dinner seven nights a week
1 train to Christopher Street station; A, C, E, B, D, F, V trains to West 4th Street station

Housed in a beautiful landmarked carriage house on a quiet, lovely street in the West Village, this place is by now an institution. It's also easy to miss; with no exterior sign, just those white-washed walls and big bay window mark the way. You enter past the piano, the bar to your left; the rooms spread up and around, and all are characterized by period charm (this was, after all, Aaron Burr's carriage house). For years the place's claim to fame was being billed in nearly every publication as one of New York's most romantic restaurants, whatever that means. Okay, it's quaint: the dining rooms are candlelit and of a period; they possess not one but two working fireplaces and a live piano player; the views are of a private garden mews. But these days you'd better have more than that going for you to make it in this town. And, happily, this place now does. After serving mediocre food from a menu that hadn't changed in what seemed like decades, in 2007 the owners decided it was time to hit the refresh button. Initially they brought in the peripatetic and talented chef Gary Robbins, post–Biltmore Room, post–Tea House, pre–Sheraton Square, He was followed by Craig Hopson, who had been for years the chef de cuisine at Picholine uptown. I stopped by in early 2008 to find a nearly entirely new menu, and for the most part it was very, very good. That said, late in 2008, Craig left this kitchen to take over as the new chef at Le Cirque, but what follows describes a meal I had while he was there, and to a large degree, the kind of food coming out of the kitchen these days as well. The night I was there, the place was packed with young couples who must have been in the know. It looked like date night for the NYU senior class, table after table of couples, so romantic. Perhaps it had been featured in a *Sex in the City* episode, or maybe they all had been reading their parents' diaries: "You were conceived the night we had that bottle of Bordeaux with the beef Wellington at One if . . ."

Well, the beef Wellington is still on the menu, the only holdover. These days it is an individual piece of filet, cooked to order, wrapped in good thin puff pastry, and layered with a fine mushroom duxelles and some foie gras foam for good measure. My starter that night was a winner, a boneless, lightly smoked quail set over house-made jícama kimchi. Here the fine diced jicama was substituting for the normal choice of white daikon radish, but the kimchi spice profile was there, and it worked beautifully, drizzled with a crunchy peanut aioli—nice textures and flavors that worked in layers.

The item billed as wild mushroom and Parmesan crumble was a bit less successful. The dish was plated in a ring at the center of the plate. The crumble was a straightforward savory streusel, redolent of good Parmesan, but the amount of the slightly floury streusel overshadowed the fine sautéed mushrooms set beneath it. The plate was drizzled with aged balsamic and looked better than it tasted. On the other hand, the Gruyère gnocchi were lovely, garnished with excellent canned French snails, slow-cooked yellowfoot mushrooms, and shaved botarga. Another winner was the fresh Gulf shrimp, still partially in their shells, served perfectly cooked with fresh hearts of palm and a broth infused with kaffir lime and sweet carrots. Spanish mackerel, a delicious fish rarely seen on Western menus, here is pan-seared and set atop a sweet and sour eggplant puree, then, with a nod to this fish's popularity in the Orient, seasoned with a touch of mint and very good sesame oil.

The desserts these days, in keeping with the rest of the menu, are much better than before. A dense, moist apple butter milk cake arrives with a scoop of lovely cheesecake ice cream, drizzled with caramel. The kumquat baba is fresh, airy, and yeasty, imbued with mixed citrus syrups, and topped with lozenges of blood orange, tangelo, and sweet orange. The soufflés are worth the wait. The wine list is good and improving. The staff, many of whom have been here quite a while, are trying hard to keep up with the changes in the kitchen. One if by Land is now a player, and with food this good in a room this nice with those fresh flowers, candlelight, and tinkling piano, it's only up to you to provide the romance.

Oriental Garden

212-619-0085

14 Elizabeth Street, between
Bayard and Canal Streets

Casual

Reservations only for parties
of six or more

Inexpensive to moderate

Cash only

Lunch and dinner seven days
a week

6, J, M, Z, N, Q, R, W trains to
Canal Street station

The chef-owner of Momofuku and Ssam Bar, David Chang, told me about this place. He loved it and thought I would. I do. Next to Ping's, it may be the best seafood restaurant in Manhattan's Chinatown. Many foodies and fans of Chinese cooking now feel that the "other" two Chinatowns in New York, Flushing, Queens, and Sunset Park, Brooklyn, have eclipsed the traditional downtown Manhattan neighborhood in terms of energy and quality, but I still love coming here. When I first moved to New York in 1982 I had an illegal sublet in a lovely Mitchell-Lama building nearby on Greenwich Street, and on my one day off I'd wander to Chinatown to buy great, cheap ingredients and cook dinner at home. On days when I had a few extra dollars, which was a rare treat, I'd eat there as well. Those were the days in the early 1980s when cheaper bars served good, cold 50-cent beers, and the restaurants were real bargains too. Well, the 50-cent beers are long gone, but the restaurants are still a bargain. If you want value in New York, hop on the subway and get off at Canal Street

This place specializes in seafood. Some of it is excellent, and most of it is very good. You'll walk past some species in the fish tanks up front that may end up on your plate soon thereafter. My favorites, which I seem to order on every visit, include the great razor clams in black bean sauce—or anything in black bean sauce, for that matter. Pan-fried noodles with assorted seafood is a lovely spin on the traditional lo mein varieties. Get the West Coast geoduck clams, the belly here fried. I think they surpass my best memories from my youth of trips to Howard Johnson's, whose fried clam strips were excellent, or at least I thought so then. Whole steamed black bass arrives with the fish presented as it should be, slow-cooked, tender, on the bone, and full of flavor. Black bass is a sweet-fleshed fish, one of the best from our waters, and the minimal treatment here is just perfect. Avoid the fried dishes; recently they have seemed to my taste uncharacteristically gummy and even bland. While they do a great dim sum business here too, I found some of the won ton wrappers to be a bit undercooked and some of the fillings underseasoned.

A few years back they changed management, and old-timers claim it was better before. Lacking that reference point, I've found my meals here to be good, sometimes very, very good. They have a short, forgettable wine list, some beers, and sake. The room can get very loud and the service is up and down, but overall it is still a favorite of mine for seafood. If you order well, you'll leave with a full belly and a smile on your face.

Orsay

212-517-6400
1057 Lexington Avenue,
 at 75th Street
Casual
Reservations
Moderate to expensive
All major credit cards accepted
Lunch and dinner Monday–
 Saturday, brunch and dinner
 Sunday
6 train to 77th Street station

Orsay sits squarely on the northeast corner of Lexington Avenue and 75th Street, where for many years Mortimer's did a brisk business under the watchful eye of owner Glenn Bernbaum and his pet dog, Swifty, until Glenn's passing in 1998. Mortimer's was always packed with New York society types like Nan Kempner and Pat Buckley, who seemed to dine there daily, sharing the room and the mediocre food with the usual assortment of Upper East Side ladies who lunch and trust fund lackeys. Enter veteran New York restaurateur Jean de Noyer (who also runs the popular La Goulue nearby), who transformed the space into a beautiful belle époque dining room straight off the rue Royale, complete with a menu that now makes this place well worth a visit.

You enter off Lexington into a lovely room lit by art nouveau chandeliers, the high ceiling framed by molded art nouveau arches, mahogany-paneled walls, rows of comfortable banquettes separated by etched glass, and a floor of hand-laid Italian tiles. To the back left sits a zinc bar; to the far right, weather allowing, there is outdoor seating on 75th Street, and upstairs is a coat check and a private dining room as well. The kitchen is run by Jason Hicks, a young British chef who started his career in his hometown at the age of 15. Now in his mid-thirties, he worked in London, Scotland, Australia, and New Zealand prior to coming to New York a decade ago.

The menu is mostly straightforward bistro fare, but he breaks from the traditional and often repetitive menu offerings typically found in this genre by adding two signature sections to the menu; one features a variety of tartares, and the other is called "jars and preserves," a selection of slow-cooked savory dishes all served in glass mason jars. Start any meal with the sardine escabèche and you can't go wrong. Inside this jar are layers of plump, thick, boneless sardine filets, cooked by the initial heat and then the acidity of the marinade, redolent of Banyuls vinegar and olive oil, and served with toast points. Or try the jar of coarse-ground thick-textured duck pâté, served with traditional cornichons and mustard, or the chicken liver and foie gras parfait under a lid of cassis jelly. Other appetizers include house-made boudin blanc set beside a salad of beluga lentils with a sauce spiked with calvados, or in cold weather a bowl of poacher's broth, a rich chicken and venison consommé garnished with pheasant and duck meat, alongside pearl barley and a dice of mixed root vegetables.

For main courses, try the Chatham cod pot roast. Here the thick, flaky filet is served barigoule-style, with lobster and artichokes in a scented fish broth. Beef cheeks are prepared Bourguignon-style, braised with red wine in a rich veal stock, garnished with poached marrow, and set alongside a lovely celery root puree. All the steaks, strip, loin, filet, and hanger, are cut from Herefordshire cattle, the chef's favorite, and are dense, well marbled, and sure to please, set alongside a pile of frites that rate among the best in all New York. Should you be in the mood, there are wonderful chilled seafood platters and those tartares as main courses, including an excellent steak tartare; a Japanese-style tuna tartare spiked with wasabi, sesame oil, and sesame seeds, with bits of tempura for crunch; or my favorite, the niçoise, made from diced raw salmon paired with a traditional garnish of diced boiled potato, haricots verts, cornichons, chopped hard-boiled egg, and pesto.

Desserts are what you would expect: a great example of the classic tarte Tatin, warm profiteroles drizzled with chocolate, crème caramel, and ice creams and sorbets. Should they have it on the menu, don't miss the milk chocolate tart with sea salt and Ovaltine ice cream. The wine list is very good—heavy on French producers, of course, and getting better with the recent addition of sommelier Romain Ambrosi to the roster. Ambrosi worked at Ducasse New York for several years and brings great polish and pedigree to this seasoned team, so don't be afraid to ask his suggestions for pairing wines with your meal.

Ouest

212-580-8700
2315 Broadway, at 84th Street
Casual
Reservations
Expensive
All major credit cards accepted
Dinner Monday–Saturday,
   brunch and dinner Sunday
1 train to 86th Street station

Born in Ithaca, New York, and raised by a single mom, Tom Valenti had an early culinary inspiration: his grandmother. He was a lackluster student, and after high school he started work for the leading French chef in that area. A few years later he would find himself employed as the personal chef for a wealthy family in Westchester, whose only caveat was "don't cook the same thing twice." Armed with their fancy kitchen, an unlimited budget, and dozens of their cookbooks, he made this his private training laboratory. From there he worked for Guy Savoy in a short-lived venture in Greenwich, Connecticut, then headed off to Guy Savoy in Paris to learn pastry. While he was waiting at the airport for his plane home, fate intervened. In one of those great, only-in-the-movies moments, he spotted Daniel Johannes, who was then the sommelier at Montrachet, who in turn introduced him to another young American on his way home as well: none other than the young and then unknown Alfred Portale. Valenti would become Portale's first sous-chef at Gotham Bar and Grill, way back when the plates were still black. He was one of the many in a long line of talented chefs who would train under Portale at Gotham.

I first tasted Valenti's food when he was the chef at Alison on Dominick. Alison Hurt too had worked in the front of the house at Gotham, and opened her tiny restaurant in the most unlikely spot: a one-way street, 100 yards long, steps from the Holland Tunnel entrance. Only in New York would this place work. Somehow people found the place and figured out a way to get there, and get there they did; the restaurant did very well. Valenti was given glowing reviews for his earthy, rustic fare, and that braised leg of lamb is still on his menu today, 20 years later.

Valenti's food at Ouest is neither subtle nor light. The menu is comprised of roasts, pan sautés, and braises that carry well-developed flavors, the result of long and slow cooking. Sometimes these can be a bit heavy on the animal fat component, but I like that too. The key to the roasts and braises is that they can be done, in fact must be done, ahead of time, and as such are easy-to-serve time savers for this tiny open kitchen.

It's a big, noisy, two-tiered L-shaped room, entered through a narrow bar area. Actually it's two separate addresses that were combined to create one space, previously a storefront coffee shop on Broadway and a dry cleaner on 84th Street. Packed since it opened, Ouest has been a huge success and was a harbinger for change as the first new restaurant since Picholine to put the Upper West Side on the culinary map as a place for fine dining.

The food is rustic and flavorful, from great meatloaf and short ribs to medium-rare tuna, sturgeon topped with egg and lardons, tripe, and those signature lamb shanks. Desserts follow the homey theme and are worth a try should you have any room. The wine list is good, the service civilized, the place always packed and noisy. And who knows—maybe you'll bump into Bill Clinton, Kevin Bacon, or your neighbor from West End Avenue.

Pakistani Tea House

212-240-9800
176 Church Street, between
    Duane and Reade Streets
Casual, BYOB
No reservations
Inexpensive
All major credit cards accepted
Seven days a week, 24 hours
    a day
A, C, 1, 2, 3 trains to Chambers
    Street station

Traveling downtown on the number 2 train one morning, I fell into a food-related conversation with a very nice young lady from Bombay who told me about this great hole-in-the-wall on Church Street. I had mentioned that I liked Haandi on Lexington Avenue, and she said this place downtown had the same vibe and the same type of no-frills home-cooking style. She was right on. A sure sign of a good ethnic eatery is when a large number of expats eat there on a regular basis, and this place, like Haandi, is full of Pakistani and Indian livery drivers on break. If you can get past the bright fluorescent lights and abundance of Formica and linoleum, head straight for the cafeteria-style steam table.

They have fresh-baked naan all day long, the meats are certified halal, and you'll find a good selection of vegetarian choices every day. Since there are fewer than 20 seats, takeout may be an option. Try the chicken tikka; here it is really good, as are the balti gosht beef, hot Goan fish curry, and nearly any of the many vegetarian dishes. I especially like what they do with cauliflower. As the menu changes from day to day, it's hard to recommend specific dishes that appear only from time to time, but if you're feeling adventurous, check the place out; you won't be disappointed.

The Palm

212-687-2953
837 Second Avenue, between
    44th and 45th Streets
Casual
Reservations
Expensive
All major credit cards accepted
Lunch and dinner Monday–
    Friday, dinner Saturday
4, 5, 6, 7, S trains to Grand
    Central station

It's very easy to overlook a place like this in New York. These days the restaurant scene moves at a pace like it never has before. Each year, a dozen very good restaurants open and vie for the title of restaurant of the year. The cooking keeps getting better all over town, and the public can't get enough of it. So places like the Palm, which seemingly have been here forever, tend to get lost in the shuffle or are considered passé by the younger generation—places that their parents may have liked or where older celebrities hang out but which aren't worth a visit. To them I say nonsense. This place, taking up the first two floors of an old tenement walk-up on the west side of Second Avenue, is not only very good but just loaded with history. If the restaurant L'Ami Louis matters to Parisians and fans of the bistro genre worldwide, then the Palm should be afforded that same reverence here and be considered as part of the great steakhouse story.

Opened in 1926 by grandparents of the current owners, the Bozzi and Ganzi families, it was to have been an Italian restaurant named Parma, the hometown of both families. But the clerk at the New York office where they registered the name misunderstood them and thought they said Palm, not Parma. In any case the menu then featured Italian classics, but customers kept ordering steaks and lobsters too. There was a good butcher nearby, and they would send the waiters there all night to buy individual steaks until finally they put steak and lobster on the menu. This area had a lot of steakhouses in those days: Christ Cella, Pietro's, the Pen and Pencil, Bruno's, and Manny Wolf's, to name just a few. Many of New York's daily newspapers were headquartered nearby as well, hence the cartoons on the walls, which were essentially a barter deal between the owners and the regulars, who were running up tabs they couldn't pay. These names are lost on most today, but some of the cartoonists are legends: Bill Keane's "Family Circus," Dik and Chris Browne's "Hagar the Horrible," Mort Walker's "Beetle Bailey," Matt Weil and "Popeye," and so on. While all the other Palms around the country are good, this one is the original, the cartoons are real, and the place just reeks of New York history.

So how's the food? Better than you think, I bet. Back in the day, the excellent food critic for the *New York Times*, Mimi Sheraton, awarded the place three stars, and to this day, I think the food is very good for what it is. Take a simple dish like veal Parmesan. Here they cut thin veal scallops from the top round, then pound them thin, bread and sauté them to order, and top them with muenster cheese. The tomato sauce is made from imported San Marzano tomatoes. The corporate executive chef, Tony Tammero, hails from New York's Hell's Kitchen neighborhood and started here as a teenager washing pots. For years, all the chefs and waiters were Italian immigrants. Tony worked his way up, but the concept is still the same: buy really good ingredients and present them in a straightforward manner. The steaks are prime and dry-aged and the lobsters fresh. The menu is old school; if you stick with steaks, pasta, and lobster, you'll eat exceptionally well, and the portions are huge. Steak à la Stone was invented here: a simple sauté of sliced sirloin heaped over sautéed onions and peppers, it was named after the film director Oliver Stone's father, who ordered it all the time.

If you have room for dessert, the portions here are huge; order a slice of carrot cake and you get a quarter of a cake. Be prepared for doggy bags. The drinks are strong and the staff all seasoned professionals, so if you're looking for a true original New York steakhouse, put the Palm on your short list of the best of the best. If you've never been there or it's been a while, I think you'll be surprised.

Pamplona

212-213-2328
37 East 28th Street, between
Park Avenue South and
Madison Avenue
Casual
Reservations
Moderate
All major credit cards accepted
Lunch and dinner Monday–
Friday, dinner Saturday
6 train to 28th Street station;
N, R, W trains to 28th Street
station

Chef-owner Alex Urena is a great New York story. His father worked in the kitchen at the River Café back when Charlie Palmer was the chef there, and while still in his teens, Urena was hired as a pot washer. He worked his way up off the pot sink into the prep kitchen, then onto the hot line, and up the brigade, followed by stints in some very good kitchens as a cook and a sous-chef prior to breaking into the realm of chefdom first at Marseille for Simon Oren and then briefly at Suba for Yann de Rochefort. This space was originally opened as Urena in 2006, a more formal and ambitious project that for a variety of reasons had to be closed, revamped, essentially taken downmarket somewhat, and then reopened as Pamplona in 2007. It's noteworthy at this point in time that Alex is one of the very few Dominicans to step up to the plate, assume the job of executive chef, and then open his own restaurant. The greater Hispanic community for years has been the backbone of many New York restaurant kitchens. From the 1950s through the 1970s it was initially just Puerto Ricans. Then came the wave of Dominican immigrants, many of whom found kitchen jobs. This was followed by populations from Ecuador, El Salvador, and now a new generation of Mexicans, all an integral part of the restaurant kitchen scene, a group of solid workers who rarely choose to run their own kitchens, preferring instead to be among the best and most reliable support staff. I'm not certain why this is; a lack of role models, perhaps. In any case, with chefs like   Alex stepping up, I hope it will be the beginning of a new trend.

The food here is straightforward and fairly priced. This stretch of 28th Street approached from the west side is bleak; the neighborhood really is a transitional area, mostly office buildings, parking lots, and delicatessens that close at night. The space itself is a challenge, long and narrow, with the bar and some seating up front, the dining room opening up with an aisle down the center, and seating against both walls, all the way to the rear. When busy, it can get very loud, and décor and service are not the strong suit. But put up with a few bumps, and two people can eat well here for under $100.

Start with skewers of chorizo and shrimp over toast with a schmear of goat cheese, or the fried little balls of Iberico and manchego cheese flavored with chorizo, crisped on the outside from a light coating of beer batter, liquid at the center. The salt cod croquettes are worth a try, as is a nice plate of patatas bravas (diced potatoes), fried and then drizzled with paprika-laced aioli. The dish billed as lasana de txanguro turns out to be thin ravioli skins, one below and one set loosely on top of a flavorful mix of creamy lump crabmeat laced with a good salsa verde. For main courses, the hamburger is very good, made from ground beef, suckling pig, and chorizo, aggressively seasoned and set on a nice custom-made bun, accompanied by chunky, thick fries. Chicken breast is cooked sous vide, tender and moist atop a puree of leeks and truffle oil, and the plate finished with a nice pile of quick-sautéed oyster mushrooms.

The desserts are all fairly simple but satisfying. Fried churros come with a Valrhona chocolate dipping sauce; a low-fat ice cream is frozen, breaded, and fried, and set next to a small scoop of mint-and-orange-laced ice cream. The wine list is small but all the selections work with the food. Clearly this is a labor of love for the chef, as he has no backers save his family and wife, who also works the floor some nights. While it's a retreat from the more ambitious restaurant it was originally opened as, I suspect this space and menu will do very well in the neighborhood, and it is well worth the trip should you be looking for a different take on Spanish food from a talented young chef.

Pam Real Thai

212-333-7500
404 West 49th Street,
   between Ninth and Tenth
   Avenues
Casual
No reservations
Inexpensive to moderate
Cash only
Lunch and dinner seven days
   a week
C, E trains to 50th Street
   station; N, R, W trains to
   49th Street station

Considered by many, myself included, to be among the best Thai restaurants in New York, this place is the creation of Pam Panyasiri, the chef-owner. She hails from northern Thailand, where the food is a bit less spiced than in the southern regions. The room is small and adequate, with a few posters on the walls, and when busy it can get very loud. But who cares? If the food is good, I'm in. And here the food is indeed very good. The menu is a large document, but to my mind the best dishes are the curries, custom blends that deliver flavor in long-lasting layers. Service is good; Pam's son Timmy often works the floor, so it's a straight-up family business, usually a good sign in my book.

Start with the durian in season; the fruit may be stinky and ugly, but when its delicate sweet flesh is removed and set over sticky pineapple rice, the dish is addictive. Or start with (and maybe end with) the amazing oxtail soup. Rich and packed with flavor, the bowl arrives topped with big sprigs of fresh cilantro and deep-fried shallots. The broth below delivers spoonful after spoonful of flavor. This is Thai soul food. The green papaya salad is a perfect little dish, blending contrasting flavors and textures from the sweet fruit to the acid of lime juice, a hint of garlic, some tomato and green beans, and then the crunch of peanuts and those tiny dried shrimp. For the brave, try the entrée listed as gang tai pla, where fermented fish kidneys are stir-fried with vegetables, turmeric, and lime leaves, then bound in a hot chili paste; order this one extra spicy and be prepared for fireworks. They serve beer and wine, and if you order the food hot, you'll definitely need the beer. It's seemingly always busy and crowded, and they do have a cash-only policy, but it's well worth it.

Park Avenue Winter

(or Park Avenue Spring, Summer, or Autumn, depending on season)

212-644-1900
100 East 63rd Street, between Park and Lexington Avenues
Casual to dressy
Reservations
Expensive
All major credit cards accepted
Lunch and dinner Monday–Friday, brunch and dinner Saturday and Sunday
F train to 63rd Street station; 4, 5, 6, N, R, W trains to Lexington Avenue/59th Street station

With the Smith & Wollensky group sold, Alan Stillman and his son Michael can for the moment concentrate on their New York holdings. To that end, a few years back they tapped the talented young chef Craig Koketsu, a California native who had been cooking in New York for nearly a decade, most recently with chef Christian Delouvrier at the last great incarnation of Lespinasse. His first gig with the Stillman clan was to take over as chef for the Manhattan Ocean Club, which was later turned into Quality Meats, where he created a good, reliable modern steakhouse concept. But it is here in this space, with this broader seasonally driven menu, that he can really open his wings and cook. The theme here reminds one of the grand Four Seasons on Park Avenue, which broke this same ground when it opened back in 1959: essentially to change the look of the place, the décor, the uniforms, and the menu four times a year, based on the current season. This is a bit of a conceit these days in a city where most good chefs change their menus all the time based on market-driven ingredients and the weather, but we will let that pass for now.

What matters is that the food here is very, very good. I've followed Craig's career, and he's got a fine mind and deft touch for mixing flavors and textures, especially the use of citrus fruits, fresh herbs, heat from peppers, and acids to impart lightness and clarity in dishes, where other chefs may steer toward heavier stock-based reductions and butter or cream. Take, for example, the starter of tiger prawns. The crustaceans are held together with fitted discs of kataifi, then flash-fried, the dough crisp and light against the shrimp. The whole is placed above tiny lozenges of blood orange swimming in a clear, sharp ceviche-style broth accented with brunoise carrot, hot pepper, grapefruit juice, and elderflowers, topped with a sprinkle of micro greens. In each bite you have crispness and crunch, then the flavor of good clean shrimp balanced with the various acidic components, playing off each other to cleanse the palate. A starter of fluke sashimi is cut paper-thin and layered over a pool of yuzu-based broth, accented with persimmons and crunchy diced roast cashews. The clean fish taste gives way to the acid fruit, and then the richness, salt, and fat of the flavorful cashews have you digging in for more. The fluke was paired with a good Heidsieck "blue top" Champagne. Another great starter from the 2007–8 winter menu was the modernized French onion soup, here made with a delicious, rich clear beef broth, enriched with oxtail and topped with a Gruyère crouton, as good an example of this classic dish as I've had anywhere. A ravioli of porcini is paired with wilted Swiss chard over a pool of gorgonzola cream. Again off that menu, a perfectly cooked filet of red snapper, the meat with the proteins just set, almost custard-like, is encased in a cornbread crust, the richness of the fish set off by a simple citrus salad. The grilled veal chop is topped with lightly gratinéed herbed garlic bread crumbs, and it shares the plate with a mound of dry-sautéed chanterelles and royal trumpet mushrooms. Surprisingly, the showstopper was a simple steak dish, in this case Brandt beef via the La Frieda boys, dry-aged, absolutely screaming with the taste of great beef at its best, and full of minerality from the unique diet these Holsteins enjoy.

Richard Leach is the pastry chef, a veteran on the New York scene, once dubbed "the Pythagoras of pastry," and a real talent. While I should have ordered the coconut angel food cake with caramel panna cotta and coconut-curry sorbet, I opted instead for the warm chocolate flourless cake with peanut brittle mousse, garnished with strands of pulled sugar rising off the plate. The flavors were clean, rich, and satisfying. The wine list is very good. Alan Stillman is a noted collector, though as to be expected with the Park Avenue address, bargains are few and far between. The staff is young and good, though the all-white uniforms they were wearing paired with the all-white room had an oddly sterile effect. The crowd is very Upper East Side, not my scene nor my favorite part of the city; on most nights it could double as a casting call for *Nip and Tuck*, with tables of distracted older couples with heavily jeweled hands who seem to be constantly checking their BlackBerrys while scanning the room for familiar faces, fussing about where they are sitting, and asking for sauce on the side, various steamed vegetables, and silly menu substitutions. That said, it's easily one of the best restaurants in this part of town. Catch it on a good night and order wisely, and it can be one of the best in the city.

Pastrami Queen

212-734-1500
1125 Lexington Avenue,
   at 78th Street
Casual
No reservations
Inexpensive to moderate
All major credit cards accepted
Seven days a week 10 AM–1 AM
6 train to 77th Street station

Believe it or not, in a city with a Jewish population of over 2 million, delicatessens are not doing very well. It's getting harder and harder to find a good deli, specifically one that serves good pastrami and corned beef, not the pink, rubbery, watery, salty, flabby commercial stuff that so often masquerades for the real thing these days. There are maybe a half dozen places left where you can get this, and Pastrami Queen happens to be one of them. Originally based in Queens, it recently moved across the East River and changed genders, but the pastrami served here is still top-notch. The menu is big; the place itself isn't, with most tables downstairs and a few more up on the mezzanine. It is billed as a real kosher restaurant; I'm not going to get into a discussion of what is and isn't considered kosher, or really kosher, or glatt kosher, who recognizes which rabbi, and all that, as it gets very complicated very fast. But they don't serve dairy here, harking back to kosher restaurants like the old and lamentably gone Ratner's deli.

The pastrami here is among the best in the city, as are the corned beef, tongue (divided into two cuts, center and tip), brisket, and chopped liver. They do combo sandwiches, triple-deckers, hot open-faced sandwiches, and full dinners as well. Both the chicken in the pot and the flanken in the pot are worth the trip in cooler weather. Stuffed cabbage is lovely, and while the Roumanian steak may not be as good as Sammy's downtown, here it's still darn tasty. Potato pancakes, which could be a meal in themselves, arrive crisp and moist, three to an order, with a dark brown tinge to the surface, and a side of applesauce. Service is good, and somehow this food screams for Dr. Brown's sodas, which they will gladly supply.

Patsy's

212-247-3491
236 West 56th Street,
   between Broadway and
   Eighth Avenue
Casual to dressy
Reservations
Expensive
All major credit cards accepted
Lunch and dinner seven days
   a week
1, A, C, B, D trains to 59th
   Street/Columbus Circle
   station; N, Q, R, W trains to
   57th Street station

The two big red neon signs and red canvas awning, landmarks visible from blocks away, tell the story. While restaurants like Peasant, Insieme, Babbo, Caffé Falai, and Bellavitae represent a modern version of Italian cuisine in New York, Patsy's is pure old-school New York City Neapolitan. Family-run at this same location for over 50 years, the kitchen is now in the hands of Sal Scognamillo, while his father, Joe, who was for many years the head chef, works the dining room. The story goes that Joe got his start in the kitchen here at the age of seven, under the tutelage of his father, the original Patsy (short for Pasquale). It appears that not much has changed in three generations, and that's not a bad thing. After all, this is the kind of cooking that most Americans, if they were lucky, grew up eating and calling Italian food—dishes like clams casino, mozzarella in carozza, eggplant Parmigiana, fettuccine Alfredo, chicken cacciatore, and lobster fra diavolo, all rich, hearty, and well seasoned. Patsy's was purportedly a favorite haunt of Frank Sinatra, and these days, it's popular with Tony Danza, and a host of other celebrities; I suspect many come here as much for the nostalgia as the food. There are two dining rooms spread over two floors, the upper accessed by a mirrored spiral staircase at the rear of the main room. The tables are well spaced, the lighting tends toward bright, and the service is very good, as much of the wait staff has been here for years and knows all the regulars. On a recent visit last winter, early one Friday night before a concert, I dined with my sons and their friends. We were seated upstairs opposite a large table of 12 or more people spread across a banquette. The group, perhaps an extended family, represented four generations from grandparents, older couples, their children, and four little ones who from time to time grew restless and squirmy as kids will during a long meal. It felt like home, or someplace in Brooklyn, with the parents walking the kids around the dining room in between courses, and no one minded; that's the kind of place this is—a restaurant where people come for birthdays or anniversaries or to show out-of-towners a slice of the real New York.

Honestly, most of the food is just okay, solid, and old school, but some of it rises to very good. Spiedini alla Romana at $16, alternating layers of good Italian bread and fresh mozzarella, fried and served with a tangy anchovy butter, is gooey, salty, fishy, and delicious. Fresh escarole here is sautéed with crushed garlic, gaeta olives, raisins, pine nuts, and capers, bathed in olive oil, then topped with seasoned bread crumbs and baked until the crumbs form a crisp top layer. The eggplant parmigiana, $19 and good for sharing, is presented centered on the plate, a thick wedge cut from a larger baking dish, the layers of creamy-smooth baked eggplant alternating with melted mozzarella cheese and a rich tomato sauce. One of my favorite seafood entrees here is the stuffed calamari, a bit expensive at $29, but worth it considering the labor involved. Two medium squid are served on a good spicy fra diavolo sauce, redolent of the squid that it was cooked with. The stuffing is a fine, well-seasoned mix of lobster and crab laced with pine nuts, the whole thing tasty; mop up the remaining sauce with whatever bread is available on the table.

For pasta, try the bucatini all'amatriciana, $21, the chewy long pasta set in a thick, reduced tomato sauce flecked with chunks of bacon, sliced

prosciutto, diced onions, and a chiffonade of fresh basil. The potato gnocchi in meat sauce is very good, as is the manicotti, stuffed with a mixture
of three cheeses and baked in a good hearty tomato sauce. The veal dishes
are traditional and good, either chops served in sauce or cutlets sautéed or
rolled and stuffed. I love the hard-to-find tripe alla Napoletana, a bargain
at $23, slow-braised in a tomato sauce thick with onions and prosciutto,
and finished with green peas.

Desserts are traditional; the baba au rhum is good, the various sponge
cake creations arrive moist with rum syrup, and the cannoli is good as
well. The lunch menu is nearly identical to the dinner menu, with smaller
portions and lower prices. The pre-theater menu is priced at $49 per
person for four courses, and there are daily specials worth checking out as
well. The wine list is decent but pricy, but overall, if you are in this theater
district neighborhood and yearn for very good, old-style Italian cooking
in a nice room with attentive service, come to Patsy's. Who knows, maybe
you'll become a regular too.

Payard Bistro

212-717-5252
1032 Lexington Avenue,
  directly to the rear
Casual to dressy
Reservations
Moderate to expensive
All major credit cards accepted
Lunch and dinner Monday–
  Saturday
6 train to 77th Street station

This is a sleeper of a restaurant. The chef,
Philippe Bertineau, runs a great kitchen here,
the food is consistently very good, the dining
room well run, the room itself a charm, and the
desserts—well, now really, you don't have to ask.
I should mention that Philippe is married to
Odette Fada, the chef at San Domenico, and if
they ever open a place together, watch out. The
room spreads out over two floors and is lush and gilded. David Rockwell
does belle époque replete with banquettes in a fine striped fabric, dark
wood paneling, brass chandeliers, antique mirrors, and drama. When
packed, it's noisy, but then again this is a bistro. If you're looking for seriously good classical French cooking look no further. There are fewer and
fewer places like this around, and I'll take this over Balthazar any day of
the week.

For lunch you can do well with just a soup and a plate of the excellent
coarse-ground house pâté, or hand-cut steak tartare, well seasoned and
served with crisp frites. Or go light with just a simple frisée lardon salad
and a little bite of the tempting desserts, say a perfect éclair.

For dinner start with the warm, thin tart of sliced Maine diver scallops,
set atop tender slow-braised leeks and a salad of watercress and frisée,
glossed with a black truffle vinaigrette. If you're a fan of chilled foie gras,
try the terrine here, sliced to reveal the pink blush at its center, with just

a dollop of house-made pear-onion chutney, and thick, chewy grilled toast in between bites. For one main course, thick slabs of fresh cod from Chatham are sautéed, then baked briefly until the delicate protein is just cooked, firm yet moist. It's set above a puree of curried cauliflower and alongside a tangle of Tuscan kale tossed with hon shimeji mushrooms and rainbow cauliflower florets. The sauce of reduced mussel liquor is flecked with crunchy crosnes and chopped herbs, then lightly bound with good butter. In the winter, wild boar shank is marinated in red wine overnight and then braised in that same wine and paired with glossy braised red cabbage and quince. Even humble chicken here is good, the breast stuffed and moist, the skin crisp and golden, served with garlicky mashed potatoes and a good, clean chicken-mushroom jus. Good sides can be had; try the traditional french fries or crunchy haricots verts sautéed with shallots.

Of course they do tasting menus, which allow the chef to play around with smaller portions and combinations, and after 3 PM they even serve a great formal high tea. Desserts are, as expected, among the best anywhere in New York. If you have a big table, consider the $21 dessert tasting selection. The wine list is deep but pricey. The service is good in an old-school way. All in all, you'd be hard pressed to find better classical French cooking in a more convivial dining room anywhere else in New York.

Peacock Alley

212-872-4895
301 Park Avenue, between 50th and 51st Streets, in the lobby of the Waldorf-Astoria
Dressy
Reservations
Moderate to expensive
All major credit cards accepted
Breakfast, lunch, and dinner seven days a week
6 train to 51st Street station; E, V trains to 5th Avenue/ 53rd Street or Lexington Avenue/53rd Street station

Don't roll your eyes—the food here can be very good. Over the last decade, some very talented chefs have come through this kitchen: Laurent Manrique, followed by Laurent Gras, and then Cédric Tovar. The problem is the setting. A recent renovation places the main dining room just off the hotel lobby by that famous Waldorf clock, so while you eat, you get to observe the comings and goings of tourists; great spot for a detective or a hit man, lousy for a date. They do have some tables out back behind the bar, and while you have no view except for that bar and a few turned-off flat-screen televisions, it would be my preference. The walls are gold and gilded, the ceiling the same. Peacocks from that famous mural are now framed here and there by way of decoration. This is now a Hilton property, true, but the Waldorf-Astoria is also a piece of New York history, the last great old-time hotel that still is operated exclusively as a hotel. It traces its roots back to the late 1800s, when there were two hotels, the Waldorf and the Astoria, located on 34th Street on the lot where the Empire State building now stands. They were connected by a walkway dubbed "Peacock Alley" for the dandies who were out to see and be seen. When the Waldorf was reborn here on Park Avenue, the long hallway connecting the front and back was dubbed Peacock Alley again.

This restaurant opened in the 1960s but closed for five years in the post-9/11 era, reopening in late 2005 with its current renovation. But let's talk food. The cooking is thoughtful and accurate. Starters include a decent tuna tartare, rich and set off by the presence of a tangerine-cilantro vinaigrette and crisp fried shallots, a good study in contrasting flavors and texture in an otherwise ubiquitous dish. Chile-seared scallops arrived cooked through and well seasoned, the two pieces set atop a delicious mound of marinated chanterelles and piquillo peppers. One night, a special of poached warm oysters covered with an odd-tasting turnip puree left me wondering what in the world the kitchen was thinking; the puree overwhelmed the oysters, and the flavors didn't seem to belong together in the first place. Instead try the pistachio-encrusted seared foie gras with a lychee marmalade, or the combination of seared sweetbreads and slow-braised pork belly, sauced with an interesting yuzu-espresso vinaigrette.

For mains, a thick slab of fresh Atlantic halibut arrives perfectly cooked, the proteins just congealed, tender, flavorful, and flaky, the top tasting of the soy marinade where it spent its last few hours, and sauced with a dollop of ethereal pure white celeriac mousseline, with edamame and sautéed chanterelles. A Niman Ranch pork chop comes just pink at its center, garnished with guanciale, stuffed braised romaine, and a good earthy parsnip puree. They offer very good vegetable and starch sides, and the menu is devised so there is something here for everyone. One recent night, two middle-aged couples sat down at the table next to mine, and one of the gentlemen reviewed the menu and put it down after just a few seconds. When his wife asked what was wrong, he said, "Nothing, dear, I've found what I want: a good steak, some sautéed spinach, and mashed potatoes."

Desserts are good. Nancy Olsson, now at Gramercy Tavern, used to be here. Try the chocolate feuillantine served with crispy rice-cereal-laced chocolate sorbet, the poached pear flavored with lemongrass and ginger, or a small mascarpone millefeuille with chocolate sauce and a boule of cinnamon ice cream.

Maddeningly, the wine list is entirely too short for a restaurant of this caliber, the document barely four pages long, and short on variety and value. Service is good, especially for a hotel dining room. Again, eat out back unless you want ringside seats to a hotel lobby. Choose well, and this can be a very good restaurant.

Pearl Oyster Bar

212-691-8211
18 Cornelia Street, between
  Bleecker and 6th Streets
Casual
Reservations
Moderate
Visa and MasterCard accepted
Lunch Monday–Friday, dinner
  Saturday
A, C, E, B, D, F, V trains to West
  4th Street station

Chef-owner Rebecca Charles grew up in suburban New Rochelle, Westchester County. Her father was a TV sitcom writer for *The Dick Van Dyke Show*, which was based on the life of a suburban sitcom writer living in New Rochelle; as many a professor has advised his or her students, write what you know. To which I will add a new twist: cook what you know. Rebecca's family summered in the very WASPy enclave of Kennebunkport, Maine, staying in the only hotel where Jews were permitted. Those happy, sun-washed memories of playing on the beach followed by meals of steamers and lobster, grilled fish, shoestring potatoes, blueberry pie, and apple brown Betty remained with her. Fast-forward to the tale of how this place came to be: she was broke, coming off a relationship that ended badly, and found herself stranded in San Francisco at Swan's Oyster Bar, where she had an epiphany—she'd open a place just like that in New York, with a Maine feel to it. And so it came to be a few years later that she and her partner at the time, Mary Redding, now owner of the nearly identical Mary's Fish Camp a few blocks away, opened what was to be the first of many New York City crab shacks. I'll let other folks duke it out as to which is better, Mary's or Pearl; I like them both plenty.

This is seafood cooked without pretense, simple preparations that work, two or three things per plate that taste fine and don't go out of their way to dazzle you—in short, my kind of food. If well-prepared simple seafood is what you're looking for, you won't be disappointed. The food is very good, the service is reliable, and the room, even though it has doubled in size since opening, is still cramped, with small tables shoehorned in here and there and chairs that are not terribly comfortable. In the summer, with the open kitchen in the rear, the place tends to be hot, and the A/C units leak. In the winter it's just okay, with the door opening and closing, blowing cold air into the room. But look past all this; the place is packed nightly with a line out the door, fans who know that this is some of the best seafood to be found anywhere in New York.

The signature dish is the lobster roll. They go through hundreds of pounds of cleaned lobster meat every week and, with kitchen space limited, have instructed Slavin, the big fish purveyor out of Brooklyn, how to custom-cook and shell the meat for them. Chunks of this sweet meat are lightly bound in Hellmann's mayonnaise. To that a little diced celery is added, some scallions, salt, pepper, a touch of this and that, then it's plunked into the center of a warm, buttery, just-out-of-the-pan sautéed Pepperidge Farm hot dog roll, alongside a pile of shoestring potatoes. How can you go wrong? But try the rest of the menu. It's all very good, divided into three parts: chilled seafood, small plates, and large plates.

For starters I like salt-crusted shrimp, à la Chinatown, served with a rémoulade of carrot and celeriac, or oysters and clams on the half shell with a glass of Sancerre from Daniel Chotard. Plump, meaty crab cakes are good too, as are the crispy, addictive fried oysters, set back in their shells with a dollop of tartar sauce for each bite. A thick New England clam chowder has chunks of bacon, and a big bowl of Prince Edward Island mussels arrives in a lovely reduction of mussel liquor, white wine, and mustard, bound in heavy cream. Among the large plates I like the grouper, set next to sautéed fresh corn mixed with red peppers, or the dry-seared plump sea scallops, of course the lobster roll, or the whole grilled fish of the day.

Desserts are good, homey, and house-made. Fruit pies in season, with ice cream, are a great way to finish a meal here. The wine list is small but well chosen, long on whites, with many options offered by the glass each day for $7 to $8, and most bottles priced between $30 and $50.

Peasant

212-965-9511
194 Elizabeth Street, between Prince and Spring Streets
Casual
Moderate to expensive
Reservations recommended
All major credit cards accepted
Dinner seven nights a week
6 train to Spring Street station; N, R, W to Prince Street station

I'd heard about Peasant. The place got a fair amount of very positive press, but I wasn't sure what to make of it. Then a funny thing happened: over the space of just a few weeks, a variety of well-known chefs whose opinions I trust all told me I had to go there for a meal, that I'd like it. One night it was Karen and David Waltuck, the owners of Chanterelle; they raved, saying it was one of their favorite restaurants. Shortly after that was Eric Ripert of Bernardin, then Christian Delouvrier of Lespinasse (who's now working in Florida), then the guys in the kitchen at Ducasse. So I went, and they were right. The reason chefs love this place is chef-owner Frank DeCarlo's style of food: mostly rustic Italian, and specifically Pugliese-style with a focus on Bari, as in great seafood, a lot of it cooked in big wood-fired ovens. It's simple, bold, flavorful food, featuring lots of Adriatic seafood, pastas, and roasts, emerging on sizzling platters from those custom-made brick ovens, the centerpieces of the open kitchen at the rear of the dining room.

DeCarlo, an Italian American kid born in Newark and raised in Mountainside, New Jersey, worked in some typically average Jersey restaurants as a kid. He was not the type who would have been selected as most likely to succeed, but then again most chefs I know were all crazy kids. He landed a job at Il Cortile back in the 1970s, when that was one of the best Italian kitchens in New York. He spoke neither Italian nor Spanish, the only two languages used in that kitchen, but he worked hard, kept his mouth shut, and worked his way up the line. After Il Cortile, he took off for Bari, Italy, where the chef from Il Cortile had come from, to work for a few years and immerse himself in that style of Italian regional cooking. He returned home, graduated from Peter Kump's cooking school, worked here and there in New York, and then returned to Italy for another three-year stint, where he honed his style. Back in New York he spent some time baking in the kitchen at Le Cirque when Alain Sailhac was the chef, and then was hired by Pino Luongo, followed by a stint at Circa and then Mazzei. In opening his own place, he wanted to cook rustic, simple, down-to-earth southern Italian roots food. When I'm traveling in Italy, this is often the food that I'm most impressed by: great ingredients prepared simply, food that isn't the least bit fussy but tastes wonderful.

Peasant was a garage before De Carlo got the space, and it had no gas lines. De Carlo lives in Little Italy and was walking to work one day up Elizabeth Street when the owner of the building, an elderly Chinese woman, was putting up a For Rent sign. He was going to help her hang it but decided to negotiate and rent the space for himself instead. They poured four inches of new concrete for the floor, braced and partially renovated the basement, and built the kitchen out back, past the exterior wall, where there had been an open storage area. When they opened, all the stoves were custom-made and wood-burning, which sounded like a good, quaint idea but didn't work for volume. So they kept the big ovens and added a pasta cooker and a gas stove, with three wok-style burners for quick cooking and sautéing. De Carlo works on that stove while his cooks tend to the brick oven. It's great to know that these days there are still chefs who cook for each diner, and he's back there, in full view of the room, signature white napkin tied back covering his hair, tending to the pots and pans, his face illuminated by the bursts of flame shooting out of the open burners he prefers to work with.

The large dining room is open, with high ceilings, brick walls, a bar on one side by the entrance, and ample seating on brushed aluminum military-issue chairs set before simple bare solid wood tables. When the room is full and the kitchen is busy, it has a certain inescapable drama. Each meal starts with crusty bread from Sullivan Street Bakery and a small bowl of fresh cow's milk ricotta from Di Palo; that sets the tone, simple and perfect.

The entire menu is written in Italian, but in a ritual unique to this spot, your server will translate the entire menu, item by item for you, without being asked, as well as answer any questions you may have. In season they have an excellent salad of the bitter Italian green puntarella, paired traditionally with white anchovies, with the addition of marinated onions and slices of radish, tossed with radicchio and arugula in a bracing vinaigrette. A trio of baked fresh sardines comes out of the wood-burning oven crisp yet moist, sprinkled with sea salt, fresh thyme, and olive oil. I love high-quality European jarred or canned tuna, a delicacy that bears no resemblance to the common brands sold here in our supermarkets in terms of species, cut, processing method, or flavor. An appetizer here billed as fagioli Toscani con tonno pairs firm-fleshed, slow-braised Tuscan beans with arugula and chunks of Callipo brand Italian tuna. Just before the plate leaves the kitchen, it is drizzled with fruity Tuscan oil. A table next to mine didn't eat theirs; they were expecting it to be yet another medium-rare, chilled fresh tuna loin and were disappointed to find the imported, jarred variety. To my taste, this style of glass-packed tuna from Europe is preferable to pan-seared tuna loin. With its better flavor and buttery texture, the jarred tuna is what they should be using for salade niçoise as well.

Razor clams are topped with seasoned bread crumbs and baked in a casserole with fresh thyme and white wine, finished with a splash of olive oil; they couldn't be better, tender and oceanic under those crisp crumbs. The dish called "polpi in purgatorio" is tender grilled octopus, courtesy of Octopus Garden on Avenue U in Brooklyn, the supplier of choice for all the greats. Here it is baked en casserole in an oil laced with hot pepper. When you're done with the octopus, dip your bread in the oil and don't waste a drop. Pasta with four clams arrived with a sauce of reduced clam broth and olive oil clinging to the al dente house-made pasta, the clams in their shells—perhaps the best linguine with clams in all New York. Wide-cut maltagliati are served with braised rabbit and a reduction of the braising liquid that glosses the pasta. Whole fish, varying with the season, are baked in the wood-burning oven and served with sea salt and olive oil. Osso buco is made with lamb shanks rather than veal and is rich, moist, and full of lamb flavor in a dense, complex jus. Lamb appears in another guise, this time the boneless leg tied and roasted on a spit, then sliced and paired with creamy polenta, ringed with jus and topped with herbed, grilled radicchio. Roast baby suckling pig is slow-cooked whole on a spit, carved, and served in sections over fingerling potatoes simmered in milk, with some of that milk drizzled over the whole dish.

Desserts are house-made, simple but good: fruit pies in the summer season, an excellent panna cotta with figs paired with a glass of vin santo, and on the light side, a pistachio gelato full of that nut's often elusive flavor. On the heartier side, bread pudding arrives with white chocolate gelato topped with caramel, and individual fruit tarts big enough for three people come topped with a scoop of ice cream. The wine list has gotten bigger and better over the years and features lots of lovely wines from small producers, especially those in southern Italy. Service is casual but good; many of the wait staff have been here for years and know the food and the kitchen pacing by heart. Honestly, I've never had a bad plate here.

Peking Duck House

212-227-1810
28 Mott Street, between
  Pell Street and the Bowery
  (and elsewhere)
Casual
Reservations
Moderate
All major credit cards accepted
Lunch and dinner seven days
  a week
6, J, M, Z, N, Q, R, W trains to
  Canal Street station

For years this place was a few doors down, where Ping's now stands. The new space, opened in 2004, is nicer, cleaner, and brighter than the old one. But the duck has always been worth the trip; of course, with a name like Peking Duck House, it had better be good. Few other places execute this dish as well as they do here. Some of the side dishes are good—the dry crispy string beans with minced pork and garlic, the chilled jellyfish appetizer, and the braised Asian eggplant, to name a few—but come here for the duck. By now we all know the bird, with its mahogany crisped skin, the thin layer of fat, and the moist, succulent flesh sliced thin, with a bit of skin attached to seemingly every piece. Place a few slices of this delicious meat in one of the warm, thin crêpe-like pancakes. To this add a little sliced cucumber, some sliced scallions, and a dab of hoisin sauce, roll it up, and devour. This is a great dish that I have to have every few months, regardless of the season. The duck is served for a minimum of two people at under $40, and with a side dish or two is more than enough food for any appetite.

They have a liquor license, and beer works well with this dish. The staff is friendly, the new room is clean and comfortable, and the duck about as good as it gets in New York. There's another branch on East 53rd Street as well.

Perbacco

212-253-2038
234 East 4th Street, between
  Avenue A and Avenue B
Casual
No reservations
Moderate
All major credit cards accepted
Dinner Monday–Friday, brunch
  and dinner on weekends
F, V trains to Second Avenue
  station

It's funny sometimes how you hear about new restaurants in New York—blogs, print reviews, phone calls from insiders. I first heard about Perbacco from an older chap I know at the New York Athletic Club, who lives just steps off Fifth Avenue on the Upper East Side. He was a major voice-over talent for decades, has traveled abroad extensively, and knows good food. Then Josh Ozersky raved about it when he was still at Grub Street. This was followed by a glowing review from Frank Bruni at the *New York Times*. So okay, I get it, guys—it's good, it's new, and I'll have to try it. So try it I did, and as it happens, they were all correct. The chef is a young Italian, Simone Bonelli, from Modena in the north. He's young, ambitious, and likes to tinker around with things, as most young chefs these days seem to do. The space is tiny, with brick walls, a little bar, and around 40 seats, including those at the bar and along a communal table made from what appears to be a long wooden Campari sign.

During a summer meal when there was some sidewalk seating available, I had a nice appetizer of burrata wrapped in bresaola, under which was tucked a slice of summer truffle, set over a small pool of pesto made from arugula. Another take with cheese featured grilled, smoked scamorza, a firmer and drier version of mozzarella from the Molise region of Italy, set over radicchio and studded with rendered bacon bits. My dining companion had an appetizer of grilled scallops with speck, sautéed red onions, and thin strips of raw zucchini, sprinkled with salt and drizzled with very good olive oil. A pasta dish I loved featured plump, airy gnocchi made from both potatoes and a chickpea puree, tossed with sautéed shrimp and diced zucchini, bound in an herbaceous pesto. In colder months, go for the thick whole-wheat pappardelle with braised lamb shank and a rich tomato-based braising liquid. Another pasta dish we loved was baked, studded with speck again, bound in a good cheesy béchamel sauce, and then laced with a border of truffled foam that melds its way into the plate as you dine.

The menu allows you to mix and match small plates, some simple, like the starter of fried calamari with house-made tartar sauce and little meatballs as they are done in Italy, rolled small, deep-fried and served with a simple tomato sauce. There are good pastas and a few larger, traditional mains of various local and imported fish, organic chicken, and specials that are usually winners. The wine list is almost all Italian and mostly in the $30–$50 range. The short dessert list is good. My favorite to date has been the pistachio semifreddo, light yet full of flavor. Service is friendly, and for modern, innovative avant-garde Italian cooking, or just good straightforward Italian cooking, Perbacco is a winner.

Per Se

212-823-9335
10 Columbus Circle, on the fourth floor of the Time Warner Building
Dressy
Expensive
All major credit cards accepted
Reservations required, only taken one month in advance
Dinner seven nights a week, lunch Friday–Sunday
1, A, C, B, D trains to 59 Street/ Columbus Circle station; N, Q, R, W trains to 57th Street station

To my mind, on any given night, Per Se vies for the title of Best in NYC. Expensive? Absolutely. Fussy presentation and tiny portions? Indeed. Three-plus hours for a meal? Easily. But for foodies of a certain stripe, it's a must-visit. Keller's fans are legion, and I'm one of them.

F. Scott Fitzgerald was dead wrong when he said that there was no such thing as a second act in America. Per Se is proof of that. Thomas Keller worked his way up the ranks in New York City alongside many chefs of his generation, and many recall him not as a young genius but as a regular line cook, somewhere in the middle of the pack. He passed an early stint with the very young Daniel Boulud at the Westbury, a year in this kitchen, a year in another; he was good but not a standout. When he did get his first head chef job, he was like many young chefs at that time: inexperienced, young, and opinionated, with the arrogance of youth. His first big break came when he opened Rakel down on Varick Street, with Tom Colicchio as his sous-chef. The food was decent, some days very good, but the place failed for a variety of reasons, not the least of which was the then risky though pioneering location and an odd room design. After that, he left town, heading for L.A., where he worked for a while as the executive chef at Checkers, basically treading water, his career in stasis. He knew he wanted one more chance, one more thing, so he cobbled together dozens of investors and purchased an existing, quirky upstate restaurant in the wine country, the French Laundry in Yountville. This was to be his last stand; at that point he was 37 years old and had been cooking since he was a kid, and he told me once that if it didn't work, he'd quit the business and go be a beach bum in Tahiti. Well, the rest is history. The French Laundry is arguably the best restaurant in the country, and Keller is America's most celebrated chef.

As things go, Steve Ross was a frequent customer, and when the huge Time Warner Building deal was sealed, they wanted Thomas Keller on board as the anchor tenant, the jewel in the crown of what would later be known as the Restaurant Collection. Who knows what his business deal is? Does he pay rent or not? And if so, how much? Well, I don't know, and it's not my business, but I do know that the place cost an estimated $14 million to build out.

The space, designed by Adam Tihany, is a chef's dream come true. The sprawling white-tiled kitchens total well over half of the usable total square footage, unheard of in New York restaurant real estate. And as a centerpiece in the main service kitchen, set beneath soaring 20-foot ceilings and walls of white tile, sits a custom-made $100,000 Bonnet stove. There are not just one but two big prep kitchens, each outfitted with the best equipment money can buy: Rational combi ovens, dozens of stainless sous-vide water baths calibrated to the tenth of a degree, vacuum machines, and high-tech gadgets galore. There is a chocolate room, a pastry room, a bread baking room; many walls are lined with spotless stainless-steel reach-in refrigerators, each containing neat stacks of precisely labeled and dated ingredients, prepped and raw, cured and cooked, all in their own see-through plastic containers. But beyond all that, what really separates this place from any other million-dollar flashy kitchen is the work ethic. Here you'll find a most refined and focused kitchen culture under the direction of the day-to-day chef, Jonathan Benno, that sets the tone for what takes place each night for service: near perfection.

Coming back to New York was risky, and Keller knew that. His reputation hung in the balance. So to ensure success, he closed the French Laundry for a much-needed renovation and brought the entire West Coast staff east to train the new New York staff. Cooks worked together and learned the recipes, the technique, the Keller style. The front of the house studied the menus, perfected the casual style of service, and even took ballet classes to learn how to move together gracefully in the dining room. They invited chef friends over for the soft openings. All went as planned, but five days after the hard opening, disaster struck: an electrical fire in the walls closed the place for months. Now Keller had to rebook thousands of reservations and reopen two restaurants on two coasts simultaneously, while keeping all these unemployed workers on his payroll.

Somehow he did it. After they reopened, I was walking through the New York kitchen and noticed that all the screen savers on the computers read "Four stars," indicating what they knew they needed from the *New York Times*. Four months later, in the first big post-summer September review from the *Times,* they got their four stars.

While in the planning process, Adam Tihany asked Thomas Keller what he wanted the room to look like. His answer: "I want to look as good as the Four Seasons fifty years from now." You enter off the fourth-floor mezzanine though automatic thick glass doors. Coats are checked. If you need to wait for your guest, there is a small lounge area with leather sofas, chairs, a table or two, and a bar as well. The main room seats only

75 or so people and is spread over two levels: the upper level has an interior space that's slightly raised to ensure a park view, and the lower level is a half-moon-shaped room centered by a modern fireplace. The ceiling is high, the walls shades of beige. Facing the park on the interior wall, there is a small sculpture made of rough-hewn pieces of wood arranged horizontally, the odd shapes suggesting driftwood. Lamps are covered by beige shades, each imprinted with various laundry symbols. Tables are well spaced, chairs extremely comfortable; this is a very civilized dining room. The staff, and there are loads of them, walk that fine line between too much and just enough, coming out on the just enough side more often than not. They are extremely well trained and know the menu, and to a degree the wines as well.

Spend any time with the cooks in the kitchen and you'll realize why this place is so different. They work slowly, methodically, with the emphasis on precision, accuracy, and cleanliness—in short, with finesse, a term Keller loves to use. The normal constraints of food cost don't exist here. They use only the best of the best cuts; for example, the heavily marbled calotte is removed from the rib eye and used as a steak. Organic eggs, specifically from the Jidori breed of hen, are courtesy of a rabbi upstate. Snails, when they appear on the menu, are the fresh variety, not canned, and are farm-raised in California. When soft-shell crabs are in season, they utilize only the centermost portion, roughly the size of a nickel. With filets of fish, they only use the uniform center cuts. The trim, and there is lots of it, becomes the staff meal, or perhaps a mousse somewhere else on the menu. The technique is very French, and though there's a distinct nod to the classics, the food on the plate is utterly modern.

A tasting menu back in May 2004 was half vegetarian and half from the normal chef's menu, and was preceded by six different types of amuse-bouche before the first course of spring onion soup, strewn with tiny "vermicelli" of onion confit, garnished with a dark green globe of chive mousse. I had the house standard oysters and pearls, a Keller signature of pearl tapioca sabayon with Island Creek oysters and a spoonful of Osetra caviar riding the top. With this we drank a Sato no Homare Junmai Ginjo sake. Next up we had long, thin pasta-esque ribbons of crunchy jicama coated with a rich creamy Hass avocado emulsion, played against tart cubes of Persian lime gelée, all accented by micro cilantro sprouts. Hen-of-the-woods mushrooms appeared next, slow-cooked alongside red-wine-glazed Walla Walla shallots and a small fork-turn of Savoyard spinach, all bathed in a rich reduction of red wine and port. I had the "peach Melba," a torchon of cured Moulard duck foie gras set with a thin layer of glass-clear peach gelée, pickled white peaches, marinated red onion, tiny melba toasts of brioche, and nubbins of crunchy Carolina rice. With this plate, you choose from a selection of six various sea salts. For the wine, here they paired a Kiralyudvar Tokaji Cuvée Ilona 2004. I could go on and on, but you get the idea: each plate is a stand-alone masterpiece, requiring hours if not days of labor.

The dessert, courtesy of Sébastien Rouxel, one of the best working anywhere, included two sorbets, one of English cucumber with a cream cheese bavarois and brunoise of various melons that had been marinated, the other a verjus sorbet with a vanilla sablé Breton, a thin sheet of gelée accented by Szechuan peppercorns, and a sauce of crème fraîche. The last act was a Valrhona chocolate velours filled with a ginger-infused custard and a schmear of Meyer lemon granita, while my guest had the chocolate temptation, a mini-construct with no fewer than five individual elements: a hazelnut streusel with condensed milk sorbet, a milk chocolate crémeux, sweetened salted hazelnuts, and a pain au lait sauce, complemented by two glasses of Chambers Rosewood Muscat, Rutherglen.

One could argue as to whether the food at the French Laundry is better, in that Thomas Keller spends most of his time there, visiting the New York kitchen seven or eight days a month, but I don't have the budget to fly back and forth to compare meals. Let's just say that this is as good as it gets for fine dining in New York.

Persepolis

212-535-1100
1407 Second Avenue, between 73rd and 74th Streets
Casual
Reservations
Moderate
All major cards
Lunch and dinner seven days a week
6 train to 77th Street station

To answer a question I don't recall ever having been asked, Persepolis may be the best Persian restaurant in Manhattan. An Iranian ex-pat told me about the place one day as we shared a subway downtown. I love hearing about restaurants, especially ethnic ones, from folks who really get the food—the natives, so to speak. So on his advice I tried it, and I liked it. I also like the fact that, as happens in New York, the chef here, San Sethachutkul, is Thai and learned Persian cooking right here in New York, mostly in this very kitchen as a line cook, then as the sous-chef, prior to taking over the reins as chef and partner. The cuisine of Persia is one of the oldest on the planet and has had broad influence, from the Mediterranean to India, in terms of style and ingredients.

Throughout the menu you'll find eggplant in various guises, as well as yogurt, tahini, cucumber, tabouli, loads of kebabs made from marinated lamb and beef, as well as chicken, a smattering of seafood, and a few very nice vegetarian entree choices. On one visit when I could not make up my mind, I went with a starter billed as an eggplant trio, as I just love what can be done with eggplant in various cultural settings. This plate combined three dishes: baba, where eggplant is first roasted and then chopped fine and combined with walnuts; mirza, where the vegetable is braised in a tomato sauce and finished with creamy yogurt; and a version that was simply sautéed with onion and various freshly ground spices. Fresh house-made yogurt can be had combined with fresh spinach and loads of garlic, or studded with cucumber and mint. A plate of tabouli is a good choice in the summer, with fresh in-season tomatoes and loads of chopped parsley and mint, bathed in olive oil and lemon juice. Another good starter had roasted beets tossed with chunks of feta cheese, pistachios, and a vinaigrette that included preserved sour cherries.

Kebabs, when done well, as they are here, can be a treat. The shandji kebab has meat taken from the loin or rack, marinated in saffron, then grilled and served with eggplant puree and yogurt. The kebabs of chicken and ground meat arrived moist, flavorful, and well charred. The vegetarian plate listed as gaimah badam joon arrived as a large plate festooned with slow-braised eggplant and split peas redolent of cinnamon and citrus, framed by a rich tomato-based sauce.

The wine list is decent and includes a collection of more expensive bottles from the cellar. Some of the oldest vineyards in the world can be found throughout the Middle East, and legend has it that the Syrah varietal was born here. Service is very good, as is often the case when the owners, Kaz Bayali and his business partner, Parvez Eliaas, are active and working on the floor day to day.

Petrossian Boutique and Café

212-245-2217
911 Seventh Avenue, between 57th and 58th Streets
Casual
No reservations
Moderate
All major credit cards accepted
Breakfast, lunch and dinner Monday–Friday, brunch and dinner Saturday and Sunday
N, Q, R, W trains to 57th Street station; 1, A, C, B, D trains to 59th Street/Columbus Circle station

When I'm in the mood for a quiet breakfast in the European tradition, this is my favorite place in all New York. While I love my bacon and eggs, pancakes, French toast, and side orders of sausage, scrapple, and ham, here at Petrossian it's about great little pastries, superb croissants, and the ideal pain au chocolat, all served with great coffee and fresh-squeezed orange juice in a small, quiet room with refined and attentive service. The name Petrossian is synonymous worldwide with superb caviar, smoked salmon, and foie gras, but in this location they run a jewel of a French pastry shop. Just steps from Carnegie Hall and a few blocks from Lincoln Center and Central Park, housed on the ground floor of the stunning, landmarked Alwyn Court apartment building, breakfast is served after 8 AM, lunch from

11:30, and recently they added one early dinner seating, which is a first-rate pre-theater option. But I go for breakfast.

A selection of the excellent pastries is displayed fresh each morning in a two-tiered display case in the front window. You enter a long narrow space. On the right, on a chilled white marble slab, they hand-pack caviar and slice smoked salmon to order. To the left, more pastries are on display, as well as fine baguettes, a good variety of fresh-baked, organic breads, croissants, simple sandwiches, quiche, and assorted muffins. Should you need a quick little gift, the loose chocolates sold by the piece, cookie samplers, assorted jarred preserved fruits and conserves, and tinned pâtés are wonderful. Meals are taken in the rear of the store, up a few steps in a little square room lined with banquettes that overlooks the retail space. Curtained walls feature original art that changes regularly.

The French-born pastry chef, Catherine Lahitette, produces a wonderful selection of traditional pastries and viennoiserie before dawn each morning. Prior to Petrossian, she worked at the four-star Lespinasse, and her pedigree shows; her pastries are some of the best in the city. She is not well known, but I'd rank her work far ahead of some of the big-name pastry chefs in town. I've spent time with her downstairs in that small kitchen, where she works from her own handwritten recipes collected in several well-worn (and well-guarded) spiral notebooks. Let's start with something ubiquitous as a reference point: muffins. In my experience, virtually all the breakfast muffins I encounter are way too big—muffins on steroids—and seriously undercooked. For whatever reason Americans have grown used to eating certain pastries undercooked; yes, they are very moist, but they also taste like raw dough and are tough to digest. By contrast, here you'll find a selection of muffins as they should be prepared: corn, lemon poppy, cranberry almond, blueberry, bran with raisins, apple walnut, all roughly three inches high and an inch and a half in diameter. They are perfectly cooked, moist, beautifully colored on the exterior, and feature only natural flavorings: citrus zest, cornmeal, puree of apples, whole and ground nuts. Try any of her selections and let that be the standard by which you judge muffins from that point on.

Her compact, rectangular lemon financier is rich, firm, and buttery, full of bold lemon flavor and laced with vanilla. The croissants here are made with pure butter (which I find less and less to be the case these days, as shortening is much less expensive and certainly easier to work with; however, you can tell the difference instantly when you bite them, as butter melts in your mouth, while shortening always leaves an odd greasy film on your palate). The paper-thin crust of the exterior is crisp against the swirling cloudlike interior. Like Danish and puff pastry, croissants are made from a laminated dough with 81 alternating layers of butter and flour. In the hot oven, the heat turns the moisture in the butter into steam, creating a feather-light interior. On a good day, when the air is dry, the crisp outer shell nearly explodes when you first bite it, showering you with small shards of that brown crust, and leaving your fingers lightly coated with butter—yum! The pain au chocolat is made with that same croissant dough, this time rolled and stuffed with two pieces of semisweet chocolate. They are a superb snack, and nearly the only thing that one of my sons ever eats there.

If you're not in the mood for pastry, try the Greek breakfast, a small bowl of rich, creamy Greek yogurt, buttery smooth and slightly sour, topped with granola and drizzled with honey. This comes with coffee, a pitcher of heated milk, and a brimming glass of fresh-squeezed orange juice, all for eight bucks. Should you order chocolate milk, here it is made with steamed hot milk and melted chocolate. If you need eggs for breakfast, have the eggs Benedict. Or treat yourself to the crisp waffles made to order with ice cream and fruit. Other choices are the signature smoked salmon and a so-so bagel. I'd opt instead for the croissant, the French standby of a sliced half baguette slathered with jam and butter, or for you big spenders a caviar tasting with blinis.

It's a shame to go alone, as this place is best enjoyed with a small crowd where you can order many things and share them. And don't be surprised if you spot Le Bernardin's executive chef, Eric Ripert, picking up a croissant there on his way to work.

Picholine

212-724-8585
35 West 64th Street,
 between Central Park West
 and Columbus Avenue
Dressy
Reservations
Expensive
All major credit cards accepted
Dinner seven nights a week
1 train to 66th Street station;
 B, C trains to 72nd Street
 station

Picholine was the first serious restaurant to open on the Upper West Side after the demise of Andiamo a few years earlier. Yes, there was Café des Artistes, but it had been there forever and really wasn't all that good anymore. The man behind Picholine was chef Terrance Brennan. Though still young, he was a veteran New York chef with over a dozen years under his belt cooking at some very good restaurants. Born in Annandale, Virginia, to restaurateur parents, he started in the business at the age of 13. He moved to D.C. to work, and then spent a few years as a stagier in Europe, working in excellent kitchens: Taillevent, Le Tour d'Argent, Le Moulin de Mougins, and Le Gavroche, to name a few. After coming to New York, he worked at the Westbury and Annabelle's and as a saucier under Alain Sailhac at Le Cirque before opening Prix Fixe. In between jobs he did some consulting, and that was how he found this place, coming in as a hired hand to rescue a failing operation. He eventually bought it in 1993 and turned it around. Opened on a shoestring budget, Picholine was initially just an upscale neighborhood restaurant, with simple furniture, inexpensive flatware, decent service, but always very good food. The restaurant is located a short block from Lincoln Center, and Brennan knew that he could get one full seating in before 7:15 six nights a week most weeks; anything after that was gravy. Brennan's cooking was good, the dishes accurately prepared, and soon the crowds came. So did the critics, and within a short time he had two stars, followed by a third from the *New York Times*.

His kitchen is physically poorly laid out, small, oddly shaped, hot, and in need of a total renovation, but the food that emerges from these antiquated and cramped quarters is wonderful. There have been a few chefs who oversee the operation from day to day, as Brennan has several projects that keep him busy and out of this kitchen. But Brennan oversees the menu, which hasn't changed much in terms of direction over the years and can be described as modern yet classically based French cooking, beautifully presented, flavorful, and accurately seasoned. Thankfully, the dining room, once stuffy and dated, received a much-needed renovation in the summer of 2006.

On a recent summer menu, a salad of peekytoe crab arrived with the meat moist and mounded in a large quenelle, set next to grapefruit and mint gelée, a fresh grapefruit lozenge, grapefruit-Campari granita, with a toss of micro cilantro leaves over the top. A fat, tall cylinder of foie gras arrives chilled, wrapped in a thin skin of duck prosciutto beside a mound of small dice of green apple gelée and a drizzle of black truffle vinaigrette. A surprisingly big appetizer was a lightly battered sautéed soft-shell crab paired with paper-thin slices of crisp pork belly and a crab tamarind sauce. Off a fall menu a thick steak of wild sturgeon comes atop sauerkraut made from rutabaga, in a pool of red wine mustard butter sauce. His artichoke variations are lovely, mixing crispy fried leaves with paper-thin slices of the raw heart and puree garnished with cèpes, socca (a Provençal touch made from fried chickpea flour), and arugula salad. From Florida, they have fresh frog legs that are stuffed with diced pork and tempura-battered, set above a kimchi of celery and a creamy spiced aioli. Best of all was the soft-cooked egg, the protein just set after 45 minutes at a very low temperature, then served atop fresh morels, shaved asparagus, garlic croutons, and a delicious rich sauce. Some days they offer a classical dish as a special, and his pike quenelles set on sauce Nantua bring back fond memories of La Caravelle in its heyday. Diver scallops are larded with slivers of whole black truffle, sautéed medium rare, and set on a bed of black truffle risotto and salsify mousseline, drizzled with a foie gras vinaigrette. A signature dish is his sea urchin panna cotta with osetra caviar, oceanic gelée, and seaweed.

His cheese course, the work of the now famous Max McCalman, is splendid, with more than 60 cheeses presented on a trolley. Many of these cheeses have been brought to perfect ripeness in his custom-made temperature-controlled caves on Ninth Avenue. Brennan and McCalman were at the forefront of the cheese cart movement, which is so popular among serious restaurants these days. Though I usually go with cheese, desserts are excellent. They do a lovely terrine of apple confit with cranberry gelée, spiced crème fraîche, and walnut praline, though on a recent night, my warm caramel apple brioche spent a few seconds too long in the microwave. The rhubarb float with yogurt sorbet and rhubarb Linzer cookies was just fine. Or pair great Fourme d'Ambert with Sauternes sabayon and pear marmalade.

The crowd tends to be older, the wine list is expensive but very good, the room is a tad stuffy and too formal for my tastes, and most gentlemen wear jackets, but the food and the location, convenient to Lincoln Center, make it a no-brainer for pre- or post-theater dining. In spite of Brennan's numerous other projects around town, this is still one of the best restaurants in the neighborhood, if not the best.

Ping's

212-602-9988
22 Mott Street, between
  Worth and Mosco Streets
Casual
Reservations
Moderate
All major credit cards accepted
Seven days a week 10 AM–
  midnight
6, J, M, Z, N, Q, R, W trains to
  Canal Street station

Chef Chuen Ping Hui first came to notice in the mid-1990s, preparing excellent dim sum at that old standard on the Bowery, Say Eng Look. A native of Hong Kong, he was born to a poor family and started working in construction as a young teenager. Guess why he was fired from that job: for eating too much during lunch break. No dummy, he got a job in a restaurant where that would be less of an issue. After emigrating to New York and cooking around town while still barely in his twenties, he became a rising star in the Chinese community and was tapped to open his own place in Queens. The first Ping's was an instant hit. This, his first Manhattan restaurant, is located on the site of the old Peking Duck House, which has now moved a few doors to the west on Mott Street. There are two dining rooms on two floors, and the place is usually very busy. Bright, clean, and not as noisy as most spots down here, this is an excellent choice for Hong Kong–style food, and especially seafood. The fish swimming in the huge fish tanks may indeed turn up as your dinner.

This cuisine is sometimes described as new Cantonese, a style that emphasizes natural flavors, steaming, and the liberal use of garlic, ginger, scallions, and the signature XO sauce. The term XO comes from the Cognac and Armagnac labels, and here it is meant to suggest a level of expense, luxury, and uniqueness. At Ping's, they make their own, which includes over a dozen ingredients, such as dried scallops, dried squid, fresh garlic, fish roe, and chile peppers, to name a few. This sauce is a very dark brown and finds its way into many dishes. Among my favorites is the simple steamed fresh oyster on the half shell, topped with a spoon of XO. Another favorite is a dish using jicama, a non-Chinese ingredient, but Ping loves the texture. Here it is combined with long-cut Chinese chives, dried squid cut julienne, baby silver fish (similar to whitebait), and dried jellyfish. These are all quick-sautéed and then sauced. The dish is texturally complex, with loads of snap and crunch, and much good, clean flavor in every bite.

The woks they use here were custom-made and are some of the hottest I've ever seen—they must be 50,000 BTU each. The heat is adjusted by a metallic lever placed knee high, where the oven door would be in a traditional stove. The lever moves from the twelve o'clock position to the three o'clock position, and Ping and his cooks use their left leg to adjust the heat as they cook. All the cut ingredients are portioned and brought to the cook for each dish in small bowls, and the cooks in turn add them in sequence, constantly tossing and turning the contents in the wok. At the end, when all is ready, a little sauce is added, and a touch of starch. Each cook has three or four different starches ready at hand, premixed with water, so all they need to do is flick a pinch of the slurry into the pan, toss it once or twice to coat, and cook. The sauce is thickened instantly, the dish plated in seconds, and the food is on its way out to the dining room.

Dungeness crab with black bean sauce is addictive. Lobster cut in chunks, still in the shell, is sautéed with garlic, ginger, and scallions, lightly sauced, and served with pan-fried noodles, again a lovely dish. Another house specialty is fresh lobster, taken live from the tank and served minutes later over ice as lobster sashimi, complete with soy sauce and wasabi. (It's no surprise that Ping is a big fan of Nobu.) Abalone is braised and served in a rich brown sauce, and steamed whole fish arrives garnished with scallions, ginger, soy sauce, and a touch of vinegar, the meat falling off the bones and perfectly cooked. For lighter fare, try the hot pot of fresh shrimp, scallops, and soft bean curd, served as a bubbling casserole. For meat lovers, they have great braised tripe, Chinese-style beef spare ribs, and honey-roasted quail.

They serve beer, and tea works well too. Desserts are an afterthought; try Baskin-Robbins across the street if you're in the mood for something sweet afterward. Many feel that the Queens branch is better, and I'm told by Chinese friends that the quality of Chinese restaurants in general is better these days in Queens. But that's okay; I feel lucky to have this place nearby.

The Pink Teacup

212-807-6755
42 Grove Street, between Bleecker and Bedford Streets
Casual
No reservations
Moderate
Cash only
Tuesday–Thursday 8 AM–midnight, Friday–Sunday 8 AM–1 AM
1 train to Christopher Street station; A, C, E, B, D, F, V trains to West 4th Street station

In business since 1954, opened then by Mary Raye and now run by her niece Seretta, Seretta's daughter, and Raye's grandniece Lisa, this place still serves the same authentic, family-style southern cooking, based on Raye's recipes. Don't miss out on the lovely little homemade desserts as well. If you're looking for decent soul food south of 110th Street, this may be your best bet. The walls are pink, the tables are made of Formica, the furniture is sheathed in pink vinyl, and the entire space is a bit cramped; it's cash only, and they don't take reservations. But order the crisp-skinned fried chicken or the smothered pork chops and a side of greens, and all is well with the world. They do a very nice breakfast. If you're in the mood, try the fried chicken with corn or apple fritters; you won't need lunch, trust me. For lunch, they do the breakfast menu plus some good burgers and sandwiches, but for dinner come hungry and with friends and try the fried chicken, ham hocks, smothered steak, beef tips over rice, or pot roast, with a side of greens, creamy mac and cheese, biscuits, or decent grits.

Save room for the banana cream pie, peach cobbler, coconut cake, or bread pudding. They don't serve alcohol but have good lemonade and unsweetened or sweetened iced tea. Service is friendly and the place is down-home for real; these days, delivering that plus good soul food in Greenwich Village makes it a thumbs-up for me.

Pio Pio

212-426-5800

1746 First Avenue, between
   90th and 91st Streets
   (and elsewhere)

Casual

No reservations

Inexpensive

All major credit cards accepted

Lunch and dinner seven days
   a week

4, 5, 6 trains to 86th Street
   station; 6 train to 96th Street
   station

What started in Queens as a good cheap Peruvian restaurant is now a mini-chain, with stores here and on the Upper West Side as well. I'm told that this one is better than the one across town, which is rather hard to fathom, as the simple menu is a relatively easy formula to duplicate, but we'll leave that for another discussion. The place is tiny, so expect to wait in line during normal dinner hours, but if you're looking for good cheap eats, this place is all that. The main event is the rotisserie chicken, marinated overnight in a mixture of beer and spices, I'm told, prior to being placed on the rotisserie. You can order a quarter bird, a half bird, or a whole bird for a mere $8, which is what I would suggest, as any leftovers make great sandwiches or salads the next day. The meat is moist and surprisingly flavorful as far as commodity birds go.

The Peruvian combo includes a whole chicken plus an order of large fries and an avocado salad for $20, but the fries aren't really any good. Instead opt for the matador special: an entire bird, rice and beans, avocado salad, salchipapas (a mix of deep-fried sliced hot dogs and french fries), and tostones (flattened fried plantains, a Dominican specialty)—surely there is enough food here for three or four people for $28. There is a nice, spicy mayonnaise-based sauce for the chicken should you need more flavor for your bird. Of course the salad is iceberg, which I actually like, especially when consumed with spicy or big-flavored foods. Ask for your fried calamari well done, or you may risk getting them rather pale and soggy. The sangria is decent, and beer works fine with this food. The crowd is local and young, and to their credit they know a good deal when they find it.

Pizza Suprema

212-594-8939

413 Eighth Avenue, at 31st
   Street

Casual

No reservations

Inexpensive

All major credit cards accepted

Lunch and dinner seven days
   a week

1, 2, 3, A, C, E, N, Q, R, W, B,
   D, F, V trains to 34th Street
   station

Back in the day when I was a young chef coming up, I also boxed a lot at Gleason's Gym, which was right around the corner from here. This area has mostly bars catering to construction workers, local office types, groups wafting in and out of the Garden for concerts or sporting events, and residents of New Jersey and Long Island on their way home from work via Penn Station. What it is short on is good places to eat, so I was surprised when a friend recommended I try this place. I'd walked past it literally a thousand times and never considered going in. What I found was a darned good pizzeria amid the otherwise middling assortment of sports and beer bars, 99-cent stores, and fast-food joints.

I especially liked the white pizza topped with ricotta and mozzarella cheeses, and the broccoli rabe version as well. The calzones are a meal in themselves. To that, add their Roman stuffed pie, where between two layers of pizza dough is a filling that contains pepperoni, sausage, ham, and cheese, or the rich, dense, chewy Sicilian pie, strewn with onions and dusted with pecorino cheese. The lasagna may be forgettable, but if you're in need of a quick bite before a show at the Garden (where they serve awful pizza at luxury prices) or on your way home via Penn Station, you could do far worse, especially in this neighborhood.

Pop Burger

212-414-8686
58-60 Ninth Avenue, between 14th and 15th Streets
No reservations
Casual
Inexpensive
All major credit cards accepted
Sunday–Wednesday 11 AM–2 AM, Thursday–Saturday 11 AM–5 AM
A, C, E trains to 14th Street station; L train to Eighth Avenue station

As the tale goes, there once was a restaurant on the Lower East Side, Café Tabac, that catered the cocktail party for the opening of the movie *Bull Durham*. In attendance there would be a mix of professional baseball players, movie stars, producers, agents, and hangers-on. The food had to be good, user-friendly, and bite-size for passing on trays and stand-up eating. Thus the two-bite burger served on a custom brioche bun was born. It was such a hit that years later Roy Liebenthal would hire a serious chef and open Pop Burger, filled day and night with crowds yearning for more. It didn't hurt that this neighborhood would become a magnet for a generation of young, single hipsters prowling the area's eateries, as years back another generation prowled the club scene.

Go when it's busy and the flame-broiled burgers are straight off the grill. The fresh ground meat comes daily from the venerable New York meat house Ottomanelli. The burgers are hand-formed here—nothing frozen, nothing prefab, no junk. The brioche buns are straight from the ovens of Tom Cat Bakery. To that add a slice of fresh tomato, a few leaves of lettuce, and the mystery schmear, a Russian-dressing-like blend of secret ingredients, including mayonnaise mixed with hot sauce. The fries and onion rings are packaged and frozen, but that said, they are still very good, and considering the volume this place does, I can't see them making these by hand. For vegetarians, they make a great deep-fried portobello mushroom burger that vies for best veggie burger in New York

City. The place is packed late at night, especially on weekends, and there is a big bar scene during those hours in the back lounge. Figure $15 per person for three burgers, fries, and a soda.

Primola

212-758-1775
1226 Second Avenue, between 63rd and 64th Streets
Casual to dressy
Reservations
Moderate to expensive
All major credit cards accepted
Lunch and dinner Monday–Friday, dinner Saturday and Sunday
F train to Lexington Avenue/63rd Street station; 4, 5, 6, N, R, W trains to Lexington Avenue/59th Street station

Tucked away amidst the many bars and mediocre restaurants in this East Side location, Primola has been drawing crowds nightly and serving solidly good food since it opened in 1986. Under the watchful eye of owner Juliano Zuliani, the dining room fills with regulars who often don't even seem to require a menu. The room is non-descript, with yellow and white walls over blond wood wainscoting, the walls dotted with Italian posters and an assortment of watercolors, and the tables spaced reasonably well apart.

The menu is a large document, and there are also nightly specials that can be very good. The starter plate of excellent bresaola arrives with the cured dried meat sliced paper-thin and topped with a smattering of lightly dressed arugula. The meat below is drizzled with extra-virgin olive oil and a touch of lemon juice, whose light acidity adds polish to the dish and brings the various flavors together. The beef carpaccio is good, but this dish can be found everywhere these days. Instead try the grilled mozzarella with prosciutto and endive, or the simple but delicious bowl of littleneck clams and mussels in an herbaceous wine and garlic broth. The minestrone here is a reminder of what that simple Italian pistou variation can be, and on a cold winter night it's a pleasure. The pasta section is large, and they have a pasta special every day as well. Keep it simple and you'll do fine. Try the penne carrettiera, the pasta al dente, the sauce a simple tomato base with the addition of olives, capers, and fresh basil. Add a pinch of pecorino cheese and I think you'll be happy. Another good choice is the i chicchi della nonna, little spinach dumplings served in a light cream sauce.

Fish in old-style Italian restaurants can be hit-or-miss, as the menus tend to favor meat and veal especially, but the whole fish of the day here is reliable, as are the misto de pesce, a seafood combination, fried and steamed, set over a pool of light tomato sauce, or the fried combination of squid and imported red shrimp. If you insist on veal, try the Abruzzese-style thinly pounded medallions accompanied by prosciutto, baby peas, and sage, or the thick chop, bone in, with black truffles and assorted wild mushrooms—the mild meat, a good carrier of other flavors, does the trick here. I'm not crazy about the chicken dishes, which seemed over-cooked and dry to me. The pan-seared, Florentine-style porterhouse was good, as was the veal kidney with pork sausage, for offal fans.

As I've stated before, Italian desserts are not my thing and never have been. Opt instead for fruit and cheese and save a glass of wine to go with that course. The wine list is good, mostly priced fairly, with some good bargains among the less well known Nebbiolo varieties. Service is friendly and efficient under the watchful eye of Zuliani. In the last five years, we've seen some of the best Italian restaurants ever to open in New York, popping up around town, mostly downtown of course, featuring modern, delicious, carefully prepared food, made from the freshest ingredients, and cooked by young and ambitious chefs. That said, Primola stands as a reminder that you can still eat very well east of Fifth Avenue and north of 57th Street.

Province

Note: This venue is closed.

212-925-1205
305 Church Street, at Walker Street
Casual
No reservations
Inexpensive
All major credit cards accepted
Monday–Saturday 11 AM–9 PM
A, C, E trains to Canal Street station; 1 train to Franklin Street station

New York has gone sandwich crazy, with the likes of 'Wichcraft, the resurrection of Eisenberg's, the various hamburger iterations around town such as Shake Shack and Pop Burger, the Bread outposts, the banh mi craze, panini, and now the lovely stuffed mantou served at Province. There is something universal about bread; at its heart it is the ultimate peasant food, and the possibilities seem to be endless. Here the steamed buns are derived from the traditional mantou (also called mo or momo), a simple steamed bun hugely popular in China's northeastern Shanxi province. This agrarian region has an abundance of wheat, vegetable farming, and deciduous fruit trees. Mantou, sort of a Chinese version of the famed Parker House roll, are a big part of the culture there and are frequently used in ceremonies, weddings, birthdays, and New Year's celebrations. The steamed bun offered here is studded with black or white sesame seeds and a variety of very tasty fillings, all for under $4 apiece. You pick the fillings, from BBQ pork shoulder to grilled chicken, pulled duck, braised pork, or diced braised short ribs, all combined with a spread of either hoisin or sweet bean sauce, cilantro, kimchi, and crunchy pickled cucumber. How, I ask, can you go wrong with any of those combinations on a warm steamed bun? Like the Vietnamese banh mi, these are addictive, and two will be required to put a dent in most reasonable appetites.

Prune

212-677-6221
54 East 1st Street, between
  First and Second Avenues
Casual attire
Reservations recommended
Moderate
All major credit cards accepted
Lunch and dinner Monday–
  Friday, brunch and dinner
  Saturday and Sunday
F, V trains to Second Avenue
  station

Prune is Gabrielle Hamilton's restaurant, reflecting her personality and sensibilities. She's the chef and owner, and she cooks what she likes to eat, which are big, clean, robust flavors. It's the kind of New York restaurant I'm partial to, a chef's restaurant. The bare-bones style of the place, the music selection off her iPod, the menu, the servers, the cooks, and even the clientele somehow reflect Hamilton's vision of what she wanted this place to be. One hopes New York will always have places like this, artsy, funky, hip, smart, and without compromise. Though these days I wonder.

When she first took the place over, it had been Casanis, which the owner abandoned seemingly overnight, leaving food in the refrigerators and booze at the bar. She should have hired a hazmat team to clean the space, but I'll spare you the details. They cleaned it up, changed a few things, and opened for business, not quite knowing what to expect. Hamilton, in truth, was a reluctant chef. Well educated and from an artsy family, a graduate of Hampshire College with a master's in fiction writing, she was supporting herself doing odds-and-ends cooking—catering mostly, grunt work, not fun stuff. She was not one of these starry-eyed 30-somethings walking away from a great job to peel carrots for $6 an hour in a four-star kitchen. I actually thought in the early days at Prune that Hamilton didn't like running the place that much. When I first met her, she was cooking on the line and impressed me as a sort of culinary sprite, tall and rangy, with two red-blond braids tucked behind her ears and streaming halfway down her back.

The room is tiny, with most seating at the simple wooden banquettes along one wall, where space is so tight that getting in and out requires that others cooperate and get up from their seats to allow you to maneuver. The place does have a Parisian hole-in-the-wall feel. There are a few tables scattered about up front, and a cute, private two-top behind the door as it opens, with one larger table downstairs as well. A long mirror flanks one side, the bar the other. In general it's downtown funky, rustic, and irresistible.

The food Hamilton cooks is big, rich, and aggressive: roast marrow bones, deep-fried sweetbreads, monkfish liver, braised pork shank, and lamb shoulder. Even her vegetable sides grab you by the collar: celery with meat sauce, thick sheaths of soft green cabbage tossed with a reduction of their own cooking liquid and bound with butter and salted anchovies, cauliflower with capers and brown butter, and a wonderful mixed salad consisting of bitter greens tossed in extra-virgin olive oil and lemon juice. I'm surprised more chefs don't work with monkfish liver, as it is delicious and a good substitute for foie gras. Here it is served sautéed warm and custard-like, with sea salt and warm buttered toast, a great starter combining richness with a certain briny edge. Italian wedding soup on cold nights is a winner, as are the chunks of crispy fried sweetbreads with a rich bacon and caper butter.

Braised heritage pork shanks are served on a bed of braised white beans and garlic sausage, cassoulet style. Lamb shoulder, again braised, is full of flavor, paired with tomatoes and lemon. Whole grilled fish is presented simply, with a garnish of fennel oil and coarse sea salt. And a grilled prime rib appears in retro form, topped with a cylinder of maître d'hôtel butter. Sweetbreads are braised, skinned, pressed, and finally deep-fried and served with a caper butter emulsion and topped with a thick strip of applewood-smoked bacon.

Service is good yet casual, the staff mostly earnest young women with tattoos and piercings who know the food and seem very happy to be working here. The wine list is relatively modest, filled with mostly Old World wines from very good small producers; you'd be hard pressed to find a bad bottle in the mix. If you can't get a table, you can eat in the cute bar area and enjoy the vibe.

Public

212-343-7011
210 Elizabeth Street, between Prince and Spring Streets
Casual
Reservations
Moderate to expensive
All major credit cards accepted
Dinner Monday–Friday, brunch and dinner Saturday and Sunday
6 train to Spring Street station; N, R, W trains to Prince Street station

This is yet another one of those places that I'd walked past dozens of times on my way to somewhere else, usually to dinner at Peasant, which is located a few doors down on the same side of Elizabeth Street. It always seemed busy, but the crowd skewed young, the sound track was too loud, and what was most visible from the street was the bar-lounge area, which seemed way too clubby for me. That all changed when the publicist for the place at the time badgered me into going with her for dinner there one night. The food turned out to be way better than I'd thought it would be, and, in a way, with that clubby scene, better than it has to be. The chef is Brad Farmerie, an American who trained in London and cooks what he calls Australasian cuisine, a menu loaded with ingredients from Australia and New Zealand, cooked in a pan-Asian style, and it's better than it sounds on paper.

The place is long on design, an early effort by the AvroKO group, who transformed the space from what it had been, a commercial bakery, into what it is, a multilevel spectacle that evokes a mailroom, wine cellar, and lounge, all done up in a mix of rough-hewn and polished textures, with natural wood and earth tones lit by custom-designed hanging bare light bulbs. You step up from the street past the mailroom-themed entrance. Behind that is the main dining room. The ceiling is high, the feel postindustrial, recycling bits and pieces of the place's past, such as the heavy sliding metal doors, the skylight, and the exposed arched brick ceiling. To the right, you step down into the bar and lounge, which was once a loading dock, I presume; behind that is a room billed as the back lounge, which has a fireplace and is mostly lit by candles. The other side of the space to the left of the main room is a separate sleek wine bar and dining room.

The menu arrives on a clipboard, looking like some sort of office supply reorder form. On it you'll see listed kangaroo, pink sea trout from Tasmania, and snapper and venison, both from New Zealand, sharing the bill of fare with local diver scallops and line-caught swordfish. The kangaroo dish is a winner, the meat moist and rich-tasting, sliced thin and then spread over a falafel cake, garnished with a sort of green pepper chutney. The scallops, big and sweet, were grilled and set over crème fraîche with fried green plantain as garnish and textural contrast. Striped bass was pan-seared, the skin crisped and sauced with a Thai-influenced spiced eggplant relish known as prik num. A cut of lamb new to me, called a chump—taken from the rear end of the loin, I'm told—is served medium-rare as ordered; it was plated with polenta studded with goat cheese and grilled vegetables. Roasted duck, the meat rich and fatty, played off well against pickled chiles and crunchy bok choy.

For dessert, try the pavlova, here made with whipped cream drizzled with banana-flavored caramel. They do a huge brunch business on weekends; try their version of eggs Benedict, which swaps out the Canadian bacon for tea-smoked salmon and spikes the hollandaise with yuzu. The wine list is, as expected, mostly New World but very good; not surprisingly, it pairs well with the heavily spiced, hot, sweet, salty, and sour flavors that come into play in many of the dishes. When it's busy the service lags, but the young staff do their best to keep up, and overall, the design-centric space, the food, and the feel of the place come together as effective, even transformative for the doubters among us, among whom I once was.

Rack and Soul

212-222-4800
2818 Broadway, at 109th Street
Casual
No reservations
Moderate
All major credit cards accepted
Lunch and dinner seven days
  a week
1 train to Cathedral
  Parkway/110th Street station

This is one of the best places in New York for BBQ. It's a very smoky, rich style, with the meat tasting of wood, and I like it a lot. There are three people behind this story: Michael Eberstadt, who runs Slice of Harlem and Bayou further uptown; Charles Gabriel, of Charles' Southern Style Kitchen up on Frederick Douglass Boulevard; and John Wheeler, the pit master out of Mississippi. Truth be known, none of them is there very often; they pop in and out to check on things, but the folks who run it day to day are doing a fine job following the various chefs' instructions. The room looks like a converted diner, running along 109th Street. There is takeout available all day long and seating for around 80 people in red vinyl booths. Service is good and friendly, and the menu is self-explanatory.

Once seated, you'll receive a small plate of their very sweet, warm, and tender biscuits to munch on while sorting through the menu. Chicken is offered fried, smothered, and BBQ. They also do BBQ short ribs of beef, which are wonderful, and baby back ribs in quarter or half racks. To this add nice, moist, smoky pulled pork, rich and tender braised oxtails, fried catfish, and various combo platters, which is where I tend to gravitate, as I can never make up my mind and settle on one thing. The ribs are as they should be, the meat a deep red from long slow smoking, moist, and falling-off-the-bone tender. The BBQ chicken wings will have you chewing, gnawing, scraping, and licking your fingers. Sides are decent. The greens can be watery; the mac and cheese lacks seasoning and can seem tired; skip the broccoli and asparagus; candied yams have the emphasis on candied; black-eyed peas are in a good rich sauce; and they even offer a Belgian waffle, to create, I suppose, your own version of chicken and waffles.

Desserts are nothing special, but the red velvet cake seems appropriate, and they push the banana pudding. I'm not sure why, though; it's basically a trifle, with layers of roulade smashed together with pastry cream and (sometimes) ripe sliced bananas. The wine list is not good, but they have a half dozen good beers, including Abita, a hard-to-find crisp amber brew from Louisiana that works just fine with all that smoke. All in all, the location is convenient and the BBQ is well worth the trip.

Ramen Setagaya

212-529-2740
141 First Avenue, at 9th Street
Casual
No reservations
Inexpensive
Cash only
Lunch and dinner seven days
a week
6 train to Astor Place station;
N, R, W trains to 8th Street
station

Opened in 2007, this is the first U.S. outpost of a Japanese restaurant chain of the same name, and the results so far are good. It's the brainchild of chef Tsukasa Maejima, who has several identical shops in the Setagaya ward of Tokyo. The room is small and rather spare, with a flat-screen TV broadcasting Japanese content, a sound track of Japanese pop, and usually a dozen or two Japanese expats reading the paper, taking it all in. The broth is shiso-style, based on salt (rather than miso or soy), and is accented with things like dried scallop oil, seaweed, braised pork, chicken, mushrooms, scallions, ginger, little dried Asian anchovies, and other seafood. Additionally, they finish the dishes by sprinkling them with sesame seeds, dried powdered scallops, fried onion, and a few drops of grapeseed oil. While I don't profess to be a ramen expert, I did love the movie *Tampopo* and have seen it many times. I have frequented a few ramen places over the years, and good clean broth, good stir-ins, and great chewy noodles are a hard combo to beat—healthy fast food for under $10 a pop. My favorite to date may be the chashu, or fatty pork, sliced thick, then grilled and served atop the broth and noodles, with the addition of half a soft-cooked egg. Yum. A light dinner, a tasty lunch, a midafternoon winter snack, or whatever you call it—it's all good. Those noodles come in three sizes or thicknesses, as explained on the menu, but honestly, I can't really tell them apart. There are a few other side dishes, but the ramen and the broth are the stars of the show and the reason to go here in the first place. Give it a try; it's already one of my favorite inexpensive noodle houses in New York City.

Rao's

212-722-6709
455 East 114th Street,
between First Avenue and
Pleasant Avenue
Casual
Reservations required
Moderate
Visa and MasterCard accepted
Dinner Monday–Friday
6 train to 116th Street station

So why, you may ask, do I write about a restaurant that is nearly impossible to get into? Well, it certainly is part of the New York scene, and as best I can tell, it's the longest-running restaurant continuously operated by the same family in the same location in the entire country, and that's saying something. There are less than a dozen tables, and each one in theory is reserved by someone each and every night. Truth is, a lot of the regulars eat here at least a few times a month all year long, year after year. Should one of those regulars opt not to go on their regular night, they can then "give" that reservation to a friend to use for the evening.

Way back when, this part of East Harlem was an Italian neighborhood. The restaurant sits a block away from the historic Our Lady of Mount Carmel church and the Museum of Roman Catholic History, opposite the old Benjamin Franklin High School, and across the street from Thomas Jefferson Park, and is just a stone's throw from the FDR and the East River. Little is left of the old neighborhood, and the highrise Jefferson Houses projects loom to the west, covering much of the area between 112th and 115th, running from Third to First Avenues. But Rao's has hung on, and each night the limos line up. The owners, Ron Straci, a labor law attorney, and Frank Pellegrino, who among other things played an FBI supervisor on *The Sopranos*, are there nightly presiding over the dining room, which is lit partially by the ever-present Christmas lights. Nick (the Vest) Zaloumis has been the bartender nightly since 1976 and knows all the regulars and what they drink.

So should you get in, here are a few suggestions: the roasted peppers are house-made, marinated in good olive oil and served with roasted pine nuts and raisins; the chilled seafood salad is very good; cabbage and sausage are paired with al dente penne pasta; the lemon chicken can easily be split for two; the plump juicy meatballs, Grandma's recipe, are an excellent side dish; all the pastas are good; and the veal dishes, as expected, are large and satisfying. If you can get a table, go, and I think you'll be pleasantly surprised. There are a lot of very good Italian restaurants in New York, but should you be able to get a table here one night, it's worth the trek uptown for the scene and the exclusivity, the occasional movie star sighting, or just to watch a bunch of middle-aged guys who may or may not be in the mob.

The Redhead

212-533-6212
349 East 13th Street, between First and Second Avenues
Casual
Reservations taken only for parties of five or more before 6:30 PM or after 9 PM
Moderate
All major credit cards accepted
Dinner only, Monday through Saturday
L train to First Avenue station; 4, 5, 6, L, N, Q, R, W trains to 14th Street/Union Square station

What started as a bar with a restaurant in a holding pattern offering a dinner menu Thursdays only, has now morphed into a one-day-a-week bar (Sundays only) with a six-day-a-week restaurant, serving familiar, homey, American comfort foods. The road to success is often a winding one, and in the New York restaurant world even more so. The chef, Meg Grace, was cooking at MOMA uptown, and her partners, Rob Larcom and Gregg Nelson, were both working in the industry here in New York as well. They all kept their day jobs and took over a former bar and music venue, reopening it as a bar where Meg would come in one day a week, Thursdays, to cook dinner.

The food was good, word got out, and in mid-2008, Meg took the plunge, quit her job uptown, and now is cooking to a packed house nearly every night. The cooking is solid, featuring some very nice ingredients simply prepared in an accessible style. Order the bacon peanut brittle and house-made waffle-cut potato chips with an onion dip as starters with a drink while you're still deciding on the rest of your order. A winning interpretation of a Caesar salad here featured long leaves of fresh romaine dressed in a creamy, briny cloak, topped with a single large, round crouton into which a sunnyside-up egg nestles, sprinkled with salt, pepper, and flash-fried capers.

Her shrimp and grits alone are worth the trip. It's all about ingredients again—the grits come courtesy of Anson Mills and are creamy and delicious, topped with three large sautéed shrimp, sliced andouille, and a sauce that tasted like brown butter and reduced shrimp stock, flecked with diced tomato and chives. Another winner was the small rectangular tart made of crab and leeks sauced with a mushroom cream sauce studded with fresh mushrooms. Like Hill Country, she gets her all-beef sausage from Kreuz Market in Texas. Here the sausage arrives at your table plated with a warm, soft house-made pretzel, a nod to their German ancestry. Like me, she plays around with fried chicken recipes. Sometimes the chicken is brined overnight and then coated thinly with just seasoned flour; other times she offers it as I prefer, with a thick, crusty buttermilk-and-flour coating, garnished with a small salad and lemon-flavored corn bread. Her bacon cheeseburger destroys the Bistro burger at Corner Bistro. Duck confit, though paint-by-number, is good here. And I liked the simple sautéed Berkshire pork chop, plated with house-made sauerkraut and a few spoons of buttery pork jus, simple and satisfying. In the summer, a plate billed as corn and chanterelle ravioli is really broad pasta noodles strewn around fresh corn cut off the cob and sautéed with chanterelles in a light butter cream sauce, flecked with parsley.

In a play on Ho-Ho's, a chocolate roulade is rolled around a creamy filling flavored with caramel and sea salt. In-season berry buckles and berry-topped biscuit-style puddings come with ice cream made with good Greek yogurt. In cooler months, try her sticky toffee pudding cake. They have some interesting house cocktails, beer, and wine. Service is friendly. In hard times like these, I appreciate places like this, where what you spent and how good and enjoyable it all was seem to fall perfectly in line.

Resto

212-685-5585
111 East 29th Street,
   between Third and
   Lexington Avenues
Casual
Reservations
Moderate
All major credit cards accepted
Dinner Tuesday–Sunday,
   brunch Saturday and Sunday
6, N, R, W trains to 23rd Street
   station

Resto, a restaurant that in part is devoted to exploring the highlights of Belgian cuisine, opened in the fall of 2006 to great acclaim. Good review followed good review, and over time the kitchen has just gotten better. The chef then, Ryan Skeen, now at Irving Mill, hailed from Portland, Oregon, had worked here in New York City with Zak Pelaccio prior to stepping out into the limelight, with this being his first solo effort. The room is the familiar restaurant rectangle, not too narrow, with walls painted off-white and a brand-new pressed tin ceiling; it's well lit (maybe too well lit) with large globe-style lamps hanging at regular intervals and wall sconces lending some additional wattage. The bar is to the right, the room spread out beyond it, and the kitchen through the swinging doors to the rear. The crowd for the most part is young, and as the evening wears on it can get loud, but this is a fun place to eat regardless.

Owner Christian Pappanicholas loves Belgian beer. Who doesn't? But for him, that was reason enough to open a restaurant devoted to Belgian-inspired dishes. The beverage list includes no fewer than five dozen beers from Belgium as well as a decent assortment of wines from around the world, but in truth beer works well with much of this meat-rich menu. Though Ryan left in 2008, I still find the food here good and worth the trip.

While they do have fish, and it is often prepared simply and well, this is a meat eater's destination, and fatty, heavy, odd cuts at that, not your standard steakhouse loin cuts. Start with the chef's version of bitter ballen, little ground veal and Gruyère meatballs made with the addition of pâte choux folded into the mix, which are then lightly dusted with potato flour and deep-fried, crisp and moist—yet another great mini meatball to add to the meatball/slider renaissance these days in town. On the lighter side, they have sautéed scallops with Brussels sprouts and a crisp little chickpea waffle, or chargrilled octopus paired with grapefruit sections. Try the deviled eggs, which also seem to be making a comeback these days. Here they are presented atop "pork toast"—braised, pressed, chilled, then deep-fried—for another wallop of flavor and fat. Each day there is a variety of house-made sausage preparations, made from humanely raised pork, beef, and lamb. The rich meats, often fatty and often fried or grilled, set the stage, and this is when the good Belgian beers start to come in handy.

For entrees, beef cheeks are served flamande-style, slowly braised in good beer and loaded with sweet carrots, or you may want to opt for any one of the half-dozen versions of steamed mussels and frites, my favorites being the ones steamed with Witt ale and the debal curry version. The hamburgers are really good; I just wish they were a little thicker, as patties that are too thin tend to cook past medium doneness. They are formed from a house-made mix of beef cheek, hanger steak, and ground pork at a nearly 70/30 meat-to-fat mix, served on little rolls with diced pickled onions and mayonnaise—great burgers. I wish the fries came cooked with more color; they are nearly white, for some odd reason. Though his spiced lamb ribs drive some folks crazy—they sell quite a few each night—I found them salty and too much work for the pale reward.

For dessert, should you have room, try the pain perdu or the simple Dutch-baby waffles sprinkled with powdered sugar and grated lemon. Overall the prices are easy on the wallet, the food good, the beer great, the crowd fun. In this part of town, Resto is a much-needed addition.

Rickshaw Dumpling Bar

212-924-9220
61 West 23rd Street,
  between Fifth and Sixth
  Avenues (and elsewhere)
Casual
No reservations
Inexpensive
All major credit cards accepted
Lunch and dinner seven days
  a week
F, V, N, R, W trains to 23rd
  Street station

If you build up an appetite shopping for a new iPod at nearby Tekserve, drop in here for a great quick meal. The brainchild of Kenny Lao, who worked for a while as special projects director (what does that mean anyway?) for impresario Drew Nieporent's Myriad Group, this place is a welcome addition to the neighborhood. (There's another location near NYU.) Lao hired Michelin-starred New York veteran chef Anita Lo, of Annisa in the Village, to consult, and what they ended up with is a very nice, clean, modern dumpling house for a new generation of dumpling eaters. It's a great concept, fast, cheap, and tasty. The menu overhead pretty much explains everything. Want just dumplings? Then you have half a dozen choices, either steamed or fried, from the classic pork-filled to a low-carb option that's wrapped in tofu and even a very nice (albeit a bit sweet) vegetarian version. Six dumplings cost $4.96; nine will set you back $6.95. If you want your dumplings served in a nice hot noodle soup, add $3. If you want a salad too, that's another $3. You can add to this sides of miso soup for $2, edamame with Japanese pepper salt for $3, or a decent chile-sesame noodle salad for $4. You can wash it all down with a green tea milkshake, Meyer lemonade, iced tea, hot tea, or soda for another couple of bucks. So it's the fast-food format, but the fast food here is very good. In short, it's hard to go wrong here. The place is very clean, the dumplings are very fresh and well made, and at these prices, you won't care if your $249 80GB iPod lasts barely a year.

Roberto Passon

212-582-5599

741 Ninth Avenue, at 50th Street

Casual

Reservations

Moderate

All major credit cards accepted

Lunch and dinner Monday–Friday, brunch and dinner Saturday and Sunday

C, E, 1 trains to 50th Street station

The great pastry chef and chocolatier Jacques Torres told me about this place. He lives in the area and eats here frequently. Since my first visit I've loved the simplicity of the food, the good service, and the easy-to-take bill at the end of the meal. The chef-proprietor, Roberto Passon, a native of Friuli, Italy, north of Venice, worked previously at Le Zie and Le Zoccole before setting out on his own and opening here in Hell's Kitchen. Though many love the feel of this part of town, it's never been my favorite. Ninth Avenue is still gritty and lined with undistinguished eateries mingled with bodegas and odd clothing stores. But this place stands out like a beacon, literally. The awning is bright yellow, as are the interior walls. The welcome at the door is genuine, and the food is good.

The menu is a mixed Italian bag with an emphasis on Venetian cooking, especially the fish, which are prepared simply and pared down. The appetizers and salads are all priced well under $10 apiece, and some are very good. Fried calamari are crisp, nearly greaseless, and white, as they often are in Italy. The octopus with boiled potatoes and chopped chives swims in good olive oil. The tuna niçoise could be a meal in itself on a hot summer night, good tuna served over fresh salad greens tossed with string beans, diced potatoes, hard-boiled egg, and olives; a good piece of crusty bread and a glass of rosé round it out perfectly. The warm beet salad too is a favorite, garnished with string beans, braised leeks, and a medallion of Montrachet cheese. In cooler months, the orzo and bean soup is a great, hearty starter, full-flavored and filling.

With well over a dozen pastas on the menu, it can be hit-or-miss depending on the night. Any of the broad noodles offered with the rich meat ragù are good. Taglierini with lamb, pappardelle with venison, or garganelli with osso buco are examples of this style. Ziti Bolognese too is a safe bet, as is the fusilli with chunks of smoky bacon, tossed with slightly bitter braised radicchio. White asparagus are wrapped in prosciutto and then topped with a sauce of brown butter, grated Parmesan cheese, and, as if that were not enough, a soft poached egg. In a nod to its Venetian concept, they do a good, hard-to-find calf's liver Venetian style, with sweet caramelized onions and a touch of vinegar for contrast. Fish offerings change with the season, but I like the striped bass paired with hearty, garlicky broccoli rabe, oven-roasted potatoes, and a sauce made from large caper berries, olive oil, and lime juice. On the lighter side, poached grouper is set in a saffron-accented Tokaji-based broth, with clams, mussels, and their juice as well.

Desserts are okay, never a strong suit for me in Italian restaurants. The appetizers are priced in the single digits and low teens, and few entrées are north of $20, making this a great spot for value and good cooking. The service can be erratic, as is the case in many of the city's smaller eateries, and the place can be loud when it is packed, but if you can overlook these minor inconveniencies and concentrate on the good food and fair prices, you'll leave a happy camper.

RUB BBQ

212-524-4300
208 West 23rd Street,
   between Seventh and
   Eighth Avenues
Casual
No reservations
Moderate
All major credit cards accepted
Lunch and dinner seven days
   a week
1, C, E, F, V, N, R, W trains to
   23rd Street station

In my opinion, one that is shared by many, this place serves some of the very best BBQ in New York City. One Tuesday night a few years back, my phone rang. It was Josh Ozersky, who used to write for *New York* magazine's online column "Grub Street." He was at RUB with a crowd including Ed Levine and Jeffrey Steingarten, among other major New York foodies, eating a slow-smoked prime rib just out of the oven. I couldn't make it for that meal, but a few weeks later a bunch of us, including Josh, the ringleader, took over the back tables, and the chef sent out course after course of great BBQ, ending with slow-smoked whole mutton. Since then I've been in and out of RUB a lot, as Dan's Chelsea Guitars is just next door, and the BBQ siren song is irresistible.

This restaurant comes to New York courtesy of the combined efforts of Kansas City barbecue legend Paul Kirk, the consultant, lecturer, and member of the BBQ Hall of Fame, and the day-to-day owner-operator who lives upstairs, local boy Andrew Fischel from Roslyn, Long Island. Fischel started to cook BBQ as a young suburban kid, experimenting in his backyard, mainly in an attempt to make a better brisket than Mom's. Those experiments plus loads of travel around the country bring us some of the best BBQ in the area.

On any given Monday, after a typically busy weekend, all four of his custom-made smokers are packed full with beef ribs, beef brisket, pork ribs, whole chickens, chicken wings, whole ducks, turkey breasts, sausage, pork butts, pastrami, and who knows what else. They do lunch and dinner seven days a week. At night it gets real busy, especially on the weekends. This barbecue is Kansas City–style, dry-rubbed, then slow-smoked to develop a very smoky exterior. The characteristic red char makes it about a quarter inch into the meat.

The sandwiches are all good. Try the chopped beef, featuring Black Angus brisket tossed with spicy sauce on a soft bun, or the burnt ends, an assortment of tidbits from the ends of the brisket, the deckle cut (also known as the point), twice cooked and really crunchy, smoky, and satisfying. His pastrami is traditionally dry-marinated with loads of coriander seeds and peppercorns and then slow-smoked, but never steamed, so this is a bit dryer and chewier than what you'll get at a traditional deli, but it's very, very good. It certainly can hold its own against the best traditional styles in this town. They have a full bar, and beer and wine as well. If you're looking for really good BBQ in New York, you must put this place at the top of your list.

Ruben's Empanadas

212-692-5330
4 Fulton Street, between Cliff and Gold Streets (and elsewhere)
Casual
No reservations
Inexpensive
Cash only
Lunch and dinner Monday–Saturday
2, 3 trains to Fulton Street station; A, C, J, M, Z trains to Broadway/Nassau Street station

There are at least three or four of these scattered around lower Manhattan these days under the same ownership, and all are good and cheap. Here you get the Argentine take on the empanada. The dough is flour-based, not corn-based, and baked, not fried, they are light and fluffy, and the fillings are good. Beef is the classic, with the seasoned ground meat mixed with onions and raisins. There are also fillings such as chunks of cod mixed with tomato, shrimp in Creole sauce, and ham and cheese. For breakfast they offer a Western, with scrambled eggs, onions, peppers, and cheese; supposedly this is good hangover food, and judging by some of the crowds I've seen here in the East Village location during late mornings, many have tried it. My favorite is the Argentine sausage, combining ground beef and braised pork in a red wine sauce. Round all this out with a few sides such as decent rice and beans, okay black bean soup, salsa cruda, or chimichurri, all washed down with iced tea or coffee, soda, or canned fruit juices. The empanadas are all priced below $4 apiece and many reasonable folks find two to be a meal, though just as many, less reasonable perhaps, can eat three or more at a sitting.

Rue 57

212-307-5656
50 West 57th Street, at the
  corner of Sixth Avenue
Casual
Reservations
Moderate to expensive
All major credit cards accepted
Lunch and dinner seven days
  a week
F, N, Q, R, W trains to 57th
  Street station

The awnings outside suggest that this is not only a brasserie but a sushi joint as well, and strange as it sounds, it's true. Sam Hazen is the corporate chef behind this scheme, with Marc Packer and a few other investors who also run the ever-popular Tao around the corner and several other spots around town. Hazen is a veteran New York chef who cut his teeth years ago under J. J. Rachou at La Côte Basque, and since then has been working steadily in the city for well over two decades. The space is housed in what until recently was a business and hotel district, and it's a location where many others had failed, including Lucky's, the previous tenant, but Hazen has created a very decent restaurant here, and it is usually packed with a mix of New Yorkers and tourists. So don't be surprised if at first glance it seems like just another busy midtown tourist trap with a line of customers spilling out the door and outdoor seating on both Sixth Avenue and 57th Street—don't you just love a side of bus fumes with your pinot noir?

But be brave, step inside, excuse the booming music, and you'll be surprised how well you can eat. The sushi and sashimi are decent and handmade to order at the sushi bar on the far end. The place sprawls over two floors connected by a sweeping stairway in the center. There are enough polished wood, tiled floors, and old mirrors to convince you of its New York faux-brasserie pedigree. The sushi idea, as incongruous as it seems, comes from the fact that brasseries traditionally serve big chilled shellfish platters, and Hazen had worked at several of the B. R. Guest properties where they serve sushi in a nontraditional setting—think Blue Water Grill. From the outset there were constraints with the kitchen size, so the shellfish platters became sushi. They tapped sushi chef Charlie Oh from Planet Sushi to help them set it all up, and it took a strain off the downstairs kitchen in the same way the shellfish platters at brasseries are assembled elsewhere and take pressure off the main kitchen. It's all about volume management in New York.

The sushi, as mentioned, is good, offered by the piece for $3 to $7, or by the platter starting at around $25 per person. Salads too are a nice way to start, with a very good Cobb salad, and another of lentils and frisée. I like the steak frites here. The meat is aged and flavorful, and the frites are excellent, served hot and crisp, wrapped upright in conical paper set in a stainless holder. The sirloin burger is one of the best burgers in town and a great bargain at $12.50, topped with a choice of good cheeses and served with that stack of excellent fries. I've also enjoyed the potato-crusted salmon, the simple roast chicken, and sides of crunchy haricots verts sautéed with shallots. The wine list is okay, and they have a decent selection of beers bottled and on tap. Desserts are good—split the banana upside-down sundae and you'll leave with a smile on your face.

Salumeria Rosi

212-877-4800
283 Amsterdam Avenue, between 73rd and 74th Streets
Casual
Reservations
Moderate
All major credit cards accepted
Lunch and dinner seven days a week from 11 AM
1, 2, 3, B, C trains to 72nd Street station

Chef Cesare Casella has been a fixture on the New York restaurant scene for some time via his restaurants Beppe and Maremma, both now closed. He's also the dean of the Italian Culinary Academy, part of the French Culinary Institute downtown. He's vivacious, passionate, and a lover of Italian food and cooking, but perhaps is not the best businessman, a trait he shares with many chefs. In this venture he has partnered with the Rosi family, producers of excellent salumi, based in Parma, Italy. This small 35-seat outpost reminds one of the little places found all over cities such as Florence or Parma. There is a small bar, a retail area for take-out orders of salumi, and an area with small tables ideal for the casual, simple, Italian comfort food served up here.

You must start with salumi: prosciutto crudo San Daniele, prosciutto cotto, which is cooked by steam, or prosciutto arrosto, a boneless, roasted version. Move on to the buttery sliced mortadella, parma cotto (again, a seasoned, cooked ham), Tuscan porchetta, or lightly smoked speck from the Alto Adige. The torta di porri is a small flaky pastry tart filled with leeks and pancetta with Parmigiano cheese; in the winter opt for the tripe stew, or try costina, Tuscan-style spare ribs braised with tomato, rosemary, and loads of garlic. Light starters can be ordered in combination to make up a meal—try a seven-bean salad bathed in rich olive oil, or roasted Brussels sprouts with sliced pancetta and chopped garlic, or chunks of Romanesco cauliflower topped with a gratin of crumbs and fresh parsely.

For large, heavier plates, they always have a seasonal risotto, a few simple pasta dishes, and, when available, a dish hard to find in America: imported bitter puntarella greens, from the chicory family, sautéed with anchovies, garlic, lemon, and olive oil.

The wine list is really good too, with many obscure small producers and glasses for under $10. Prosecco goes very well with salumi, and once past that, the choices of white include a delicious, almost salty Vermentino from Sardegna, Greco di Tufo from Campania, and Gewürztraminer from Alto Adige. For reds there are Nero d'Avola from Sicily, Montefalco from Umbria, and Morellino di Scansano from Tuscany. None of these is a household name, and all are excellent, which is another good reason to visit. Service is fine, and the prices more than fair for the quality and uniqueness of the offerings.

San Domenico

Note: Since Tony May passed the baton to his daughter Marissa, the restaurant has moved south to 26th Street and Lexington in mid 2009 with the same team in the kitchen and on the floor. The new space is larger, the setting more casual and modern, and the menu designed to allow the diner lots of choices, pairing smaller plates with more traditional regional Italian offerings.

212-265-5959
240 Central Park South,
off Columbus Circle
Dressy
Reservations
Expensive
All major credit cards accepted
Lunch and dinner Monday–
  Friday, dinner Saturday,
  brunch and dinner Sunday
1, A, C, B, D trains to 59th
  Street/Columbus Circle
  station; N, Q, R, W trains to
  57th Street station

Tony May, the man behind San Domenico, has been active in the New York restaurant scene for well over four decades. He's a pro, and his chef, Odette Fada, is one of the best practitioners of Italian cuisine working in New York City. These days Tony's daughter, Melissa, is there more than he is, and she's gradually taking over the reins. The crowd tends to be moneyed and a tad on the gray side, and the prices are high, but I hope a younger crowd soon discovers just how good this place really is. Back when there were no good restaurants in this area, which was most of the 1980s and 1990s, when the old New York Coliseum sat in mothballs and only tourists in horse-drawn carriages ventured near, they were putting out some of the best Italian food in the city, and still are. These days the neighborhood has radically changed, due in no small part to the completion of the Time Warner complex nearby. There are quite a few great restaurants a stone's throw from here, but San Domenico is still a standout. The menu prices start in the high teens and low twenties for appetizers, pastas are nearly all in the same range or higher, and entrees drift into the thirties and beyond, but the level of cooking and fine ingredients largely warrant the price structure.

You enter off Central Park South past the small bar to the right and a coatroom, then down a few steps into the large square room. From the front, and most seats facing that direction, you have a park view via the busy sidewalk. Service is good; some of the characters on the floor are a bit odd, but that gives the place some of its personality.

Start with the excellent appetizer of steamed Prince Edward Island mussels in a reduction of their broth, polished with parsley and a parsley puree, and set over creamy cannellini beans. In the warmer months, botarga, a Sicilian specialty that is essentially salted, pressed, and preserved mullet roe, is shaved over halved cherry tomatoes, micro greens, sections of orange, and chopped Tropea onions, for a great mix of citrus, crunch, and brine. Good grilled octopus arrives well charred and set atop a smooth puree of rosemary-scented cicerchie bean puree, a nice play on contrasting textures.

All the pastas here are first-rate, and most are homemade from 00 flour and farm eggs. In the fall, you simply must have the uovo, a rather obscure and hard-to-find pasta, offered in perfect form here. It is an experience you'll long remember. A single fist-sized raviolo arrives filled with seasoned ricotta cheese, and in the center is a barely cooked egg yolk. It is sprinkled with grated Parmigiano Reggiano cheese, then topped with browned butter and showered with freshly shaved white truffles. Cut into the center, and the yolk runs free into the brown butter. The pasta is chewy, the ricotta creamy and rich, the white truffles pungent, and the whole effect is a rich burst of flavors unique to this dish. An Abruzzese specialty, spaghettoni alla chitarra, is made from hand-cut pasta dough that is especially rich due to the use of just egg yolks in the recipe (a dozen or more per pound), cut thick, and tossed with a delicious, simple sauce of fresh tomato and basil. Here the simplicity of the dish reveals why great pasta, done well, is so sublime. If you happen to be here on a Monday, order the special of spaghetti cacio e pepe, again a simple yet lovely dish pairing nearly sauceless pasta tossed with grated pecorino cheese and fresh-ground black pepper. There is always a risotto of the day, and the stuffed lamb agnolotti served in a lamb ragù is a good cold-weather choice as well.

Daily specials vary with season, but trust Odette; you're in good hands with nearly everything this kitchen turns out. For main courses, if they have it, I suggest the Sicilian red prawns with tender braised cannellini, or the Chilean sea bass set over a pool of tomato zucchini broth swimming around a small mound of Sicilian couscous. The saddle of rabbit is good, and if you're hungry and want meat, the beefsteak Florentine-style for two is well worth it, as good an example of this served anywhere, cooked and served in cast iron with roast vegetables—just allow a little extra time.

The wine list is very good, deep, very Italian, and expensive. But with some help from the headwaiter, you can find some good value there as well. For dessert I like the light panna cotta with fresh berries and reduced balsamic glaze, or the upside-down apple tart with caramelized apple sauce.

Sapporo

212-869-8972
152 West 49th Street, between
  Sixth and Seventh Avenues
Casual
No reservations
Moderate
Cash only
Lunch and dinner seven days
  a week
N, R, W trains to 49th Street
  station; 1 train to 50th Street
  station

I was introduced to this place years ago by Yuji Kobayashi, a senior executive of the Nozaki Corporation, the owners of the Geisha brand line of food products and, at that time, a large Japanese food importer, with offices in the area with whom I did business. The place has been here for well over 30 years and is usually full of Japanese expats and Japanese tourists in search of authentic Japanese food and a good value. This is a tough restaurant neighborhood because there are so many choices, and mostly bad. So Sapporo is a standout. The room is larger than it looks, going deep into the building, or you can sit at the open bar facing the kitchen and watch the chefs at work.

For lunch, the noodle soups are very good, the broths rich and clean-tasting, the ramen noodles fresh and chewy, and all priced well below $10 a bowl, many in the $7–$8 range. Sautéed noodles too are excellent, served with a small green salad on the side. The plump gyoza are standouts. Crisp, meaty, and nearly greaseless, these dumplings are pan-fried pot-sticker style, crisp on one side only, the skins thin, light, and almost translucent. They are among the best to be found anywhere in the city, and six pieces for under $5 makes them even more appealing. The items listed as teishoku (which translates literally as "set meal") include soup and rice. Try the katsu dan, a panko-crusted pork cutlet. Cooked in stages, first it is deep-fried until crisp. It is then placed in a thin, small black steel pan and covered with a beaten egg, and a lid is put on top, allowing the scrambled egg to coat the cutlet. Then the whole thing is placed over a bowl of steaming sticky rice. It's perfect hangover food.

Start with the gyoza, finish with katsu dan, wash it all down with sake or beer, and you'll be out with a tip for less than $20, a bargain anywhere, especially here in this Times Square theater district neighborhood.

Sarge's Deli

212-679-0442
548 Third Avenue, between
  36th and 37th Streets
Casual
No reservations
Inexpensive
All major credit cards accepted
Seven days a week, 24 hours
  a day
6 train to 33rd Street station

These days Murray Hill is still a sleepy, midtown backwater with few great eateries and even less nightlife, but Sarge's, open 24 hours, is one of the city's best little secrets. At breakfast it's a mix of local businesspeople on their way to work. Late breakfasts and lunch cater to the work-at-home crowd, mothers with strollers, more business types, cabbies, cops, and students. Around

5 PM in stroll the area's many senior citizens, followed by families and couples. And at 3 AM some nights, the club set arrives for a quick meal on their way home from a night out on the town.

The menu is huge, and most of it is very good considering its size, but what I go for are those dishes that are becoming harder and harder to find in New York. Take, for example, their exemplary corned beef hash. Where else can you get that these days? (I know of a diner in the theater district that shall go unnamed where the wait staff periodically breaks into song, microphones in hand, complete with karaoke tracks booming over the sound system behind them. It's like a surreal *American Idol* audition. Anyway, this place claims to have real corned beef hash, and even boasts "not from a can" on the menu. Not only is it directly from a can, but it tastes like bad dog food.) Have Sarge's, the genuine article, for breakfast at $10.95 with two poached eggs, and skip lunch because you won't need it. They serve those kinds of breakfasts here: pastrami, salami, bologna, and tongue omelets, matzo brei with applesauce, Nova Scotia salmon and onions with scrambled eggs, an assortment of plump rolled and stuffed deli omelets cooked in individual egg pans (as opposed to the flat or folded variety that come off a grill), and of course bagels and smoked fish.

The pastrami sandwich here is very, very good, as are the corned beef, tongue, and brisket. For dinner try the Roumanian steak sandwich, a skirt steak served on top of garlic bread, topped with Bermuda onions and tomato, with a side of fries for $16.95. Or go for the hot brisket served on a latke with a side of applesauce. They have blintzes, kugel, kasha varnishkas, egg barley and mushrooms, boiled flanken, and a great chicken in the pot with a nice matzo ball. The wait staff are all seasoned veterans, the room is bright and clean, and the prices are more than fair, so what are you waiting for?

Sassy's Sliders

212-828-6900
1530 Third Avenue, at 86th
   Street
Casual, mostly takeout
No reservations
Inexpensive
All major credit cards accepted
Seven days a week 11 AM–11 PM
4, 5, 6 trains to 86th Street station

I know some will disagree, but the tiny burgers here are decent, the fries are better than decent, and the place is cheap. Yeah, it's a White Castle rip-off, to be sure. It is the brainchild of Michael Ronis, who helped open Carmine's and Virgil's, so not surprisingly, this too is an imitation of a familiar genre, in this case an old-fashioned burger joint. It's a funky little spot under a brightly lit awning that does mostly takeout and delivery. Inside there is a little counter with some stools. During normal lunch and dinner hours the place is packed with locals, students, bargain hunters, and folks who love White Castle but know there's none around for miles. The burgers come in three varieties—beef, turkey, or vegetable—and cost $1.09 apiece. If you want cheese, add 12 cents per. Fries, the skin-on variety, cost $2.49 for a large order. Order the combo platter and you'll get four burgers, a large fry, and a large soda for $7.29. Original, no. Great, no. Good and cheap, yes.

Savoy

212-219-8570
70 Prince Street, at Crosby Street
Casual
Reservations
Moderate to expensive
All major credit cards accepted
Lunch and dinner Monday–
Saturday, dinner Sunday
N, R, W trains to Prince Street
station; B, D, F, V trains to
Broadway/Lafayette station;
6 train to Spring Street
station

Housed in a squat, two-story antique building on the cobblestone corner of Prince and Crosby, this place has been a standout since it opened in 1990. The building itself is one of the oldest in the area and dates back to the 1820s, when it was a barbershop downstairs and a residence upstairs. You can still see the original red-and-white striped barber pole just inside the entrance. Post-barbershop, it was transformed into a sort of simple, neighborhood diner back in the 1920s, when this corner of SoHo/NoLIta was basically all industrial lighting manufacturing. It continued to exist as a diner until Peter Hoffman took it over in 1990. Peter sprang from the Jewish intellectual branch of the great New York culinary tree. Other chefs of that school include Barry Wine, David Waltuck, and Bobby Pritzker, to name a few. Peter worked for Barry back at the Quilted Giraffe, then spent some time in the kitchen of Hubert's with Len Allison and Karen Hubert. Peter was a pioneer in what today is known as market cuisine. He has been shopping for menu ingredients at greenmarkets, most notably Union Square, since they began, cooking seasonal dishes with intellect and simplicity.

You enter off the street into the downstairs dining room, with the horseshoe-shaped bar at the front center. When the weather allows, the windows open out to the street, giving a sense of space in this small room. Covering the ceiling is a fine copper-colored metal. Below hang some small spotlights that at night illuminate the space. To the rear, along the side wall, is a nice working fireplace; the kitchen is a few steps beyond that. The kitchen space itself is difficult, small and tight, with bearing walls right where you don't want them. That the food that comes out of it is as good as it is serves as a testimonial to the chef's ingenuity at using every square inch of space to its utmost. There is a nice upstairs dining room as well, with its own fireplace, and it seems after several visits that this room tends to be a bit quieter, though noise really isn't an issue anywhere here. They serve food continuously throughout the day, and I've been here at 3 PM on many a weekday and people are still streaming in, sometimes even waiting for a table. The crowd is diverse, from young hipsters to their well-heeled parents, and it's not uncommon to hear French, Spanish, or German being spoken at a table nearby.

For lunch and that midafternoon crowd, they have a menu of small plates designed to be eaten based on interest and appetite. They are all $5 apiece, and if you're hungry, you can pair any combination of three for $12. To that add a good assortment of soups and salads, a great BLT, and a very, very good burger, with twice-fried french fries and homemade ketchup with a hint of roasted red pepper. The dinner menu is more traditional, offering eight or nine appetizers including soup, a choice of six or seven entrees, and several à la carte side orders such as creamy polenta, sautéed greens with garlic chile oil and preserved lemon, and roasted Brussels sprouts with crisped bacon.

Start with the braised pork belly, from a heritage-stock pig, the belly meat white-pink, moist, and tender. The skin is removed, sliced thin, flash-fried to make it extra crispy, and set over a julienne of Asian pear, celery root, and smoky blue cheese. The house-made charcuterie plate combines thin slices of mortadella, rabbit rillette, duck pâté, bresaola, and liver mousse, garnished with house-made butter pickles. On the lighter side, the roast beet salad is a favorite, plated with crunchy arugula and a piece of good goat cheese. House-made pork sausage is grilled, then sliced and set atop a small pile of braised beluga lentils, with a black radish salad and a spoonful of apricot mustard.

Fish and meats change with the season. One night, a big, thick Montauk fluke found its way to the kitchen, where it was poached in a saffron-flecked fish broth, then set atop braised root vegetables, with a small ladleful of the poaching liquid functioning as the tasty sauce. A suckling pig from Vermont was boned out whole, rubbed with garlic and herbs, rolled, wrapped, and tied, then flash-fried to crisp the skin before being slow-roasted in the oven. The roulade was sliced and set over polenta and garnished with Gala apples, a bacon-onion marmalade, quick-sautéed fresh kale, and roasted, seasoned pecans. Striped bass, another great local fish here, is cooked almost entirely on the skin side to crisp it up, then finished briefly flesh side down and served with a medley of roasted shallots, Brussels sprouts, and double-smoked bacon.

Desserts are good, homey, and simple: a nice trifle with salted caramel and chocolate, or a very good crème brûlée that is finished in the working dining room fireplace with an old-fashioned salamander. The well-selected wine list offers value in every price range, especially $30–$50.

Service is good and attentive; the crew is young and casual without being silly. All the fish and meat come from organic, sustainable sources—grass-fed cattle from small producers, fish from local fishermen, vegetables from organic growers and local farms—and overall the place is an absolute joy at any time of day.

Sea Grill

212-332-7610
**19 West 49th Street,
  on Rockefeller Plaza**
Dressy
Reservations required
Expensive
All major credit cards accepted
Lunch and dinner Monday–
  Friday, dinner Saturday
B, D, F, V trains to 47th–50th
  Street/Rockefeller Center
  station

It's easy to dismiss this restaurant as an over-priced tourist destination, with its prime Rockefeller Center location, ringside seats to the gold Prometheus (and the Christmas tree and skating rink in season), but that would be a mistake. This is one of the best seafood restaurants in New York. The chef for years was the seasoned veteran Ed Brown, who now has his own place on 81st Street, just off Central Park West. Taking over is Jawn Chasteen, who worked closely with Ed for three years.

Service is professional, and the food is modern, intelligent, straightforward, and well executed. The minimalist treatment of very fresh fish shows their understanding that when fish is very fresh, it needs little embellishment and does well on its own, simply cooked and seasoned correctly. A traditional large menu is offered, as well as a smaller daily menu broken down into five groups: small plates, salads, plates, plancha special, and side plates.

Under the small-plates section, I love the rich chowder of lobster, shrimp, and clams; it is a great example of what very good chowder can be in the right hands, lifting this often leaden, starchy genre into the realm of truly great soups. If it's on the menu, try the wonderful lobster salad with fresh Hawaiian hearts of palm, all bathed in a yuzu vinaigrette, a nice foil that helps polish and refine the richness of the ingredients. The crispy, greaseless panko-crusted fried oysters are set on a bed of honey mustard oil and topped with paper-thin slices of scallion greens. There is always a good selection of salad options that vary with the season, such as a roasted beet carpaccio with lamb's tongue lettuce and a classic walnut vinaigrette, or a plate of the freshest tiny grilled calamari, with a pine nut and garlic crust and tossed with arugula and a fruity extra-virgin Tuscan olive oil. There is always an interesting selection of ceviches and tuna and salmon tartares, as well as excellent sushi and sashimi, prepared by the in-house sushi chef. In summer months, when you're seated outdoors, what better starter or main course than a tier of sparkling chilled seafood, priced in size gradations that includes, per your choice, a selection of oysters, clams, mussels, shrimp, crabmeat salad, and lobster, with a trio of dipping sauces?

As expected in any good seafood restaurant, the main courses vary by seasonal availability, but don't miss the featured "day boat specials" seared à la plancha. This Spanish method of cooking utilizes a very thick square grill with a stainless-steel surface that holds a constant temperature and is ideal for the quick, accurate cooking smaller cuts of seafood require. More and more well-equipped kitchens in New York are using these to great results and serving fish that combine a well-seared exterior with a moist, firm-textured interior at just the correct point of doneness. In season, they offer cod, halibut, grouper, monkfish, black bass, barramundi, or snapper, paired with grilled or sautéed spinach and a simple light emulsion sauce. They are not afraid to grill whole fish here on the bone in the European style. On a recent visit, our table shared a superb daurade, cooked whole and boned tableside. Salmon filets are grilled, and the fatty flesh plays well off the sauce of apple cider broth, studded with Nueske's double-smoked bacon, garnished with pumpkin-corn blini. Marinated house-roasted red peppers, tossed with spaghetti squash and a brilliant green fresh parsley emulsion, make for a colorful and delicious vegetarian alternative.

Desserts are of the American variety and vary with the season. These include a great key lime pie, a terrific tarte Tatin made with quince and topped with calvados ice cream, or my favorite, the rich steamed Valrhona chocolate pudding set next to a ball of pistachio ice cream. The wine list—heavy on whites, of course—is carefully chosen and matches the food very well; the staff are helpful with pairings should you need guidance.

2nd Avenue Deli

212-677-0606
162 East 33rd Street,
 between Third Avenue and
 Lexington Avenue
Casual
No reservations
Moderate
All major credit cards accepted
Seven days a week, 24 hours
 a day
B, D, F, V, N, Q, R, W trains to
 34th Street station; 6 train to
 33rd Street station

When the original 2nd Avenue Deli closed back in 2005, it was really bad news for New Yorkers who loved delis, because it left us with nothing. The place had been in business since 1954 and had a loyal and passionate following, myself included. Yeah, Katz's is great, but essentially it's a sandwich shop, and while Carnegie does make some great sandwiches, notably the pastrami, corned beef, and turkey, the rest of the menu is really hit-or-miss. So everyone I knew in the foodie world was psyched when Jeremy Lebewohl, son of the legendary original 2nd Avenue Deli owner, Jack, decided to reopen this place—no longer on Second Avenue, but who's quibbling? The new space is smaller and bright and clean, with a copper ceiling and lots of white tile and wood trim. They now have a liquor license, and the food so far seems to be good as well, though the longtime chef from the old place didn't return. To me, the food, I'm sorry to report, isn't quite what it once was in the old days.

The menu is a little different; some of the older-style heavy items are gone, and they now serve smoked fish, which they never did before. When you're seated, you're given a small dish of gribenes (crisp sautéed salted chicken skin) and fried onions to munch on. That plus a martini and I'm in trouble. The sandwiches are very, very good, not huge like at Carnegie, and sliced by machine, not by hand like at Katz's, but darn good. I've tried the chicken soup, and it's first-rate, though I'm not sure they use beef shanks like at the old place to make the stock. The matzo balls too are the genuine item, and the gefilte fish is about as good as it gets in restaurants. The sturdy, dense mushroom barley soup, enriched with dried porcini powder, is a cure for virtually anything from a cold to depression.

As of this writing, it's still early and a work in progress, but a good deal of the old staff returned to work here. My money says that within a few months, certainly by the time this book is published, anyone who wants to schlep over to East 33rd Street will have reason to celebrate. We finally have a great deli back in town.

Sfoglia

212-831-1402
1402 Lexington Avenue,
at 92nd Street
Casual
Reservations
Moderate
All major credit cards accepted
Lunch and dinner Monday–
Saturday
4, 5, 6 trains to 86th Street station

When Sfoglia first opened in 2006, the husband-and-wife proprietors Ron Suhanosky and Colleen Marnell-Suhanosky had dish towels as napkins, 10 tables, no liquor license or PR firm, and another place they ran in Nantucket. In other words, it seemed more like a youthful whim than a serious first effort in the febrile New York market. Well, that whim of a project turned into one of the most popular restaurants on the Upper East Side, because the food is that good. There's now a very decent wine list and a line out the door every night. The room is still spare, as it was in the beginning, lit by three chandeliers and decorated with bowls of fruit and an odd assortment of rural memorabilia, including a stuffed bird set above the kitchen door. But what comes out of the kitchen is very, very good food.

You enter the restaurant off Lexington Avenue; a large plate glass window is etched with the restaurant name. Past the bar you'll find the open farmhouse-style dining room, replete with painted brick walls, hanging copper pans, and mismatched tables and chairs. The menu is small and changes a few times a month, reflecting the chef's curiosity and the seasonal nature of ingredients. Like most talented chefs these days, Ron has a palate that's driven by the market, and his cooking shows great balance and restraint. While this place has been compared to a few other Italian eateries in town, the style of cooking reminds me of Savoy downtown, where sheer simplicity produces great results. While other chefs strive for more, more, more—more ingredients, more technique, more everything—here less is more, as it is in Italy.

A good reference point may be Colleen's excellent house-baked bread, a cross between focaccia and ciabatta, airy and light but chewy and full of flavor. It's the perfect mate for the house-roasted peppers, cheese, and salumi that make up one of the simple starters. Or start with any of the pasta selections: the broad pappardelle tossed with a rich, concentrated Bolognese sauce, or the great gnocchi made with butternut squash and blended with creamy cannellini beans and braised leeks. On a recent visit I had the pork scaloppine, lightly coated with pine nuts and pan-sautéed, the meat rich and moist, the pine nuts toasted and playing beautifully off the meat, and the sauce a simple caper-based house-made mayonnaise.

The dessert list, like the rest of the menu, is short but makes up for its brevity with quality. The milk chocolate espresso semifreddo is nice. If you're full, just opt for a plate of the house cookies or good, smooth, rich-flavored gelati. These days, small chef-driven restaurants are all the rage downtown, but it appears that the Suhanoskys succeeded with much the same idea a few years back, way up on the northern reaches of the crusty Upper East Side. As long as they keep cooking at this level, it will remain one of the best restaurants around these parts for some time to come.

Shaffer City

212-255-9827
5 West 21st Street, between Fifth and Sixth Avenues
Casual
Reservations
Moderate
All major credit cards accepted
Lunch and dinner Monday–Friday, dinner Saturday
1, F, V, N, R, W trains to 23rd Street station

If you love oysters on the half shell, there aren't a whole lot of places in New York where you can get such a good selection in such a casual setting. Grand Central Oyster Bar is another excellent choice that comes to mind, but that's buried in the basement of Grand Central Station, while this little bar/restaurant is right in the middle of Chelsea. You enter off the north side of 21st Street, steps from Fifth Avenue, the bar and its nice lit fish tank to your left, with seating to the right and plenty more in the two more-formal, nautical-themed dining rooms out back. The owner, Jay Shaffer, loves seafood, and aside from oysters you can do well here with items like the lightly breaded, pan-sautéed crab cakes. But it's oysters that first drew me in the door. Up front by the bar, packed in long stainless-steel inserts loaded with ice, a broad selection of East and West Coast varieties is featured every day: Blue Points, Peconics, Blue Islands, and their own signature Shaffer's Cove, all from Long Island; the sweet Buzzards Bay variety from Cape Cod; Narragansetts from Connecticut; Pemaquids from Maine; Wellfleets from Massachusetts; and Pickle Point, Malpeques, and French hooters, all from Canada. From the West Coast, there are the sweeter, less salty varieties such as Cortez Island, Sinku, Denman Island, Elkhorn, and Fanny Bay, all from British Columbia, and the famous Kumomoto, Hama Hama, Skookums, and Hood Canal, all from Washington State's waters. Ranging in price between $2 and $2.50 apiece, they are a great way to start a meal, or you can create a meal around them. The fried squid, fried oysters, and chowder are good as well. For traditional main courses, the blackened salmon over andouille-studded polenta is good, as are the pan-seared scallops. So if you're yearning for oysters washed down with a good selection of beer or wine and you're anywhere near this part of town, this is the place to go.

Shorty's

212-967-3055
576 Ninth Avenue, between
41st and 42nd Streets
Casual
Inexpensive
No reservations
All major credit cards accepted
Lunch and dinner seven days
a week
A, C, E, 1, 2, 3, 7, N, R, Q, W, S
trains to 42nd Street station

Originally opened as the first New York City outpost of the wildly popular Philadelphia chain Tony Luke's, it became Shorty's back in 2006 when the owner, Evan Stein, realized he had a bad deal with the founder, Tony Luke. Stein, a Philadelphia native, apparently has always wanted to bring great cheesesteaks to New York, and in a way he's succeeded. I'm from Philly, and I've never understood the fascination with this sandwich. I mean, they're okay, but never great, and often barely mediocre. The meat, usually frozen South American rib eye, is sliced thin while still frozen, then allowed to sweat (cook), piled high over a flat-top grill. This steamed, sliced meat is then heaped on a soft, long roll and topped with Cheez Whiz and a few other options—and that's it, a simple meat sandwich invented in South Philadelphia years ago. So maybe Shorty's has the best cheesesteaks in New York. If you're of a certain age and have had enough to drink, maybe they are amazing. For me, Shorty's best sandwich is the roast pork with sautéed broccoli rabe and provolone cheese.

When it became Shorty's, the owner also increased the size of the dining room, which was previously almost nonexistent. The kitchen was designed by Tony Luke himself, and it was way too big. Stein realized this once he opened and recovered that space to enlarge the dining room and make it more comfortable. At the same time he also broadened the menu, adding soups, salads, and a few other sandwiches, and now the place is a pretty decent restaurant hangout for this area of town. The cheesesteaks are as good as you'll find in New York, the menu is decent, they have beer and wine, and the place is a good, casual, bargain-priced choice as these things go today in New York.

Shorty's 32

212-375-8275
199 Prince Street, between
  Sullivan and Thompson
  Streets
Casual
No reservations
Moderate
All major credit cards accepted
Dinner seven nights a week
C, E trains to Spring Street station;
  1 train to Houston Street
  station

In what appears to be a encouraging mini-trend these days, chefs who have worked valuable, long apprenticeships in top New York kitchens are now opening their own, usually very intimate restaurants with very small kitchens where, out of love for cooking and/or sheer necessity, they find themselves the head cook, often with a supporting team of just one or two others. This is a good thing, as chefs should cook. It's what they've been trained to do, and after years of working under the tutelage of others adept at this same task, they've learned good basics and good technique. Think Little Owl, the Spotted Pig, Dell'Anima, Bar Blanc, and Market Table, to name just a few recent examples.

And so here in this far west corner of SoHo, in a little kitchen with a little dining room, Josh Eden is living his dream. The place is named after him (it's a nickname—he is indeed short), and the place has 32 seats. He worked for a dozen years with the Jean-Georges Vongerichten team at various locations, including JoJo and 66. Now on his own, he knows the limitations of the small kitchen and staff, and so he offers us a rather limited but well-rounded menu of good simple dishes, priced well. The room is small, with a little bar to your left as you enter, the balance of the square room dimly lit by the many little hanging lamps dangling from the ceiling. The place has been packed since it opened, and by 7 PM it's always full and noisy too. But younger people these days like it that way, so who am I to complain? The great sound track played in the dining room is courtesy of Josh, and I can also tell you that on a recent visit backstage to the main kitchen at WD-50 during afternoon prep, they were playing his iPod mixes as well.

One recent meal started with a rich, thick soup made with roasted squash and ham, for $7 a real winner. The fresh cavatelli with arugula and wild mushroom ragù seemed a little soupy to me; perhaps the pan jus needed another 30 seconds of heat to reduce a bit more to the correct consistency, but it was hard to complain about the excellent braised, crisped pork belly set atop a salad of perfectly cooked and seasoned cranberry beans. In a crab cake variation here, they are rolled out like little logs, breaded, and deep-fried as crab sticks, full of good crabmeat flavor and served with a basil rémoulade dipping sauce.

For main courses, skate was given a southern Italian twist. Here the delicate meat is browned first, but only on one side; then the filet is smothered with a thick tomato sauce chock full of caramelized onions and baked in the oven for a few minutes before being topped with crisped bacon. Long, thin, toasted, crusty slices of baguette are added to the plate to soak up the good sauce, a winner for sure at $18. The house burger, weighing in at 8 ounces, is also an easy choice, arriving with a stack of perfect, crisp fries, stacked tall in a paper cone and garnished with homemade pickles; at $14, this is a good plate of food. Another night I had the cod. Here it is served in an original style, combing the familiar flavors of French onion soup. The cod itself was pan-sautéed, then briefly baked, cooked perfectly, flaky, white, and very moist. The thick, center-cut filet was set atop a toasted slice of good bread, then sauced with a rich, oniony broth redolent of Gruyère cheese and enriched by the addition of wilted Swiss chard. This was a simple yet effective dish, the cod meat flaky and mild but tending toward bland; the onion soup treatment gives the fish a good background chorus of flavors, both sweet and rich, and the whole worked well when taken together. They have a very nice roast chicken; you receive half of a large bird, more than enough for most. There's also a wet-aged, grass-fed strip steak and, in cooler months, braised short ribs for the meat lovers in the crowd.

Desserts are simple but satisfying. I love the pan-toasted pound cake with berries and whipped cream, and the chocolate bread pudding served with sliced bananas across the top and nice caramel ice cream. Service is fine, the staff small but enthusiastic. The wine list is limited but good and growing, with value present as per the rest of the menu. All in all, with prices this fair and cooking this good, I suspect Shorty's 32 will have a long run.

Sip Sak

212-583-1900

928 Second Avenue, between 49th and 50th Streets

Casual

No reservations

Inexpensive to moderate

Cash only

Lunch and dinner seven days a week

6 train to 51st Street station; E, V to Lexington Avenue/ 53rd Street station

Orhan Yegen has been the man behind several very good Turkish restaurants in New York, starting with Turkish Kitchen, then Effendi, Deniz, Dervish, Beyoglu, and Taksim. His latest venture is Sip Sak, which loosely translated means "fast," but the food here is anything but fast food. Like many other great ethnic cuisines, Turkish food in New York does not get the respect or attention that it deserves. If you've ever traveled around Turkey, Algeria, or Morocco, the land, soil, sky, ocean, and scenery will remind you of Spain, Portugal, Greece, and, to a degree, parts of southern Italy as well. They share many of the same crops, like fresh olives (and delicious olive oils), lemons, capers, eggplant, and peppers; the same fish, such as daurade, branzino, sardines, and anchovies; the same grazing animals; and much the same weather and growing seasons. Turkish food layers these flavors in each dish and offers meals featuring many small plates, mezzes, nearly all delicious and driven by ingredients.

A good example of this here is the eggplant salad. Whole eggplants are first charred on the outside, then baked until tender, allowed to cool, peeled, and deseeded. This smoky eggplant meat is whipped with garlic puree, lemon juice, and loads of good green olive oil to create a delicious, silky puree, polished by the acid from the lemon juice. The taramasalata blends pink cod roe with a touch of garlic puree, cubed white bread briefly soaked in milk, fresh lemon juice, and a good dose of olive oil, folded together to create a smooth, rich, fishy spread that will disappear off the table, slathered on the good, fluffy pita bread served with it. The hummus served here is well above average, as are the stuffed meatballs and various gyro plates. Chicken can be overcooked, as can the fish. It's hit-or-miss with the main courses, but with prices no higher than $15 per plate, I suppose we can live with that.

The wine list is not very good; stick with beer or bring your own wine. The service here varies wildly. I've had many acquaintances complain to me that the staff and owner were rude. Yegen is a character. Think of him as a Turkish version of Kenny Shopsin: talented, irascible, opinionated, and incendiary. It's his place, he makes the rules, and if you don't like it, get lost. That said, for food this good and at these prices, I'll put up with a little abuse if I have to—that's why they invented the iPod.

Smith & Wollensky

212-753-1530
797 Third Avenue, at 49th
   Street
Casual to business
Reservations
Expensive
All major credit cards accepted
Lunch and dinner seven days
   a week
6 train to 51st Street station;
   E, V to Lexington Avenue/
   53rd Street station

Great ideas have to start somewhere, and in this case it was all about meeting girls. The year was 1965, and Alan Stillman, the owner and creator of the Smith & Wollensky chain, was in his mid-twenties and single, living in Manhattan, and simply wanted to meet airline stewardesses. He knew many of these attractive young ladies lived on the Upper East Side, a short trip to both JFK and LaGuardia airports, and so decided to buy a cheap shots-and-beer bar in the neighborhood and turn it into something else, mainly a place where he could meet girls. He did all the above, and that bar became the very first T.G.I. Friday's, opened with the help of a $5,000 loan from his mother. The rest, as they say, is history. T.G.I. Friday's did very well and spawned countless franchises, and eventually Stillman sold the chain. In the interim he also opened a Thursday's, a Wednesday's, and a Tuesday's, and while running these establishments, which were mainly clubs and bars, he grew up and got the restaurant bug.

Always on the lookout for potential restaurant locations, he'd often walk past the shuttered but legendary Manny Wolf's Chophouse on the corner of Third Avenue and 49th Street. Manny Wolf's had been a fixture on the New York restaurant scene for years, originally on the Lower East Side, then moving to the Upper East Side, right next to the elegant Café Chambord. They had a good long run, but by the mid-1970s, Manny's was history: the building was vacant, the roof leaked, and it needed a complete renovation. So in the winter of 1976 Alan Stillman purchased this historic two-story building, which had originally been built as a buggy whip factory in the 1800s, and restored it to its former glory as a white-tablecloth restaurant, opening in the winter of 1977 as the very first Smith & Wollensky.

But all did not go as planned. Stillman and his longtime business partner and fellow restaurateur, Ben Benson, had just assumed the place would be packed. Why not? All their other places had done well. But this would be a different scenario. The surrounding neighborhood had no shortage of great steakhouses—the Pen and Pencil, Christ Cella, the Palm, and Pietro's, to name just a few. Business was so bad in the first six months, they actually put the place up for sale. Their first break came that summer, by coincidence really, when all the other steakhouses in the neighborhood closed for the month of August, as they habitually did, and steak lovers simply had nowhere else to go. By September the crowds at

Smith & Wollensky had doubled, they were making money, and a star was born. These days there are Smith & Wollensky steakhouses in every major American city, 17 restaurants in all, but let's talk about the flagship in New York.

First of all, this place is always busy—lunch and dinner, every day, all year long. It is one of the highest-grossing à la carte restaurants in the country, so they must be doing something right. It is built along classical steakhouse lines, very masculine and clubby, with loads of dark wood paneling, high-backed leather banquettes, and heavy brass lamps. There are throngs of hale and hearty types, mostly men in suits, knives in hand, martinis before them, napkins tucked beneath their chins. The restaurant sprawls over two floors, with nary a bad table in the house. The large kitchen is on the first floor in the rear. Most nights, a crowd three deep can be found waiting for their tables at the bar to the left of the entrance. The menu is large and has something for everybody, except vegetarians. For years they would routinely take out expensive full-page ads in the *New York Times* depicting a single enormous steak knife with text reading, "Terrifying vegetarians for over 25 years."

Appetizers are predictable but all good examples of the genre: wedge salads, shrimp cocktails with either three or four huge shrimp, a good lump crab cocktail, thin slices of smoked salmon done pastrami-style, great split pea soup, or a lobster cocktail for the big spenders. But who goes to steakhouses for appetizers? They are really the warm-up acts prior to the main event, beef.

The steaks here—USDA prime and dry-aged for a minimum of 21 days—are uniformly good and accurately charbroiled. I usually order the New York strip, dense and well marbled, and full of beef flavor. That said, all the other cuts are excellent. For filet lovers, they deliver a well-turned-out filet au poivre. The sirloin is very good; the prime rib is dependable, and except for the end cuts, which go fast, they usually have several degrees of doneness to choose from. For folks who want to share, they have a double sirloin and a châteaubriand taken from the fat end of the filet.

Should you not want steak, try the veal chops, excellent triple-cut Colorado lamb chops, the daily butcher's special, lemon pepper chicken, or the hard-to-find calf's liver done a variety of ways. For seafood lovers, lobsters start at 3 pounds. There are good-quality fish steaks—tuna, salmon, swordfish— purchased fresh daily from the Fulton Market and cut in thick, boneless slabs. Crab cakes are big, moist, and meaty, and don't pass up the soft-shells in late spring and early summer.

I often find desserts a bit much after one of these meals, but here, unlike at many steakhouses, they actually employ a pastry chef who makes all the desserts from scratch, and it shows. The desserts, in true steakhouse style, are big and rich and don't hold anything back. For the brave or fool-ish, go ahead and order dessert. Try the tall wedge of moist carrot cake with cream cheese icing, the classic eight-layer chocolate mousse cake, the fluffy all-white coconut layer cake, bourbon pecan pie, deep-dish apple brown Betty with vanilla ice cream, or the classic profiteroles with warm chocolate sauce drizzled over them.

Service here is excellent. Most of the staff have been here for years and know the regulars by name, yet strangers and tourists are treated well. The 100 percent American wine list is excellent. Stillman is an avid wine collector, and the list shows that off. Aside from the usual winemakers—Cakebread, Chalk Hill, Grgich, Heitz, Jordan, and Mondavi—they fea-ture some wonderful hard-to-find gems such as Kluge Estates New World red from Virginia, WesMar pinot noir from the Russian River Valley, and the fine CE2V Meritage from Napa.

Smith's

212-260-0100
79 MacDougal Street,
   between Bleecker and
   West Houston Streets
Casual
Reservations
Moderate
All major credit cards accepted
Dinner seven nights a week
1 train to Houston Street station;
   A, C, E, B, D, F, V trains to
   West 4th Street station

Located on this funny little block in the south-ernmost fringes of the Village are an old private Italian gun club, the Tiro a Segno, then the res-taurant Villa Mosconi, followed by a large asphalt playground designed for handball and basketball taking up the entire corner of West Houston between MacDougal and Sixth Ave-nue. Smith's space used to be Trattoria Dante until Danny Abrams of Red Cat, the Harrison, and the Mermaid Inn acquired the lease. He installed Pablo Romero in the kitchen, fresh off years of cooking with David Bouley and Jean-Georges Vongerichten, and seemingly ready for his own kitchen. As of this writing, the results are mostly good and a new chef, Doug Psaltis, is on board. The place opened in late 2007 and was very busy from the start. The space is essentially three very different rooms. You enter into the bar and lounge area, where you can have a drink while waiting for your table or grab a table there. The other dining room connects the front to the back bar and resembles an old train car. It is narrow, with a beveled mirrored ceiling, banquettes lining one wall, and a row of small two-tops lining the other. At the back is tucked away a bar proper. The theme is black and white; the space is done in those colors, and the wait staff are dressed to match.

The menu is broken down into several categories: appetizers, seasonal starters, entrees, and accompaniments (essentially à la carte sides). The choices are all good and put together in an interesting lineup. A starter of charred Cape Cod baby squid was mostly accurate—that they came from Cape Cod I can't vouch for, but I wouldn't call them baby squid, just smallish winter squid instead. They were quick-cooked, then tossed with lemon confit, chopped pitted olives, and sliced pancetta—a good dish, clean, bright flavors showcasing good ingredients. The artichoke pasta too was good; sliced artichoke hearts were folded into good fresh pasta, presented in one long curl folded off a large serving fork, French style, in a sauce studded with diced black truffle, truffle oil (which I don't like much), Parmigiano Reggiano, and crisped prosciutto, all good solid flavors.

Boneless pork loin, when taken from good stock like these Berkshire chops, can be delicious. My dish had a medium-rare chop set alongside a braised pork cheek, and a nice combination of celery root and apple puree to round it all out. The entree of striped bass was disappointingly small, either taken off the tail section of a larger fish or perhaps simply taken from a filet of the smaller, less desirable farm-raised variety. It was cooked well, skin side crisped and served over hearty flageolet and guanciale stew, but the fish portion couldn't have been more than 3 or 4 ounces, and I was wanting more.

Among the sides try the Anson Mills polenta, made from those excellent South Carolina grits, creamy and delicious—but please hold the darn truffle oil. Another side taken from the seasonal starters was a roasted, peeled, marinated eggplant, the flesh soft, set in an acid-based brine, accented with piquillo peppers, raisins, and sherry vinegar.

The menu gives you the flexibility to mix and match starches and sides and create an interesting meal around the entree choices, though be careful because ordering that way can get expensive in a hurry. The wine list was okay, not great, and considering the neighborhood and the menu prices, I thought it was top-heavy and could use more food-friendly wines in the $20–$40 range. The staff was good; the place had just recently opened, so they need to work out the kinks. I suspect it will do well, as the team assembled behind it are by now New York veterans. And because Chef Psaltis, who is young, still likes to cook and is eager to make his mark, the food is better than ever.

Socarrat Paella Bar

212-462-1000
259 West 19th Street, between
   Seventh and Eighth Avenues
Casual
No reservations
Moderate
All major credit cards accepted
Dinner seven nights a week
   from 5 PM
1 train to 18th Street station;
   C, E, F, V, N, R, W trains to
   23rd Street station

Jesus Manso of La Nacional opened this spot in the summer of 2008 with chef Felipe Camarillo doing the day-to-day cooking. It's a great addition to the neighborhood—casual, moderately priced, with very good food to match the setting. I'm not certain who the designer was, but the feel of the place evokes comparisons with Allen & Delancy, Freeman's, and Elettaria, and by that I mean farmhouse, rustic, casual, even romantic in spite of the cramped quarters. And cramped it is, with just 20-some seats and no waiting area to speak of. Diners are seated at one long communal table running down the center of the room. Depending on who got there before you, you may sit facing your companions or alongside them. Not to worry—once the food arrives, you'll all be happy.

The paella is first-rate, and at last count there were eight varieties to choose from. The standard is made with chicken, beef, shrimp, cuttlefish, mussels, clams and green beans. A vegetarian version is full of asparagus, zucchini, artichoke hearts, mushrooms, and tomatoes. There is another all-meat one with pork, chicken, duck, and chorizo, and two made not with rice but with noodles known as fideua. If you want to keep it on the lighter side, you can easily make a meal of the small tapas plates. Excellent braised pork belly comes with roasted potatoes and a dab of date puree. Salt cod is silky over white beans as a salad or as a brandade, blended with potatoes and good olive oil. For a light late-night meal just order the Iberico ham, aged 24 months, silky and delicious, with a small plate of shrimp in hot garlic oil, a small bowl of sautéed chorizo chunks, and crispy fried artichokes. Service is fine, the wine list is short but good, with some decent sherry as well, and of course they also serve beer.

Solera

212-644-1166
216 East 53rd Street, between
   Second and Third Avenues
Casual
Reservations
Moderate to expensive
All major credit cards accepted
Lunch and dinner Monday–
   Friday, dinner Saturday
6 train to 51st Street station;
   E, V to Lexington Avenue/
   53rd Street station

Years back, the very talented chef Dominick Cerrone opened this restaurant after his tenure as the opening sous-chef at Le Bernardin. The food then, as now, was very good, but the timing wasn't. New York was not ready for serious Spanish food, and so the place struggled. These days, in part thanks to chef Ferran Adrià and how he has popularized all things Spanish, good Spanish cooking can be had in more than a few places around town, and this is one of them. There is a tapas bar, with a good sherry list to match the food, and at the regular tables a Spanish menu and an all-Spanish wine list to match. The room is rather formal, the floor a mix of terra-cotta and carpet. Bentwood chairs are set before linen-covered tables beneath an arched ceiling. The walls are painted a creamy yellow, with natural wood trim framing the ceiling, doors, and windows.

The menu is good but has a few clunkers. Stick with the traditional-sounding Spanish country cooking and avoid the fancier French-influenced dishes, and you'll do fine. The starter of mixed fried and marinated seafood is a good choice, as is the garlic shrimp. Pair either with a glass of albariño and you'll be happy. The paella is a good version of this classic, but I prefer the leek-wrapped monkfish with bone marrow and a red-wine-based sauce, or the braised rabbit Jerez-style with snails.

The wait staff are a tad stiff and to some can come off as snooty, but the cooking is solid, and the wine list matches well to the food. An alternative idea is to sit at the long wooden bar and just eat tapas. It's more casual, and you can sample lots of good food, like the excellent, creamy, garlicky white beans studded with chunks of good chorizo, the fried squid, or the stuffed piquillo peppers. The sherry list that pairs with the tapas menu is impressive. While I prefer the scene and food at Suba downtown, if you live in this neighborhood and need to eat nearby, it's the best Spanish food for miles.

Soto

212-414-3088
357 Sixth Avenue, between
West 4th Street and
Washington Place
Casual
Reservations
Expensive
All major credit cards accepted
Dinner Monday–Saturday
A, C, E, B, D, F, V trains to West
4th Street station; 1 train to
Christopher Street station

After this place opened in 2007, I walked by a few times before I knew what it was. I'm familiar with the block, live in the neighborhood, and often walk this side of Sixth Avenue en route between my guitar store on Carmine Street and Citarella, a few blocks to the north. Here you'll find head shops, tattoo parlors, inexpensive takeout, and then this little white storefront with the small square peepholes set into the frosted glass front window. Inside, it's all white and blond wood set over the stone floor. The architect, Hiro Tsuruta, also did Momofuku and ChikaLicious, and here the word "spare" comes to mind. Chef-owner Sotohiro Kosugi, a slender, third-generation sushi chef who arrived in New York by way of Atlanta, already has quite a following here. You'll find him here each night working at the small sushi bar, and he's usually the first to greet you as you enter. The room is small, with seating for just over 40, with the sushi bar seating seven, a few tables in the center, and a strip of two-top banquettes lining the far wall.

The menu is comprised of sushi and inventive plays of raw and cooked fish, many prepared by the chef's wife, Maho, who works in the kitchen. The portions are very small, the food is very pretty, and usually the flavors are built in multiple layers and textures. Take the dish of chayutoro tuna tartare: hand-cut, this fatty, rich fish is blended with caviar, seasoned with chives, sesame, ponzu, and dried ginger, formed into a disk, then topped with a thin spread of smooth, creamy guacamole, rich on rich, with the other accents emerging slowly. Crunchy horse mackerel tataki is stacked up and woven with purple shiso blossoms; sea urchin is wrapped in squid, seasoned with nori, and topped with a raw quail egg; and the delicious, sweet red shrimp tartare is seasoned with tobiko (flying fish eggs) and yuzu, then topped with a spoonful of foamed soy. The hot food continues along the same lines, with inventive and quirky pairings that suggest a good deal of work and thought behind them. Sea urchin again crops up, this time in a version of new Japanese comfort food, the rich orange orb set in a shiitake mushroom broth, with black bean milk skin as counterpoint. New Zealand sea bream is briefly steamed, then sauced simply with a ginger and scallion oil. Shrimp cakes are deep-fried and topped with shiitake mushroom caps. Lobster is steamed and presented with a sea urchin mousse, smoked sea urchin, lotus root, and caviar.

The 12-piece sushi omakase is a relative bargain at $56, and for dinner I'd recommend the 15-course meal that can be had for $80. Is this place already among the best in the city? Is it as good as Sushi Yasuda? No, not yet, but it's not far off the mark, and it's still young. This is not a traditional sushi/sashimi restaurant, and don't think of asking for soy sauce and wasabi. Prepare to spend a few dollars, place yourself in the chef's hands, and you'll be rewarded.

Sparks Steak House

212-687-4855
210 East 46th Street, between
 Second and Third Avenues
Dressy
Reservations
Expensive
All major credit cards accepted
Lunch and dinner Monday–
 Friday, dinner Saturday
4, 5, 6, 7, S trains to 42nd
 Street/Grand Central station

Always a popular place, Sparks was made even more so by the pre-Christmas mob assassination of "Big Paulie" Castellano and his associate Thomas Bilotti on the curb directly in front of the restaurant on December 16, 1985. Castellano had just emerged from the car, and John Gotti was parked half a block away watching safely from his own town car. The shooters, stationed across the street and wearing trench coats and Russian Cossack hats, fired away, and when the job was done they hightailed it down Second Avenue to the getaway car and escaped into the crush of midtown Christmas traffic. The restaurant kept serving dinner to a full house that night, and it's continued to pack them in every night since. You'll need reservations, and when the place is busy, expect to wait at the cozy wooden bar until your table is ready—more on that later.

As at most steakhouses, the food is retro, and the steak's quality can vary radically from night to night, meal to meal, and even during the same meal. Part of this is due to the fact that excellent-quality American corn-fed, dry-aged prime meat is harder and harder to come by. The demand exceeds the supply, so many places are aging for shorter periods or aging "wet," which is not the same as dry-aging. But you don't come here for culinary inspiration, you come to take part in a quintessential New York restaurant scene: tables full of guys in suits, a lot of booze being consumed, noise, pinky rings, heavy watches, and a very decent wine list if you have the money to spare. The sprawling rooms are somewhat cramped and rather dark and clubby, with heavy-framed oil paintings, much dark wood paneling, and etched glass, but that just adds to the old-boy feel of the place.

If you require an appetizer, skip the hot ones, as I've found none to be good, but go for the chilled shrimp cocktail if that's your thing. Here they are served peeled and deveined, lying horizontally on a plate, with lettuce and cocktail sauce. The lump crabmeat is good too, but let's face it, that product comes into the place already cooked and cleaned. But at least they buy good jumbo lump and serve it fresh. Sometimes the cold appetizers arrive too cold, as in pre-plated and right out of the refrigerator, but that's the way these old-time steakhouses do things. Other options are the Caesar salad or the spinach salad—both are okay.

Getting to the main courses, stick with the big steaks or lobster. The main event is the prime shell sirloin. On a good night the filet mignon is tender but mild, a nice piece of meat, but it can vary. I've never liked their hash browns, which resemble rösti potatoes more than anything else. If you need fish, order the lobster, as it's the best thing they have from the ocean, but if you're not in a lobster mood, then try the halibut, salmon, or swordfish; with these thicker, firmer pieces the odds are better that they won't arrive too overcooked, which is what happens to most of the fish here. Vegetables? Well, this is a steakhouse, so asparagus is available nearly all year long with a vinaigrette; tomatoes too, in and out of season.

Desserts, again like the starters, are hit-or-miss, mostly miss. Maybe opt for the cheesecake or berries and cream. Skip the rest of them and have instead a great glass of port or dessert wine from the deep wine list. One of the strengths here is that wine list—expensive, yes, but much better than most around town.

When Ruth Reichl reviewed this place for the *New York Times* back in 1998, she watched one night as a befuddled Kurt Vonnegut and Albert Finney waited near the bar for over half an hour for a table and then left. If this kind of thing can happen here to famous people with reservations, the rest of us should be prepared to wait too, even with a reservation. That said, once you are seated, the service is good from the old-school professionals who work the floor. Is this New York's best steakhouse? No, I think not, but on a good night it's somewhere darn near the top.

Spigolo

212-744-1100
1561 Second Avenue,
    at 81st Street
Casual
Reservations
Moderate
All major credit cards accepted
Dinner seven nights a week
6 train to 77th Street station

The Upper East Side is home to many Italian restaurants, too many really, and most are average or worse. New Yorkers have always loved Italian food and most Upper East Siders don't cook at home much, so this part of town was always full of choices for breakfast, lunch, and dinner. So I'll assume that Heather and Scott Fratangelo, who live in the neighborhood, had that in mind when they decided to open Spigolo in 2004. The room is small, with just under 30 seats and a few more at the bar; the walls are brick and the tables are plain wood, with cushioned wooden chairs set before them. As it is on the northwest corner of the block, there is good light from two exposures, plus hanging brass lamps above the room as night falls. I have a weakness for restaurants run by couples, but there's good reason: the shared passion and vision some couples are able to bring to the business often translates to tightly focused restaurants with consistently good or better-than-good food, and service to match. Think Chanterelle, Peasant, Sfoglia, and Al di La, to name a few. Here he does the cooking, and she does the baking and also can be found in the dining room at night.

The menu starts with a selection of salumi, including good prosciutto, bresaola, sopressata, and coppa that can be had individually for $13 a plate, or—a better idea—the full assortment for $17. Beyond that, they offer clams and oysters on the half shell, sold by the piece, as well as a good tuna tartare studded with capers. Other starters include a nice plate of grilled jumbo shrimp sauced with rich jus, served with farro, pine nuts, and raisins bound with good olive oil, and topped with chopped parsley. Or there is the crunchy shaved celery combined with sharp gorgonzola and pecans and tossed in an apple-cider-based vinaigrette.

But if you're a pasta lover, all of this is little more than a distraction, as the pasta is the best thing they do here. The gnocchi are light and airy, made from sheep's milk, poached, then tossed in a butter-based sauce flecked with herbs and crisped pancetta, with flash-sautéed radicchio as a crunchy, bitter foil for the richness and texture of the other ingredients. Fettuccine is seasoned with lemon zest in the pasta itself and tossed with an arugula and herb-based pesto. Strozzapreti ("priest choker"), essentially a form of cavatelli, is tossed with wild mushrooms pan-sautéed in butter, flecked with herbs, then topped with pecorino, the tangy sheep's milk grating cheese. This could be dinner, like all the pastas here, but then you'd miss some more great food. So a dining strategy for two may be to share an appetizer and a pasta, and then two main courses.

In the winter months, breast of veal is braised and, to my mind, an equal to the pork belly variations so popular today around town. The braising liquid is reduced as a sauce and the plate is rounded out with butternut squash puree and wilted escarole, a lovely combination. A good strip steak topped with compound herb butter and set with garlicky broccoli rabe does the trick. Cod is pan-roasted, then plated with Romanesco cauliflower puree and an artichoke-based caponata. To round things out, they offer a selection of sides: sautéed broccoli rabe, creamy polenta enriched with melted fontina cheese, escarole, and squash puree with pecans.

Save room for desserts—they are worth it. The ginger pudding with vanilla gelato is lovely, as are the caramel affogato with warm bombolini and the Italian doughnuts. The staff is friendly and casual and knows the food. The wine list is small but works well with the food served here. To my mind, this is easily one of the best Italian restaurants in this part of town. Needless to say, with the small room and limited seating, reservations are hard to come by, but be patient because it's well worth the wait.

The Spotted Pig

212-620-0393

314 West 11th Street, at the corner of Greenwich Street

Casual

No reservations

Moderate to expensive

All major credit cards accepted

Lunch and dinner seven days a week, kitchen open till 4 AM

1 train to Christopher Street station; A, C, E, 1, 2, 3 trains to 14th Street station

I didn't want to like the Spotted Pig. I tried, really tried, to hate it. Part of Mario Batali's ever-expanding empire and located just south of the totally overrated meatpacking district dining scene, the restaurant was very hyped when it opened. It's always very crowded, noisy, and packed with young hipsters, and it's one of those places that for some strange reason doesn't take reservations. So you either show up for dinner at 6 PM or, should you arrive at a more civilized hour, expect to place your name on a list and wait, wait, wait. But after attending a private party there and several dinner visits, I was smitten. The food is really very good and the service gracious. The place rocks. Yes, you must endure a wait and noise, but it's worth it.

The two dining rooms, spread over two floors, are small and rather cramped but have a certain charm about them. This space used to be Le Zoo, but with a little touch-up and lots of pig decorations, the owner and brains behind the concept, Ken Friedman, tapped chef April Bloomfield, who had worked at London's River Café and then most recently at Alice Waters' Chez Panisse before bringing her British gastropub cuisine to the West Village. What is gastropub cuisine? I don't really know; when I used to visit London, the pub food sucked, though it's much better now. But let's talk about what April cooks here.

The menu is broken down as follows: bar snacks, plates, entrees, and sides. You can mix and match and almost never go wrong. The duck egg with botarga, priced at $3, arrives on a small plate, the egg hard-boiled, split, topped with botarga, and drizzled with excellent extra-virgin olive oil. The dish listed on the menu as chicken liver toast is actually beautifully seasoned sautéed chicken liver, chopped and blended with caramelized onion, redolent of great olive oil, spread high and thick on pieces of crusty grilled bread. This chicken liver is up there with Russ and Daughters and Barney Greengrass, it's that good. From the plates section, the rich and delicious stew of squid, potatoes, and fennel, seasoned with a bright aioli, made me want to rush home and try to re-create it for my family. Smoked haddock chowder too is excellent, the creamy broth rich with haddock and laced with finely diced carrots, celery, and what appears to be tiny tapioca, all finished with chopped parsley and homemade chowder crackers. Be brave and try the salad of crispy pig's ear with trévise in a lemon-caper dressing. The pig ear is deep-fried, all crunch and full of flavor from the acidic vinaigrette, the bitter greens a good foil for its richness. The gnudi, made of sheep's milk ricotta, are legendary and perhaps only surpassed by those once served at the now shuttered Dona uptown. They are lovely, cloudlike little dumplings set in a pool of beurre noisette accented with sage. Among the entrees, the burger is solid, topped with Roquefort cheese and accompanied by a pile of shoestring potatoes, perfect beer food. Calf's liver is very good, as are the monkfish, the rack of lamb, and the steak that occasionally makes its way onto the menu.

Desserts keep pace with the rest of the meal: the ginger cake is excellent, the lemon and lime tart straddles the line between sweet and sour, and the crème Catalan is a good choice as well. The wine list and beers are fairly priced and chosen well to work with the hearty food. They have good wines by the glass as well. The service is genuine and efficient without being silly. The wait staff is simply deluged by customers; taking into consideration the volume and the constant running up and down the steps, it's really a minor miracle. Your best bet may be a late lunch when the small dining room downstairs is half full and bathed in afternoon sunlight. It takes on the feel of a little Parisian hole-in-the-wall, with a few tables of tourists and locals chatting, sipping wine, and passing the afternoon in style. So this place I didn't want to like is now a favorite haunt.

Suba

Note: This venue is closed.

212-982-5714
109 Ludlow Street, just north of Delancey Street
Casual
Reservations
Moderate
All major credit cards accepted
Dinner seven nights a week
F, J, M, Z trains to Delancey/ Essex Street station

In many ways, Suba can be offered as a perfect example of exactly what is going right with the New York restaurant scene these days. It is emblematic of several converging trends, starting with the transformation of the depths of the Lower East Side from hardscrabble tenements in a down-and-out neighborhood to what it is today, an über-chic place where everyone under a certain age now wants to live. To that add the energy and vision of a new generation of young, talented chefs. Suba sits mostly below street level in the basement space of a standard five-story walk-up tenement across from a banal brick parking garage on a dreary strip of Ludlow Street. You enter off the street into a small front room with a half dozen tables and a bar midway in, but the real dining space is below, accessed via a postindustrial metal staircase that turns right and then right again, leading you into a room set above and surrounded by a slow-moving pool of water. The winning interior design is the work of the Meyer Davis Studio. The brick walls of the main dining room are painted white and lit from below, through the water. The shimmering, subterranean effect is calming and otherworldly, and somehow keeps the noise level very low as well. The ceiling is crossed with exposed metal I-beams, and the furniture is low-set, modern, and comfortable, with tables for two that are easily paired into groups of four, six, eight, or more. Just be careful not to place your purse too far from your chair, or it may fall into the water. The crowd, as expected in the neighborhood, is attractive, energetic, and young.

The food is excellent, courtesy of chef Seamus Mullen. A Vermont native, he's worked in California and Philadelphia, done a stint with Floyd Cardoz at Eleven Madison, and then spent nearly a half dozen years working around Spain, including with Jordi Villa in Barcelona, Andoni Aduriz in San Sebastian, and Xavier Pellicer back in Barcelona, before coming back to New York to work a stint at Brasserie 8½, where his current business partner discovered him. That person is Yann de Rochefort, who also runs Boqueria with Mullen. Suba takes the Spanish tapas theme offered at Boqueria and ups the ante, offering some very refined dishes in a broader and far more ambitious menu. The restaurant has undergone several transformations over the last five years. Chefs and concepts have come and gone; Alex Urena was there for a while, and since then the kitchen has been completely redone. I'd venture to say that these days, Suba is among the very best restaurants in the increasingly crowded field in this Lower East Side neighborhood.

An amuse-bouche one night was a firm cube of pressed pork belly set atop a cube of seared melon on a skewer. It was a one-bite wonder, releasing a great mix of clean flavors, rich notes right behind them. Another night it was a single Malpeque oyster, removed from the shell and served with a celery broth and quartered baby heirloom tomatoes, drizzled with an artisanal Spanish olive oil redolent of toasted pecans—again, clean, fresh layers of well-defined flavors.

The menu is divided into three sections: tapas, or small plates; media raciones, slightly larger ones; and arroces, half a dozen dishes designed around short-grain rice. The croquetas, similar to the ones at Boqueria, are very good one-bite affairs. Fried crisp and set atop complementary purées, they are a good way to begin. One day there was lightly breaded and bound crabmeat—essentially a mini crab cake—next to a croquette of creamy Valdeón goat cheese melded with bacon, set over a date puree and another fritter redolent of roasted red pepper. Spiced lamb meatballs, cooked medium rare, are served en brochette, paired with salsa verde. A stunning crudo of sushi-grade New Zealand snapper, the meat rich, almost fatty, was tossed with tkemali (sour plum), early spring garlic scapes, roasted baby beets, and candied pine nuts, and drizzled with Moroccan argan oil. The textures and flavors played off one another beautifully. My favorite dish, and one of the best I'd had that year, was simply billed as cuttlefish à la plancha; it arrived in an oblong bowl with that fish both cooked and raw, shaved into long, thin noodles like shards, tossed with perfectly fresh English peas, diced apples, and a chiffonade of mint in a clear, dark jus made of fish fumet enhanced with brown chicken stock. The crunch and sweetness of the peas against the rich fish meat and the mint and apple notes added a certain lightness, and the sauce packed a lot of flavor. The entirety all came together as proof that great ingredients, simplicity, and restraint have their rewards.

Any dish with pork belly is a must. Here, the Berkshire variety, crisp-skinned, sits alongside smoked fingerling potatoes, crunchy Savoy cabbage, and small balls of Macoun apple. The rice dishes are enough to be a main course. Arroz cremoso pairs creamy short-grained rice in the risotto style with fine, crisp diced pork belly, spring peas, manchego cheese, and a mint pistou, with a tangle of pea tendrils set atop the bowl. Arroz de bacalao pairs that same creamy rice with basil, sweet lychee meat, and an item billed as salt cod tripe.

For dessert, try the addictive chocolate-filled warm fried doughnuts set beside horchata ice cream; ice cream served in a rocks glass and drizzled with sherry; or the simple poached peach with vanilla cream. The wine list, put together by Roger Kugler, is very good and works well with this dynamic menu. Service is good, the room lovely and unusual, and the food alone well worth the trip to this reemerging part of New York City.

Sueños

212-243-1333
311 West 17th Street, between Eighth and Ninth Avenues
Casual
Reservations
Moderate
All major credit cards accepted
Dinner Tuesday–Sunday
1, 2, 3, A, C, E trains to 14th Street station; L train to Eighth Avenue station; 1 train to 18th Street station

Most of the Mexican restaurants in Manhattan are mediocre margarita joints at best, with a few exceptions. Sueños stands at the head of that pack. It is the brainchild of chef Sue Torres, who worked previously at Rocking Horse. The scene at this subterranean spot is casual and convivial. This is a neighborhood spot, usually packed by 8 PM, and FYI, they do make very good margaritas as well.

For starters, the shredded beef mini tacos are fun, as are the sweet plantain and drunken goat cheese empanadas. If for no other reason, go there for the thin, long quesadillas, flavored with sautéed huitlacoche, a very rare naturally occurring mold that grows on corn and lends an unforgettable flavor, perhaps like the first time you tasted fresh truffles. Or try the chorizo quesadillas, filled with that signature sausage, diced potatoes, and chile rajas, and accented with sliced McIntosh apples. Chile-rubbed roasted goat is tender and redolent of garlic. The tortillas are made as they should be, one by one, all night long. The chicken enchiladas use organic birds, and another favorite is the chile Mecco stewed pork tacos, messy and delicious. If you want to go whole hog, they have a great $50 chile tasting that's as educational as it is delicious in terms of exploring what can be done with chiles and how different they can be in each dish. I'm sure somewhere in Queens or scattered about remote Brooklyn zip codes there are great authentic Mexican restaurants to serve the increasing New York Mexican expat community, but for now, Sueños does fine by me.

Sushi Yasuda

212-972-1001
204 East 43rd Street, between Second and Third Avenues
Casual to dressy
Reservations
Expensive
All major credit cards accepted
Lunch Monday–Friday, dinner Saturday
4, 5, 6, 7, S trains to 42nd Street/Grand Central station

Considered by many to be among the very best sushi restaurants in New York City, this place has no sign, no name on the window, nothing that stands out on this dreary block of parking lots heading east toward the United Nations. There is just a simple black and white Gyotako fish print on the humble awning above the door that lets you know you're at the right place. The greeter is not the most polite chap; "perfunctory" describes him best. Arrive early and you may be told to wait until just around the time your table was booked for. Arrive late and you may have been bumped altogether. Don't be late—the place is very, very popular, and reservations are hard to come by. They book the tables for dinner mostly on the basis of a 90-minute turn. In other words, after an hour and a half, you may be asked to leave. That's okay, because for most of those 90 minutes, you'll have a chance to eat some of the best sushi and sashimi you may ever have.

The chef, Naomichi Yasuda, works the counter. Prior to opening this store, Yasuda had worked for years at Hatsuhana, one of the great old sushi houses in this city. He's usually the one at the far right, a compact, middle-aged man for whom this is a calling. He hails from a small fishing village called Chikura, where as a young man during high school he spent an entire year studying oysters for a school project. His passion for fish—buying it, aging it, cutting it, and offering his customers the best cuts from the best fish—is one of the things that make this place a real standout. For his rice, he uses three varieties and then two different vinegars to season it. Each piece of nigiri arrives on warm rice, barely held together, and topped with glistening, often translucent cuts of impeccably fresh, clean-tasting fish. My suggestion is to sit at the bar and have a dialogue with any of the chefs working the counter. Please, please do not use any additional soy sauce or wasabi here; each piece of fish comes seasoned by the chef and hence requires no additional sauce whatsoever. Let them know what you enjoy and what you'd like to spend per person, and let them take care of you.

For my first visit, I was the guest of several acquaintances who work for a boutique Japanese food importer. We were at the bar, a few stools down from where Chef Yasuda works, but were able to keep up a conversation with him nonetheless. This was good—he learned that I too am fascinated with oysters and that we are both black belts in Kyokushinkai karate as well. Between dojo tales and fish talk, the time flew by. The room is bright, with the sushi bar to the right and tables to the left. The space is well lit, allowing guests to see the fish. The walls are mostly paneled with blond wood, the bar area spotless—none of the surroundings distracts you from the fish being served.

In the chef's hands the sushi is delivered in small flights, usually two or three pieces of nigiri or sashimi together, in some cases specimens of the same species from different locales or different cuts of the same fish for comparison. One night we had three types of salmon nigiri—wild king salmon from the Copper River, sockeye salmon, and yellow salmon—each with its own unique flavor profile. This was followed by two preparations of eel, one of the chef's specialties, then a flight of tuna with different levels of fattiness, including a silky piece from the top of the tail known as hagashi yoro. Then came a flight of mackerel, followed by another of a white fish from Japan that I was not familiar with. The chef is known to age his fish when appropriate; not all fish are best ultra-fresh, so for some varieties, just like for meat or cheese, he prefers to buy them, ice them down, and wait until they are perfect.

On another occasion, he presented me with two types of uni, an orangey ochre one from California, plump and custard-like, and another from Russia that was an odd gray-green, less texturally pleasant but with an amazingly long finish, the strong nuanced flavor much more pronounced than its California sibling's. Generally speaking, that's the story here: pop the fish in your mouth in one bite, start to chew, and marvel at the layers of flavor and texture, the slow release, and the length of the finish that the fish leaves in your mouth. The only other sensation like this that I know of is with great wines that start as one thing, then change, and change again. Sometimes a full 60 seconds later you've got a silly smile on your face expressing the pure pleasure and amusement of what is going on inside your mouth and nose.

The hot dishes are not to be missed—monkfish liver with ponzu, clams in broth, and various fried parts of fish as well— but I go mainly for the raw food. This is a hard act to beat anywhere in New York, at any price.

Tabla

212-889-0677
11 Madison Avenue,
    at 24th Street
Casual
Reservations
Expensive
All major credit cards accepted
Lunch and dinner Monday–
    Friday, dinner Saturday and
    Sunday
6 train to 23rd Street station

Easily one of the most interesting Indian restaurants in town, Tabla takes traditional Indian culinary reference points and melds them into a modern fusion-style menu full of good food, bold flavors, lots of spices, and pleasant surprises. Danny Meyer has a nose for talent and has consistently attracted excellent chefs to cook at his various restaurant projects, which conceptually differ from one another, with Tabla as the most unusual jewel in his by-now-considerable crown. The opening chef, Floyd Cardoz, is still in the kitchen; over a decade later, the place has just gotten better under his hand. Manhattan is underserved by Indian restaurants; I'm not sure why that is, but it's true, and there are just a few that operate anywhere near this level. For less expensive dining options and down-home style cooking, hit the places nearby along Lexington, but for serious, thoughtful cooking, great service, and a well-laid-out beverage program to go with it, Tabla is unique.

Early reviews were all great. Ruth Reichl glowingly awarded it three stars back in 1999, and Hal Rubenstein, then critic for *New York* magazine, praised it as well, but initially I wasn't as enamored. On my early visits, the food seemed hit-and-miss, occasionally a bit clichéd, and Floyd seemed to be playing his cards too close to the vest. Indian by birth, Goan specifically, Floyd worked in some great kitchens, among them a long stint at Lespinasse during the Gray Kunz era. But he's settled in here and is cooking with more confidence than ever. The restaurant is a success, and that allows him to relax and have fun, cooking dishes like he makes at home for his family, just fancier here.

There are two spaces inside, the "bread bar" downstairs, which is more casual and less expensive, and the main dining room upstairs. The bread bar menu is a good introduction to his food, home-style Indian street food. Over the last few visits I've really liked the chunky eggplant bharta, served with an assortment of breads with which to pair it. The spiced onion rings are addictive, and the pan-seared scallops laced with chunks of fresh coconut over a spiced vegetable puree were great. The upstairs room is pricier and the food more complex, but still the idea remains: layers of flavors, sweetness melded with acidity, loads of freshly ground spices, and a balance of Western ingredients. I love crab cakes and am often disappointed with them at most restaurants; not here, where chunks of the sweet meat are lightly bound and served formed into a crisped disk alongside an avocado salad and tamarind chutney. In season, the rawa-crusted soft shells are crisped on the exterior and moist at the center, with sautéed oyster mushrooms, garlic scapes, and coconut korma. Maybe one of the best lunch items is the chicken tikka Cobb salad. Most Cobb salads are little more than mediocre country club food, but this one is really fun to eat, the chicken spiced and tender, the salad cut from hearts of romaine, the blue cheese probably Maytag, and the bacon chunky, smoky, and delicious. A great example of his border melding is an item from the dinner menu billed as Goan sausage and poached egg; what arrives is a dish of thick, toothsome bucatini pasta, celery cut from the sweet center portion, chunks of sausage, fava beans, and shaved botarga, all bound by that soft, slow-cooked egg. Surely this must be a dish from the forgotten Goan invasion and occupation of southern Italy.

His nice flaked halibut with peppery wild watercress, offset with watermelon curry and a good dose of lime, paired beautifully with a glass of Laurent Chatenay chenin blanc from the Loire. Spice-crusted beef strip loin, crisped and tasting of ground coriander, mustard seeds, and peppercorns, was served with morel mushrooms, baby lettuce salad, and horseradish raita, paired with a 2006 Campo Reale nero d'Avola from Sicily, which worked beautifully with the plate, as would a great Zinfandel.

For dessert the banana mousse cake is lovely. Just when I though I'd never have another crème brûlée, the one served here, flavored with coconut and served with tamarind sauce, a scoop of coconut ice cream, and a carrot sorbet, had me swooning. Service, as in all of Meyer's places, is spot-on. The food here is better than ever, and the wine list matches the food, which is a hard trick to pull off. For my money, this may be one of the best contemporary Indian restaurants anywhere in America.

Taboon

212-713-0271
773 Tenth Avenue, between 52nd and 53rd Streets
Casual
Reservations
Moderate
All major credit cards accepted
Lunch and dinner Monday–Friday, dinner Saturday and Sunday
C, E trains to 50th Street station; N, R, W trains to 49th Street station

Though this spot is a little west of what may be considered the traditional theater district, the 5 PM seating on weekdays makes this a good choice for pre-theater dining. Chef Haim Cohen is the man behind this operation, and though billed as Mediterranean, it's really an Israeli restaurant. The L-shaped room has a long bar, which is a comfortable place to take a meal, and tables are set either near the wood oven or in the room adjacent to it. The walls are white-painted brick, the sound track courtesy of an iPod, and the crowd a mix of Middle Eastern expats and fans of this interesting food.

The name comes from the traditional wood-fired brick oven used here for, among other things, the great flatbreads that are part of each meal. The breads, with an assortment of spreads, are reason enough to visit Taboon. The golden-topped, crisp-bottomed house focaccia arrives warm and gleaming, brushed with olive oil, and encrusted with a bit of sea salt, sage, and fresh rosemary. Pair it with the tzatziki, a mix of rich, sour Greek yogurt, swirls of sliced cucumber, za'atar (a Middle Eastern spice mix), finely chopped garlic, and a hint of fresh mint, and watch the focaccia disappear. Another good choice is the hummus, here a big bowl of chickpea puree studded with some whole chickpeas, ringed with good olive oil, and redolent of lemon, cumin, and jalapeño peppers. Sautéed calamari at $7.50 arrives on a layer of shaved raw fennel laced with good yogurt. Octopus is quick-grilled, charred and smoky. Plump Mediterranean sardines share a plate with Moroccan salt-preserved lemons, pine nuts, spicy harissa paste, and a salad of roasted beets.

For main courses, the item billed as lamb osso bucco is really a braised whole lamb shank set alongside chewy farro, peas, and interesting Persian lemon sauce. Short ribs here are done in a style known as tchouma, slow-braised, fork-tender, seasoned with Moroccan spice mix, and paired with very good couscous, butternut squash, and black lentils. Each day there is a fish special, or opt for the ubiquitous farm-raised branzino, baked whole, or the more interesting halibut, baked with tomatoes, roasted peppers, chickpeas, more Moroccan spices, and accents of fresh cilantro. The wine list is short but decent, and service is fine. With the food big on bold flavors, in this neighborhood you could do far worse.

Tailor

212-334-5182
525 Broome Street, between
  Sixth Avenue and
  Thompson Street
Casual
Reservations
Moderate
All major credit cards accepted
Dinner seven nights a week
C, E trains to Spring Street
  station

Along with Pichet Ong, Johnny Iuzzini, Iacopo Falai, and Will Goldfarb, to name a few, Sam Mason emerged as one of a small crew of 30-something rock star pastry chefs working in New York. They have come to define an era in which pastry chefs are not just household names but also seem driven to open their own restaurants, stretching the borders of the traditional pastry kitchen. Sam rose to prominence as the pastry chef at WD-50 prior to opening this spot in the fall of 2007. In its early days I wasn't quite sure what exactly Tailor was trying to be. A restaurant? A lounge is more like it. Well, as I've said many times before, it takes time to get it right, and Tailor is a case in point. Initially, this was a lounge with very good small plates of food, but you often left still hungry. The critics, and the public to a large degree, didn't get it. Then Sam changed things: the plates got bigger. The cooking then and now is still excellent, but these days, the food and flow of the meal resembles a more traditional delivery of courses, smaller appetizers followed by seriously well-portioned mains. In fact, on a recent visit in late 2008, I had one of the best meals I'd had all year in New York right here at Tailor. You enter off Broome, the front of the space sheathed in industrial wired glass, the upstairs dining room squarish, with exposed steel beams. On one side is a brick wall, and the other wall is covered in a beige fabric. Custom lights are hung off metal arms, their exposed Edison-style tungsten bulbs reminiscent of antique subway lighting. Beige leather chairs are set before dark wood tables with no linens, just the place settings and a swatch of leather decorated with a squat crystal square holding a nice arrangement of dried flowers. The sound track is hip, probably off an iPod. The wait staff, in purposely mismatched outfits—some in ties, other not, some in pants, others in skirts—are all young, earnest, and doing their best. Downstairs is the bar and lounge proper, where the sound track is louder and the lighting lower, and one assumes the plan is for the space to be filled each night with the young, the hip, the restless, and the monied, downing the excellent cocktails created just for this venue. During the early evening, the crowd tends to be older and quieter and upstairs is busier than down, but as the night progresses both rooms fill, the kids come in, the noise level rises, and for some, I suppose, the fun begins. It should be noted that Eben Freemen, formerly the bartender at WD-50, has created the signature cocktails for Tailor, which to my mind rates as among the best cocktail programs in Manhattan for this restaurant or any restaurant/ lounge for that matter, on par with the best at Death & Co., PDT, Apotheke, Pegu Club, or Little Branch.

Once you're seated, the menus arrive; the first part of the document lists foods broken down simply in three sections: 1) appetizers, 2) mains, 3) desserts. This is a change from the opening menu where the lines between courses were blurred, listing various menu items as either sweet or salty. The cocktail list is impressive, boasting several single-bottle specialties like the pumpernickel raisin scotch, tobacco bourbon, root beer rye, huitlacoche mescal, and lemon verbena rum. Were that not enough, there are a dozen house cocktails also of considerable interest, like the Bazooka, made from vodka, bubble gum cordial, and house sour; the delicious Pan Pacific, made from shochu, Thai basil, calamansi, and coconut water; the oddly named Blood and Sand, combining scotch, sweet vermouth, orange head, and Redbach; and the Waylon, named after the country great Waylon Jennings, blending bourbon, smoked Coke syrup, and preserved lemon. One of the most delicious drinks I've ever had anywhere was the "Butternut and Falernum," a modern drink with a nod to Tiki cocktail culture. It was late fall, and Eben wanted something that suggested the cold winter season heading into the holidays. So he worked together with Sam, which is often how things are done here, as collaborations, discussing ideas and then charting a course as to the best ways to get the desired results. They oven roasted butternut squash meat, then pureed it in a Vitamixer, adding a good amount of brown butter. Then through a process known as Liquid Nitrogen clarification, they froze the whole mixture and allowed it to thaw slowly over several days, during which time the fat from the butter rose to the top, but the milk solids and good brown butter flavor remained in the puree. This way the fat was removed, and once free of the fat layer, the puree was mixed with the flavors of Falernum, ginger, clove, vanilla, allspice, and a touch of citrus; the alcohol was a very good rum, served very chilled neat, and consumed slowly in a small martini glass. Health reasons notwithstanding, one could make a pretty darn interesting evening ordering solely from the cocktail list and going no further, but then you'd miss the food.

Initially when asked what I thought of the place, I'd relay that I considered it as more of a culinary way station, somewhere between a great bar and small cocktail party, serving the best canapés you've ever had with the best drinks you'd ever tasted. From the appetizer side the big winner was the foie gras peanut butter terrine. The plate arrives with four thin slices of dark brown terrine set with a single paper-thin, glass-like pane of candied pear, ground peanuts, cocoa powder, and foam of some sort or another. The flavors of foie gras and peanut butter actually work together as well as the textures do. I recall once being served delicious quenelles of fattened goose liver mousse at Antoine Westermann's great restaurant Le Buerehiesel in Strasbourg, and noticing how much it resembled creamy peanut butter. Thirty years later they meet here on my plate. Off another old menu, three small spoonfuls of peekytoe crab are laced with fresh pineapple and topped with snow-white pine nut foam, the plate dotted with basil oil. The foam, as usual, I could live without, but the sweetness of the crab played well off the pineapple, with the basil providing a little needed lift.

Artic char is cured with rye whisky, then plated sliced thin with dill cream, fried capers, and red onions. Veal is served with marrow that has been formed into pearl-sized balls, a thin crust of Parmesan cheese, and a huckleberry puree. Individual skirt steaks are layered and bound with meat glue, then sautéed like a thick steak, and served medium rare, with a silky puree of cauliflower, English peas, and a dusting of cocoa. The workhouse beef brisket is braised in bourbon Waylon Jennings style, the braising liquid reduced and used as the sauce, and garnishes include sweet potato puree and fresh cranberries. If it's on the menu, don't miss the carryover from the opening days—the delicious pork belly braised and then crisped, served with miso butterscotch and artichokes. The desserts, as expected, are mostly great. Lemon curd made without eggs is tart and sweet, served with lemon crisp, fresh blackberries, and a Thai basil meringue. Summer peaches are paired with tomatoes—a great idea— alongside ricotta puree and an intensely flavored black sesame caramel. Caramel panna cotta is rich, like butterscotch, and the corn sorbet makes you wonder why more pastry chefs haven't tried that out before.

Kudos to Sam and Eben; with the recent changes in the menu over 2008, I'd consider this restaurant as one of the most innovative, interesting, and satisfying restaurants in New York if you're willing to think out of the box a bit. The food is great, as is the cocktail program and wine and beer selection should you go that route, and the general vibe both upstairs and down.

Takahachi

212-505-6524
85 Avenue A, at East 6th
 Street (and elsewhere)
Casual
Reservations
Moderate to expensive
All major credit cards accepted
Lunch and dinner Monday–
 Friday, dinner Saturday and
 Sunday
F, V trains to Lower East Side/
 Second Avenue station

The original Takahachi opened on the Lower East Side in the early days, pioneers indeed. The owner, a short, fit fellow named Hero, was a professional rock climber prior to settling into this career. Both locations of this restaurant represent good value in the world of New York sushi. The sushi men here are all older, all Japanese, classically trained, and thoroughly professional. They work clean and fast.

The menu carries your typical staples: two miso soups, one soy-based with bonito, the other made from mushroom broth; all your favorite sushi rolls; maki, both large and small; good, clean, greaseless, crispy tempura; sashimi sold by the piece; lunch specials; donburi; and an assortment of salads to round things out. But if you look hard or ask, they also carry a good selection of seasonal imported Japanese specialties. Here, for the first time, I had raw octopus—opaque, shimmering disks, soft and chewy, and a good rich flavor. It helps to ask if there are any special items on any given night.

Overall, the freshness of the fish, the accuracy of the knife work and seasoning, and the good service make it a standout in a town with a lot of other choices. There has been a movement of late to certify Japanese-run sushi places where the chefs and cooks are all properly trained. Should that happen, this will be among those on the list. As a footnote, the head sushi chef of the Tribeca location is also an excellent potter, so the small ceramic plates, dishes, assorted tableware, and cups are all his creations.

Tamarind

212-674-7400

41–43 East 22nd Street,
 between Park Avenue
 South and Broadway

Casual

Reservations

Moderate to expensive

All major credit cards accepted

Lunch and dinner seven days
 a week

6, N, R, W, trains to 23rd Street
 station

The fact that this is one of the best Indian restaurants to open in a long time should come as no surprise. The man behind it is Avtar Walia, who honed his craft as part owner of the famed Dawat uptown. The chef he initially chose to run the place was the visionary Raji Jallepalli-Reiss, a woman of considerable talents who also ran her own great restaurant in Memphis, Raji, but passed away a few years ago at the age of 52 after battling stomach cancer. That New York only had her company briefly is sad, but the restaurant is still in very good hands these days and stands as a legacy to her years here.

Raji hailed from southern India, but the cooking here is more from the north and laced with a French accent, very much her doing. This is a good place to come with a crowd so that you can order lots of dishes and pass plates to taste. Start with the raj kachori, little croquette-like patties, similar to pooris, filled with chickpeas and then dipped in sweet and sour tamarind sauce; the saag paneer, with melting soft cubes of farmer cheese set in a spinach sauce; or the shrimp balchau, a Goan specialty, pairing shrimp with a spicy masala sauce studded with chunks of tomato.

Much of the best work comes out of the tandoors. They were imported and handmade, and to my eyes as a Western cook are very interesting cooking appliances. These clay-lined vessels can trace their roots back 3,000 years to ancient Persia, where they were used exclusively for breads. One of the great advantages to the tandoor is that it allows fast, oil-free cooking, and many varieties of items can be cooked together at the same time. Breads can simply be packed onto the side walls along the rim, where they cook in minutes and develop a nice charred flavor. Items placed lower in the ovens cook faster, as the temperatures near the bottom can be in the 1,000°–1,400°F range, a searing heat similar to our traditional Western broilers. By placing items on long metal skewers, a good tandoor chef can prepare many meals at the same time, adjusting angles and directions, lifting and turning the skewers up and down, checking for doneness, and working on several tables' worth of dishes at once. Thanks to a kitchen window, the chefs' cooking prowess with the tandoor is on display here.

As the cooking is quick, most of the items cooked in the tandoor are marinated in advance to develop a more complex flavor. Lamb chops emerge juicy, medium rare, and beautifully seared on the outside, and shrimp are plump and firm, as are the noorani kabab, chunks of boneless chicken redolent of saffron. That same chunked chicken flavored with basil is dubbed tulsi malai kabab. Whole lobster tail dusted with tandoori spices emerges charred and delicious, as is the Cornish game hen with tamarind.

There is a good selection of seafood done in a Franco-Indian style, like the pan-seared tuna loin in a crust of tomato seeds, or the jumbo lobster tail set atop shiitake mushrooms, laced with onions and garlic and bathed in a beurre-blanc-like sauce. Better to stick with the traditional items like shrimp moiley, a Chennai-style specialty with shrimp simmered in a sauce of coconut milk, curry leaves, and smoked tamarind, or the mixed fish curry stew, served in a coconut milk curry broth. Traditional stews are all excellent. Rogan josh features goat in a cardamom sauce, lamb vindaloo has tender braised lamb chunks submerged in a thick and powerful sauce, and saag ghost has lamb again, this time braised with spinach leaves and loads of ginger.

The breads are addictive. The naan come straight out of the oven, moist, chewy, and full of flavor; roti is a whole-wheat option. The huge crisp poori, a whole-wheat bread, is deep-fried in a wok and arrives like a giant orb at your table. For dessert, try the unusual rasmalai, sweet cheese dumplings flavored with saffron and cardamom. The wine list, with over 200 bottles and a good selection by the glass, is matched very well with the food, which is among the best of any Indian eateries in New York. Service is fine, and I'd recommend this place as an upscale, dressed-up alterative to Curry Hill (Lexington Avenue) or the East Village's 6th Street budget options.

Telepan

212-580-4300
72 West 69th Street, between Central Park West and Columbus Avenue
Casual
Reservations
Moderate to expensive
All major credit cards accepted
Dinner Monday and Tuesday, lunch and dinner Wednesday–Friday, brunch and dinner Saturday and Sunday
1 train to 66th Street/Lincoln Center station; 1, 2, 3, B, C trains to 72nd Street

Chef Bill Telepan has been cooking in New York for over two decades. Years back he was a sous-chef for Alfred Portale at Gotham, where Portale's confidence allowed him to start the habit he continues to this day, taking nights and weekends off on a regular basis. Telepan then went on to be the opening chef at a few places on the Upper West Side before settling into a long run as the chef at Judson Grill, earning three stars there prior to its closing. Wanting to open his own place, he floated around in culinary limbo for a few years waiting for the right deal. The wait was worth it. This space had been Santa Fe, a neighborhood fixture serving okay food with a busy bar scene. Reopened as Telepan in the fall of 2005, it's been busier than ever, serving very good food in a completely remodeled space. Cast rightly or wrongly as a farmer's market chef, Telepan does let ingredients drive his cooking, but then, so do all good chefs, don't they? The menu is broken down into three section: appetizers, midcourses, and entrees. I suppose this allows diners to create three-course menus in any way they see fit. They offer both four- and five-course tasting menus priced at $64 and $74 respectively, which in today's market is a pretty darned good deal. Add roughly $50 to each to include wine.

A good starter might be the delicious house-smoked brook trout served here with buckwheat blini and black radish sour cream. Sweet Nantucket Bay scallops are served with slow-roasted garlic, sautéed hedgehog mushrooms, wilted baby spinach, and toast points. In the colder months, I love to sit at the bar with a good glass of Madiran, nibbling on the marinated beet salad with fresh guanciale, garnished with two small breaded disks of pied de cochon and a salad of mâche in a good vinaigrette.

The robiola-stuffed tortellini served in a light broth with summer vegetables is nice, as is the duet of a lightly breaded, crisp-fried soft-shell crab and a small crab cake with a small salad of arugula. In cooler months, opt for the great heritage-stock pork, a plate that often contains various cuts of the excellent meat cooked in different manners, the grilled chop paired with black-eyed peas and long-braised collard greens, or the hanger steak brushed with a bone marrow glaze and served with great garlicky potato hash.

Desserts are straightforward and homey, such as a peach cream buttermilk panna cotta with a scoop of peach sorbet and a thin crisp sesame tuile, or the great olive oil box cake, moist and dense and served with raspberry sauce. The wine list is good and fairly priced, and service too, as in most chef-run restaurants, is attentive. While there are now a few more very good restaurants on the Upper West Side, Telepan is still, years after it first opened, among the best.

Tia Pol

212-675-8805
205 Tenth Avenue, between 22nd and 23rd Streets
Casual
No reservations
Inexpensive to moderate
All major credit cards accepted
Dinner on Monday, lunch and dinner Tuesday–Sunday
C, E trains to 23rd Street station

It's not easy being Tia Pol. Like the youngest child of a large family, this tiny slip of a restaurant is easy to overlook in the red-hot High Line gallery district, where the prevailing school of restaurant style favors the grand, bordering on ostentatious. Amidst a slew of enormous gilded spaces with soaring ceilings, dramatic entryways, eye-catching staircases, glittering chandeliers, and walls made of water bottles, where jumbo kitchens crank out overdesigned and overpriced food to match, humble little Tia Pol stands for qualities rare in this business today: consistency, value, and quality.

Neighboring Morimoto, Buddakan, and Del Posto are all stadium-size spaces put together by stadium-size egos, enlisting big-name architects, designers, and publicists. By contrast, Tia Pol, barely bigger than your average squash court, was opened on a shoestring budget, the food courtesy of a husband-and-wife team who both oversee the kitchen. Bigger isn't always better, especially in the restaurant business, and in this mere 15 feet of storefront, you'll find some of the best tapas in New York.

Chef Alex Raij, whom the owners found on Craigslist, shared the kitchen responsibilities with her Basque husband, Eder Montero, and their love of good food, good ingredients, and good wines come through in most every plate. Tapas are at heart simple and ingredient-driven, and that's what you get here, with an all-Spanish wine list to match, featuring a great selection of sherry, usually over a dozen by the bottle, with four or five by the glass. The space has brick walls and a high ceiling, with heat pipes wrapped in thick hemp cord; a bar up front seats nine guests, and is a very comfortable place to dine. Total seating is around 30, with small tables to the rear past the bar in the narrower section of the room, near the semi-open kitchen. The staff is friendly, and they know the food well. The menu is divided into sections: soups, hot plates, cold plates, sandwiches at lunch, and specials. The prices range from the single digits to the low teens for most of the plates; entrees tend to be a little more. If you don't get carried away, as I do, you can eat well with a good glass of wine for under $40 a person.

Periwinkles, those little snails of the sea that in America grow on rocky shores and in salt marshes, are served warm in a bowl in the manner of "barrio chino," as in Chinatown-style. Coated with a mix of ground ginger, scallions, and coriander, the little gastropods are delicious. Ham croquettes arrive two to the plate, perfect little brown cylinders, crisp, greaseless, and warm, soft at the center, and redolent of white truffle oil and ham. Chorizo, a bargain at $6, arrives as the genuine article, a medium-sized bowl brimming with warm slices of that good Spanish-style sausage swimming in a little pool of sherry. Ask for bread on the side to swab up that broth. Fava bean puree arrives with a slight green tint, the beans cooked, ground, and passed through a fine sieve, then blended with Beyos cheese and stacked high on slices of baguette. Paquetitas arrive as three triangles of excellent ham folded over artichokes and manchego cheese, glistening with good Spanish olive oil.

One of my all-time favorites is the carpaccio of oyster mushrooms. Here they are cut in thin scallop shapes, spread over the plate, and then topped with diced manchego cheese, tomato concassé, chopped parsley, and delicious Marcona almonds, all drizzled again with great olive oil. The meatiness of the mushrooms plays well against the buttery richness of the cheese, the tomato provides a little needed acid, and olive oil contributes fruit tones and a certain nutty quality—a perfect flavor bridge to meld with those crunchy almonds, whose flavor and texture work like an exclamation point. In the colder months, the braised specials—veal cheeks, suckling pig glazed with sherry and honey, rabbit, pork shoulder, or lamb—are all fine, Spanish comfort food.

The wines work very well with the meat section of the menu, especially the braised meats. I really liked the hard-to-find 2005 Ameztoi Txakolina, at $9 a glass or $34 a bottle. This is a bright, polished white wine made from Hondarribi grapes, fermented in stainless-steel tanks, with citrus accents and a hint of salt, suggesting the vineyard's location right off the ocean. Or there is the Joan d'Anguera La Planella, a dense, chewy red with dark fruit and some spice on the finish, made from a mix of carignan, grenache, cabernet sauvignon, and syrah, for $9.50 a glass or $36 a bottle. Desserts are simple and homey; you can't go wrong with the classic orange-flavored flan or fried dates set beneath two scoops of vanilla ice cream. One night on a whim I tried the lemon foam with figs; I hate foam, but I liked this. Come hungry, come with friends, order a lot of food, and share.

Tiffin Wallah

212-685-7301
127 East 28th Street, between Lexington Avenue and Park Avenue South
Casual
Reservations
Inexpensive to moderate
All major credit cards accepted
Lunch and dinner seven days a week
6, N, R, W trains to 28th Street station

Pradeep Shinde opened this restaurant in 2007 right around the corner from his other spot, the very good Chennai Garden. The space is bright and rather cheery; some of the other spots around here are long on food and very short on atmosphere. The menu is all vegetarian and kosher, and they are planning a great delivery system for everything from individual meals to a week's worth of dinners, cooked and brought to your apartment. It should be mentioned that the name of the place refers to tiffin wallahs, delivery boys in India who schlep light meals, known locally as tiffins, by bicycle from housewives to their spouses at work. In this neighborhood you have to be inexpensive to survive, so they have a $6 lunch buffet, and most meals can be had for under $20 per person.

The menu starts with a few decent soups and moves on to the tiffins, which, as they sound, are light starter courses that should be shared at the table; order with variety in mind. Try the thali, a selection of small plates arranged around a tray for sharing. Here they serve four different kinds of thali: the eponymous tiffin wallah, gujarathi, South Indian, and sapadu. I've had both the South Indian and the tiffin wallah, and as I recall, they contained a broad mix, from pappadum and soft breads to great rice pilaf, chickpea stew studded with tomatoes, rasam soup, raita, smooth spinach curry with cubes of paneer, a large dosa filled with soft potatoes, fried and steamed lentil cakes, good coconut chutney rice pudding, and a simple but delicious dessert known as badam halwah and made from ghee, almonds, sugar, and saffron. The breads are good, especially the stuffed paratha. Dosas arrive with a broad selection of sides and dips, again all good for sharing. Curries are broken down into two styles, Gujarati, from a region of predominantly vegetarians, and Punjabi, heavy on dairy, especially butter, ghee, and paneer. From the Punjab I love the alu gobi, where cauliflower is slow-cooked with potatoes and tomatoes to form a great vegetarian stew.

Add a selection of breads and some chutneys, and simply order what sounds good to you. If I ever consider vegetarianism as a way of life, I'll probably move to India. A little closer to home, it's hard to beat this place for health and value; the food is prepared with passion, and the prices are among the lowest in town.

Tiny's Giant Sandwich Shop

212-982-1690
129 Rivington Street, between Norfolk and Suffolk Streets
Casual
No reservations
Inexpensive
Cash only
Seven days a week noon–10 PM
J, M, Z trains to Essex Street station

This is a perennial favorite slacker hangout, for good reason: smart kids on tight budgets know a good thing when they find it. The sandwiches are good, catering to the typical Lower East Side demographic, with a fair amount of vegetarian choices, but I prefer the ones with meat between the bread. The menu may offer only sandwiches, salads, and desserts, but there's something here for everyone. The sandwiches can be ordered whole or by the half, which for many may be enough, as they are big. If you're going retro, try the really good roast beef, served hot, slathered in onions and provolone cheese, with a choice of add-ons such as roasted red peppers and portobello mushrooms. Or try the chicken parm, swimming in tomato sauce, topped with melted mozzarella, and served on good semolina bread. The tuna melt is a classic, and the Big Mack Daddy I'd take over many burgers served around town. But the Big Mack Daddy is a veggie burger, with cheddar, tofu bacon, lettuce, tomato, pickles, and ketchup—ask for some of Tiny's famous chipotle mayo too—all in a brioche bun. With a veggie burger this good, I could go meatless for a while at least. They only serve soda, but they have Gus's all natural and Brooklyn Cream, which goes with everything on the menu in my book, and don't forget to order a Rice

Krispies treat for dessert. The place is usually busy, as it only seats 20-some customers, but turnover is fast, so wait and enjoy.

Tocqueville

212-647-1515
1 East 15th Street, between Fifth Avenue and Union Square
Casual to dressy
Reservations
Expensive
All major credit cards accepted
Lunch and dinner Monday–Saturday
4, 5, 6, L, N, Q, R, W trains to 14th Street/Union Square station

By now you've gotten the idea that I like restaurants run by hands-on chef-owners, so Tocqueville is right up my alley. Run by the husband-and-wife team of Brazilian-born chef Marco Moreira and his wife, Jo-Ann Makovitsky, who presides over the dining room, it is in every sense a family affair. The couple met years back while both were working at Dean and DeLuca. Jo-Ann, it is worth mentioning, is also a trained professional chef who graduated from cooking school and cut her teeth in great New York restaurants like La Caravelle when Chef Fessaguet was still there, where she worked alongside Michael Romano, Tadashi Ono, David Ruggiero, and other young up-and-coming chefs of that era. Jo-Ann and Marco founded and ran a catering company together, then opened the original Tocqueville in 2000, just down the block. When this space became available, they pounced on it. It was bigger but not too big, having been a therapist's office. During the early stages of construction, while the space was still wide-open, they installed a beautiful, huge Bonnet stove in the center of the subterranean kitchen; they built the space around it. The main dining room is set toward the back of the space, past the entrance vestibule and the beautiful, long onyx bar. The room is roughly square in shape, with a high ceiling, comfortable seating, and well-spaced tables clad in white linen, all softly lit with a chandelier at the center of the room and candles on each table. The wait staff enters and exits the room at the rear, which keeps traffic flow to a minimum. Upstairs there is a small mezzanine that overlooks the main room and is perfect for little private parties. The feel of the dining room is in keeping with the times and the general movement of restaurants downtown, a modern, casual standard, somewhere between formal and yet not quite so. On any given night the room may be three-quarters full of men in suits and well-dressed women, but there is no dress code, so a young couple in jeans and T-shirts is just as welcome and will feel perfectly comfortable in this mix. The sound track comes off an iPod, where fado, classic jazz, and world music share the bill, further adding to the idea that you can have fun here.

And you can also eat very well. The menu is à la carte, with appetizers starting in the low teens and entrees in the high twenties. They offer both a five-course tasting for just under $100 and a seven-course menu for around $125. A salad of soft butter lettuce arrives piled high like an Easter bonnet, though a tad overdressed with a creamy vinaigrette emulsion accented with chamomile. The broad green leaves are mixed with sweet william petals and saffron-pickled lotus root. Excellent calf's tongue is presented in two guises, braised and then smoked and sliced thin, and set on its own confit alongside a "napoleon" of creamy celeriac puree layered between crispy disks of pommes galette, with sautéed mustard greens and sprinkles of fennel pollen rounding out the plate. Hmm, fennel pollen—they didn't do this at the old Caravelle, did they? Fresh California sea urchin is paired with great chewy, homemade angel hair pasta, carbonara style, perhaps a bit salty for some tastes. Here, the lobes of the urchin meat are intermingled with a rich, dark sauce, one assumes made of that same oceanic invertebrate, pureed and combined with soy sauce and shellfish stock reduction. It is then thickened with egg yolks, laced with lime zest, and garnished with sea lettuce. In the early spring, green asparagus is paired with white asparagus and topped with a truffled vinaigrette and chips of toasted *Tuber aestivum*, or summer truffles.

For main courses, four or five fish dishes are offered, with as many meat options. If they have scallops, try them. These are big, thick, fresh, pan-seared dry scallops, sweet and clear tasting. A recent spring menu paired three big scallops with a sautéed slab of fresh foie gras, set over a mix of cèpes, artichokes, fava beans, and a crunchy raw brunoise of Fuji apples in a pool of cider vinegar gastrique. Fennel pollen again finds its way into a dish of local, wild-caught striped bass, and toasted fennel seeds accompany a slow-cooked confit of red snapper, with excellent Spanish arbequina olive oil from Catalonia, all on a smooth puree of wild baby spinach. A meat special one night of baby pig four ways was a bit too thought-out for my taste. The tiny bone-in chops were thin, cold, and dry; the shoulder confit was very good; the roulade was okay, but the lemon myrtle accents were almost a jarring note in the forcemeat, though the accompanying spaetzle and Swiss chard were perfectly fine—this is why restaurants need to streamline six-pan pickups. Opt instead for the odd but delicious combo of the 60-second sirloin steak, cut thin, rare, and seared on both sides, with its sidekick, the 24-hour slow-cooked beef rib pot roast, soft and rich. The balance of the plate is rounded out by glazed root vegetables and smoked mashed potatoes.

The desserts keep pace with the good food that precedes them. The black walnut and brown butter financier is served with a lovely Armagnac raisin ice cream and a poached Seckel pear. A creamy rich cheesecake comes accented with toasted wattleseed, a new spice providing a new twist for an old classic. All the ice creams are turned fresh for service and are delicious. The wine list is a good document—decent selections abound at all price levels—and the staff are helpful at pairings, with a sommelier on hand should you need one. As is the case with any good establishment, as this restaurant matures, it only gets better.

Tout Va Bien

212-265-0190
311 West 51st Street, between
    Eighth and Ninth Avenues
Casual
Reservations
Moderate
All major credit cards accepted
Lunch and dinner seven days
    a week
C, E trains to 50th Street station

In business now for more than 60 years, Tout Va Bien is one of the last of the old-guard French bistros remaining in New York. René Pujol, just a few doors down the street, was another of these family-owned French eateries that traced its roots back to the 1940s and 1950s, but sadly Pujol was recently sold, and under its new owners it is not the same. Every time I eat at Tout Va Bien, it reminds me of the many small family-run restaurants in the working-class districts of Paris and small towns throughout France. And when I say family, I mean it literally and figuratively. Aside from the ownership, most of the staff have been here for years, raised families together, take meals together, and come from the same towns in France.

The square room is well lit, with 30 or so seats, a nice bar, a TV that's always on and usually tuned to sports, and a French pop soundtrack, and everyone seems to know everyone else by first name. While it's a great choice for pre-theater dining, it's also a very good choice for simple plates of home-style French food at any time. Under their big neon sign, you step down from 51st Street into this small room with red checkered tablecloths, red vinyl banquettes, fake wood paneling, and walls lined with French movie posters and signed head shots of Broadway stars. For many years it was run by a couple from Marseille, Nina and Carlo Migliaccio, who passed the torch on to Jean-Pierre Touchard, a Breton, who changed little about the place and usually can be found in his long blue apron working behind the bar with his son Michael. That they own the building and several more in this neighborhood means that this place may well remain a theater district fixture for some time to come.

The menu is typical of the genre. The starters, all priced well under $10, feature a few leafy salads with good vinaigrette, asparagus or endive in season, snails in their shells with a garlic butter, chilled herring, sardines, clams raw or baked, shrimp cocktail, white beans with onions, thin slices of head cheese topped with grated onions and a small salad, a very decent onion soup, and a good whole artichoke vinaigrette. The main courses, all priced in the mid-teens, include a more than decent version of beef Bourguignon. The coq au vin sometimes can be dry; instead be brave and try the delicious and hard-to-find tripe à la Caen. This braise features tender chunks of tripe mixed with carrots and onions and set in a rich beef-based sauce, enriched with calf's foot and marrow bone, all laced with Calvados. I used to be able to eat food like this for dinner, but now I prefer it at lunch. Ditto the tête de veau, here served off a separate plate where the warm braised meat is wrapped in a clean white napkin, all the parts (need I name them?) lined up with boiled potato and carrots; it's served with a generous portion of sauce gribiche on the side. For the less adventurous, stick with the tried and true: filet mignon with sauce madiera, pork chops with sautéed mushrooms, a simple roast Cornish hen, or even dinner omelets. The fries are good too.

During the midafternoon, between services, staff from other French restaurants including Le Bernardin hang out here to talk, smoke, and watch soccer in season; after 10 PM, many cooks and waiters from New York's French expat community stop by at the bar for a beer or two, catch up on things, and wind down. There are a few tables outside, set just below the sidewalk, that are very nice, and if no one tells the mayor, you can still smoke out here; just bring your own Gauloise.

Trestle on Tenth

212-645-5659
242 Tenth Avenue,
   at 24th Street
Casual
Reservations
Moderate
All major credit cards accepted
Lunch and dinner Tuesday–
   Friday, dinner Saturday–
   Monday
C, E trains to 23rd Street station

Chef-owner Ralf Kuettel took over the space of a restaurant that had formerly been here for years and years, Chelsea Commons. Trestle fits into the neighborhood well, with its exposed brick walls, wide plank wood floors, small bar at the front, and open garden in the back when weather permits. The heavy wooden tables are rustic, and the room's simplicity sets the tone for the straightforward cooking that comes out of the kitchen. The exposed brick walls are adorned by a rotation of art supplied by local artists. Essentially Kuettel, who was born, raised, and trained in Switzerland, cooks food he likes to eat. I've visited Switzerland numerous times, and each region tends to reflect its neighbor's culinary genetics: in Basel, the German style; in Lausanne, the French; and to a degree in Ticino, an Italian style as well. During my first trip here, I knew I'd like the place when I saw not only a great crépinette of braised pork shoulder and Savoy cabbage on the menu, but also a terrine made from oxtail and pigs' feet, and even roast kidney.

Though the room is warm and inviting, the food alone is worth a trek. You can start with that great flavorful crépinette, the braised rich pork held together by a thin film of caul fat, the cabbage providing a clean crunch and sweet relief to the meat's richness. The terrine of oxtail and pigs' feet is rich and gelatinous, very good. For lighter fare, skip the generic field greens and start with the far more interesting salad of butter leaf lettuce with crisped bacon and a buttermilk-based creamy dressing, or the house-made gravlax of Arctic char with a sliced radish salad and pieces of good pumpernickel bread. The sautéed sweetbreads served in a puff pastry shell topped with hedgehog mushrooms could double as a light entree. I miss this kind of food, rarely found anywhere in town these days. A recent visit paired halibut with shrimp and cockles in a thyme-scented shellfish broth studded with portobello mushrooms and savory potato dumplings.

Lamb saddle was roasted medium rare and set atop a tangle of delicious, slow-cooked mustard greens and braised cipollini onions. Don't miss ordering a side dish or two. The broccoli rabe with chunks of speck is delicious, as is the gratinée of pizokel dumplings under melted Gruyère or the pressed fingerling potatoes sopping with good olive oil.

The wine list is excellent—no surprise here, as the chef spent a few years working at a decent wine store, offering further training for an already well-trained palate. The list is interesting, with a broad assortment of excellent wines from small producers and varietals rarely seen here in New York, all sold at prices that rarely exceed double retail. In short, for under $50 a bottle you have a great selection to choose from. I should point out that the chef's wife is Juliet Pope, the wine director at Gramercy Tavern, which boasts a superb list as well. Desserts here are okay, not great. If you have room, try the walnut nusstorte with fresh whipped cream, probably his mother's recipe. I only wish New York these days had more of these restaurants, where chefs gladly work in the kitchen and cook with heart and soul every day.

Tribeca Grill

212-941-3900
375 Greenwich Street, at Franklin Street
Casual
Reservations
Moderate to expensive
All major credit cards accepted
Lunch and dinner seven days a week
1 train to Franklin Street station

This was Drew Nieporent's second venture after Montrachet, and according to him, it was this restaurant that was the tipping point in terms of Tribeca's transformation into a restaurant scene. He was there from the beginning, night after night, so who am I to disagree? It's all the way west on Greenwich Street, in the shadow of the former World Trade Center and across the street from 310 Greenwich Street, the southernmost of three nondescript Mitchell-Lama high-rises. The neighborhood was in transition, but just barely, and this part of town was very quiet at night and on weekends. The buzz behind the place was impressive; the co-owner was Robert De Niro, and other investors included Sean Penn, Bill Murray, Ed Harris, Russell Simmons, Christopher Walken, Harvey and Bob Weinstein, and Mikhail Baryshnikov, as a partial list. Needless to say, the press were there from the start.

The space is one big square room. The centerpiece that anchors it all is the imposing square bar from the old Maxwell's Plum, which Nieporent bought at auction, removed, and reconstructed piece by piece. That bar is a tribute of sorts, as Nieporent worked at Maxwell's in its heyday and at Tavern on the Green as well, both owned by the larger-than-life Warner LeRoy, an impresario from the 1970s and 1980s who has since passed on. Brick walls surround you, punctuated by framed art, some it by Mr. De Niro Sr., an accomplished painter on the New York scene from the 1950s and 1960s. The industrial poured-concrete ceiling and exposed plumbing and ductwork are vestiges from the space's past as a working warehouse.

When they first opened, no one had any idea how many covers to expect—50, maybe 100—but from the start it was very busy, and Drew began to add more tables every night to accommodate the crowds. The opening chef, Don Pintabona, had no idea what to plan for, but each night it was busier than the last. At one point Pintabona finally asked Nieporent, "How many seats do we have?" He wasn't sure, but on busy nights these days, they'll do 400-plus meals. The food is not great but okay. I like it for out-of-towners or families. It reminds me of eating at Julien, Vaudeville, or Flo in Paris. The crowds are always a blend of downtown locals, guys in suits from the nearby offices, tourists, young college types, and families. But it is at its core a very New York place. The scale of it all, the noise, the consistently well-prepared food, the good wait staff, and the occasional celebrity spotting make for a fun time. When the weather is good they have a few tables outside facing Greenwich Street, which can be very nice as well. That's where I sneak my cigars—so far no tickets from Bloomberg.

The menu is big, and if you select carefully, you can eat well. I like the salads and cold plates as starters. Crispy arugula is paired with imported buffalo mozzarella and roasted red and yellow peppers. The seared tuna, cooked rare, is cut in little squares and set next to a decent version of sesame noodles and pickled vegetables. Coconut-crusted rock shrimp, deep-fried and served with a curry sauce and lemongrass-spiked yogurt, are good bar food. Braised short ribs are set in a pool of consommé scented with horseradish, a good foil to the meat's richness, and garnished with foie gras and porcini ravioli. Sturdy Alaskan halibut takes a Provençal turn here, served with a black olive tapenade, ratatouille, artichoke mousse, and preserved lemon confit.

Desserts are okay too, a bit retro. The banana tart with milk chocolate malt ice cream works, as does the chocolate, peanut butter, and hazelnut cake with a scoop of vanilla ice cream. The wine list is very good, as one would expect at any of Nieporent's Myriad Group restaurants, and there is a good selection of beers on tap. Service is always good; the ever-present management sees to that. But more than anything else, the attraction here is the convivial feel of the place, that on a good night when the place is jumping and in walks a few of the Knicks, the Jets, the Giants, or an entertainer in town promoting their latest gig, you've got ringside seats to a happening New York scene.

Txikito

212-242-4730
240 Ninth Avenue, between
  24th and 25th Streets
Casual
No reservations
Inexpensive to moderate
All major credit cards accepted
Dinner from 5 PM, closed
  Monday
1, C, E, F, V, N, R, W trains to
  23rd Street station

I first met Alex Raij and her husband, Eder Montero, back when they ran and cooked at Tía Pol and El Quinto Pino, both first-rate tapas bars. They have since severed their business relationship with those two spots and now have this lovely little store to call their own. In opening Txikito (pronounced "chic-ee-toe," which means "little"), they turned their eye to the little-known cuisine of the Basque country. If you've never seen the Basque region of Spain, known as Pais Vasco, it's remote, rugged, and beautiful, and has its own ancient language, Euskera, some of which you'll find on the menu here and may require translation. If you're looking for traditional paella or straight-up tapas, go to Socarrat or Boqueria in the same neighborhood, but if you're looking for something different, try this spot. The room is small, square, and rough-hewn, with a rustic, industrial feel to it. There is a small bar, which is a fine place to eat, as are any of the little tables arranged to fill the room.

The far-reaching menu is broken down into a few sections, starting with cured olives and house-made potato chips, and moving on through Basque canapés, followed by cold and hot items. It is a surprisingly large document, listing 37 different menu items, so there is something for everyone. I've always liked grilled cheese in any form, whether it's the French croque-monsieur or the American version; here it is billed as txiki txanpi, and comes as a classic miniature Pullman loaf of white bread sliced, filled with grilled shrimp and cheese, then grilled crisp and warm, served four pieces to a plate for under $10. Another variation is the bocata, a warm sandwich mixing sliced pork belly (essentially uncured bacon) with melted cheese, or the arraultz, an open-face Basque answer to the Egg McMuffin. Soft sliced bread forms the bottom, onto which they arrange julienned chorizo sausage over a spread of sofrito marmalade, the whole topped with a sunnyside-up quail egg. I only eat good canned tuna, like Callipo from Italy, so when I saw a tuna sandwich on the menu here, I pounced. They use the Serrats brand, which was new to me, but is made from the same small Mediterranean albacore tuna found in the region. The meat is rich and clean-tasting, here bound with just a touch of piquillo pepper oil and onion, served in a small submarine-shaped roll; for $8 it may be the perfect lunch, with a good glass of rosé to wash it down.

For heartier fare, go for the morcilla, where it appears the blood sausage meat is removed from its casing and stuffed into a crunchy wrapper somewhere between spring roll skins and flattened brioche. It is rolled into a tube shape, deep-fried, then sliced and served crisp and warm—a Basque pig-in-blanket, I suppose. Squid is sliced into thin ribbons and quick-grilled on the plancha. It is sprinkled with thin strips of sweet sautéed onion, drizzled with good olive oil, and topped with a few toasted pine nuts—a winner. On my last visit during a cold day in the winter of 2009, I had a plate of txarripatak, pig trotters blended with braised tripe, slow-cooked beef tendon, and chickpeas and seasoned with choricero pepper—a perfect meal for lovers of offal.

The wine and sherry list is all Basque and many varietals were new to me, but prices are on the low end and they offer flights of small pours as well. If you have room for dessert, I've always liked simple, light custards such as panna cotta to finish big meals. Try the cuajada, a thin milk-based custard topped with orange honey and walnuts. Service is fine, and I'm glad to have Raij and Montero back cooking in Manhattan.

Una Pizzeria Napoletana

212-477-9950
349 East 12th Street, between
First and Second Avenues
Casual
No reservations
Moderate to expensive for pizza
Cash only
Thursday–Sunday 5 PM until
the dough runs out
L train to First Avenue station;
6 train to Astor Place station

Think of what Al Yeganeh has been to soup, Rob Kaufelt to the New York cheese scene, and Dan Barber to local, organic ingredients, and you'll begin to understand what Anthony Mangieri is to the New York pizza scene. In plain English, this guy is a pizza freak. He makes the rules, you follow them. He closes each day when he runs out of dough. Sorry, that may be 8 PM on a Saturday, but that's just the way it is. He charges more than anybody else per square inch of pie, makes no bones about it, and offers only four kinds of pizza, all served whole—you cut them yourself. Add to that a printed document that amounts to a pizza manifesto, and you get the idea. It's his store, it's his passion, and though it all sounds a little nutty, it works perfectly for me. Bakers by breed are a passionate bunch. Dough is organic, alive. It changes each and every day with different ambient temperatures and humidity, different flour, the change in seasons, and the different ways in which the yeast reacts. It can't be rushed. It helps to be a little crazy when you're a baker, and Anthony Mangieri was a baker before he turned his eyes to pizza. Born and raised in Point Pleasant, New Jersey, he recalls coming to New York as a kid with his mom and eating great pizza at John's on Bleecker and Totonno's. Prior to opening in Manhattan in 2004 he had a great pizzeria in Point Pleasant. He travels frequently to Naples, and it is from that historical port town, where pizza purportedly was invented, that he derives his inspiration.

His is a pure Neapolitan-style pizza. The wheat flour used is stone ground and neither bleached nor bromated. The sea salt comes from one source in Sicily. The dough is naturally fermented and kneaded by hand—no machines ever touch it. The initial fermentation takes 24 hours, and then it is knocked down, docked, portioned out, and formed into balls that again ferment naturally, taking 12 more hours. The tomatoes for the sauce are real San Marzanos, and the mozzarella is authentic buffalo mozzarella, flown in fresh twice a week. To this add only extra-virgin olive oil, fresh basil, and the four pie varieties: marinara, with just tomatoes, olive oil, herbs, and garlic; Margherita, with tomatoes, buffalo mozzarella, basil, and olive oil; bianca, with mozzarella, olive oil, and basil; and filetti, made with fresh cherry tomatoes, buffalo mozzarella, basil, and olive oil.

The oven used is custom-made of brick and fired by wood alone, no gas, no coal. All of this excellence, however, comes at a price. A 12-inch pie costs $16.95. Add a few dollars more for a beverage and you can easily spend upward of $20 per person for pizza. Crazy? No, not really. The problem we have in America is that pizza historically has been categorized as a cheap food. Once you get used to paying a couple bucks a slice at your corner joint or $12 for two pies from those big chains, the prices here seem outrageous. But the pizza at your corner joint really isn't very good. So I look at it this way: at good restaurants I've had many appetizers that cost $15 or more and were not worth half that, and I've had many forgettable meals that cost twice that or more, so in the grand scheme of things, for $17, this pizza really is one of the very best you'll ever have.

The crust is thin but has a good bite from the gluten development and slow fermentation time. The sauce is excellent and the cheese unimpeachable, as are the olive oil, hand-chopped garlic, and fresh basil leaves. As is the case with most Italian food, it's all about ingredients, and the simplest dishes require the best ingredients. Here you have all that, from the dough to the toppings to the oven they are cooked in—and the crazy man in charge, for whom this is such a passion. Worth it? Yes. And I'd say we're lucky to have it too.

Uncle Nick's Greek

212-245-7992
747 Ninth Avenue, between
50th and 51st Streets
Casual
Reservations
Moderate
All major credit cards accepted
Lunch and dinner seven days
week
N, R, W trains to 49th Street
station; C, E trains to 50th
Street station

If you're looking for good, inexpensive, simple Greek food in a bright, friendly taverna, this may be just the place for you. As you walk into this well-lit restaurant, the open kitchen is to your right, where the staff are busy grilling whole fish and sending out the many small plates that start your meal. The room has no real charm to it, but the staff are good, service is fine, and the prices are very reasonable. If you order right, you can eat well for 30 bucks a head.

Stick with the simple appetizers. The dips are a good choice—not done with the same finesse as at, say, Molyvos a few blocks east, but good just the same. Tzatziki packs a garlic kick against cool cucumber. Taramasalata, made from pink fish roe, is very good too, as are the skordalia and the roasted-eggplant-based melitzanosalata. Move on to a plate of those big white Greek lima beans called gigantes, tender, meaty, and dressed with good olive oil, or the fried eggplant or zucchini sticks with skordalia. Or opt for the grilled octopus, sautéed sweetbreads, or great little spicy meatballs called keftedakia. For main courses, stick with whole grilled fish that is simply splashed with a bit of lemon juice, topped with some sea salt and maybe a touch of dried oregano; just ask them not to overcook it, which happens frequently. Snapper is a good choice, as is the porgy, a local favorite of mine, if they have it. If you need meat, stick with the various kebabs or the interesting bifteki, a sort of Greek-spiced sirloin burger.

The wine list is short but decent. Ask the waiters—they know the food and wine. If you still have room, try the rice pudding, which is actually very good. Not the most romantic place to eat, but for flavor and value, it's a find.

Union Square Café

212-243-4020
213 East 16th Street, between Union Square Park and Fifth Avenue
Casual to dressy
Reservations
Moderate to expensive
All major credit cards accepted
Lunch and dinner seven days a week
4, 5, 6, L, N, Q, R, W trains to 14th Street/Union Square station

Over the years I spent writing and compiling this book, I never meant to include Union Square Café. Though it's enduringly popular for legions of New Yorkers, I've never been a fan and have had too many mediocre meals there to change my mind. Then on one last visit, really a business meeting, I was swayed by my meal, first of excellent pasta flecked with cod and breadcrumbs, followed by an entree of perfectly cooked Chatham cod barigoule-style in a very rich, butter-thickened herbal broth studded with artichokes. It was late winter, we had a one o'clock reservation, and the place was still three-quarters full well after 2 PM when a waitress—not our waitress, just another on that busy floor who has been there forever—came by the table to say hi to me and remembered what I'd had the last time I was there, nearly a year before, when she was my waitress. Well, that made an impression. Hospitality is really what owner Danny Meyer does best. No one gets it more right than he, and that's true at all his restaurants around town. The fact that he opened this place more than 20 years ago, when he was still a very young man, is rather amazing as well. A St. Louis native, Meyer has left his mark on the New York City dining scene like few other impresarios before him—credit where credit is due.

That said, I've often felt that while his front of the house was so strong, his kitchens always performed just enough to be good, never great, with the lone exception of Gramercy and maybe now Eleven Madison, while his prices walked a fine line between too expensive and the high range of just barely acceptable. Perhaps Meyer knows that most diners understand great service, but far fewer really understand great food. Great service and average food keep you in business. Great food with average service . . . well, you're toast. He knows his audience well and is aware of what he can serve them and how much he can charge, and he knows the press too, whom he plays like a fiddle. No one in New York gets more gratuitous press than he.

You enter Union Square Café off 16th Street, always to a deft greeting by the hostess. Here you'll find the bar area, which is a great place for a casual lunch or dinner. There are a few tables scattered about that front room, both by the street and to the rear, but the main room is to the left. The staff are happy and well trained. They know the wine list, will recite all the specials in detail, and can field any menu questions that you may have, easily walking that the fine line between casually friendly and too much so. This was also true here in the 1990s, when dining room service was at its lowest point in history: hostesses around the city were downright belligerent and wait staff at their least informed and nastiest. But they have always been tops here.

The food, on the other hand, has been hit-or-miss. Part of it is the sheer volume that place does every day. Michael Romano was the chef here for many years, having replaced Ali Barker, who was the chef for the first three years. Romano is a seasoned pro, having worked in some of New York's best kitchens; just prior to this gig, he was the chef at the famed French restaurant La Caravelle. Romano is still with the Union Square Hospitality Group, now as the executive chef for the whole organization, and his replacement in 2007 at the restaurant was Carmen Quagliata, who has done a great job filling those big shoes and keeping the food consistent, seasonal, and for the most part interesting. But, like his predecessor, he has a lot of cooks in the kitchen here. He needs them to keep up with the volume, and a lot of them are recent culinary grads who just need more training, experience, and supervision.

Order carefully and you can dine well. Skip the gummy gnocchi and start with the spaghetti with flaked cod, one of the best starters they have. Al dente pasta is tossed with crunchy sautéed bread crumbs bound with garlic and olive oil, redolent of parsley, red pepper flakes, and broccoli rabe, with bits and pieces of excellent shredded cod laced through the dish. My grandmother made something like this, and I've never been able to replicate it. The version here is very close. A salad special of thin-sliced blood oranges flecked with ricotta salata, toasted pine nuts, and micro arugula drizzled with excellent olive oil was a standout as well. The aforementioned Chatham cod, seared crisp and then baked, was perfectly cooked, flaky, almost custard-like, set in a thick pool of buttery artichoke ragout, garnished with leaves of earthy Swiss chard and fingerling potatoes. This is an example of the kitchen at its finest. To round out the menu for the masses, they have good steaks, fish, lamb chops, chicken, and duck. The sides vary in quality, however.

The desserts are better than average. The wine list is excellent, as should be expected with the buying power that Danny Meyer has these days. But like so many great restaurants from the 1980s, this place can seem stuck in a culinary time warp. The level of cooking has just gotten better and better all over town, and what was once great is now merely average.

Utsav Festive India

212-575-2525
1185 Sixth Avenue, between 46th and 47th Streets
Casual
Reservations
Moderate
All major credit cards accepted
Lunch and dinner seven days a week
B, D, F trains to 47th–50th Streets/Rockefeller Center station; N, R, W trains to 49th Street station; 1 train to 50th Street station

Opened a few years back, this restaurant is located on the second floor overlooking a small plaza on 46th Street. The opening chef was Walter D'Rozario, who had been a chef at Bay Leaf a few blocks north on 56th prior to this gig. The menu is big and ambitious and the food, for the most part, simply tastes great. Skip the bar downstairs; it's rather depressing, and they offer only a small selection from the menu, such as chicken wings, smaller tandoori kabobs, and Indian flatbreads just warm from the grill or the tandoor. Upstairs is the main room, with brightly colored walls and tables with both green and white tablecloths.

The $17 lunch buffet is a great deal, and for dinner you can eat well for less than $25 per person. I loved the lamb shanks braised Kashmiri-style, the jumbo shrimp flavored with coriander and mint, and the chicken tikka masala. The Goan chicken vindaloo is good and reasonably hot, and the slow-braised lamb gosht pasanda is a winner, the tender lamb chunks dressed in a thick sauce redolent of star anise, fennel, and other spices. From the tandoor, try the big shrimp with green chutney, or the baby lamb chops, most likely from New Zealand, marinated in lots of freshly grated ginger. Vegetarians will be happy too, with a large selection including excellent fried okra, dal Bukhara, a tomato-based stew of black lentils and kidney beans, or the excellent paneer with chunks of white cheese tossed with well-spiced tomato sauce and studded with green and red bell peppers.

Vai Restaurant and Wine Bar

212-362-4500
225 West 77th Street, between Amsterdam and Broadway
Casual
Reservations
Moderate
All major cards
Dinner seven nights a week from 5 PM
1 train to 79th Street station; B, C trains to 81st Street station; 1, 2, 3 trains to 72nd Street station

This little restaurant and wine bar opened in 2008 in an Upper West Side neighborhood that is finally getting some very decent dining options. The owner, a Brooklynite named Vincent Chirico, worked years back for Marcus Samuelsson at Aquavit. Samuelsson was impressed by the young man's drive and abilities and would later help him in arranging a trip to France that included a *stage* at Georges Blanc's great restaurant in Vonnas, France. That three-star training is not lost here, though the food and near bargain price points at Vai are very much in keeping with these tough times. The restaurant is divided into two small rooms, one with a bar, the other just tables. The space was formerly a pita place, as I recall. Seating is tight, but the room fills quickly and has a good neighborhood feel to it throughout the night with a diverse group of ages and ethnicities, all here for the good cooking, very good wine list, and moderate prices.

Start with the small plates of crudo, thin-sliced raw fish Venetian-style, drizzled with extra-virgin olive oil, a splash of lemon juice, and a sprinkle of sea salt. Or start with the baked clams topped with toasted bread crumbs and bits of finely diced chorizo. Sautéed sea scallops were fresh, plump, and cooked properly. The grilled calamari with capers and a sauce made from preserved lemon was another good starter. If you're in the mood for meat, opt for the charcuterie plate of excellent prosciutto, speck, bresaola, and Serrano ham, or the square little individual pizzette, offered with a variety of toppings.

Salads, in keeping with the theme, are both simple and satisfying: thin-sliced pears tossed with bitter frisée, goat cheese, and pistachios; golden beets with diced firm ricotta salata; buttery Boston lettuce with fried prosciutto and creamy sweet gorgonzola. Pasta courses are decent and priced in the low teens. For main courses, the grilled deboned farm-raised branzino was clean-tasting and fresh, and the pork rib chop is a deal at $18. The crispy fried artichoke side dish rounds things out.

The wine list is small but very good. A glass of the Canevari Prosecco works with the salumi or crudo to start the meal. With your seafood choices, try the hard-to-find Picpoul de Pinet from southern France at $11 per glass, or the lovely Mustilli Falanghina from Campania for just under $50 per bottle. The list includes both New and Old World styles of winemaking. Good choices for reds include a 2007 Arboreto Montepulciano d'Abruzzo at $34, a nice sturdy primitivo from Puglia at $38 a bottle, and from France, a full-bodied Côtes du Rhône Domaine Galevan at $46. Most bottles are under $50, by the glass around $10, and they even have a good, short list of dessert wines and ports to choose from. Service is efficient, Chirico is almost always on the floor and is a gracious, flirty host, and in these times of tight wallets, Vai is a welcome addition to a neighborhood that is finally being well served by good dining options.

Vanessa's Dumpling House

212-625-8008

118 Eldridge Street, between Broome and Grand Streets (and elsewhere)

Casual

No reservations

Cash only

Seven days a week 7:30 AM–9 PM

J, M, Z trains to Bowery station; N, R, W trains to Prince Street station

If there were a category for great New York bargains, Vanessa's Dumpling House would be the headliner, offering perhaps the best bang for the buck in all of Manhattan. It used to be a tiny storefront with a steady line out the door, but they've expanded and now offer tables for dining in, though the lines are still there. (There's also a branch on East 14th Street between Second and Third Avenues.) The decor is barebones, but with food this good and this cheap, who cares? For $5 you can eat very, very well. The cooks work off three wok-like stoves, but these have thick flat steel bottoms. Two of them are nonstop dumpling producers, where the chefs can load an entire half sheet pan's worth of dumplings onto the surface, and then with combination of hot oil and steam bang out 50 or so perfect pot-stickers every five minutes, crisp and crunchy on the bottom, steamed and delicate on the top. You'll pay $1 for four dumplings and can top them with a red-hot sauce, a soy-vinegar mix, or both if you choose. They offer chive and pork, vegetable and pork, or just vegetable, steamed or fried. Eight dumplings in soup will set you back a whopping $2. The other wok usually is occupied producing sesame pancakes, which are pizza-shaped and pan-fried before your eyes. The fried dough rises to about two inches in height and is golden brown on both sides. Topped with sesame seeds, they are then cut into wedges and served plain or stuffed with some kind of braised beef. For $1.50, it makes a heck of a snack. They also stuff these with vegetables or pork as well. If you live in the city or want to take some home, they sell the same dumplings frozen, 50 pieces for $5 and 100 pieces for $8. For a $5 bill, you simply can't beat this place.

Via Emilia

212-505-3072

47 East 21st Street, between Broadway and Park Avenue South

Casual

No reservations

Moderate

Cash only

Lunch and dinner Monday–Friday, dinner Saturday

6, N, R, W trains to 23rd Street station

This section of Park Avenue South has been an odd culinary neighborhood for some time now, with some very good restaurants, Gramercy Tavern leading the pack, mixing in with the big-box restaurants, which tend to be terrible. I'm talking about places like City Crab, TanDa, Olive, Angelo & Maxie's, Dos Caminos, and those watering-hole restaurants with huge bars and bar crowds, vestiges of the bar/pickup scene so popular during the late 1990s. Set amidst all this, you'll find Via Emilia, a small, unpretentious, and serious eatery, moderately priced, that survives even though it does not take credit cards. The menu celebrates the food of the Emilia-Romagna region of Italy, not as well known as Tuscany, to its immediate south, but, like many places in Italy, an area loaded with great food, wine, and cheese. The major cities are Modena, Bologna, Ferrara, and Parma, and if you've visited any of these, you've dined well.

Start here with a plate of the delicate boiled pork sausage cotechino served over well-seasoned lentils, simple and satisfying. Or opt for the signature tagliatelle Bolognese, a lovely starter that could also be the main event. The pasta is handmade, light, and airy, cooked perfectly. The meat sauce served with it brings the dish together as a whole and reminds me of what makes great pasta so memorable. The lasagna, a dish I am loath to order in fear of the leaden slab that may arrive before me, here is on cue. Instead of the usual SUV-shaped version, towering and slathered in cheese, I found it to be smaller, lower, and svelte, the pasta layers made from fresh egg dough, the meat sauce good too, and the béchamel sauce that binds it all perfect and creamy, redolent of good Parmesan cheese. Some come just for the stuffed pasta, a house specialty, like the large tortelloni, on fall days filled with a sweet pumpkin puree and bathed in a rich cream reduction, or the tortellini stuffed with chicken, prosciutto, and ricotta and served in a rich chicken broth.

If not pasta, then start with an order of borlengo, a specialty of the Panaro Valley region, essentially a crêpe filled with lardo, pancetta, and grated cheese, sautéed and folded—salty, simple, satisfying, and delicious. Or the gnocco fritto, fried dough balls served with good salumi. There are only a few main courses. One is usually a bluefish dish over roasted vegetables that I don't like much. I prefer bluefish when they are small, under one or two pounds, and cleaner-tasting. Opt instead for the grilled skirt steak. But in truth you'd be better served to order several appetizers to share and a great pasta for the main course, even if that's not how they do it in Italy.

Desserts are okay, service is fine, the rooms small, the staff attentive, and the wine list derived from exclusively regional wines. If you're not a fan of Lambrusco, think again. They are some very interesting wines when well made, and the selection here is excellent. These light, fizzy, refreshing wines work beautifully with the food, especially the salumi and the salty, fatty, and fried dishes.

Via Quadronno

212-650-9880
25 East 73rd Street, between
Fifth and Madison Avenues
Casual
No reservations
Moderate
All major credit cards accepted
Lunch and dinner seven days
a week
6 train to 68th Street or 77th
Street station

This place could be considered a café or a wine bar, and they serve some of the best espresso in the city, with a good assortment of gelati as well. I'm not a huge fan of Italian pastry, but the ones here are pretty darned good, though not as good as the simple sandwiches. I get the impression that many regulars—typical stuffy Upper East Side types, to be honest—come here for cappuccino, espresso, and various sweets, but I prefer the simple panini and the one- and two-ingredient sandwiches offered up on the small menu. There's a decent selection of wines by the glass. The room is very nice, with earth-tone walls, simple arts-and-crafts decorations, comfortable wood-backed banquettes, a mural depicting a seaside view from a columned window, and loads of wine bottles in wooden racks and set on tables.

In this part of town bargains are hard to come by, but you can have a nice lunch here of sandwiches, cheese, and wine for around $20 per person and feel like there was actual value there. The bread they use is custom-made for the place and perfect for small sandwiches. The meats, as in Europe, are used sparingly but are of very good quality: simple boiled ham, mortadella, pork and beef salami, and rose-hued sopressata that here comes in two styles, lean and fatty. Open-face sandwiches are a specialty, topped with smoked salmon or (even better) just salmon roe, grated botarga, pâté, or Italian tuna with artichoke hearts. The panini selection is big, and you can put together many combinations, weird-sounding but good-tasting Prague-style ham with brie, fontina and a slice of pâté or speck, brie and pâté, or the lighter bresaola, arugula, and hearts of palm.

To this add salad, some cold plates, and decent soups. You can have a good lunch, a light dinner, a between-meals post-museum snack, or just a cup of darned good coffee and their signature deconstructed tiramisu, discovered by owner Paolo Della Puppa while dining in Italy. Here they simply take fresh-baked ladyfingers and serve them with coffee alongside a creamy mix of mascarpone cheese and zabaglione dusted with bitter cocoa for dipping—a great midday treat or shared dessert after a meal.

Villa Mosconi

212-673-0390

69 MacDougal Street, between Bleecker and Houston Streets

Casual

Reservations

Moderate

All major credit cards accepted

Lunch and dinner Monday–Saturday

A, C, E, B, D, F, V trains to West 4th Street station; 1 train to Houston Street station

Pietro Mosconi is always there. He's the kind of chef who arrives early, preps all day, and cooks on the line, and that's what makes this place what it is. Each day he makes his own pasta in the basement, butchers his own meat and fish, trims mushrooms, and prepares soups and stocks. He may have the best steaks available in any Italian restaurant, prime, dry-aged, and very well marbled. The food is straightforward and simple, and while some presentations are clunky, like the huge braised portobello caps drowning in a balsamic glaze, most are spot-on. He serves good imported Italian prosciutto, anchovies with house-roasted peppers, fresh mozzarella with tomatoes in season, clams in several guises, and a very good baked stuffed artichoke. The food is old-school, Old World, and humble, but honest.

Pastas, especially the ones he turns by hand, are very good. On one recent visit, he had vongole as a special. These are tiny clams from south-central Italy, paired with linguine, garlic, olive oil, and chopped parsley. My family agreed we had not had this dish prepared this well since we were in Amalfi years back. The meatballs are very good, the basic marinara made from San Marzano tomatoes. Tortellini are stuffed with meat, Roman-style, and the handmade ravioli, manicotti, and cannelloni are all just fine. By the way, the pasta portions are large and priced between $10.50 and $12.50. It helps that he owns the building. Meats are good. Chicken is done in all those familiar ways—Parmigiana, cacciatore, Bolognese—cooked to order. The veal he butchers and pounds is a better choice, done any number of ways—al limone, pizzaiola, marsala—though a bit oversauced for my taste. But those great steaks rule the day. Start with a pasta, then have the bistecca al ferri, grilled sirloin, with a side of spinach, escarole, or broccoli rabe, and you can't go wrong.

Desserts are good, big, and sweet—spumoni, ricotta tortes, rum cake, zabaglione, cannoli. All in all, this represents a dying breed of old-style, chef-run Italian eateries that hark back to the turn of the century in New York. If you're looking for great retro food, fine service, and a slice of what this neighborhood used to be like, go no further.

Waverly Restaurant

212-675-3181

385 Sixth Avenue, between
Waverly Place and 8th Street

Casual

No reservations

Inexpensive

Cash only

Seven days a week, 24 hours
a day

A, C, E, B, D, F, V trains to West
4th Street station; 1 train to
Christopher Street station

If you're looking for one of the last great 24-hour diners in New York, this is it, even though it's decidedly not a classic rail-car-style diner. It's more of an old-school neighborhood restaurant featuring a huge menu that caters to locals, students, and—as you can assume by the collection of old head shots that grace the walls—at one point legions of actors, actresses, and local artists who were once a larger part of the greater Greenwich Village community. These days, gentrification has taken a toll on places like this, which are reminiscent of an older, gentler time in New York City. The West Village still has a heck of a lot of very good restaurants and some good old-time bars and clubs, but stretches of Sixth and Seventh Avenues and Hudson are increasingly home to the cleaner, higher-rent-paying, national corporate tenants landlords prefer, such as banks, clothing stores, chain drugstores, and of course Starbucks. Just check out the first few blocks of Bleecker between Abingdon Square, where it starts, and West 10th, a few blocks down—it's all Marc Jacobs, Ralph Lauren, and their ilk. So how refreshing, then, to find a place like the Waverly, with good service, fair prices, decent food, and a real sense of place. Plus it's open 24 hours.

The menu reads like they just couldn't say no to any classic American menu item from the middle of the last century. The sheer combination of eggs, sides, egg sandwiches, omelets, low-cholesterol omelets, Belgian waffles, French toast, bagelry (their own choice of vernacular), pancake variations, toast, muffins, cereal, and juice runs into the hundreds. Then starts the list of burgers—beef, turkey, and veggie. There are club sandwiches and melts, a little Greek section with gyros, souvlaki, and spinach pie, and then pages' worth of classics such as roast beef, pastrami, veal Parmigiana and other Italian items, salads, chicken croquettes, shrimp scampi, meatloaf, roast turkey, filet of sole, broiled halibut . . . How about a Roumanian steak with two stuffed shrimp? I kid you not, that's a menu item. And please leave room for dessert; they have 30-plus items listed on the menu. I know this sounds insane, but where else can you find this?

So what should you order? Well, if you're sober and it's still morning, the egg dishes are all decent. For lunch, the meatloaf is too, as are the burgers. At 3 AM, you can either start a new day with a breakfast combo, or perhaps go whole hog and order the stick-to-your-ribs pasticchio, a casserole of baked macaroni studded with ground beef and bound with a nice thick béchamel, followed by a slice of banana cream pie. Sounds like a surefire cure for the potential "was out way too late and drank way too much" hangover.

WD-50

212-477-2900
50 Clinton Street, between
   Stanton and Rivington
   Streets
Casual
Reservations
Moderate to expensive
All major credit cards accepted
Dinner Monday–Saturday
F, J, M, Z train to Essex/
   Delancey Street station

Wylie Dufresne, seemingly a household name among foodies around the country these days and some years back winner of the James Beard Rising Star Chef award, has had a relatively quick ascent to the top. This is due in no small part to the combination of a tireless work ethic, a real talent for cooking, and a passionate intellectual curiosity that drives him to constantly tinker. Part chef, part mad scientist, he stands at the forefront of the most modern of culinary movements, the one started by the Spanish chef Ferran Adrià and dubbed by others "molecular gastronomy." Molecular gastronomy is to cuisine what modern art, starting with Cubism, was to the art world. Since early history, painting was taking what one saw and rendering it recognizably on canvas. Then, starting with Cubism, artists began to turn the familiar into the barely recognizable, and abstract art took it further. By way of example, one of Wylie's early creations was deep-fried mayonnaise; more recently was his foie gras "knot." What was wrong with excellent mayonnaise or a foie gras terrine in their usual forms? Well, tinkerers tinker. To my mind, early on the food was hit-or-miss in maybe equal proportions, and some nights it seemed as though your dinner was his experiment, but of late the food has matured and the mistakes appear less frequently, if at all. For sheer culinary innovation, you'd be hard pressed to find a more avant-garde kitchen in the city or anywhere else in this country.

Dufresne grew up in the business, and after he graduated from college went on to attend and graduate from cooking school and then train with Jean-Georges Vongerichten at Jean Georges. He's smart and curious, and he works hard at his craft each day in this kitchen, with a very strong crew playing with the latest gadgets and combinations. You're more likely to find dishes made with hydrocolloids. methylcellulose, liquid nitrogen, and modified cornstarch than dishes served with chopped parsley.

From the street, a door made from large blond planks announces you're here. Enter past the bar area to the main room, square and comfortable, with high-backed banquettes and a warm vibe in spite of the sleek modern look of it. They have a small private party room surrounded by wine bottles as well. The staff are very good, well-trained devotees; Dufresne's father is often on the premises, supervising the front of the house. Once you're seated, as if to set the tone from the start, each table is given a small wooden box containing paper-thin sesame crisps, as opposed to the more standard dinner rolls served elsewhere. When the plates arrive, surprise follows surprise. The dish billed as carrot coconut sunny side up is plated like an egg. The yolk, like any free-range hen's egg, is deep orange, but is made from carrot, and the white is a coconut emulsion, the flavors clean, complementary, and distinct. He plays a lot with foie gras. A few years back, were you to order it, a small hockey-puck-shaped disc would arrive turned on its side, set over what appears to be freeze-dried crumbled peas, candied olive, and micro greens. So far, so good; it appears to be a standard torchon-style preparation. But cut into it and the center of the foie gras puck contains beet juice that bleeds onto the plate. The flavors worked well, the concept was sound, and it was a dish you were likely to find nowhere else. You'd find that fried mayonnaise on the plate of beef tongue. The mayonnaise reminded me of the classic cromesquis from modern French cooking, flash-fried crisp and crunchy on the outside while liquid at the center. It sits next to a small mound of well turned-out, thin-sliced beef tongue and a schmear of tomato molasses, with a garnish of ground nuts.

Eggs Benedict gets the complete makeover treatment as well. The plate arrives with the yolks having been poached in plastic forms, then cut into thick little disks. Hollandaise gets the mayonnaise treatment and is breaded with English muffin crumbs and deep-fried. Canadian bacon cut paper-thin is slow-cooked on a silicone baking mat until it becomes a mere crisp. So there you have it: the egg, the muffin, the sauce, the bacon, all reinvented, and it actually tastes great. But I'm still not sure that I wouldn't take a correctly poached egg atop artisan Canadian bacon on a Thomas's English muffin with a dollop of perfectly made whole-butter Hollandaise instead of this. Then again, things must move forward, especially in the culinary world, and that is the whole point here.

Pastry here follows the same code and has always been exceptional. One of my all-time favorites was the rich, thin slab of shortbread book-ended by a scoop of perfect jasmine ice cream, a poached, almost confit-style banana slice, and saffron gelée. The wine list is a strong, modern, well-assembled document. The crowd skews young and enthusiastic; this is after all the Lower East Side, and Dufresne and his team reign supreme. Imitators abound, but no one to date in New York can match his creative, inventive style, with results that are worth eating and coming back for time and again. From the outset I've never warmed to this school of cooking. I prefer food I can recognize on my plate, but should you have an interest in modern experimental cuisine then this is the place to come, and of late it's well worth all the effort and accolades.

'Wichcraft

212-780-0577
60 East 8th Street, at Mercer
Street (and elsewhere)
Casual
No reservations
Moderate
All major credit cards accepted
Breakfast, lunch, and early
dinner seven days a week
N, R, W trains to 8th Street
station; 6 train to Astor Place
station

What chef Tom Colicchio's Craftsteak did for the steakhouse, his 'Wichcraft does for the sandwich shop. Take a classic America culinary idiom and bring it into the modern era. If you want a great old-style sandwich shop, visit Eisenberg's; if you want the modern version, try 'Wichcraft. Conceived by Tom and his partners in this venture, Jeffrey Zurofsky and Sisha Ortuzar, the idea was to create sandwiches that are delicious, fun to eat, and even interesting to think about. Working chefs often have to grab a bite here and there as they can during the day; rarely can they sit down for a meal. It's also not at all uncommon for chefs and cooks who handle food all day and tend to get bored to whip up oddball creations in part for sustenance and in part for amusement. The menu here suggests that process may have been at play.

Take, for example, the warm sandwich billed as grilled Gruyère. Essentially this is onion soup taken apart and put back together between slices of bread. What we have is good rye bread slathered with a dose of warm caramelized onions and a slice of melted Gruyère cheese. Add a little rich beef stock and put it in a bowl, and you get the idea—this is an onion soup sandwich. Or how about the one billed as slow-roasted pork with red cabbage? Again I can see the staff at a good restaurant with some of the night's special left over—what to do? Well, roast pork certainly goes with braised red cabbage. Add a little mustard, some sliced hot peppers, put the whole thing between some good soft ciabatta, and there you have it—the dinner special as a sandwich. Fan of niçoise salad? Try the marinated white anchovy sandwich, where those briny Mediterranean fish are spread out over crunchy bitter frisée, slathered with a soft-cooked egg, and then placed on good, crusty country bread and spread with salsa verde and roasted onion. Simple offerings include a great triple-decker PB&J on fresh-baked Pullman-loaf white bread, or the roasted turkey with avocado, bacon, onion relish, and aioli on soft ciabatta. One of my other favorites is the mortadella layered with sautéed mushrooms and black olive mayonnaise on sourdough.

The menu is divided into breakfast offerings, cold and hot sandwiches, soups, sides, half a sandwich and bowl of soup, and some excellent pastry as well, for many years courtesy of the great baker at Craft, Karen DeMasco, who recently left to work on her first book and spend more time with her young children. But her style remains. Don't miss the peanut butter and chocolate 'creamwich, or the brownies. All the sandwiches are under $10, and the beverage selection is nonalcoholic but very good, with loads of top-quality soda, tea, and fruit spritzers.

Wolfgang's Steakhouse

212-889-3369
4 Park Avenue, at 33rd Street
Casual to dressy
Reservations
Expensive
All major credit cards accepted
Lunch and dinner Monday–
Friday, dinner Saturday and
Sunday
6 train to 33rd Street station

If imitation is the sincerest form of flattery, the family that owns Peter Luger's should be very happy. Well, give Wolfgang's some credit—this was, after all, the first of many deliberate, unapologetic Peter Luger simulacra. Opened to much acclaim in 2004, Wolfgang's is run by none other than Wolfgang Zwiener, an old-school natural charmer and 40-year veteran of Peter Luger's dining room, and his son, Peter Zwiener. Actually it was Peter's idea. Wolfgang was ready to retire and move to Florida when Peter, a recently laid-off banker with too much free time on his hands, had two great ideas: he wanted to open a steakhouse, and Dad should run it with him. The result: a Xerox of Peter Luger's on this side of the East River. The menus are virtually identical, the serving plates are (surprise, surprise) the very same Buffalo China Co. pattern and shape used by Luger's, several members of the floor staff are longtime Luger veterans, and the style of cooking and service . . . well, you guessed it. In a way, that's good news for some, as you save the cab fare to Brooklyn, and the meat Wolfgang's cooks is the genuine article, USDA prime, dry-aged, almost, and I mean almost, as nice as the meat served at Luger's, which is saying a lot.

That beautiful meat receives the same blunt treatment it is accorded in Williamsburg, cooked in an old-style 1,100°F radiant broiler, burnt on the outside, removed, then sliced while just half cooked, to be finished off when the table is ready by being topped with a dose of clarified butter and thrust back under those broilers until the thing goes positively incendiary, and then and only then brought out into the dining room still smoking and sizzling in a pool of butter, beef fat, and blood, where it is plated tableside slice by slice. As with Luger's, the beauty of this cooking method is completely lost on me, but apparently not on others, as both places are packed all the time. People just love this shtick.

Located steps off Park Avenue in midtown, this was the old dining room of the Vanderbilt Hotel. Recently street-level windows have been added, bringing in more light from behind the bar area on the avenue side, but it is still somehow a bit cramped and claustrophobic. This is one of the few dining rooms in the city featuring decorative Guastavino tiles that cover the entire vaulted ceiling. While strikingly beautiful to look at, they are an acoustical nightmare. Once the room is half full, which happens about ten minutes after it opens every day, it is impossible to have a conversation without yelling. But it appears that noise in steakhouses isn't a bad thing, as I've heard few complaints. There is a small, long, narrow room off to the far back side of the main dining room that is even noisier when full and should be avoided if you didn't think to carry earplugs. Bring your handheld device and you can text-message your dining companions.

The various seafood cocktails are all fine for what they are. In true steakhouse style, that usually means seriously overcooked to begin with and then served too cold straight out of the refrigerator, where they were undoubtedly waiting pre-plated and ready to go. The shrimp cocktail arrives in this fashion, but aside from the flaws previously mentioned, the big shrimp are okay, dipped in a hot cocktail sauce or washed down with a few martinis. Jumbo lump crabmeat is just that. The lobster, hmmm . . . if you thought those shrimp were overcooked, just wait until you try the lobster. The oysters can be good in season, and crab cakes are fine. But if you want to throw all dietary caution out the window, order the grilled sizzling Canadian bacon at $2.50 a slice, which arrives at your table as nearly 3 ounces of thick, chewy, charbroiled slabs of excellent crispy bacon, guaranteed to get you right over the daily dietary allowance for both sodium and cholesterol before the steak arrives. These places are not for the faint of heart. The salads, as per usual, are forgettable; go right for the meat and potatoes, and you'll come away smiling.

The meat is genuinely very good. The potato sides reliably accomplish their supporting role. Hash browns are crunchy, crusty, and moist at the center. The German potatoes, slathered in caramelized onions, and home fries are decent. Vegetables? You can name them by heart. The creamed spinach is okay but is better elsewhere in town, like at Ben Benson's, for example. There is steamed or boiled broccoli, and yes, asparagus is in season all year long.

Desserts, all uniformly mediocre, are purchased from somewhere else and can be skipped unless you absolutely have to have something sweet. The wine list was really bad when they first opened but is now only half bad. The service is okay, better if you're a regular and they know you, but after all, this is a New York steakhouse, so what did you expect?

Wondee Siam 2

212-286-1726
813 Ninth Avenue, between 53rd and 54th Streets (and elsewhere)
Casual
Reservations
Moderate
All major credit cards accepted
Lunch and dinner seven days a week
1, C, E trains to 50th Street station; N, R, W trains to 49th Street station

What started as a cramped, seemingly always packed takeout-only joint across the street has now expanded to include a branch on Third Avenue on the Upper East Side and this less cramped but seemingly always busy little 30-seat sit-down operation in the area of town with the highest concentration of good Thai restaurants. Some say that Pam Real Thai Food isn't what it used to be, but who knows? I like it, but I like it here too. I have never been to Thailand, and even if I had, I'm still not sure that would make me an expert on Thai food or cooking. New Yorkers love to say that the Thai restaurants here are good for New York, wink wink nod nod, and that you have to visit some favorite place in Bangkok or whatever. Hey, Italian food usually tastes different in Italy, and French food tastes different in France, so I just figure that when you travel halfway around the world to open a restaurant in a foreign city, it's going be a bit different than what you'd do at home, or could do, for that matter. So we'll leave the whole discussion of authentic ethnic cooking for that part of the foodie press who sweat those details. If it tastes good, I'm in. And for the most part, everything here tastes real good in the Thai way, covering all the corners of taste at once: hot, salty, sweet, and sour.

Take the duck salad from the old menu, billed as ped kra prow, where the duck was somehow pressed thin and crisped like bacon, then set over a salad of pineapple, minced cashews, lime juice, and hot chiles, with loads of flavor and texture. Or start with the surprisingly spicy chicken pad Thai. The broad noodles are not as sweet as elsewhere in town and give not a hint of the slow-burn spice reaction that follows. Another good starter with duck present as the protein was the yum ped yang; this salad arrived piled high on the plate, Portale-esque, with slices of boneless crisped duck mixed with lettuce leaves, fresh cilantro, sliced green apples, red onions, thinly sliced hot peppers, chunks of fresh pineapple, minced cashews, and again a vinaigrette based on fresh lime juice. I can't resist deep-fried whole fish, so I always order the one billed as pla la prig, arriving with the head on, set over a lettuce leaf, and smothered with a thick, hot chile-based sauce studded with garlic, mushrooms, and sliced bell peppers. Duck kra prow is another winner here, the duck sliced and tossed with loads of caramelized onions, fresh Thai basil, chile, and what I think may have been sweet soy sauce or perhaps oyster sauce. The noodles are all good, especially the key mao ta lay, which resembles chow fun served in Chinatown. The thick broad noodles, deliciously starchy and slimy, are mixed with seafood and chiles.

Service is good. They serve beer and wine, but stick with beer or any milk-based drink if you order hot food, as that's the only relief from real chile burn. In short, if you can get in, try it; it's one of the three or four best Thai places in the area for sure.

Woo Chon

212-695-0676
10 West 36th Street, between Fifth and Sixth Avenues
Casual
Reservations
Moderate
All major credit cards accepted
Lunch seven days a week
B, D, F, V, N, Q, R, W trains to 34th Street station

This is among the oldest Korean restaurants in this neighborhood, one of the originals. The cooking is solid, often very good. The upstairs and downstairs rooms are basically similar, and there is a second small room upstairs for private parties that accommodates 20 to 30 people. The rooms feature lots of natural dark wood, with the tables and chairs in typically ornamented Korean style. The walls are papered with pages of handwritten Korean texts. Service is good and polite. Occasionally the Korean-English barrier is a problem, but with food this good, I can overlook minor issues like that.

The menu is large and uniformly well prepared by the all-female kitchen staff, overseen by the diminutive owner, Yon Suk Choi, who seems to be in the kitchen all day every day. Over regular visits spread over a dozen years, I've never had a bad meal here. As is the case with good Chinese restaurants featuring large menus, it's best to come here with friends. This way you can order lots of different plates and share. Start with the complimentary ban chan, often a half-dozen small plates, each with a few bites of kim chee, cooked or pickled vegetables, preserved fish, and other specialties. Follow this with the hanjongshik menu, which is a tasting menu featuring a soup course, a fish course, grilled short ribs, and numerous side dishes. I always order the seafood or kimchi pajun, which is a large sautéed pancake made from bean flour and long shreds of scallion, studded with shrimp, oysters, and fresh peppers, sliced like a pizza and dipped in a mixture of soy sauce and rice vinegar.

All the dumplings are winners, either meat or fish, steamed or pan-fried. Another great starter is the vegetarian japchae, transparent amber sweet potato noodles tossed with mixed julienned vegetables and mushrooms, coated with a light soy and sesame oil sauce. Koreans make wonderful family-style soups that are really meals in themselves. The kalbi tang is a rich beef broth with chunks of short ribs. This flavorful meat is braised tender and served still clinging to the bone, accompanied by rice noodles and large chunks of braised white daikon radish, which acts as a foil to the richness of the meat and broth. Or try the seafood soups, stews really: either the daegu maewoon tang or the haemul soon tofu, spicy rich broths featuring cod and mixed seafood and served with dollops of soft tofu, each again a perfect meal in itself. There is the mandoo guk, a rich meat broth served with poached dumplings and vegetables.

Each table is equipped with a BBQ grill in the center, so if it's traditional Korean BBQ you want, try the galbi, marinated sliced beef short ribs, grilled at the center of the table. I like to wrap the grilled meat in lettuce leaves with a dab of seasoned bean paste and rice and eat them like a wrap. Or try the yukwe, a Korean version of steak tartare made with hand-cut julienned flank steak tossed with dark caramel soy sauce and topped with a raw egg yolk to mix in. They feature some wonderful hard-to-find dishes here, including several cold buckwheat noodle preparations, which are another specialty of this restaurant. In the summer months when it's hot out and I don't want tableside BBQ, I love to eat tosok guksoo jaengban, chilled buckwheat noodles with sliced lean beef brisket and vegetables in a spicy chilled broth. The naeg myun can be prepared either mild or spicy, buckwheat noodles served with sliced brisket and assorted pickled vegetables. The ojingau bokeum is an aggressively seasoned stir-fry of buckwheat noodles with julienned vegetables and squid, served on a rectangular ceramic tile. Pork lovers will enjoy the jaeyuk kimchi with pork, with steamed tofu to cool the palate down.

Wu Liang Ye

212-398-2308
36 West 48th Street, between
   Fifth and Sixth Avenues
Casual
Reservations
Inexpensive to moderate
All major credit cards accepted
Lunch and dinner seven days
   a week
B, D, F, V trains to 47th–50th
   Streets/Rockefeller Center
   station; N, R, W trains to
   49th Street station

This is a hard place to find, located upstairs off the street on the parlor floor of a small commercial brownstone, midblock on a busy stretch of 48th Street in the heart of the diamond district. I must have walked past it a hundred times until friends suggested I try it, and I'm glad I did. Climb the steps up from the street and into the two dining rooms, the first with a small bar and the second, a little more formal, just beyond it. This is easily one of the best Sichuan restaurants to be found in New York. Decidedly old-school, the wait staff are nearly middle-aged men, dressed in black pants, white shirts, and black vests, who between shifts can be seen doing some light kitchen prep in the dining room. The lunch menu offered weekdays is priced at $6.95, which also makes this one of the great bargains to be had in midtown. The menu is broken down into several categories: Sichuan delicacies and appetizers (nearly all of which are excellent, and many very hot and spicy), followed by an assortment of soups, rice, and noodle dishes, including very good chilled noodles with sesame vinaigrette and a great brisket of beef with noodles in a soup. This is followed by poultry, meat, seafood, and vegetable sections, and yet another list of entrees billed as "chef's signatures." Among the latter, the chef's ma po tofu, a heaping dish of fresh tofu tossed in a spicy black bean and red chili sauce mixing minced pork with scallions, onions, and green pepper, is a bargain at $9.95. Braised beef filet with Napa cabbage and chile is another great choice and a steal at $13.95.

Among the Sichuan specialties, the ox tongue and tripe with roasted chile-peanut vinaigrette is wonderful, as is the steamed fresh bacon, really a double-cooked pork belly served with a garlic-soy-based sauce. The appetizer of sliced conch is tender and richly flavored, paired with a red chile oil dipping sauce. Six crisp, plump, porky fried dumplings arrive with a vinegar-based soy dipping sauce. Dan dan noodles arrive in a bowl, a heap of plain white bare noodles topped with Chinese water spinach and minced pork. Start stirring them together and you bring up the red chile oil, which is set beneath the noodles in the bowl; the blandness of the chewy noodles is satisfyingly offset by the hot oil, the spinach provides a bit of relief, and the minced pork rounds the whole thing out. It's as good a stand-alone plate of noodles as you'll find anywhere.

Service is good, and they have a full bar, a small wine list, and some good beers. All in all, this is one of the best Chinese restaurants to be found anywhere in New York, including Chinatown proper, and a whole lot better than many of the more highly touted, overpriced eateries.

X.O. Kitchen

212-965-8645
148 Hester Street, between the Bowery and Elizabeth Street
Casual
No reservations
Inexpensive
Cash only
Breakfast, lunch, and dinner seven days a week
B, D trains to Grand Street station; 6, J, M, Z, N, Q, R, W trains to Canal Street station

While technically this is a Hong Kong–style restaurant, it's more Hong Kong meets the global food movement. The big, odd-shaped, purple-trimmed sign announces you're there, and once you're inside, the menu is very long and a bit confusing. It's as if the chefs spent time working in some of New York's Western kitchens and brought that experience back here to X.O. How else to explain the spaghetti section, baked clams with cream pasta, baked escargot French style, or the udon with teriyaki? The good news is that most of it tastes really good and the prices are very low. I'm a sucker for salt-baked shrimp or squid, and here they arrive in a pile, warm, lightly breaded, chewy, and salty. Try the fish balls (what are they made of?) with curry sauce. Order the razor clams with black bean sauce, available only on the Chinese menu, the clam meat a perfect vehicle to carry the lovely chunky black bean sauce. I like the taro cake, flecked with chopped vegetables and served with a mysterious black dipping sauce, though I'll agree it's an acquired taste, but the chicken teriyaki, fried and then sliced over sauce, is really decent.

While I'm not a fan of congee, friends who are tell me this place is better than Congee Village, and any of the "over rice" combinations are winning. Try the salted fish, fried rice, or braised stew beef with Chinese vegetables. Let's be honest—I'm not Chinese, I really can't cook in this style all that well, and I don't dissect this food while I'm out to eat, wondering how they made it. I just go for the wow factor. If it tastes good, I'm in. The service is good, and the room is small and always busy, but with food this good at these prices I'll wait and endure.

Yakitori Totto

212-245-4555
251 West 55th Street, between Broadway and Eighth Avenue
Casual
Reservations
Moderate
All major credit cards accepted
Dinner Monday–Wednesday and Saturday 5:30 PM–1 AM, Thursday and Friday until 3 AM; Sunday until midnight.
N, Q, R, W trains to 57th Street station; 1, A, C, B, D trains to 59th Street/Columbus Circle station

Located up a short flight of stairs above Sugiyama, both restaurants celebrate Japanese cuisine, but from different ends of the spectrum. Sugiyama is all about kaiseki, subtlety, small plates, and finesse, and this place is about izakaya, good drinks, small plates, and grilled meat on skewers, chicken mainly. Chicken breast meat, chicken dark meat, chicken livers, crispy skin, tail, and even something billed as "soft knee bone" share the bill. Expect your chicken here to be served medium rare. Don't be wimpy about it—give it a try. The birds they use are all top-shelf, organic, and free range, and experience suggests they're clean and salmonella-free. They even offer a chicken sashimi that's a revelation, dipped in a mix of soy sauce, vinegar, and minced garlic; it is delicious, the creamy texture melding into a sweet, mild, organic, almost grassy flavor. The menu is big and includes tofu-based dishes, fried chicken (well done, of course), rice-based dishes, and even omelets. The crowd tends to be male and Japanese, but it can be a good mix, including foodies on the prowl. On weekends, the kitchen stays open past 1 AM, and if you're hungry after a catching a play nearby, a concert at Carnegie Hall, or the late set at Iridium, this is a great place to hang out, drink, and eat tasty small plates of delicious, albeit occasionally weird, food. That said, don't go hungry or eat too many plates; it can get expensive, as everything is à la carte.

Yeah Shanghai Deluxe

212-566-4884
65 Bayard Street, between
 Mott and Elizabeth Streets
Casual
Reservations
Inexpensive to moderate
Cash only
Lunch and dinner seven days
 a week
6, J, M, Z, N, Q, R, W trains to
 Canal Street station

This strip of Bayard Street now has several of Chinatown's best Shanghai-style restaurants, including Moon House next door and New Green Bo right across the street. If the line is too long at any of these, try one of the others. I'm not in the business of saying who is better, just that they'd all be very good choices. Ignore the dumpling makers hard at work in the front window and the little bridge and rock garden you walk over upon entering. Within this bright, clean, carpeted dining room, there is some very good food to be had. I'm told by locals that the place is often full of Chinese natives who speak with a Shanghai accent, and that some of the staff came directly from Shanghai as well. The soup dumplings are great, of course. Chrysanthemum fish, silly as it sounds, is very good. They take a whole fish, bone in, score the flesh in two directions, dust it in cornstarch, and deep-fry it so that it sort of opens up and blooms. It's easy to separate the meat from the bones this way as well. All the dumplings, steamed or fried, are very good, freshly made, and clean-flavored. Northern-style chicken is sort of like pulled BBQ, with meat taken off the bones and then topped with its skin and served with a dipping sauce. Try any of the eel dishes, especially the eel with chives, the delicious, rich, moist meat bathed in an excellent sauce; it will make you wonder why we don't see this fish on more menus all over town.

Zoë

212-966-6722
90 Prince Street, between
 Broadway and Mercer Street
Casual
Reservations
Moderate to expensive
All major credit cards accepted
Lunch and dinner Monday–
 Friday, brunch and dinner
 Saturday and Sunday
N, R, W trains to Prince Street
 station; 6 train to Spring
 Street station; B, D, F, V
 trains to Broadway/Lafayette
 Street station

Way back when, before Soho became the overpriced designer shopping mall that it is today, there once was a neighborhood, and normal people lived, shopped, and ate there. Steve and Thalia Loffredo had both worked in the restaurant business, he in Boston and she at the Pierre in New York. They met and married, and this was their first and to date most successful restaurant venture together. Named after their daughter, it was a family affair, with Steve's dad and relatives doing a lot of the construction, even building the tables for the place, part of which, it turns out, used to be the dining room/cafeteria for the workers who used to toil away upstairs, stitching together clothes when this part of town was industrial and these cast-iron buildings often housed factories or light manufacturing of one sort or another. The tiled floors and walls are part of the original building.

This was one of the first restaurants in New York to feature an open kitchen, as Steve and Thalia had traveled out to the West Coast prior to opening and were impressed by what they had seen there, in terms of both modern restaurant design and the West Coast wine scene. They had one of the very first wine lists in New York to feature exclusively American wines and to post Robert Parker scores with each listing, along with the price. The menu, trendy back then, is much more mainstream these days, with simple fare cooked well, seasoned well, and priced accordingly.

A good starter is the crispy calamari, which has been on the menu forever and for good reason, as it is better by far than the version served at most Italian restaurants. Here the pile of squid rings arrives golden brown, with a good crunch and paired with a hot, salty, sweet, and sour Vietnamese dipping sauce. The layered spinach salad too has been on the menu a long time; order it and you'll be pleased. Formed using a large ring mold, layers of tasty baby spinach leaves alternate with thin, hand-shaved crimini mushrooms and idiazábal cheese and are dressed with an excellent vinaigrette made from pistachio oil and lemon juice.

For main courses, the filet of organic salmon arrives next to a mound of potato puree, scented with the often-underrated summer truffles, Oregon morels tossed with fava beans, and glazed baby carrots. The East Coast pan roast features local seafood, including Chatham cod, littleneck clams, mussels, and squid, braised together. To this dish they add fregula, a Sardinian pasta that resembles large balls of couscous and which sponges up the pan juices very well, the whole accented by slices of braised fresh fennel and charred tomatoes. For lunch they have one of the best burgers in town, with good beers to wash it down.

Desserts are house-made and very decent. I'm a sucker for coconut layer cake, and theirs is darn good, as is the strawberries-and-cream sundae, layers of dense moist lemon pound cake slathered with lemon cream and accompanied by a scoop of mascarpone gelato and a drizzle of strawberry coulis. As noted, the wine list is all-American, a better idea in 1992 than it is today; I hope that someday soon they'll break the mold and offer many of the good bargains and interesting wines available from beyond our shores.

Soho has changed an awful lot since 1992, mainly for the worse, as it increasingly resembles an urban version of the Mall at Short Hills. Thankfully, Zoë remains a steady, reliable outpost for very good modern food, with service to match.

BAKERIES
and DESSERT
SPECIALTY
SHOPS

Absolute Bagels

212-932-2052
2788 Broadway, between
107th and 108th Streets
Casual
No reservations
Inexpensive
All major credit cards accepted
Seven days a week 6 AM–9 PM
1 train to 110th Street station

In what is becoming more and more common, a family of recent immigrants opened a store for New Yorkers making a very New York product—in this case bagels. But the bagels at Absolute stand among the very best in the city. Run by a Thai family that learned their craft at the excellent Ess-a-Bagel, Absolute Bagels is worth the trip uptown. These run on the big side, and they're chewy on the outside, with a silky, firm, but soft crust, and of course are soft within, with a very nice flavor profile—not as sweet as H&H's, and a bit richer-tasting. While you can take out, they also have a dozen or so tables and serve bagels and nearly all the toppings you'll need. The staff is well trained and friendly, but be prepared, especially on weekends, for the crowds. They bake all day long, so the selection is usually broad, with my favorites being the plain, cinnamon raisin, sesame, and poppy seed. Put it on your top-10 list of bagel places in New York.

Bouchon Bakery

212-823-9366
10 Columbus Circle, in the
Time Warner Building,
third-floor mezzanine
Casual
Reservations
Inexpensive to moderate
All major credit cards accepted
Monday–Friday 8 AM–9 PM,
Saturday 10 AM–9 PM, Sunday
10 AM–7 PM
1, A, C, B, D trains to 59th Street/
Columbus Circle station;
N, Q, R, W trains to 57th
Street station

It's small, but it's superb. Sébastien Rouxel, the pastry chef at Per Se, and one of the most talented in the country, oversees all the production. Not surprisingly, here you'll find some of the best baked goods in all New York City. The croissant is perfection, and the pain au chocolat the same. To that add amazing old-fashioned sticky buns, great Danish, wonderful fruit tarts, and fabulous muffins, and that's just for starters. The TKO, Thomas Keller's version of a giant Oreo, is a lovely snack, as are the giant peanut butter cookies, little chocolate bouchons (deep, rich, and satisfying), perfect madeleines, financiers, and macaroons, especially the caramel macaroons. The assortment of more formal, dinner-style desserts is small but well focused, and the quality nearly without peer in New York. In 2006, they started with a small line of custom, house-made chocolate that stands among the best in the city. There is additional seating in the third-floor mezzanine, where simple lunches and early dinners are served. This isn't Per Se—it's not meant to be—but it's a nice, moderately priced alternative for a lunch or pre-theater dinner should you be nearby. They are open for breakfast, lunch, and early dinner, the coffee is fresh, and the staff is well trained; in short, this place is a little jewel.

Buttercup Bake Shop

212-550-1111
973 Second Avenue, between
   51st and 52nd Streets
   (and elsewhere)
Casual
No reservations
Moderate
All major credit cards accepted
Monday–Friday 8 AM–10 PM,
   Saturday 10 AM–10 PM,
   Sunday 10 AM–7 PM
6 train to 51st Street station

The New York cupcake wars—where did it all start, anyway? Perhaps it was at Magnolia on Bleecker. Jennifer Appel, who owns Buttercup, was a partner at Magnolia back in the day. Billy Reece, who now runs Billy's in Chelsea, also worked at Magnolia. Ditto Peg and Deb of Sugar Sweet Sunshine on Rivington, and Mark Libertini, who owns the Little Cupcake Bakeshop in Bay Ridge, Brooklyn. So many bakers, so many hungry New Yorkers to feed, so many cupcakes to choose from. Who's the best? Who knows? Depends on the day, I suppose. Cupcakes are funny little things. Often the cake, though baked fresh, can seem dry and crumbly, and though the icing is paramount, often it's spread a little too thick, and the ratio between cake and icing is wrong. Truth is, I've had great and terrible cupcakes from every bakery in the city at different times, and sometimes even on the same day.

But I do like Buttercup, and I especially love the coconut layer cake. While Jennifer Appel's plans for franchising have yet to materialize, this flagship location is well worth a visit. The cupcakes, iced with delicious buttercream, are very good and sell for under $2 apiece. They also feature nearly a dozen layer cakes, including a two-layer apple walnut, three-layer carrot, three-layer German chocolate, red velvet, and the southern Lady Baltimore cake, with the great, shiny boiled seven-minute frosting favored by none other than former First Lady Laura Bush. (This information comes through Bill Yosses, who worked a stint as the White House pastry chef during the second George W. Bush administration.) The cheesecakes are all very good, as are the seasonal pies, such as the strawberry-rhubarb, lemon meringue, and pumpkin. It's a very decent bakeshop and a destination in this neighborhood.

Ceci-Cela

212-274-9179
55 Spring Street, between
   Lafayette and Mulberry
   Streets
Casual
No reservations
Moderate
All major credit cards accepted
Seven days a week 7 AM–10 PM
6 train to Spring Street station

Pastry Chef Laurent Dupal runs this little NoLita outpost, offering simple pastry in a quirky little store. At Ceci-Cela, which is more casual Parisian patisserie than Ladurée knock-off, everything is made from scratch; in Dupal's kitchen you'll find flour, butter, eggs, sugar, cream, chocolate, fruit, and the best flavorings. He was born in Nancy, France, and started studying baking at the age of 13. His technique is classically based, and his work shows an eye for excellence in detail combined with a very good palate.

I always try a croissant first to judge a French bakery; the simple things are the hardest to do, and croissants are no exception. My New York favorites are found at Bouchon, Petrossian, and Payard, all uptown. The croissants served here are decent, all butter-crisped on the bottom, with a tissue-thin, shell-like cover and a beautiful fluffy center, coiled and twisted when pulled out from the ends. Not as sweet as the ones at Petrossian, nor as crisp as at Bouchon, but still very good. They also do fruit-filled crêpes, which are nice for breakfast or a light snack, salads, quiche, and sandwiches on good crusty baguettes or softer crumbly brioche. I like the ham, butter, and pickle on a baguette for a quick meal on the run at midday. The cakes and tarts are very good; try the individual banana chocolate cake, with layers of banana mousse and chocolate mouse alternating between good vanilla sponge cake, the whole enrobed in shiny couverture and topped with sliced banana. Some days after dinner at home I wish I'd stopped by his place and picked up an individual bergamot-flavored crème brûlée, so simple and so good. To this add fruit tarts, good Linzer torte, meringue, buttery madeleines in both plain and pistachio flavors, palmiers, cookies, truffles, and specialty cakes to order. All in all, this is one of the best bakeries downtown.

ChikaLicious

212-995-9511
203 East 10th Street, between First and Second Avenues
Casual
No reservations
Moderate
Visa and MasterCard accepted
Thursday–Sunday 3 PM–10:45 PM
6 train to Astor Place; L train to First Avenue

Opened in 2003 as an early dessert-only project by the husband-and-wife team of Don and Chika Tillman, with the help of Donna Ryan in the kitchen, they expanded in 2007 with the takeout-only ChikaLicious Puddin' to accommodate all the business. Room4Dessert may be long gone, and pastry chefs such as Sam Mason, Pichet Ong, and Jehangir Mehta are now blurring the lines between sweet and savory with their newest projects, but this place sets out to do what it did from the start: offer a nice, small dessert-only menu with wines to match. I can only assume that the concept is for folks to have dinner out or at home and then come here for the final course. To that end, it works perfectly, even romantically. The room is lit from above and done mostly in white, with stools set before a bar, the open kitchen just before you on the opposite side. You can choose dessert flights and wines to pair with them and watch your plates being created. In most good à la carte restaurants, the desserts average a minimum of $10 per plate. To that add a glass of port or a dessert wine and you're at $20 in a hurry. Here you get three small plates with a dessert wine pairing for $19, roughly the same price.

A recent menu included a beautiful plate with a section of poached pear set alongside a "salad" of fine julienne of crunchy Asian pear and a small scoop of rich, creamy lemon verbena ice cream paired with a slightly fizzy and sweet 2006 Saracco moscato d'Asti. A rich, dense cornmeal pound cake was served warm and plated with sweet corn ice cream and two peeled grapes floating in a pool of Asti; here another great Italian dessert wine, a 2005 Banfi brachetto d'Acqui, worked well. The dark, dense warm chocolate tart with pink peppercorn ice cream and red wine sauce has fans all over town, as well it should. Taken with a small pour of Graham's Six Grapes Reserve Port, that alone is worth the trip. If the wait is too long, as it can be many nights and weekends at the main branch, which has just 20 seats along with its sit-down bar, the takeout-only shop always has great brioche bread pudding, apple bread pudding, and killer chocolate pudding that you can enjoy in the privacy of your own home.

Cupcake Café

212-465-1530
545 Ninth Avenue, between
   40th and 41st Streets
   (and elsewhere)
Casual
No reservations
Inexpensive
Cash only
Monday–Saturday 7 AM–7 PM,
   Sunday 9 AM–5 PM
A, C, E trains to 42nd Street station

Opened originally as a bakery in 1988 by Ann Warren, for 18 years this little jewel of a bakeshop existed on what was then a very dicey strip of Ninth Avenue in the high thirties. During that time, the place became an institution, while the surrounding neighborhood was changing very fast. With the back end of the Port Authority just to its north, a butcher and a cigar store a few feet away, surrounded by fish markets and funky vegetable markets across the street, and bathed in that urban perfume of exhaust from the seemingly constant stream of traffic backed up outside the Lincoln Tunnel, this place really stood out, and it still does, though now it has moved across the street and a block to the north. You'll still find it offers some of the cutest little cupcakes to be found anywhere.

The cake itself is usually moist and rich in flavor, and the buttercream thick and sweet, but the shop's strong suit is the beautiful floral designs on the cupcakes, which cost between $2 and $3 apiece. Anyone who's done cake decoration will recognize the steady hands at work here—the floral patterns adorning each cupcake are made from custom-colored buttercream and hand-piped blossom by blossom. This is labor-intensive stuff. The shop offers cakes made with the same attention to detail for $30, and special-order wedding cakes are $8 a slice. They also have wonderful homemade doughnuts. There is an 18th Street location as well, tucked within the Books of Wonder bookstore. It's a splendid place for moms and dads to settle down with their children, reading together and sharing great sweets.

Ess-a-Bagel

212-260-2252
359 First Avenue, at 21st Street
(and elsewhere)
Casual
No reservations
Inexpensive
All major credit cards accepted
Monday–Friday 6:30 AM–10 PM,
Saturday and Sunday 8 AM–5 PM
6 train to 23rd Street station;
L train to First Avenue station

Opened in 1976 by the Wilpon and Wenzelberg families, Ess-a-Bagel is considered by many to be the best bagel shop in Manhattan. I won't argue; the bagels here put most others to shame. The families' roots as bakers can be traced back generations to Austria, and the hand-rolled beauties here would make Grandma and Grandpa proud. The interior is circa 1970-some-thing, with a silly chandelier and funky chairs and tables, and the service can be gruff, but who cares—it's all about the bagels. These bagels are on the big side and have just the right balance of chewy and soft, great flavor capped off with a super crust. With two East Side locations, this is the go-to bagel place for this or any other part of town. A classic old-school appetizing store, Ess-a-Bagel carries coffee, assorted salads, and many flavored cream cheese spreads, as well as some very good cakes, rugelach, and seasonal specialties. While there are more and more lousy bagel places opening up every day, Ess-a-Bagel stands at the top in my mind, along with the others outlined on these pages.

Ferrara Bakery and Café

212-226-6150
195 Grand Street, between
Mott and Mulberry Streets
Casual
No reservations
Inexpensive
All major credit cards accepted
Sunday–Friday 8 AM–midnight,
Saturday 8 AM–1AM
6 train to Spring Street station,
6, J, M, Z, N, Q, R, W, trains
to Canal Street station

This is billed as America's first espresso bar and pasticceria. I won't argue. What I do know is that this place has been an anchor for what's left of the old Little Italy neighborhood, centered around the intersection of Mulberry and Grand. Opened in 1892 and still family-run, Ferrara is justifiably a New York City institution. Sad to say, in the minds of many it is probably also dis-missed as a tourist trap, overrated or not what it used to be and therefore not worth visiting, but that view is incorrect. Ernest and Peter Lepore run the place these days, and in many ways it hasn't changed a bit in the last hundred years. Beyond the sparkling-clean mirrored, tiled, and wood-trimmed dining room lies the vast production kitchen. What would surprise many is that they still bake everything right here on the premises. In the back you'll find the nuts and bolts of a good bakery: sacks of flour, 50-pound blocks of butter, three different sugars, slabs of chocolate in various forms, large flour-dusted worktables, mixers, sheeters, ovens, and chocolate-tempering machines. My point is that they work from scratch—no mixes, no frozen junk, no shortcuts.

Take, for example, Ferrara's tiramisu. This dessert is so popular and so often poorly done that I'm loath to write about it at all. But here they make the ladyfingers from scratch, piped out individually and baked on large sheet pans. The filling, which consists of mascarpone, eggs, sugar, coffee, and a touch of brandy, is made the old-fashioned way, separating the yolks from the whites, whipping, cooking, folding, and blending, and the result is as good a tiramisu as you'll find anywhere. Torrone are perfect, and the sfogliatelle are crisp and chewy with a deep flavor, maybe the best in the city. Their cannoli have few peers as well, the dough fried over a copper mold, then allowed to cool before the pastry cream filling is piped in to order. They're crisp and crumbly on the outside and rich and creamy in the center. The pasticciotto ricotta, or individual Italian ricotta cheesecake, is wonderful, and the truffle pastry is a must for chocolate lovers. I even like the silly lobster tail, which is a large cone of puff pastry filled with pastry cream. Espresso arrives hot and foamy, and they scoop a dozen varieties of gelato. I still think the place is a classic. I've never been a huge fan of Italian desserts, but these are among the best in New York, along with DiRoberti's and Veniero's.

Grom Gelato

646-290-7233
2165 Broadway, at 76th Street
(and elsewhere)
Casual
No reservations
Moderate
All major credit cards accepted
Monday–Thursday noon–11 PM,
Friday and Saturday noon–
1 AM, Sunday noon–midnight
1, 2, 3 trains to 72nd Street station

One of the best food shopping blocks in New York just got better. With Fairway and Citarella only a few doors away, now make room for Grom. When they opened, advertising free tastes for the first few days, the lines snaked down the block, and people waited hours—yes, hours—for the free samples. These days you pay, and pay dearly; the stuff isn't cheap, but it's worth every penny. Grom was founded in Turin, Italy, in 2003 by Guido Martinetti, a former winemaker, and Federico Grom, who had worked in finance. Lamenting the lack of true handmade gelato, they took matters into their own hands and opened what they felt was a pure gelato store. Inspired by the slow-foods movement, they sought out rare, organic, and artisanal ingredients for their pure taste.

The chocolate gelato, dark and rich, uses only French Valrhona; the hazelnut is flavored with nuts from the Langhe region; the pistachio, a brilliant and difficult flavor to capture, uses nuts from Bronte; beans for the coffee flavor come only from the Antigua region of Guatemala; and the lemon flavor comes from those huge Sfusato lemons found only on the Amalfi coast, the ones used for the best limoncello. The sorbetti flavors are all made with Lurisia mineral water, sourced from the Italian

Alps. You get the idea. All the product is made in Italy and shipped here every few days in a liquid state and then frozen into gelato on site, ensuring the best quality. Concerned that future growth would be limited by the ability to obtain great ingredients, the pair recently purchased 20 acres in Piedmont, Italy, in order to grow their own organic fruit.

It's a small storefront, with large blue letters above the entrance spelling out the name. The line forms on the sidewalk; as it winds its way indoors, you pass lovely large photos of the select ingredients on your way to the counter. The flavors change, but they usually have vanilla, extra-dark chocolate, regular chocolate, hazelnut, pistachio, zabaglione, cinnamon, stracciatella, gianduja, and cappuccino gelato; lemon, red grapefruit, and coconut sorbet; and lemon or almond Sicilian granita. Prices start at $4.75 for a small scoop and go up from there. Expensive, sure, but the quality and richness of the flavors combined with the creamy, perfect mouthfeel make them worth every penny. If you've never had great gelato, make this your reference point.

H&H Bagels

212-595-8003
2239 Broadway, between
  79th and 80th Street
  (and elsewhere)
Casual
No reservations
Inexpensive
All major credit cards accepted
Seven days a week, 24 hours
  a day
1 train to 79th Street station

Is there an actual answer to the question of who makes the best bagels in New York? New Yorkers get downright silly over stuff like this. The fact is that H&H has to be at the top of any list. In one of those great New York cross-cultural stories, H&H was opened in 1972 by Helmer Toro, a native of Puerto Rico, and his brother-in-law, Hector Hernandez. Their goal was to make the best traditional bagels, and the formula remains the same today. The bagels are made fresh all day long, and yes, sometimes there isn't enough salt in the cinnamon raisin, or the plain bagels are too white, but whatever—for the most part, these are the real deal, expensive but worth it. On weekends there is a line out the door to get in. Once inside, you'll see why. The air is hot and moist and smells like fresh bagels. To the left, there is a refrigerator case with beverages and schmears; to the rear are the cash registers and the heart of the place, the ovens.

These bagels, like all good bagels, are kettle-poached prior to baking. That's what gives them the smooth, shiny surface and chewy, dense texture. They are not too big and blimp-like, as you find elsewhere around town and in the suburbs. They are the right size and, when warm out of the oven, irresistible.

They have a second retail location at 639 West 46th Street, right off the West Side Highway, which is where they do the wholesale baking too. It's right next to a very good car wash, so should you find yourself on your way uptown on the West Side, out to Westchester, Connecticut, upstate New York, or northern New Jersey, get your car washed and pick up a dozen bagels while you're at it. Just watch out for those cops writing $100 seatbelt tickets at the tunnel entrance—don't these guys have anything better to do?

How Sweet It Is

212-777-0408
157 Allen Street, at Rivington Street
Casual
No reservations
Inexpensive
All major credit cards accepted
Sunday–Wednesday 8 AM–9 PM, Thursday–Saturday 8 AM–11 PM
F, V trains to Second Avenue station

Two enterprising and talented young ladies, Ellen Sternau, who had been the pastry chef at the River Café, and Beth Pilar, a food stylist, teamed up initially to form a small catering company, and turned the commercial space they'd rented into this nice little pastry shop. The selection is relatively small, but the quality is very good. There are a few seats for those who want coffee, pastry, and a place to sit, but mostly this is a take-out bakery. On any given day you'll find lovely rugelach, little butter cookies, Linzer torte, and even miniature bananas Foster in cake form. Add to that scones, muffins, small individual fruit tarts, layer cakes, cupcakes, and an assortment of viennoiserie. If you ask, they make little ice cream sandwiches with their cookies and various flavors of Capogiro gelato. It seems, at least for now, that they love what they are doing. They still do catering, but from a space down the block, so this is the "fun" project, one assumes. In any case, for good, old-fashioned, homemade pastry at very reasonable prices, stop by if you're in the area—it's well worth a visit.

Kyotofu

212-974-6012
705 Ninth Avenue, between 48th and 49th Streets
Casual
Reservations
Moderate
All major credit cards accepted
Tuesday, Wednesday, and Sunday noon–12:30 AM, Thursday–Saturday noon–1:30 AM
1, C, E trains to 50th Street station; N, R, W trains to 49th Street station

Designed after a chain of similar cafés in Japan, Kyotofu is a great spot for serious cupcakes, serious snacking, light dining, or late-night people-watching with great cocktails and even better desserts. A jewel of a room, it's also very romantic, done up in shades of off-white with a polished bare wood floor, high-backed, fluffed-up banquettes, tables designed for couples to face each other, and a minimalist aesthetic, all cast in a soft golden light that bathes the room from recessed fixtures. They offer a small menu of savory dishes, including a great soy burger served on a brioche bun with a side of lotus root chips, and the really good meaty alternative, the Kurobuta Puff, a fancy pig–in-the-blanket Japanese-style, essentially a puff-pastry-wrapped Berkshire pork sausage.

The chef, Ritsuko Yamaguchi, does wonders creating excellent sweets based on tofu, melding Asian flavors with Western ones. A good example is the light cheesecake—while it contains a bit of good old-fashioned cream cheese, it's mostly silken tofu flavored with a little sansho pepper and wrapped in a black sesame crust. Speaking of black sesame, try her pudding made of the same seed. I've never been a big frozen yogurt fan, but I do like soft-serve, and here they do a great one made entirely from soy milk. A favorite is the chocolate paired with white sesame. For no extra charge they'll throw in a few spoons of mugi-choco, a crunchy, chocolate-covered puffed barley, reminiscent of children's cereals but much better. Their cupcakes are some of the best in town, and brunch here is well worth the trek just for the dorayaki honey pancakes served with a sweet red bean sauce and garnished with lozenges of blood orange and black currants soaked in shochu.

Lady M Cake Boutique

212-452-2222
41 East 78th Street, between Madison and Park Avenues
Casual
Reservations
Moderate to expensive
All major credit cards accepted
Monday–Friday 10 AM–7 PM, Saturday 11 AM–7 PM, Sunday 11 AM–6 PM
6 train to 77th Street station

My favorite waiter at Petrossian told me about this place one day during breakfast, when I was complimenting him on one of the restaurant's new pastries. I hadn't heard about Lady M, so that very day I went up to check the place out. This old-money section of the Upper East Side can be daunting. Walking past buildings such as 740 Park, billed as "the world's richest apartment building," gives most of us a sense that we don't really belong here. It doesn't help that nearly everyone you walk past is impeccably dressed, carefully groomed, bejeweled, and seemingly without a care. Do any of these people have a job? Well, enough about that. Lady M fits right in: jewel-box sleek, all done in white, brightly lit, and clean, clean, clean. The narrow space has a counter running down the right side, filled with pastry and other offerings, and a few tables to the left. The staff is actually quite nice, genuine, and helpful.

The pastry is indeed very good, though I'm not certain what the overall business plan is for this place. All the baking is done in a commercial kitchen in Long Island City. They do mail-order, and at the moment this is their only retail shop. The signature cake is a classic, the Lady M mille crêpes, essentially a few dozen paper-thin crêpes stacked between thin layers of lightened pastry cream, the top crepe lightly brûléed. At once light and rich, sweet but not cloying, the brûlée at the top is just enough of a counterpoint to all the softness and air below. You can buy the whole thing for $65, a great idea for a party, or just enjoy a slice at one of the tables here at the store after a long day shopping in the neighborhood. During strawberry season, they have an excellent alternative to commercial strawberry shortcake. The montagne de fraises features thin-sliced fresh strawberries adorning a very light vanilla sponge, slathered with whipped cream and topped with caramelized Italian meringue—yummy. Tired of New York cheesecake? Try the fromage blanc gâteau here, essentially a variation on the icebox style using fromage blanc lightened with whipped cream, bound by a little gelatin, flavored with a hint of lemon zest, and topped with a fresh blueberry compote. Each day there is a small selection of sandwiches offered, as well as tea, coffee, and Champagne by the glass, should the spirit move you. All in all, it's one of the best pastry shops in New York, though there is something a bit clinical about the place. Super-clean, neat, white, but with no kitchen, it somehow seems to lack a soul, the sense that behind it all there is a passionate baker and not just some very well-trained drones across the river working long hours. They deliver all around New York and, for an extra charge, ship overnight frozen around the country as well.

Lady Mendl's Tea Salon

212-533-4600
56 Irving Place, between
17th and 18th Streets
Casual
Reservations required
Moderate
All major credit cards accepted
Wednesday–Friday seatings
at 3 and 5 PM, weekends at
noon, 2:30, and 5 PM
4, 5, 6, L, N, Q, R, W trains to
14th Street/Union Square
station

If you're a fan of formal high tea, this is the place, located within the historic Inn at Irving Place, a brownstone built in 1834 that houses Casa Mono and Cibar as well. The rooms are period and gilded—therefore perfect, I assume, for the serious tea crowd. Edith Wharton would have felt right at home with the fresh flowers, pink and white decor, lit candles, fine bone china, and silver to match. As to the tea part, I can claim no particular expertise, nor do I find afternoon tea to be romantic, but apparently some do. The tea selection is traditional and tends naturally to be a bit British, featuring English breakfast, Earl Grey, Ceylon, and Darjeeling, along with chai, chamomile, and other varieties.

Skip the simple mixed green salad, which, frankly, can be had anywhere, but if you're in the mood, the crustless tea sandwiches are nice, dainty examples of this idiom: smoked salmon with dill cream cheese on good, chewy pumpernickel bread; sliced cucumbers on brioche, slathered with mint crème fraîche; decent goat cheese with sun-dried tomatoes on seven-grain bread (not my favorite); and smoked turkey with cranberries on brioche, for a remembrance of Thanksgiving leftovers all year long. Scones are crumbly, moist, and fresh, served with clotted cream and good fruit preserves. The 25-layer crêpe cake I love, but I'm not so crazy about the rather ordinary cakes served daily with fresh berries. You can mostly skip the cookies and the chocolate-covered strawberries that follow.

Along with tea, each guest will receive a glass of Champagne. Again, I must confess that high tea is not my thing, nor are finger sandwiches at 3 PM, but after a good friend dragged me here one day, I can certainly see the appeal for those who somehow see the excitement in old rooms, hushed conversation, tea, and nibbling.

La Tropézienne

212-860-5324
2131 First Avenue, between 109th and 110th Streets
Casual
No reservations
Inexpensive
Cash only
Seven days a week 6 AM–8 PM
6 train to 110th Street station

I have no idea how this great little pastry shop, run by the husband-and-wife team of Roger and Mebe since it opened in 1991, found itself moored here, located on the far fringes of the upper, upper reaches of the Upper East Side, essentially the barrio. I only heard about it when Ron Silver, the owner of Bubby's, told me of it one day during a pie demonstration he was doing for Viking at the 92nd Street Y. Rao's sits a few blocks north, and there are some good tacos nearby at the El Paso Taqueria, but food-wise that's about all she wrote up here. That point established, this is one standout pastry shop, and because it is essentially a neighborhood joint, the prices are so cheap it's crazy. Last time I was there, the excellent croissants were $1 apiece, and these are very, very good croissants. They have takeout as well as room for sit-down.

The menu is eclectic but has some real winners, such as the Tropézienne itself, a sugared sweet brioche split and slathered with rum-flavored crème légère. Thank goodness I don't live nearby, or I fear I'd make it a regular part of my diet. The fruit tarts and layer cakes are all first-class as well. Each day they have some hot food too, as well as sandwiches and quiche. The baguettes are good, the croissants come in a variety of flavors and fillings, and there are brioche in various guises, éclairs, fruit tarts, individual cookies, and the usual mix of baked-from-scratch goodies. All in all, if you live anywhere near here, make this a must visit.

Levain Bakery

212-874-6080
167 West 74th Street,
between Amsterdam and
Columbus Avenues
Casual
No reservations
Inexpensive
All major credit cards accepted
Monday–Saturday 8 AM–7 PM,
Sunday 9 AM–7 PM
1, 2, 3 trains to 72nd Street station

I stumbled upon this place one day after shopping at Citarella and then running over to Nancy's, around the corner, for a few good bottles of wine. It's a tiny slip of a bakeshop on the basement floor of a nondescript building in the middle of the block. The whole place can't be more than 600 square feet, if that, including all the prep area and ovens. Most of the baking is done in an old gas-fired pizza oven, right behind the counter. The baked goods are hit-and-miss, with some of the smaller rolls being the best choices, but what they are famous for, thanks to an article in the *New York Times,* are their huge chocolate chip cookies. Either you love them or you don't. Most love them, but I'm on the fence. To their credit, they are big, moist, and yummy. As a criticism, they are not quite cooked at the center, and I hate the taste of raw dough, which is so common in a lot of American retail and wholesale baking. Maybe people have just gotten used to this, but raw is raw. The cookies weigh a good six ounces, and aside from chocolate chip, they have oatmeal raisin, chocolate chip walnut, and dark chocolate with peanut butter chips. They now have a second store in the Hamptons and a booming mail-order business. If you like your cookies huge, chewy, sweet, and a bit on the raw side, you'll be in heaven here.

Little Pie Company

212-736-4780
424 West 43rd Street, between
Ninth and Tenth Avenues
(and elsewhere)
Casual
No reservations
Moderate
All major credit cards accepted
Monday–Friday 8 AM–8 PM,
Saturday 10 AM–6 PM, Sunday
11 AM–6 PM
A, C, E trains to 42nd Street/
Port Authority Bus Terminal
station

The great pastry chef, cookbook author, and baking instructor Nick Malgieri told me about this place, so I had to check it out. He was right, as often he is in matters concerning pastry. Founded at this location in 1985, they also have another branch downstairs in Grand Central Station. The baked goods sold here are all very, very good. From old-fashioned apple pies to their sour cream walnut, lemon meringue, key lime, sugarless peach cherry, cheesecakes, cherry pie, Mississippi mud pies, pumpkin pie, and a truly great pecan pie, you really can't go wrong. The crusts are flaky, perfectly cooked, and flavorful, the fillings all natural, and the pies as good, I suspect, as you'll find at any great county fair bake-off in America. If you're looking for a classic pie for a holiday meal or as a gift, or if you're entertaining and don't want to bake, look no further.

Their pies are among the best you'll find anywhere in New York, including most restaurants. They also have a small selection of other items, including great quiche, muffins, seasonal breads, lemon pound cake, cupcakes, and moist, rich, dense sour cream coffee cake. The apple-sauce carrot cake is to die for; the apple turnovers too. I even love the chicken pot pie; where else can I get one of those to go in New York?

Magnolia Bakery

212-462-2572
401 Bleecker Street, at West 11th Street
Casual
No reservations
Moderate
All major credit cards accepted
Sunday–Thursday 9 AM–11:30 PM, Friday and Saturday 9 AM–12:30 AM
1, 2, 3 trains to 14th Street station; 1 train to Christopher Street station

Give them credit: this is the place that gave birth to many of the other cupcake bakeries now operating in New York. Originally opened in 1996 by Jennifer Appel and Allysa Torey, this is where it all started. For whatever reason, and there are many—it was, after all, featured on *Sex and the City* and in a funny *Saturday Night Live* skit—there is a line out the door seemingly all day and night. Don't even bother going near the place on weekend nights—I live in the same West Village neighborhood, and on my postprandial wanderings, I am amazed to see 30 or more folks lined up out the door and around the corner in what could be a half-hour wait for a cupcake. And while they wait, they get to watch the icing girl in the window—well, usually it's a girl—manning her triple KitchenAids of buttercream and spreading it thick on the recently baked cakes. Sometimes the cupcakes here are just wonderful, and other times they can be dry and the sugar in the butter-cream too granular. With the kind of volume they do, rumored to be over 3,000 cupcakes sold each day, and the staffing challenges familiar to all New York businesses, consistency is hard to come by.

I suggest you visit during the midafternoon, when there is just a small line, if any (barring the daily *Sex and the City* bus tour crowd). They sell their cupcakes by the piece, around $2 a pop depending on the flavors. You serve yourself, picking the varieties you want from the half-sheet pans up front, loading your own little folded carton, and using the waxed paper sheets to keep your hands clean. Aside from the varieties up front in the window, chocolate or vanilla cake smeared with a few colored icing options, they also have some other baked specialties behind the counter, but it's the cupcakes that they line up for, so go see for yourself. And while you're at it, wander southeast down Bleecker and see just how much this neighborhood has changed since 1996. These days, with Marc Jacobs and Ralph Lauren outposts and lovely antique stores, it reminds me more of a trendy Parisian neighborhood than anywhere else in the city.

Murray's Bagels

212-462-2830
500 Sixth Avenue, between
12th and 13th Streets
(and elsewhere)
Casual
No reservations
Inexpensive
All major credit cards accepted
Seven days a week 6:45 AM–9 PM
F, V trains to 14th Street station;
L train to Sixth Avenue station

Murray's delivers what are consistently among the best, chewiest bagels in New York City. The bagels are classic, old-school, shiny orbs, the kind you can only dream of once you leave this city, with a glutinous, chewy crust, and when cut open they reveal a great bagel aroma that is hard to describe. Go buy a good bagel, cut it open with a serrated knife, and you'll see what I mean. I must say that of late, since 2007, I've noticed that the bagels at Murray's seem to have grown too big. They seem overproofed, and that is a huge drawback. I'm not certain why this is, but when the hole in a bagel virtually disappears and the thickness gets too great, you're talking suburban bagels. If this pattern continues, they won't be in the next edition of this book. There is a lot of variety and bagels are baked fresh all day long, while ample spreads, smoked fish, salads, and meats are provided to pair them with. There's good nova, very good whitefish salad, pastrami courtesy of the Carnegie Deli, and decent strong coffee to wash it all down. If you live in midtown east, you have Ess-a-Bagel, but if you live in Chelsea or the Village, there's no need to look past Murray's for that bagel and a schmear when you're in the mood. Quality here does vary a bit, and on a few occasions the bagels seemed to lack that certain something, but those are the rare days.

Payard Patisserie

212-717-5252
1032 Lexington Avenue,
between 73rd and 74th
Streets
Casual to dressy
No reservations
Moderate to expensive
All major credit cards accepted
Monday–Saturday 7 AM–11 PM;
tea served 3:30–5 PM
6 train to 77th Street station

François Payard is one of the best pastry chefs practicing in America today, and New York is lucky to have him. He had worked in some of the best kitchens in the city prior to opening up his own shop here in the heart of the Upper East Side. This is superb, old-school pastry at its finest; think Fauchon in Paris during in the 1980s. For my money, this is the best pastry shop in the city in terms of quality, consistency, execution, freshness, and variety. You enter off Lexington Avenue into the salon, behind which is housed his excellent bistro (see Payard Bistro review, page 237). The well-lit room is Belle Epoque, with a high ceiling, marble floors and counters, bronze accents, wood paneling, and polished glass displays holding a large selection of classical French desserts along with some of Payard's own inventions. Seating is limited to the coffee bar and a few small round tables throughout the room.

The pastries on display are fine examples of the craft, showing what can be done in the right hands with flour, butter, eggs, cream, chocolate, vanilla, and other natural flavorings and fruit. A telltale sign of the overall quality are the macaroons; varieties sold here include chocolate, coffee, coconut, raspberry, gingerbread, passion fruit, and pistachio, to name a few. All of them here are topped with perfectly formed meringue domes, no cracks, bumps, or other flaws. This is much harder to achieve than you might think. The éclairs are heaven, and all the chocolate desserts feature perfectly tempered couverture, with its signature glossy surface, unblemished and smooth as glass. Aside from well-known classics including the Opéra, the sachertorte, the St. Honoré, and such, they have items like the Chinon, made with pistachio dacquoise and cherry gelée on a thin hazelnut wafer, or the Japonais, made with yuzu-flavored cream and milk chocolate mousse on a sacher-style biscuit. The simple lemon tart is perfection, finding the right balance in the curd between sweet and sour, and with a light, flaky, buttery crust. There are also the Menton, a cream cheese and mandarin orange mousse on a base of moist carrot cake; the baba au rhum, rich, moist, and yeasty; the Louvre, made with chocolate and hazelnut mousse; and the great varieties of buttery sugar cookies. Of course, the croissant and pain au chocolat are among the best in New York.

There is not enough room to write about all the great offerings here. I can only assure you that this is a must-visit, worth traveling well out of your way for. The chocolates sold by piece and weight are superb, the hot chocolate offered in the colder months is lovely, rich, and satisfying, and the pastries, all of them, are of a quality level matched at only a few other pastry shops in town, and nowhere else is there this much to choose from.

Podunk

212-677-7722
231 East 5th Street, between the Bowery and Second Avenue
Casual
No reservations
Moderate
Cash only
Tuesday–Sunday 11 AM–9 PM
6 train to Astor Place station; F, V trains to Second Avenue station

I'm not really a tea person—I drink coffee—but tearooms such as Podunk may change my mind. The owner, Elspeth Treadwell, serves great tea and really good homemade sweet and savory items alike in this tiny slip of a store in the East Village. This Minnesota native and self-taught home baker bailed from her former corporate gig to follow her dream and open this beguiling little gem. A striped awning with blue letters welcomes you; the room is small and rustic, the decor a mix of antiques and vintage furniture. The tea varieties are plentiful, including some of the best iced tea I've ever had in the summer. The homemade pastries in the little display case are all very good, with a slight nod to the Nordic tribe by way of her moist, flavorful cardamom ring, or the dense-grained bread served with some of the savory dishes.

The prices aren't cheap; full tea is $12 for one person or $22 for two, and it comes in either "nibbler" or "rustic" versions, where you can pair sweets and savory dishes as you please. The scones, buttery cookies, toasted coconut cake, and fruit tarts are all fresh-tasting, homey, and well made, as are the homemade jams, jellies, and tea sandwiches. They serve whatever they have coming out of the oven. If you arrive early enough, they may still be baking a good deal of what will become the menu. From beef Wellington and onion tarts to mini cupcakes, the offerings are eclectic but genuinely homemade, humble, and good. And for that alone it's worth a trip.

Be prepared: no cell phones or laptops are permitted. Save them for your neighborhood coffee shop. Here they are after the cool tea vibe. The owner has her rules and does not allow tipping, as it is mostly self-service, but in a sense you can say it's built into the price. In any case, the Old World charm of the place, great teas, lovely food, and serene atmosphere should have you coming back for more once you've tried it. For a variety of reasons, Elspeth's personality among them, this may be the Shopsin's of tearooms, which is fine with me. Take that, Starbucks!

Veniero's

212-674 7070
342 East 11th Street,
    between First and Second
    Avenues
Casual
No reservations
Inexpensive to moderate
All major credit cards accepted
Sunday–Thursday 8 AM–midnight,
    Friday and Saturday 8 AM–1 AM
6 train to Astor Place station;
    L train to First Avenue station

As New York City's various neighborhoods slowly lose their ethnic and individual identities to gentrification and the empires of Starbucks, CVS, and bank branches, I live in fear that someday Veniero's will close too. I mean, we're down to something like two or three classic delis, and with Veniero's and Ferrara, there are now only two great Italian bakeries in a city that once had hundreds. This is a first-class operation that's been doing it all from scratch since 1894—same family, same recipes, same emphasis on quality. As a kid growing up in Philadelphia, I remember that we too had some great local bakeries, such as Termini Brothers in South Philly and little neighborhood places all over town, and when you walked in the door, they smelled just like Veniero's—the scent of pine nuts and almond paste, mixed with cannoli and cream, rum cakes and sfogliatelle.

This place is an institution that speaks to another era, when things moved more slowly, traditions mattered, and people grew up, married, had kids, and raised those children in the same neighborhoods. It's another generation, a New York that really no longer exists except in memory, and so for that reason—and also for their great pastry—this place should be on your list for Italian desserts. The room is classic, with the black-and-white tiled floor, the stained-glass window, the long marble counter, and the rows upon rows of Italian specialty pastries lined up on display. Come here after dinner in Chinatown and have a great espresso, some gelato, a cannoli, or a sfogliatelle, and remember why these community-based ethnic pastry shops were so good in the first place. Great service, great pastries, fair prices, and a welcoming smile—that's enough for me.

CHOCOLATE
STORES

Among the most recent developments in the New York culinary scene is the arrival of great chocolate shops and serious chocolatiers. We've always had a few good chocolate stores in Rockefeller Center and on the Upper East Side as well as the second-tier, larger retail brands such as Godiva (which really doesn't count, as that chocolate is lousy), but for connoisseurs of chocolate, New York has finally arrived as a world-class city for nibbling. Europeans, specifically the French, Belgians, Swiss, and English, have had a love affair with great handmade chocolate for some time, but for years chocolate in America was relegated to inexpensive candy bars and poorly made holiday specialty selections in fancy boxes. Fortunately, when we as a people decide we like something, we move fast, as we now have in our love affair with great chocolate.

What constitutes great chocolate? The best manufacturers source the beans carefully from around the world and then supervise the fermentation, drying, grading, roasting, grinding, and milling stages. Next come conching, a process that develops chocolate's characteristic flavor and texture, and tempering, which gives it a smooth finish. Well-produced chocolate has a bright, glass-like sheen and can be worked thin but firm, resulting in the finished product having a good snap when bitten and literally melting in your mouth. Once you've seen great bonbons—they look like jewels—and tasted them, you'll know the difference. Poorly made commercial chocolates tend to be gray and mottled. The chocolate itself crumbles, has no snap, and can even feel granular in your mouth. Among the greats, there is some debate about what makes the best chocolate, and so now we'll get into a little philosophy. Some chocolatiers use beans from only a single source, and the resulting chocolates are prized for their unique terroir and character. Others find that by blending beans from multiple sources they ensure a more consistent product. I'll let someone else referee that fight. I just want great-tasting chocolate, and that can be had from both camps.

Top-tier chocolates are not cheap to produce, so expect to pay a few dollars or more per piece. However, with chocolates this great, one needs only a bite or two, as the flavors are long, deep, and satisfying. During my most successful weight-loss diet ever, during which I lost over 30 pounds, I allowed myself a few bites of great chocolate, from either artisanal bars or bonbons, each night. As they say, everything in moderation. Better two or three amazing bites than a 6-ounce bar of junk. I'm not a chocolate snob, so the following list includes some of the best chocolate stores to be found anywhere in the country as well as some other all-time favorites that are just very New York and hence are worthy of a visit for different reasons.

Bouchon Bakery

212-823-9363
10 Columbus Circle, in the Time Warner Building, third floor
Expensive
All major credit cards accepted
Monday–Friday 8 AM–9 PM, Saturday 10 AM–9 PM, Sunday 10 AM–7 PM
1, A, C, B, D trains to 59th Street/ Columbus Circle station; N, Q, R, W trains to 57th Street station

Though not technically a chocolate store, starting in the fall of 2006, the small take-out section of Bouchon Bakery (see page 55 and 350) began selling some of the best chocolates in the city. The pastry chef for Per Se, Sebastien Rouxell, is one of the finest pastry chefs working in America today. A French native raised in the beautiful Loire Valley, he is classically trained and has worked at some great restaurants, including the French Laundry. His chocolates are offered by the piece and in small boxes as well. The selection varies from day to day, but the quality and workmanship are stunning. The couverture is tempered perfectly, the outer layer shines like polished glass, and those thin crusts snap when you bite them. The fillings for the truffles are a silky ganache. The flavored chocolates usually include bourbon, épice (which contains a touch of jalapeño pepper along with other spices), lemon, almond, coconut, raspberry, single-origin dark chocolate, and my favorite, sea salt and caramel. Enrobed in either milk or dark chocolate, these are sold by the individual piece, half dozen, or full dozen. While you're there for chocolates, be sure to grab a few pastries as well, which I can assure you are some of the best available in New York, and in America for that matter.

Christopher Norman Chocolates

212-402 1243
60 New Street, between Exchange Place and Beaver Street
Expensive
Casual
Monday–Saturday 10 AM–7 PM
J, M, Z trains to Broad Street station; 2, 3, 4, 5 trains to Wall Street station; 1, R, W trains to Rector Street station

Way downtown, steps off Wall Street, in this old history-rich part of Manhattan with its dark, narrow cobblestone alleys flanked by tall office and bank buildings, sits this little store offering a fine selection of house-made chocolates and specialties. It was started as a hobby in the early 1990s by John Down and Joe Guiliano, both artists by profession, which you can still appreciate in the fine hand and attention to visual design and detail of the chocolates, some of which are indeed hand-painted and made in the rear part of this salon. But unlike some chocolates that look better than they taste, here it's all about chocolate sourcing, chocolate as craft, as taste. Chocoholic friends raved about the place, so I stopped by and found, as usual, that they were right. The store is small, clean, and well designed and lit, and offers an assortment of chocolates and beverages, including great hot chocolate in the colder months. The chocolates made here have intense, clean flavors, from the truffles through the individual bars. The selection changes almost daily, but nearly all I've sampled were beautifully made, had rich balanced flavors, and were as attractive to look at as they were enjoyable to eat.

Food Emporium Bridgemarket Store, Chocolate Section

212-752-5836
405 East 59th Street, between First Avenue and Sutton Place, under the Queensboro Bridge
Moderate to expensive
Monday–Friday 7 AM –11 PM, weekends 8 AM –11 PM
4, 5, 6, N, R, W trains to Lexington Avenue/59th Street station

Yes, you read correctly. It's hard to imagine a world-class chocolate selection as part of any New York supermarket, but the chocolates sold by the piece here are among the best anywhere in the city. Not surprisingly it turns out that the GM of Food Emporium, Hans Heer, a Swiss native, is also something of a chocolate freak. This is his baby, and you'll find a very broad selection of domestic and imported chocolates, bonbons, candies, truffles, and bars, delivered daily from around the world. Producers include Bernard Castelain, Michel Cluizel, Schönenberger, Tschirren, Coppeneur, Knipschildt, Felchlin, Green and Black, Lake Champlain, Christopher Elbow, and Vosges. It even has its own Valrhona boutique. They run chocolate tasting clinics from time to time as well.

Jacques Torres Chocolate

212-414-2462
350 Hudson Street, at King Street (and elsewhere)
Expensive
All major credit cards accepted
Monday–Saturday 10 AM–8 PM, Sunday 10 AM–6 PM
1 train to Houston Street station

Jacques Torres was one of the great pastry chefs working in New York City before he turned his eyes to chocolate and became one of the early pioneers of the artisan chocolate movement. He had the courage and vision to open his first store on Water Street in the Dumbo section of Brooklyn long before that neighborhood became a chic address. He did so, interestingly, with no investors, just his own money and ambition, and the gamble paid off. The store on Hudson Street is part retail, part factory, where shipments of beans arrive daily and are roasted, shelled, conched, and eventually turned into the lovely confections sold in the glass cases before you. You can choose among his great truffle varieties, bars of varying sweetness and cocoa purity, great hot chocolate on cooler days, and sculptures in season. He makes great Easter bunnies, and approaching Valentine's Day, the line goes out the door. He brings a pastry chef's palate to his work—the flavors are clean and mostly traditional. They do serious volume, and he mixes the bean varieties and sources to create a consistent blend all year long. In 2008 he opened a new branch on the Upper West Side at 73rd and Amsterdam, and I suspect he will continue to open satellite stores throughout the metro area in the coming years, making it even easier to get his great-tasting chocolates no matter where you live.

Kee's Chocolates

212-334-3384
80 Thompson Street, between
   Broome and Spring Streets
Moderate
All major credit cards accepted
Monday–Friday 9 AM–7 PM,
   Saturday and Sunday
   11 AM–7 PM
C, E trains to Spring Street station

Ever want to quit your corporate job, follow your dream, and maybe open a teeny-weeny chocolate store in SoHo? That's what Kee Ling Tong did when she opened this small shop in July 2002. She had a serious interest in chocolate, and she bailed out of the corporate world to attend the French Culinary Institute. What started as a flower and chocolate store swiftly turned into just a chocolate store, and her loyal fans around the city are passionate, ranking this among the best. You enter this tiny storefront, and not surprisingly, it smells like chocolate. She's there right out front in the open, alongside the display case, stirring, tempering, and shaping the chocolates by hand.

The goods here are truly made fresh daily, and often the most popular flavors sell out by midafternoon. Typically there are a dozen or so varieties, neatly stacked in the glass display next to some very well-made macaroons. There is a mix of rolled truffles and molded, filled bonbons, including orange, coconut, and blood orange truffles. White-chocolate-covered cognac, green tea, pistachio, jasmine, and tiramisu flavors round it out. Perhaps the most popular item is the tall six-sided piece flavored with crème brûlée and covered with dark chocolate, indeed delicious and original, as is the key lime, a mix of milk and dark chocolate ganache flavored with that southern fruit and enrobed in a crisp dark-chocolate couverture. Other favorites of mine are the honey saffron, ginger, kaffir lime, jasmine truffle, orange confit, yuzu, and dark chocolate with smoked salt. They sell for $2 apiece and are worth twice that. Try a sesame macaroon while you're at it—lovely.

La Maison du Chocolat

212-265-9404
30 Rockefeller Plaza, at 49th Street (and elsewhere)
Expensive
All major credit cards accepted
Monday–Friday 9:30 AM–7 PM, Saturday 10 AM–7 PM, Sunday 11 AM–6 PM
B, D, F, V trains to 47th–50th Streets/Rockefeller Center station

The chocolates here are all made in Paris and air-shipped to New York nearly every day. Robert Linxe is the creator of this brand, which was launched in Paris in 1977, where they have more than a half dozen locations, as well as stores in London, Cannes, Tokyo, and New York. The workmanship is excellent, the quality control top-notch, and the selection broad. A hallmark of this brand is the use of chocolates with no more than 65% cocoa; hence they are on the sweet and smooth side, without any hint of the bitterness often found in the upper 80% cocoa range. They also offer an unusual experience, dubbed Le Parcours Initiatique, for groups of fewer than 15 people: for $60 a head, you get to sample pairings of different chocolates, pastries, and beverages and learn about what makes chocolate great and why. The Madison Avenue location has a small, very elegant tea salon in the rear that is a great place to pass some time eating lovely small pastries or chocolates while pretending to be in Paris. The prices are high, but the quality warrants the expense.

All the truffles feature creamy-smooth and rich ganache. The Habanera collection is a delight, including milk chocolate flavored with mirabelle plum and dark chocolate with vine peaches. My favorites are the mendiants, delicious milk chocolate studded with roasted almonds, pistachios, hazelnuts, raisins, and confit orange rind—pure, grown-up heaven. The caramels too are insanely good, creamy and smooth, not too sweet, buttery, and flavored with pure vanilla, chocolate, chocolate and almonds, chocolate and pistachio, coffee, and coffee and hazelnuts. Frankly, you can't go wrong here—all the chocolates, bars, truffles, other sweets, and pastry are beyond reproach. And in the cooler months, try their chocolate milk. It brings me back to Fauchon, off the rue Royale in Paris, and those ladies in the long blue coats who made the best chocolate milk I'd ever tasted.

Li-Lac Chocolates

212-274-7374
40 Eighth Avenue, just north of Jane Street
Moderate
All major credit cards accepted
Monday–Friday 10 AM–8 PM, Saturday noon–6 PM, Sunday 11 AM–6 PM
1, 2, 3, A, C, E trains to 14th Street station

Originally opened in 1923, for years this place was a fixture on Christopher Street, just off Bleecker, but a number of years back they moved to this strip of Eighth Avenue, a few blocks south of 14th Street. They still offer some very nice, old-style, hand-dipped chocolates, sold by the piece. In a way it reminds me of the old-fashioned candy stores of years gone by, when youngsters could walk in with a little pocket change and buy individual pieces of candy. Chocolate making has come a long way since then, but they still have decent caramels and truffles, loads of those cream-filled surprises, foil-wrapped chocolate-covered apples, and chocolates in the shapes of brownstones, high-rises, animals, dinosaurs, the Statue of Liberty, trains, baseballs . . . you name it. It's a paradise for kids, and those of us who are still kids at heart. They have their own line of chocolate bars too, studded with almonds, walnuts, cashews, or pecans, as well as cream-filled log-shaped rolls, caramels, nut bars, cream-filled patties, and mint bars. Did I mention homemade fudge and chocolate-covered Oreos and graham crackers? And the prices are very reasonable. Most of what I just mentioned is in the $2–$3 range. They do mail order as well. One visit, and I think you'll be a customer for life. Who needs Milky Ways and Mars Bars when you have Li-Lac?

Martine's Chocolates

212-705-2347
59th Street and Lexington Avenue, in Bloomingdale's on the sixth floor (and elsewhere)
Moderate to expensive
All major credit cards accepted
Monday–Friday 10 AM–8:30 PM, Saturday 10 AM–7 PM, Sunday 11 AM–7 PM
N, Q, R, W trains to 59th Street/Lexington Avenue station

A few years back Martine Leventer opened this little store dedicated to making great handmade chocolates that recalled the best of her childhood in France. The French love their chocolates—these little stores are everywhere you turn in Paris, and every little town has one or two. The chocolates are sold by the piece, and then packaged in her signature pink ballotin boxes, very French. The selection varies with the seasons and holidays, and you can also do special orders in advance, such as monograms, logos, or perhaps a little message. Individual pieces, boxes as large as 72 pieces, and nearly everything in between are available. The workers prepare the chocolates out in the open kitchen, like a few other places in town, which adds to the experience.

The daily varieties include filled chocolates, some with brandied cherries, others with ganache, hazelnuts, or soft caramel. There are hand-rolled truffles and buttery caramels, raspberry dark chocolate and milk chocolate, marzipan shapes, and even a few oddities such as the piano-shaped caramel-filled chocolate, the mini Benji filled with pecans and caramel, dried apricots dipped in chocolate, and the classic orangette, a confit of orange rind dipped in dark chocolate. Essentially, there is some-thing here for everyone at every age, and the quality is very, very good.

Michel Cluizel

212-477-7335
888 Broadway at 19th Street, in ABC Carpet and Home
Expensive
All major credit cards accepted
Monday–Saturday 10 AM–8 PM, Sunday 11 AM–6:30 PM
4, 5, 6, L, N, Q, R, W trains to 14th Street/Union Square station

Ask the real chocolate freaks in New York who's the best there is, and the name Michel Cluizel is sure to come up. Certainly he is one of the finest chocolatiers in the country, and we're happy to have him here in New York. Though I hate the location inside that big boxy store, it is what it is, and I go there in spite of the journey. The store in Paris, at 201 rue Saint-Honoré, is a gem, and knowing that makes this location a little worse. But close your eyes, open your mouth, and taste the chocolate, and any misgivings melt away instantly. This is surely chocolate heaven, or one of them. As with some other producers, these chocolates are made elsewhere, in this case Nor-mandy, France, and shipped here. Like very few others, he sources the best beans from around the world and then ferments, dries, roasts, and grinds them himself. He's a purist and uses only a few ingredients: cocoa mass, sugar, cocoa butter, and natural flavorings, with no emulsifier, veg-etable oil, or butter whatsoever. The vast majority of chocolate makers use some emulsifier, usually soy lecithin, as it makes the chocolate easier to work with, but not here. His single-origin chocolates emphasize terroir (like in wines and olive oils), the result of microclimates and soil. Others prefer blends, as they are more consistent, but not this chocolate maker.

The shop carries bars, which are essential to any good home pastry chef or chocolate lover. Each bar lists the cocoa percentage and blend or country of origin. There are bars flavored with natural orange, almond, hazelnut, and milk chocolate, and single-origin bars. The tour de force noir infiniti, at 99% pure and conched to butter-like smoothness, is a revelation. They have truffles, of course, and great filled chocolates. I love the one with Armagnac and dried plums. Another carries the light, polished flavor of lemon zest. To this add raspberry, whiskey, nuts, and caramel—the usual suspects. If they have them, don't ignore the chocolate-covered cherries, which are first soaked in kirsch and meant to be consumed in one bite. Pull off the stem with your front teeth and then chew; the flavors release in order, the kirsch first, then the chocolate, and then ripe fruit, but be careful, as these cherries have pits. They sell chocolates by the piece or the box, and best of all, you can sit at the long, curving bar and try some desserts. They have a liquor license, so you can pair chocolates and drinks, or just try one of the great offerings from the menu. The chocolate chestnut, decadent with framboise, is ridiculously good, the chocolate mousse an epiphany, dark-chocolate-laced crullers . . . well, you get the idea. Oh, and did I mention the chocolate milk?

Myzel

212-245-4233
140 West 55th Street,
between Sixth and
Seventh Avenues
Moderate
All major credit cards accepted
Seven days a week 10 AM–7 PM
N, Q, R, W trains to 57th Street
station

Some will argue that Myzel should not have been included in this guide, but obviously I disagree. Granted, they should not be classified under chocolate stores, as their chocolates aren't very good, but they should be in a category that doesn't exist in this book, such as candy stores or jelly bean heavens. Whatever you call it, I love the place because it is so out of the past and funky, and they have loads of old-school candy. Nearly across the street from the City Center Theater and around the corner from Carnegie Hall, the whole space is tiny—maybe 200 square feet—loaded with dolls and candy, and usually with a little old lady behind the counter. How can you knock a place with jelly beans that taste like cream soda, key lime, and peanut butter? Their roasted nuts, sold by weight, aren't bad either. Skip the fresh-scooped ice cream, though.

Pierre Marcolini

212-755-5150
485 Park Avenue, between
58th and 59th Streets
Expensive
All major credit cards accepted
Monday–Saturday 10 AM–7 PM
4, 5, 6, N, R, W trains to 59th
Street/Lexington Avenue
station

These fine chocolates are made in Belgium by Pierre Marcolini and his brigade and flown here daily. He is one of just a few certified chocolatiers in the world, which assures you that he purchases only the best beans, roasts them on the premises, and makes his own couverture (and everything else, of course) from scratch. He has won some major awards in Europe and is recognized as one of the premier chocolate makers in the world. The products in the small store are close to perfect. I happened to stumble upon this place shortly after the opening in February 2005; I did a double-take walking down that familiar block as I noticed something new. The store manager was very kind, explaining to me who Pierre was (I hadn't known) and allowing me to taste a few of these fabulous chocolates without any pressure to purchase anything.

Here you'll find truffles, bars, and the unique filled little wafer-like numbers called palets fins. There are thin, delicate chocolate squares containing caramel made from chestnut honey, or almond praline and milk chocolate. An eight-piece box will set you back $20, but if ever chocolates were worth it, these are. For a great chocolate education, buy the small box billed as "world flavors"; for $17 you get 7 pieces, one each from a different single source such as Ecuador, Java, or Madagascar, with tasting notes. He also carries those little jelly-like pâtes de fruit that the French and Belgians are so crazy about, though I'm not. Add macaroons, bars, and seasonal items, as well as coffee and tea, and of course amazing hot chocolate. Everything is packaged in splendid little black boxes and tied with silky ribbons. What the store lacks in square footage it more than makes up for in quality; this is one of the best chocolate stores in America.

Richart

Note: As of this printing, Richart is in the process of moving to a new location; address and hours to be announced. Visit their Web site at www.richart-chocolates.com for more.

1-888-RICHART
Expensive
All major credit cards accepted

Working out of his studio in the historic town of Lyon, Michel Richart is considered among the best in France. Like many others who use air freight to expand their business, his chocolates are all produced there and then flown to his various retail locations around the globe. In terms of quality, he is a perfectionist, sourcing only the best chocolate, 70% cocoa minimum, exclusively from Venezuelan criollo beans, then conching it to an unheard-of texture, 12 to 20 microns, resulting in an incredibly smooth chocolate. In terms of style and flavoring, he is a modernist, which some scorn as inappropriate and showy.

The flavors are bold and direct. The selection is broken down by category: roasted, fruity, citrus, herbal, floral, spiced, and balsamic. One of my favorites is the bergamot ganache; the ganache uses heavy cream from Normandy, and the bergamot flavor is pure and surreal. The chocolates billed as fruit coulis pack a wallop of flavor. These include kumquat, citrus essence, and orange zest. The product line continues with roasted flavors incorporating nuts, caramel, and coffee, and moves on to herbal jasmine, basil, thyme, and the stunningly good anise and fennel ganache. The black chocolate–balsamic licorice and vanilla ganache are equally good. If you're really feeling experimental, try the curry or ginger flavors. The designs on the exteriors are playful and modern as well, using colors and geometric shapes on the topmost portion of each piece. Elegantly packaged, boldly flavored, and thoroughly modern, these are expensive, though to my mind, they're well worth every penny.

Teuscher Chocolates

212-246-4416
670 Fifth Avenue, between
  49th and 50th Streets
Expensive
All major credit cards accepted
Seven days a week 10 AM–6 PM,
  Thursday to 7 PM
B, D, F, V trains to 47th–50th
  Streets/Rockefeller Center
  station; E, V to 53rd Street/
  Fifth Avenue station

No one will argue that Swiss don't know chocolate. Dolf Teuscher opened this business in Switzerland more than 70 years ago, and to this day the chocolates are still handmade there and shipped to the various Teuscher stores around the world. This is an older style of chocolate making, classical and perhaps a tad dated for today's ever-growing fans of all things chocolate.

The store too seems a bit out of the past, with displays of bright "fantasy" flowers, chocolates in stacks, and lots of pretty gift boxes and ribbons. But the work is solid and the chocolate tempered perfectly, with good shine on the exterior and a nice snap when bitten. The selection too is a bit old-school, consisting mainly of truffles, pralines, and specialty chocolates filled with creams or nuts. They have sugar-free chocolates, and they do wedding gifts and a big mail-order business. It's interesting for its type, but I prefer La Maison de Chocolat just a few blocks to the north for their varieties.

WINE
BARS

Of all the experiences involved in dining out, perhaps the most intimidating can be ordering wine. The wine lists themselves are not helpful, and the larger the list, the more daunting the task becomes. Customarily they are broken down into broad categories—sparkling, red, white, rosé—then countries of origin, regions within the countries, producers, and specific vintages. So how do you begin to make a good decision on which of more than 350 choices will work with the food you just ordered? Sommeliers and waiters can be very helpful, but if you're not careful, you may find yourself spending much more than you bargained for.

Familiarizing yourself with wines simply involves drinking them and pairing wine with food. Never forget that wine is made not to be sipped by itself but to be consumed alongside meals. To develop a trained palate for food, it's all about exposure. You need to dine out, cook, sample different cuisines, and experiment. Over time you learn, and you simply get better at it. It's the same story with wine. Experiment at home, pair different wines with a variety of foods, and remember what you liked, what you didn't, and why some wines worked so well with certain foods and others didn't. There is no better way to do this, and at bargain prices too, than by frequenting any of the dozens of excellent wine bars that have sprung up all around New York over the last decade. As wine bars exist solely to match food and wine, the staff are well trained, know the wines and food, and can be very helpful. You'll find dozens of wines available by the glass, paired with delicious, simple plates chosen to complement them. Expect to pay between $5 and $10 per glass, with food often priced in the single digits to the mid-teens. As educations go, this is a bargain.

Accademia di Vino

212-888-6333
**1081 Third Avenue,
at 64th Street**
Casual
Reservations
Moderate
All major credit cards accepted
Seven days a week, noon–2 PM
and 5–11 PM
F train to Lexington Avenue/
63rd Street station; 6 train to
68th Street station

Situated below street level, this cellaresque spot seems to be a natural space for a serious wine bar. The team that opened 'Cesca on the Upper West Side a few years back, owner and wine expert Anthony Mazzola and his chef, Kevin Garcia, tapped John Fanning to act as general manager to run this spot on a day-to-day basis as they go back and forth. They opened on August 15, 2007, a date each year when seemingly everything in Italy is closed for the Feast of the Assumption. This address has seen many businesses fail over the years, but I suspect this team will get it right. You enter off the street to the upstairs bar-level lounge, with seating available at the bar and at the tables across from it, as well as a few spots outdoors, weather permitting. The main dining room is found below, down a flight of stairs.

The menu boasts nearly 500 wines, mostly of Italian origin, 20 or so a night available by the glass, paired with a broad selection of smaller plates and a bigger special each night of the week. Start with one of a half-dozen good proseccos and a plate of salumi, or any of a dozen or more small sandwiches—the soft, triangular tramezzini; the grilled panini, filled with cheeses, cured meats, and arugula; and my favorite, the roast peppers and roast pork duo. The lengthy menu continues through hot and cold starters and snacks, some familiar—gnocchi, roasted peppers, fried Roman-style artichokes, and eggplant caponata—and others less so, like the good selection of fresh ripened cheese each day, the calamari that are breaded and broiled, not deep-fried as they so often are, and the addictive little fritters studded with prosciutto and Parmesan cheese. Add a broad, seasonal salad selection, carpaccios of meat and fish, crudos, hand-chopped tartares of meat and fish, more than a half-dozen grilled pizzas, a variety of pasta selections, and, should you have any room left for more, another half-dozen main courses.

Prices range from the single digits to the teens for the starters, small plates, pizza, and pasta offerings. The grilled pizza is one of the better versions in town, chewy and flavorful, with good-quality toppings. The main courses range from the high twenties to the low thirties, with the daily specials on the lower end of that scale. The thick yet tender rolled and braised braciole, a Sunday night plate one day, was very good. On Saturday nights, it's a simple roast lamb, just like you see all over southern Italy. The wine list, while Italian-centric, is impressive, with choices from the mid-twenties up to the big bucks for those Super Tuscan hybrids and older vintage Barolos. The ambition and scope of the menu should move this entry away from the wine bar category and into the restaurant section, but Accademia di Vino is essentially a great wine bar with a restaurant wrapped around it.

Aroma Kitchen and Wine Bar

212-375-0100
36 East 4th Street, between Lafayette Street and the Bowery
Casual
Reservations
Moderate
All major credit cards accepted
Monday–Friday noon–midnight, Saturday and Sunday 6 PM– midnight
N, R, W trains to 8th Street station; 6 train to Bleecker Street station; B, D, F, V trains to Broadway/Lafayette Street station

This decent little wine bar is run by a couple, Alexandra Degiorgio, originally from Malta, and Vito Polosa, a native of Potenza, Basilicata, deep in the south of Italy. The small but good wine list is entirely Italian, and offers some good finds from small producers. Last I was there in 2007, the chef was Chris Daly. His pastry chef was Shawn Darling, and that may have been the entire kitchen staff, less a pot washer. The food is simple but works well with the wine list, as it should.

You can begin with a good glass of prosecco from Silvano Follador; dry and slightly fizzy, it works well with a plate of rosemary-scented olives, cheeses, salumi, or the simple salad of sunchokes, squash, and beets and artichokes. Cavatelli or pappardelle are dressed in a rich Bolognese sauce. Pick any sangiovese they have, or perhaps a Montepulciano; either one works well with this dish. Baked squid is stuffed with shrimp, capers, almonds, and parsley; reach for the lovely Neapolitan Greco di Tufo if they still have it on the menu, or the Tiburzi Brigante. Order the Daisyfield roast pork chop medium or medium rare, a good piece of meat served with escarole and potatoes, and try it with the Cascina La Ghersa rosé from Piedmont, made with barbera grapes, or the Fattoria di Valiano chianti classico, a single-vineyard, hand-harvested gem from Tuscany. You can order wines by the flight, and sample four glasses of smaller pours for $20. If the main room fills up, there is an additional dining room downstairs to the rear, nearly subterranean, with an antique European feel, an open beamed ceiling, a decoratively painted stone floor, and one long communal table made from heavy old planks that Vito found at a demolition site a few blocks away, hauled here, and refinished. It's a great space for a small party; racks of wine line one wall, candles light the room at night, and the kitchen is on the same floor.

Desserts too are good. Try the gianduja panna cotta, a light but flavorful plate. Vanilla bread pudding is hard to resist, as is the Sicilian pistachio crème brûlée. The menu, while small, does not overreach, the wines are all fairly priced, and the owners are on hand most every day for each service, which ensures a certain level of welcome and competence. Overall this is a fine place to while away some time alone with a book or with friends over good food and wine.

Bar @ États-Unis

212-396-9928
247 East 81st Street, between
Second and Third Avenues
Casual
No reservations
Inexpensive
All major credit cards accepted
Monday–Friday noon–midnight
4, 5, 6 trains to 86th Street
station; 6 train to 77th Street
station

Run by a father-and-son team, this little hole-in-the-wall happens to be a great wine bar. With a half-dozen seats at the bar and a few more at the banquettes along the wall, this cubbyhole of a room may be the smallest wine bar in all New York. It is the offshoot of its big brother, the original États-Unis restaurant directly across the street. The Bar @ États-Unis shares most of its prepared food and interesting wine list with the original location, but the bar is a more casual setting, geared for lighter meals and wines by the glass. There is no cooking done here; they have no kitchen, just a toaster oven, a panini press, and bowls for mixing salads, with some of the food coming from the restaurant kitchen across the street. Although it sounds odd for a wine bar, they make an excellent guacamole from scratch that works very well with any of their sparkling wines. I recently paired it with the dry Colli Trevigiani prosecco, an excellent example of how crisp and bright good prosecco can be when not sweetened artificially. The Caesar salad is another good starter, topped with fresh grated Parmesan and redolent of anchovies. There is always a soup of the day, or try one of their simple terrines.

Entree choices include a fish special, usually straightforward and reliable, a choice of panini, and in the colder months a stew of beef or lamb or a braised Niman Ranch pork shoulder. The wine list is printed daily and features 20 or so wines by the glass, including a good sparkling selection where you may find that great prosecco, nonvintage Champagnes, and even several hard-to-find, wonderful sparkling ciders from Normandy. On a recent visit, I had a great silky Sancerre, Fournier Père et Fils Les Belles Vignes 2002, with my starter, a roasted beet salad course, followed by a wonderfully open, soft, and round St. Chinian from the Languedoc, Château Fontanche Cuvée Pierre Antoine 2001, with a navarin of lamb. The menus and wines vary daily, as they should, but the staff are very helpful in guiding you with pairings that work.

Bar Jamón

212-253-2773
125 East 17th Street,
between Irving Place and
Third Avenue
Casual
No reservations
Moderate
All major credit cards accepted
Monday–Friday 5 PM–2 AM,
Saturday and Sunday
noon–2 AM
4, 5, 6, L, N, R, Q, W trains to
14th Street/Union Square
station; L train to Third
Avenue station

This is perhaps the smallest wine bar in town. It has to be under 400 square feet, and was originally opened by the folks that ran Verbena just around the corner (now Casa Mono, which, like Bar Jamón, is part of the highly successful Mario Batali/Joe Bastianich empire). Past the little window display of fruits and jarred preserves, you enter the tiny dining room and bar area. A small sign announces, as the name implies, that this is a ham bar, specializing in cured meats, regional cheeses, olives, and a comprehensive selection of the best wines from Spain—all good news and mostly true. While sometimes it seems the place is packed with the spillover from Casa Mono, that's sad, as the food here—prepared by Andy Nusser, sharing a kitchen and cooks with the other restaurant—stands on its own and is quite good.

The space, as mentioned, is tiny, with the bar and a few long tables parallel to it, with seating for maybe 15 total guests. In the spirit of tapas bars, here you order a succession of small plates and pair wines as you choose. Try the small salad of greens, anchovies, and smoky chorizo; a slice of the creamy potato omelet; the tortilla; or any of the thin-sliced aged Spanish hams, washed down with a good glass of chilled vino verde. The pickled sardines are good, but the pickled pigeon was a dish that I didn't think worked too well. Opt instead for the good canned tuna with a salad, gazpacho style, or the cured pork tenderloin known as lomo. The wines change frequently, but as we've come to expect with these Batali-Bastianich partnerships, they are all very well selected and fairly priced. Off hours it's a good, fun hangout, but I would not recommend it for a romantic night out unless your idea of romance is a date shared with 15 total strangers in a room not much bigger than a phone booth.

Bar Veloce

212-260-3200
175 Second Avenue, at 11th
Street (and elsewhere)
Casual
No reservations
Inexpensive
All major credit cards accepted
Seven days a week 5 PM–3 AM
L train to Third Avenue station;
6 train to Astor Place station

I've lost count of how many branches of Bar Veloce there are now—maybe five? But the first one I visited was the original on Second Avenue in the East Village. It's a tiny, well-designed slip of a store, barely 15 feet wide, with a sleek bar and a row of stools before a tiny wall-mounted table. The two owners, Frederick Twomey and Chris Cannon, met while working at Remi. Cannon also had a piece of Judson Grill when it was open, and is one of the partners behind the highly regarded Convivio in Tudor City. Not surprisingly, they know wine and how to capture a vibe. The blond wood bar, backlit display of wine bottles, candles, and soft lighting throughout give the place a pleasant glow. They have a few dozen wines open by the bottle every day, mostly Italian, and serve good simple food to nibble on while drinking. The place was at one point a late-night hangout for chefs and restaurant workers.

They offer simple panini, plates of cheese and cured meats, and a few sweets. The wines change often and are mostly priced between $8 and $12 a pour. The sandwiches are good, layering speck with taleggio cheese and grappa-cured apples in one, or prosciutto with mushrooms and truffle oil in another. The bartenders wear dress shirts, ties, and lab coats, and the place has a younger crowd, lending a hip East Village feel to the festivities. If you're in the mood for a late-night snack, find yourself early for a feature at Cinema Village East a few doors down, or just want to check out some interesting Italian wines and have a good nibble, this is the place.

Casellula Wine and Cheese

212-247-8137
401 West 52nd Street, between
 Ninth and Tenth Avenues
Casual
No reservations
Moderate
All major credit cards accepted
Seven days a week, 5 PM until late
1, C, E trains to 50th Street
 station; N, R, W trains to
 49th Street station

On this northwestern fringe of Hell's Kitchen, you'll find a lovely little space to sit and repair after a busy day. Should you like wine and cheese, you've hit the lotto, as that is what this place does best. Their name says it all: they like cheese, really, a lot, and they buy it fresh and nearly daily thanks to cheesemeister Tia Keenan. The wine list is good, small, tight, and well organized, and pairs well with dishes like stuffed pappadew peppers with buffalo mozzarella, peppers, and speck; bigger plates include a duck confit salad, and sandwiches made from "pig's ass" (that's a quote) or braised short ribs with provolone. The room is small and square, with a very friendly staff, and the standouts, aside from the simple food, are the really great cheeses offered with the wines. Divided by style—fresh, bloomy, and soft-ripened, cooked and pressed, washed and blue—they are offered by the piece, plate, or flight with custom-made accompaniments, little fruit purees, or savory baked items. If you like cheese and wine, this place is a standout not just for the neighborhood but in the entire city.

Centovini

212-219-2113
25 West Houston Street,
between Greene and
Mercer Streets
Casual
Reservations
Moderate
All major credit cards accepted
Monday–Friday noon–3 PM and
5:30–11 PM, Saturday noon–
4 PM and 5:30–11 PM, Sunday
noon–4 PM and 5:30–10 PM
N, R, W trains to Prince Street
station; B, D, F, V trains to
Broadway/Lafayette Street
station

The owners of Moss, a design store in SoHo, and the restaurateurs behind I Trulli collaborated to create this very good though expensive wine bar on the northern fringes of SoHo. The space is small and has a European feel to it, with a long white marble bar lit by colorful Venetian glass hanging lamps, and the bar stools are made of sleek stainless steel and white leather. The dining room features small black tables, black chairs, gray walls dotted with large framed portraits, and bottles of wine stored in cubicles above the brass coat rack that runs the length of the wall. The place has evolved over the years and has gotten much better. The cooking is mostly southern Italian, though dishes such as cotechino Modenese, a sausage specialty, can also be found on the menu. They have a good, large selection by both the glass and the bottle. The prices per glass run a little high, which is made even more obvious by the fact that they own the adjacent retail store, where the bottle prices are usually identical to the prices of two glasses of wine, sometimes less. That said, you can eat well here, sampling some great food paired with a variety of well-chosen wines, for well under $50 per person.

The opening chef, Patti Jackson, keeps the food pairings good and simple. As at so many small restaurants in Italy, the pastas are made fresh each day by the proprietor's mother, in this case Addolorata Marzovilla. The lunch and dinner menus are broken down into simple categories: antipasti, panini, primi, and secondi. Start with chunks of the salty, mildly acidic Roman sheep's-milk specialty, pecorino cheese, paired with thin slices of cured speck, or the creamy burratina, a salty, peppery buffalo mozzarella flown in twice a week from Italy, paired with house-roasted peppers and chunks of excellent cured culatello-style ham. For pasta, if it's on the menu, order the cavatelli with broccoli rabe, swimming in good olive oil and garlic. This is as good as the one my grandmother used to make. Chewy hand-cut maccheroncini comes with a rich Bolognese sauce dotted with peas. Both these pastas sell for $18 each and are as good as or better than many versions served all over town for nearly twice the money.

In the summer, I love the Sicilian tuna salad, sort of a Sicilian tuna niçoise, combining rich, brown-red canned tuna loin with haricots verts, pickled eggs, and roasted beets. In the late winter and spring they offer imported puntarelle, a delicious Italian vegetable from the chicory family, tossed with chanterelle mushrooms, sliced culatello, and fried quail eggs, easily a meal in itself. In the colder months, they have braised meats, veal cheeks and the like, all good. In the summer, the fare is lighter. The wine list changes often but is very good, though, as mentioned, it's a bit on the expensive side. All in all, if you're hungry and in the SoHo area shopping, you could do far worse than to settle here for a few hours to repair.

Enoteca I Trulli

212-481-7372
124 East 27th Street, between
  Lexington Avenue and
  Park Avenue South
Casual
No reservations
Inexpensive to moderate
All major credit cards accepted
Lunch Monday–Friday noon–3 PM,
  dinner Monday–Thursday
  5:30–10:30 PM, Friday 5:30–11,
  Saturday 5–11, Sunday 5–10
6 train to 28th Street station

An offshoot of the decent Pugliese restaurant next door, Enoteca I Trulli showcases the wines of Italy, mostly the deep south, with some very decent food to pair with it. Nicola Marzovilla and Charles Scicolone's wine bar has a minimum of 40 bottles a day available to sample. You can choose your selections by the glass or by the flight, which is a great way to taste a lot of wine. Here they pour three 2-ounce glasses per flight, priced in the $10–$13 range. Sit at the marble bar or the small tables across from it and order simple plates from the short but excellent menu.

If you liked anything you had, you can probably buy a bottle at Vino at 121 East 27th Street, which is run by the same team. The wines run the gamut from big Barolos and brunellos to barberas, barbarescos, chiantis, traminers, falanghinas, and proseccos. The selection is well put together, and the food simple—plates of salumi, cheeses, olives, simple pastas, soups, and appetizers from the kitchen next door at I Trulli make this place a lovely spot to pass a few hours, expanding your palate while eating well at the same time.

Flute

212-529-7870
40 East 20th Street, between
  Park Avenue South and
  Broadway (and elsewhere)
Casual
Reservations
Moderate to expensive
All major credit cards accepted
Sunday–Wednesday 5 PM–2
  AM, Thursday to 3 AM, Friday
  and Saturday to 4 AM
6, N, R, W trains to 23rd Street
  station

As if you couldn't guess from the name, this is New York's only full-blown Champagne bar. And judging by the hours it is open, it answers one nagging question: where can you go at 1 AM on Sunday night to sip Champagne by the glass? Seriously, if you are in the mood and have the money, this is a great place to go to nibble on food and drop some serious cash on good bubbly. The owner and architect behind the idea is a Frenchman, Hervé Rousseau, who now runs two such establishments in New York, this and another on West 54th Street. I'd walked past the Gramercy location hundreds of times, as it sits just down the street from Gramercy Tavern. The place has the look and feel of a private club, or a hangout for wealthy frat boys, so it took me years to walk in and give it a try. What you'll find is a darned good selection of Champagnes and sparkling wines: more than 120 by the bottle (including an impressive selection of great vintage and nonvintage Champagnes) and over a dozen or so by the glass, as well as some good Champagne-based cocktails. During the year, they also offer a fair amount of Champagne-tasting classes and events.

Food choices are limited to little nibbles, but you can sample spring rolls, some excellent caviar courtesy of Petrossian, chocolates from Maison du Chocolat, or, should you desire, strawberries dipped in whipped cream. The space is spread out over three levels, with an upstairs lounge featuring little private candlelit seating areas that lend themselves to established romantics. The main floor is more a singles scene, replete with live jazz Sundays and Wednesdays, a DJ on the weekends, and guys and gals on the hunt most every night. So if you're in the mood for a rare Bollinger RD and have a few hundred bucks just waiting to be spent, this is your spot.

'inoteca

212-614-0473
98 Rivington Street,
    at Ludlow Street
Casual
No reservations
Inexpensive to moderate
All major credit cards accepted
Monday–Friday noon–3 AM,
    Saturday and Sunday 10 AM–
    3 AM
F, J, M, Z trains to Delancey/
    Essex Street station

I'm not certain if 'inoteca should be considered a wine bar or a restaurant, but I'll take my cue from the owners, three guys who worked at Lupa, 'ino, and Otto, who named this place as a play on the Italian word *enoteca*, "wine bar." It's been packed since it opened, and for good reason. The wines they pour are well selected and well priced, and the food, basically little plates of this and that, work nicely with the wines. The scene is mostly downtown, skewing young and hip, but don't be surprised to find serious wine geeks here passionately discussing terroir, malolactic fermentation, and stainless steel versus oak.

The big, open corner room is simple, with plenty of natural light by day and good views to the street. The bar and tables are all natural wood, rough-hewn, and rustic. The food, most of it in the $7–$12 range, consists of bite-sized portions served on small white plates. The menu is divided into sections, with an emphasis on sandwiches of various types: standard tramezzini, open-faced bruschetta, and warm panini. They have a nice plate of cured meats and a decent prosciutto, both of which work very well with the good prosecco they pour. A fine assortment of cheeses includes good crumbled dry Parmigiano Reggiano, cacciocavalo, fresh buffalo mozzarella, and pecorino. Small salad plates vary by season, but they usually have roasted beets with orange and mint, grilled squid mixed with white beans and loads of excellent olive oil, arugula with bresaola, and tomatoes in season. Desserts are simple—the panna cotta is enjoyable, as is the warm, runny Nutella panini.

Le Bateau Ivre

212-583-0579
230 East 51st Street, between Second and Third Avenues
Casual
Reservations
Moderate
All major credit cards accepted
Seven days a week 8 AM–4 AM
6 train to 51st Street station;
E, V trains to Lexington Avenue/53rd Street station

Opened in 1999, this is one of New York's more interesting wine bars. First off, they carry well over 250 selections, many of those by the glass. The wines are all French and are divided by region, then by white, red, rosé, and Champagnes. To this add a few beers, some ports and dessert wines, and a full menu all day and night. Can't make up your mind? Try the tasting tray with five 3-ounce glasses for $20, or nine for $35. The selection is impressive, with $300 Burgundies alongside humble Bourgueils, a 1983 Petrus for $1,100, and a lovely 2004 Faugères from Abbaye Sylva Plana for $10.50 a glass.

The food is mostly decent too, such as a good onion soup gratinée, mussels steamed with white wine, and clams and oysters on the half shell, as well as other chilled seafood specialties, half a lobster, and such. Crusty Poîlane-style country breads are served with decent pâté, assorted cheeses, and a good croque monsieur. If you're in the mood for heavier fare, the lamb chops are good, as are the duck confit and the hand-cut fries. In the warmer months, tables are arranged on the sidewalk, and as the place fills, it is a most pleasant way to spend a night: sampling very good wines by the glass, with decent food to match, and doing some people-watching, New York style.

Morrell Wine Bar

212-262-7700
1 Rockefeller Plaza, between Fifth and Sixth Avenues, across from the skating rink
Casual
Reservations
Moderate
All major credit cards accepted
Monday–Saturday 11:30 AM–midnight, Sunday 11:30 AM–6 PM
B, D, F, V trains to 47th–50th Streets/Rockefeller Center station

The Morrell family has been a fixture on the New York City wine scene for several generations. With retail roots going back to the 1950s, they now are a leading auction house and have added a wonderful wine bar to their list of services. Tucked right next to their retail shop, the wine bar takes advantage of this fabulous setting, and weather permitting, the outdoor seating is some of the best in town. The muscular art deco architecture throughout Rockefeller Center is stunning. It's hard to imagine a better place to sit down and enjoy a simple meal with a few glasses of great wine.

The interior of the wine bar is small and sleek, with the little bar to your right, table seating around it, and a stairway to the left, leading to more seats and tables on the open mezzanine above. I prefer whenever possible to sit outside at one of the dozen or so umbrella-shaded tables and take it all in. In the spring, summer, and fall, there are flowers, an occasional art installation, and a seasonal Greenmarket, while traffic on this strip of 49th tends to be light. In the winter, with the Christmas tree, the skating rink, and that piped-in music, add a touch of snow and it's magical. Or maybe it's the 2,000-bottle wine list or the 100-plus wines available daily by the glass at $8 and up.

The kitchen upstairs is tiny, thanks to the building's landmark status they were allowed no gas to cook with nor hoods to vent. Yet from this closet-sized, all-electric kitchen, you can choose from an assortment of appetizers and main courses done surprisingly well and designed with wine in mind. Smoked meats and fish are paired with seasonal fruits and salads, a daily selection of cheeses, oysters served chilled on the half shell, roasted beets drizzled with good olive oil, a silky terrine of foie gras, a very decent onion tart, plates of charcuterie, and steak tartare to begin your meal. Follow that with a bowl of truffle and mushroom risotto, good simple pastas, braised veal cheeks, lamb stew, juicy pan-seared Muscovy duck breast, or a filet of dorade.

Desserts are simple but good: puddings, cobblers, fruit tarts, and assorted biscotti, all screaming for a glass of wine. To that end, they offer no less than a dozen varieties of vintage and nonvintage sparkling wines, from domestic Iron Horse Blanc de Noirs for $11 and a Banfi Brachetto d'Acqui from Italy at $12 to a stunning 1992 Dom Pérignon for $36. That's the beauty of this place—you can come on a budget and just sample some interesting wines with good food, or you can make it an occasion, celebrate a birthday or anniversary, and drink some amazing wines by the glass that you might never try if you had to buy a whole bottle—say, a Corton-Charlemagne Grand Cru from Frédéric Magnien for $58 per glass, or a Phelps Insignia, vintage Opus One, a Pisoni Testarossa, a 1993 Latour, or Ornellaia from Tuscany at $52 a pour. Finish the night with a 20-year-old port, amazing Vidal ice wine from Canada, or the rare Austrian Kracher Trockenbeerenauslese, aged for 16 months in new oak, for $40, and walk off into a New York night you'll never forget.

Nectar Wine Bar

212-961-9622
2235 Frederick Douglass
   Boulevard (Eighth
   Avenue), between 120th
   and 121st Streets
Casual
Moderate
All major cards
Seven days a week 5 PM–1 AM
2, 3, A, C, B, D trains to 125th
   Street station

The proprietors of this fine little wine bar also own Harlem Vintage, a great wine store literally next door. The feel of the place is modern, with a gray concrete floor, a half-moon-shaped white bar, and a wall painted burgundy, and there are a handful of tables set about the room. The wine list is interesting, favoring Europe and America, but full of surprises nonetheless. Both owners hold MBAs and were drawn to the wine business because, well, they love wine—reason enough for me. On any given day, you'll find a selection of bubbly as well as nearly three dozen wines by the glass, most around $10. To go with the wine, they offer a very decent selection of cheeses and salumi with crusty bread, good foils for both the red and white wines poured here. As with many of the modern smaller wine stores and wine bars, the selection comes from smaller producers as well. So it's not at all uncommon to buy a bottle or try a glass, return in a month or two, and find that it's gone, out of stock until the next vintage arrives. All the better, as this makes us leave our familiar wine comfort zone and experiment with new producers, new varietals, and new countries of origin, expanding our palates at the same time.

Peasant Wine Bar

212-965-9511
194 Elizabeth Street, down
   the steep steps next to
   Peasant
Casual
Reservations recommended
Moderate to expensive
All major credit cards accepted
Tuesday–Sunday 6 PM–2 AM
6 train to Spring Street station,
   N, R, W trains to Prince
   Street station

Peasant tends to be a very busy restaurant and is often hard to get into, especially on short notice, but here, just below it, you have an excellent alternative. Climb down the steep steps off the sidewalk, push open the antique wooden door, and the subterranean world of Peasant Wine Bar is before you. Lit by bare bulbs and candles, this place is like stepping off Elizabeth Street and into a friend's 18th-century barn in the countryside of southern Italy. Chef Frank DeCarlo built this place himself, a few hours at a time, usually late at night after work upstairs. The project took him a few years. He did the masonry, put together some of the old wooden tables, laid out the bar, and put up the walls. The tables, arranged communal-style, consist of long, unadorned planks of wood, some literally cut from half a tree, with the bark still exposed on the bottom. The wooden chairs are simple and rustic, a mix and match from antique stores, Dumpsters, and DeCarlo's mother's barn in Mountainside. The bar is at the rear, with seating for 8 to 10 more, and features an all-Italian wine list with many good selections by the glass, and even more by the bottle.

What makes this place shine is the food. Unlike most wine bars that have a limited kitchen, if any, and hence can only offer simple cold dishes, salads, cheeses, pâtés, and pressed sandwiches off an electric hot plate, the food here all comes from that great kitchen upstairs. That's correct: down here you get to eat Peasant's food, cooked in the same kitchen, with wine by the glass and no noisy crowds. In some ways, I may prefer this room, especially early in the evening when you can dine down here with just a few others and read a book, or have a quiet conversation with friends. Order the cold salumi with cheese and fruit plate, and what arrives is a large platter featuring quartered figs in season, mixed with melon, strawberries, pineapple, and hard fruit, along with chunks of hard, soft, and runny cheeses and thin-sliced bresaola, Italian prosciutto, and hot spiced salami and mortadella. This could be a late-night meal in itself, accompanied by the good, fresh, crusty bread from Sullivan Street Bakery and washed down with a glass of chilled prosecco. Try the same great baked sardines as they have upstairs, or the octopus baked in oil, paired with a good, straw-colored gravina. The small pizzas served here are a perfect match for the light, fruity barbera wines. Desserts also come from the same kitchen, and after dinner and espresso, try a glass or two of grappa, moscato, or malvasia, to brace yourself before climbing those steps back up into the New York night. The food here may be the best of any wine bar in New York. Add the rustic feel and the good wines, and you have a winner.

Sakagura

212-953-7253
211 East 43rd Street, between Second and Third Avenues, B1 level (basement)
Casual
Reservations
Moderate
All major credit cards accepted
Lunch and dinner Monday–Friday, dinner Saturday and Sunday
4, 5, 6, 7, S trains to 42nd Street/Grand Central station

Nearly impossible to identify from the street, as there is just a small sign fastened at knee level to the front of the office building that it inhabits, this is more speakeasy than traditional wine bar. You enter through the building's bright, fluorescent-lit lobby, and then descend the service steps, past the boiler room, beneath much ductwork, and past walls of white-painted cinder blocks, to this subterranean sake bar, which just happens to boast one of the best collections in the country.
With more than 200 sake varieties to choose from, Sakagura attracts Japanese expats and Western fans of casual Japanese food and great sake.

After several visits, it occurred to me that this is the Japanese version of a tapas bar, with a good menu of small plates designed to work with sake. The room is long and features backlit rice paper panels and much natural wood. To the left, there is a long, polished wooden bar that accommodates well over a dozen guests. On my first visit, we had already had dinner across the street at Yasuda Sushi and were really just there for a nibble. We started with an order of onsen tomago, essentially a small bowl of cold soup, the broth tasting of dashi, those smoky bonito flakes, and in it swam a slow-poached egg, salmon roe, and a piece of sea urchin. Though a small wooden spoon was placed beside it, it was best to just drink it down in a few flavorful gulps. I'm told that this slow-cooked egg style hails from the Japanese hot springs, where it is customary to cook whole eggs in their shells directly in the springs themselves, and also common to have this dish for breakfast. We moved on to a dish that consisted of thin, see-through crispy wafers, made from a tight weave of cooked, pressed fish resembling miniature anchovies, served with a spicy dipping sauce. The udon noodles are good, as are the soy-braised pork belly and the gyutan, tender braised veal tongue, served with miso. Grilled Asian eggplant comes with three dipping sauces, and thin sections of pre-sliced, well-marbled beef arrive raw, to be cooked on a hot black stone set on the table, along with a soy-based dipping sauce. They carry a good selection of preserved roots, mushrooms, and mountain vegetables that come in small ceramic bowls for serious nibbling. Of course, the real star is the sake collection, and this is a great place to familiarize yourself with the many various styles available in the United States these days.

Terroir

646-602-1300
413 East 12th Street, between
First Avenue and Avenue A
Casual
No reservations
Moderate
All major credit cards accepted
Dinner seven days a week
from 5 PM
L train to First Avenue station;
6 train to Astor Place station

Brought to you by the team responsible for Hearth and Insieme, this is a great addition to the New York wine bar scene. The food for the most part comes from the kitchen of Hearth, which is around the corner, and that really is why this place works as well as it does. The space is small, square, and cramped, with a bar area and communal tables. Most nights it's packed, as it should be, offering very good home-style cooking paired with a seriously well thought-out wine list. One night during the summer of 2008 I bumped into the owner, Paul Grieco, who was there checking in with co-owner and chef Marco Canora, both sporting lick-and-paste Riesling tattoos on their forearms. Paul then proceeded to pair every dish I ordered with a Riesling to prove his point that this is one of the most versatile wines on the planet. Point made. Beyond Riesling you'll find a well-honed selection of wines in the tongue-in-cheek list, contained in what is essentially a high-school-style three-ring notebook. But don't be fooled by the sophomoric wit at play here; it's a very serious list with an entire page devoted to the little-known Austrian winemaker Johannes Hirsch. Paul is a wine lover and iconoclast, and Old World here is mixed with New. Nearly all the wines offered by glass or bottle are winners, and many will be eye-openers as well. The food is simple and very good, such as panini, meatballs both braised in tomato sauce and fried as they do in Italy, pork and lamb steaks, simple salads, bruschetta, and his famous deep-fried sausage with sage leaves.

Xai Xai

212-541-9241
365 West 51st Street, between
Eighth and Ninth Avenues
Casual
No reservations
Moderate
All major credit cards accepted
Seven days a week 4 PM–2 AM
C, E trains to 50th Street
station; N, R, W trains to
49th Street station

A great addition to this neighborhood, Xai Xai was opened by three partners to introduce New Yorkers to the wines and cuisine of South Africa. The wine scene in South Africa has grown quite a bit in the last 30 years as Old World producers explore New World climates and match varietals to soil, altitude, and terroir in general. The South African wine scene has been around for a while, starting with the Dutch, specifically the Dutch governor Simon Van der Stel, who planted the famed Constantia vineyard, which in its day produced wines that were a match for Bordeaux's famed Yquem dessert wines; Van der Stel's name was given to the Stellenbosch varietal. In 1972, the South African government introduced a system for specific regions, varietals, and wines of origin, similar to what was in place throughout Europe.

The room here at Xai Xai is rustic and lovely. Rough-hewn cypress-wood pillars, the exposed-beam ceiling, natural red brick walls, and lots of stucco create the theme throughout the space. Candles provide a lot of the light, and the word *romantic* comes to mind. The list is entirely South African, and the style of these wines is very big, as expected from a place with a warm climate and an extremely long growing season. The reds—a mix of pinotage, which was created in South Africa years ago as a viticultural cross, and the better-known European varietals, including merlot, shiraz, cabernet sauvignon, and syrah—are big, juicy, ripe wines, with abundant fruit and alcohol. The whites, including sparkling choices from Graham Beck and Pierre Jordan, include the familiar varietals: sauvignon blanc, chenin blanc, viognier, chardonnay, riesling, gewürztraminer, and blends. With nearly 100 wines to choose from, many by the glass, this is a great place to familiarize yourself with South African wines if you don't already know them. The food is interesting. Ostrich finds its way onto the menu, as do fresh-shucked oysters, meat pies, the jerky-like biltong saamies, and an assortment of boerewors and local sausages.

WINE
SHOPS

Astor Wines and Spirits

212-674-7500
399 Lafayette Street,
    at East 4th Street
Wines and spirits
Moderate
All major credit cards accepted
Open Monday–Saturday 9 AM–
    9 PM, Sunday noon–6 PM
6 train to Astor Place or
    Bleecker Street stations; B,
    D, F, V trains to Broadway-
    Lafayette station

The recent move across the street and half a block south has doubled the square footage of this legendary store. It's been an East Village institution for years, and for good reason. They have a great selection of wines, at all price points, from all over the planet. The new space gives them room for, among other things, a small, temperature-controlled enclosure for 500 "fragile" bottles. To that add what's billed as New York's largest sake selection, kept at its optimal temperature, 40°F.

Upstairs, next to Serafina restaurant, is the brand-new Astor Center, where they hold excellent tastings and lectures and have space as well for chef- and wine-themed dinners and discussions. Should you feel in need of research, they have a small library filled with wine literature, or you can just ask the staff, which has always been the store's greatest asset as far as I'm concerned. (How do the young kids who work here know so much about wine, anyway? Most of their contemporaries are out late drinking Jell-O shots, while they're talking biodynamic vineyards, natural yeasts, and malolactic fermentation.)

The wines are organized by country, and as you're strolling the polished wood floors, your biggest problem will be limiting your purchases. They have weekly wine tastings, weekly sales, and a great list of very drinkable bottles for under $10, many, many more exceptional choices in the $10–$30 range, and an entire section of organic wines.

Best Cellars

212-426-4200
1291 Lexington Avenue,
    between 86th and 87th
    Streets (and elsewhere)
Wines and spirits
Inexpensive to moderate
All major credit cards accepted
Open Monday–Saturday 9:30 AM–
    9 PM, Sunday noon–8 PM
4, 5, 6 trains to 86th Street
    station

Josh Wesson and Richard Marmet opened this, the first of several stores under this name, in 1996. I had worked with Josh briefly when I was the chef and he was in charge of the wine program at Brive. Back then, in 1986, he was an up-and-coming sommelier on the New York restaurant scene. He morphed into a consultant, writer, and then store owner, and the concept he and his partner have come up with here is as sound today as it was a decade ago: basically, you come in, tell them what you are planning for dinner, and for less than $20 you'll leave with a good bottle, likely to match well with the food. And isn't that what wine shopping is supposed to be about?

The space was designed by the Rockwell Group, and the spare lines, concrete floor, and informed staff set the tone. Their good variety of wines is categorized by style, such as soft, juicy, luscious, fizzy, smooth, and sweet. We're all a little smarter about wine than we were a decade ago, so to my mind, they should lose the silly descriptive adjectives and divide the wines by varietals—but the idea of assembling a large selection of good-value wines, in some instances actually having wines made just for this store, makes a lot of sense.

Bottlerocket Wine and Spirit

212-929-2323
5 West 19th Street, between Fifth and Sixth Avenues
Wines and spirits
Moderate
All major credit cards accepted
Monday–Saturday 11 AM–8 PM, Sunday noon–6 PM
N, R, W, F, V trains to 23rd Street station

As best I can tell, owner Tom Geniesse opened this store as a labor of love. He had been in TV before, he had an Internet company, which he sold, and now he owns this lovely little shop in Chelsea. He lives nearby and is in and out of the store all day long, running back and forth to be with his small children whenever he can. There is even a small kids' play area in the store, if you happen to be shopping with yours in tow. The store is bright, well lit from the high loft-style ceilings above. The wines, 365 different choices, are divided by country of origin down the right side of the store and then laid out alphabetically. Tom believes, as do I, that wine-buying decisions should be driven by what you are eating, so the wines are also displayed in the center of the shop in kiosks, assembled by themes such as Chinese takeout, sushi, steak, seafood, organic, biodynamic, and then further descriptions such as light or heavy. There's even a gift section, organized by occasion, recipient, and price. The idea of this new generation of wine stores is to make it easier for the consumer to pair wines with food. Essentially they are here to demystify the whole buying process, a welcome development for consumers. There are frequent in-store tastings and deals on mixed cases all the time, such as the "Find the Love Holiday Champagne Tasting" half case, where you'll find six bottles of bubbly from five countries of origin, with tasting notes, grape varietals, brief explanations, and even place mats to arrange the glasses in order of sampling sequence, to create a perfect, formal at-home Champagne-tasting party. Sounds like a great gift idea, no?

Chambers Street Wines

212-227-1434
160 Chambers Street,
 between Hudson and
 Greenwich Streets
Wines and spirits
Moderate
All major credit cards accepted
Monday–Saturday 10 AM–9 PM,
 Sunday noon–7 PM
1, 2, 3 trains to Chambers
 Street station

Opening any business, especially a small retail business, involves a certain leap of faith. Chambers Street Wines opened in June 2001. Summers in New York are predictably slow, as most locals leave the city for as much of July and August as they can; things are even less busy downtown, which is not exactly a mecca for tourists. Then came 9/11—and the shop's location is just a few short blocks from where the Twin Towers were. As you can imagine, the next couple of years were a struggle. But co-owners David Lillie and Jamie Wolff stuck it out, and these days the place is doing better than ever. Lillie and Wolff are very knowledgeable wine guys, with a passion for the varietals produced in the Loire Valley. David is one of the foremost experts in the United States on the Loire Valley region's producers, soil, and microclimate, and Jamie too loved the region, having had a house there for a while, allowing him to travel back and forth often. What makes this Loire Valley focus especially appealing is that this region of France is still not very well known in this country. The wines are excellent, and as a kicker, Robert Parker doesn't think much of them, so availability is strong and prices are very reasonable considering the quality.

The styles vary greatly across the Loire Valley region, from bone-dry whites such as muscadet, grown in the Sèvre-et-Maine region, to the youthful robust reds from Chinon and Bourgueil, best drunk young, and sometimes even slightly chilled. Vouvray can run from dry through semisweet to the sweet side, and is a soft, wonderfully food-friendly white made entirely from the chenin blanc grape; when made well, it can age for decades. From the upper Loire they have Pouilly and Sancerre, derived from the sauvignon blanc grape, easy-drinking young wines that match especially well with food. Recently I sampled two bottles of 2005 muscadet from the passionate vigneron Marc Ollivier's Domaine de la Pépière, including his single-vineyard old-vines Clos des Briords. These wines were an excellent match not just for oysters but also for shellfish in general and most white fish. They were priced at $10 and $13, respectively, absolute bargains.

Beyond the Loire, they stock a great selection from Italy as well. From the well-known producer Valentini, they carry the big, bold Montepulciano d'Abruzzo Cerasuolo. From the lesser-known but brilliant winemaker Emidio Pepe, Chambers carries examples of small-batch artisanal Montepulciano bottles, going back through the early 1970s. Pepe's wines, even his young ones, are must-haves if you're interested in seeing what comes from a winemaker striving for purity of style and the most natural of methods. Barolos that age well, and in fact need aging, are well represented here. The selection is vast, going as far back as Giacomo Conterno's 1974 Riserva Monfortino.

The broader selection rounds out with very good wines from Germany, Australia, Austria, and of course all regions of France. They guarantee their stock here, so should you shell out the big bucks for an older vintage that turns out to have gone south, this is one of the few places where you will get a credit. The staff, as we've come to expect in these types of stores, are very helpful; they're basically all wine geeks. Just tell them what you are having for dinner, give them a price range, and let them pair the wine. Note to all underpaid restaurant workers: should you be employed as a cook or otherwise be in the restaurant business, they will give you a 10% discount.

Columbus Circle Wine and Liquor

212-247-0764
**1802 Broadway, between
58th Street and Central
Park South**
Wines and spirits
Moderate
All major credit cards accepted
Monday–Saturday 8 AM–9 PM,
Sunday noon–6 PM
1, A, C, B, D trains to 59th
Street/Columbus Circle
station; N, Q, R, W trains to
57th Street station

For many years this was an under-the-radar store located just a few blocks south of its current location. The old store had the look and feel of a generic midtown liquor store, the entrance under a huge red neon sign that spelled out LIQUOR, where cheap, generic wines shared the shelves with some very good choices as well as pints of vodka and sloe gin. The new store is better laid out and much more modern. Step in and you'll find a well thought-out selection of wines from around the world, at prices that should fit most budgets, from $500 bottles of Haut-Brion to Australian factory wines priced in the single digits, with much to choose from in between. The selection is global—most good regions of France are well represented, ditto for Italy and Spain—and the staff is very helpful when asked. Should you need a good bottle of Scotch or eau de vie, they have that too. When shopping at the Time Warner Center Whole Foods nearby, I often find myself crossing Broadway to visit this store and pair a wine for that night's dinner.

Crossroads Wines and Liquors

212-924-3060
55 West 14th Street, between Fifth and Sixth Avenues
Wines and spirits
Moderate
All major credit cards accepted
Monday–Saturday 9 AM–8 PM
4, 5, 6, L, N, Q, R, W trains to 14th Street/Union Square station; F, V trains to 14th Street station; L train to Sixth Avenue station

This place was highly recommended to me on the advice of master sommelier Roger Dagorn. Who am I to argue? He's always right. Yet Crossroads is the kind of store that a certain type of wine geek likes to dismiss because it carries low-priced, commercially produced wines such as, say, Yellow Tail. If they sell *that* kind of stuff (you know, nod nod, wink wink), they can't be a serious store. Well, Crossroads sells a ton of Yellow Tail every week, and last time I checked it not only helped to pay the rent but also allowed them to discount some very good wines. As one of the staffers told me recently, many of the middle-aged Burgundy-quaffing oenophiles today started on Boone's Farm, Lancer's, and Mateus decades ago. So whatever it takes to get people to start drinking wine, fine. Let them develop better palates as time goes by.

If you know what you are looking for, Crossroads is a great source for solid-quality discount wines. They have many good producers as well as some popular swill. The store is small and cluttered and the staff typically introverted and harried, but if you're nice to them, they're nice back. They carry a solid selection of wines from around the world with an increasingly good focus on organics and biodynamic wines. The wines are displayed all over the place, from floor to ceiling, many standing upright in a kind of random order, as if someone set a case of Burgundy on the floor and then that just became the Burgundy section. Of special interest here is their California pinot noir selection, considered by many to be one of the best in New York. They also have a great selection of Scotch and some darn good rums as well.

Crush Wine and Spirits

212-980-9463
153 East 57th Street, between Lexington and Third Avenues
Wines and spirits
Moderate to expensive, with some rare collectible wines
All major credit cards accepted
Monday–Saturday 10 AM–9 PM, Sunday noon–6 PM (closed summer Sundays)
4, 5, 6, N, R, W trains to Lexington Avenue/59th Street station

Opened to much acclaim in February 2005, this store was the brainchild of restaurateur Drew Nieporent and two acquaintances, real estate developer Josh Guberman and Nieporent's long-time friend Robert Schagrin, a passionate wine collector who owns an antique and high-end pop culture collectibles store named Gotta Have It, located next door. The 3,200-square-foot space is heavy on design, with the entire right wall featuring an undulating backlit display of thousands of horizontal wine bottles, organized by grape variety.

The impressive assortment runs from whites in the front to reds as you head toward the rear. Lyle Fass, the wine director, came from Chambers Street Wines downtown and is a well-respected wine geek. His explanation of how to decode German wine labels left me even more confused than before he started. The selection here is impressive. This is not a bargain hunter's store. That said, if you're looking for good wines in the $20–$50 range or rare bottles, it's a real find. The selection is broad, mixing Old World–style wines with New World darlings, but there's really not a bad bottle in the entire store. Yes, you pay a premium, but while the discount stores may offer bargains for savvy wine buyers who know labels, producers, and vintages, they often are also full of wines that you probably don't want to drink. Here, every bottle is good, and many are very good.

To the rear left of the space is "the cube," a 500-square-foot, temperature-controlled, glassed-in vault featuring rare, collectible auction-grade wines, set over a special floor designed so that dropped bottles don't break but bounce instead. It works; I've tested it. Just off "the cube" they also have a great tasting room with daily pours. Here you'll sit on heavy leather chairs before 200-year-old oak tables and taste wines out of very good crystal glasses. The tastings are free of charge and open to the public, and they represent an exceptional way to learn about wines, develop your palate, and speak with other wine lovers. The staff, as expected, are all walking, talking wine experts, many of whom have trained at other New York stores and are very helpful in pairing wines with foods to match your budget. Keep in mind, this is East 57th Street, and most of the stores in this neighborhood cater to customers who have more money than they know what to do with.

Discovery Wines

212-674-7833
10 Avenue A, between Houston and East 2nd Streets
Wines and spirits
Inexpensive to moderate
All major credit cards accepted
Monday–Saturday 11 AM–10 PM,
Sunday 2–8 PM
F, V trains to Second Avenue station

Of the new-generation wine stores around town, places that seriously want to help you pick the right bottle and demystify the whole experience, Discovery is one of the best. Part of the reason is the store layout, which is wide, well lit, open, and very user-friendly. The space spreads out deep into the building, with high ceilings, polished wood floors, and row after row of wine bottles set upright so that you can read the labels. The staff, as expected these days in any good wine store, consists mainly of wine lovers who are more than happy to share their experience and dispense advice when asked for pairings. But this shop has another thing going for it: grab any bottle that looks interesting, walk it over to a kiosk equipped with a bar code scanner, and voilà—you'll have a full description of the wine, grape varietals used, flavor profiles, and even food pairings. Now *that's* a new wine store concept.

There are three partners behind this operation: Ellisa Cooper, a Kentucky native and event planner; Anthony White, a former software executive, film instructor at Columbia, and then wine buyer for another store; and Scott Reiner, who grew up in the Bahamas, was in banking, and then started collecting wines. He and White do all the buying for the store. They seek out small independent producers, essentially artisan winemakers, while carrying wines from larger producers as long as the juice drinks well. To survive in this neighborhood, they also have a lot of very drinkable wines at right around the $10 price point. They host monthly wine tastings on Fridays and Saturdays, and they make the space available for parties, corporate events, and weddings, a nod there to Cooper's background. If you live anywhere nearby, pay them a visit. It's a great shopping experience, the selection is good and broad, and the prices, especially at the low end, are very fair.

Garnet Wines

212-772-3211
929 Lexington Avenue,
   between 68th and 69th
   Streets
Wines and spirits
Moderate
All major credit cards accepted
Monday–Saturday 9 AM–9 PM,
   Sunday noon–6 PM
6 train to 68th Street station

The place may look like a dump from the outside, but if you know what you're looking for, there are many great bargains stowed away on these dusty shelves. Recently I asked the esteemed "sommelier to sommeliers" Roger Dagorn, whose palate is one of the most respected on the planet, where he shops, and he replied without hesitation, and to my surprise, "Garnet, of course." It helps that he knows exactly which cru he's looking for, as they stock more than 6,000 bottles, but the secret here is good purchasing and volume. They buy large quantities and turn them over fast, working on a smaller margin than many other retailers. Most folks I know who live up here swear by the place. They have a great selection of Champagne and sparkling wines and even a decent supply of Armagnac, one of my favorite ways to end a meal, including numerous offerings from Château de Laubade: a blended VSOP for $34 or, should the mood strike you, the wonderfully soft and approachable 1965 for a mere $155.

Harlem Vintage

212-866-9463

2235 Frederick Douglass
  Boulevard (Eighth
  Avenue), between 120th
  and 121st Streets

Wines and spirits

Moderate

All major credit cards accepted

Monday–Thursday 11 AM–9 PM,
  Friday and Saturday 11 AM–
  10 PM, Sunday noon–6 PM

2, 3, A, C, B, D trains to 125th
  Street station

Opened a few years back by a couple of wine lovers with day jobs, this store has become perhaps the best wine shop in the area of Harlem. It has a rustic country feel to it, with loads of natural exposed wood, stone, and easy-to-peruse display shelving. Most bottles fall into the $10–$25 range, in keeping with neighborhood feel. The selection is broad and features wines from Old and New World producers. Each month they hold in-store pairings featuring cheeses, chocolates, fruit, and wine for $25 per person. While some of the neighborhood old-timers resent places like this in ever-gentrifying Harlem, business is solid, they have a loyal following, and they have recently opened a popular wine bar next door. Surely if I lived in the neighborhood, this would be my go-to wine store. The staff is friendly, knows the wines well, and will work within your budget, or mine, which is the $10–$20 zone. On a recent visit I grabbed a lovely aromatic bottle of Chiorri Sangiovese for $15.99 to pair with a tomato-sauce-based dinner, a bargain-priced chenin blanc by Indaba for $9.99, and a complex and delicious Savennières, "La Jalousie," by Closel, a smaller producer that has been run by women for nearly a century and shows how good chenin blanc can be, with ripe fruit on the nose and tongue and a dry, crisp, minerally finish—though it broke the bank at $21.99, this is a great food-friendly wine.

Is-Wine

212-254-7800

24 West 8th Street, between
  MacDougal Street and
  Fifth Avenue

Wine and spirits

Moderate

All major credit cards accepted

Monday–Saturday 11 AM–10 PM,
  Sunday noon–7 PM

N, R, W trains to 8th Street
  station; A, C, E, B, D, F, V trains
  to West 4th Street station

This stretch of 8th Street is really trying to reinvent itself these days as a retail destination. What once had been the home to many an inexpensive store featuring T-shirts, head shop paraphernalia, and discount sneakers and shoes is now is showing signs of new life, with interesting little stores like this, plus a few decent restaurants as well. Is-Wine has a small but focused selection that changes with the seasons and availability, as many of the small producers that it champions don't make that many cases of wine. For some that may prove to be a disappointment, as it's quite possible to find a wine here, drink it a few weeks later, return to buy a case, and find that it's all been sold out and you have to wait for next year's vintage. That's the case with many of these smaller stores that represent smaller producers. But what you can do is explain to the staff why you liked that wine so much, and they'll have a few other new options for you to explore, often expanding your palate and wine knowledge in the process. Like all good wine stores, this place is about pairing wine with food, so it's helpful to have an idea of what you may want to be eating and how it will be prepared, and with that, the staff can choose a good wine for you in any price range.

Nearly every Saturday they have a free in-store tasting, another great way to expand your palate. For the most part, you're going to find Old World wines here, that is to say, wines from all around Europe made with an emphasis on grape varietals and terroir. They do not carry wines from big producers, and only a smallish selection from California, New York State, New Zealand, Australia, South America, or South Africa. For what they offer, the selection is good and presents decent value; they offer case discounts as well, and delivery is available. The staff is very friendly and helpful, and they even have a few big leather chairs in which to sit and ponder.

Italian Wine Merchants

212-473-2323
108 East 16th Street, between
Irving Place and Park
Avenue South
Wines and spirits
Moderate to expensive
All major credit cards accepted
Monday–Friday 10 AM–7 PM,
Saturday 11 AM–7 PM
4, 5, 6, L, N, Q, R, W to 14th
Street/Union Square station

This store is part of the Mario Batali–Joe Bastianich partnership. Here they partnered with the Italian guru Sergio Esposito, a former sommelier turned consultant, newsletter author, and portfolio expert. Like Le Dû's Wines in the far West Village, Sergio and his team are here to help wealthy buyers put together carefully selected, deep cellars of rare and collectible Italian wines. That said, it's also a great source for very good Italian wines from small producers virtually unknown outside Italy and a small cadre of professionals. They have a good e-newsletter and offer frequent in-store tastings and classes that are well worth attending. I recently discovered a great Vino Nobile di Montepulciano from a small producer, Robert Kengelbacher, who works only 4 hectares of vineyard, which is planted with the native prugnolo clone. The 2003, which I had in 2007, was an absolute stunner, though not cheap at $35.75, but a great example of how good this wine can be.

Julian Niccolini, co-owner of the Four Seasons and a huge fan of brunello wines, got me thinking big, so for an occasion I purchased a bottle of the 2001 La Casa from Tenuta Caparzo, established in the late 1960s. Here they draw from another small vineyard, just 5 hectares, for a amazingly concentrated wine with serious tannin and aging potential.

Only 100 cases made their way to the United States. At $70, it's a splurge, but I'd drink this against many wines at two and three times the price.

From up north in Friuli, a bargain white from Silvio Jermann, the crisp, delicious Vinnae, sells for just $22. From outside Naples, the falanghina from Sogno Due is lovely, with great crisp fruit and mineral layers, at under $30 a bottle. It's easy to be intimidated here, as the wines tend to be pricey, but give the sales staff your budget and food pairing and I'll bet you walk away with a very pleasant surprise. They may be heavy on the high end, but the overall quality of the selection speaks for itself.

Le Dû's Wines

212-924-6999
600 Washington Street, between Morton and Leroy Streets
Wines and spirits
Moderate
All major credit cards accepted
Monday–Saturday 11 AM–9 PM, Sunday 1 PM to 7 PM
1 train to Houston Street station

Jean-Luc Le Dû gained much notoriety during his years of service as the head sommelier and wine director at the venerable restaurant Daniel. A dark-haired, affable, energetic native of Brittany, his passion for wine has earned him many awards (James Beard, *Wine Spectator*, etc.) and has allowed him to travel and taste. This store is the culmination of that experience. Located on the ground floor of a new apartment building just a block from the Hudson River in the far West Village, the space is bright, clean, uncluttered, and designed for easy shopping. The wines are broken down by varietals and countries. The displays are easy to navigate, with the inventory stacked vertically beneath display bottles tilted slightly on chest-level shelves, the prices are easy to read, and the system is self-explanatory.

The wines are mostly from France, Italy, Germany, Austria, Portugal, Spain, the United States, and New Zealand, with focused selections from each country. While you can certainly find some very good choices in the $10–$20 range, the emphasis here tends to be on wines of a higher caliber, and of course correspondingly higher price points. This is a store well suited for serious wine enthusiasts. Not surprisingly, the selection is especially strong from the Burgundy region, arguably an area where the most interesting wines are being made today. It's hard to find bargains in Burgundy, but the Fourrier Gevrey-Chambertin Vieilles Vignes for $28.99 is a great buy. There are a few less expensive bottles, but Burgundies are not bargain wines, and the prices go up quickly into the hundreds. Just next to the Burgundies, you'll find a tightly edited collection of Italian reds: nebbiolos, barbarescos, Barolos, and those big Amarones. For those of us on a tight budget, the dolcetto d'Alba from Vietti is a lovely example of this grape for under $20 a bottle. Domestic pinot noirs, mostly from California, include the hard-to-find Favia La Josefina from John Bucher.

There is a surprisingly good selection of those controversial California zinfandels, including seven selections alone just from Turley. From the Rhône, he carries more than 20 varieties of Châteauneuf-du-Pape, huge wines and a personal favorite of Jean-Luc.

In the summer months he has a dozen or so rosés. Among white wines, there are very good choices from all regions of France, especially Chablis, the Loire Valley, and Alsace, and many others from Italy, Spain, Germany, and New Zealand. You won't find a bad bottle of wine in this store, and the staff is very knowledgeable and helpful in terms of pairing wines with food. Additionally, they have tastings nearly every week in the back room, which range in price accordingly depending on what they are pouring (never more than eight bottles). This is a great way to develop your palate, interact with the staff, ask questions, and expand your knowledge base.

Moore Brothers Wine Company

212-375-1575
33 East 20th Street, between Broadway and Park Avenue South
Wines and spirits
Inexpensive to moderate
All major credit cards accepted
Monday–Friday 11 AM–9 PM, Saturday 10 AM–8 PM, Sunday noon–6 PM
6, N, R, W trains to 23rd Street station

Greg Moore was the head sommelier for years at Le Bec-Fin in my hometown, Philadelphia. For those who don't know, Le Bec-Fin has been considered the best restaurant in that city for well over three decades, and its chef, Georges Perrier, a culinary king. What Moore learned there has come in handy—in this store, unlike many others with broad global selections and variety, the focus is strictly on small European producers, and even then, only those from France, Germany, and Italy. This is his third store, with the flagship location being in (of all places) Pennsauken, New Jersey, and the second shop in Wilmington, Delaware. The New York store is kept at 56°F year round, which in the hot, steamy New York summer is welcome relief, but during the cooler months not so much, so they'll give you a little coat to wear should you need to linger. Not only is the store at cellar temperature, but all his wines are shipped in 20-foot refrigerated containers kept at that temperature, a practice far more common now than it used to be, to ensure that the wines never bake in the summer heat nor freeze in the winter on the long journey from various European ports to American docks, then warehouses, and finally his shop. One of wine's worst enemies is variations in temperature; here the bottles never experience that.

If you're like me, when you're confronted with a new label, you might turn to the back of the bottle to see who the importer is. Mad Rose, Skurnik, and Lynch are all good, trusted, familiar names, and to my experience often a guarantee of quality. Here the wines mostly come mainly from just two importers I've grown to trust as well: Fleet Street and Wine Traditions. These are judicious buyers who seek out and champion small producers, often with very limited production but offering great value. Most of the wines here are right in my price range, and prove the point that you can have excellent wines for between $10 and $20 a bottle.

They have tasting and cheese-and-wine events, and the staff are all passionate and informed. For my money, this is one of the most interesting little wine shops in town. You'd be hard pressed to walk out with just an average bottle. More likely, you'd uncork a very pleasant surprise.

Nancy's

212-877-4040
313 Columbus Avenue, between 74th and 75th Streets
Wines and spirits
Moderate
All major credit cards accepted
Monday–Saturday 10 AM–8 PM, Sunday noon–6 PM
1, 2, 3, B, C trains to 72nd Street station

Actually the full name of this store is Nancy's Wines for Food, which is a perfect way to describe what they sell and how they do it. I lived half a block away in that same neighborhood for much of the 1980s, but Nancy's didn't arrive until the early 1990s, after I'd left. This little storefront has now become one of my favorite wine shops in New York City. Nancy Maniscalco is usually there behind the counter. She's the tall, thin, quiet one with the glasses, by appearance more schoolmistress than gonzo wine queen, but get her started about wine and she sparkles. In her previous career she did administrative work for an accounting firm, loved wines as a hobby, and was sick of going into wine stores where the salespeople might just as well have been selling chewing gum (that's her line, by the way). To remedy this, she took the leap, opened her own place, works there daily, and has well-trained, passionate staff who are all very knowledgeable.

The selection here isn't that big, and the space itself is small: a room in the front with whites and rosés, and a smaller room out back with reds from around the world. Every bottle has its own three-by-five card with a few sentences describing the wine. The comments are written by Nancy and a few other staff members, but the broader point is that they taste each and every bottle of the wine they sell. One of her ever-present seasoned floor staff, Evan Spingarn, has even coauthored a very good wine guide. Like many of the better wine stores in the city, they favor small-batch producers who make wines that taste of the place they come from, wines made by talented winemakers for whom wine making is art, not artifice. Her specialty is German wines, specifically rieslings. She's done for rieslings what Chambers Street has done for Loire Valley wine: pick a great but less-celebrated wine-producing region featuring food-friendly, well-crafted wines that in many cases are serious bargains, and promote them while educating the public as to their merit.

Once the staff gets to know you, what you cook, and how you eat, they can put together cases of wines that almost always work perfectly at home. If you're looking for a 1961 Cheval Blanc, a Crozes-Hermitage, or a nine-liter bottle of Veuve Clicquot, go to Sherry-Lehmann or Morrell, but if you want a great selection of food-friendly wines in the $10–$25 range, you'd be hard pressed to do any better than here.

Sakaya

212-505-7253
324 East 9th Street, between
  First and Second Avenues
Sake
Moderate to expensive
All major credit cards accepted
Monday–Saturday noon–8 PM,
  Sunday noon–6 PM
6 train to Astor Place station;
  N, R, W trains to 8th Street
  station

If you are a fan of sake, than add this store to your list of places you must visit. Sake, it seems, is finally getting its due, with the great selection at Astor Place, good representation on better wine lists and at a few other retail stores in New York, and now this store, which is devoted entirely to fine sake. The space is minimal and spare, with lots of natural wood and shelves that display bottles upright. The husband-and-wife team who run it, former *Food and Wine* publisher Rick Smith and Hiroko Furukawa, are passionate about the subject, and often both are present at the store to help explain things. It opened in late 2007 with a base collection of about 80 sake varieties, and by the time this book hits the streets, I'm certain that number will have nearly doubled, with everything from little starter 300-ml bottles to the giant 1.8-liter ishobin.

In addition to sake varieties, they also sell sake serving sets, a few books, and a small selection of shochu, a higher-alcohol spirit variety also made from rice. This store features artisanal sakes from Japan, many from small producers that have not been available for sale here in the United States before. It would be helpful to do a bit of research prior to your first visit, as all the labels are written in Japanese, and differentiating the styles, while relatively simple once you understand the basics, can be confusing for the novice. That said, the staff and owners are very helpful, and they will have regular sake tastings to help speed the learning curve along. Please note that sake does not just have to be paired with Japanese food; it works very well with certain Western dishes too.

September Wines & Spirits

212-388-0770

100 Stanton Street, at the
corner of Ludlow Street

Wines and spirits

Moderate

All major credit cards accepted

Monday–Thursday 11 AM–10 PM,
Friday 11 AM–11 PM, Saturday
noon–11 PM, Sunday 1–8 PM

F, V trains to Second Avenue
station

Just around the corner from Katz's Deli and Ludlow Guitars lies September Wines, on the northwest corner of Stanton and Ludlow. The small store, which opened in 2005, is a welcome addition to this ever-changing neighborhood, once gritty and now chic. The selection here is limited but well chosen, with a focus on small producers, many of whom practice eco-friendly winemaking. The owner, Steve Flynn, formerly a documentary filmmaker, has traveled the globe extensively and has a passion for wine. This store, like many of the smaller wine stores opening around town, is a singular expression of the owner's vision. The simple displays are arranged by wine type and country and offer some hard-to-find selections from countries one does not normally consider as wine producers, including a decent merlot from Brazil, a very nice petit syrah from Mexico, a riesling from Slovenia, a cinsault from Morocco, a cabernet from India, and a wonderful red from the Bekka Valley of Lebanon—Château Musar from Gaston Hochar, a blend of cabernet sauvignon, cinsault, and carignan.

Among his organic selections, you'll find a 2003 Joguet Chinon Rouge from the Loire Valley of France: its loads of ripe berries, decent body, and soft tannins make for a great, food-friendly wine. A bargain at $11.99, the deep garnet Montepulciano d'Abruzzo from Valle Reale, made from vines planted in 1999 in a national park in Abruzzi, comes loaded with tons of dark fruit, a perfect match for roasts in the colder months. For regular customers they keep a file on your likes and dislikes, aiding the staff in your choices. (I'm told they do not share this list with Homeland Security or the CIA.) He also stocks a good selection of whisky and artisanal vodka, should you have the need.

Union Square Wines

212-675-8100
140 Fourth Avenue,
at 13th Street
Wines and spirits
Moderate
All major credit cards accepted
Monday–Saturday 9 AM–10 PM,
Sunday noon–7 PM
4, 5, 6, L, N, Q, R, W trains to
14th Street/Union Square
station

For many years they were housed opposite Union Square in a two-story space that was a great location. They moved here in 2006; it's a more modern, user-friendly layout, and they expanded the footprint and added a very fancy little wine-tasting machine imported from Italy. The Enomatic system, pumped with argon gas, can handle up to 48 open bottles, dispensing 15 ml pours at the swipe of a special card. And how do you get those cards? You buy wine here, and for each dollar you spend, you get points on your card toward tastings. It's a great idea for two reasons. One is simply that this store carries a great selection of wines from around the world, and the other is their very friendly staff to help you make decisions. Forget Trader Joe's around the corner on 14th—this place is a must-visit if you've been shopping at the Union Square Greenmarket or at Whole Foods nearby on 14th Street. Like all the good stores, they have tastings and a monthly selection of staff picks right by the door when you walk in. They have a decent sake selection, and while they do have good bottles in the lower range, their strength may lie in the $20–$50 range. There you'll find some great wines from all over the planet. They have a pretty darned good, regularly updated Web site as well, where you can browse by vintage, price, and country of origin. These days retail wine stores need every edge they can get over the competition, and here they have that cool machine, the great Web site, a user-friendly layout, and a really smart staff to answer your questions. In short, this is one very good shop.

Vino Italian Wine and Spirits

800-965-8466
121 East 27th Street, between
Park Avenue South and
Lexington Avenue
Wines and spirits
Moderate
All major credit cards accepted
Monday–Saturday noon–9 PM,
Sunday noon–8 PM
6, N, R, W trains to 28th Street
station

Since opening in 2000, this has been one of the best stores in New York for Italian wines and spirits. The selection is the work of owner Nicola Marzovilla and wine director Charles Scicolone and is impressive at all price points. From hard-to-find bitters to artisanal grappa and everything in between, if you're a fan of Italian wines, put this store on your list. They feature in-store tastings weekly and usually have a promotion linked to the event, such as 10%–20% off the wines they are pouring. Additionally, they offer wine classes monthly, by reservation only. The shopping experience is pleasant. Above the wood floors, the wines are displayed on glass shelves set into custom-made cases that line the walls, as well as on display on the rustic natural-wood tables placed around the room. The staff, as is the case in all good wine stores, knows the product. From Gaja's Super Tuscans to modest sangiovese blends or the previously impossible-to-find Lini Lambruscos, if you're looking to expand your knowledge and palate about Italian wines, or simply pick up a good bottle, this store is a find.

Winesby.com

212-242-5144
23 Jones Street, between West 4th and Bleecker Streets
Wines and spirits
Moderate
All major credit cards accepted
Monday–Saturday 11:30 AM–7:30 PM
A, C, E, B, D, F, V trains to West 4th Street station; 1 train to Christopher Street station

This tiny store has a loose, ramshackle feel to it, with opened cases of wine lying on the floor and an assortment of bottles set on small shelves. Initially a Web-site-only wine business (hence the .com name), the store became a retail location in 2000. What they lack in architectural flourishes, they more than make up for with a tightly focused selection of great organic and biodynamic wines from around the world, many in the $10–$20 range. Owner Jeff Hock personally selects wines that are great with food and ready to drink right now. That is an important distinction, as for most of us, that's really how we buy wine: to drink it soon, if not that night, not to lay it down in the cellar until it's ready five or ten years from now. The Web site is helpful, and you'll see that the wines are divided by sections like boutique, organic, and screw caps. (Screw caps are perfectly fine—even better than cork, in fact, as screw caps don't result in "corked" wines, which are far more common than people think.)

The organic California Coyne Mourvèdre 2004 is a stunner, paired with a good steak or grilled lamb chops. Or reach for the wine called VRAC, an $11 screw-cap chardonnay blend from eight villages within the Mâcon region—either one may be the perfect way to convince you that you should shop here more often. The VRAC red, a Rhône blend, is a lovely wine loaded with dried-cherry punch and dark fruit, slightly herbal, with decent minerality; it's lovely with light foods too. This store is a little treat for real wine lovers.

Wine Therapy

212-625-2999

171 Elizabeth Street, between Kenmare and Spring Streets

Wines and spirits

Moderate

All major credit cards accepted

Monday–Thursday 11 AM–10 PM, Friday and Saturday 11 AM–11 PM, Sunday noon–9 PM

N, R, W trains to Prince Street station; 6 train to Spring Street station; J, M trains to Bowery station

This tiny store is a great addition to the ever-expanding NoLIta culinary scene. It was opened in the fall of 2005 by French expat Jean-Baptiste Humbert, who lives upstairs with his family; his wife runs the salon just next door in the same building. This may be the smallest wine store in New York, but the selection is focused and reasonably priced. With rents what they are in NoLIta these days, and so many young people living there on what must be a tight budget for most, a great selection of bottles under $20 makes sense for this neighborhood store. The staff is small and friendly and shares the owner's passion for good wines. The Francophile iPod soundtrack makes shopping here all the more fun.

MARKETS

New York City is a treasure trove of ingredients from far and near. Thanks to the city's ethnic diversity, the public's interest in new cuisines, and the amount of money spent on food items each year, the food shopping here just keeps getting better. Paralleling the growth in the restaurant scene, the market scene has exploded over the last 10 to 20 years. First we had a Whole Foods supermarket in Chelsea, and now branches of that chain are popping up around the city. There are also the ethnic markets along Lexington Avenue in the twenties, on Ninth Avenue in the high thirties, along the stretch of Bleecker between Seventh Avenue and Carmine Street, and in the Essex Street Market. Plus of course there's Fairway, Citarella, Zabar's, Gourmet Garage, and the many other great independent retailers to be found all over town. This list is partial, as new stores keep opening, but nonetheless it should prove helpful in locating most everything you'll need to stock your pantry or simply prepare a great meal at home.

Chelsea Market

75 Ninth Avenue, between 15th and 16th Streets

Restaurants/retail

Prices vary

Credit card acceptance varies

Monday–Friday 7 AM–9 PM, weekends 10 AM–8 PM, but individual store hours vary

A, C, E trains to 14th Street station; L to Eighth Avenue station

Though construction started decades earlier, this piecemeal project was finally completed in 1929 as a working factory for the National Biscuit Company (Nabisco), formerly the New York Biscuit Company, and was designed by their in-house architect, Louis N. Wirshing Jr. The merger of two large competitors in 1898 resulted in a baking behemoth, with 114 separate bakeries and more than 400 commercial ovens that produced graham crackers, oyster crackers, lemon drops, and ginger snaps, and it was here in this building that the first Oreo was ever baked, circa 1912. The structure starts on Ninth Avenue and runs the full block through to Tenth, effectively connecting the factories' baking and storage space to the old High Line railroad on Tenth Avenue (which is now being converted into a public park).

Purchased in the late 1990s by real estate visionary Irwin Cohen, who supervised the beautiful renovations, the space's ground floor is now home to a free-flowing 800-foot-long concourse, weaving through the building and linking the retail stores, while upstairs you'll find the offices and kitchen stage sets for the Food Network, Oxygen, Sterling Sound, NY1, and Major League Baseball Productions. The exterior on Ninth Avenue is faced in old brick, bound by brass spandrels, with a wavy glass-and-steel canopy covering the main entrance. As you walk through the ground-floor retail space, you'll see sections of the building's skeleton as a design element left on display: handrails fashioned from rebar and an upside-down fountain of sorts with water flowing from a large industrial drainpipe. There are stone sculptures and recycled objects hanging on the walls, along with photography and original art. The stores, and their workplaces as well, are all visible from this hall via floor-to-ceiling glass panels. If you're really lucky, maybe you'll even bump into Rachael Ray.

It's hit-or-miss as far as shopping goes. The restaurants are average at best, and some of the retail spaces are like others that can be found anywhere in town. But several are well worth the trip.

AMY'S BREAD
212-462-4338

Amy's Bread is a good place to start. This was Amy Scherber's second store, but as the space is large, this is where much of the baking gets done for the other satellite locations and her wholesale business. Scherber started baking bread years ago at the short-lived but very good restaurant Mondrian. It just so happens that was also the place where a young chef named Tom Colicchio began to build his reputation. She worked at a few bakeries in France and then in 1992 opened Amy's Bread on Ninth Avenue. Her breads are very good, especially the larger loaves studded with nuts and olives. At some point they expanded into cakes, pastries, and sandwiches, all very good as well, and she bakes one of the best red velvet cakes in New York.

BUON ITALIA
212-633-9090

This L-shaped store is a great place to hunt for top-quality and hard-to-find Italian ingredients. Start with the one-kilo bags of Setaro pasta from Naples. This is some of the best dried pasta on the market, and a bargain at around $6 a one-kilo bag. They have a good, small selection of Italian tomatoes, from DOP San Marzano to great brands from Puglia and Campagna. These are all small-batch runs, really the best examples of Mediterranean tomato flavor. This market is where I buy my European-packed albacore tuna, mostly glass packs that are wonderful. If you've never used these, you should try them. The glass packs have a clean, fresh flavor, with no metallic overtones. If you want to splurge on olive oil, try the fruity, bright Colle di Bellavista from Tuscany, or the thick and almost chewy dark green Lucrezio from Puglia. They have several offerings from Mancianti, a superb producer from Umbria, as well as excellent examples from Lombardy, Sicily, Liguria, and Campania. If you've never thought of olives as bearing distinct individual regional characteristics (like grapes in winemaking), compare these oils and you'll see how different they are from one another. To this add a good selection of Arborio rice, sardines, anchovies in various forms, and those great little cans of Flot tuna, a bargain at just over $2 apiece. In the rear of the store, they cut good cold meats (sold by weight), make great sandwiches, have prepared foods to go (also sold by weight), and even have a table or two tucked away in the corner, a great place to eat and read in privacy.

THE LOBSTER PLACE
212-255-5672

This small seafood market is well worth the trip. I shop here all the time and have been impressed with the quality and prices. In the fall of 2008, they renovated and slightly expanded the retail footprint. All the fish, laid out on ice, has been very fresh each and every time I've been there. The selection is much bigger than their little outpost on Bleecker Street, and it usually includes several salmon options—wild caught and farm raised—fluke, flounder, swordfish, tilefish, clams, mussels, shrimp, oysters, dry scallops, catfish, skate, and whole fish as well as red snapper, branzino, and black bass. This is the offshoot of a wholesale operation run under the same name that sells more than a million pounds of lobster a year to New York restaurants, so it's no surprise that the quality of the fish at their retail shops in town is impeccable. They have some great choices in partially prepared meals as well, including crab cakes, stuffed shrimp, and filets of various fish that are breaded and seasoned, marinated, or placed on skewers, all ready to be cooked and requiring no further work. The blackened grouper is very nice, as are the swordfish or monkfish kebabs, coconut-crusted mahi-mahi, panko-breaded summer flounder, and crab cakes. Overall, this is one of the best seafood retail stores in New York, though, as expected, you pay for the quality.

Sarabeth's

212-989-2424

I remember when Sarabeth Levine opened her original place on Amsterdam Avenue and how good the baked goods, the fruit jams, and the restaurant were. At some point she sold most of the locations and opened a few more, such as the one on Central Park South, but to me, none has that same magic. Here in the Chelsea store, though, it's almost like stepping back in time. They have a few tables for sit-down meals and a menu that is small but very good. Exemplary eggs and omelets, creamy porridge, and those delicious pumpkin waffles and oatmeal pancakes, though, are available only on weekends. The cakes, muffins, and preserves are all lovely little specimens of what can be done, should you take the time to do it right.

Citarella

212-874-0383
2135 Broadway, at 75th
  Street (and elsewhere)
Retail supermarket
Moderate to expensive
All major credit cards accepted
Monday–Saturday 7 AM–9 PM,
  Sunday 9 AM–7 PM
1, 2, 3 trains to 72nd Street
  Station

To this day, Citarella is one of the premier fish markets in New York, with a great selection of the freshest fish from all over the planet. The fish are displayed on crushed ice, stretching the entire width of the store at its rear. On any given day, they have a half dozen varieties of fresh oysters in their shells from both coasts. The oysters sit next to razor clams, huge green mussels from New Zealand, sea urchins, Maryland jumbo lump crabmeat, and cooked and raw shrimp. For salmon lovers, they carry a variety of wild-caught Alaskan, organic, and farm-raised salmon from around the world, along with whole striped bass, skate, squid, dry scallops, monkfish, fluke, flounder, black bass, and halibut from our waters, and whole sardines, bar, loup de mer, rouget, and St. Pierre, all on the bone, imported from the Mediterranean. I spend weekends in Cape May, New Jersey, and so can eat great fish all year long right off the boats, and yet I am amazed at how

Citarella offers so many varieties that all seem straight-off-the-dock fresh. Cheap, no, but worth the price.

Next to Lobel's, they have some of the best prime, dry-aged meat, including well-marbled strips, short loins and ribeyes, onglet, tri-tip, and skirt steak. There's also cubed meats for stew, organic meats, Colorado lamb, ground meats, veal sweetbreads, pork, and a good selection of organic and free-range poultry as well. The butchers behind the counters know the customers and are very accommodating. Just past the entrance they have prepared foods to go (which are just okay), a good selection of breads from various New York bakeries, a small array of assorted vegetables (you're better off at Fairway), and a limited but well-selected variety of imported and domestic olive oils and specialty vinegars. Near the fresh fish display, they carry a small but very good selection of imported tinned fish. Try the Flot brand of tuna, from Sicily, at $1.99 for 3 ounces packed in olive oil; you'll never eat Bumblebee again.

Upstairs you'll find hand-cut smoked salmon, sable, whitefish, and chubs next to caviar, foie gras, and a good selection of deli meats, dried sausage, and imported prosciutto, all sliced by order and sold by weight. They also have bulk olives, a great cheese selection, and hard-to-find specialties including imported glass-packed goose fat, a must for homemade confit. There's a broad offering of cakes, pies, tarts, and other dessert options, many baked from the recipes of Bill Yosses, formerly of Bouley and later executive pastry chef at the White House. While that great new Whole Foods has opened just a few blocks to the south, and Fairway beckons next door, I'd argue that Citarella has them all beat when it comes to the freshest fish and well-marbled, dry-aged meats, albeit at a few dollars more per pound than the competition. It's invariably one of my first choices for shopping anywhere in town.

Deluxe Food Market

212-925-5766
79 Elizabeth Street, between Hester and Grand Streets
Fresh meat, fish, groceries, prepared foods
Inexpensive to moderate
Cash only
Seven days a week 7 AM–9:30 PM
6, J, M, Z, N, Q, R, W trains to Canal Street station

Straightaway, this place amazes me. This long, narrow store runs through the entire block, so you can enter on Elizabeth and exit onto Mott, or the other way around. Within these walls, you'll have so much selection it's hard to believe—from prepared food to eat in or take out to a selection of fish, meat, marinated delicacies, and semi-preserved items. They offer not just pigs' feet but boneless pigs' feet, along with every imaginable cut from every imaginable species—nothing is wasted here. Traditional cuts include all the steaks, such as hanger steak, flank, and thin-sliced ribeye, but there are also inexpensive oxtails and an array of offal. To this add Chinese sausage, beef and veal bones, fresh quail, and the hard-to-find black chicken, also known as silkies.

The fish selection is very good and very fresh, with everything from salmon, tuna, cod, and whiting to baby octopus, live eels, and frogs, and at prices a fraction of what they'd be uptown. In another cooler, they feature partially prepared, marinated fish, and meat all ready for the oven or the grill—not just a time saver but flavorful and at prices that are nearly impossible to beat in Manhattan. The hot food is good too: six big steamed pork buns for $2, roast duck, scallion pancakes, steamed and fried wontons, soups—you name it, all good and cheap. Due to the store's size, prices, and great selection, expect a crowd any time of day. But that to me is part of the charm. You'll be elbow to elbow with a Chinese grandmother holding the hand of her small granddaughter, vying for the attention of the plentiful staff, most of whom actually speak some English. Once you've seen the place and are familiar with the offerings, this could be a one-stop shopping destination for most dinner needs.

Despana Brand Foods

212-219-5050

408 Broome Street, between Lafayette and Cleveland Streets

Specialty foods from Spain

Moderate to expensive

All major credit cards accepted

Monday–Saturday 11 AM–8 PM, Sundays 11 AM–5 PM

J, M trains to Bowery station; 6, J, M, Z, N, Q, R, W trains to Canal Street station

This may possibly be the best store in New York City for Spanish ingredients, and did I mention great sandwiches as well? From great olive oils and vinegars to Marcona almonds, canned albacore tuna, sardines, mussels, true Cantabrico anchovies, single-source honey, roasted and peeled organic chestnuts, Iberico ham, a very good cheese selection, and fresh saffron, it's here. There are also great sweets such as traditional flan, churros dusted with powdered sugar or dipped in melted chocolate, and hand-cut Spanish turrones and nougats. Prepared foods are of high quality as well. In a pinch and need some easy items for entertaining? Try the savory little tarts, wedges of potato and egg tortilla, croquettes, roasted peppers, and superb sandwiches. In the European tradition, small sandwiches are composed of just a few simple ingredients, but always of the highest quality, and set within good bread slathered in good olive oil. Chorizo with manchego cheese is yummy. Canned ventresca tuna, fatty, hand-cut slices cut from the albacore loin, are paired with piquillo pepper and fresh tomatoes in season. And they have maybe the best ham sandwich on the planet, made with ribbon-like slices of Pata Negra ham on a ciabatta-like bread with a drizzle of fruity, nutty Spanish extra-virgin olive oil.

DiPalo's

212-226-1033
206 Grand Street, at Mott Street
Cheese and other Italian specialty ingredients
Moderate
All major credit cards accepted
Monday–Saturday 9 AM–6:30 PM, Sunday till 3:30 PM
6, J, M, Z, N, Q, R, W trains to Canal Street station

Though there are better all-around cheese stores—Murray's, Artisanal, Fairway—I don't think anyone, including DiPalo's competition, would argue that the selection of Italian cheeses available here isn't the best in the city. They make their own fresh mozzarella and fresh ricotta and have Italian mozzarella di bufala flown in at least twice a week. This is a family business, where you'll often find Sammy, his brother, Lou, and Lou's wife behind the counter all at once, slicing, weighing, and packaging cheese for their devoted longtime customers. Lou's son is also in the business and was trained in Italy, where he spent the better part of four years tasting and learning about the best Italian ingredients. In 2008 and early 2009, they finally expanded westward, taking over two stores that were neighbors. Here you'll find a great little Italian wine-only shop and more Italian specialties. If you need Parmigiano, they have half a dozen varieties of Reggiano, plus Grana. Need Ribiola? No problem. Pecorino, over a dozen choices. Speck or great prosciutto? You've come to the right store. Past the great cheese and meat selections, add a superb assortment of olive oils, often from very small producers, along with vinegars, pastas, anchovies, mustards, fruits, canned tomatoes—you name it. When it comes to Italian specialties, this little store probably not only has everything but also carries the best available for export. If you can, visit this place on the weekdays, as on weekends and around any holiday the line goes out the door and around the corner. It should be mentioned that DiPalo's supplies many of the best Italian restaurants in New York with cheese, especially rich creamy imported ricottas. With a long lease in place, as of 2008 a new and expanded retail space that doubles the square footage, a small but focused Italian wine shop next door, and a younger generation eager to take over, the New York food scene will be all the richer with DiPalo's in its foreseeable future.

Essex Street Market

212-312-3603
80-120 Essex Street, between
Delancey and Rivington
Streets
Restaurants/retail
Prices vary
All major credit cards accepted
Monday–Saturday 8 AM–6 PM
F, J, M, Z trains to Essex Street/
Delancey Street station

Let's say you have a recipe that requires fresh breadfruit, recaro leaf, whiting, pigs' feet, yautia root, single-vineyard artisanal extra-virgin Spanish olive oil, perfectly aged Vermont farmhouse cheddar cheese, and a bottle of kosher wine, plus you need a cheap pair of jeans . . . and oh yeah, a haircut. This is the place. This 15,000-square-foot space houses dozens of retailers and is run by the city's Economic Development Corporation. A half-dozen years ago the place was half empty; now it's nearly fully rented, with new applications coming in every day. Like Arthur Avenue in the Bronx, the Essex Street Market was Fiorello La Guardia's brilliant idea, intended to get pushcarts off the street and turn the peddlers into vendors, all under one roof. Over the years, as the neighborhood changed, it went from Jewish to Puerto Rican to what it is today, a mixed bag skewing younger and richer all the time. And so it is that the market is a perfect snapshot of what this neighborhood was, what it is now, and where it's headed.

BATISTA GROCERY

212-254-0796

Just next to Saxelby's is the far larger and older Batista Market. Here you'll find plenty of Hispanic canned goods and dried goods, grains, fruits, salt cod (bacalao), and the hard-to-find herb recaro, which is very close to fresh cilantro in flavor but has long fern-shaped leaves. They have sweet Scotch bonnet peppers, yuca root, and kabocha squash, as well as the usual fresh produce found around town, but here at discount prices. For many years, this neighborhood was very Hispanic, mainly Puerto Rican, and this stall and a few others like it in the market cater seemingly exclusively to that broader Latino community. Canned and dried beans sit next to spice mixes and canned fish and tomatoes. The selection of high-quality fresh and preserved foods here is hard to beat anywhere outside of the barrio or Washington Heights.

FORMAGGIO ESSEX

212-982-8200

In the rear, this is one of my favorite stalls, featuring a good selection of imported cheese as well as artisanal olive oils and an amazing Jerez reserve sherry vinegar. The back wall is all cheeses, and the selection is very good. The rest of the space features an assortment of little culinary wonders, odds and ends from here and there, all carefully selected and hard to find elsewhere. The Turkish-born owner, Ihsan Gurdal, and his wife, Valerie, run this shop, and one in Boston as well. His contacts include friends at the famed spice market in Istanbul. The store is run by Maximillian Shrem, who is a real foodie and knows every product in the store very well. Here you'll find sea salts from all over Europe, slender one-kilo boxes of fine Italian spaghetti and vermicelli from Molino Pastificio, bags of pastas from Rustichella d'Abruzzo, Marcona almonds, assorted jars of dated, specific-flower French honey, and jams from the Ardèche region— in short, a great little selection of hard-to-find goodies for your pantry. You won't find a single product here that doesn't come with some excellent story and culinary pedigree.

JEFFREY'S MEATS
212-475-6521

In addition to Luis Meats, where cows' feet, pigs' feet, and blood sausage sit right next to ground chuck and assorted cubed stew meats, one of the more interesting stalls is that run by butcher Jeffrey Ruhalter. He's a fourth-generation Lower East Side butcher whose family once ran a store nearby at 188 Orchard Street before coming here in 1939. You'll find prime dry-aged beef and ducks from D'Artagnan alongside tripe, ground chuck, and inexpensive but top-quality stew meats. These guys were here back in the days when a high percentage of the purchases at this market were made with food stamps, not C-notes. Ruhalter is a link to the old Jewish roots of this market and the community. He reminded me one day that back in the 1930s, new arriving immigrants were told by the authorities on Ellis Island to visit this market in order to find ingredients from home and also to help establish themselves in this bustling neighborhood, make contacts, and locate relatives or familiar faces from their hometown who could help them get a job or an apartment. Stop by and meet Ruhalter. He's not shy, and he's a great source of information on meat and this neighborhood.

NEW STAR FISH MARKET
212-475-8365

RAINBO'S FISH MARKET
212-982-8585

These two fishmongers are decent, not great, but on a recent visit the fresh whiting looked very nice, completely cleaned and boneless at $3.99 per pound; there were also grouper at $5.99 and some very decent tilefish at $6.99, less than half what they would cost uptown. The selection varies with the season. Rainbo's also sells muffins, pies, and tarts, and you can order specialty cakes.

SAXELBY CHEESEMONGERS

212-228-8204

Enter through the southernmost door of the market, and right in front of you is Saxelby Cheesemongers. Ann Saxelby had worked for years at the great Murray's Cheese on Bleecker Street before opening this tiny kiosk of a shop back in 2005. Prior to her stint at Murray's, Saxelby worked as a cheesemaker at Cato Corner Farm in Connecticut, and she spent half a year abroad in Europe, some of that time with slow-food folks, before bringing her passion to the Essex Market. She features a well-focused variety of cheeses from American farmstead producers. The selection is small but jewel-like, varying with the season. When Saxelby herself is not there in the flesh, the staff are very helpful and have great product knowledge. Here you'll find great cheddars and goat's-milk cheeses from New England, blues from out west, and some interesting finds from the flyover states in between. She also has great milk from an upstate dairy—try it for a reminder of what milk used to taste like.

Faicco's Pork Store

212-243-1974
260 Bleecker Street, between Carmine and Leroy Streets
Meats
Inexpensive
All major credit cards accepted
Tuesday–Thursday 8:30 AM–6 PM, Friday to 7 PM, Saturday to 6 PM, Sunday 9 AM–2 PM
1 train to Christopher Street station; A, C, E, B, D, F, V trains to West 4th Street station

Pronounced "fee-ack-os," this is one of the best pork stores in Manhattan. If you're looking for great sausage, pork for roasting, cutlets, various cured meats, and other Italian specialties, this is the place. It reminds me of the kind of pork stores that were once much more common in East Coast cities with Italian neighborhoods. Walk in, and you can just smell it: fresh sausage, fennel seed, and aged cheeses. This strip of Bleecker Street is a shopping mecca, with Murray's Cheese right next store, the Lobster Place on the other side, and Amy's Bread a few doors down. Along with those at Giovanni Esposito & Sons in Hell's Kitchen, these are the best sausages made in Manhattan, including hard-to-find items such as the big fat cotechino that is a specialty of Apulian cuisine. You'll find superb, house-made pork sausage, hot and sweet, in various thicknesses, and those lovely little sausage rings in lamb casings, filled with cheese and herbs and held together with long, thin wooden skewers. Plump, well-seasoned, tied braciole made of beef or pork, stuffed pork chops, a few decent cuts of steak, and pre-breaded chicken and pork cutlets are all ready to take home and cook. In the rear they have a small counter with some prepared food to go, which is very decent and very convenient: lightly breaded, greaseless fried chicken and pork cutlets, lasagna, and some days good stromboli, as well as balls of just-made fresh and smoked mozzarella and an assortment of whole olives. They carry a good array of imported canned tomatoes, good-quality Italian dried pasta, cheeses both whole and grated, and other Italian specialties and breads. Stop by and you'll see why they have been in business so long.

Fairway Market

212-595-1888
2127 Broadway, between
74th and 75th Streets
(and elsewhere)
Retail supermarket
Moderate
All major credit cards accepted
Seven days a week 9 AM–9 PM
1, 2, 3 trains to 72nd Street station

It's hard to believe it, but Fairway recently celebrated its 50th anniversary. I lived a block away for years during the 1980s, and the place was wildly popular then. In those days it was essentially a discount produce store, with some canned goods, bagels, and, oddly, one of the best cheese counters in the city, courtesy of Steve Jenkins. As the neighborhood gentrified, they got more serious, and when Citarella next door expanded, it became a war. There used to be a D'Agostino's between the two stores, and you'd get your produce from Fairway, your fish at Citarella, and soap at D'Agostino's. Then Citarella started selling meat, as did Fairway. Citarella expanded upstairs, and Fairway took over the D'Agostino's space, greatly increasing its footprint. At its core, Fairway is still a great discount fresh produce store, but to that add a well-selected range of mainly imported specialties—oils, vinegars, canned fish— as well as discount traditional supermarket items. The meat is still better at Citarella, but the prices here are significantly lower and the quality a close second place. They carry Murray's chickens, an excellent local brand of fresh, clean poultry. While the fish counter cannot equal the one at Citarella, the prices here are more reasonable. The cheese counter is still great. Upstairs via an elevator are more shopping and a decent small café that serves breakfast, lunch, and early dinners. The place is an Upper West Side landmark and by 6 PM on any given day is a mob scene. The lines move fast, the staff are mostly veterans, and the place is a real slice of New York shopping at its finest. They have other stores, including one uptown in Harlem, a newish one in Red Hook, Brooklyn, and one on Long Island, and in 2006 they took on some additional investors and are now poised for greater expansion into the outer boroughs and the surrounding suburbs as well.

Florence Meat Market

212-242-6531
5 Jones Street, between
Bleecker and West 4th
Streets
Hand-cut gourmet meats
Moderate
All major credit cards accepted
Tuesday–Friday 8:30 AM–6:30
PM, Saturday 8 AM–6 PM
A, C, E, B, D, F, V trains to West
4th Street station; 1 train to
Christopher Street station

In a neighborhood already rich with great ingredient stores, Florence still delivers after all these years. A reminder of what the term "neighborhood butcher" used to mean, this is still a humble little storefront with a sawdust-strewn floor and a small counter where the meats are cut by hand to order. And it was here that a little history was made when the butcher, teacher, meat man extraordinaire, and longtime owner of the shop, Jack Ubaldi, coined the term "Newport steak," which is the cut he took from the sirloin tri-tip. Once he discovered this great-tasting, inexpensive steak, he didn't know what to call it, as this cut had never been marketed before. He got the idea for the name while watching a TV commercial for Newport cigarettes, which had a triangular on-screen logo at the time. "That's it. I'll call it a Newport steak." And so a star was born. These days the butcher in charge and current owner, Benny Pizzuco, burly and bearded, mans the knives and the meats. The quality is excellent, the meats are prime or top-quality choice, the lamb is from Colorado or other domestic sources, and the service can't be beat, as they really cut all steaks and chops to order any way you like them. With Citarella, Ottomanelli, and Faicco's just a few blocks away, Greenwich Village has a wealth of great choices for excellent hand-cut meat.

Food Emporium Bridgemarket Store

212-752-5836
405 East 59th Street, between
First Avenue and
Sutton Place, under the
Queensboro Bridge
Groceries, specialty foods,
chocolates
Moderate to expensive
Monday–Friday 7 AM –11 PM,
weekends 8 AM –11 PM
4, 5, 6, N, R, W trains to
Lexington Avenue/59th Street
station

Food Emporium is a division of the Great Atlantic and Pacific Tea Company, aka A&P, and they also own Waldbaum's, Super Fresh, and the recently purchased Pathmark, but Food Emporium represents their best effort to date at upscale shopping. There are more than 20 locations in Manhattan, but this store is the jewel in the crown, though geographically remote, tucked away on the far end of East 59th Street, hard against the East River. It's worth the trek. Manhattan is underserved by its indoor food markets, partially due to the simple fact that commercial rents here are far and away the highest in the nation. We have great independents like Citarella and Fairway, some decent shopping at Essex Street Market and Chelsea Market, and greenmarkets in season as well, but none of the retail spaces are anywhere near as glorious as this. Like the Grand Central Oyster Bar, this room is one of the few public or private spaces sheathed in decorative Guastavino tiles. The ceiling soars, the space is open, and the feel reminds one of the great food courts of Europe, especially Harrods food hall at Knightsbridge, which is not a coincidence. The man behind this store and in charge of overseeing the growth and direction of the chain is Hans Heer, a Swiss native whose previous post was at Harrods in London. He travels abroad frequently in search of new items and producers, and the shelves are a testament to his commitment to quality. Here you can find your usual laundry detergent, toothpaste, and toilet paper alongside an excellent selection of gourmet specialties, charcuterie, foie gras, smoked duck breast, Berkshire pork chops, USDA prime meat, Black Angus beef, farmstead cheeses, condiments, pasta, artisan olive oils, and vinegars.

Giovanni Esposito & Sons

212-868-4142
500 Ninth Avenue,
    at 38th Street
Meats
Inexpensive
All major credit cards accepted
Monday–Saturday 8 AM–6 PM
A, C, E trains to 42nd Street
    station

This was one of the last remaining old-time, family-run businesses on this strip of Ninth Avenue, in what used to be called Hell's Kitchen. Recently the business was sold, but the recipes are the same and the quality still ranks at the top in this genre of old-school pork stores. The original Giovanni moved from Naples to New York in the early 1900s and had a pork store on Mulberry Street in Little Italy. He returned home in 1924 to join the military, but after the rise of Mussolini, he left Italy once more and brought his entire family back to Manhattan with him. The store opened in this location in 1933, and is today run by the affable Robert Esposito. This is still a great part of town for ingredient shopping, with the spice market International Grocery just up the street; Manganaro's a block south; and Stiles Farmer's Market a few blocks up and across the street.

These days you can't just be a pork store, so they sell chicken, beef, and lamb as well, but I come for the Italian-style sausage. There is really no excuse to buy the stuff in the supermarket; it's awful. So what's the difference, you ask? The meat they use, the percentage of fat, and finally how it's butchered, ground, and seasoned. The mass-produced sausage has a higher fat content, is made from all trim derived from all over the animal, tends to have much more cartilage and even chips of bones in the finished product, and flat out doesn't taste nearly as good. Here the butchers work in smaller batches, wielding sharp knives on fresh pork shoulder. They take their time and produce well-trimmed meat that is then cubed, chilled, marinated, ground, and stuffed into casings in small batches. They offer both hot and sweet as well as rings in smaller and thinner casings, along with varieties that incorporate cheese and herbs in the mix. The other meats here are good as well, especially the pork cuts. Along with Faicco's on Bleecker Street, here you'll find some of the best sausage available in New York—it's well worth the trip.

Gramercy Meat Market

212-481-1114
383 Second Avenue, between 21st and 22nd Streets
Meats and prepared meals to go
Moderate
All major credit cards accepted
Seven days a week 9 AM–7:30 PM
6 train to 23rd Street station

This place opened originally a few years back as the French Butcher, and the man behind the scheme was in fact a very good French butcher. His name was Arnaud Carré, and he had been for many years the butcher at the New York restaurant Les Halles, where I first met him; he now is rumored to have moved to Thailand, but the store continues in his tradition. Europeans butcher cattle differently than we do. The loin cuts are identical, as are the filet mignon, strips, ribeyes, etc., but where we grind or cube the balance of the animal for hamburger and stew meat, they dig for buried treasure. The American beef business is huge and is a large part of the heavily government-subsidized commodity farming agroindustry that keeps proteins cheap and plentiful. In Europe, cattle are scarce and grass-fed, and every piece of meat gets used to its best and highest value. So one day Carré showed me how he takes down a carcass like a surgeon, revealing cuts such as the poire, the pavé, the paleron, and the fausse-araignée. They are small cuts, just one per animal, but prized, and they make for a nice meal simply grilled or pan-seared and eaten medium rare. Gramercy Meat Market also now offers a good selection of free-range, organic, and grass-fed beef. These days the place is run by Antero Pereira, who studied under Carré and continues to provide very good meat, and some prepared meals as well to go.

The prices are fair, not cheap, but the meat is of good quality, and they are more than happy to do specialty cuts, cut steaks to order, and prepare, trim, season, and tie roasts as you need them.

Greenmarkets

212-788-7476
http://www.cenyc.org

Over the last decade, the Greenmarket scene has vastly improved in Manhattan, the outer boroughs, and throughout the country, for that matter. Part of it has to do with the raised public awareness of and interest in eating good, seasonal produce and organic and locally grown ingredients whenever possible. In many cases these markets have helped smaller farmers keep the farm by allowing them to sell directly to end users who are willing to pay a premium for quality, flavor, and freshness. Call it the Whole Foods effect, if you will, but what was once considered the province of patchouli-scented, Birkenstock-wearing hippies is now very mainstream.

The list below is partial, as new markets sprout up all the time. Of these markets, I use Union Square the most, as I live nearby, and it still is the biggest and most diverse of all in Manhattan. Most chefs I know use Union Square as well. If you're going to visit Union Square, the best selection of foods is found on Wednesdays and Saturdays, though the place can be a total zoo on Saturdays when the weather is cooperating. You'll find everything from artisanal cow's, goat's, and sheep's milk cheeses to organic fruits and vegetables, herbs, leafy greens, garlic, dozens of tomato varieties, the Rick's Picks line of pickles, wonderful poultry, fish fresh from Montauk (often caught within 24 hours of being trucked down here), organic turkey, beef, eggs, great pretzels, jellies, jams, breads, and baked goods. In short, the Union Square Greenmarket is a foodie's paradise. The list below of Manhattan locations is loosely geographic, starting downtown and heading uptown.

ABINGDON SQUARE
West 12th Street and Eighth Avenue
Saturday 8 AM–2 PM
Year round

BOWLING GREEN
Broadway and Battery Park Place
Tuesday and Thursday 8 AM–5 PM
Year round

CITY HALL
Chambers Street and Centre Street
Tuesday and Friday 8 AM–3 PM
June to December

FEDERAL PLAZA
Broadway and Thomas Street
Friday 8 AM–4 PM
Year round

HARLEM
West 144th Street and Lenox Avenue
Tuesday 8 AM–3 PM
July to October

I.S. 144
West 77th Street and Columbus Avenue
Sunday 10 AM–5 PM
Year round

LAFAYETTE STREET
Lafayette Street and Spring Street
Thursday 8 AM–5 PM
July to October

175TH STREET
West 175th Street and Broadway
Thursday 8 AM–6 PM
July to December

P.S. 234
Greenwich Street and Chambers Street
Saturday 8 AM–3 PM
Year round

SHEFFIELD PLAZA
West 57th Street and Ninth Avenue
Wednesday and Saturday 8 AM–6 PM
May to December

St. Mark's Church

East 10th Street and Second Avenue

Tuesday 8 AM–7 PM

June to December

Tompkins Square

7th Street and Avenue A

Sunday 8 AM–5 PM

Year round

Union Square

East 17th Street and Broadway

Monday, Wednesday, Friday, and Saturday
    8 AM–6 PM

Year round

Verdi Square

West 72nd Street and Broadway

Saturday 8 AM–5 PM

June to December

Washington Market Park

Greenwich Street and Chambers Street

Wednesday 8 AM–3 PM

April to December

West 97th Street

West 97th Street, between Amsterdam and
    Columbus Avenues

Friday 8 AM–2 PM

Year round

Han Ah Rheum

212-695-3283
25 West 32nd Street, between
    Fifth and Sixth Avenues
Korean specialties
Inexpensive
All major credit cards accepted
Seven days a week 9 AM–9 PM
N, Q, R, W, B, D, F, V, 1, 2, 3
    trains to 34th Street station

This strip of 32nd Street is the epicenter of Koreatown, Manhattan. Some say that the Korean food is now better in a few North Jersey towns or in Queens; if I lived there, I'd shop and eat there, but I don't. So if you live or work in Manhattan and want to cook Korean food, need Korean ingredients, or just want to see what a Korean grocery store looks like, look no further. Past the automatic doors, the store spreads deep and wide into this two-story space. The basement is for employees only and storage, but the ground floor has a large assortment of anything needed for the Korean pantry. Immediately to the right as you enter are 25- and 50-pound bags of Asian-style short-grain rice. Past that, small refrigerators are filled with Korean soft drinks and then little containers of kim chee and everything imaginable that can be pickled. Beyond that is an assortment of dried and preserved roots, all sorts of bean curds both soft and firm, and a multitude of pepper pastes. To the rear is a good fish counter and a very good meat counter, with some of the best buys on short ribs, cut thick and thin, anywhere in Manhattan. Koreans love short ribs and use them for all sorts of dishes.

The center of the store has reach-in freezers with some great meal-in-a-hurry solutions, including tasty frozen dumplings, wontons, and noodles. They have a great selection of soy sauces, various styles of rice vinegar, bean pastes, and other Korean condiments essential for a good homemade Korean meal. Up front on the way to the checkout are some nice Korean snack foods and pastries. Try the ones made from brown sticky rice studded with nuts and dried fruit, the soft little rice flour balls with red bean paste filling, or the doughy ones shaped like small walnuts with a nut-like paste at the center. None is too sweet, and each is interesting in its own way.

Integral Yoga Natural Foods

212-243-2642
229 West 13th Street, between Seventh and Greenwich Avenues
Retail supermarket, health food and vegetarian items
Inexpensive to moderate
All major credit cards accepted
Seven days a week 8 AM–8:30 PM
1, 2, 3, A, C, E trains to 14th Street station; L train to Eighth Avenue station

I'd walked past this place dozens of times when I lived in the neighborhood; I'm not a yoga kind of guy, though I probably should be. But it seemed honest, earnest, and humble, and I'm kind of a hippie at heart, so one day I wandered in just to see what was going on in there. I expected chanting, incense, thick braids, baggy clothes, and patchouli, but what I found was a pretty darned good old-fashioned (circa 1970s in any good college town) health food store. Let's face it, before Whole Foods came in and cornered the market, it was places like this all over the country that serviced the health-conscious, vegan, vegetarian, and natural-food crowds. They have a daily selection of pre-made sandwiches, hot and cold soups, and salads, hot and cold prepared foods to go, a good selection of fresh produce in season, whole-wheat pastas, grains, rice, dried and fresh fruits and nuts, legumes in various and sundry forms, and all kinds of tofu products. They even have organic, enviro-friendly cosmetics, shampoos, skin care products, and the like. To that, add a juice bar and a good selection of frozen ingredients and meal solutions. I'm told that it is essentially a nonprofit store, with all the proceeds going to an organization that promotes yoga and the lifestyle founded by Sri Swami Satchidananda, who also founded the Integral Yoga Institute, located right next door. For over 30 years they've been at it, and as far as I can tell they are now established, with a big and dedicated clientele, as one of the best stores for vegans and vegetarians in New York.

International Grocery

212-279-1000
543 Ninth Avenue,
at 40th Street
Dry ingredients like spices
and grains, oils, and Greek
specialty ingredients
Inexpensive
All major credit cards accepted
Monday-Saturday 8 AM–6:30 PM
A, C, E trains to 42nd Street/
Port Authority Bus Terminal
station

Here you'll find half a dozen varieties of cornmeal at three pounds for $1.50, including an unusual white cornmeal used for baking by African immigrants who trek from all over the city to purchase hundreds of pounds a week. If you look carefully, you'll find tucked away amid the bulk spices the very hard-to-find imported dried Greek white elephant bean, which looks like a large, flat lima bean. After some soaking and slow cooking in a stew or with aromatics, this bean has a unique firm but silken consistency. There are one-pound canisters of natural sea salts at prices that are a fraction of what they charge uptown: Spanish paprika at 99 cents for 4 ounces, pure onion powder and garlic powder at 75 cents for 4 ounces, bulk celery salt, and several varieties of whole black peppercorns at giveaway prices. Not only are these sold for far less than what you'd pay for those name-brand spices in the supermarket, but they're so much fresher here too.

Italian Food Center

212-925-2954
186 Grand Street,
at Mulberry Street
Italian specialties and
sandwiches for take-out only
Inexpensive to moderate
All major credit cards accepted
Seven days a week 10 AM–2 AM
6, J, M, Z, N, Q, R, W, trains to
Canal Street station

When I was a child in Philadelphia, there were Italian delis like this all over the place. You could just walk in the door and you knew it was good by the smell. There are still a fair number of places like this in Brooklyn and the Bronx, but in Manhattan, especially in what's left of Little Italy, this is about the last one. It's narrow and a bit cluttered, but they have a really good selection of Italian goods, from pasta to canned tuna, San Marzano tomatoes, anchovies, roasted peppers, and the like. But what I come here for are the sandwiches. Made to order on good bread, these are some of the best Italian-style heroes (or hoagies, to use the Philadelphia term) you'll find in town. They have silly names, but the one billed as the New Yorker is a good reference point: slices of good prosciutto, Genoa salami, dry provolone, and pickled mushrooms with a good splash of olive oil make for a heck of a nice lunch. If you want prepared food to go, they have a good small selection of that here as well. Like other little stores, they carry trays of eggplant Parmesan sold by weight, breaded fried chicken cutlets, pork chops in various guises, chicken rollatini, and of course sausage and peppers. Mostly I come here for the sandwiches, though, which are stuffed with top-quality cold cuts, drizzled with olive oil, and almost always consumed on the fly on the way home.

Joe's Dairy

212-677-8780
156 Sullivan Street, between West Houston and Prince Street
Italian cheeses, some house-made
Inexpensive
Cash only
Tuesday–Saturday, 9 AM–6 PM
C, E trains to Spring Street station; 1 train to Houston Street station

A tiny little storefront of just a few hundred square feet tucked away on what seems like a little New York side street, Joe's Dairy sells some of the best fresh mozzarella and ricotta in the city, not to mention great homemade sandwiches. Got the recession blues? Stop by for the smoked mozzarella sandwich with roasted red peppers served on fresh semolina bread. Set on the ground floor of a humble red brick walk-up tenement, the signage out front in red, white, and green announces *Latticini Freschi*, and it delivers on the promise of fresh house-made cheese. For years this was run by Joe Aiello. These days Anthony Campanelli runs the shop, but the fresh cheese is still the draw. They have a selection of other cheeses, some salumi, and some olives, all of which are fine, but if you are looking for fresh mozzarella, salted, unsalted, or smoked, or great inexpensive sandwiches, this is the place.

Kalustyan's

212-685-3451
123 Lexington Avenue, between 28th and 29th Streets
Herbs, spices, grains, and other dry ingredients
Moderate
All major credit cards accepted
Monday–Saturday 10 AM–8 PM, Sunday 11 AM–7 PM
6 train to 28th Street station

Kalustyan's takes its name from back when this neighborhood was primarily Armenian, in the 1950s and 1960s. These days the area is the epicenter of Manhattan's Indian, Pakistani, and Bangladeshi communities, with some very good restaurants and two of the best spice and ingredient stores in the country, namely, Kalustyan's and Sinha Trading, right next door. Kalustyan's owner, Aziz Osmani, is a gracious host, always smiling and patient with my many stupid questions. He runs several good restaurants here too, notably Curry Leaf, a few doors down, and Rice, right across the street. Spices are crucial to all Indian cuisine, and freshness is most important. What separates this store from so many others in the business is that Osmani brings in spices from around the world in whole form, then properly stores them in bulk in his warehouse in New Jersey and grinds them only as needed, after which they are immediately sealed and sent to this store for sale.

These are top-quality spices in their purest, freshest form, with no additives, shortcuts, or cheap fill. And his prices are complete bargains. Compared to what you pay for stale, tasteless name-brand spices in the supermarket, here you'll find the real thing, full of freshness and flavor, at a fraction of the cost. It's no surprise that many top chefs flock to the place, as do foodies in the know, and of course the greater New York metro Middle Eastern and South Asian expat communities. Kalyustan's Web site is very good and kept up to date, and they do a brisk mail-order business as well. This little store, maybe 25 feet wide and barely two stories tall, stocks more than 4,000 items, many of which are nearly impossible to find elsewhere, on spotless shelves, stacked floor to ceiling.

Kam Kuo Food

212-349-3097
7 Mott Street
Chinese retail
Inexpensive
All major credit cards accepted
Seven days a week 10 AM
6, J, M, Z, N, Q, R, W trains to
Canal Street station

There are a few big Chinese retail stores in Chinatown proper that seem to sell everything, from wall art to tea cups and saucers, and Kam Kuo is one of them. While they carry meat, produce, and some fish, I think you do better at the stores and stalls nearby that specialize in such ingredients. Come here for odds and ends and frozen Chinese oddities with no English labeling. (How can they import and sell these items?) Like a mini version of Kam Man, around the corner, this is a sort of Chinese version of a food-based five-and-dime store, or what they used to be. On these shelves you'll find lots of teas, some dried herbs, assorted ginseng varieties, dried mushrooms, 10-gallon plastic buckets of hydrating roots, and assorted oddities. Upstairs it's mostly utensils, woks, and the like.

Kam Man Foods

212-571-0330
**250 Canal Street, between
Mott and Mulberry Streets**
Chinese retail
Inexpensive
Cash only
Seven days a week 8:30 AM–8:45 PM
6, J, M, Z, N, Q, R, W trains to
Canal Street station

When I first moved to New York, this place used to fascinate me. On my day off, with very little cash to spare, I'd walk from my apartment on Greenwich Street and shop for exotic ingredients for dinner at home. Chinatown was then, and still is, one of the great bargain shopping areas remaining in New York. This place is spread out over two floors. You enter past the street-level windows, where they have some pretty darned good BBQ pork hanging next to crisped duck, all ready to be hacked into portions and sold by weight. I figure this is sort of a Chinese version of Trader Joe's, with everything from canned and frozen foods to plates, chopsticks, and woks upstairs, and a full meat and fish counter to boot. Unless you're very savvy about ingredients, you may find the whole thing confusing. How many different varieties of soy sauce are there, anyway? That said, if you're looking to get started as a budding Chinese home cook, this place offers one-stop shopping to prepare your basic pantry, with everything from oyster sauce and sesame oil to dried shiitakes, seaweed, sea cucumbers soaking in white plastic bins, hundreds of types of fresh and dried noodles, fresh wonton skins and everything you'll need to place between them, and even the pans and steamers to cook them in. If you like food shopping, put this place on your list for the fun of it. It's worth a visit even if just to window-shop.

Lobel's of New York

212-737-1372
1096 Madison Avenue, between 82nd and 83rd Streets
Gourmet meats
Expensive
All major credit cards accepted
Monday-Saturday 8 AM–6 PM; closed Saturdays in July and August
4, 5, 6 trains to 86th Street station

What can I tell you about Lobel's? First, I rarely shop here because it is so darn expensive. That said, they may very well have the best retail meat in all New York City, if you don't mind spending big bucks, and I mean *big* bucks. They survive— well, actually, thrive—off the simple fact that in this neighborhood, which is perhaps the most well-heeled area of the genteel Upper East Side, it seems that no one is watching pennies. The meat they purchase is the first and highest grade within the prime designation, and often costs 10% more than the next grade of prime just below it. They sell Certified Black Angus meat, the designation ensuring that all the cattle used must be at least 50% Black Angus stock by breeding. By paying more and carefully selecting each and every carcass, Lobel's ensures that its dry-aged steaks are the gold standard, and they should be at these prices. The family can trace its roots in the cattle and butchering business to the 1840s in Austria, where Nathan Lobel got started. Today, five generations later, David, Evan, and Mark run the store, which has been at this location for more than 50 years.

The store is a simple, unpretentious place, wood-paneled, with stuffed animal heads hanging on the walls and two or three aproned butchers working the counter. Aside from the superb steaks, they have excellent free-range chicken, goose, duck, and Cornish game hen. The lamb they sell is grass-fed Rocky Mountain free-range; the pork is either Berkshire heritage or pastured, vegetarian, grain-fed, antibiotic-free Duroc pigs from Vande Rose Farms in Iowa. They sell Wagyu beef, milk-fed veal, and naturally raised prime beef, as well as great homemade hot dogs and sausages. For those in a hurry they sell homemade cooked meatballs, beef stew, BBQ ribs, pot pies, pot roast, roasted whole chickens, and even fried chicken to go. This is to my mind the best butcher shop in America for those who can afford it.

Murray's Cheese

212-243-3289
254 Bleecker Street, between Morton and Leroy Streets
Cheese and other specialties
Moderate to expensive
All major credit cards accepted
Monday–Saturday 8 AM–8 PM, Sunday 10 AM–7 PM
A, C, E, B, D, F ,V trains to West 4th Street station; 1 train to Christopher Street station

Murray's is the oldest continuously operating cheese store in New York, in business for well over 65 years in this same neighborhood. Its owner, New Jersey–born Rob Kaufelt, grew up in the grocery business, and is to cheese what Billy Graham is to Christianity: an evangelist. He even sells a T-shirt that reads "You've got a friend in cheeses." He's been profiled in the *New Yorker* and written about often in the *New York Times*, so I'll spare you all the background details and cut to the chase. In this little storefront you'll find one of the best selections of cheese from around the world. Rob and his buyers travel most of the year, tasting batch after batch of cheese and selecting specific wheels that they like. Like Terrance Brennan at Artisanal (let's not go into who was first), Rob has installed climate-controlled caves below Bleecker Street where cheese is allowed to mature to perfect ripeness. This process, known as affinage, was unheard-of in New York until just a few years ago. It allows Rob to bring in cheeses at various stages of ripeness, segregate them by type, and store them in custom-designed walk-in coolers until they are perfectly ready for consumption. Then and only then will they be brought upstairs for sale. Looking for a perfect Abbaye de Cîteaux, a delicious soft raw cow's milk cheese from Burgundy? They have it at $32.99 a pound. How about the terrific triple-cream Fleur-de-Lis from chef John Folse's Bittersweet Plantation Dairy in Gonzales, Louisiana? This soft ripe beauty is made from the milk of Guernsey cows, has a 75% butterfat content, and when available sells for $15.99 a pound—a steal. You'll find organic cheeses from the famed Cowgirl Creamery in beautiful coastal Point Reyes Station, California, perfect little raw goat's-milk Mâconnais cheeses from Burgundy at $6.99 apiece, and wedges of the nutty, burnt-butter Vacche Rosse Reggiano, made from milk of the rare red cows of Italy. They have cheese classes, free tastings, suggestions for wine pairings, seminars, and a staff that is as dedicated as its owner to spreading the gospel. Mixed in with the cheese are bulk packs of excellent Italian pastas sold by weight, breads, oils, tomatoes, and assorted hard-to-find ingredients.

Myers of Keswick

212-691-4194
634 Hudson Street, between Horatio and Jane Streets
British specialty ingredients
Moderate
Seven days a week 10 AM–7 PM
American Express and cash only
A, C, E, 1, 2, 3 trains to 14th Street station; L train to Eighth Avenue station

I live just a few blocks away, and early on as I explored the neighborhood I stumbled upon this curiosity. Its business card says it all: framed by two mini images of the Union Jack is the text "England's Glory, Myers of Keswick: Pork Pies, Cumberland Sausage." On display are not just the British flag but stacked cans of Heinz baked beans for the British market, Baxters soups, Wilkin and Sons' Tiptree preserves, Burgess chutney and mushroom ketchup, and tea, tea, and more tea. The owner, Peter Myers, is usually in the back room making his signature fresh sausage and savory meat pies. Many a day I'd just waltz in and ask what was warm and just out of the oven. If you're not familiar with British specialties, meat pies are ground seasoned meats combined with various vegetables and then wrapped in flaky pie crusts. The shop offers meat pies in several sizes, chicken and mushroom pies, sausage rolls, steak and kidney pies, shepherd's pies, Scotch eggs, and Cornish pasties. Nearly all these items are under $5 apiece, and with a small salad they make a great lunch or light dinner. Of course they have fresh scones too, but my all-time favorite things here are the great fresh sausages. The chipolatas at $5.95 a pound are some of the best breakfast sausage I've ever had—fresh and clean-tasting, mildly seasoned, and perfectly blended. If you've ever had brunch at Balthazar or Pastis, they use the same sausage there. The bangers and Cumberland sausage are more aggressively seasoned, and twice the size too; on weekends they sell a pork, leek, and ginger sausage as well. If you're looking for black pudding, they have that, as well as Danish and Irish bacon, some specialty cheeses, butters, and snacks for that taste of home for British expats. If you are a fan of mincemeat pies, stop by and place your order between Thanksgiving and Christmas, the only time of year they sell this specialty; it's among the best I've ever had anywhere. The employees all seem to have British accents and are almost painfully polite and cheery.

Olivier & Co.

646-230-8373
249 Bleecker Street, between
Cornelia and Leroy Streets
Oils
Moderate to expensive
All major credit cards accepted
Monday–Saturday 9 AM–7 PM,
Sunday noon to 6 PM
A, C, E, B, D, F, V trains to West
4th Street station; 1 train to
Christopher Street station

I'd walked past this tiny jewel of a store for years, as my habit had been to walk down the south side of Bleecker, the Murray's Cheese, Faicco's, and Lobster Place side. But one day this place just caught my eye, as it shares a name with the excellent florist who used to supply the restaurant Daniel, among others, with their beautiful floral arrangements. To my surprise, within this tiny store they had one of the best collections of olive oils to be found anywhere in New York, or the entire United States, for that matter: small, artisanal oils from the south of France, Italy, Spain, and elsewhere, many dated and coded with information about the harvest, the year, and the specific olive variety. Some are flavored, most are not, and all are lovely. These oils come packed in dark glass or small tins and are offered at prices that at first may cause sticker shock. But great oil is expensive to make, and a few drops go a long way. There is usually a good selection of oils to sample for free, and the staff can help match an oil and a producer's style with what you like. If you think you know good oil, think again, and stop by this place for some schooling.

O. Ottamanelli Meats

212-675-4217
285 Bleecker Street, just
south of Seventh Avenue,
near Jones Street
Meats
Moderate
All major credit cards accepted
Seven days a week 10 AM–7 PM
1 train to Christopher Street
station; A, C, E, D, B, F, V trains
to West 4th Street station

This great old-school butcher shop is run by four elderly brothers: Joe, Jerry, Frank, and Peter. Usually two or three of them are behind the counter at any given time. It was their father, Onofrio, who founded the store back in the 1930s. The prices are more than fair, the meat is very good, and they really still do butcher their own beef, grind their own meat (makes for great burgers), and prepare their own sausages. Though the neighborhood has gentrified and Bleecker Street is now home to froufrou fashion boutiques, this place is run the way it was back when it opened. The meat is cut and trimmed to order, and they fabricate unusual cuts such as the flatiron steak, taken from the chuck. I was there one day when the butcher was taking down an entire chuck on the butcher block out back. I asked one of the brothers if they sold flatiron, and of course he said yes. Then he told me they used to call it "chicken steak" back in the day. He proceeded to cut small slices for a regular customer and told me that he would seam it out for me to use as a quick steak, and that it was also great slow-cooked in tomato sauce. They do holiday roasts and have a nice line of individually frozen cuts of delicious bison meat from out west. The lamb is hormone-free, grass-fed, and shipped fresh, not frozen, from Australia, and the veal is white and milk-fed. Whether you need one small steak for dinner or a standing rib roast for a dozen guests, this is the kind of place that makes you wish butchers were found more frequently around town. With Faicco's down the street and Florence around the corner, you should be able to find any cut you're looking for here or just a few steps away.

Pino's Prime Meats

212-475-8234
149 Sullivan Street, between
  Houston and Prince Streets
Meats
Moderate
Cash only
Monday–Saturday
  8:30 AM–6:30 PM
1 train to Houston Street station;
  C, E trains to Spring Street
  station

I wish I could remember who told me about this place. I know it was a chef who said he shopped there on his days off, but that's all I can recall. So on that advice I stopped by and discovered a very good butcher shop that has been here for decades under various owners. It's now run by Pino Cinquemani, a Sicilian immigrant whose family has been in the butchering business for generations and had worked for other butchers around town before taking over this space in 1990. It's bare-bones but what a good butcher shop should be. The storefront is humble and narrow, with a simple stenciled sign on the window announcing the name, address, and phone number. The prices are on the blackboard, and hams hang from the ceiling. The butchers who work the counter are real live butchers, not the make-believe kind found all over town, and they work in front of you with cleavers, saws, and long slicing knives. The meat is cut, for the most part, to order, and if it's advice you're after, they'll talk to you all you need about which cuts are best for what and how to cook them. Here you'll find everything from nicely marbled prime and choice meats to great sausage (including the Moroccan merguez), legs of lamb, baby lamb, lamb chops, and very good poultry. The art of the butcher is going fast, and places such as this, where that craft still thrives, are real treasures, to my mind. The meat may cost a few dollars more than elsewhere, but it's worth the difference; the quality of the meat here is way above what is sold at most other stores in town. And you can talk to the butcher or Pino himself and learn about less expensive, delicious cuts such as the Newport steak and the lifter.

Raffetto's

212-777-1261
144 West Houston Street,
at MacDougal Street
House-made pasta
Inexpensive
Cash only
Tuesday–Saturday 9 AM–6 PM
1 train to Houston Street station;
A, C, E, B, D, F, V trains to
West 4th Street station

Here is one of the last old-school pasta makers left in Manhattan, echoing the Italian roots in this part of Greenwich Village. Within a block you have Pino's butcher shop and Joe's Dairy just across Houston, all destinations for serious foodies looking for quality ingredients. Raffetto's has been at this location for over a hundred years, run by the same family with the same recipes and even the same old pasta machine out back. These days Andrew looks after the store, and his brother Richard oversees the wholesale operation in Jersey, but little else has changed. If you're looking for fresh-cut, hand-made pasta or excellent ravioli, you've come to the right place. As with Lou Di Palo's excellent cheese store on Grand, you can count on your fingers the number of stores like this that have survived over the years. It doesn't hurt that they have a big, beautiful commercial wholesale facility in northern New Jersey to serve all the wholesale accounts, restaurants, and supermarket retail demand, but this place is the epicenter. They have extruded pasta such as penne and radiatore, as well as cavatelli, gnocchi, and even polenta, and also premade pasta-based meals including pasta sauces that are all restaurant-quality. The staff is lovely, and the pastas made here stand alongside the best made by anyone in any of the boroughs.

Russ & Daughters

212-475-4880
179 East Houston Street,
between Allen and
Orchard Streets
Appetizing store, specialty
ingredients
Moderate to expensive
All major credit cards accepted
Monday–Saturday 9 AM–7 PM,
Sunday 8 AM–5:30 PM
F, V trains to Second Avenue
station

This place is a New York institution. For four generations, this family (well, actually it's two families) has been buying and dispensing some of the best cured herring, smoked fish, and other appetizing items to New Yorkers who care about quality. The business started back when the founder sold herring off a pushcart. They have been here on Houston Street since 1914. How many businesses survive two generations, let alone four? Years back these types of stores were as common in this neighborhood as Starbucks is today, but institutions like this have been falling by the wayside for years now. The term "appetizing store" comes from kosher dietary law: whereas regular delicatessens were allowed to sell meat and meat-based dishes, appetizing stores carried only fish—smoked, cured, pickled, whatever. The only other place that offers quality as consistent as Russ & Daughters is Barney Greengrass (see the Restaurants section).

These days Mark Federman, the man who ran the place single-handedly from the late 1960s until recently, has been joined by his nephew, Josh Russ, and most recently his lovely daughter, Nikki. I can't tell you how thrilled I am that these two youngsters have showed up on the scene, energetic and willing to continue to carry on this great tradition well into the foreseeable future. It doesn't hurt either that they own the building. Mark was an attorney when he rejoined the business four decades ago, and now Josh, a former engineer for Silicon Valley powerhouses, is joined by Nikki, with a master's from Yale. Both realized they had herring in their blood.

Herring is one of the real specialties here, and they have no fewer than a dozen varieties, from your basic rollmops to schmaltz style, herring in cream, herring with onions, Danish style (my favorite), curried, Swedish dill, and chopped. All are delicious and at their prime. To this add a great selection of smoked salmon, from your basic eastern Nova to Scottish smoked, Gaspé, wild western, Balik, Norwegian, kippered, Baltic style, belly lox, center loin cut, and hot-smoked "baked" salmon. They buy very well and very carefully, inspecting each delivery to ensure that each and every day, the sliced salmon you purchase here is the best on the market—fatty, fresh, and fully smoked and cured. If it's caviar you need, you've come to the right place. They offer everything from the best imports available, to American transmontanus and paddlefish roe—they have it all. Of course they carry sable, whitefish, chubs, and a big variety of flavored cream cheeses, fish salads, and other schmears. And lest I forget, here too you'll find what's arguably one of the best chopped livers in all New York. Across from the fish aisle is a little selection of candied fruits, handmade chocolates, and varieties of halvah. There's cured fish and then there's great cured fish, and if you know the difference, come here and be rewarded. If you don't know the difference, then you should, so come here for an education.

Simchik Meats

212-888-2299
944 First Avenue, at 52nd Street
Meats
Moderate
All major credit cards accepted
Monday–Friday 8 AM–7 PM,
    Saturday 8 AM–6 PM
E, V trains to 53rd Street/
    Lexington Avenue station

While the far-east midtown location is not terribly convenient, this store is very good and well worth a detour. Lenny Simchik carries very good-quality beef, cut to order, and side dishes that are fully prepared and oven-ready as well, to make dinner solutions that much easier. This little spot, barely 400 square feet, has been a butcher shop for well over a century. This is no fancy place. An air conditioner with a little drain hose sits above the entrance, and the storefront is brick with a small awning above the plate-glass window, but the service and the meats are top-notch. The meats, including veal, are all beautifully sourced, cut, and trimmed; they carry premium chickens and very good eggs too. If you need small roasts, they will cut and tie those for you. Even the burger meat, which they grind in-house, is super; here it is a mix of spiced veal and lamb. Should you want it delivered, they do that by bicycle, covering the East Side south to 34th Street and north to 79th. Neighborhood butchers, once common, are now very rare, and this little jewel with its quality meats and personal service embodies all that was once great about the classic butcher shops.

The Vinegar Factory

212-987-0885
431 East 91st Street, between York and First Avenues
Retail supermarket, specialty ingredients
Moderate
All major credit cards accepted
Seven days a week 7 AM–9 PM
6 train to 96th Street station

Opened in 1993 by Eli Zabar of the famed New York food family, this was to be Fairway, Citarella, and Dean and DeLuca all rolled into one. His original partners were the folks from Gourmet Garage, but that partnership ended quickly, and since then it's been his baby solo. He also runs the lovely but absurdly expensive E.A.T. restaurant and take-out, further west of this spot. The selection here is worth the trip, and the prices are not nearly as bad as one might think, due to the far-east location just off York Avenue. That said, as in most big stores with lots of items, you have to shop carefully. The produce is mostly good, though a tad expensive. The fish selection is better than most, not as good as Citarella's but cheaper. Ditto the meat counter. I don't buy prepared foods to go, but they have a big selection here, and they appear for the most part decent. Some of the baked goods are better than decent: apple pie, coconut layer cake, pecan pie, and the bread selection. The smoked fish counter, surprisingly, features mostly the pre-packaged and pre-sliced stuff. The prepared soups, on the other hand, are a strong point here, full of flavor and for the most part made from scratch. If I lived nearby, I'd shop here often, but there have been a lot of changes in retail since 1993, and for individual ingredients such as cheese, bread, fish, or meat, better alternatives are plentiful.

Whole Foods

212-823-9600
10 Columbus Circle, in the
Time Warner Center
(and elsewhere)
Retail supermarket with
organics and traditional
offerings
Moderate
All major credit cards accepted
Seven days a week 8 AM–9 PM
1, A, C, B, D trains to 59th
Street/Columbus Circle
station; N, Q, R, W trains to
57th Street station

While the Chelsea location was the first Whole Foods in New York City, the opening of the flagship store in the basement of the Time Warner Center was a major statement. This was New York City's first real supermarket. Real estate is precious here, and historically the city's supermarkets have been dreary, tight, crowded affairs, with low ceilings, limited inventory, and zero charm. Walk into any of the older Red Apple, Gristede's, or Associated stores, and you'll see what I mean. So when Whole Foods leased this 50,000-square-foot space, it was huge news. The day they opened, they had security guards and senior management directing traffic at the top of the escalator leading to the store. Literally, there was a line out the door just to get in and take a peek. Their second week in business, this location became the highest-grossing store in the entire chain, racking up well over a million dollars in sales per week. During off hours, it is a pleasure to shop here. Space, space, space—the aisles are wide, the ceilings are high, the store is bright and clean, and two people can actually maneuver shopping carts down the same aisle in opposite directions with room to spare, which is quite a novelty in New York.

The produce is good, with an emphasis on organics, but well over half is from traditional farms as well. The displays are kept fresh and stacked high, and the staff is helpful. Of course, this place is expensive compared to ordinary supermarkets, but that has not stopped the chain from growing at record rates year after year, as most customers appear willing to pay more for the selection, the organics, and the concept in general. The fish selection is good—not as good as Citarella's, but few are. The items on sale usually represent very good value. They emphasize line-caught and wild fish, as well as farm-raised, and do not carry species that are in danger of being overfished. Their humane animal practices include not selling live lobsters here or at any other location nationwide. Organic dairy is available, as well as a nice variety of high-quality yogurt, both imported and domestic. They carry a full line of pasta, beans, sauces, oils, and grains, and even a good selection of green household cleaners. The meat counter is well stocked with a variety of options. Choice beef is sold next to prime and dry-aged choice—an odd decision, in my mind: why dry-age choice meat but not prime? But that's what they do here. They also have good beef from Niman Ranch, which comes from organic, free-range, grass-fed cattle; buffalo steaks, which are some of the best in New York; and a full line of both traditional and organic pork, lamb, poultry, and house-made sausage.

They do a huge business in prepared foods to go—there's even a sushi counter—and ample seating in the front portion of the store, to take a meal relaxed and sitting down. The whole rotisserie-cooked chicken is one of the great bargains in town for a quick meal solution. To this add an in-house bakery as well as a good selection of breads from other New York bakers, such as great crusty loaves from Sullivan Street and Balthazar. The cheese selection is good; ditto for the fresh whole-bean coffees. There is a full cosmetics, bath, and vitamin section as well. By 5:30 on any given day the place is packed, but they have a good system; though the lines can get very long, they move quickly, and note that there are separate lines for customers with 10 items or less. All in all, New York has embraced Whole Foods, and in many ways, they have raised the bar for retail food shopping.

Yorkville Meat Emporium

212-628-5147
1560 Second Avenue, at 81st Street
Smoked, cured meats
Moderate
All major credit cards accepted
Monday–Saturday 8 AM–7 PM, Sunday 9 AM–6 PM
6 train to 77th Street station

This is one of the last licensed smokehouses in Manhattan. A Hungarian meat market, it has some good smoked meats and a short and rather odd selection of Hungarian items as well. The garlic salami, smoked Gyulai sausage, smoked and double-smoked bacon, smoked pork butt, pork shoulder, pork ribs, and great ham hocks are surely worth the trek. They also have prepared food to go, mostly stews of beef and veal; goulash, of course, made from beef, veal, and once in a while tripe; Szekely goulash made with sauerkraut; fried pork cutlets; roast pork butt; meatballs; sour cherry soup; excellent house-made liverwurst; stuffed cabbage; and even decent chicken soup. In the refrigerated display case they keep feta cheese from Bulgaria, pork lard, rendered duck fat for confit, several cheeses, and even butter from the Jana Valley. Piled on top of the counters here and there are jarred and canned Hungarian specialties, such as fruit syrups, fruit preserves, tinned and house-made sauerkraut, pickles, and dried egg noodles. The staff is not too friendly, but once you get their attention, they will get what you need, answer questions, and make correct change. The store is a bit odd overall, but with Starbucks and CVS spreading everywhere, I'll take odd any day.

Zabar's

212-496-1234
2245 Broadway, at 80th Street
Retail supermarket
Moderate
All major credit cards accepted
Monday–Friday 8 AM–7:30 PM,
Saturday 8 AM–8 PM, Sunday
9 AM–6 PM
1 train to 79th Street station

What can be said about Zabar's, a longtime landmark in this Upper West Side neighborhood, that hasn't been said already? Dating back to 1934, this is a quintessential New York story: immigrants, hard work, determination, aggressive business practices. It's still essentially run by the same family, plus Murray Klein, three generations later. Originally housed in a smaller, Tudor-style building, the space these days sprawls over two floors and breaks nearly every retail record for dollar sales per square foot. What started as an appetizing store years back now sells nearly everything, it seems; there's even a great kitchen and housewares section upstairs. Cluttered and often way too crowded, the place has displays from floor to ceiling.

The smoked-fish counter is good, very good, but to my mind not as good as that at Barney Greengrass, a few blocks to the north, or at Russ & Daughters, on Houston. They have a great selection of coffee, both whole beans and ground, at very fair prices. The takeout food varies, of course, but is generally tasty and made with fresh ingredients to a high standard. For cheese, you're better off at Fairway, Murray's, Artisanal, or DiPalo's. For chocolates and some specialty or seasonal packaged sweets, be careful; they are brilliant buyers and are known in the industry for getting deals on items that are somewhat past their prime, which explains to some extent the amazingly cheap prices they offer to the public. As someone once said, if it's too good to be true, it probably isn't. That said, the store is a must-visit if you're anywhere near this neighborhood, and they are open 365 days a year to boot. I know Zabar's fan base is fiercely loyal, but to my mind, its heyday is behind it. Even so, it is still one of the great stores in New York for the smart shopper who knows good merchandise and can spot a good deal.

CHEAP EATS—$25 AND UNDER

Tough economic times call for creative solutions. While this book already has a lot of restaurants categorized as "moderate" and "inexpensive," I wanted to include a little section of great places, many of which are small and casual, while some are take-out only, but all of them offer great value for roughly $25.00 per person or less. It should also be noted that due to the difficult economic environment we are all experiencing, many restaurants are running "restaurant week" pricing all year long for lunch, which translates to $24.07 for three courses, plus tax and tip. Beyond this promotion, other deals abound all over town, so it's worth calling restaurants in advance to find out what they may be offering in terms of promotions, discounts, special menus, and any other incentives they may have to draw in customers.

Alfanoonse

8 Maiden Lane

212-528-4669

When I used to do live radio six days a week, many of them from the studios of WOR nearby on Broadway, I'd pop in here for a quick a falafel sandwich and was never disappointed. What started as a takeout-only joint nearby expanded to this 50-seat BYOB spot due in great part to the quality of the food and word-of-mouth reputation. The Middle Eastern menu features shawarma, various kebabs, baba ghanoush, meat and vegetable pies, and vegetarian platters. I also like the rice pudding and bizarre custard pudding with chocolate.

Akdeniz

19 West 46th Street

212-575-2307

In a neighborhood chock full of restaurants, mostly all bad, it's easy to view this part of town as a culinary flyover. But once in a while New York will surprise you. Akdeniz is a decent and inexpensive Turkish restaurant specializing in good vegetarian dishes and seafood. For starters, the babaghannouj is smoky and rich and the cacik (the cucumber yogurt mix scented with garlic and laced with chopped mint and dill) a good foil. Kebabs, lamb chops, and chicken in various guises are available, but I'd opt for the whole grilled fish on the bone—sea bass, trout, snapper, or dorade—all farm-raised but good especially cooked this way fresh off the grill. The wine list is short but okay, with a few notables from Turkey like the white Beyaz or Cankaya. For dessert, the Turkish pudding or kadayif are good options.

Ariyoshi

226 East 53rd Street

212-319-3940

Think of this as a midtown discount Izakaya, essentially a Japanese pub with great little plates. Start with the good plump gyoza dumplings or various yakitori, and move on to the small plate of greaseless, crisp-fried squid tentacles and a bowl of house-made miso known as moro, delicious with good udon. Nato, made with fermented soybean, is an acquired taste for sure but one that I love; here it is paired with grated daikon, fine julienne of black seaweed, and a sprinkle of tempura crumbs set in a broth. In one simple dish, you have crunch, brine, funk, and wheat-based noodles to round out the chorus. With beer and sake to wash it all down, expect to dine alongside many Japanese businessmen by 8 PM on most nights.

Cabrito

50 Carmine Street

212-929-5050

This space, which is just a few steps down the block from Rick Kelly's excellent custom guitar store, has turn over a few times. Prior to Cabrito, it was the short-lived Bar Fry, Josh DeChellises' homage to tempura, which was not the best showcase for his talents. The tempura was often way too greasy, the menu monochromatic, the room way too noisy, and the service awful. So in comes, Cabrito with a lower price point, painted tiled walls, and a more user-friendly neighborhood format. You can't miss the place; look for the hanging pink goat atop the doorway that has already been swiped and returned by some mischievous locals. The food is Mexican, good, and cheap. The signature baby goat has received mixed praise, but the rest of the menu is solid. Starters run from the single digits to low teens and include the rib-sticking re-fried beans studded with bacon and house-made chorizo. Tacos are $5.00 to $6.00 a piece. My favorite may be the rarely seen combination of braised tongue with avocado and salsa. Their tradition Pueblan sandwiches are great, filled with either marinated pork, grilled skirt steak, or fried chicken cutlet. Good-sized main courses top out in the high teens and include a nice dish of braised pork ribs with grits and fried corn tortillas. To this add a good selection of beer and tequila, and you get the idea: good drinks, good tasting food, easy on the wallet.

Café el Portal

174 Elizabeth Street

212-226-4642

Ignacio Carballido and his mom run this little subterranean store. She oversees the kitchen, and the food is good, simple, inexpensive, and homey. If it's on the menu, try the quesadilla made with huitlacoche, an acquired taste derived from ground corn that has a unique edible fungus. There are good chile rellenos, a decent range of tacos, burritos, quesadillas, enchiladas, and a really good rich tres leche cake to finish it all off. They do not serve alcohol, so be prepared to bring your own.

Co.

230 Ninth Avenue

212-243-1105

Opened in early 2009, Co. is the brainchild of the great New York bread-man Jim Leahy of Sullivan Street Bakery and no-knead fame. His part-ners here are none other than Jean-Georges Vongerichten and Phil Suarez, aka, JJ Inc. The dining room seats around 50, and the custom-made oven cranking out between 700 and 900 degrees comes from Modena, Italy. The pizza, cooked in under 2 minutes with a good char and sometimes too many black blisters, is generally very good, though I do think that Jim gets a bit carried away with some of his goofier topping ideas. Brussels sprouts on pizza? Now please, Jim. That said, Jim is a serious baker, and Co. is a place for serious pies. I love the simple Amalfi for $9.00, adorned with just crushed tomato, anchovies, pitted green olives, and chili pepper flakes, or the ham and cheese laced with caraway, topped with pecorino, gruyere, buffalo mozzarella, and shards of prosciutto. To complete your meal, they have good salad and vegetable sides, and they offer beer, have a good small wine list, and even have a few desserts should you be so inclined.

Community Food and Juice

2893 Broadway

212-665-2800

Everyone I know that lives anywhere near here, which is to say the Upper West Side northward through Harlem, just loves this place. And what's not to love? Though urban New York by location, there is something very Bay Area about the scene. Think Berkeley, as in organic, certified green, no bottled water (just filtered in re-useable containers), really solid cook-ing, great friendly service, and inexpensive, market-driven seasonal food to boot. From breakfast through dinner, they've got you covered. Start your day with good fair-trade coffee and house-made granola, blueberry pancakes, or brioche French Toast. For lunch, try the famous bowl of beets with creamy whipped goat cheese and toasted pistachios or the rice or udon bowls, veggie burger, or natural grass-fed beef burger. For dinner, shrimp pot stickers, really good crab cakes and any of the salads make for good starters. Also, seasonal house ravioli or panko-crisped chicken both come in under the $20.00 mark. My favorite desserts of theirs are the Key lime meringue pie and the dulce de leche sundae. With a full bar and food this good, it's well worth the trek uptown anytime for a visit.

Dok Suni's

119 First Avenue

212-477-9506

I usually get my Korean fix stepping off the N, Q, R, or W at 34th and walking south two blocks, but should you find yourself in the East Village, Dok Suni's will do just fine. Run by a mom-and-daughter team, the room is always busy. The food, especially the more traditional Korean side of it, is very good. There is a hip soundtrack, and not surprisingly, unlike their midtown counterparts, the place is packed with that Gen "X" and "Y" crowd living nearby. The good-sized menu is in English mostly, mixing traditional dishes with some new wave, fusion concepts. Their dumplings are good, and the kim chee pancake dipped in soy and vinegar is good to share. Essentially there is something here for everyone—noodle lovers, vegetarians, meat heads—and very good options as well, such as hot and spicy broiled squid, redolent of that ubiquitous red pepper paste, or the dish billed as fish jun, a white-fleshed fish egg, battered and then pan sautéed, served with a soy vinegar dipping sauce. A full bar is available, but beer or roast barley tea works best with this food.

Je'Bon Noodle House

15 St. Mark's Place

212 388 1313

As New York has gone noodle crazy, with everyone from Jean-Georges Vongerichten to David Chang getting in the game, I'm surprised this place doesn't get more press. It's good, consistent, and cheap. The theme is Asian noodles in various guises, with a good amount of variety. Everyone raves about the "silver needles," pan fried and tossed with minced pork shrimp, julienned carrot, egg, and onion, but I like the Singapore-style chow mei fun laced with curry or the combo fish ball and beef ball in chicken broth just as well. They have sushi, Japanese-style skewer plates, and a good beer list, as well as a broad range of interesting salads, with nearly nothing on the menu save the sushi for more than $10.00.

Keste Pizza & Vino

271 Bleecker Street

212-243-1500

Yet another great new pizza spot opened in early 2009, this one in the West Village, not far from John's and a few other Bleecker Street joints that aren't half bad as well. Keste sits next to Matt Uminoff Guitars, and one day as I was eyeing a vintage Les Paul I couldn't afford in the window,

I noticed something new right next door. In I marched. The long narrow room seats around 50, with the open kitchen and oven to the rear. Initially they had no liquor license, but beer was available right across the street at a deli. The menu offers a small a variety of pizza all coming from a custom-made, imported oven, as well as a few daily pizza specials, with some salads and side dishes. The ingredients for the pies are top notch: imported flour, San Marzano tomatoes, buffalo mozzarella, Sicilian sea salt, all sourced by the proud Pizzaiolo Roberto Caporuscio, who can be found forming the pies and manning the ovens most nights. The result here is a good, inexpensive, casual pizza spot as one might find anywhere in Southern Italy.

Lan Zhou

144 East Broadway

212-566-6933

I love good noodles in any culture and in any guise; ditto for dumplings, and those are the two best reasons to visit this spot. For around $5.00, you can get a great bowl of soup filled with chewy, addictive, hand-pulled noodles, and for less than half that price, eight, that's right eight, boiled pork and chive dumplings. Twelve dumplings will set you back $3.00. Bring your own beer and be advised that the décor is awful, the lighting fluorescent, and the staff less than vigilant, but the noodle maker performs in open view, and dinner for two can easily be done for well under $15.00.

Maoz

38 Union Square East (and others throughout city)

212 260 1988

A Middle Eastern vegetarian restaurant with several locations flaunting some of the best falafel in town; space is tight, the seating communal, but if you can look past that, they offer some very tasty and inexpensive salads, sandwiches, and entrees, and many qualify as vegan. For $10.00, the Maoz Royal is a sandwich filled with roasted eggplant, hummus, chopped lettuce, onions, cucumbers, and finished with fresh limejuice and a side of fries. Or mix and match falafel with various sides and a soft drink, and you can eat well for around $ 10.00 per person.

Margon

136 West 46th Street

212-354-5013

I discovered this place after wandering about, post guitar shopping just north of here on 48th Street. I walked past, did a double take, and went in. The cashier is by the door with the sandwich maker, with the dining room itself to the rear. What you have here is a great little Cuban hole-in-the-wall set in the midst of the Theater District, located mid-block on the south side of 46th between Broadway and Sixth Avenue. Margon offers eat-in and take-out options. Always busy at lunch, service here is cafeteria style. Sandwiches, especially the signature Cubano and the roast pork pernil, are very good, as are the hot items available daily from the steam table. Chicken soup studded with potatoes and chicken pieces and the fish soup are rich and satisfying. If you're really hungry, go for the palomilla, a nice-sized cut of beef taken from the top butt served with chopped onions, shards of garlic, and loads of lime juice. I love the stews here too, combining offal and lesser cuts; the ones made from oxtail, tripe, and pigs feet are totally worth the trip. Check out the daily specials: on Tuesdays they feature chicken chicharones and on Wednesdays Cuban fried pork "masas de puerco fritas." And save room for the flan or rice pudding for dessert.

Philly Slims

Various locations

789 Ninth Avenue

212-333-3042

As a Philadelphia native, I grew up eating cheese steaks, loads of them, and yet I've never quite figured out why people are so passionate about them. From time to time, I make them at home for my kids and must say that there is a certain something—beef, cheese, ketchup, salt, pepper, and maybe a few add-ons—resulting in a hot sandwich that is very satisfying on a basic level. That said, New York only has a few decent cheese steak joints that give this Philadelphia specialty its just due. For under $10.00, here in Hell's Kitchen, you can have a cheese steak and a drink and for another buck or two enjoy a Tastycake for dessert. Philly Slims is one of the best cheese steak options outside of Philadelphia.

Pho Grand

277 Grand Street

212-965-5366

The name may hint at the rent, the key money, or what they spent on "renovation," as I'm not exactly sure what this place was before it was Pho Grand. The cedar walls that line the dining room suggest a giant sauna or perhaps an upstate ski lodge, but whatever, it's a good choice for pho and other Vietnamese specialties with a budget in mind. The signature soups come in around $6.00 to $7.00 a pop. Your pho choices include a good broth redolent of Chinese five spice, studded with various cuts of meat such as the navel, which is the same cut used in pastrami, to the leaner eye round, or thinly sliced, julienned tripe, to chewy, gelatinous beef tendon, my favorite. To this, add great noodles dishes, a small multiple squid section of the menu with options listed at $7.95, and on to shrimp, beef, and chicken choices. On a recent visit I had dish billed as bo nuong vi, in which thin slices of beef are sautéed then combined with pickled carrots, sliced radish, and finely chopped mint, all wrapped in rice paper and simply eaten with the addition of a dipping chili sauce… yum!

Pinche Taqueria

27 Mott Street (plus other locations)

212-625-0090

This diminutive space is a long, narrow room with natural red and painted brick walls and an open kitchen. Food may be served on disposable plates and aluminum foil takeout containers, but Pinche vies for being one the best taquerias in town, including La Esquina a few doors down. The tortillas are house-made, and the fried fish tacos supposedly made from line-caught Mahi Mahi are excellent. The decent burritos (not huge, but adequate and good), yucca fries, and the very good, slow-cooked pork carnitas are a few of the highlights. While the Mission District food police may not approve, to my mind the chow served here, washed down with good beer or a glass or two of wine, at these prices is worth the trip.

Porchetta

110 East 7th Street

212-777-2151

Chef Sara Jenkins has been cooking around NYC for years now. Prior to this she ran 50 Carmine. She lived in Italy for most of her youth and really knows authentic Italian food. Here at Porchetta, the premise is simple. It's basically a one-dish restaurant, a food stall essentially, the kind one might find traveling through Italy but rarely if ever here. It's counter service only, with a few seats if you can snag them, but worth it regardless. Porchetta is simply Heritage breed, boneless Hampshire pork loin that is first slathered with chopped garlic, rosemary, fennel pollen, a generous dose of salt and fresh pepper, and a few other herbs and encased in rich fatty Hampshire pork belly, tied together and slow roasted. The result features crisped skin, alternating in layers with the meat and fat, served as a standalone with lovely little roasted potatoes or as a sandwich set within Sullivan Street ciabatta rolls, with a great bitter chicory salad thrown in to cover the vegetable group from the food pyramid. Simple, satisfying, and delicious.

Wilfie & Nell

228 West 4th Street

212-242-2990

Greenwich Village has some great food shopping and restaurants catering to British ex-pats or Americans looking for specialties from the British Isles: Meyer's of Keswick, A Salt & Battery, and Tea and Sympathy, to name a few. Add Wilfie & Nell to that list. April Bloomfield may have helped re-invented the gastropub scene in NYC with her Spotted Pig a few blocks away, but this place stays true to the more traditional model. Though primarily a bar, the cooking here is very good, from the soups like bacon studded split pea, to deep fried Scotch Eggs, house-made fried potatoes served with malt vinegar, and even a great grilled cheese. It's in the sourcing of ingredients that you notice that this place is special. In the case of that grilled cheese, the Tallegio cheese is from nearby Murray's and the bread from Blue Ribbon. They offer a choice of pastry clad meat pies and those stuffed, savory offerings the Brits love, like the crumbly delicious Cornish pasties. A great selection of beer rounds out the options.

Index by Neighborhood

Index by Price Range